the ONION® AD NAUSEAM

Fanfare for the Area Man

COMPLETE NEWS ARCHIVES • VOLUME 15

This book uses invented names in all stories, except notable public figures who are the subjects of satire. Any other use of real names is accidental and coincidental.

Published by Three Rivers Press, New York, New York.
Member of the Crown Publishing Group, a division of Random House, Inc.
www.crownpublishing.com

Three Rivers Press and the Tugboat design are registered trademarks of Random House, Inc.

The material in this work previously appeared in *The Onion*.

Printed in the United States of America

Design by The Onion

Library of Congress Cataloging-in-Publication Data is available upon request.

ISBN 1-4000-5455-9

10 9 8 7 6 5 4 3 2 1

First Edition

PHOTO CREDITS

p. 1, Ad; p. 86, Toomey; p. 109, Nicastro; p. 120, Gerald; p. 129, Schwann; p. 135, Scanlon; p. 165, Marchand; p. 171, Wilmot; p. 175, Dieber; p. 181, Treat; p. 195, Gary; p. 105, Woods; p. 222, Hebert; p. 223, Bellisle; p. 230, Dassle: Mike Loew/Onion Photos. p. 1, Mudslide: Rayell Call/Getty. p. 1, Kevin Bacon: Robin Platzer/Getty. p. 1, Terrorists; p. 11, Planes; p. 14, Winona Ryder; p. 19, Ashcroft; p. 43 and 67, Kim Jong-Il; p. 53, Truck; p. 61, Sosa; p. 68, Jackson; p. 97, MOAB, Troops; p. 103, Bush; p. 104, Dion; p. 115, Hussein; p. 146, Blair; p. 158, Hope; p. 166, Bombing; p. 187, Sharon and Abbas; p. 208, Sadat, Carter, Begin; p. 217, Larry Flint; p. 247, Bush and Students; p. 254, Siegfried: Getty. p. 1, Molly Ringwald: Matthew Peyton/Getty. p. 1 and 4, Dishwashers; p. 2, Renter; p. 3, Pinter; p. 5, Visine; p. 10, Equation; p. 12, Peavey; p. 13, Marxists; p. 15, Burdon; p. 16, Dishes; p. 19, Schram, Dressler; p. 20, Dunn; p. 24, Markham; p. 25, Patek; p. 26, Driesen; p. 32, Foster; p. 37, Successories, Ghost; p. 41, Bill of Rights; p. 43, Tamagotchi, Room, Condom, Tudor; p. 44, Hollins; p. 47, Food; p. 49, Object, Robot, Ladder; p. 50 and 110, Groznic; p. 51, Schaffner; p. 55, Mahaffrey, Phone; p. 56, Glenn; p. 57, Debate Team; p. 62, Peltz; p. 65, R2D2; p. 66, Lynne; p. 67, Dice, Friends; p. 73, Butler, Laundromat; p. 74, Winger; p. 75, Thompson; p. 79, Pedestrians, Employee, Sadecki; p. 81, Couple; p. 87, Cop; p. 90, Delsman; p. 91, Flowers; p. 93, Riesman; p. 98, Eckert; p. 99, Blynn; p. 103, DVD, Malveaux; p. 104, Dunst; p. 105, Neuwirth; p. 109, Toy; p. 111, Ghosts; p. 115, Strauss; p. 119, Domer; p. 121, Saltines, DVD Collection, Pearle; p. 122, DeVries; p. 127, Garden, Taco Bell; p. 128, Kanner; p. 133, Pool, Staff; p. 137, Eppard; p. 139, Perssen; p. 140, Adams; p. 144, Gunther; p. 145, Tolbert; p. 146, Russo; p. 147, Iwanski, Lundback; p. 151, Cat, Catalog; p. 155, CD; p. 156, Kenniff; p. 158, Crewes; p. 163, Anthology, Rogowski; p. 169, Haley, Beer; p. 172, Haley; p. 174, Roberts; p. 175, Man, Lunch, Son; p. 176, Hume; p. 178, Board; p. 181, Giant Girl, LeBarge, Cart; p. 186, Chips; p. 187, Painting, Body, Higby; p. 189, Zimmerman; p. 193, Brooks, Bacardi, Triplet; p. 199, Turlock; p. 201, Traden, Mistress; p. 205, Magnet; p. 206, Harnack; p. 207, Menu; p. 210, Jacobs; p. 211, Ellis, Gummy Bear; p. 212, Lascowicz; p. 213, Romans; p. 217, Pants, Nielsen; p. 223, Scientist, Tacos: Chad Nackers/Onion Photos. p. 5, Physicist: Tom Shaw/Getty. p. 5, Republicans; p. 94, Van Gogh: Bill Greenblatt/Getty. p. 5, Armey; p. 123, Hitchens: Richard Ellis/Getty. p. 9, Errico and Ausmus; p. 49, Maurer: Denise Thompson/Onion Photos. p. 13, Ray Charles; p. 217, Huffington, Coleman, Bustamante: Frederick M. Brown/Getty. p. 13, Beltway Sniper Game: Kirk Brillion/Onion Graphics. p. 17, Game Expo; p. 67, Ashcroft; p. 188, Kraft Foods; p. 224, Tower: David McNew/Getty. p. 19, Strokes: Sebastian Artz/Getty. p. 31, Crocodile Hunter; p. 80, Duct Tape; p. 98, Hangar: Justin Sullivan/Getty. p. 31, Mall: Mark Erickson/Getty. p. 32, Thurmond; p. 37, Bush; p. 45, Dinosaur; p. 109, Bush and Aznar; p. 169, Republicans: Mark Wilson/Getty. p. 34, Store: Mark Simons/Getty. p. 46, Missiles: Chung Sung-Jun/Getty. p. 50, Wine Taster: David Silverman/Getty. p. 55, U.N. Inspectors; p. 211, Aid: Scott Peterson/Getty. p. 58, Nunez; p. 115, Girl, Troops; p. 116, Search; p. 193, Taco Bell; p. 235, Bombs: Joe Raedle/Getty. p. 61, Gondola: Clive Brunskill/Getty. p. 61, Johnson: Todd Warshaw/Getty. p. 61, Bonds: Harry How/Getty. p. 61, Rodriguez; p. 134, Brown: Arnaldo Magnani/Getty. p. 62, AOL-Time Warner; p. 194, New York Times Building: Adam Rountree/Getty. p. 74, Affleck and Lopez: Mel Bouzad/Getty. p. 79, Dirty Soldier: Robert Nickelsberg/Getty. p. 82, Hutchinson: Karen Cooper/Getty. p. 82, Allard; p. 133, Bush; p. 151, Frist; p. 175, Bush; p. 199 and 203, Kerry; p. 241, Williams: Alex Wong/Getty. p. 83, Restroom: Billy Stickland/Getty. p. 85, Barrymore: Mario Magnani/Getty. p. 85, Troop: Anthony Suau/Getty. p. 85, Stamp: Manny Ceneta/Getty. p. 86, Sheen: Frazer Harrison/Getty. p. 88, E.T. The Extra-Terrestrial: B. McBroom/Universal Studios/Zuma. p. 88, Playboy: Playboy/Getty. p. 88, Charlie's Angels: Darren Michaels/Getty. p. 88, Kissing: UK Press/Getty. p. 91, Keith: Adele Starr/Getty. p. 91, Merger; p. 170, Clinton: Stan Honda/AFP. p. 97, U.N.; p. 128, Bloomberg: Spencer Platt/Getty. p. 101, Home: Scott Nelson/Getty. p. 109, *American Idol*: Michel Boutefeu/Getty. p. 115, Robot: John Chiasson/Getty. p. 117, *Norah's New Nose*; p. 118, Cottonball; p. 159, Chipmunk; p. 169, Nudes; p. 223, Recyclables; p. 249, Brown: Maria Schneider/Onion Graphics. p. 121, Riot: Jason Kirk/Getty. p. 123, Cops; p. 161, Homeless; p. 244, Body: Don Murray/Getty. p. 127, Syrians; p. 221, Team: Salah Malkawi/Getty. p. 127, Press Conference: Stefan Zaklin/Getty. p. 131, Syrians: Chris Hondros/Getty. p. 132, Grady; p. 170, Curran: Joe Garden/Onion Photos. p. 139, Chimp: Robert Mora/Getty. p. 141, Sale: Norman Ng/KRT. p. 148, Sum-41: Scott Harrison/Getty. p. 151, Fans: Otto Greule Jr./Getty. p. 152, Bush: Jason Connel/Getty. p. 157, Ruzek; p. 241, Asshole: Carol Kolb/Onion Photos. p. 163, Franks: Tim Sloan/Getty. p. 164, Powell; p. 187, Powell: Evan Agostini/Getty. p. 176, Potter Fans: Jimin Lai/Getty. p. 177, Stoddard: Preeti Parasharami/Onion Photos. p. 182, Concert: Erik S. Lesser/Getty. p. 205, Bryant: J. Emilio Flores/Getty. p. 205, Cheney; p. 256, Bush and Dog: Paul J. Richards/Getty. p. 205, Hearing: Michael Porro/Getty. p. 206, Gray Davis; p. 217, Dave Grayvis: David Paul Morris/Getty. p. 211, Asimo: Junko Kimura/Getty. p. 212, Computer Café: Jonathan Elderfield/Getty. p. 217, Red Hot Chili Peppers: Frank Micelotta/Getty. p. 217, Schwarzenegger; p. 248, Affleck and Lopez: Kevin Winter/Getty. p. 217, Peter Ueberroth: Vince Bucci/Getty. p. 217, Foreman: Anthony Harvey/Getty. p. 218, Gay TV: Scott Gries/Getty. p. 223, Latifah: Pious Utomi Ekpei/AFP/Getty. p. 223, Burning Man: Stephen Ferry/Getty. p. 225, Friedman: Christine Carlson/Onion Photos. p. 235, Girl: Paula Brownstein/Getty. p. 235, Parade: Lee Roth/Star Max. p. 236, Consumers; p. 260, Troops: Tim Boyle/Getty. p. 254, NYSE: Stephen Chernin/Getty.

NEWS

Phone-Sex Ad Masturbated To For 0 Cents A Minute

see LOCAL page 11C

Mudslide Kind Of Fun Until The Dying Part

see LOCAL page 3C

Mask Probably Bush

see HALLOWEEN page 11B

Man Unwilling To Discuss Lifetime Denny's Ban

see LOCAL page 9C

STATshot

A look at the numbers that shape your world.

Claimed Vs. Actual Causes Of Scars

1. Alligator attack/Shoehorn mishap
2. World's Strongest Man contest/ Pie-eating contest
3. Downhill skiing/ Stepped on Lego
4. Stigmata/High-five gone awry
5. Rock climbing/Rock tumbling
6. Rescued child from house fire/ Flaming-marshmallow incident

THE ONION • $2.00 US • $3.00 CAN

the ONION®

VOLUME 38 ISSUE 40 AMERICA'S FINEST NEWS SOURCE™ 31 OCT.–6 NOV. 2002

THE WAR ON TERROR

Kevin Bacon Linked To Al-Qaeda

U.S. Students Lead World In Detention

UNITED NATIONS—With one in 25 students currently in detention, on suspension, or otherwise held after school on charges, the U.S. leads the world in disciplinary action against schoolchildren, the U.N. Human Rights Commission reported Monday.

"There is a disturbing trend in the corrective measures taken by contemporary American educators," the report read. "The United States is requiring its students to do time in the guidance counselor or principal's office three times as often as the average Westernized nation. No other country incarcerates its young at anywhere near that rate."

Detailed in the 922-page document is an alarming pattern of arbitrary

and discriminatory enforcement, uneven interpretation of rules, and unfair punishment disproportionate to the transgression.

"It is an accepted, almost universally acknowledged fact that detention in America is class-based," UNHRC chief David Ottersen said. "If you are a member of the upper classes, especially a senior, you have little or nothing to fear. You can hit the teacher with a spitball in broad daylight, and you won't do time. But if you're a lower-class student, a freshman or sophomore, look out."

The report also found that U.S. detention facilities place a far greater emphasis on isolation and punishment than on rehabilitation.

"We have case study after case study of detainees being forced to sit silently with their heads down on their desks, sometimes for hours at a time," Ottersen said. "How does this help prepare a child for a return to the classroom? A class clown needs to be given the tools necessary for success

see STUDENTS page 5

Dishwasher Thinks He's Mentoring Younger Dishwasher

GAINESVILLE, FL—Gordon Polone, 49, a dishwasher at Smitty's Family Restaurant since 1991, has taken new hire Craig Garrick, 19, under his wing, patiently mentoring him in the ways of washing dishes.

"I've been washing dishes at one restaurant or another for half my life," Polone said Tuesday. "If anyone is qualified to show Craig the ropes, it'd be me."

"I know this dish station inside and out, that's for sure," Polone continued. "When I started here, we didn't even have this fancy new Hobart [industrial dishwashing machine]. We had an earlier-model Hobart. That was way the hell back when Dale was manager."

Polone, who has trained an estimated 30 dishwashers during his 11 years at Smitty's, said he is more than happy to pass on his knowledge to the next generation of plate-scrubbers.

"It's not too much extra work training a new guy, and Craig seems pretty on the ball about the whole thing," Polone said. "I only had to show him how to load the racks the one time, and after that, he had it down like he'd been doing it for weeks."

Though he has only been working with Garrick for

see DISHWASHER page 4

Above: Polone and his protégé.

North Korean Nukes

Last week, it was revealed that North Korea has secretly been pursuing a nuclear-weapons program. What do *you* think?

"While it appears that North Korea may indeed have The Bomb, it remains unclear whether they have The Food."

Gene Franke
Systems Analyst

"Don't worry: It's probably just a bootleg bomb that won't work anyway."

Bill Cullums
Delivery Driver

"My remarks on this matter will be brief, as the only stereotype I know of Koreans is that they eat dogs."

Valerie Schmidt
Florist

"This news really burns me up. In fact, it vaporizes me into my component subatomic particles, leaving the soil around me lifeless and radioactive for millennia."

Marcia Martz
Homemaker

"I just pray that this does not interfere with the Koreans' important work animating *The Simpsons*."

Christopher Sims
Lawyer

"North Korea may have a few nukes, but we have more than 12,000. That should make everyone feel safer."

Eddie Rutt
Cashier

Playboy's Overhaul

Losing readers to *Maxim* and other "lad" magazines, *Playboy* plans a major editorial overhaul. Among the upcoming changes:

- Scaling back from boobies, boobies, boobies to just boobies, boobies
- Enlisting top writers like Don DeLillo and David Foster Wallace to write articles about cool new gadgets and gear
- Aggressively referring to men as "guys"
- Creating special section where WB actresses have opportunity to give their wholesome images an unexpected jolt
- Explaining that magazine is not porn but a "men's lifestyle magazine" in introductory Letter To The Reader's Girlfriend
- Audiophile column tells you how to get girls to nearly undress in front of the right stereo equipment
- Stealing *New Yorker* staff writer Seymour Hersh, having him write comprehensive piece on history of the thong
- Finding out what's in *FHM*, doing that

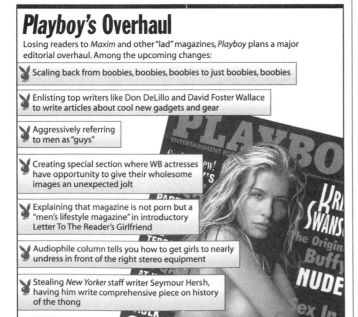

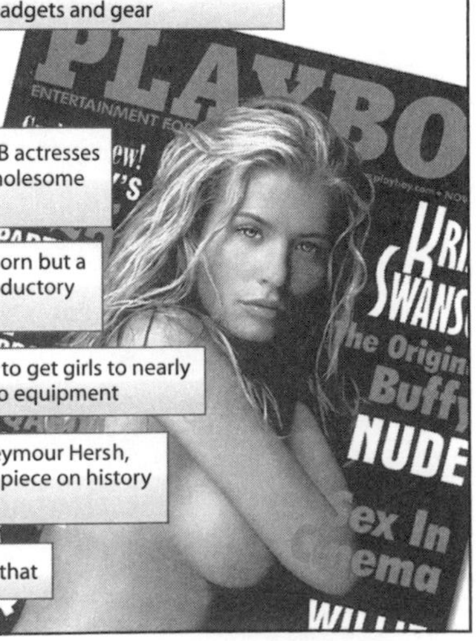

the ONION®
America's Finest News Source.™

Herman Ulysses Zweibel
Founder

T. Herman Zweibel
Publisher Emeritus
J. Phineas Zweibel
Publisher
Maxwell Prescott Zweibel
Editor-In-Chief

Would You Like To Give A Dollar To Prove You Don't Hate Crippled Kids?

By Bill Renter

Good afternoon, sir. Do you have a minute to discuss something of vital importance? I'm canvassing this neighborhood collecting donations for the Tersbury Group. We're an organization dedicated to helping mentally and physically handicapped children here in the community lead better lives. If you don't mind my being blunt, sir, may I ask whether you hate crippled kids? Wonderful, I'm so glad I was right about you. Now, would you be willing to donate a dollar to our organization to prove that you don't?

Anyone can just say they don't hate crippled kids, but it takes a special kind of person to put their money where their mouth is; a person who doesn't want everyone on the street to know they're too cheap and selfish to part with one measly dollar to help those far less fortunate than themselves.

I don't mean to pressure you, but the Tersbury Group is an extremely worthwhile cause that's in dire need of funds. So if you could find it in your heart to pull some spare change from the pocket of that expensive-looking suit, it would be much appreciated by the crippled children you claim not to hate.

Perhaps before you decide to donate, you'd like to hear a bit more about the Tersbury Group and its programs. We have three fully staffed locations that provide medical attention, equipment, and life-skills programs that help crippled children in the community live better lives. We are also developing a new living facility where crippled children can practice life skills and independent living. As you can imagine, all of this is expensive but very important. It takes the generosity of people who don't hoard their every last penny to make such endeavors a reality. Do you count yourself among these people, sir?

Anyone can just say they don't hate crippled kids, but it takes a special kind of person to put their money where their mouth is.

Your donation doesn't just go toward equipment, medicine, and services. We also use it to take these children on fun, spirit-lifting trips, such as to the children's museum and petting zoo. These outings may not mean much to healthy people like yourself, but to a poor crippled child who must drag his or her lifeless limbs through life, it means the world. Without generous donations from folks like you, these kids are going to spend their sad little lives staring at the same four walls every day.

Perhaps you'd like to take this pamphlet with you. Don't worry, it's free of charge.

Perhaps you'd like to take this pamphlet with you. Don't worry, it's free of charge. It explains a little bit more about what we here at the Tersbury Group do, and it even has some photos of our kids, so you can see exactly who you'd be helping with your dollar. There's even a donation envelope, should you later decide that you don't despise crippled kids and would like to mail in a check.

I know money is tight these days, but if you think about it, a dollar isn't really going to make much difference in the way you live your life. What's a dollar for a person like you, anyway? A candy bar? A can of soda? But for these poor children, that same one dollar goes a long way. Of course, you could always just walk away from me on the two good, strong legs God gave you. But wouldn't it be nice to walk away knowing you did something nice for the crippled children you purport not to loathe?

I'm sorry—I didn't realize you were waiting for a date to arrive. Sorry to bother you at a time like this. I hope things work out for you and your lady friend. You realize, of course, that without the proper medical attention your dollar would bring, many of these children will probably not live to see their first crush, much less a first date.

If you'd like to wait until your date arrives to make your donation, I would understand. Not everyone likes to selflessly donate money to children who can barely walk or breathe under their own power without getting credit. I'd be more than happy to wait so you can make a big show of it in front of some girl you're trying to impress, if that's what it takes. Ø

RELATIONSHIPS

Man Feels 19 Again After Not Getting Laid

SANTA CRUZ, CA—Jason Pinter, a 33-year-old data-systems specialist who has not had sex in eight months, reported Tuesday that the celibacy streak has made him feel 19 again.

"Wow, talk about déjà vu," said Pinter, staring longingly at an attractive woman at Murphy's Pub. "All this not-getting-laid really takes me back."

Pinter has not been intimate with a woman since early February, when Claire Sundberg, his girlfriend of four years, broke up with him. He called the past eight months "the longest dry spell since just after high school" and "a real blast from the past."

"I lost my virginity right after I turned 20 and have pretty much had a girlfriend or something ever since," Pinter said. "Even though it's like I'm reliving my days as a horny, frustrated teenager all over again, this time I know exactly what I'm missing. So in a way, it's actually worse."

Since the breakup with Sundberg, Pinter's interactions with women have been characterized by nervousness, a fear of eye contact, and an inability to make natural, charming conversation. Such insecurities have remained dormant, or at least been kept under control, for the past 14 years.

"I keep having flashbacks to my old freshman dorm," Pinter said. "The other night, I was awkwardly trying to chat up this woman at a bar and, I swear, I could almost smell that combination of stale pizza, old socks, and my roommate's Drakkar Noir."

Pinter's sexless streak has triggered other memories of his late-teenage years.

"I keep having flashbacks to my old freshman dorm," Pinter said. "The other night, I was awkwardly trying to chat up this woman at a bar and, I swear, I could almost smell that combination of stale pizza, old socks, and my roommate's Drakkar Noir."

"I got home last night and had the urge to listen to [Jane's Addiction's] *Nothing's Shocking*," Pinter said. "I haven't listened to that album in, like, 10 years, but then I remembered how I used to listen to it whenever I came home drunk and alone in college. It really transported me back to that time when the whole world seemed fresh and new and I couldn't get a hand job to save my life."

Above: The nostalgically celibate Pinter.

Even the dating advice Pinter has received of late takes him back.

"My friends at work have been telling me to be myself and not act so desperate," Pinter said. "I don't need to hear that. It's the same old shit I heard back in high school, like when I had a huge crush on Desiree from French class, and my friend Kristin used to give me that sort of advice during her weekly pep talks. I wonder what Desiree's up to these days."

While Pinter's past inability to get laid stemmed from a lack of sexual experience and his chronic acne, today the cause lies largely with Sundberg.

"Claire dumping me, that really did some serious damage to my self-esteem," Pinter said. "I haven't felt this insecure and self-conscious around girls since I was lab partners with Brittany Ellis, the leader of the pom-

see LAID page 6

NEWS IN BRIEF

Adam Sandler Fans Disappointed By Intelligent, Nuanced Performance

LOS ANGELES—Adam Sandler fans across the nation expressed deep disappointment in the new film *Punch-Drunk Love*, which features an intelligent, nuanced lead performance by the comedian. "He didn't even do his funny high-pitched 'retardo guy' voice," said college student Bradley Sanderson, 19, after seeing the critically lauded film Tuesday. "And what was with all that textured, multi-dimensional character-development shit?" Similarly let down was fan Bob Trotta: "I didn't pay $9 to see Adam Sandler wrestle with some psychological crisis. He could have at least put a trash-can lid on his head and gone, 'I'm Crazy Trash Head! Gimme some candy!' How hard would that have been?"

Daytime-Talk-Show Mixup Leads To 1,000-Pound-Man Makeover

NEW YORK—In a mix-up Ricki Lake producers called "deeply regrettable," 1,000-pound Willard Hoskins, 37, was removed from his Paramus, NJ, home by forklift and transported to the posh Richard Stein Salon on Madison Avenue for a thorough beauty makeover Monday. "Let's see Willard's stunning new look!" Lake told the studio audience as Hoskins was wheeled out in a sequined black garment made from two king-size bed sheets to the accompaniment of throbbing disco music. "Wow, you look great!" The episode is believed to be daytime television's worst mix-up since Maury Povich sent a group of disfigured children to boot camp in 1999.

Plan 'L' Switched To

BEREA, KY—Plans A, B, C, D, E, F, G, H, I, J, and K having failed, David Zenger resorted to "Plan L" in his efforts to move an air conditioner from the garage to the house Tuesday. "Okay, here we go," Zenger said to himself. "If I wrap the air conditioner in bubble wrap and then balance it on a basketball, I can spin-roll it into the house." Previous failed attempts to move the air conditioner involved a pair of bungee cords, a bag of marbles, and a bottle of Crisco cooking oil.

Visible Panty Line Discussed Like It's Cancer

ABILENE, TX—During a trip to the mall Monday, Melissa Gilham and Tiffany Cornell discussed a fellow mall patron's visible panty line as if it were cancer. "Oh my God, look at that," a shaken Gilham told Cornell outside Suncoast Video, where the panty line was first sighted. "Somebody really needs to sit her down and have a talk about that. Doesn't she have any friends?" Added Cornell: "Maybe we could chip in and buy her a thong." The pair's horror deepened when they faintly made out the panties' flower print through the woman's white pants.

Woman Mad Boyfriend Not Jealous She Danced With Other Guy

WEST LAFAYETTE, IN—Deborah Raskin, 20, became angry Saturday when boyfriend Kris Barros failed to become jealous over her dancing with another guy. "She was being all quiet and staring at the wall, and she wouldn't tell me what it was all about," Barros said shortly after leaving the party. "Finally, I realized, shit, I was supposed to get all mad and make some big scene because she danced with that one dude before." Barros promised Raskin that he would make more of an effort to be jealous in the future. Ø

DISHWASHER from page 1

three days, Polone has already begun the long process of passing along the many secrets he has absorbed in his years of washing dishes.

"A roasting pan that they cooked meatloaf in is about as tough as they get, especially since [Smitty's lead cook] Perry [Tuscan] likes it with a crispy bottom," Polone explained to his trainee. "Those pans, you want to soak them for half an hour minimum, in really hot water with lots of soap, before you get to the scraping, or else you're just wasting elbow grease. You could soak it overnight to loosen things up, but I honestly wouldn't recommend that unless you're opening the next day, because you don't want to get on some other dishwasher's shit list."

"Sunday dinner rush is the real trial by fire," Polone said. "That's six hours of bus tubs coming in non-stop. You have to learn to time everything so you can start the machine, load up another rack while it's running, and then have the new rack all ready to load after you take out the clean rack."

Polone said that, while seemingly simple, the dishwashing trade is fraught with hazards and hurdles.

"I've got some stories that would curl your hair, believe me," Polone told Garrick, who half-listened while twirling his apron strings. "One time at this place in Orlando, we were short-staffed, and I had to do all the dishes myself. Just as we were closing, this party of 15 comes in. Now, you'd think I'd be screwed, but about half an hour earlier, I'd overheard the host confirming their reservation over the phone, so I had a bit of lead time. The lesson there is, always stay on top of what's going on out front. Awareness is key."

Though Garrick has shown himself to be bright and a quick study, Polone stressed to his disciple that he faces a long road to mastery of his craft.

"Even after you get the nuts and bolts down, there's little things you have to pick up to get through the busy shifts," Polone told him. "Sunday dinner rush is the real trial by fire. That's maybe six hours of bus tubs coming in non-stop. You have to learn to time everything so you can start the machine, load up another rack while it's running, and then have the new rack all ready to load after you take out the clean rack."

Added Polone, "You're not supposed to use the dirty rack to push the clean rack out, because of health codes."

According to Polone, once Garrick can handle the rigors of a Sunday second shift on his own, he will be well on his way.

Above: Polone demonstrates one of his many tricks of the trade.

"If Craig gets Sundays down, he can pretty much run the dish station on his own," Polone said. "Still, there's always going to be new stuff for him to learn. Like how to refill the soap and sanitizer reservoirs and prime the lines. Then there's all the politics, like getting along well with the chefs so they'll bring you their dirty pots right away, before all that stuff gets dried up and has to be scraped. There's always something new."

Reflecting on the vast body of dishwashing knowledge he has accumulated over the years, Polone expressed a strong sense of pride.

"I suppose I could write a whole big book on dishwashing," Polone said, "except I don't have a computer or anything, and it's not the kind of thing you can pick up from just reading about it."

"Hey, I teach 'em so good, maybe I should open some big dishwashing school and get rich," Polone added. "Nah, I'm just kidding."

Asked for comment on his experience training under Polone, Garrick said, "Whatever."

the ONION presents

Headache-Relief Tips

Millions of Americans regularly suffer from headaches.
Here are some tips to help prevent them and ease the pain:

- Though disputed by conventional Western medicine, the ancient Chinese art of kneecap-smashing may distract you from your headache.
- The surest method of headache prevention is to develop a working time machine, go back to 1988, and marry a different woman who doesn't nag your ass into the ground about where you were all night and who was there with you and were you drinking.
- No matter how bad your head hurts, do not under any circumstances attempt to remove it.
- Many popular herbal headache remedies exist, including valerian and kava kava, but be advised that they don't do shit.
- Headaches can get so bad that, in some cases, doctors prescribe morphine or methadone. A better way to look at this is that headaches can get so good that doctors prescribe morphine or methadone.
- If you have a severe headache, you likely have five or six throbbing red lightning bolts behind your sinuses. Neutralize them with a soothing, bluish, glowing orb.
- A key to headache prevention is avoiding getting Starship's "We Built This City" stuck in your head.
- If you suffer from recurring headache pain, you probably have a tumor or something. Man, am I glad I'm not you.
- If you suspect that your headache is a migraine, ask yourself: Does the prospect of having a double-barreled shotgun inserted in your anus and discharged fill you with thoughts of blessed, eternal relief? If so, it's probably a migraine.
- Headache sufferers, be advised that episodes can easily be triggered by stress, improper diet, or people constantly chiming in with their useless fucking headache advice.

STUDENTS from page 1

Above: One of the millions of U.S. students currently serving time.

upon his or her release from detention, not some pointless heads-down-for-the-whole-period punishment.”

Even more disturbing, a whopping 82 percent of detained American students are repeat offenders. This stands in sharp contrast to Germany, where only one detainee in 50 serves a second sentence in the same school year.

“The American detention system is a revolving door,” Ottersen said. “It is not a deterrent. It's a badge of honor for some of these kids. We've got kids in detention now who are 10 years old and are going to be in and out of there until they're 18. Then what? And what about the kid who goes in not knowing how serious it is and comes out with a blot on his permanent record and a newfound knowledge of how to flush cherry bombs down the toilet?”

The report reflected many human-rights advocates' beliefs about U.S. detention policy.

“The American educational justice system is deeply flawed, perhaps beyond repair,” said Roberta Leigh of Amnesty International. “Fifteen percent of U.S. students are African-American, but they make up more than half of all detained students. The U.S. expulsion rate is six times that of Canada and 15 times that of Japan. How can we call ourselves the world's leading democracy in the face of those figures?”

“The American detention system is a revolving door,” Ottersen said. “It is not a deterrent. It's a badge of honor for some of these kids.”

Many American educators disputed the report's findings.

“What works for the rest of the world doesn't necessarily work for America,” U.S. Secretary of Education Rod Paige said. “The only effective means of maintaining order is to equip our educators with broad discretionary powers. To strip them of their punitive authority would lead to a sharp rise in inappropriate behavior and, inevitably, a nationwide decline in school spirit. We as a nation cannot afford this.”

Added Paige: “Detention in this country is necessary, humane, and effective. Our motivation, especially in cases of recidivism, is to get these kids away from the general student population. Since the 1950s, we've been more successful than not at halting the spread of shenanigans, tomfoolery, and clowning around. Can France or Britain say the same? I don't think so.”

WET NURSE from page 2

amounts of blood. Passersby were amazed by the unusually large amounts of blood. Passersby were amazed by the unusually large amounts of blood. Passersby were amazed by the unusually large amounts of blood. Passersby were amazed by the unusually large amounts of blood. Passersby were amazed by the unusually large amounts of blood. Passersby were amazed by the unusually large amounts of blood. Passersby were amazed by the unusually large amounts of blood. Passersby were

Just let me know if you don't want me to joke about your missing eye.

amazed by the unusually large amounts of blood. Passersby were amazed by the unusually large amounts of blood. Passersby were amazed by the unusually large amounts of blood. Passersby were amazed by the unusually large amounts of blood. Passersby were amazed by the unusually large amounts of blood. Passersby were amazed by the unusually large amounts of blood. Passersby were amazed by the unusually large amounts of blood. Passersby were

see WET NURSE page 8

COMMUNITY VOICES

I Gotta Drop A Few Pounds

Hola, amigos. It's been a long time since I rapped at ya, but I been workin' for a living, taking what they're giving, all that. Actually, to be honest, I ain't been working all that hard lately. As you well know, I left my bullshit coat-check job for greener pastures: sitting around on my ass and enjoying the finer things.

The Cruise
By Jim Anchower

I wasn't even thinking about getting a job for, like, a month or so, figuring I'd just coast on my nest egg. But what I didn't account for was a $150 ticket for an improper left turn. Improper left turn, my ass! The lines on the road were so faded, I couldn't even tell there was supposed to be a turn lane! Next thing I know, I see the rollers, and this pig slaps me with the $150 fine. I'm going to court to contest it, but, barring a miracle, I gotta assume that money's spent and gone.

I started putting on my REO jeans and, for some reason, they didn't fit. A little tight is okay—gives the ladies something to think about—but when I got them all the way up, I couldn't even button them. I thought they must've shrunk or something, but I hadn't washed them since last year's show.

Actually, it *is* spent and gone, 'cause me and Wes blew that much seeing REO Speedwagon at the Dane County Coliseum.

I don't ever miss a Speedwagon show. Last year, I saw them put on the best show ever at the Winnebago County Fair. They busted out “Riding The Storm Out.” They let go with “Don't Let Her Go.” They ran with “Take It On The Run.” They brought the rock so good, the audience was drunk on the music. I was pretty drunk on beer, too, but I could tell there was something moving me

see ANCHOWER page 6

ANCHOWER from page 5

besides the Miller. So you can bet old Jim wasn't missing out on Kevin Cronin and the boys this year.

For me, going to see the Wagon is like going to church. I mean, I got my own rituals for the occasion. I always

I figured I had time to grab some beers before they hit the stage. I made my way to concessions, and the line was really long. By the time I got to the front, I heard some opening guitar licks and the crowd went nuts. I reached into my pockets to get my money in a big hurry, and my belt broke. It was a relief at first, because the thing was pinching me like some old lady's girdle.

listen to *Hi Infidelity* in the car on the way. I get there a half-hour early so I can burn one and chug a beer. But most important, I always wear my special pair of REO Speedwagon jeans. Once, in 10th grade, I wrote "REO" on the left ass pocket in red pen, and ever since, I've never seen Kevin and the boys without them. If I lost my cassette of *Hi Infidelity*, that would suck my rod, but it wouldn't be the worst thing—I could always make do with the greatest-hits tape. But, man, a Gary Richrath solo is nothing without the comfort of those jeans.

For whatever reason, REO was opening for Foreigner. Now, I got nothing against Foreigner, but it just didn't seem right that they got top billing over Champaign's finest. Anyhow, Wes was picking me up in 15 minutes, and I started getting ready, which meant rocking out to "Time For Me To Fly." I started putting on my REO jeans and, for some reason, they didn't fit. A little tight is okay—gives the ladies something to think about—but when I got them all the way up, I couldn't even button them. I thought they must've shrunk or something, but I hadn't washed them since last year's show. There was only one other explanation: I must have put on some pounds since then.

Well, you know Jim Anchower wasn't going down that easy. No pants were going to tell me what to do, even if they were my lucky Speedwagon jeans. I left the top unbuttoned and pulled the zipper up as high as it would go. Then I dug out an old belt and punched a new hole at the end. It wasn't the most comfortable thing, but I figured it was worth the sacrifice.

Wes showed up, and we got to the Coliseum with about five minutes to spare. REO knows how to keep a crowd waiting, so I figured I had time to grab some beers before they hit the stage. I made my way to concessions, and the line was really long. By the time I got to the front, I heard some opening guitar licks and the crowd went nuts. I reached into my pockets to get my money in a big hurry, and my belt broke. It was a relief at first, because the thing was pinching me like some old lady's girdle.

I picked up the four beers and headed back to our seats, but halfway there, I felt the zipper starting to slip. I had my hands full of brew, so I couldn't stop and zip up. About 50 feet from my seat, my jeans started to drop. Three steps later, they gave way and came down just below my ass. I was wearing a clean pair of drawers and didn't want to miss any of the show, so I kept on.

By the time I got to my row, the jeans had fallen past my knees, and I was taking baby steps. It looked like I was gonna make it, but just as I'm getting to my seat, this assmunch steps on the jeans, and I take a spill. My cups go flying, and I land in a puddle of beer. So now I'm soaked from head to toe, my pants are around my ankles, and

So, like Kevin sings, you gotta keep rollin' with the changes. If I'm going to fit back into my jeans, I need a man's job where I'm doing something with my hands. Lifting and toting, that kind of shit—the kind of good, hard work where I can burn off my gut.

everyone's looking at me like I'm either a perv or a retard. I felt like a tool, but no way was I missing out on the show. I yanked my pants up as good as I could and sat next to Wes. He was about to ask if I could get more beer, but he took one look at me and thought better of it.

The whole time REO was playing, it felt like I was wearing a pair of denim diapers filled with beer and coliseum dirt. REO still rocked out, but I was too uncomfortable to get into it like I usually do. As soon as they finished, Wes and I took off, even though he wanted to stay for Foreigner.

When I got home and took a long hot shower, I took a good look at my beer belly. It had gotten pretty out of control. Now, I ain't one of those pretty boys who's all into looks, but I got some self-respect. I figure all that time sitting on my ass at the museum coatroom made me soft. That and playing my new Game Cube all the time. And drinking a lot of beer. And eating pizzas.

So, like Kevin sings, you gotta keep rollin' with the changes. If I'm going to fit back into my jeans, I need a man's job where I'm doing something with my hands. Lifting and toting, that kind of shit—the kind of good, hard work where I can burn off my gut. If you hear of anything where I can get some good scratch and not sit on my can all day, let me know. Only I ain't washing cars. Not with winter coming up. That shit's for the birds. ∅

HOROSCOPES

Your Horoscope

By Lloyd Schumner Sr.
Retired Machinist and
A.A.P.B.-Certified Astrologer

Aries: (March 21–April 19)
Just so you know: A blood drive is not necessarily a success just because you've set records for the laundry bill.

Taurus: (April 20–May 20)
You've always thought of your life as original, but it turns out to be identical to that of the daughter of a young couple from Leinster, Ireland, in the mid-1700s.

Gemini: (May 21–June 21)
In spite of everything, you'll manage to stay on the good side of your wife, the trained-seal woman, the trombonist, and the Las Vegas Fire Department.

Cancer: (June 22–July 22)
Change is ahead, but don't worry: A year from now, you won't be able to remember a life outside of Army desert field hospital #740.

Leo: (July 23–Aug. 22)
You're getting the feeling that your underlings are doing all the work. Maybe you shouldn't have gone with Cheney.

Virgo: (Aug. 23–Sept. 22)
After 36 hours of beatings fail to wrest a confession out of you, Interpol will just forge your signature.

Libra: (Sept. 23–Oct. 23)
It may seem like it's all wrapped up neatly, but admit it: You still have no idea who killed the chauffeur.

Scorpio: (Oct. 24–Nov. 21)
Scientists are slowly abandoning the idea of the infinite universe in favor of one that's merely big enough for your mother's fat ass.

Sagittarius: (Nov. 22–Dec. 21)
You will be struck down by horror and anguish when you learn that the events chronicled in the song "Wreck Of The Edmund Fitzgerald" really happened.

Capricorn: (Dec. 22–Jan. 19)
You've finally achieved the personal and financial independence that will allow you to fulfill your life's craziest dream: to dance naked on the Berlin Wall.

Aquarius: (Jan. 20–Feb. 18)
You have no empathy or compassion, and are mystified by motivations other than raw personal ambition. Enjoy Harvard Business School.

Pisces: (Feb. 19–March 20)
You will spend another week putting off the inevitable unpleasantness, but, come to think of it, that's life.

LAID from page 3

pom squad. The only way I could feel like a bigger loser is if I got into my Honda Civic and cruised the local strip with my rocket-club buddies, like I used to do right after I got my driver's license."

"In order to have sex, you have to be confident in your sexuality, or at least appear confident," Pinter continued. "But in order to be confident, you have to have sex. It's, like, this Catch-22 sexual-confidence loop that I spent all of high school and half of college trying to break. And now I have to break it all over again."

Though he has ruled out hiring a prostitute or taking out an ad in the personals, Pinter said he wonders if he'll ever break his celibacy cycle.

"I keep trying to remember what I was doing right in my early 20s," Pinter said. "After I started having sex, things just seemed to fall into place. Now, I somehow feel like I'm right back where I started. Maybe I'm just doomed to never have sex."

Added Pinter: "Whoa, that's something I haven't said in a while." ∅

NEWS

Dog Doesn't Realize He Just Graduated

see PETS page 9C

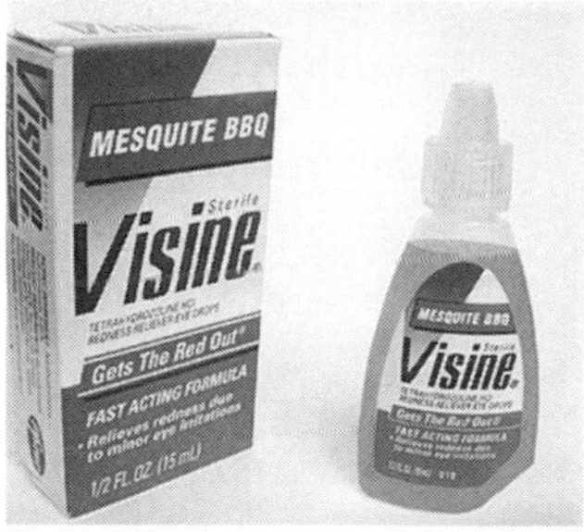

Mesquite BBQ Visine Selling Poorly Outside Texas

see PRODUCTS page 2D

Prisoner Sort Of Expected To Get Raped More Often

see LOCAL page 15A

STATshot

A look at the numbers that shape your world.

Worst-Selling Fat-Free Foods

1. Donuthings
2. Ben & Jerry's gourmet ice
3. Fennel jerky
4. Fruitility
5. Oreo E-mmm-pty Boxes
6. Tastee-Chew Food Strips from 3M
7. Vegetables
8. I'm Having Very Little Difficulty Believing It's Not Butter

THE ONION • $2.00 US • $3.00 CAN

the ONION®

VOLUME 38 ISSUE 41 AMERICA'S FINEST NEWS SOURCE™ 7–13 NOVEMBER 2002

India's Top Physicists Develop Plan To Get The Hell Out Of India

Above: Chattopadhyay answers reporters' questions.

NEW DELHI, INDIA—Months of research and development by a team of India's top physicists have resulted in an ambitious plan to get them the hell out of the overcrowded, impoverished nuclear powderkeg, sources revealed Monday.

"It has been a long road, but our many nights of hard work have finally paid off," said team leader Dr. Birendra Chattopadhyay, 2001 winner of a Shanti Swarup Bhatnagar Prize, the country's top science award. "We couldn't be happier with our findings: It is not only legal, but economically viable for us to leave India by December."

The plan, which includes complex mathematical calculations on the cost of transportation out of India, as well as detailed projections regarding residency and employment prospects in the U.S., Canada, or Europe, represents the fulfillment of a "lifelong dream" for Chattopadhyay.

"I have been working toward this breakthrough all my life," Chattopadhyay said. "India is the second most populous country in the world, with a 30 percent poverty rate, a 52 percent literacy rate, and debts that swallow

see INDIA page 10

Republicans Mount Campaign To Rename Alzheimer's 'Reagan's Disease'

Above: Armey urges his fellow legislators to rename Alzheimer's to honor Reagan.

WASHINGTON, DC—Seeking to honor the former president and longtime Alzheimer's sufferer, congressional Republicans have mounted a campaign to rename Alzheimer's "Reagan's Disease."

Reagan

"No one is more strongly associated with this degenerative brain disease than Ronald Reagan, the man who restored pride to America and single-handedly ended the Cold War," said House Majority Leader Dick Armey,

see REAGAN page 11

Second-Grade Teacher Overhyping Third Grade

BERWICK, PA—April Niles, a second-grade teacher at Benjamin Franklin Elementary School, is constantly overhyping the third grade, warning her students that "expectations will be very different next year."

"If you think [third-grade teacher] Mrs. [Bobbie] Shuler is going to stand for this kind of nonsense, you're wrong as can be," Niles said. "If she catches you kicking a desk or running in the hall, you get one warning, and then it's off to the principal. So you'd better clean up your act, because you're in for a rude awakening when you get to third grade."

Niles, 43, frequently invokes the mysterious, unknown realm of the third grade as a means of maintaining order in her classroom. She has used the tactic to get her students to stand in a straight line, remain silent during fire drills, and pay close atten-

see TEACHER page 11

Above: The third-grade-fixated Niles works with a pair of her second-graders.

The Russian Theater Raid

During a hostage rescue, Russian authorities pumped gas into a Moscow theater, killing 116 of the 800-plus captives. What do *you* think of the controversial move?

Jamie Koss
Librarian

"I can't say I'm shocked. Killing Russians has always been what Russia does best."

Oscar Riggins
Delivery Driver

"Just answer this: Were the captors terrorists? Okay, what about the people who killed the hostages, were they terrorists? How about the victims?"

Reggie Simms
Systems Analyst

"Now that the siege is over, the surviving hostages can get back to watching *Nord-Ost*. I think they left off at the part where Vasily was about to propose to Svetlana."

Meredith Dietz
Teacher

"This is the worst thing ever to happen in Russia."

Oleg Yashin
Russian Official

"I trust that the Russians handled this correctly. No doubt we'll soon learn that every gas victim was actually a Chechen collaborator. Yes. This is what we will find."

Gordon Lenox
Roofer

"All I can say is, somebody had better answer to the United States about this."

The Lynyrd Skynyrd Crash

October marked the 25th anniversary of the 1977 plane crash that claimed the lives of three Lynyrd Skynyrd members. How are fans marking the occasion?

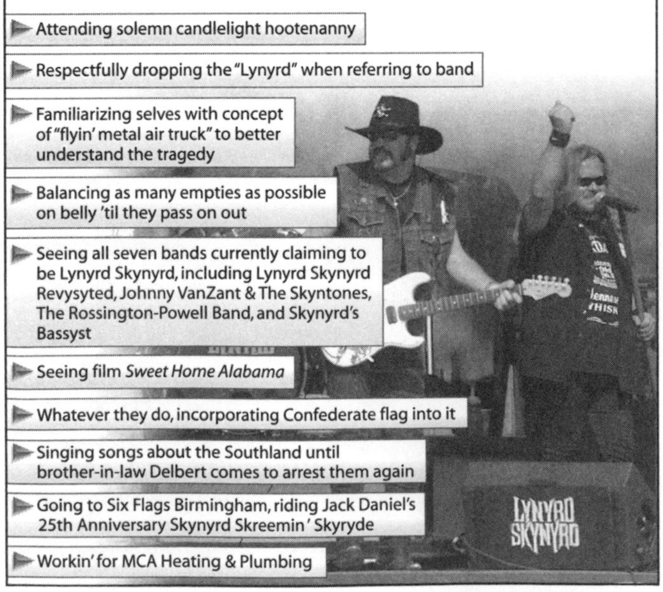

- Attending solemn candlelight hootenanny
- Respectfully dropping the "Lynyrd" when referring to band
- Familiarizing selves with concept of "flyin' metal air truck" to better understand the tragedy
- Balancing as many empties as possible on belly 'til they pass on out
- Seeing all seven bands currently claiming to be Lynyrd Skynyrd, including Lynyrd Skynyrd Revysyted, Johnny VanZant & The Skyntones, The Rossington-Powell Band, and Skynyrd's Bassyst
- Seeing film *Sweet Home Alabama*
- Whatever they do, incorporating Confederate flag into it
- Singing songs about the Southland until brother-in-law Delbert comes to arrest them again
- Going to Six Flags Birmingham, riding Jack Daniel's 25th Anniversary Skynyrd Skreemin' Skyryde
- Workin' for MCA Heating & Plumbing

the ONION®
America's Finest News Source.™

Herman Ulysses Zweibel
Founder

T. Herman Zweibel
Publisher Emeritus
J. Phineas Zweibel
Publisher
Maxwell Prescott Zweibel
Editor-In-Chief

Just Wait 'Til I Get These Fucking Rubber Bands Off

Oh, man. You just caught yourself a whole mess of trouble, pal. Believe it. I don't think you realize who you're dealing with here. You might have me in the tank for now, but just wait 'til I get these fucking rubber bands off.

By Freddie The Lobster

That was some cheap move, capturing me in some trap. You didn't have the guts to come looking for me yourself, 'cause you know you wouldn't last five minutes in the depths where I live. But you knew exactly what would make me come sniffing around, and you set me up good. Well, chalk one up for you, mister, and enjoy it, 'cause it's the only one you're gonna get.

Come on. Take the fucking rubber bands off, I fucking dare you. Just the left one, the one on my little claw. I'll make you wish you were never born.

I know what you think of me. I disgust you. You don't like my kind. I'm a bottom feeder, no better than a cockroach. "You should see how they live, what they eat," you say. "They use those claws mostly on each other, fighting over the women. And their

Pound for pound, you just bit off more than you could chew. Better take off that fancy dinner jacket, pal. We're going at it hammer and tongs, you and me. And when the steam clears, there's only gonna be one of us moving.

brains are tiny." Well, I'll tell you one thing: My brains are a hell of a lot bigger than your balls, you trap-using pussy.

And they say we're the spineless ones.

You thought you were in control, but now you're not so sure. Can you really afford to do this? Am I going to be more trouble than I'm worth? Well, pally, it's gonna be a hell of a lot of work, I guarantee you that. More than you've ever had for a piece of tail. You thought you wanted the biggest and best, but now you're realizing that, pound for pound, you just bit off more than you could chew. Better take off that fancy dinner jacket, pal. We're going at it hammer and tongs, you and me. And when the steam clears, there's only gonna be one of us moving.

Come on. Take the fucking rubber bands off, I fucking dare you. Just the left one, the one on my little claw. I'll make you wish you were never born.

So come on. Take the rubber bands off. Take them off, Mr. Fancy. I'm feeling salty. Mano a mano, sucker. Let's go.

Leaving them on, huh? I knew it. I knew you were too big a coward to square off with me on a level playing field. And giving me to your woman to play with first! That takes the cake. Say, is that supposed to be me on your bib? It better fucking not be. I've never worn a fruity mustache or a fucking chef's hat in my life. Or rubber bands, either. I'd kill you with my two bare claws, if only I had the chance.

I don't know why you dragged me and those other guys in here. I'm sure you had your reasons. Maybe that's how you get your kicks—lure us in, set the table for a nice night, then get things simmering. You turn the heat up gradually, figuring we might not even notice at first. Then, you think, we'll show our true colors, maybe even squeal. Well, I ain't never gonna squeal. And I might get steamed, but I'll never get soft. You better have some special stuff if you want to crack me. I don't crack easy. And you won't hear a peep outta me no matter what you do. That story's for the sob sisters and the tourists.

I'm giving you one last chance. We can do this the gentlemanly way, both of us with our appendages free, or we can do it the ugly way. You wanna see things get ugly? Because I promise that they will if you come anywhere near me with those tongs. Rubber bands or no rubber bands, you are going down, buddy. I am one bad example of my type, and it won't be me in deep dip when this is all over.

Oh, you asshole. You gutless pansy. You can bite my ass. Ø

Frat-Guy Boyfriend Not Like The Other Frat Guys

LAWRENCE, KS—According to University of Kansas sophomore Christine Errico, boyfriend and Sigma Epsilon member Troy Ausmus is "totally different" from the typical fraternity member.

"Most frat guys can be pretty obnoxious, especially around women," said Errico, 19. "But Troy's not like that at all. If one of his brothers makes some lewd comment or something, Troy will tell him to cool it when I'm around. Even though he still parties pretty hard, he almost always sets aside one night a week just for us."

"Even though he still parties pretty hard, he almost always sets aside one night a week just for us," Errico said.

Errico and Ausmus met on Sept. 27 at a Sigma Epsilon mixer and "immediately clicked."

"I was really thinking of not dating frat guys anymore," Errico said. "But then I met Troy in line for the keg, and he was just so funny, cute, and nice that I couldn't help but be attracted to him."

Unlike most fraternity men Errico has met, Ausmus seems to know exactly what he wants to do in life.

"Most frat guys don't have any direction," Errico said. "But Troy is a business major, and he's totally serious about getting out in the real world and having a career that will make him a lot of money. He's always talking about stuff he wants to get, like a Beemer, a house on the beach, and a plasma-screen TV. I just know he's going to do really well after college. Most of Troy's brothers want the same stuff, but they're too lazy. Troy totally has his head on straight. He even already has some connections lined up with some Sig Ep alums."

Errico said Ausmus further defies the frat-guy stereotype by not fearing commitment.

"Most frat guys just want to get drunk and get laid," Errico said. "Troy told me that even though he used to chase after any drunken skank at a party, those days are long gone. He's looking for something a little deeper."

Also separating Ausmus from his fellow Greeks, Errico said, is the fact that he did not pressure her to have sex the night they met.

"Troy walked me home to make sure I was safe, because I was pretty trashed, but he didn't even try to get me into bed," Errico said. "That's when I knew he was different. He said later that he didn't try anything because I'd puked all over myself on the way home, but I know better."

Above: Errico and Ausmus.

Other Sigma Epsilon members agreed that Ausmus is a great guy who is clearly unlike the other frat guys.

"Troy's cool," fraternity brother Marcus Glynn said. "He's totally down for whatever: He can put away the vodka like nobody's business, and if there's chicks to mack on, he's there. Wait—did you say Troy Schultz or Troy Ausmus? Actually, I guess it doesn't matter. They're both kinda like that."

Sigma Epsilon president Todd Bohnert had similarly high praise for Ausmus.

"Troy's a total player," Bohnert said. "These days, it's some chick named, I think, Christine. He's always talking about what a great lay she is and all the crazy shit she likes to do in bed. He's so smooth, it's sick. He knows exactly what they want to hear." ⌀

NEWS IN BRIEF

Vacationer Checks Weather Report For Hometown

SAN FRANCISCO—Vacationing with her husband Tuesday, Judy Keck, 34, scanned *The San Francisco Examiner* over breakfast, looking for news about the weather in her hometown of Norfolk, VA, some 2,700 miles away. "Looks like it's starting to get nippy there," Keck said of the coastal Virginia city she will not return to for 10 days. "Bummer about the drizzling." Upon returning to her hotel room, Keck turned on The Weather Channel to check Norfolk's extended five-day forecast.

Hippie Very Involved In Hippie Non-Sports

AUSTIN, TX—According to acquaintances of the 22-year-old hippie, Chad Beresford is a frequent participant in hacky sack, frisbee, and other hippie non-sports. "Chad's way into all that stuff: juggling, devil sticks, and yo-yo tricks," friend Aimee Kolkos said Tuesday. "From stilt-walking to unicycling, there isn't a non-competitive, stoner-friendly quasi-non-sport he hasn't tried."

Teen Anxious For Cigarette Addiction To Kick In

EVANSVILLE, IN—Ashleigh Davis, 14, who started smoking three weeks ago, "can't wait" for her cigarette addiction to kick in. "Right now, I'm smoking, like, four or five cigarettes a day, but I definitely don't feel like I'm hooked yet," Davis said Tuesday. "That's gonna be so cool when the nicotine kicks in, and I have to, like, sneak out of restaurants and stuff for a fix."

Tract Writer Cites God, Jack Chick As Influences

STILLWATER, OK—Robert Welton, founder and sole employee of Inspired Word Christian Tracts, cites God and Jack Chick as the two biggest influences on his work. "God is the one I owe the most to. Everything I write draws on something of His," Welton, 44, told reporters Tuesday. "But Jack Chick, he showed the tract-writing world how to do it. Everything from *This Was Your Life* to *Sin Busters* to the ongoing Bible Tract series are pretty much the gold standard." Welton added that Mohammed and Buddha are in their graves, but Christ's grave is empty.

Director's Commentary For *One Night At McCool's* Trails Off After 20 Minutes

LOS ANGELES—Director Harald Zwart's commentary track on the recently released *One Night At McCool's* DVD trails off after 20 minutes, sources reported Tuesday. "This scene, I remember... we set things up to... look right and all, but I, well... you know..." Zwart said some 18 minutes into the track. "This, uh..." The remainder of the commentary features long stretches of silence, occasionally broken by coughing or throat-clearing.

Former Couple To Remain Friends Until One Finds New Sex Partner

MCMINNVILLE, OR—Bryce Tornquist and Stephanie Herrick, whose three-year relationship ended in August, are remaining close friends until one of them finds a new sex partner. "We still have a lot in common, and it's really nice to have someone around who knows you so well," the 26-year-old Tornquist said Tuesday. "So, until one of us is having sex with somebody else, it really works out for both of us." Tornquist added that he really, really hopes to be the one to find a new sex partner first. ⌀

INDIA from page 7

80 percent of her gross domestic product. Figure in our continuing conflicts with Pakistan, and you can see why I was so passionately devoted to this project."

In addition to imagining access to

The team spent a majority of the past three years developing the top-secret plan, dubbed the Manhattan Or Maybe London Project, overlooking no details.

modern scientific equipment and adequate funding for his research, physicist Dr. Kolluru Sree Krishna theorized what it would be like to live in a country without a caste system.

"Facts and figures point to many new opportunities for me and my family," said Krishna, as he loaded his possessions into boxes in preparation for his move to Boston, where he will teach at MIT. "Though India is a democracy, the will of the largely uneducated non-voting population has little effect on the decisions of lawmakers, and the bureaucracy put in place by the raj continues to cripple our economy. Correction... *their* economy."

The team spent a majority of the past three years developing the top-secret plan, dubbed the Manhattan Or Maybe London Project, overlooking no details.

"We met some setbacks along the way, such as getting [team member] Amitabha [Patel] out of his contract at the Indian Institute of Technology," Chattopadhyay said. "But our vigilance paid off. Our findings show conclusively that I am going to live in a city where clean, potable water is readily available."

For all their success, the physicists said their project got off to a slow start.

"We simply could not find an answer to our original research question: 'Now, why exactly are we here again?'" said Dr. Prashant Goswami of the Centre for Mathematical Modeling and Computer Simulation. "After months of studying the subsistence-level existence of the average Indian, who lacks modern amenities like electricity and running water and is ever threatened by drought, flood, famine, and disease, we were at a dead end."

The team, however, pressed on.

"As an astro-particle physicist, most of my work is theoretical," Goswami said. "So I applied abstract thinking to the project, imagining a place where I had access to a wealth of goods and services."

Finally, on Oct. 7, the team had a breakthrough.

"I was in Germany talking to Dr. Li

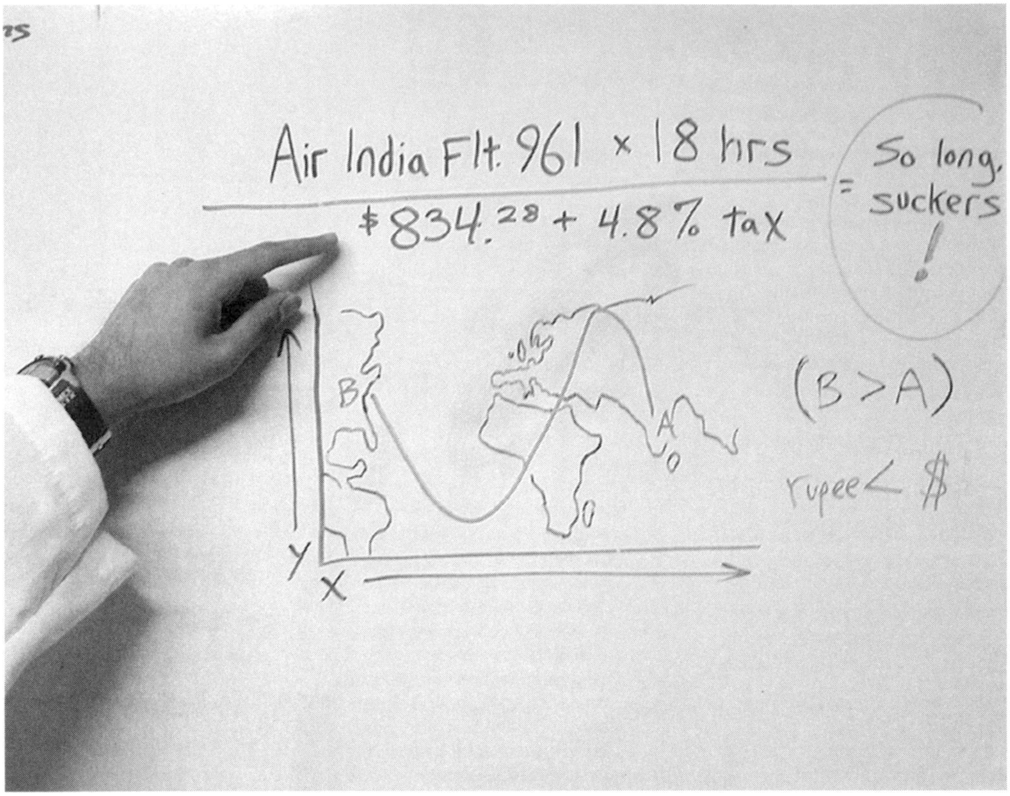

Above: Dr. Amitabha Patel works on an equation.

Hongzhi, a physicist who had moved from China, when it hit me," Chattopadhyay said. "Apply the solution that worked so well for Li to my own problem. I couldn't get through to Amitabha because, as always, the

"We simply could not find an answer to our original research question: 'Now, why exactly are we here again?'"

phones were down in New Delhi, but I knew I had the answer: Get the fuck out. Now."

Upon making the breakthrough in Germany, Chattopadhyay immediately began working 16-hour days to complete additional research in the areas of visa application, airplane tickets, and employment opportunities overseas. He also began gathering data on school districts, as well as cardboard boxes and packing tape.

In spite of their success, Chattopadhyay and the others are not resting on their laurels.

"There still remain many questions I wish to answer," Chattopadhyay said. "Is Nature supersymmetric, and if so, how is supersymmetry broken? Why does the universe appear to have one time and three space dimensions? And do I really have to wait another four weeks to get out of this godforsaken place?"

TUFTED from page 5

amounts of blood. Passersby were amazed by the unusually large amounts of blood. Passersby were amazed by the unusually large

I'm young, ambitious, and hungry for tacos.

amounts of blood. Passersby were amazed by the unusually large amounts of blood. Passersby were amazed by the unusually large amounts of blood. Passersby were amazed by the unusually large amounts of blood. Passersby were amazed by the unusually large amounts of blood. Passersby were amazed by the unusually large amounts of blood. Passersby were amazed by the unusually large amounts of blood. Passersby were amazed by the unusually large amounts of blood. Passersby were amazed by the unusually large amounts of blood. Passersby were amazed by the unusually large amounts of blood. Passersby were amazed by the unusually large amounts of blood.Passersby were

see TUFTED page 64

TEACHER from page 7

tion to math lessons.

"You'd all better get your subtraction down, because next year you're going to need it for long division," said Niles, seeking to quell student chatter during a math lesson. "You're going to be dividing single-digit numbers into three-digit numbers, which requires subtraction, and I know for a fact that Mrs. Shuler is not going to wait for you to catch up on things you should've learned this year."

Niles is also quick to point out the many exciting perks that await the class.

"Next year, you're going to get to hold your own lunch tickets, just like in the upper grades," Niles told her students during a recent lunch period. "Won't that be exciting?"

While Niles occasionally uses the third grade as an intimidation tactic, she also uses it as a reward.

"I really envy you," Niles said after

"Next year, you're going to get to hold your own lunch tickets, just like in the upper grades," Niles told her students during a recent lunch period. "Won't that be exciting?"

her entire class passed a test on Pennsylvania history. "When you get to third grade, you'll get to go see these places we're learning about. You'll get to go to Philadelphia to see the Liberty Bell, and you'll get to learn more about our state's history. Maybe you'll even go to Harrisburg. I know last year's third-graders did."

Even the class pet, a hermit crab named Crabby, has given Niles occasion to describe what lies ahead for her students.

"I know how much you love Crabby," Niles said. "Well, you're all going to love next year, because Mrs. Shuler's class has a gerbil. And how well you care for Crabby this year can make all the difference. If you do really well, you can be the one to take care of the gerbil."

Though most faculty members are indifferent toward Niles' constant talk of the third grade, one teacher is concerned.

"I certainly hope those kids don't come into my class with unreasonable expectations," Shuler said. "I don't want the third grade to become a bogeyman or promised land to these kids. I just want them to come in with good attitudes and open minds, because I have a lot to teach them before they get to the really hard stuff in the fourth grade." ⊘

REAGAN from page 7

speaking before the House Tuesday. "For all he has given this country, this is the least we can give back."

Armey, co-sponsor of HR 3461, the Reagan's Disease Renaming Bill, is

"How fitting it would be to name this disease after Reagan, who has so valiantly battled it since the early 1980s," Andrusko said.

backed by the American Ronald Reagan Recognition Group (ARRRG), a coalition of citizens and business leaders who have championed the cause for more than five years.

"Approximately four million Americans are afflicted with Alzheimer's, and another 37 million know someone suffering from it," said Armey, reading a statement prepared by ARRRG. "To put the name of this great leader on the tips of all these tongues would be a fitting tribute, indeed."

Republicans have already honored Reagan by naming or renaming hundreds of public works—including highways, libraries, parks, hospitals, and federal buildings—after him. In 1998, Washington National Airport was renamed Ronald Reagan Washington National Airport. The following year, construction was completed on the Ronald Reagan International Trade Center, the largest government building in Washington.

"When someone drives past the Ronald W. Reagan Federal Courthouse in Santa Ana or Ronald Reagan High School in San Antonio, they are reminded of the contributions of this great man," ARRRG spokesman James Andrusko said. "How fitting it would be to name this disease after Reagan, who has so valiantly battled it since the early 1980s."

Armey and other GOP lawmakers hope to change the disease's name in time for Reagan's 92nd birthday on Feb. 6, 2003.

"Just as Lou Gehrig's Disease calls to mind the Iron Horse and his legendary achievements on the baseball field, Reagan's Disease will remind Americans of the Great Communicator and his countless achievements in the field of politics," U.S. Sen. Richard Lugar (R-IN) said. "I can't think of an Alzheimer's sufferer more richly deserving of this honor than one of the greatest presidents of all time, Mr. Ronald Wilson Reagan."

"President Reagan may not be capable of understanding this honor," Lugar continued. "But we owe it to him nonetheless."

In 1995, Reagan revealed his fight with Alzheimer's in a letter to the American people, then retired from public life to privately battle the illness.

"Though Reagan first disclosed that he had Alzheimer's in 1995, it's clear that he suffered the onset of the disease long before then," said Dr. Jim Hollis, the president's personal physician. "There is no test to diagnose Alzheimer's in its early stages, so symptoms like memory loss and confusion are often wrongly attributed to normal aging. Obviously, this was the case with Reagan, judging by his behavior during the Iran-Contra hearings."

Hollis said that early symptoms of Alzheimer's, including repetition of statements and mild disorientation, are often subtle. Advanced symptoms, however, are more pronounced, including inability to recall recent major life events, delusions, depression, agitation, hallucinations, belligerence, and violent behavior.

"Reagan," Hollis said. "Definitely Reagan."

According to Alzheimer's Association president Diane Watros, though the name change may result in temporary inconvenience, the group fully supports it.

"This can only help raise awareness, which will, in turn, lead to increases in federal research funding to find a cure," Watros said. "Some may see it as unnecessary and pandering, even a slap in the face to Alois Alzheimer, the scientist who discovered the disease in 1906, but he's dead and long forgotten, unlike The Gipper."

Watros said she hopes the renaming

"President Reagan may not be capable of understanding this honor," Lugar continued. "But we owe it to him nonetheless."

will result in improvements in quality of care for those who suffer from the disease.

"As it is, health-care workers look at an Alzheimer's sufferer and only see someone who can no longer perform such basic functions as eating, dressing, and bathing, someone who spends most of his or her day babbling nonsensically or just staring off blankly into the distance," Watros said. "But in the future, they will look at this same person and be reminded of Ronald Reagan." ⊘

Above: Planes are readied for departure at Reagan National Airport.

COMMUNITY VOICES

I'll Try Anything With A Detached Air Of Superiority

By Christopher Peavey

I'm a pretty sophisticated, well-educated person. I went to Wesleyan, where I got my B.A. in comparative literature. I listen to *This American Life* on NPR. I've traveled abroad fairly extensively and even spent a year living in London. Given all this, you'd think I might be a little staid and stodgy, that I'd shun certain activities because I'm too good for that sort of thing. That is completely untrue. The reality is, I'll try anything with a detached air of superiority.

A few weeks ago, my friend Curtis organized a bowling party for his birthday. Can you imagine anything more tacky and all-American? But, contrary to what you might think, I was more than game for it. I even bought a personalized bowling shirt so I could fit in with the common folk. I only bowled a 76, but I loved it. The people there were so into it, some of them actually did little dances when they got a strike. There was this one guy I called "One-Fist," because after every frame, he'd pump his fist in the air like some blue-collar Billy Idol. Never in my life have I had such a great time participating in townie culture while simultaneously sneering at it from a distance.

A few weeks ago, my friend Curtis organized a bowling party for his birthday. Can you imagine anything more tacky and all-American? But, contrary to what you might think, I was more than game for it. I even bought a personalized bowling shirt so I could fit in with the common folk.

I guess that's just who I am. I'm open to anything, no matter how pedestrian or mainstream it may be. Last year, I decided to dive headfirst into the realm of the unwashed masses by attending a professional football game. What better way to experience the hive mind than by communing with 70,000 drunken, frostbitten Americans who are only too happy to blow their meager wages cheering on their date-raping, steroid-enhanced gridiron heroes? I don't even remember which teams were playing. All I remember is yelling my head off while surrounded by a sea of jersey-wearing telephone repairmen and electricians, all the while thinking, "This is so authentic!"

A true snob would never waste his time with something like that, but I am able to see the charm of my inferiors' sad little diversions.

I must admit, some of the mind-numbingly lame stuff I've exposed myself to has actually grown on me. I used to go to rummage sales for the sociological thrill of seeing commoners eagerly scrounge through their fellow commoners' crude, mass-produced possessions. You'd see all sorts of amusing parts and parcels from people's tiny lives. After a while, though, I started to enjoy finding good bargains. I even began collecting completed Paint-By-Numbers pictures. My favorite so far is a rabbit where the "artist" confused two of the colors, resulting in what I strongly suspect is the world's only purple-eyed hare. A true snob would never waste his time with something like that, but I am able to see the charm of my inferiors' sad little diversions.

When you think about it, it's really the mundane things that make life interesting. Attending pro-wrestling matches, shopping at the mall, riding a Greyhound bus, eating at McDonald's, seeing conventionally crowd-pleasing movies like *My Big Fat Greek Wedding*—such things may seem like lowbrow wastes of time, but they really help one maintain a sense of oneself. If you can do such things and still maintain your sense of haughty superiority, you've done more than merely lived. You've tasted the sickly sweet nectar that life has to offer and said, "I am above this. I am better than this. This is beneath me, but I will still do it because I'm open-minded enough to try anything and look down my nose at it at least once." Ø

HOROSCOPES

Your Horoscope

By Lloyd Schumner Sr.
Retired Machinist and
A.A.P.B.-Certified Astrologer

Aries: (March 21–April 19)
After a grisly incident next week, specialists will need to use your dental records to identify all your cavities.

Taurus: (April 20–May 20)
The forgiveness of the Lord is nigh-infinite. Unfortunately for you, the "nigh" part seems to include animal mutilation, child vandalism, and personal arson.

Gemini: (May 21–June 21)
Just so you know what to tell the doctor: Separation anxiety is not what you feel when all your major joints are separated.

Cancer: (June 22–July 22)
Your natural abilities will be put to good use when you are chosen by leaders of 12 countries to head the U.N. Insecurity Council.

Leo: (July 23–Aug. 22)
Next thing you know, Old Jed's a millionaire, but you'll be damned if you can figure out how he did it.

Virgo: (Aug. 23–Sept. 22)
Your small town will ban all dancing after witnessing your ungainly attempts at that "Ketchup Song" dance.

Libra: (Sept. 23–Oct. 23)
The stars would love to help you realize your cosmic destiny, but they got their copy of Grand Theft Auto: Vice City, and it's freakin' awesome.

Scorpio: (Oct. 24–Nov. 21)
In spite of your complaints about how undignified it was and your repeated professions of shame, you still kind of enjoyed sleeping with the fat girl.

Sagittarius: (Nov. 22–Dec. 21)
A soon-to-be-released university study will show that you are less likely to refuse offers of drugs than anyone in the known universe.

Capricorn: (Dec. 22–Jan. 19)
You will be surprised by the lack of approval you elicit after saying "Don't blame me, I voted for Nader."

Aquarius: (Jan. 20–Feb. 18)
Though Boyle's Third Law is certainly important, you don't need to apply it to every situation you encounter.

Pisces: (Feb. 19–March 20)
The judge will declare a mistrial in your capital-murder case—not for any legal reason, but out of a desire to listen to Lou Reed's *Mistrial*.

KHMER EMPIRE from page 3

amounts of blood. Passersby were amazed by the unusually large amounts of blood. Passersby were amazed by the unusually large amounts of blood. Passersby were amazed by the unusually large amounts of blood. Passersby were amazed by the unusually large amounts of blood. Passersby were amazed by the unusually large amounts of blood. Passersby were amazed by the unusually large amounts of blood. Passersby were amazed by the unusually large amounts of blood. Passersby were amazed by the unusually large amounts of blood. Passersby were amazed by the unusually large amounts of blood. Passersby were amazed by the unusually large amounts of blood. Passersby were amazed by the unusually large amounts of blood. Passersby were amazed by the unusually large amounts of blood. Passersby were amazed by the unusually large amounts of blood. Passersby were amazed by the unusually large amounts of blood. Passersby were amazed by the unusually large amounts of blood. Passersby were amazed by the unusually large amounts of blood. Passersby were amazed by the unusually large amounts of blood. Passersby were amazed by the unusually large

Let us now praise Famous Footwear.

amounts of blood. Passersby were amazed by the unusually large amounts of blood. Passersby were amazed by the unusually large amounts of blood. Passersby were amazed by the unusually large amounts of blood. Passersby were amazed by the unusually large amounts of blood. Passersby were amazed by the unusually large amounts of blood. Passersby were amazed by the unusually large amounts of blood. Passersby were amazed by the unusually large amounts of blood. Passersby were

see KHMER EMPIRE page 31

the ONION®

VOLUME 38 ISSUE 42 AMERICA'S FINEST NEWS SOURCE™ 14–20 NOVEMBER 2002

NEWS

Crude But Functional Starbucks Hewn From Rock Facing

see LOCAL page 5E

Ray Charles Signs Def Leppard Album

see PEOPLE page 9D

Sweatpants-Wearing Man Needs Rolling Papers

see LOCAL page 2E

STATshot

A look at the numbers that shape your world.

What Are We Trapped Under?

1. Poverty line
2. Layers of fat
3. Collapsed sofa-cushion fort
4. Mountain of paperwork (figuratively)
5. Husband's sleeping, sexually spent body
6. Mountain of paperwork (literally)
7. Crushing weight of own incompetence

THE ONION • $2.00 US • $3.00 CAN

Supreme Court Makes Pact To Lose Virginity By End Of Year

WASHINGTON, DC—By an 8-1 vote Monday, the members of the U.S. Supreme Court collectively resolved to lose their virginity by Dec. 31, 2002.

"Whereas neither this judicial body, nor the bodies of any of its nine members, has ever been touched in an intimate manner, it is wholly appropriate for us to become men and women via acts of sexual congress, and this on a deadline described by the completion of the year 2002," wrote Justice Anthony Kennedy, voicing the majority opinion. "The only caveat is: There *are* no caveats."

The pact was first proposed on Oct. 23, when Kennedy and Justice Antonin Scalia were bullied by a coalition of prominent congressional jocks led by Sen. Jim Bunning (R-KY).

"The legislators in question were stepping on our robes and coughing the word 'fag' and carrying out a variety of other acts that, while not unconstitutional, would unequivocally be construed as mean," Kennedy said. "The final straw came when Sen. Susan Collins (R-ME) told me she thought I was cute and said to meet her at the Jefferson Memorial dressed as a cowboy so we could make out."

Above: The court's nine virgins.

After complying with Collins'

see SUPREME COURT page 17

'Beltway Sniper' Video-Game Release Delayed Out Of Respect For Victims

REDWOOD CITY, CA—Video-game developer Pixxel Arts announced Monday that it will delay the release of Beltway Sniper: Silent Strike out of respect for the victims of the recent D.C.-area shootings.

Based on the sniper attacks linked to suspects John Muhammad and John Lee Malvo, Beltway Sniper: Silent Strike was slated to hit store shelves Nov. 15. Last Friday, however, Pixxel top brass made the decision to postpone the game's release until March 2003.

"Upon discussing the matter internally, we decided that it would be inappropriate to unleash the intense sniping action and white-knuckle stealth gameplay of Beltway Sniper at this time," Pixxel Arts president Davis Con-

see VIDEO GAME page 17

Above: A scene from Beltway Sniper: Silent Strike.

Marxists' Apartment A Microcosm Of Why Marxism Doesn't Work

Above: Marxists Kirk Dorff and Josh Foyle.

AMHERST, MA—The filthy, disorganized apartment shared by three members of the Amherst College Marxist Society is a microcosm of why the social and economic utopia described in the writings of Karl Marx will never come to fruition, sources reported Monday.

"The history of society is the inexorable history of class struggle," said sixth-year undergraduate Kirk Dorff, 23, resting his feet on a coffee table cluttered with unpaid bills, crusted cereal bowls, and bongwater-stained socialist pamphlets. "The stage is set for the final struggle between the bourgeoisie and the proletariat, the true productive class. We're well aware of that here at 514 W. Elm Street, unlike other apartments on this supposedly intellectual campus."

Upon moving in together at the beginning of the fall 2001 semester, Dorff, Josh Foyle, and Tom Eaves sat down and devised an egalitarian system for harmonious living. Each individual roommate would be assigned a task, which he would be required to carry out on a predetermined day of the week. A bulletin

see MARXISM page 16

Republicans Take The Senate

In last Tuesday's midterm elections, Republicans retook the U.S. Senate, giving them control of both houses of Congress. What do *you* think?

"You know, they say people get the government they deserve, but I don't recall knife-raping any retarded nuns."

Jared Andruss
Shipping Clerk

"I'm confused. It was my understanding that the Democrats had already rolled over and died after Sept. 11."

Elaine Dorner
Speech Pathologist

"Don't blame me, I voted for the Green Party. Hee hee hee! Aren't I the dickens?"

Melissa Kendall
Student

"The American people have spoken. And they have said, 'Duhhh, I likes chockomut ice cream.'"

Rodney Garn
Systems Analyst

"On the bright side, the Democrats did triumphantly retake the Kansas governorship."

Thom Abboud
Cashier

"Gosh, that election really sucked. Well, at least it'll probably be the last one we ever have."

Raymond Thatcher
Architect

Winona Ryder's Probation

Last week, Winona Ryder was convicted of shoplifting $5,500 worth of merchandise from a Beverly Hills Saks Fifth Avenue. What are the terms of her probation?

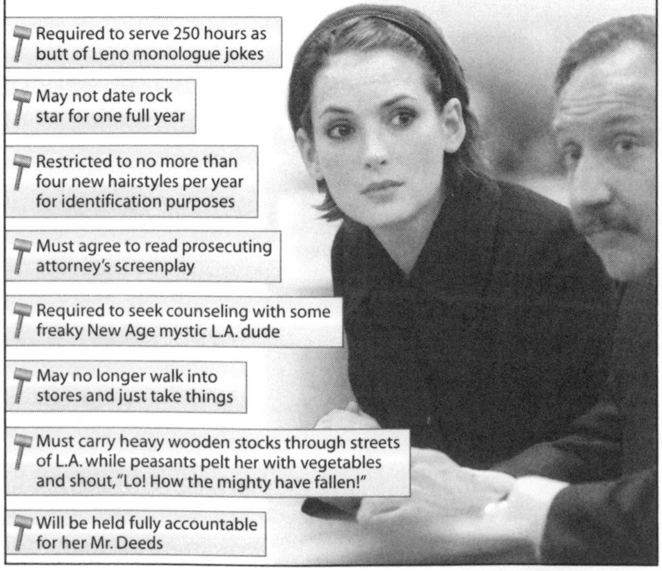

- Required to serve 250 hours as butt of Leno monologue jokes
- May not date rock star for one full year
- Restricted to no more than four new hairstyles per year for identification purposes
- Must agree to read prosecuting attorney's screenplay
- Required to seek counseling with some freaky New Age mystic L.A. dude
- May no longer walk into stores and just take things
- Must carry heavy wooden stocks through streets of L.A. while peasants pelt her with vegetables and shout, "Lo! How the mighty have fallen!"
- Will be held fully accountable for her Mr. Deeds

the ONION®
America's Finest News Source.™
Herman Ulysses Zweibel
Founder
T. Herman Zweibel
Publisher Emeritus
J. Phineas Zweibel
Publisher
Maxwell Prescott Zweibel
Editor-In-Chief

Depends Ain't So Damn Dependable

By Lenny Gramsched

Lately, I've been getting pretty tired of having to change my pants constantly. It's no fun having to go put on a pair of fresh trousers every time a dog barks or a door slams too loud.

So, the other day, I was watching TV in the nursing home's rec room when one of those Depends commercials came on. You know, the ones with the happy-looking gray-haired couples riding bicycles. They seemed to really be enjoying the diapers, so, figuring it was worth a shot, I headed over to the local Walgreens and picked myself up a 12-pack.

When I got back to the senior center, I strapped a pair on, and at first, it seemed pretty promising: Snug around the legs with plenty of room for cargo in the back, the Depends felt like they just might be the answer to my troubles.

But I quickly found out that Depends ain't so damn dependable. I don't know what those confounded things are made of, but I didn't have them on more than 30 minutes before they fell halfway to my knees, sopping wet and stained the color of lemonade.

I was more than a little irate. After all, I could have spent that money on Brach's sourballs or a new *TV Guide*. My mind set on a full refund and no

I started having major problems with the Depends on Friday, which is taco day at the nursing home.

less, I headed straight back to the Walgreens.

After a barrage of questions that, I must say, were very personal, the lady at the photo-finishing counter determined that I had put on the Depends incorrectly. She said I was supposed to have the plastic side with the wetness-check strips on the outside, not the inside.

For the next few days, her advice seemed to do the trick: With my new-found understanding of how to properly put on the undergarment, I was able to successfully manipulate the various straps, buttons, and sticky strips each morning and be worry-free until sometime in the middle of the day. At that point, I simply had to remove the diaper, its innards loaded down with waste materials but its outside dry and shiny, and toss it into the garbage. Then I simply replaced it with a fresh one from my late wife's macramé bag, and presto, I was set through the start of the CBS prime-time line-up.

Unfortunately, the smooth sailing did not last: I started having major problems with the Depends on Friday, which is taco day at the nursing home. While they had worked fine on

When I got back to the senior center, I strapped a pair on, and at first, it seemed pretty promising: Snug around the legs with plenty of room for cargo in the back, the Depends felt like they just might be the answer to my troubles.

typical "light flow" days—three urinations at five-hour intervals and a small defecation in the evening—they were not equipped to handle a Friday load, which is almost always much heavier, what with my difficulties digesting meat.

An hour after a nice lunch consisting of a taco, fruit cup, and scooter pie, the trouble began. I barely made it back to my room when I felt a warm, spongy feeling creeping down my leg. Sure enough, on my good dress slacks, there was a yellow line running from my privates to my slippers, with an enormous brown circle in the back. Apparently, the Depends' safety straps had collapsed under the weight of what I consider to be merely a medium-sized defecation.

Furious, I marched right back into the Walgreens and demanded my money back, placing the offending article on the checkout counter, thoughtfully placed inside a Denny's doggie-bag I'd been saving under my bed. After some discussion, the store manager agreed to give me my refund, and I left with my $8.99 in hand.

I will shop at Walgreens again, because I feel they have a good return policy—within 14 days with receipt and your full money back—but I'll tell you this: You'll never catch me diaper-shopping in the "adult needs" section again. Me and Depends, we're through. Ø

LOCAL

Area Man Buying Not So Much A Soft Drink As An Image

SOUTHFIELD, MI—In a move Coca-Cola marketing executives called "a clear sign of our branding success," highway worker Chuck Burdon, 37, purchased a two-liter Diet Coke during his lunch break Tuesday, buying not so much a soft drink as an image.

"Let me tell you, I was mighty thirsty after all that paving," a refreshed Burdon told reporters. "Yet on a subconscious, psychological level, I wanted more than mere rehydration or refreshment. I craved an image. I craved being imbued with the sort of fun, carefree spirit seen in Diet Coke commercials. I also wished to feel like I was part of a larger community of discriminating, likeminded consumers who have the good taste to choose the world's most widely consumed diet cola and not some inferior, lower-priced off-brand."

Standing in the soda aisle of a supermarket near the construction site, Burdon was confronted with a vast array of soft-drink choices, each projecting its own distinct image for consumers to identify with and project onto themselves through the acts of purchase and consumption.

Standing in the soda aisle of a supermarket near the construction site, Burdon was confronted with a vast array of soft-drink choices, each projecting its own distinct image for consumers to identify with and project onto themselves through the acts of purchase and consumption. According to Burdon, key to his decision to choose Diet Coke was the memory of a 1994 television spot featuring model-actor Lucky Vanous as a construction worker who excites young, single women by shirtlessly consuming a can of the soft drink.

"Back when that ad was on TV, me and the other construction workers made a lot of jokes about it," Burdon said. "I think my purchase was partially motivated by a desire to recapture the relative whimsy of those days before Allied Construction owner Bud Wanamaker died and the new owners mismanaged it into the ground. That, as well as the more basic desire to liken myself to the sexy Vanous via our mutual enjoyment of Diet Coke."

Burdon freely admitted that image was more of a motivating factor than the needs of his parched body.

"To be honest, selecting a caffeinated drink ran counter to my physical needs at the time, given the diuretic effects of caffeine," Burdon said. "If my only goal were rehydration, I would have done better with Gatorade or Sprite or, at the very least, Caffeine-Free Diet Coke. Or, I suppose, tap water."

Above: Burdon with the soft drink whose branding image most strongly resonates with him.

Despite the negative side effects of caffeine, particularly for a manual laborer, Burdon said he is averse to consuming caffeine-free soft drinks.

"To appear on the construction site drinking a beverage that is both calorie- and caffeine-free would be an emasculating blow to my carefully cultivated image as a burly, rough-and-tumble working-class type," Burdon said. "The sight of me consuming such a soft drink would diminish the respect I enjoy from my professional peer group by casting a light of skepticism upon my masculinity and even

see SOFT DRINK page 16

NEWS IN BRIEF

Teen Newsweek Reports North Korea Is The Bomb

NEW YORK—According to the new issue of *Teen Newsweek*, a fledgling *Newsweek* spin-off aimed at younger readers, North Korea is the bomb. "An in-depth investigation of Pyongyang's shopping and recreational options has provided incontrovertible evidence that North Korea is, like, totally the bomb, from its delicious food to its way-inexpensive electronics," *Teen Newsweek* reported. It remains unknown how the nation came to possess bomb-being technology.

Senator Mix-A-Lot Sponsors Titties-On-Glass Legislation

WASHINGTON, DC—Seeking to stem a four-year decline in freaky Yolandas throwing they titties on U.S. glass, U.S. Sen. Mix-A-Lot (B-WA) introduced sweeping new putting-'em-on-glass legislation Tuesday. "Now listen up, Uncle Sam / I wanna see soul sistas pressin' that ham / Make me say damn / I wanna rear-end 'em / So I'm callin' a Senate referendum / Bounce by the ounce don't make no fun / I'll take 'em by the ton, son," Mix-A-Lot said. "Don't hand this bill down to no committees / 'Cause Mix don't wait on monster titties / Note to my colleague Tom Daschle / That if the babies be gettin' bashful / No melons droppin' on my windshield / So get them nudie laws repealed." Mix-A-Lot then gave props to the authors of H.R. 1610, from which several key clauses were sampled.

History Channel Admits To Profiting From Nazi Documentaries

NEW YORK—The History Channel confessed Monday that it used Nazi footage to fatten its coffers. "The time has come to bring our network's shameful legacy to light," History Channel president Warren Brabender said. "Over the past 10 years, more than $300 million in ad revenue has been generated through the airing of Nazi documentaries." The channel will likely be required to pay reparations to Americans who viewed the atrocities.

Christian Slater Dropped From List Of Names To Drop

HOLLYWOOD, CA—Citing a rapidly lowering profile, the National Name Drop Index announced the removal of actor Christian Slater from the list of celebrity names to casually reference Tuesday. "Taking into account his lack of major roles since 1998's *Very Bad Things* and the flaccid box office of last year's *Windtalkers*, we have no choice but to classify Slater's name as undroppable until further notice," NNDI director Don Hall said. "Until Slater gains at least a supporting role in a hit feature or a lead role in a TV series, he is relegated to Dean Cain Memorial Limbo."

Upper-Middle-Class Woman Worries There's Better Coffee She Doesn't Know About

DEERFIELD, IL—Upper-middle-class homemaker Irene Risser expressed fear Monday that there exists a gourmet coffee superior to the brands she currently buys. "I have Kona Coffee's peaberry flavor, which is really terrific, and I also like to buy Sumatran Rainforest," Risser said. "But I still worry that somewhere out there, someone has better, more expensive coffee than I do." Risser then went on the Internet to search for $25-a-pound breakfast blends. Ø

MARXISM from page 13

board in the kitchen was chosen as the spot for household announcements, and to track reimbursements for common goods like toothpaste and toilet paper.

"We were creating an exciting new model for living," said Dorff, stubbing his cigarette into an ashtray that had not been emptied in six days. "It was like we were dismantling the apparatus of the state right within our own living space."

In spite of the roommates' optimism, the system began to break down soon after its establishment. To settle disputes, the roommates held weekly meetings of the "Committee of Three."

"I brought up that I thought it was total bullshit that I'm, like, the only one who ever cooks around here, yet I have to do the dishes, too," said Foyle, unaware of just how much the apartment underscores the infeasibility of scientific socialism as outlined in *Das Kapital*. "So we decided that if I cook, someone else has to do the dishes. We were going to rotate bathroom-cleaning duty, but then Kirk kept skipping his week, so we had to give him the duty of taking out the garbage instead. But now he has a class on Tuesday nights, so we switched that with the mopping."

After weeks of complaining that he was the only one who knew how to clean "halfway decent," Foyle began scaling back his efforts, mirroring the sort of production problems experienced in the U.S.S.R. and other Soviet bloc nations.

The roommates have also tried to implement a food-sharing system, with similarly poor results. The dream of equal distribution of shared goods quickly gave way to pilferage, misallocation, and hoarding.

At an Oct. 7 meeting of the Committee of Three, more duties and a point system were added. Two months later, however, the duty chart is all but forgotten and the shopping list is several pages long.

The roommates have also tried to implement a food-sharing system, with similarly poor results. The dream of equal distribution of shared goods quickly gave way to pilferage, misallocation, and hoarding.

"I bought the peanut butter the first four times, and this Organic Farms shit isn't cheap," Eaves said. "So ever since, I've been keeping it in my dresser drawer. If Kirk wants to make himself a sandwich, he can run to the corner store and buy some Jif."

Another failed experiment involves the cigarettes bought collectively. Disagreements constantly arose over who smoked more than his fair share of the group's supply of American Spirit Blues, and the roommates now hide individually purchased packs from each other—especially late at night, when shortages are frequent.

The situation is familiar to Donald Browning, author of *Das Kouch: A History Of College Marxism, 1970-1998.*

"When workers willfully become less productive, the economy of the household suffers," Browning said. "But in a society where a range of ability naturally exists, someone is bound to object to picking up the slack for others and end up getting all pissy, like Josh does."

According to Browning, the group's lack of productivity pervades their lives, with roommates encouraging each other to skip class or work to sit on the couch smoking pot and talking politics.

"A spirit of free-market competition in the house would likely result in better incomes or better grades," Browning said. "Then, instead of being hated and ostracized by the world at large as socialist countries usually are, they could maintain effective diplomacy with their landlord, their parents, and Kirk's boss who cut back his hours at Shaman Drum Books."

"I bought the peanut butter the first four times, and this Organic Farms shit isn't cheap," Eaves said.

The lack of funds and the resulting scarcity breeds not only discontent, but also corruption. Although collectivism only works when all parties contribute to the fullest extent, Foyle hid the existence of a $245 paycheck from roommates so he would not have to pay his back rent, in essence refusing to participate in the forced voluntary taxation that is key to socialism. Even worse, Dorff, who is entrusted with bill collection and payment, recently pocketed $30, a theft he claimed was "for the heating bill" but was put toward buying drinks later that night.

"As is human nature, power tends to corrupt even the noblest of men," Browning said. "The more power the collective has over the lives of the individuals, as is the case in this household, the more he who is in charge of distribution has to gain by being unscrupulous. These Marxists will soon realize they overestimated how much control they would like 514 W. Elm as an entity to have." Ø

Above: Dishes and seminal Marxist tracts pile up in the kitchen sink.

SOFT DRINK from page 15

my sexuality."

Moments before making his purchasing decision, Burdon said he was almost swayed by the memory of a Diet Coke With Lemon billboard featuring an attractive woman puckering her lips. In the end, however, he rejected the soda for similar gender-identity reasons.

"I must admit that my desire to associate myself with such a woman was a powerful temptation," Burdon said. "Nevertheless, the perception of diet soda, an already somewhat feminine product, infused with lemon flavor signified on the packaging by the girlish color yellow, was a bit too rife with feminine overtones for my purposes. I felt that I would be more likely to attract such a woman by reinforcing my masculinity with a lemonless soft drink than by drinking the same female-oriented beverage as her."

Though Burdon spotted a bottle of Pepsi Blue, a drink he greatly enjoyed upon first tasting it in a Safeway parking lot in August, he ruled out the beverage as a possibility for at-work consumption.

"Drinking an adolescent-targeted, convention-flouting, candy-colored fantasia beverage like Pepsi Blue would paint me as an aging and pathetic man desperate to appear youthful and virile," Burdon said. "From its flavor blend to the cheekily angular lettering on the label, Pepsi Blue projects an image far too cutting-edge and impudently rebellious to convincingly mesh with the reality of my 37-year-old self. I purchase soft drinks to identify with a somewhat realistic lifestyle archetype, not retreat into an outright delusional fantasy." Ø

VIDEO GAME from page 13

way said. "Out of respect for the victims of this horrific killing spree and their loved ones, we are delaying release of the mind-blowing first-person shooter until early next year."

According to Rich Koslow, editor of GamePro magazine, Beltway Sniper:

"I had a chance to play it myself at Pixxel's offices, and it's as close as you can come to real-life experience short of actually being Muhammad or Malvo himself," Koslow said.

Silent Strike was expected to be one of the hottest video-game releases of the holiday season. Available for Nintendo Gamecube, PlayStation 2, Xbox, and PC, the game enables players to wander through an ultra-realistic suburban D.C. landscape shooting innocent passersby.

"Beltway Sniper is everything you've heard and more," Koslow said. "I recently had a chance to play it myself at Pixxel's offices, and it's as close as you can come to real-life experience short of actually being Muhammad or Malvo himself."

In spite of the strong buzz surrounding the game, Conway said Pixxel Arts is committed to holding off releasing Beltway Sniper "until the wounds from the tragedy have begun to heal." He stressed that the delay has nothing to do with any problems with the game itself.

"I want people to understand that

Above: A Pixxel representative demonstrates Beltway Sniper at a recent video-game-industry convention.

the delay is strictly a product of our deep and profound compassion for those affected by this tragedy," Conway said. "The game itself is ready to go and, believe me, it more than delivers: The mind-blowing, fully rendered 3-D graphics feature both first- and third- person modes, and the special SneakScope View enables players to track their targets with deadly precision while still keeping an eye out for police. Once enough time has passed and we as a nation have put these events behind us, I am confident that gamers will find the strength to move on to more than 20 thrilling levels of stealth-shooter action."

Though disappointed by the delay, software programmers at Pixxel Arts said they fully support the decision.

"This was clearly the right thing to do—it's just too soon," programmer Russell Sperber said. "No one is ready for the realistic wound-channel modeling or rifle-bullet ballistics right now, but by the time March rolls around, they'll go nuts over it. That and the unlockable extra levels, the 'Create A Cryptic Note' feature, and the 'Play As The Cops' mode. And, of course, we'll be expanding the Create-A-Sniper feature, in which you can put yourself or your friends in a tree outside a strip-mall parking lot and take aim at the customers exiting such stores as Ponderosa, T.J. Maxx, and Jo-Ann Fabrics."

As new details of the sniper case unfold, Pixxel Arts has agreed to work in tandem with D.C.-area law enforcement.

"We've been in regular communication with the various police forces involved in the case," Conway said. "They've been very helpful, both with regard to how to respectfully approach this event and how to make the gameplay as realistic as humanly possible. In situations like this, it's crucial that you do things right."

Conway said that a percentage of the profits from sales of Beltway Sniper would be donated to the victims' families. Ø

SUPREME COURT from page 13

request, Kennedy was ambushed and pelted with eggs by several assailants, including Collins herself, who walked off holding hands with Rep. Tom Osborne (R-NE).

"She laughed and said, 'So long, virgin! Have a nice night with Mr. Right Hand,'" Kennedy said. "After that, I decided I'd had enough. It was time to take action."

The court decided to move forward with the pact later that evening when, during a late-night bonding session, Chief Justice William Rehnquist admitted to being a virgin—shattering longtime perceptions that he is the worldliest and most experienced member of the court.

"Hearing that Big Willie had never buried the gavel was a key turning point," Justice David Souter said. "It opened up our eyes and made us see how we were not alone, after all. After a period of deliberation, we arrived at a majority opinion that if we all worked together, we could overcome our nervousness and actually get laid."

"Hey, everybody!" Souter added. "We're all gonna get laid!"

The lone dissenting vote, cast by Justice Ruth Bader Ginsburg, came as a surprise to many, given her long track record of defending personal liberties. *Washington Post* judicial reporter James Klingler theorized that the vote may represent an attempt on Ginsburg's part to prevent Scalia from coupling with another woman.

"I'm not at liberty to name names, but a certain Supreme Court justice recently informed me that Ginsburg confided in her that she 'totally loves' Scalia," Klingler said. "This, I believe, is the reason she voted against the pact. But while on its surface this pact would seem to drive Ginsburg and Scalia further apart, it may well be the very thing that brings them together. Perhaps during a particularly long and difficult get-laid strategy session, Justice Ginsburg will remove her glasses and rub her tired eyes, prompting Justice Scalia to finally see the beautiful woman beneath that hard liberal exterior."

The first major test case for the pact will take place this weekend at a Judicial Branch/Daughters of the American Revolution mixer, which Justice John Paul Stevens said will be attended by some "really slutty girls" he knows from law school.

"Hearing that Big Willie had never buried the gavel was a key turning point," Justice David Souter said. "It opened up our eyes and made us see how we were not alone, after all."

"Under penalty of perjury, I swear to God, there is this one chick who is completely hot for Souter," Stevens said. "She personally attested to this fact during a conversation I recently overheard that I am not at liberty to discuss in any detail. Saturday is his night, man."

Subsequent opportunities are expected to arise at a pool party Supreme Court Marshal Pamela Talkin is slated to throw at the Alexandria Radisson over Thanksgiving break, as well as at the Judicial Branch Big Beach Bonfire on Dec. 14.

Stephen "Pee-Wee" Breyer, the most recently sworn-in justice, reported being nervous about the impending virginity loss. A close confidant, speaking on condition of anonymity, said that a trembling Breyer recently asked him, "Gee, getting it on with a real girl—what do I do?"

Not all of the justices admit to being so nervous, however. Asked to assess his prospects for losing his virginity within the next two months, a confident Scalia lifted his judicial robe and quipped, "*Res ipsa loquitur.*" Ø

Sarah Jessica Gives 'Birth In The City'!

Item! Call it Birth In The City! Or Sex In The Nursery! But whichever word you choose to alter in the title of the show, **Sarah Jessica Parker** and hubby **Matthew "Wargames" Broderick** had themselves a baby! According to my sources, the blessed newborn is named **Bueller Bradshaw Bloom Broderick**.

The Outside Scoop
By Jackie Harvey

Whew, there's a mouthful! Congratulations to the happy couple, and let's hope the little guy has the acting gene that makes his parents so entertaining to watch. One thing's for sure, though: We'll all be closely watching what Mom dresses the little fella in.

It's a whole new TV season, and Tinseltown wonderman **David E. Kelly** has done it again! For those of us who felt it deeply when Fox took **Ally McBeal** away from us, Kelly has whipped up a trio of litigious cuties. And, boy, do these Kelly girls have spunk! The show, called **girls time** (hey, I know it should be capitalized, but try telling Mr. Michelle Phifer that!), is sweet, sassy, sexy, and poised to take TV by storm, mark my words!

Item! They made another installment of **The Bachelor**, and I wasn't told? If I had known, I would have put my name at the top of the list of eligible bachelors to be considered for the show. I'll have to keep an eye on the ABC web site to register for the next one.

One thing that hasn't done very well is the new **Madonna** movie, **Swept**

If Sadaam Hussaine has weapons of mass destruction, we have to stamp him out, because he is an enemy of freedom. It is our job as the wealthiest democracy to ensure the safety of the world. I don't usually like to get political, but there's my two cents.

Away. In it, she plays a rich woman shipwrecked on a desert island with an Italian. Why did it tank, you ask? Well, it couldn't have been Madonna, since everything she touches, from **Shanghai Surprise** to **Dick Tracy**, has turned to star-studded gold. And it couldn't have been director hubby **Richie Guy**, whose first movie **Lock Stock & Barreled** was so good he made it again as **Snitch**. Hollywood, brace yourself, because it's time for a **Harvey wake-up call**! Now, you'll have to excuse me for being "politically incorrect" here, but I don't think Middle America is ready for interracial relationships yet.

I've been thinking about getting a **kitten**. I just want to share the huge amounts of love I have, and it seems like a kitten would be the perfect thing.

I was going to talk about the MTV Video Music Awards, but I forgot everything that happened during them. M&M was on, and he yelled at a puppet. Beyond that, it's all a blur.

Will we or won't we? That's the question on everyone's minds these days. Specifically, are we going to invade Iraq or not? If **Sadaam Hussaine** has weapons of mass destruction, we have to stamp him out, because he is an enemy of freedom. It is our job as the wealthiest democracy to ensure the safety of the world. I don't usually like to get political, but there's my two cents.

Call me crazy, but I've always preferred **canned peaches** to the **fresh ones**.

Pinch me, I've died and gone to diva heaven! All in a few weeks, we've gotten albums from **Faith Hill**, **LeAnn Rhymes**, **Whitney Houston**, **Shania "Mutt" Twaine**, **Mariah Carrey**, and **Jennifer "Left Eye" Lopez**. Hoo, boy, I hope I'm not forgetting anyone. Those divas can sure get fiery if they're shorted. And with all those albums to buy, there goes my mad money for the next few weeks.

Speaking of music, I've been hearing a lot about this **Napster** thing, where you download songs off the Internet without paying a penny. Well, I think that's just wrong.

Is **Robert De Niro** a busy guy or what? He's been in two movies this year, and **Analyze The Other Thing** is coming up in a few weeks, which I can't wait for, because I always wondered what happened to those characters after the first movie, and I can't ever get enough of **Billy Crystal**. Plus, the Harvey grapevine is buzzing with plenty more De Niro movies to come, including a turn as a mobster and one as a cop.

I was going to talk about the **MTV Video Music Awards**, but I forgot everything that happened during them. **M&M** was on, and he yelled at a puppet. Beyond that, it's all a blur.

Item! It's the trial of the century! All eyes are on **Celebrity Justice** (a new court show I can't get enough of) to see what's going to happen in the **Winona Ryder** shoplifting trial. The case has so many twists and turns, it's a miracle she doesn't get whiplash. And the starpower doesn't stop at the defendant's table. Word is, the jury includes such Hollywood heavyweights as **Peter Guber**, **Vicki Lawrence**, and former co-star **Michael Keaton**. With a cast like that, I can't wait for the movie version!

Is it me, or has there been nothing worth seeing in the theaters since **Sweet Home Alabama**?

In the **Harvey Buzz** department, there's going to be a new late-night talk show on ABC to replace **Politically Inaccurate**. The host? A heretofore unknown fellow named **Jiminy Kimmel**. I don't know much about him, except he was **Igor** to **Ben Stein**'s Frankenstein on **Win Ben Stein's Monkey**, he likes beer, and he was on a radio show with **Dr. Dre**. It's always great to have another late-night talk show that gets celebrities to open up about their new movies.

I watched the movie **Jackass**, and I had a really hard time following the plot. Plus, there was a guy who ate his own urine in a **snow cone**. This is what people want to watch? Forget it—I'm moving to Canada!

Well, as much as it pains me, that wraps it up for now. I have plenty more dish to dispense, but I only have so much space. I was thinking about starting up a web site so I could just let everyone get inside my head for a while, but I'm pretty strapped for time. So until next time, when you're feeling low, just remember there's a whole industry out there devoted to making you feel good: the **Magic Factory**, the entertainment industry... Hollywood! ⌀

Your Horoscope

By Lloyd Schumner Sr.
Retired Machinist and
A.A.P.B.-Certified Astrologer

Aries: (March 21–April 19)
The ever-increasing triviality of American life is good news for you and the other employees of the squirrel-waterski factory.

Taurus: (April 20–May 20)
The broken ribs, fractured skull, and dislocated shoulder won't hurt at all, mostly because you'll suffer them after being dropped by drunken pallbearers.

Gemini: (May 21–June 21)
Normally, you shouldn't blame society for your problems, but the truth is that every civilization on Earth has decided you should be publicly humiliated.

Cancer: (June 22–July 22)
You've been eating in Mexican restaurants for years now, but you still don't see how the free chips and salsa are "how they get you."

Leo: (July 23–Aug. 22)
You'll be reminded of an old cliché about warranties next Monday, your 91st day with an artificial heart.

Virgo: (Aug. 23–Sept. 22)
The interesting thing about the blood of the innocent isn't the taste or the occult power it gives you, but just how little there actually is.

Libra: (Sept. 23–Oct. 23)
You will be forced to choose between profit and dignity when creative directors tell you that your story would make a great young-adult diaper ad.

Scorpio: (Oct. 24–Nov. 21)
The importance of getting out to vote will be brought home when, in a close election, the Democrats take control of your favorite chair.

Sagittarius: (Nov. 22–Dec. 21)
You will strongly consider firing your entire PR team when your shoplifting trial fails to get the high-profile treatment it deserves.

Capricorn: (Dec. 22–Jan. 19)
Pundits will hail it as a victory for justice, if not jurisprudence, when you are sentenced to death by lethal injection for no particular reason.

Aquarius: (Jan. 20–Feb. 18)
A future filled with consequence-free lying suddenly becomes possible when you find a stylish, comfortable brand of fireproof pants.

Pisces: (Feb. 19–March 20)
Just because Ernest Borgnine hasn't spoken to you in more than 30 years doesn't necessarily mean he's angry.

Guy From The Strokes Accused Of Trying To Look Like Guy From The Strokes

see MUSIC page 9D

Pillsbury Doughboy's Image Sexed Up

see PRODUCTS page 2C

Entrepreneur Takes Gamble On First-Ever L.A. Bookstore

see BUSINESS page 10E

STATshot

A look at the numbers that shape your world.

What Was The Last Straw?

1. The "Women Of Worldcom" issue
2. The baby spilling all the coke
3. Seeing husband outside *Today Show* window with another woman
4. Having to sleep with clerk to redeem muffler coupon
5. Roommate taping over copy of *Glutton Bowl*
6. Getting caught lying about meeting local newscaster

the ONION®

VOLUME 38 ISSUE 43 AMERICA'S FINEST NEWS SOURCE™ 21–27 NOVEMBER 2003

U.S. Consumer Confidence Down, Says Guy Trying To Sell Van

BROCKWAY, PA—In more bad news for the U.S. economy, consumer confidence is down sharply this week, particularly among those in the market for a used 1994 Chevy Astro, van owner Dennis Schram reported Tuesday.

"It's a good van, with a little less than 100,000 miles on a rebuilt engine that got regular oil changes. It's got LT-package trim, a Bose cassette-stereo, and front captain's chairs, and I never smoked in it," said Schram, 43, who owns his own roofing business. "With all that, $4,200 doesn't seem like too much to ask, so I have to conclude that the average American, worried about jobs and the prospect of war with Iraq, is reluctant to spend right now."

Schram said that, in addition to the weak labor market and unstable Mideast situation, a prolonged decline in the financial markets has dampened consumer confidence and, consequently, eroded consumers' desire to buy a gently used recreational van that would make an ideal second vehicle.

see VAN page 23

Above: Schram and his 1994 Chevy Astro.

FBI: Muslim Groups In U.S. May Be Developing Nuclear Families

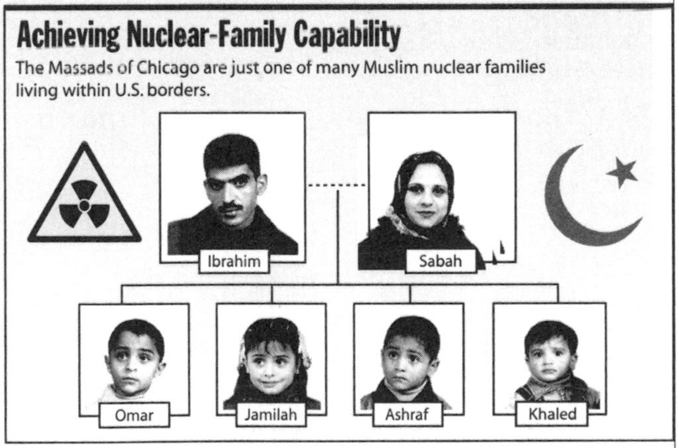

WASHINGTON, DC—According to an FBI report released Monday, "reliable and substantive evidence" exists indicating that Muslims residing in the U.S. are involved in a widespread plot to develop nuclear families.

John Ashcroft

"We possess what we believe to be credible proof that thousands of Islamic Americans, many of them Mideast-born, are attempting to acquire nuclear-family capability, often in full view of American law-enforcement authorities," said FBI director Robert Mueller, speaking before the Senate Intelligence Committee. "These nuclear families, which consist of a husband-wife core and a varied number of surrounding offspring, could potentially come into contact with other such nuclear families, creating a terrifying chain reaction of Muslim familial perpetuation."

Census Bureau statistics show that the Muslim population of the U.S. has increased dramatically in recent years. Mueller attributed much of this growth to the proliferation of nuclear families.

"Communities as diverse and far-flung as Newark, NJ, and Tulsa, OK, are being converted into breeder reactors in which Muslim nuclear

see NUCLEAR page 22

Above: The prolific Dressler.

Modern-Day Proust E-Mails Friend Six Times A Day

RUTLAND, VT—Much like the prolific 19th-century French novelist Marcel Proust, local claims adjustor Eric Dressler generates prodigious volumes of prose, chronicling the most minute details of his life and experiences in a seemingly endless stream of e-mails, friend Kevin Honig reported Monday.

"Proust devoted the last decade of his life to writing *In Search Of Lost Time*, a massive, sprawling, 3,000-page semiautobiographical work that covers 13 volumes," said Honig, Dressler's best friend since college. "Well, the way he spends half his work day sending e-mails, Eric has probably turned out at least that much. I get, like, six or seven a day without fail."

Just as the collected letters of Proust fill dozens of volumes, Dressler has stuffed Honig's Outlook Express in-

see PROUST page 23

The Bin Laden Audiotape

Last week, al-Jazeera aired an audiotape purportedly of Osama bin Laden praising the Sept. 11 attacks. What do *you* think about the possibility that bin Laden is alive?

Linda Kingery
Librarian

"I have my suspicions that this tape is older than al-Jazeera claims, mostly because of the way bin Laden peppers his speech with 'fer sure' and 'tubular.'"

Glenda Langston
Podiatrist

"You mean our bombing the crap out of Afghanistan and threatening war with Iraq hasn't softened his anti-American stance? That can't be right."

Todd Buhner
Landscaper

"Hell, that could be anyone's voice. Even *I* can do bin Laden... 'Oh, yes, I very much like to blow up the buildings, sir.' No, *you* sound Indian."

Bob Bankhead
Bus Driver

"Hey, I'm way ahead of you. I know this place down on Canal Street that had bootleg copies of the tape a week before al-Jazeera."

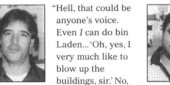

Bill Cotto
Electrical Engineer

"Bin Laden... *alive*? It's a Christmastime miracle!"

George Brantley
Systems Analyst

"I don't know which is more terrifying—that bin Laden is still alive, or that al-Qaeda may be in cahoots with Rich 'Man Of A Thousand Voices' Little."

New York City's Olympic Bid

New York is in the running to host the 2012 Summer Games. Among the NYC 2012 organizing committee's selling points:

- Free slice for every athlete
- Accessible via convenient parkways and expressways, enabling motor traffic to effortlessly glide from site to site
- Toughest anthropomorphic spokesanimal in Olympic history
- Borough of Queens, where Olympic village would be situated, is far from likely initial blast zone
- NYPD sure to provide excellent security, provided none of the African or Caribbean nations' athletes make any sudden moves
- You want a steeplechase course? We'll build you a nice fucking steeplechase course by Friday, half price
- Greek delegation can stay for free with relatives in Astoria
- NYC home to many fine restaurants and is boyhood home of Dr. Peter Rennert, who helped develop the color copier
- Survival rate expected to slightly exceed that of 1972 Munich Games

the ONION®
America's Finest News Source.™

Herman Ulysses Zweibel
Founder

T. Herman Zweibel
Publisher Emeritus
J. Phineas Zweibel
Publisher
Maxwell Prescott Zweibel
Editor-In-Chief

When I'm Feeling Blue, I Can Always Go To My Undisclosed Location

By Dick Cheney

Life can be pretty overwhelming sometimes. The daily stresses of family, friends, and being vice-president of the world's most powerful nation can get your head all twisted up. At those moments, you need a special little place that's all yours, a place where you're safe from the rest of the world. Whether it's a treehouse, a backyard tent, or an underground concrete bunker, everybody needs a place to hide away. When I'm feeling blue, I like to run off to my undisclosed location for some quality Cheney time.

When I get to my undisclosed location, nestled somewhere between Oregon and Maine, it's like all my troubles magically disappear. Even before I get inside, as the helicopter flies over the last tree-covered hill, man-made lake, craggy mountain, or expanse of desert, and I can see the razor-wire-covered embankment come over the rise, I take a deep breath and know that everything is going to be okay.

I don't know what I'd do if I didn't have my undisclosed location. I think I'd go crazy. When life gets to be too much and you really want to mull things over, it's good to have a place beneath 500 feet of solid rock where you can be alone in Secret Service-protected peace and quiet.

As a father and vice-president, I know that a lot of people depend on me. That can be a lot of pressure, but I'm no good to my family or country if I have a breakdown. That's why my undisclosed location is so important. It helps keep me sane. So when the situation with Iraq gets really bad, or my favorite uncle passes away and I have to come to terms with the cycle of life and death, I just have to go.

When times get tough and I'm feeling low, I just have to be alone in my pressure-sensitive security room with my four most trusted Secret Service agents, far away from everyone and everything, away from all the fighting, stress, and reporters. My heavily guarded subterranean lair is the only place I can truly be *me*—not Dick Cheney the husband and father, not Dick Cheney the nation's second in command, but plain old Dick Cheney. That's a feeling no one can take away from me.

Besides my guards, only one person knows where I go when I disappear: my chief of staff, Lewis Libby. He's the only one with the proper access codes and retinal scans to know how to get to me. And he rarely ever comes to find me when I get sad and hide away, because he knows how important my "bunker time" is to me.

When I disappeared after that U.S. spy plane crashed in China, Lewis came and found me. He told me how it was okay to be afraid, but that you need to stand up to those fears so they don't rule your life forever. He gave me the courage to fly back to Washington on his AH-64A/D Apache helicopter and try my best to find a diplomatic solution.

Lewis even told me about his special place, an old decommissioned Air Force base no one in Washington really goes to anymore. He says he goes there when he needs to think or just be alone. He took me to his spot,

When life gets to be too much and you really want to mull things over, it's good to have a place beneath 500 feet of solid rock where you can be alone in Secret Service-protected peace and quiet.

and we grew to be better friends. I've thought about going back there, but it's just not right. That's his spot, and I need to respect that. Besides, I wouldn't like it if I found Lewis hanging around my spot. Sometimes, a man needs to be alone in his airtight, self-sustaining shelter.

I really don't know what I'd do without my undisclosed location. It's like a second home for me, a place for me and nobody else. From the first time I was brought there, I knew it was the right nuclear-proof spot for me to clear my head and, if need be, have a good cry. Over time, it's become even more special. From the wood paneling I've had installed over the steel walls to make it more homey, to my relationship with Lieut. Daniel Parizi, who's become more than just a watch commander, I wouldn't trade my undisclosed location for anything in the world.

I've been coming to my undisclosed location less and less lately, probably because I'm getting older. But it's a good feeling to know it's there. In this cold, harsh world, it's nice to have a place you know will be there for you until the end of term. Ø

LOCAL

Mother Jealous After Reading Daughter's Diary

IRVINE, CA—Roberta Dunn, 40, experienced feelings of intense jealousy Monday after reading the diary of her 14-year-old daughter Hannah.

"I try to respect Hannah's privacy, but I also feel it's my duty as a parent to know what she's doing in her free time," said Dunn, a single mother divorced since 1994. "It turns out, unlike some people who barely have the energy to make dinner after spending all day on their feet, she's having an awful lot of fun."

Dunn said that over the past year, she has noticed Hannah "growing more and more distant" from her, spending increasing amounts of time with friends and talking on the phone. The growing alienation from her daughter prompted Dunn to seek out the journal in which Hannah records her innermost thoughts and secrets.

"Hannah's been a lot less communicative lately, and I wanted to make sure she wasn't getting into any of the typical teenage trouble, whether it be drugs or boys or whatever," said Dunn, who on Nov. 4 discovered the diary under her daughter's mattress while the girl was at the mall. "Well, she's not doing any drugs, but she did make the cheerleading team, and was picked to be class treasurer, and has a date for Tuesday's chorus trip to Six Flags Magic Mountain. Must be nice."

While Dunn was relieved to learn from the diary that Hannah's experience with alcohol and sexual activity has been limited, she couldn't help but feel angered by her white lies.

"Lying in any form is unacceptable," Dunn said. "Hannah has made it appear that when she stays at a friend's house, they're sitting around watching TV or doing homework—things me and my girlfriends used to do when I was her age. In reality, though, they're hanging out at the mall flirting with Tyler and Josh and, apparently, somebody named 'Tractor Boy.' Who is Tractor Boy?"

Said Dunn: "Unlike some people who barely have the energy to make dinner after spending all day on their feet, she's having an awful lot of fun."

After a long day at her job as a secretary at a window-treatments company, Dunn usually comes home and spends the night watching TV or catching up on housework.

"I have some friends and, yes, we do go out occasionally, but not like Hannah," Dunn said. "Every third page, there's some really exciting event—some great new band they're all into or a great new movie. I would've gone with her to see *Spider-Man* if she'd have told me it was worth seeing."

Dunn said her daughter's diary filled in some important blanks about the girl's social life. The Sept. 7 entry described a back-to-school party Hannah attended.

"Hannah said she was going to a party for somebody she knew from marching band, but she failed to say that this particular band member was 17 years old," Dunn said. "Needless to say, alcohol was served. I never got to go to any of the older kids' parties when I was in high school. And I certainly never would have written that I 'looked pretty good' in the new skirt I was wearing. Still wouldn't."

Dunn was also dismayed by an Oct. 27 entry describing a brush with drug use.

"Hannah's telling me that no one she knows does drugs, but right there on page 112, it says that some-

see DIARY page 22

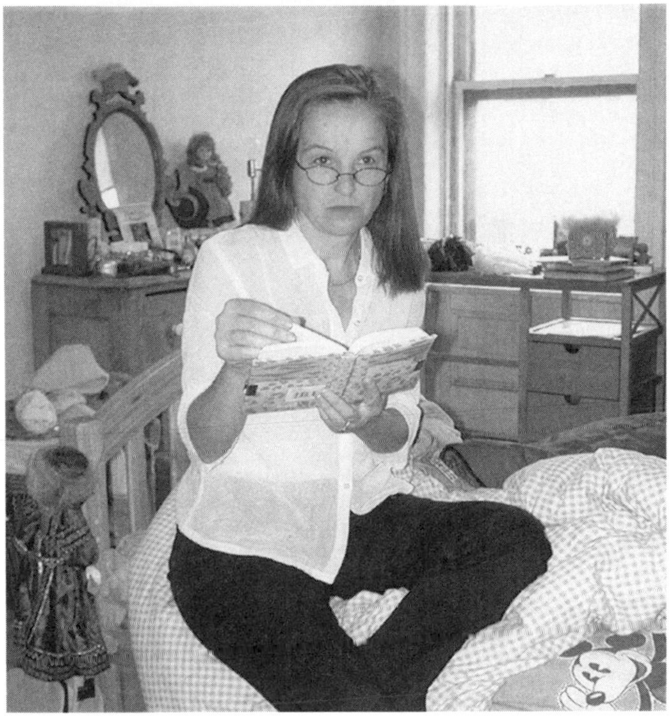

Above: Dunn in her daughter's room.

NEWS IN BRIEF

Jesus Surprises *700 Club* With Walk-On Appearance

VIRGINIA BEACH, VA—Monday's episode of the popular Christian-affairs program *The 700 Club* featured a surprise walk-on by Jesus Christ, who dropped by the set and chatted briefly with host Pat Robertson. "Pat, I can't stay long, but I just wanted to swing by and say hello to you and the whole *700 Club* gang," Christ told Robertson. "I love the show—it's just terrific in My sight. And, hey, how about this audience?" The 130 Christ fans in attendance then gave enthusiastic applause unto Him.

Drummer's Girlfriend Thinks He Should Sing

CHAPEL HILL, NC—Angie Carlson, 22, girlfriend of AstroPuffs drummer Steve Molzen, encouraged him to sing on some of the band's songs Monday. "You have such an amazing voice—just because you're the drummer doesn't mean you can't sing, too," Carlson told Molzen after a gig. "Just look at Dave Grohl." Carlson went on to ask Molzen if there has ever been a band where the drum kit was positioned at the front of the stage.

Teacher Bitches About Paycheck To Sixth-Grade Class

BOZEMAN, MT—Lakecrest Elementary School teacher Dana Frankel bitched to her sixth-graders about her "crap salary" shortly after receiving a paycheck Monday. "How am I supposed to pay for anything on this kind of income?" Frankel asked midway through a math lesson. "And now the brake pads on my Nissan need replacing. Gee, guess I'll just have to hope for the best next time I hit a red light." Frankel then got the disrupted lesson back on track by using her dwindling 401K plan as an example of negative numbers.

Infant Doing Everything In Her Power To Save Relationship

BOSTON—Eight-month-old Courtney Brindle is trying her best to save her parents' crumbling marriage, the infant reported Monday. "I put in a good hour today grabbing Daddy's finger, which I think made him feel closer to me and, by extension, to Mommy," Brindle said. "But my real dilemma is, is it better to provide lots of cute moments to fill the house with a feeling of warmth and love, or to suffer constant health problems to unite them in fear? I can't do both."

85 Percent Of U.S. Cole Slaw Remains Uneaten

WASHINGTON, DC—According to a report released Monday by the Department of Sides and Garnishes, 85 percent of U.S. cole slaw is never consumed. "Extensive surveying of restaurant bus tubs and waste bins indicates that for every 120 tons of slaw produced, only 18 tons end up eaten," the study reported. The study focused exclusively on U.S. restaurants, as there is no evidence that anyone has ever made cole slaw for home consumption.

Spy World-Famous

MONTE CARLO—Despite having a job that demands total anonymity, Colin Richards, Great Britain's number-one field operative, has somehow built a reputation as a playboy and bon vivant of world renown. "All I can say is, he must be really incredible at sneaking into places, considering everyone knows what he looks like," Monte Carlo casino owner Nigel St. Clary said. "Can you imagine how great a spy he'd be if he were unknown?"

NUCLEAR from page 19

families can be easily and cheaply produced," Mueller said. "Single Muslims who do not have nuclear families of their own are attracted by these favorable conditions."

According to Homeland Security chief Tom Ridge, unwed Muslims are crucial to the creation of nuclear families. Such individuals, Ridge said, strive to acquire certain critical materials in order to make such creation possible.

"Acquisition of wealth, education, employment, and status is key to establishing nuclear-family capability," Ridge said. "Surveillance of Muslim communities by the FBI reveals that these activities are taking place nationwide."

Quoting from the FBI report, Ridge cited the example of an unnamed Egyptian-born 24-year-old male who settled in the Bronx in 1995. Working days at a gas station owned by an uncle, the man attended nighttime business and English courses at a local community college. Upon graduation, he used his savings to acquire a partial stake in the gas station. It is believed that his hard-earned elevated social status was instrumental in his marriage to a young Iraqi-American woman whose own family immigrated to the U.S. in the late 1980s. Shortly after their wedding, the couple established a two-bedroom breeder reactor in Manhattan, where they produced two children, with another currently on the way.

"I'd like to say that this is an isolated example," Ridge said. "But the reality is, this 'Manhattan project' is the sort of thing that is occurring all across the country."

Supporting Ridge's claim, Attorney General John Ashcroft said that a June 2002 search of a home owned by a Muslim couple in Royal Oak, MI, unearthed substantial evidence of nuclear-family-building activity. Materials such as a family photo album, a baby-care book, and the discarded remnants of a used home pregnancy test were found on the premises.

"Fortunately, in that case, we were able to step in and break up the childless couple before they went nuclear," Ashcroft said. "But how many other Muslims do we have living right here in our country trying to do the same thing?"

"There are thousands of cases of marriage licenses being issued to highly suspicious Islamic couples known to harbor intentions of building nuclear families," Conrad said.

Monty Conrad, a domestic-security expert and longtime FBI consultant, said that many seemingly reputable Muslim-owned and -operated businesses funnel their profits into nuclear-family programs. Conrad has found evidence linking the proceeds from such businesses to bank deposits, food and clothing purchases, rent and mortgage payments, and other endeavors vital to creating and maintaining a nuclear family.

"Something as innocuous as a newsstand or a hole-in-the-wall falafel restaurant can be underwriting a Muslim nuclear family," Conrad said. "Shockingly, in many cases, there is no attempt to conceal it. Children can be seen behind the counter, laughing and playing as their parents and other adult relatives work."

Conrad faults the U.S. government for "willfully neglecting" the nuclear-family threat posed by Muslims living within U.S. borders.

"The government has, from the federal to local level, permitted these activities to go on right under its nose, in spite of the obvious red flags," Conrad said. "There are thousands of cases of marriage licenses being issued to highly suspicious Islamic couples known to harbor intentions of building nuclear families. Income-tax forms from some of these people even list dependents. All this is clear proof that Islamic nuclear families exist in the U.S., yet nothing is done about it. Why?"

No laws currently exist to fight the proliferation of Muslim nuclear families within the U.S. That gives such Muslims as Abdul Rahman, newly naturalized citizen and Houston resident, a virtual blank check to build a nuclear family.

"I love America," Rahman said. "There is so much more opportunity here than in Syria, and that is why I came to stay. I definitely want to build a new life here and raise a family, and so do my friends." ⊘

DIARY from page 21

one at summer camp last year was smoking pot," Dunn said. "Hannah wrote that she didn't smoke any, but I still find it disturbing that kids that young even have access to drugs. I used to smoke pot once in a while, but I haven't seen so much as a joint passed at a party in years."

Dunn also cannot help but compare her own love life to her daughter's.

"I wouldn't mind meeting someone, but I just don't really come into contact with many single men," Dunn said. "There's Jim at work, who's flirted with me on occasion, but I'm just not all that attracted to him."

In one diary entry, Hannah formed a column of "Boys Who Might Like Me," a list made up of 14 different seventh, eighth, and ninth graders.

Hannah, on the other hand, enjoys a wealth of romantic possibilities. In one diary entry, Hannah formed a column of "Boys Who Might Like Me," a list made up of 14 different seventh, eighth, and ninth graders.

"Even if you take out the names Hannah put a question mark next to, she's still got way more dating possibilities than I do," Dunn said. "It's so depressing, I almost wish I'd never violated her privacy." ⊘

the ONION presents

Bodybuilding Tips

More and more Americans are pumping iron.
Here are some tips to get your bodybuilding program on track:

- It's important to keep your lifting routine varied. If you've been saying "Oooooof" every time you lift, try switching to "Ungggggh."
- To gain respect in the gym, bludgeon with a dumbbell the first guy who offers to trade sets with you.
- Weightlifting is not just a sport for men. It is also enjoyed by many lesbos.
- A good rule of thumb for bodybuilding: If no sleeved garment fits you, you can stop.
- Doctors warn of the dangers of steroid abuse, so be a pussy and let some pussy doctor tell you what to do, pussy.
- It's true: Bodybuilding is a great way to meet, terrify, and repulse the opposite sex.
- Power up with a good meal of infants before doing any substantial lifting.
- Keep in mind that weightlifting is a physical activity. Carrying heavy emotional baggage or any other metaphorical burden will not actually improve strength.
- YOU CAN BUILD MUCSLE FAST!!! MAXMIZE YOUR PHYSIQUE! THE KEY TO SERIOUS GROWTH CAN BE YOU'RS! CLICK HERE!!!
- Remember: Flexibility is of no importance to a bodybuilder. Why turn your head when you can rotate your entire torso to achieve the same effect?
- Supplement your diet with vitamin B-12, magnesium, glutamine, amino acids, horse steroids, and zinc.
- If you are a female bodybuilder, concentrate on transforming your breasts into leathery slabs of rock-hard muscle. Guys love that.

PROUST from page 19

box with e-mails totaling thousands of pages and spanning years. The writings of each man are a winding psychological journey, weaving experiences from his everyday life with memories from the distant past.

"Clearly there is a higher purpose to these discursive ruminations," Honig said. "In describing in great detail the new dog his next-door neighbor just got, or by writing about how he was tired and just drank three cups of coffee from the vending machine down the hall, Eric is seeking to rescue these moments from the clutches of the past. Proust had the same obsession with the inexorable passage of time."

Though he does not always read the full text of the e-mails, Honig said he still appreciates his friend's ambition.

"Eric's constant search for understanding and meaning is inspirational," Honig said. "Right here in the subject line of his latest e-mail lies the eternal question, 'What's going on, dude??'"

Continued Honig: "True, Proust's narrative speaks of steeples and promenades, dinners at the Guermantes' in Paris, and a madeleine dipped in a cup of tea. Dressler's e-mails, on the other hand, tend to talk about movies he saw or that new restaurant next to West Towne Mall where you grill your own steaks. But such is the world of a 21st-century man."

Honig noted that *In Search Of Lost Time* was less a story than an "interior monologue," adding that Dressler's writing possesses the same quality.

"Eric's constant search for understanding and meaning is inspirational," Honig said. "Right here in the subject line of his latest e-mail lies the eternal question, 'What's going on, dude??'"

"In a way, Eric's e-mails aren't really even written to me at all, but to the ages," Honig said. "Why would he need to inform me that he hates the pants he's wearing that day? Obviously, he is not so much communicating a message to me as he is using metaphor and imagery to expound upon his pro-

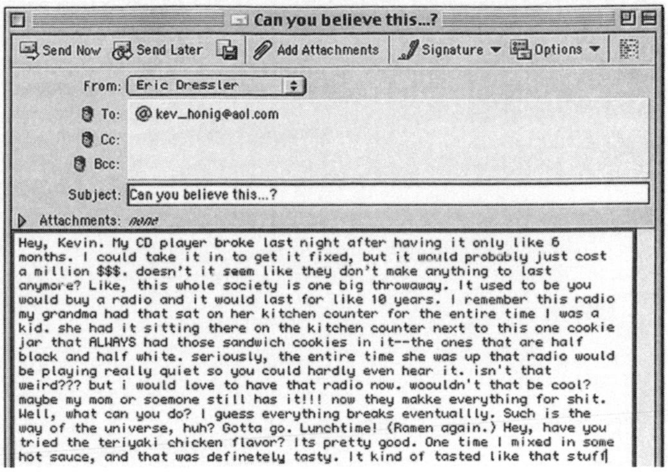
Can you believe this...?
Send Now | Send Later | Add Attachments | Signature | Options
From: Eric Dressler
To: @kev_honig@aol.com
Cc:
Bcc:
Subject: Can you believe this...?
Attachments: none

Hey, Kevin. My CD player broke last night after having it only like 6 months. I could take it in to get it fixed, but it would probably just cost a million $$$. doesn't it seem like they don't make anything to last anymore? Like, this whole society is one big throwaway. It used to be you would buy a radio and it would last for like 10 years. I remember this radio my grandma had that sat on her kitchen counter for the entire time I was a kid. she had it sitting there on the kitchen counter next to this one cookie jar that ALWAYS had those sandwich cookies in it--the ones that are half black and half white. seriously, the entire time she was up that radio would be playing really quiet so you could hardly even hear it. isn't that weird??? but i would love to have that radio now. woouldn't that be cool? maybe my mom or soemone still has it!!! now they makke everything for shit. Well, what can you do? I guess everything breaks eventuallly. Such is the way of the universe, huh? Gotta go. Lunchtime! (Ramen again.) Hey, have you tried the teriyaki chicken flavor? Its pretty good. One time I mixed in some hot sauce, and that was definetely tasty. It kind of tasted like that stuff

Above: One of Dressler's recent Proustian compositions.

tean worldview."

Dressler's writing style resembles Proust's in other ways, as well.

"In his letters, Proust often gives lengthy explanations for the most ordinary actions—an invitation to dinner might take several pages," Honig said. "Eric can sometimes take a really long time to get to the point, too. I mean, he can just say he needs his *Memento* DVD back. He doesn't have to go into the whole thing about why his sister wants to see it, and why and where they were when she asked."

Just as Proust's work is a catalog of the hundreds of characters populating his Parisian high society, Dressler's e-mails detail the activities of his family, "annoying" coworkers, and the greater Rutland community. From an e-mail message dated November 6:

"Last night at the grocery store I ran into, guess who... Donna Ramsted. She's moving to Burlington in 2 weeks, I guess. She's going to work at some business where Greg Pfeiffer is working, can't remember, some computer sorta thing. Remember when I was so hung up on her? I know it was just because I missed Diane L., but God was I pathetic. You live and learn, huh? Well, it's almost 5. See you at Lee's."

"I can hardly keep straight who all these people are," Honig said. "I really have to hand it to Eric, how he elevates the importance of certain events in his life while simultaneously revealing their essential hollowness."

Dressler and Proust are also both keen social observers. Like his literary forebear, Dressler frequently turns a critical eye to the follies and foibles of our world, in one recent case the overly litigious nature of modern man:

"Kev: was just reading the herald," read an e-mail dated Oct. 14. "Do you have a copy there? If so, gotta check out page 6. Seriously. Some guy left his snake on THE BUS and now he is suing the Greyhound people for letting it die. Isn't that so ridic??!!"

Just as some critics dismiss Proust's work as unbearably self-indulgent, Dressler is not without his detractors.

"God, Eric writes me these huge, long, rambling e-mails all the time," ex-girlfriend Julie Goldstein said. "I always feel like I should write him a decent message back, but I know I'll just get another one in a few days, so I usually just respond with something like 'Ha ha,' or 'Too bad,' or 'Funny one.' I guess he's satisfied with that. He's never complained that it's so one-sided. I guess he just feels like he's the one with all the important things to say. He always was a self-absorbed ass." ⊘

VAN from page 19

"It's a shame, because it's a great van for camping, hauling stuff, and just tooling around town," Schram said, while placing a larger "For Sale" sign in the vehicle's rear window. "Gets pretty good mileage, too, which is important at a time when most median-middle-class households—those earning $40,000 to $60,000 a year from combined income—list long-term sustainability of their current lifestyle as a primary concern."

"Actually," Schram continued, "the only problem she really has is that, like the economy, once she gets going, she can take a long time to change direction."

The feedback Schram has received from potential buyers has convinced him that the economy, not the van itself, is the problem.

"Of the calls I've received, 92.6 percent said they were unable to afford the vehicle at its current Kelley Blue Book-approved price point," Schram said. "Roughly 30 percent indicated that my price was acceptable only if I were willing to take payment in monthly installments, although nearly 15 percent said it was too high regardless. To me, that signals a lack of faith in any impending recovery from the current slump, as well as an unwillingness to make big-ticket purchases for as long as it lasts."

Brockway resident Frank Hopkins, the 7.4 percent of prospective buyers who did not consider the price too high, is expected to meet with Schram after work Monday to discuss the viability and performance history of the van. Schram said he hopes Hopkins buys the van, for the sake of all Americans.

"Although my experience may or may not be representative of a larger socioeconomic trend, my interactions with potential consumers seem to reflect the general movement toward saving extra income and away from automobile purchases," Schram said. "This is unfortunate, as it keeps currency out of healthy circulation—especially where I'm concerned—and also because this van is a lot more practical than you might think. The mileage is better than most pickups, and you can fit a whole four-by-eight sheet of plywood in the back if you take the seats out."

The feedback Schram has received from potential buyers has convinced him that the economy, not the van itself, is the problem.

Schram admitted that his decision to sell the van is a hedge against a possible Christmas downturn.

"The outlook for the holiday retail season is fairly bleak," said Schram, who traditionally sees a falloff in roofing business during the winter months. "Without an upturn in consumer spending on, say, my van, an already shaky Schram-family economic picture could worsen. That means no bike under the tree for the kids, which will just bring the mood down further. It's a self-feeding cycle, you know."

According to Schram, the U.S. economic boom of the mid- to late-'90s was driven by exuberant consumer spending, which prompted a housing boom that increased demand for skilled tradesmen like himself. As a result, Schram was able to purchase the van in 1995, a move he does not regret.

"These days, I just have to spend differently, not less," Schram said. "A drop in consumer confidence almost never causes a simple drop in overall consumer spending. What it produces is a fall in spending on durables. People put off upgrading their computer, buying a new washing machine, or buying a pre-owned van with no rust in the wheel wells—which is a real find for this part of the country, believe me."

In spite of the decrease in sales of durables, Schram said not all items suffer during economic downturns.

"The weird thing is which goods benefit, most notably 'comfort products' like chocolate, alcohol, and sundries, an effect that extends all the way to DVDs and home furnishings," Schram said. "But not used vans. Simply put, if I don't move this thing soon, I'm gonna have to take a part-time shift at The Cheese Shoppe to help pay for Christmas." ⊘

COMMUNITY VOICES

Rehab Clinics Are So Much Cooler In Europe

I'm always hearing people go on and on about how American rehab clinics are the best in the world. You gotta be kidding me! Sure, the U.S. has a few decent clinics, but after being in and out of rehab for three years on the other side of the pond, I think I'm qualified to say that rehab clinics are way cooler in Europe.

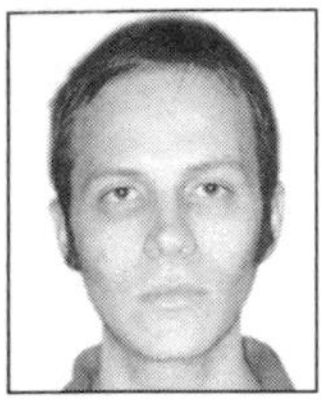

By Ellis Markham

I was in a 35-day program in Austria, trying to kick heroin, and my roommate was this 74-year-old Viennese guy named Jorg. Every morning, he'd boil up a pot of coffee, take a deep breath, and stick his hand in it. In the middle of the night, he'd be up with the shakes, sweating profusely and screaming all this crazy shit in German. I swear, man, it was like something out of a Burroughs novel. How fucking cool is that? You're not going to see shit like that in some lame clinic in Sacramento.

One of the patients on my floor, a guy who'd been there for 35 years, told me all about the history of the place, how it once survived a WWII looting when doctors told the Nazi SS that beloved opera singer Ernestine Schumann-Heink was near death and recuperating there. His stories about the clinic were so fascinating, I nearly forgot about my convulsions. Meanwhile, the only good story I've ever heard in an American

I swear, man, it was like something out of a Burroughs novel. How fucking cool is that? You're not going to see shit like that in some lame clinic in Sacramento.

rehab clinic was when some guy freaked out on PCP and lit the drapes on fire. I think it was at Horizon House in Atlanta.

I don't see how anybody could check into an American clinic when they could be rehabbing overseas. It's just so much cooler and grittier to take your methadone standing in front of a window overlooking the Rhone. You know, more... *authentic*. Over there, you're surrounded by all these colorful characters named Per and Gianfredo who'd be perfect for your movie script. I mean, who wants to detox with some guy named Brad from Cleveland Heights?

Another thing that's way cooler about the European clinics is the architecture. This one clinic I was in last summer in Rotterdam was in this building that had been there since, like, the early 1600s. I can't name one American rehab clinic that's been around since 1950—not even Hazelden. It was

I was in a 35-day program in Austria, trying to kick heroin, and my roommate was this 74-year-old Viennese guy named Jorg.

a beautiful building, too, full of old wood detailing and intricate stonework. After a week of shitting myself because I was too wracked with withdrawal pain to get up, I was finally able to check out the gargoyles on the entryway's stone façade, and I was totally blown away. Here in America, there's just no sense of culture or history like that.

It's going to be hard to go back to rehab in the U.S. and choke down the swill they call food: scrambled eggs or oatmeal for breakfast, a sandwich and chips for lunch, a dinner of meatloaf or, if the cooks are feeling wild, cheese pizza. Pitiful. Over in Europe, though, it's a whole different story. Those people know how to eat. From the golumkis in Warsaw to the pork loin smothered in locally grown olives in Madrid, Europeans know the perfect way to end a day of group therapy. The food was so good, I would do everything in my power to keep from puking all over myself during withdrawal.

One rehab center I especially enjoyed was in Nice, in the south of France. I woke up on a cot with blood pouring out of my mouth and nose, but after the bleeding stopped and I got my DTs under control, I got a chance to poke around a bit. The grounds were beautiful and, provided you weren't deemed suicidal, you could spend the day looking at the scenery or checking out the elaborate fountains that dotted the courtyard. Nice is near the sea, and if the wind is just right you can smell the salty air, which really helps you forget that all you want to do is jam needle after needle of smack into your veins.

The first time I checked into a European rehab clinic—I believe it was Prague—I thought I'd have a hard time communicating. But most of the nurses over there speak great English, or at least enough to warn you to stop trying to claw your eyes out during those first few weeks without heroin. Many of the patients spoke English and were fluent in other languages, as well. I can't tell you how many fascinating people I met while cleaning up. They all had these amazing stories about overdosing in the Czech countryside or in the Greek Isles. It was such a broadening experience, it made me want to get a Eurail pass and OD all across Europe.

Best of all, I made some great friends during my detox experiences overseas. I've even invited some of them to crash at my pad in Miami. I don't think I ever met anyone in a U.S. rehab clinic that I'd ever want to see on the outside. But that's the great thing about traveling abroad and experiencing new drug cultures. It can't help but open you up to new things. ø

HOROSCOPES

Your Horoscope

By Lloyd Schumner Sr.
Retired Machinist and
A.A.P.B.-Certified Astrologer

Aries: (March 21–April 19)
Your decision to start over with a brand-new life is admirable, but to do it properly, you should probably quit your job at Olive Garden.

Taurus: (April 20–May 20)
You aren't the kind of person who enjoys the spotlight, so it's disturbing when you discover that you actually are the center of the universe.

Gemini: (May 21–June 21)
You'll be truly surprised next week when a British gentleman teaches you the meaning of the word "bugger." Surprised, and rather disappointed.

Cancer: (June 22–July 22)
You will suffer dire consequences after toying with powerful forces you do not understand, namely gravity.

Leo: (July 23–Aug. 22)
It seems the danger is over for now, but something tells you that you haven't seen the last of that dastardly villain.

Virgo: (Aug. 23–Sept. 22)
Good things will happen when you least expect them, greatly embarrassing you while you're trying to enjoy a shit in peace.

Libra: (Sept. 23–Oct. 23)
Your impassioned speech about how use of the word "titties" is never funny will be drowned out by the shrieks of laughter at the word "titties."

Scorpio: (Oct. 24–Nov. 21)
Your defense lawyer is one of the best, but he will have a hard time blaming those 11 murders on the bossa nova, the dance of love.

Sagittarius: (Nov. 22–Dec. 21)
Having a girl pop out of the birthday cake was a fine idea, but you really should have given more thought to when the cake is cut.

Capricorn: (Dec. 22–Jan. 19)
Reality falls short of expectations when you get more—albeit larger—ass than a toilet seat.

Aquarius: (Jan. 20–Feb. 18)
If there's one lesson you've learned from the mythic, timeless sport of baseball, you have no idea what it is.

Pisces: (Feb. 19–March 20)
The awesome spiritual powers of the stars exert more influence on you than your own will, as far as that goes.

HELMUT KOHL from page 11

amounts of blood. Passersby were amazed by the unusually large amounts of blood. Passersby were amazed by the unusually large amounts of blood. Passersby were amazed by the unusually large

Fuck you and your back rub.

amounts of blood. Passersby were amazed by the unusually large amounts of blood. Passersby were amazed by the unusually large amounts of blood. Passersby were amazed by the unusually large amounts of blood. Passersby were amazed by the unusually large amounts of blood. Passersby were amazed by the unusually large amounts of blood. Passersby were amazed by the unusually large amounts of blood. Passersby were amazed by the unusually large amounts of blood. Passersby were

see HELMUT KOHL page 35

the ONION®

VOLUME 38 ISSUE 45 AMERICA'S FINEST NEWS SOURCE™ 5–11 DECEMBER 2002

NEWS

Petting-Zoo Goats Swarm Horrified 4-Year-Old

see LOCAL page 9D

With Great Suit Comes Great Responsibility

see PRODUCTS page 2C

Ten Pounds Of Phlegm Audibly Rearranged In Burger King Customer's Chest

see LOCAL page 3B

STATshot

A look at the numbers that shape your world.

Top-Selling Calendars

1. "Whoa, You're Deep" 365-Day Buddhist-Sayings Calendar
2. Women Of The Modeling Industry
3. Flags 'n' Eagles
4. Puppy Heads Grafted Onto The Bodies Of Chippendales Dancers Holding Babies
5. 732 Tits A Leap Year
6. "This Will Do" Pictures-Of-Nature Calendar

0 74470 94595 6 00

THE ONION • $2.00 US • $3.00 CAN

SCANDAL IN THE WHITE HOUSE

Report: Presidents Washington Through Bush May Have Lied About Key Matters

WASHINGTON, DC—In allegations likely to further erode Americans' faith in the office of the presidency, an independent-counsel investigation asserted Monday that presidents George Washington through George W. Bush may have lied about key matters of national import during their tenures as chief executive.

The report states that the integrity of the presidency "may have been compromised by criminal misdirection, obstruction of justice, and deliberate clouding of the truth for political advantage and/or personal gain by as many as every president since the nation's inception."

The report offers evidence linking all 42 presidents to deliberate acts of deception and dishonesty.

While conventional wisdom holds that only two U.S. presidents, Richard Nixon and Bill Clinton, have ever openly lied about anything, the report offers substantial evidence linking all 42 presidents to deliberate acts of deception and dishonesty. Among its assertions are that Thomas Jefferson lied about impregnating one of his slaves; Ulysses S. Grant deceived Congress regarding his role in the Whiskey Ring scandal; Ronald Reagan intentionally withheld key facts in the Iran-Contra Affair; Warren G. Harding told untruths during the Teapot Dome scandal; James K. Polk, Martin Van Buren, and Chester A. Arthur fibbed about the details of trade pacts; and Franklin Pierce was less than forthcoming regarding details of the Kansas-Nebraska Act.

"Shockingly, even William Henry Harrison, a president who was in office for a month and spent most of it on his deathbed, seems to have found time to lie during the famously lengthy inaugural address that would speed his demise," independent-counsel investigator James McManus said. "And so-called 'father of our

see REPORT page 29

Above: Implicated in the presidential-lying scandal are George Washington, John Adams, Thomas Jefferson, James Madison, James Monroe, John Quincy Adams, Andrew Jackson, Martin Van Buren, William Henry Harrison, John Tyler, James K. Polk, Zachary Taylor, Millard Fillmore, Franklin Pierce, James Buchanan, Abraham Lincoln, Andrew Johnson, Ulysses S. Grant, Rutherford B. Hayes, James Garfield, Chester Arthur, Grover Cleveland, Benjamin Harrison, William McKinley, Theodore Roosevelt, William H. Taft, Woodrow Wilson, Warren Harding, Calvin Coolidge, Herbert Hoover, Franklin Roosevelt, Harry Truman, Dwight Eisenhower, John Kennedy, Lyndon Johnson, Richard Nixon, Gerald Ford, Jimmy Carter, Ronald Reagan, George Bush, Bill Clinton, and George W. Bush.

Area Man Thinking Up Funny Things To Say For Next Football Game

MCKEESPORT, PA—Seeking to continue his longstanding tradition of cracking wise during NFL telecasts, diehard Pittsburgh Steelers fan Glenn Patek, 34, has already begun brainstorming quips for the team's Dec. 8 game against the Houston Texans.

"The Steelers play the awful expansion Texans, so you'd think I'd have an easy time of it," said Patek, who watches most Steelers games with friends at the Bluegill Bucket, a local tavern. "But in reality, having a big, fat target like Houston makes it tougher, because there's the temptation to resort to lazy, obvious jokes. I'd be letting Dave, Graham, Carlos, Jeannie, Tucker, Christine, and all the rest down if I resorted to obvious stuff. When you're playing a team that's

see MAN page 28

Above: Patek works on some new zingers.

Democrats In Disarray

Having lost control of the Senate and lacking a clear leader and message, the Democratic Party appears to be in disarray. What do *you* think?

"As a Democrat, I have high hopes in 2004 for Rep. Tom Lanford, a charismatic young centrist from Ohio with a clear vision for the party. Okay, I just made him up."

Marjorie Stamp
Nurse

"In this time of war, the Democrats have unselfishly recognized that America simply cannot afford to have two strong, competing parties."

Al Fanseca
Systems Analyst

"All the Democrats I've talked to know exactly what they stand for: not being Republicans."

Rick Snell
Carpenter

"The Democrats need to find a guy who can shoot lightning out of his fingertips. I'd vote for that guy."

Donald Paul
Tour Guide

"One solution to the Democrats' woes is to try to attract more fat, gray-haired white men with lots of sinister connections."

Rachel Cone
Freelance Writer

"It's not as bad as it could be. The Democrats could be desperate enough to run Walter Mondale agai—oh, shit."

Mike Ansel
Lawyer

The Cobain Diaries

Journals, a book culled from the journal entries of Kurt Cobain, recently hit bookstores. Among the revelations:

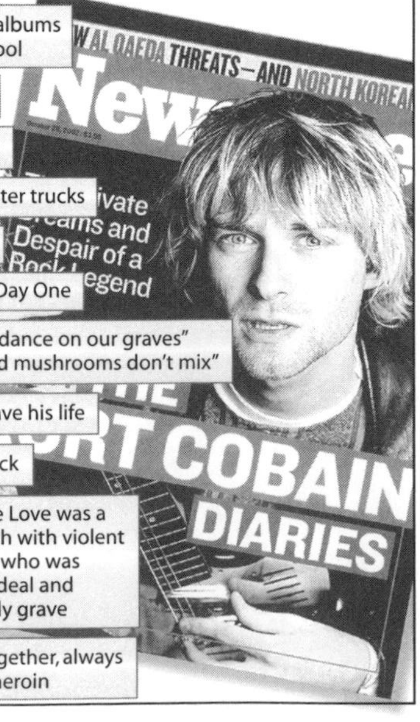

- Admitted he had all of Sonic Youth's albums only so people would think he was cool
- Smoked pot once at summer camp
- Got to sixth base with Courtney Love
- Margins filled with drawings of monster trucks
- Thought racism, sexism were wrong
- Regretted his K Records tattoo from Day One
- Aug. 8, 1987: "The cackling vampires dance on our graves" Aug. 9, 1987: "Note to self: Tequila and mushrooms don't mix"
- Couldn't spell word "restaurant" to save his life
- Was upset Hüsker Dü never wrote back
- Sometimes kinda wondered if maybe Love was a power-hungry, attention-craving bitch with violent tendencies and no discernible talent who was riding his coattails to a major record deal and would eventually drive him to an early grave
- Despite all the problems they had together, always maintained a deep, abiding love for heroin

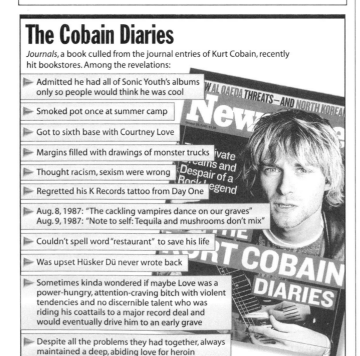

the ONION®
America's Finest News Source.™

Herman Ulysses Zweibel
Founder

T. Herman Zweibel
Publisher Emeritus
J. Phineas Zweibel
Publisher
Maxwell Prescott Zweibel
Editor-In-Chief

Forget All I Said About Me Being An Alcoholic

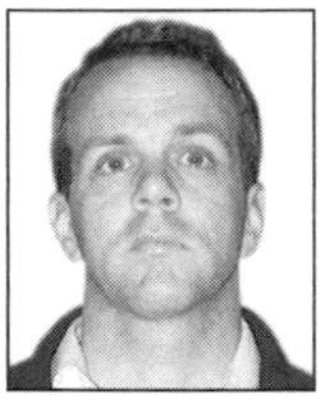

By Chris Driessen

Oh, come on, guys. Did you actually think I was serious when I said all that stuff? God, that is so funny. I was totally kidding when I said I was an alcoholic. You didn't honestly believe all that stuff I said last night about "feeling like my life was whizzing out of control," did you? It was a joke. Haven't you ever heard of "humor" before?

Yes, I realize I said, "Please help me. I need help. Don't let me drink ever again." But you didn't actually fall for that, did you? I was *drunk*. I say all sorts of crazy things when I've had a few too many. Remember when I said, "Guys, we should drive up to my hometown and hang out sometime"? I didn't mean that, either. Or when I said, "We should all chip in and buy Dan a guitar for his birthday"? I sure didn't want to do that when I woke up this morning. And all that stuff about, "I need to enter some sort of program to get cleaned up"? Yeah, right.

I know, I know. You think it was a cry for help. I think I remember saying something about being at the end of my rope. I might've even said I have no one else to turn to—that you are my best friends and that I can't go to my family with something like this.

Okay, the truth is, I do need you guys... to party with me. Man, we were so hammered last night. God, that was fun. What time did we start? It was right after work, right? We went to McMurphy's Pub for a few and then to that Cuban restaurant and had that rum with dinner, and then a couple in the car on the way back to McMurphy's. What did I have, like, eight or nine drinks? More? Damn.

Then, as I recall, we were over at Don's place, and it was at Don's that I said, "I can't do this anymore, I just can't. I've got to stop, I'm ruining my life." And you guys actually took me seriously? Talk about gullible. The whole time, I was thinking, "Oooh, I'm getting these guys so good!"

You know what a prankster I can be. You know how I sometimes fall off my chair, just to be funny, as if I'm drunk enough to fall out of my chair. And, Matt, remember that time I hit on your wife at your wedding reception? I told her that any time she gets sick of being a married woman, she could come on over to my place for a little fun on the side and no one would have to know. I knew she'd go straight to you, furious. It was all a big joke for your benefit.

Are you still trying to talk to me about this? Can we please change the subject already? Huh? What's that? A piece of paper with my signature that says, "I will not drink for the next month"? Yeah, like I need a signed piece of paper to stop drinking. What I need is a signed piece of paper to stop joking around all the time.

I said I get the shakes if I don't have a drink in the morning? I really said that? Let me guess, you fell for that one, too, hook, line, and sinker. Of course you did.

Haven't you ever heard of "humor" before? Yes, I realize I said, "Please help me. I need help. Don't let me drink ever again." But you didn't actually fall for that, did you? I was *drunk*. I say all sorts of crazy things when I've had a few too many.

Hey, did I tell you I got a call from that AA person this morning? That was so hilarious last night, how we got on the phone and called the national hotline, and they gave us the name of someone from the local group, and we called him up at 4 in the morning. Man, I love phony phone calls.

True, I did cry. And, yes, I did go into the bathroom to talk to him, and I was in there for more than an hour, and I was sobbing. But I was crying because this guy was so unbelievably pitiful, falling for the old "I need help" routine.

What? I said I'd go to the AA meeting Tuesday? Yes, Sam, I probably did ask you to please drive me there out of fear that I wouldn't have the courage to go by myself. But what you obviously didn't see is that I was totally yanking your chain.

I don't get it. You're still not laughing. Dude, lighten up.

You know what? I think maybe I need to find some friends who understand my sense of humor. It's been great knowing you guys all these years, but I'm beginning to see that you're just a little too uptight for my taste. Ø

Elderly Man Silently Wages War Against Pharmacy

AKRON, OH—Local retiree Gerald Stennis, 87, has been waging a silent war against the Copley Road Walgreens for the past two months, family members told reporters Monday.

"I don't know what his problem is," daughter Lily Bergeron said. "Every time he goes in for his medicine, there's some kind of incident. Going to Walgreens used to be the highlight of his week, because the pharmacists love him, but lately that's all changed. Last week, he knocked over a candy display. The store manager said he saw Dad kicking the candy bars down the aisle, even though he flatly denies it. I just know he's doing it on purpose."

Stennis has refused to explain his behavior, denying that there is any feud between himself and Walgreens.

"When I ask him what's going on between him and the pharmacy, he acts like I'm being crazy," Bergeron said. "That doesn't stop him from taking the manager's reserved parking spot every time he drives over there. He never did that until two months ago, so you can tell something is fishy."

Stennis' friends seem equally mystified by his strange vendetta.

"I don't know what's going on," said longtime friend Ed Bollinger, 81. "All I know is that when it's rainy, he makes a point to not wipe his feet on the mats and tracks mud all over their nice floors. If Gerry hadn't been a loyal customer for the past 15 years, I don't think they'd put up with his shenanigans."

> **"Going to Walgreens used to be the highlight of his week, because the pharmacists love him, but lately that's all changed," Bergeron said. "Last week, he knocked over a candy display."**

> **"Gerry's been complaining more and more about the Walgreens," Bollinger said. "He's been upset ever since they stopped stocking Tetley iced tea [in 1998]. But I think the final straw was when Rosalita, his favorite cashier, got fired."**

Theories regarding the source of Stennis' feud with the pharmacy vary.

"Dad got the wrong medication a few months ago," Bergeron said. "But the pharmacist himself called to tell us they'd made a mistake before Dad even got home. They even sent someone to our house to make the switch. Dad was pretty steamed over that, but that's no reason for him to keep peeling the price tags off the vitamin bottles. It has to be something else."

Bollinger said Stennis may be protesting certain store decisions.

"Gerry's been complaining more and more about the Walgreens," Bollinger said. "He's been upset ever since they stopped stocking Tetley iced tea [in 1998]. But I think the final straw was when Rosalita, his favorite cashier, got fired. That was six months ago, but I think he considered it a real slap in the face."

Above: Stennis stands before the object of his anger.

Because Stennis has been known to possess a short a temper, some family members suspect that the grudge arose from an argument with an employee.

"Lily asked me to stop in to find out if Dad had picked a fight with the

see PHARMACY page 28

NEWS IN BRIEF

Surgeon General Mills Recommends Three To Five Servings Of Froot Per Day

WASHINGTON, DC—In a report submitted Monday to the Department of Health and Human Services, Surgeon General James Mills recommended that Americans consume three to five servings of froot per day. "A crunchier, more berrilicious cousin of the fruit family, froot is vital to proper digestion and breakfast fun," Surgeon General Mills said. "Whether you're eating it straight off the vine or, ideally, in its processed 'loop' form, Americans should be sure to get plenty of froot."

Punk Band Has Something Against Local Newscaster For Some Reason

HARRISBURG, PA—Crucial Consensus, a local hardcore punk band, apparently holds a longstanding grudge against Channel 27 newsanchor Rick Wagner. "They opened with this song called 'DickLick Wagner,'" said Brad Gottesman, 17, who attended the group's Tuesday show at the Harrisburg VFW Hall. "Then they played something called 'Phlegm At Eleven,' followed by 'Wankorman' and 'Channel 666.' They really seem to hate the media—especially, for some reason, Rick Wagner."

You To Receive 15 Pounds Of Venison Sausage From Uncle

YOUR HOUSE—According to reports from your sister, your uncle has completed this year's batch of venison sausage, 15 pounds of which are now en route to your home. "[Your dad] was going on and on about how he used a different batch of seasonings this year, like cloves," your sister said. "They're thicker this year, too." Upon arrival, the complimentary meat will be placed in your basement freezer below nine pounds of last year's venison sausage.

Mom Tries To Appear Interested In Daughter's Documentary

BOISE, ID—Connie Barstow, 56, struggled Monday to appear interested in her 29-year-old daughter Andrea's just-completed independent documentary, *Incident At Round Rock*. "Is that you holding that microphone?" asked Barstow, watching her daughter's 94-minute investigation of a racially motivated 1996 beating in a small Idaho town. "I think I recognize that purple bracelet you always wear." Connie went on to say that Andrea has a lovely speaking voice and could have narrated the film herself.

FBI Director Wishes He Had Some Alien Thing To Cover Up

WASHINGTON, DC—Tired of focusing on counterfeiting operations and unsubstantiated homeland-security threats, FBI director Robert Mueller said Monday that he wishes he had some exciting alien thing to cover up. "Don't get me wrong, I know the work I do is important and necessary," Mueller said. "But, man, after a long day of reading 450-page reports on plausible areas of concern for liquor-license falsification, I really wish I could order a sweeping cover-up of reverse-engineered UFO technology." Mueller added that it would be cool just to see a real spaceman. Ø

MAN from page 25

dead-last in the NFL in total offense, you've got to get pretty creative."

Patek, who cites the dry, erudite style of ESPN anchor Kenny Mayne as his primary quipping influence, began preparing for Sunday's game by logging onto the Houston Texans' official web site.

"I've already got a bunch of stuff planned out," Patek said. "Unlike a lot of teams, there isn't a single marquee player on the entire Texans defense. So whenever a player makes a tackle, I can say, 'Man, that guy's almost good enough to play for Florida State.' Or if they throw the ball to, say, Jabar Gaffney, I could say, 'Well, you know what they say: Throw the ball to Gaffney a few hundred times, and he's eventually gonna burn you.' Or, if you can't think of anything else, you can always just sarcastically praise their 'vaunted punting game.'"

"Unlike a lot of teams, there isn't a single marquee player on the entire Texans defense," Patek said. "So whenever a player makes a tackle, I can say, 'Man, that guy's almost good enough to play for Florida State.'"

"I'm also working on a joke where I say that the Texans coaches give out those little helmet stickers whenever somebody makes a clutch play," Patek continued. "Then, when somebody at the bar points out that none of the players have any stickers, I'll say that nobody's made a big play yet."

Patek cites the dry, erudite style of ESPN anchor Kenny Mayne as his primary quipping influence.

Complicating Patek's job this week is the serious injury suffered by Pittsburgh quarterback Tommy Maddox during the team's Nov. 17 game against the Tennessee Titans.

"Kordell Stewart may end up starting at quarterback, and I've pretty much run through every Kordell joke in the book over the years," said Patek, poring over the *USA Today* sports page. "Do I joke about how he could get yanked in favor of a guy with a concussion and spinal-cord injury? I could, but I'd have to be careful."

In addition to the Steelers-Texans game, Patek is preparing jokes for Sunday's other matchups.

"We'll probably watch Falcons-Bucs, which should be pretty good," Patek said. "You can always count on someone looking dumb trying to tackle Michael Vick, or how every sportscaster loves John Lynch and Mike Alstott just because they're 'throwback' white guys. And, if I still have some steam, I'll probably invite everyone back to my place to watch the Packers-Vikes game at 8:30. Favre always gives you something to work with."

Sunday regulars at the Bluegill Bucket say Patek is always a big part of their football-viewing experience.

"Every once in a while, he'll say something that'll actually make you laugh," bar patron Tami Neff said. "I liked it when Jerry Rice caught a pass last week, and the announcers were talking about how he was the oldest receiver ever in the NFL, and Glenn said, 'When 600 years old you are, so good you will catch, hmmm?' like Yoda from *Star Wars*. I have to admit, I laughed, even though he made the exact same joke about Cris Carter a couple weeks before." ⊘

PHARMACY from page 27

manager or something," son Ryan Stennis said. "Everyone at the store seemed genuinely surprised that there were any ill feelings. Apparently, this battle Dad is fighting is completely one-sided, and he won't say what the hell is going on."

To date, Stennis' war against the pharmacy has largely consisted of petty acts of sabotage, but his daughter fears that escalation may be imminent.

"Dad's a stubborn guy," Bergeron said. "Right now, he's just doing stuff like knocking over displays and asking stock boys to see if they have any cherry-flavored Metamucil in the back and then walking out before they return. I'm just worried that one day he'll do something crazy, like pull the fire alarm."

Though Walgreens expressed an eagerness to make peace, no resolution appears to be forthcoming.

"If something is bothering Mr. Stennis, I'd be more than happy to discuss it with him," Walgreens manager Marianne Krieg said. "He's a valued customer. However, we are unsure how to make the first step toward peace, since no one has any clue what we did to upset him."

"He's doing stuff like knocking over displays and asking stock boys to see if they have any cherry-flavored Metamucil in the back and then walking out before they return," Bergeron said.

Added Krieg: "And I sure as heck would like him to stop opening the tennis-ball cans without us having to involve the police or ban him from the store." ⊘

the ONION presents

Video-Camera Tips

Video cameras are a fun and easy way to record those special moments in life. Here are some tips for getting the most out of them:

- An important rule of thumb for the video-camera novice is that everybody in the world wants to see your toddler gorge on a slice of cake.
- Pointing the camera at the TV screen it is hooked up to will create a wicked-cool "endless tunnel" effect which will blow your viewers' minds.
- If your high-end digital-video camera is not operating properly, simply throw it away and buy a new one. After all, you're made of money, Mr. I Own A High-End Digital-Video Camera.
- Don't even bother picking up the video camera until the bride is on her third drink.
- To provide viewers with an exciting, first-person point-of-view of your life, bolt the video camera directly into your skull.
- Before videotaping those priceless memories of that special someone, make sure to cover up the power-indicator light and leave the closet door slightly ajar.
- If you are acclaimed Dogme 95 director Lars von Trier, stop reading this list immediately. You need no advice on digital-camera use.
- Remember: You won't always get that perfect shot on the first try. Don't be afraid to ask the abusive, racist policeman to take it from the top.
- Endless footage of your cat wandering away from the camera while you shout its name and try unsuccessfully to get it to look at the camera is sure to delight friends and relatives.
- To allow for movement on the part of your subject, focus the camera on a point midway between the base of the breast and tip of the nipple.
- To point out the futility of existence, videotape your preschooler building an elaborate sandcastle on the beach, then pull in close to capture her facial reaction as the tide rolls in and slowly destroys her creation.

REPORT from page 25

country' George Washington is not exempt, either. A story familiar to any schoolchild tells us that, as a boy, Washington confessed to chopping down a cherry tree, saying, 'I cannot tell a lie.' Evidence suggests, however, that the entire tale may have been bogus from the start. This is doubly damning to the presidency's reputation, for it is not merely a lie, but a lie about *not* telling lies."

The report calls into question the integrity of the presidency at a particularly inopportune moment. Coming on the heels of alleged Bush Administration involvement in the Enron and WorldCom corporate scandals, as well as the "Monicagate" impeachment trial of former president Bill Clinton, the implication of every president in U.S. history will likely deepen the public's mistrust and further undermine the credibility of the nation's highest elected office.

"If these allegations turn out to be true, this country faces a crisis of confidence of unfathomable proportions," an anonymous Beltway insider said. "If the leader of the most powerful nation on Earth cannot be trusted to tell the truth, then who, in the name of God in heaven, can?"

"We are shocked by these allegations," White House press secretary Ari Fleischer said. "The president wishes to assure the public that he

"The president wishes to assure the public that he has never lied, and that every one of these accusations of lying—from the 18th century all the way to the 21st—will be thoroughly investigated and, we are confident, disproved."

has never lied, and that every one of these accusations of lying—from the 18th century all the way to the 21st—will be thoroughly investigated and, we are confident, disproved."

Calling the report "just the tip of the iceberg," McManus said incidents of lying may plague the government at all levels.

"Every day, new evidence surfaces suggesting that this lying trend is more far-reaching than we ever imagined," McManus said. "It may well extend all the way to the offices of Vice-President, Speaker of the House, Secretary of State, Secretary of Defense, Secretary of the Treasury, White House Press Secretary, secretary to the White House Press Secretary, Senator, Representative, State Assemblyman, Governor, Lieutenant Governor, County Board Supervisor, Alderperson, Mayor, Assistant to the Mayor, City Councilperson, Assistant City Councilperson, Comptroller, Town Coroner, County Librarian, and County Clerk."

On Capitol Hill, the report prompted calls for a thorough investigation of each and every allegation, from the possibility of Bush-Cheney lies regarding Haliburton during the 2000 presidential campaign all the way back to alleged lies told by the John Adams Administration regarding the Huron Indians in 1798.

"The idea that presidents and other elected officials have violated the public trust by telling lies is disturbing and deeply disappointing," U.S. Sen. Orrin Hatch (R-UT) said. "We are adopting a 'zero tolerance' position regarding the telling of untruths on the part of any politician—past, present, or future—and we will not rest until each and every lie-teller has been punished to the fullest extent of the law."

Added Hatch: "You have my solemn word on that."

Above: Four of the 137 known presidential mistresses.

BLOAT from page 16

amounts of blood. Passersby were amazed by the unusually large amounts of blood. Passersby were amazed by the unusually large amounts of blood. Passersby were amazed by the unusually large amounts of blood. Passersby were amazed by the unusually large amounts of blood. Passersby were amazed by the unusually large amounts of blood. Passersby were

John Locke, John Locke—always with the John Locke.

amazed by the unusually large amounts of blood. Passersby were amazed by the unusually large amounts of blood.Passersby were amazed by the unusually large amounts of blood.Passersby were amazed by the unusually large

see BLOAT page 44

COMMUNITY VOICES

Adventures In Babysitting

A Room Of Jean's Own
By Jean Teasdale

For me, unemployment's really not all that bad. I can easily fill the hours with my many hobbies: recording and watching my soaps, reading romance novels, and, of course, shopping! Well, more like *window* shopping these days, but I still manage to pick up a few small items here and there. For example, Pamida had a great sale on infants' onesies and sleepers, and I spent less than $10 overall!

Now, don't break out the bubbly just yet, Jeanketeers. There's no bun in the Teasdale oven! I bought them just in case a girlfriend of mine gets pregnant. When you know lots of people of child-rearing age, it's good to have baby gifts on hand for the odd shower or first birthday party and so on.

All right, I admit it: I don't always buy baby stuff for other people. In fact, the last baby shower I attended was in 1995. And, offhand, I can't think of anyone I know who's expecting. It's just that I love baby stuff sooo much! The tiny little clothes and adorable toys are irresistible to me! I even collect baby bottles and pacifiers. Sometimes, when hubby Rick is away, I take the baby stuff out of storage and spread it all around the house. You know, bottles in the sink, baby clothes hanging from doorknobs, blocks scattered on the floor—just to get a sense of what it would be like if the pitter-patter of tiny feet could be heard in our house.

I don't mean to come off as egotistical, but sometimes I think I would

When you know lots of people of child-rearing age, it's good to have baby gifts on hand for the odd shower or first birthday party and so on.

make the greatest mother ever. I just love kids sooo much, especially when they're real little. Also, I think I would make a terrific mom because I still look at the world through the innocent and wondering eyes of a child. I swear, I don't think there's a fundamental difference between myself at age 9 and myself at age 39. I can still remember all the joy and pain of childhood.

That's why my heart nearly leaped out of my chest when Miranda, the woman who lives in the apartment next door, asked me to babysit her daughter Hailey. It was totally out of

see TEASDALE page 30

TEASDALE from page 29

the blue. Apparently, her regular babysitter was sick, and she didn't want to miss her weekly church-choir practice. She said it would only be for three hours, and she would pay me $15. What I didn't say was that I would have done it for free! Hailey is the most absolutely adorable 18-month-old, with curly golden hair, rosy cheeks, and chubby little legs... Who wouldn't want to spend a few hours with that heaven-sent angel?

When I arrived for my babysitting date, I was disappointed to discover that Hailey was already asleep in her crib.

"She had a big day at her great-grandma's birthday party, and she's pretty tuckered out," Miranda said. "Lucky for you, huh? I bet she'll sleep through the night—certainly as long as you're here."

Well, I didn't consider it lucky. I'd been hoping Hailey and I could have some quality time together. When Miranda left, I sneaked into Hailey's room. Yep, sure enough, she was out like a light. For a while, I watched her

Quick as a flash, I was back in my apartment, rummaging through my special baby box. When I found what I was looking for, I grabbed my Polaroid camera and ducked back next door. (I know, I know, I shouldn't have left Hailey alone, even for a second, but this was *major*.)

coverlet gently rise and fall to her breathing. Then I went to the living room, plopped down on the sofa, and turned on the TV. Sheesh! It's just like another evening at home, I thought.

An hour crept by like molasses. I channel-surfed so much, I was practically waterlogged, and all the magazines Miranda and her out-of-town hubby Jim had to read were boring political ones like *U.S. News And World Report* and *National Geographic*. Miranda kept a two-way baby monitor in the living room so Hailey's cries and stirrings could be heard, but I didn't hear a single peep. I couldn't stand it! A precious little bundle from God was right in the very next room, and I couldn't do anything about it but sit and be on hand in case she started crying!

I couldn't do anything... or could I?

I went into the bedroom and, sure enough, Hailey was still sound asleep. Because she was lying on her stomach, I could only see one side of her face. I couldn't resist gently turning her over on her back. Her little face was so flawless and pure. She could have been one of those Anne Geddes calendar babies who wear little costumes while sound asleep.

Suddenly, inspiration seized me.

Quick as a flash, I was back in my apartment, rummaging through my special baby box. When I found what I was looking for, I grabbed my Polaroid camera and ducked back next door. (I know, I know, I shouldn't have left Hailey alone, even for a second, but this was *major*.)

Trying not to wake her, I removed Hailey's one-piece sleeper and slid it out from under her body. My heart skipped a beat when she started squirming and whimpering after a snap caught slightly against her leg, but she soon quieted down again. Whew! I'd have to make this quick. My swift work paid off, and I was pretty proud of myself when I was done. After all, it's no mean trick dressing a sleeping baby in a tiny clown outfit, complete with pointy hat!

Doesn't that sound like the most adorable thing in the world? I'd been saving the get-up for my own future daughter's first Halloween, but looking at little Hailey, I couldn't resist giving it a test run. Besides, I thought I could take a couple of Polaroids and put them in the brand-new and unused baby book I kept in my box. You know, kind of pretend that Hailey was my baby.

Well, as I pointed the camera at Hailey, I realized that something was missing. Once again, I dashed back to my apartment and came back with a tube of bright red lipstick and some old white foundation left over from a Halloween clown costume of my own from 15 years ago. I daubed the white makeup on Hailey's face and drew little red circles on her cheeks and nose. I had to be really careful with the mouth area, but I managed to thickly line it with the lipstick. (It had to be perfect, you know!) Finally, I was set to take her picture.

I wonder how Anne Geddes manages to use a flash without waking her babies. That's where she has me trumped, because as soon as my Polaroid's flash went off, Hailey's eyes snapped wide open. For a few seconds, she just looked at me dumbfounded, her eyes still focusing. Then she began screaming. (Maybe I should have aimed the camera farther away from her.)

The sound Hailey made wasn't really crying, like a baby cries. I would say it was more like panicked shrieking. Hailey sat up and rubbed her eyes, which was definitely bad, because she managed to grind in some of the makeup. Tears flowing from her tightly shut eyes, Hailey began thrashing around. I didn't know what to do! I grabbed her and headed to the bathroom to wash off some the makeup.

That's when I heard a knock at the door. I froze, terrified that it might be Miranda coming back early from choir practice.

"Are you in there, Jean? Open the hell up! You can hear that crying up and down the hall!" It was hubby Rick!

Rick had returned from Tacky's Tavern and read my note saying I was next door. When I let him in, Rick, already blotto, absolutely freaked at the sight of little Hailey, still dressed as a clown, her face all pink and smeared. Having had this silly phobia of clowns since childhood, Rick turned almost as white as Hailey's makeup! He stumbled over to the toilet and vomited! (Now I had to deal with *two* babies!)

I was just getting Rick to his feet when a foul stench filled the air. At first, I thought it was Rick, but the smell was more in Hailey's direction. You guessed it—she pooped in her diaper! Rest assured, Jeanketeers, there was no way I was going to deal with something that smelled as bad as that! (What am I, nuts?)

Well, I don't know how I did it, but in short order I shoved Rick out the door (remembering to hand the camera and photo to him so Miranda wouldn't see it), washed the makeup off Hailey's face, stuffed the clown outfit in my pocket, and got her back into her sleeper before Miranda got home. Her eyes were still red and teary, and her diaper remained soiled, but Miranda completely bought my story that Hailey had been having nightmares and couldn't sleep, and that she had filled her drawers just a few moments before Miranda walked in.

Miranda apologized and even gave me an extra $5 for my trouble. I felt guilty about lying to her, but in a way, I think I deserved that extra five based on Hailey's disturbing behavior. I mean, she just wouldn't quit screaming, even after I fixed everything! Is that normal? Well, at least I have that darling picture.

I still ardently believe that children are our future, but all the same, I think I'll have a little less Hailey in *my* future! ⌀

HOROSCOPES

Your Horoscope

By Lloyd Schumner Sr.
Retired Machinist and
A.A.P.B.-Certified Astrologer

Aries: (March 21–April 19)
Get back to the basics of family this week. Have your mother feed, bathe, and change you.

Taurus: (April 20–May 20)
Your insurance company insists that it has no obligation to insure you as long as you're still frozen in that block of ice.

Gemini: (May 21–June 21)
You will unify the disparate fields of semiotics, mathematics, and behaviorism when you prove that, if our ifs and buts were candy and nuts, we'd all have a merry Christmas.

Cancer: (June 22–July 22)
Avoid making any major business decisions this week, as you'll spend most of it out of your mind on vodka sours.

Leo: (July 23–Aug. 22)
You'll be terrified next Monday when it seems that the sky is falling, but it's merely the tail end of the Leonid meteor showers. Then comes Thursday.

Virgo: (Aug. 23–Sept. 22)
There are no blemishes on your kind, compassionate Virgo soul, but that's more than offset by the ones on your face, hands, and renal system.

Libra: (Sept. 23–Oct. 23)
You will be profoundly moved by your experiences in the next few days, but that could mean a whole lot of things.

Scorpio: (Oct. 24–Nov. 21)
The great Lions quarterback Bobby Layne will appear to you in a dream and explain why you don't deserve to have Bobby Layne appear to you in a dream.

Sagittarius: (Nov. 22–Dec. 21)
You will be caught in the greatest existential dilemma of your life when you are unable to decide if a table or radial arm saw is better for your home shop.

Capricorn: (Dec. 22–Jan. 19)
Your religion was almost right: Those you vanquished in life are waiting for you in death, but not to serve you.

Aquarius: (Jan. 20–Feb. 18)
You will turn in one of the most heroic and selfless performances of your career next Thursday, but since you're an architect, the details are pretty boring.

Pisces: (Feb. 19–March 20)
Your wife, like your jailers before her, still refuses to allow you to have belts or sharp-edged culinary utensils.

NEWS

Bush Gives France 30 Days To Speak English

see NATION page 2C

Crocodile Hunter The Same Way In Bed

see PEOPLE page 4B

Cleveland Browns Punter Endorses Cleveland Metro Bus Pass

see ADVERTISING page 14E

Killer Kinda Cute

see CRIME page 10D

STATshot

A look at the numbers that shape your world.

Least-Responsible Birth-Control Methods

1. Condom found in street
2. Twist-tie
3. Thinking of labia as "two dangling catfish heads"
4. Juicy Juice douche
5. Baby-B-Gone™ after-sex spray
6. Only sleeping with pre-pubescent partners
7. Yelling "No baby, no baby, no baby!" at moment of climax

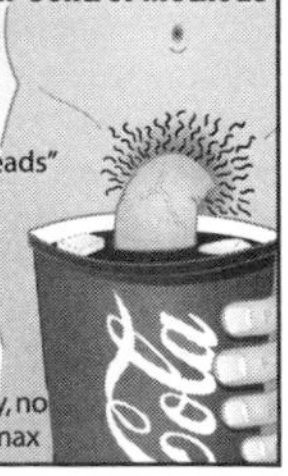

the ONION®

VOLUME 38 ISSUE 46 AMERICA'S FINEST NEWS SOURCE™ 12–18 DECEMBER 2002

Nation Afraid To Admit 9-Year-Old Disabled Poet Really Bad

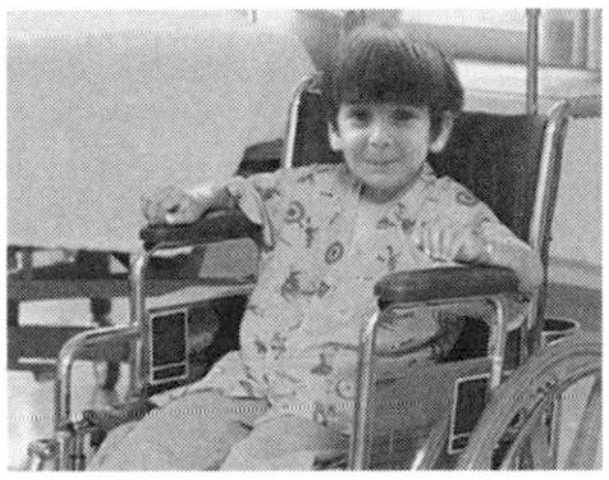

Above: Luke Petrowski, whose *Hopeweavings* (right) books have sold more than 22 million copies.

LYNDONVILLE, VT—Afflicted from birth with a rare degenerative disease, wheelchair-bound Luke Petrowski has confronted his illness by penning heartfelt verse that touches on elements vital to our lives: love, spirituality, courage, grace, and hope.

His poetry has been collected in the *Hopeweavings* book series, all of which have been *New York Times* bestsellers and stand as stirring testaments to the power of faith and love. A sought-after talk-show guest and trusted friend of religious leaders and politicians alike, this home-schooled 9-year-old from small-town Vermont pos-

see POET page 35

Mall Of Central America Looted On Opening Day

Above: Mall of Central America visitors sprint toward the "El Salvador" parking lot.

TEGUCIGALPA, HONDURAS—Less than an hour after opening its doors, the new Mall of Central America was overrun Monday by thousands of impoverished locals, who ransacked the region's largest shopping center in a smash-and-grab frenzy.

"We were simply unable to control the crowds," mall manager Jose Cepeda said. "People were drawn from miles away by our spectacular opening-day sales, product demonstrations in the beautiful glass atrium, electricity, and restroom toilet paper."

After a gala ribbon-cutting ceremony featuring a performance by Latin pop superstar Luis Miguel, the mall's doors opened to the public at 9 a.m. By 9:40, looters had begun stripping shelves of desperately needed staples.

"Many of the area's residents have lived their entire lives in cardboard shacks," Cepeda said. "I believe some of them were simply overwhelmed by the presence of so many durable goods all in one place."

The chaos escalated when a group of armed revolutionaries from the Honduran countryside raided JCPenney.

"Just after 11 a.m., machine-gun-toting marauders flooded in from the northern section of the underground parking lot and descended on JCPenney, demanding keys to the safe," mall security guard Carlos Acevedo said. "When menswear clerks refused, they fired machine guns in the air and spread out. Within minutes, they had moved to other areas of the mall, taking Camp Snoopy by force and eventually advancing their line to include all of LEGOLand."

The raid was suppressed when government forces arrived and fired tear gas and rubber bullets on the marauders, sending them

see MALL page 34

Area Mom Could Have Made Same Meal At Home For Much Cheaper

Above: Sandy Wiersma.

NAPERVILLE, IL—During an outing to Chisholm's Family Restaurant Monday, Sandy Wiersma, 43, repeatedly told her family that she could have made the same food at home for significantly less money.

"When I saw the menu, I just couldn't believe we were paying for things I easily could have made at home for a fraction of the price," Wiersma said. "It just seemed like a real waste of money to me."

After mentally calculating what it would have cost to prepare the meals ordered by herself, her husband, and their two children, Wiersma said she was "flabbergasted."

"For what we're shelling out on [son] Eric's cheeseburger and fries alone, I could have made dinner for the entire family," Wiersma said. "We all could have had nice cheeseburgers and fries, with plenty left over for baked

see MEAL page 34

Chapter 11 For Boston Archdiocese?

Already reeling from sex-abuse charges, the Boston Archdiocese is now considering filing for bankruptcy. What do *you* think?

"It's about time. I've been waiting for years to turn that downtown cathedral into a heavy-metal club."

Don Althorp
Cashier

"Well, what exactly did they do with the $2 I paid that old lady for a pecan nut bar in 1977?"

Lynette Demuth
Therapist

"Oh, no—we've all got to get together to save Christianity!"

Rob Prince
Truck Driver

"Only a miracle can save them now. Fortunately, they get lots of those."

Christine Kohl
Florist

"That's going to be one hell of a yard sale."

Rich Massena
Developer

"So now they're financially bankrupt, as well?"

Gary Williams
Systems Analyst

Strom Turns 100

On Dec. 5, U.S. Sen. Strom Thurmond (R-SC) turned 100. How did he celebrate the milestone?

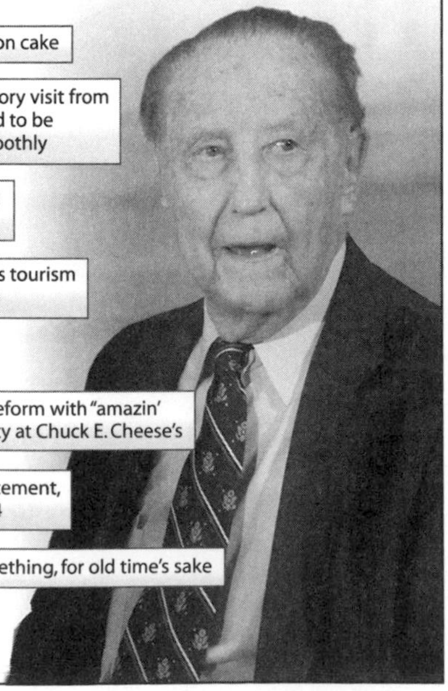

- Blew out 100 burning crosses on cake
- Received personal congratulatory visit from President Bush, who pretended to be Eisenhower so it would go smoothly
- Reflected on the cullahed guhl he kissed when he was foah
- Was placed in front of Bahamas tourism poster, told he was in Bahamas
- Shook violently
- Discussed campaign-finance reform with "amazin' singin'-talkin' bear" during party at Chuck E. Cheese's
- Welcomed his incoming replacement, Sen. Hiram Biddlebaum, age 94
- Was allowed to segregate something, for old time's sake
- Died

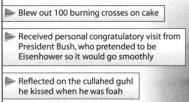

the ONION®
America's Finest News Source.™

Herman Ulysses Zweibel
Founder

T. Herman Zweibel
Publisher Emeritus
J. Phineas Zweibel
Publisher
Maxwell Prescott Zweibel
Editor-In-Chief

I Didn't Mean To Lead You On By Fucking You

By Len Foster Jr.

Hey, Lisa. Yes, I did get your phone messages, and I am so sorry I didn't get back to you right away. I'm glad you agreed to meet me for coffee, though, because we need to talk. See, I was sort of confused by some of the things you said on my voicemail: "Hey, that Kurosawa festival at the Orpheum was extended another week if you want to go." "There's a new Cuban place on Eustace Street. I'm free Thursday evening if you're interested." "Hi, Len, it's Lisa. Call me."

Since we only met last weekend, I didn't really understand all this chummy familiarity. It took me a while to figure it out, but I finally realized that a big misunderstanding had occurred: You think there's something between us. Lisa, you're a really nice, intelligent, attractive girl, and I'm truly sorry to have to say this, but I didn't mean to lead you on last weekend by fucking you.

Please don't feel embarrassed. Some of it, admittedly, is my fault. Looking back on my actions, I can see how there may have been one or two things that made you think I was reciprocating your advances. Like making out with you in that back booth of the bar for 40 minutes. Or how, when we came back to my apartment, I slowly undressed you in my bedroom. Or how I kissed the nape of your neck and shoulders and caressed your bare breasts with one hand as I stimulated your clitoris with the other. Or maybe it was that half-hour of intense cunnilingus before our extremely gratifying intercourse that gave you the wrong idea. I guess I can see how all that foreplay might have been misleading.

Lisa, please don't be offended by what I'm about to ask, but have you been with many men? If you haven't, it's okay—that's nothing to be ashamed of. It's just that, well, a more experienced woman would have quickly deduced from my body language that the fucking wasn't leading to anything. For example, as you were straddling me, I never squeezed your buttocks; I only rested my hands on them. And it's a universally understood notion that when, after climax, a man gets up to go to the bathroom, then goes back to bed and falls asleep with his body turned facing the wall, he's not interested in pursuing anything with the woman.

I sense you're upset and embarrassed, and I'm genuinely sorry. That's totally understandable. You misread the signals I was giving off. If it makes you feel any better, I, too, have misread cues plenty of times. A few months ago, I was sitting on the bus when a pretty girl came aboard. As she walked past, she made extremely brief eye contact, then sat in the seat behind me. Naturally, I thought she was hitting on me. I turned around, smiled, said hello, and began chatting her up. It wasn't long before I started putting the moves on her, but instead of returning my amorous advances, she told me to get lost. So you see, Lisa, I've been there. The only difference is that in my case, I was definitely being hit on. To this day, I firmly believe that girl was flirting, putting on the coy act. What I misread was the extent to which she was a little tease.

My point is, I know what it's like to be on the other side of that scenario. I just wish someone had set me straight like I'm doing here with you. I had to learn it the hard way.

Okay, I was hoping I wouldn't have to say this, but you've forced me to be more blunt: I don't find you sexually attractive. You're just not my type. You're definitely cute, but I prefer tall, long-torsoed women with freckles on their shoulders and small, pert breasts.

What do you mean, "That describes me perfectly"? Maybe you should find a full-length mirror and take a long, hard, honest look at yourself. Sometimes, our self-image can be severely distorted. I'm not judging you—we're all human and have our frailties. But, Lisa, you're not tall and long-torsoed. Five-feet-nine is not considered tall for a woman. Perhaps in Asia.

Look, I think we're getting into some of your personal issues that don't need to be addressed here. Indulge me on this final point, and I'll let you go. This is no great loss for you. You seem like a lovely girl, and I'm sure you'll find a man very soon. But next time, try to be more aware of what that man is thinking and feeling, and you'll spare yourself a lot of pain. From the angle at which he puts his penis in you to the way he postcoitally strokes your hair, there are many signs a man gives off that will communicate whether he's truly interested in you. The sooner you are able to read them, the happier you'll be.

So let's be friends, okay? Now, how about a hug? No? Come on, don't be like that.

Although, I must admit, your little hostility act is giving me a hard-on. What? Come on, there's no need to get upset. It's strictly a platonic hard-on. Ø

NUPTIALS

God Late For Local Wedding

CARTHAGE, MO—An embarrassed God admitted Monday that He was late for the Saturday wedding of Patrick Moore and Dina Roble, arriving halfway through the ceremony but catching "most of the important stuff."

"It was one heck of a day," God said. "Yes, I can be all places at once, but it's just so hard to keep it all straight

"I was running a bit behind and, admittedly, I probably should have left a little earlier," He said. "But I really would have made it on time if I hadn't been stupid enough to rely on that map Patrick included in the invitations. It was barely readable."

sometimes. It's been crazy all month, and this thing just came up so fast."

The ceremony that forever joined Moore, 28, and Roble, 26, in holy matrimony was held at 11 a.m. at Sacred Heart Church on Gorman Avenue in Carthage. Neither bride nor groom was aware of the Lord's tardiness.

"Religion is very important to my entire family, and Dina and I plan to raise our children in a Christian environment," Moore said. "So it was important for us to have our wedding in a Roman Catholic church, and be united under the eyes of God."

God admitted that His eyes were upon the couple for a little less than half of the ceremony—"which is a lot," said God, considering the length of the Roman Catholic liturgy.

"The Catholics go through *everything* at a wedding," God said. "There's a sermon and readings and even Communion. With the songs and the procession and the 'I do' stuff thrown in there, it takes so long. And the whole time, it's stand, sit, kneel, stand, sing, recite, sit, stand, sing, kneel, sit."

God added that the ceremony's liturgy of the Word—which includes readings from the Old and New Testaments, a responsory Psalm, the "alleluia" before the Gospel, and a Gospel reading—is nothing He hasn't already heard "billions of times."

Calling Himself "free of sin," the Lord blamed His late arrival on poor directions provided by the couple.

"I was running a bit behind and, admittedly, I probably should have left a little earlier," He said. "But I really would have made it on time if I hadn't been stupid enough to rely on that map Patrick included in the invitations. It was barely readable. Then, I come to find out that East Gorman is a totally different street than Gorman

Above: Roble and Moore, who were married Saturday in the partial presence of God (inset).

Avenue. They run parallel. So, for about 25 minutes, I'm cruising up and down East Gorman like an idiot, looking for 299—and, of course, there isn't any."

Finally, at 11:30 a.m., halfway through the ceremony, God located the small brick church. He slipped in unnoticed during the middle of the second reading.

"I came in the back, really quiet, like a thief in the night. Nobody turned around or anything, so I doubt they noticed," God said. "Besides, I am in a form no human eyes can discern, so I'd have to be pretty clumsy to get busted."

God said He does not feel a need to tell Moore and Roble that His spirit was not fully looking over them as they became husband and wife.

"Why point it out?" God said. "I got there for the exchange of the wedding vows, so, really, is any harm done?"

see GOD page 35

NEWS IN BRIEF

Conjoined Twin Hogging Kidney

SPRINGFIELD, MO—Bruce Andrusko, 27, complained loudly Monday about his conjoined twin Bryce's habit of hogging the brothers' middle kidney. "He drinks tons of beer, and that only leaves me the one kidney for everything I drink," said Bruce, who has been fused with Bryce at the torso since birth. "I'm sick of it." Bryce responded that Bruce "never seems to complain" when the beer is introduced to their shared bloodstream.

Miss Nude America Loses Title After Appearing Clothed In *Woman's Day*

OCALA, FL—Tawny Bridges, Miss Nude America 2003, was forced to relinquish her crown amid scandal Monday, when it was discovered that she had appeared clothed in a 1999 issue of *Woman's Day* magazine. "Miss Bridges has conducted herself in a wholesome manner entirely unbecoming of this title," pageant chairman Peter Taub said. "We are a non-profit pageant that provides scholarships to promising young nude women and cannot condone her decision to pose clad."

Zagat Editor A 'Nice Guy' But 'Kind Of Boring'

NEW YORK—Chris Dantley, editor of the Zagat restaurant guide for New York, received mixed reviews Monday from women who have dated him. "'Well-heeled' 'outgoing' man offers pleasant-enough company but 'loves to talk about self' and 'blows half his jokes,'" reviewers said of the 35-year-old Dantley, located on E. 81st Street near Third Avenue. "'Free smiles' and 'snappy dress' don't go far enough to offset 'strained compliments' and 'inappropriate come-hither looks.'" Dantley's midsection was also panned as "overly doughy."

Defiant Customers Refuse To Return Recalled Crib

RESTON, VA—More than 4,000 purchasers of the Babco KidSleeper crib, recalled last week amid safety concerns, are defiantly refusing to return the crib for a replacement or refund. "No way in hell am I assembling another crib," said parent Carl Bleier, 33, of Reston, VA. "If they want the thing back, too bad—it's their own damn fault for not making it right the first time." Bleier said he hopes his 14-month-old daughter Alexa gets her head stuck between the bars so he can sue their asses.

Country Music Protested In Restaurant's Kitchen

KALAMAZOO, MI—A coalition of dishwashers at the Pfaff Avenue Country Kitchen filed an official protest Tuesday against the grill crew's playing of 93.7 Hot Country on the kitchen radio. "Duuude," dishwasher spokesman Dave Stamm said. "Enough country, already." The group is calling for the radio to be switched to WKLQ 94.5, Home of the Real Rock, for the love of Christ.

Area Man Lives To Correct Pronunciation

LAWRENCE, KS—According to irritated friends and acquaintances, Jim Marder, 43, lives to correct pronunciation. "Actually, the word is 'Ant-*arc*-tic,'" Marder told coworker Amy Dennon during a conversation about polar-ice-cap melting Monday. "Don't feel bad: Pronouncing it 'Antartic' is a fairly common mistake." Said Dennon: "He's always doing that: 'Actually, the word is "affida-*vit*." "Actually, the word is "*pre*-rogative." "Actually, the word is "sher-*bet*." Every time, he plays it all casual, but you can tell he's loving it. Dick."

MALL from page 31

fleeing into the Rainforest Cafe.

The larger riot, however, was well underway. Upon hearing gunfire and seeing flames pour out of JCPenney, throngs of shoppers raced for the mall's exits, grabbing whatever merchandise they could on their way out. The mall's wooden benches were pulled up and broken into firewood. And, while no fatalities were reported, 32 shoppers were seriously injured when an overloaded glass elevator plunged three stories to the ground.

"With the addition of better-armed security personnel, good long-range rifles, and perhaps a control tower and perimeter fence, we should be back in business for the busy *Navidad* season," ASI spokeswoman Valerie Manning said.

"It all happened so fast," Sbarro employee Maria Dominguez said. "Suddenly, everyone was in the food court, grabbing anything they could, taking hot-dog buns and pretzels right off the warmers, overturning the ICEE machines. Then I heard some sort of explosion in the direction of the Build-A-Bear store, and all the lights went out."

Most of the violence and looting occurred in the first few hours, but fires fed by plastic Sam Goody shopping bags and Styrofoam TCBY cups raged long into the night.

A spokeswoman for ASI Development, the U.S. investment group that built the Mall of Central America, as well as the Mall of America in Bloomington, MN, called the episode "a small setback," vowing that the mall will reopen as soon as possible.

"With the addition of better-armed security personnel, good long-range rifles, and perhaps a control tower and perimeter fence, we should be back in business for the busy *Navidad* season," Valerie Manning said. "Actually, I'm pleased by the tremendous enthusiasm shown for the mall's merchandise. Naysayers predicted there would be no demand for high-end, brand-name retail goods in Central America, but I think they've been violently proven wrong."

Manning also expressed confidence that re-staffing the mall's stores will not be a problem.

"Although a great number of employees fled, there are vast numbers of unemployed ready to fill those positions," she said. "This time of year, Tegucigalpa is flooded with migrant laborers from the Honduran countryside, what with the work in the fields grinding to a halt during winter."

Though the average annual income in Central America is $922, Manning said she expects the mall to be a hit.

"We'll be offering on-the-spot approval for Macy's credit cards, so there will be no reason not to take advantage of their big sale on all DKNY bedding, including sheets, pillowcases, duvet covers, and shams," Manning said. "Bring the whole extended family. We're just a 12-hour canoe trip down the Pirre River and a three-day bus ride from Panama City."

Above: A shopper browses Macy's perfume department.

Manning noted that the mall has almost no competition in the immediate vicinity, other than a local market where bananas, coffee, and cacao are sold.

"We built the mall because our research indicated this area was extremely under-retailed," Manning said. "The average U.S. city has 18 square feet of retail space per person, compared to 1.2 here in Honduras. And talk about a customer base: El Salvador, Guatemala, and Costa Rica are the three most densely populated countries in the entire Western Hemisphere."

Mall visitor and father of five Andres Higuera, 37, made the trip from his slum village near Managua, Nicaragua, after hearing an ad for the grand opening on his transistor radio.

"I heard of a place with endless supplies of food and clothing," said Higuera, the soles of his only pair of shoes worn through from the trip. "I had to make the journey, for the sake of my family. It was difficult, but well worth it: Never have I seen so many Eddie Bauer rollneck sweaters." Ø

MEAL from page 31

beans and cole slaw. Plus, I would have toasted the bun just the way Eric likes it."

The restaurant outing was the idea of family patriarch Bob Wiersma, who said it served the dual purpose of "giving Mom a break" and providing a much-needed change of scenery.

"I told her, 'Don't worry about the price, Sandy,'" Bob recalled. "'Let's live it up a little.' Boy, did that backfire."

Sandy said she was upset that none of the dishes ordered were out of her culinary grasp, yet all were priced at least four times the cost of her homemade versions.

"It just seems so wasteful," Sandy said. "My chicken parmesan was $12.95, and I could have easily made it for the entire family for under $10. I could have picked up two nice chicken breasts at the Jewel for $5 and cut each one in half, making four servings. A good jar of tomato sauce would be $3, tops, and a 16-ounce box of pasta you can get for next to nothing. And I think I have everything I'd need for breading the chicken just sitting in the cupboard."

Added Sandy: "And you can bet my pasta wouldn't have been watery and overcooked."

Sandy tried to keep her worries over the cost of the dinner to herself for most of the evening. She felt compelled, however, to speak out against 12-year-old daughter Jenny's choice of a grilled-cheese sandwich as an entree.

"Mom was like, 'Why did you order that?'" Jenny said. "I told her that's what I felt like, so that's what I got.

"My chicken parmesan was $12.95, and I could have easily made it for the entire family for under $10," Sandy said.

She was freaking out, going off about how I could make a grilled cheese at home for two weeks straight for what they're charging. I was like, 'Mom, I just want a grilled cheese. Don't be such a spaz.'"

According to Jenny, Monday's incident was not the first time her mother has fretted over spending money on items she could have made herself.

"If we ask to buy a Halloween costume from a store, she has a total conniption," Jenny said. "Every year, she tells us that with a little imagination and elbow grease, we can have better costumes than the store-bought stuff. I don't know how many times I've had to be a California Raisin for Halloween because she won't let us go out and buy something cool."

Bob, the family's primary breadwinner, expressed consternation over his wife's thrifty ways.

"I keep telling her we're doing fine, moneywise," Bob said. "It's okay to spend a little to enjoy a nice night out at a restaurant. She'll agree to eat out, but then eventually, at some point in the evening, she'll say, 'You think it's worth paying $8.95 for a $2 plate of chicken fingers just to enjoy this décor? This place is nice, but it's not that nice.'"

Anxious to avoid such situations in the future, Bob said he will make an effort to only bring the family to restaurants that serve foods his wife does not know how to prepare.

Anxious to avoid such situations in the future, Bob said he will make an effort to only bring the family to restaurants that serve foods his wife does not know how to prepare.

"Next time, we'll go to a foreign place and try to pass it off as a 'family-enrichment night,'" Bob said. "There's a Chi-Chi's over in Downers Grove I've always wanted to go to, and I'm pretty sure Sandy doesn't know how to make Mexican, so it should be a more relaxed evening for us all." Ø

POET from page 31

sesses a strength of spirit that has moved and inspired millions.

Yet for all the admiration Luke has won, an unsettling, unspoken sentiment has slowly spread among the American people. Though most will scarcely dare to admit it, the consen-

"I saw Luke on *Oprah* a few months ago and was amazed by his remarkable poise and courage," said an Oklahoma homemaker, speaking on condition of anonymity. "But when I read his first *Hopeweavings* book, I couldn't deny this feeling that his poetry is actually pretty lousy."

sus is that young Luke's poetry is really, really bad.

"I saw Luke on *Oprah* a few months ago and was amazed by his remarkable poise and courage," said an Oklahoma homemaker, speaking on condition of anonymity. "But when I read his first *Hopeweavings* book, I couldn't deny this feeling that his poetry is actually pretty lousy. I feel horribly guilty saying so, but it's true."

The good intentions of Luke's poetry, coupled with his heartbreaking illness, make it difficult for Americans to recognize and acknowledge the poor quality of his work. The poems are fraught with saccharine sentimentality, slapdash mixed metaphors, and endless clichés involving rivers and the sun. One example from "What's Most Important," a poem in his most recent book, *Offering Of Hopeweavings*:

The things that are important in life / Are not wealth and fame / But the sun peering through the clouds / Its light shining on flower petals / And warming a kitten's nose / Making everything beautiful / Because that is what God wants / For us to be happy.

"Please don't hate me for what I'm about to say," said an unidentified 44-year-old male from Syracuse, NY. "I'm not against a disabled child having a creative outlet. And I don't expect Shakespeare here. But 'flower petals'? 'Warming a kitten's nose'? It's terrible. And notice how, toward the end, he always has to shoehorn in a reference to God. Almost every single poem is like that."

In "Breakfast Time," Luke likens his favorite meal of the day to spiritual redemption:

Opened my eyes to the sunrise / I can smell oatmeal and toast and juice / My favorites! / The sun's rays stream through my window / Taking away the darkness / The branches that scratched against my window all night / Are warmed in the sun's heat / Wasn't I silly to ever doubt or fear? / Mom is bringing my breakfast tray up to my room / There's oatmeal and toast / And juice! / Thank you, God, for this brand-new day / Another day to weave a new tapestry of hope.

Heaven's Not That Far Away
Another shiny morning
A big hug from Mom
My dog jumping in the grass
I love these little gifts
Making me feel special on the inside
And now I see a pretty rainbow
Right outside my window!
Yes, these are the moments
that make my hopeful spirit soar
When I know, deep in my heart
That heaven's not that far away

Above: A poem from the forthcoming *Grace Of Hopeweavings*.

"God is always near, children are always special, and the sun is forever shining," Veronica said. "I feel like somebody's cramming a rainbow down my throat."

The poem troubled a San Francisco bookstore employee, identified only as "Veronica."

"I don't consider myself some bitter, cynical crank who can't appreciate sincere sentiment," Veronica said. "But the unrelenting cheerfulness is a bit much. When I read one of these *Hopeweavings* poems, I want to open my shirt collar and go out for air. God is always near, children are always special, and the sun is forever shining. I feel like somebody's cramming a rainbow down my throat."

While Veronica and others wrestle with their guilt, Luke's fans eagerly await the January publication of his ninth book, *Grace Of Hopeweavings*.

"*Hopeweavings* books belong on every bookshelf in America," said Lubbock, TX, realtor Mary Ellen Buford. "Almost all my friends and colleagues have copies of Luke's books, and I highly recommend them to anyone. Luke is a living saint. I don't claim to get everything he writes, but that's how incredible this boy is. He has things to teach us that will take most of us a lifetime to understand."

This past April, Nicholas Farmer, 37, a technical-support specialist for a Boston telecommunications firm, attended a motivational seminar which featured Luke as a guest speaker.

"His poem about a conversation with an angel moved a lot of us to tears," Farmer said. "Watching that frail, brave little boy recite his poetry to a rapt audience is something I won't soon forget."

Moved by the experience, Farmer bought Luke's fifth book, *Hopeweavings: Heaven's Just A Hug Away*. Yet halfway through the book, even Farmer began to question its artistic merit.

"As I'm reading one of the poems—I think it was 'Another Shiny Day'—I'm thinking, can't Luke just draw pictures for his fridge?" Farmer said. "Or, better yet, not do anything artistic or spiritual at all, and just play video games? Am I just being a huge asshole? Probably." ⌀

GOD from page 33

Among the parts of the wedding God missed were the prelude, in which Roble's sister Tammy sang "Come And Journey With Me"; the processional; and the opening prayer, in which God was personally thanked for attending the ceremony.

"It was such a beautiful day," Moore said. "Everything was absolutely perfect. We were married in the presence of our friends, our family, and, of course, our God. What more could we ask for?"

Even Father Michael White, who officiated the ceremony, was unaware of God's absence, despite making numerous direct references to Him throughout.

"We always start off the ritual by welcoming God into His house and into the lives of the soon-to-be-married couple," White said during the beginning of the ceremony. "He is as central to this as the bride and groom."

God said He has "no regrets" about His tardiness.

"I really don't mind weddings—they're better than the funerals," God said. "But I've already been to 892,245 of them in the past month alone. It's not like I really needed to hear one more organ rendition of 'Nearer, My God, To Thee.'" ⌀

Oh My God, I Am So Totally Not A Fully Developed Person

Oh my God. You know what? I totally have to say something. Seriously, guys, you have to listen—this is way important. Kim? Erica? Amy? Are you listening? Okay, here it is: I am so not a fully developed person.

By Brittany Linder

Shut up, Erica, it so totally is true, and you know it.

It's like Jung says. He's all, like, the primary task of a human is fulfillment through the process of individuation and the establishment of harmony of the conscious and unconscious. That's what totally makes a person, like, whole. Except for me. I'm so not my own person, it's not even funny.

God, I can't believe I even have to say this because it's, like, so obvious. You know how individuation is, like, determination or contraction of a general nature to an individual mode of existence? How it's, like, the emergence of the individual self from the general? Well, that is so ridiculously not me, you know?

Okay, so Jung, he also was way into classifying personality types, right? He said there's, like, extroverts and introverts, and me, I am so obviously an extrovert. Anyway, so, like, the weakness of extroverts lies in their tendency toward superficiality and an overdependence on making a good

God, I can't believe I even have to say this because it's, like, so obvious. You know how individuation is, like, determination or contraction of a general nature to an individual mode of existence? How it's, like, the emergence of the individual self from the general? Well, that is so ridiculously not me, you know?

impression. Because they are well adapted to society, they usually accept popular social mores and convictions, and tend to be somewhat conventional in their judgments. They dislike being alone, regard reflection as morbid, and lack the tools for self-criticism. *Hel-lo?* Does that sound like anyone you know? I thought so.

Even though this is so clearly the case—like, how I really lack individual thoughts and opinions—my friends are still like, "Brittany, you are

Even though this is so clearly the case—like, how I really lack individual thoughts and opinions—my friends are still like, "Brittany, you are so totally the bomb."

so totally the bomb." I give my opinions on things, and people listen to me like I know what I'm talking about, but I, like, so completely do not. I mean, I'm not smart at all. Like, I am so totally one-dimensional, I can't even believe it.

If I am to develop a well-rounded personality, it's, like, essential that at some point my ego and intellect become aware of the existence of this other center of the personality—the center that contains this far greater intellect and will than the ego's center. Like, without developing the ability to become self-sufficient, there is no way I will become conscious of all the unknown potential lying dormant in the unknown parts of my psyche.

One small prob, though: I am sooo reliant on my parents, even though I'm always going off on how I can't stand them. Even more so, I'm dependent on the approval of my peer group—a group I chose specifically for its tendency to give my thoughts and actions unconditional approval. And, because I hang out pretty much exclusively with these friends and discount the opinions of those not in my peer group, I sort of get the idea I am not totally dumb. But the reality is, I, like, so totally am. Like, when I read things, I comprehend them only at the shallowest level. My opinions are just parroted reductions of things I overheard in passing or saw on TV. How sad is that?

Okay, I'm not completely dumb. I'm just really immature. I have a decent IQ, so I do have a chance of developing into a well-rounded, self-actualized person someday.

As for right now, though—oh my God. I mean, like, no friggin' way. ⌀

Your Horoscope

By Lloyd Schumner Sr.
Retired Machinist and
A.A.P.B.-Certified Astrologer

Aries: (March 21–April 19)
This holiday season is, as always, a time of terrible stress for you and the rest of the well-formed, eight-foot-tall pine trees.

Taurus: (April 20–May 20)
You would be a lot more comfortable with your home life if you knew why seven-time Winston Cup champion Richard Petty was always hanging around the place.

Gemini: (May 21–June 21)
You'll have the kind of week that makes you wish your parents had followed through on their military-school threats, but for different, sexier reasons.

Cancer: (June 22–July 22)
You'll have a thrilling adventure whose recounting will be greatly enjoyed by those willing to sit through your seizures to get to the sign language.

Leo: (July 23–Aug. 22)
You're beginning to wonder exactly who is in charge of quality control for all those treasure maps.

Virgo: (Aug. 23–Sept. 22)
You will get a good deal on a major appliance purchase, but that's about it.

Libra: (Sept. 23–Oct. 23)
An otherwise enjoyable week is shot to hell when you have several phone conversations with people from L.A.

Scorpio: (Oct. 24–Nov. 21)
You will be the toast of forensic investigators from coast to coast for your ability to really spread the ol' fluids around the murder scene.

Sagittarius: (Nov. 22–Dec. 21)
You were a cop, and a damn good one at that, but you committed the ultimate sin and testified against one of your own. Now, you must pay the price and be doomed to late-night cable syndication.

Capricorn: (Dec. 22–Jan. 19)
It's impossible for you to get more tail than a dogcatcher—partially because of your poor hygiene, but mainly because you're a dogcatcher.

Aquarius: (Jan. 20–Feb. 18)
You've never been one to take offense at accusations of arrogance, especially since they're all bullshit anyway.

Pisces: (Feb. 19–March 20)
You will abandon your search for the wisdom of the East when it turns out to be devoid of cool kung-fu moves.

ORINOCO RIVER from page 29

amounts of blood. Passersby were amazed by the unusually large amounts of blood. Passersby were amazed by the unusually large amounts of blood. Passersby were

Let me just riff a bit on this eulogy thing.

amazed by the unusually large amounts of blood. Passersby were amazed by the unusually large amounts of blood. Passersby were

see ORINOCO RIVER page 48

the ONION®

VOLUME 38 ISSUE 47 AMERICA'S FINEST NEWS SOURCE™ 19 DEC. 2002–15 JAN. 2003

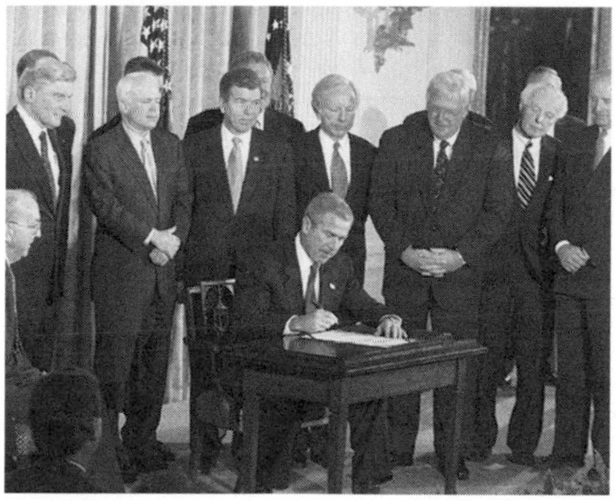

Above: As supporters look on, Bush signs the Bill Of Rights Reduction And Consolidation Act.

Bill Of Rights Pared Down To A Manageable Six

WASHINGTON, DC—Flanked by key members of Congress and his administration, President Bush approved Monday a streamlined version of the Bill of Rights that pares its 10 original amendments down to a "tight, no-nonsense" six.

A Republican initiative that went unopposed by congressional Democrats, the revised Bill of Rights provides citizens with a "more manageable" set of privacy and due-process rights by eliminating four amendments and condensing and/or restructuring five others. The Second Amendment, which protects the right to keep and bear arms, was the only article left unchanged.

see BILL OF RIGHTS page 41

Ghost Of Christmas Future Taunts Children With Visions Of PlayStation 5

SOUTHFIELD, MI—Bored with scaring elderly misers, the Ghost of Christmas Future is spending the holiday season taunting modern children with visions of Christmas 2016's hottest toy: the Sony PlayStation 5, a 2,048-bit console featuring a 45-Ghz trinary processor, CineReal graphics booster with 2-gig biotexturing, and an RSP connector for 360-degree online-immersion play.

"You know how kids are—a year is an eternity to them," the wraithlike specter said Monday during a visit to the Southfield home of 13-year-old Josh Kuehn. "So just imagine showing them something they'll have to wait 14 years for. Teasing them with a glimpse of the PS5 is the ultimate torture. They absolutely lose their minds.

see PLAYSTATION page 40

Right: The Ghost of Christmas Future offers a pair of Phoenix 10-year-olds a tantalizing glimpse of the PS5.

Above: Meyers enjoys a beer at an airport bar in Atlanta.

Frequent Flyer Knows Out-Of-The-Way Airport Bar That's Never Crowded

ATLANTA—Savvy, experienced business traveler Donald Meyers, 46, knows a great out-of-the-way bar at O'Hare Airport's "B" terminal that's never crowded, the frequent flyer said Monday during a layover in Atlanta.

Meyers, a project manager for Motorola who is on the road an average of 150 days a year, discovered the Windy City Pub during a three-hour layover at O'Hare in May 2001. He said the bar is one of his top 10 frequent-flying treats.

"I don't say this often, but visiting this little bar is actually worth extending your time between flights," Meyers said. "It's never crowded, the chairs are incredibly comfortable, and it's set back a bit from the terminal walkways, so it's not nearly as loud as your average airport bar. I'd have to put it up there with the Cheers bar at Detroit Metro and the one they used to have at the end of the United terminal at Denver's old Stapleton International."

Meyers also had high praise for Tomas Cordero, the Windy City Pub's weekday bartender.

see BAR page 40

NEWS

Putin Will Try The, How You Say, Fried Chicken

see WORLD page 4A

Successories Poster Shoplifted

see LOCAL page 3E

Cindy Lou Who Asks Why We're Invading Iraq

see LOCAL page 14E

8-Year-Old Carefully Invests Dreidel Winnings

see LOCAL page 10E

STATshot

A look at the numbers that shape your world.

How Are We Fighting The War On Terror?

1. Sending Pvt. Dale Schoepke of Elkhart, IN, to Iraq
2. Writing compelling three-part essay in *The Atlantic Monthly*
3. Watching tons of porn, which is forbidden in fundamentalist Islam
4. Keeping nails neat and trimmed
5. Tactical shopping sprees

0 74470 94595 6 00

THE ONION • $2.00 US • $3.00 CAN

Iraq And The Nuclear Option

Last week, President Bush said he would not rule out using nuclear weapons against enemies wielding weapons of mass destruction. What do *you* think?

"Well, that seems like a pretty sensible policy that won't have any negative longterm repercussions among nuclear-capable nations already wary of the U.S."

Dana Klugh
Homemaker

"That reminds me. I've got some leftover falafel I'm gonna go nuke for lunch. This is called 'displacement behavior.' It is not working."

Carl Roberts
Engineer

"It's about time we had a president who's not afraid to step up to the plate and make the biggest mistake in the history of world civilization."

Don Swartz
Systems Analyst

"It's like the late '80s all over again: A Bush threatening war, nuclear paranoia, me involved in a protracted legal battle over an alleged sex crime..."

Larry Golub
Gardener

"He's bluffing. Bush could never bring himself to deliberately nuke that many oil fields."

Cris Porter
Roofer

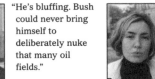

"You know the scariest thing about this whole situation? Me, neither. It's impossible to decide."

Denise Traylor
Graduate Student

Lord Of The Rings: The Two Towers

The much-anticipated second installment of the *Lord Of The Rings* series opens Wednesday. Why is there so much excitement?

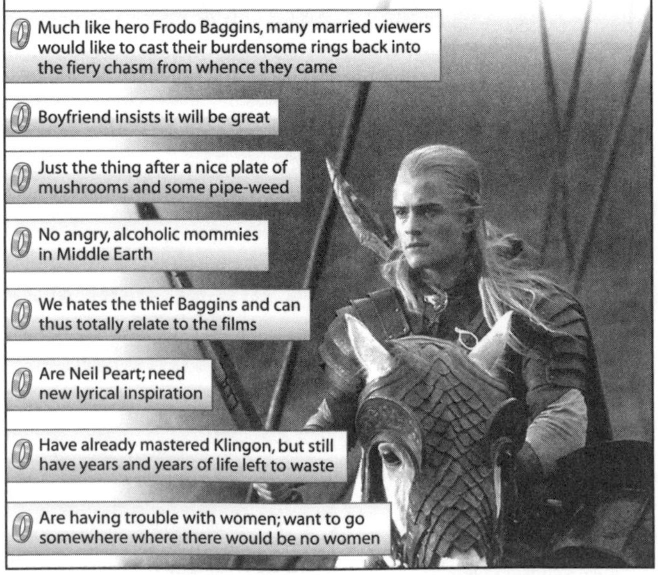

- Much like hero Frodo Baggins, many married viewers would like to cast their burdensome rings back into the fiery chasm from whence they came
- Boyfriend insists it will be great
- Just the thing after a nice plate of mushrooms and some pipe-weed
- No angry, alcoholic mommies in Middle Earth
- We hates the thief Baggins and can thus totally relate to the films
- Are Neil Peart; need new lyrical inspiration
- Have already mastered Klingon, but still have years and years of life left to waste
- Are having trouble with women; want to go somewhere where there would be no women

the ONION®
America's Finest News Source.™

Herman Ulysses Zweibel
Founder

T. Herman Zweibel
Publisher Emeritus
J. Phineas Zweibel
Publisher
Maxwell Prescott Zweibel
Editor-In-Chief

What This Town Needs Is A Really Shitty Community Newspaper

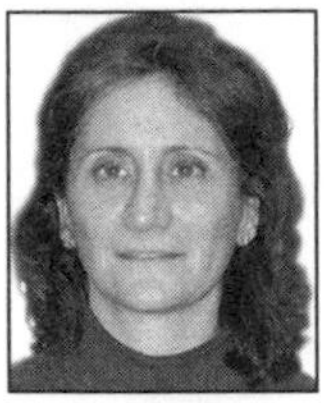

By Lorraine Ostrove

Here in Park Hills, we get *The Duluth News-Tribune*, just like people do all over the greater Duluth area. But while that major daily does a perfectly adequate job keeping the people of Park Hills in touch with the goings-on of the city at large, it doesn't speak directly to our own local community. It doesn't take into account the uniqueness of Park Hills, focusing on the people, places, and things that make our neighborhood so special. Yes, it's clear as day to me: What Park Hills needs is a really shitty community newspaper.

When the first issue of *The Park Hills Beacon* rolls off the presses next week, the people of Park Hills will finally have a mind-numbingly insipid newspaper to bind them together. Each week, the Beacon will offer the good people of Park Hills grammatically shaky, factual-error-packed articles on traffic problems, local taxpayer issues, and proposed public works projects. There will also be reports on the few trivial incidents of crime that occur in our neighborhood, but above all, we wish to highlight positive aspects of our community, no matter how grindingly dull they may be. From the Park Hills Senior Center production of *South Pacific* to the Park Hills Elementary School spelling bee, no event is too small or mundane for the *Beacon* to cover.

So what can you look forward to in the first issue? Well, the Gallery Players Theater is putting on a sub-amateur production of a play called *Locomotive*, and we're going to run a cover story with two large, blurry photos.

And how will the *Beacon* determine which local issues will be covered? That's simple: If someone in town writes an article about something they saw or heard about, that article will run.

When someone picks up a copy of *The Park Hills Beacon* from the stack in the Save-Rite entryway, they will be doing so in the spirit of building a better, more tightly knit community. What better way to foster community spirit, for example, than by scanning our ludicrously unreliable events listings? Many events occurring in the area will be included: the Oak Barrel Brew Pub's "Brew Ha-Ha" comedy night, a rummage sale at St. Mary's Episcopal Church, and a two-piece band playing at the Down Under Jazz Café. I wouldn't advise showing up at any of these, though: Nine times out of ten, the day, time, or place will be listed incorrectly. Sometimes all three! That auction at the Park Hills Convalescence Center at 8 p.m. on Dec. 24? It's actually at the Park Hills Rec Center on the 23rd. Oops, sorry.

When the first issue of *The Park Hills Beacon* rolls off the presses next week, the people of Park Hills will finally have a mind-numbingly insipid newspaper to bind them together.

So, what can you look forward to in the first issue? Well, the Gallery Players Theater is putting on a sub-amateur production of a play called *Locomotive*, and we're going to run a cover story with two large, blurry photos. The story will include a sidebar biography of the director, a woman we have all known for years, but her name will still be misspelled. Along the side of the page, we'll print ads for China Wok restaurant and Visions Eyewear Center, as well as a pleading reminder to pick up *The Park Hills Beacon* every Thursday.

Speaking of restaurants, *Beacon* readers will enjoy puffy, unexacting reviews of the handful of restaurants that everyone already knows about here in town. And each new restaurant that opens will receive a glowing review, praised either as "absolutely delicious" or "an experience not to be missed." Fat Jack's Barbeque? Absolutely delicious! Pat's Supper Club? An experience not to be missed! I think you get the idea.

That's just the tip of the iceberg. There will also be reviews of the two or three movies someone on staff happens to see, stories about sales on outdoor furniture at garden shops if

see NEWSPAPER page 41

WORKPLACE

Coworker Suicide Fails To Shatter Office

WORCESTER, MA—Last weekend's suicide of Sentinel Management Solutions employee Tom Blundell has failed to shatter the management-consulting firm's office, sources reported Tuesday.

"It's truly tragic, and our hearts go out to his loved ones," Sentinel Management Solutions president Karl Steig said Monday. "In the wake of such a shocking and violent event, however, it's important for life to go on as normally as possible. That's why we decided to keep the office open today."

Found dead in his apartment Saturday from what investigators determined to be a self-inflicted gunshot wound to the head, Blundell had worked at SMS for nearly three years as a data-entry clerk, with occasional weekend duties assisting the customer-service department. Though only two other data-entry-department employees surpassed him in seniority, Blundell was recalled by coworkers as a "recent hire" whom they never got to know particularly well.

"As hard as this has been on everyone at SMS, this has to be even harder on his family," human-resources coordinator Carol Wiese said. "Assuming he had a family, that is. I'm honestly not sure. If he had a wife and kids, he never mentioned it. And he had no dependents on his health insurance. On his employee record, he lists his father as his next of kin, so hopefully the police have contacted him already."

Right: The Sentinel Management Solutions office not rocked by the death of Blundell (above).

According to Steig, the suicide was wholly unexpected.

"We had no idea he was troubled," Steig said. "He kept to himself a lot and didn't really interact with coworkers much. Maybe if he'd reached out to us more, he would have felt less alone, but sometimes that's hard for new people."

Jon Hanschel, a customer-service representative who occasionally worked alongside Blundell, tried to recall the last time he saw him.

"It was two Saturdays ago," Hanschel said. "Or maybe the one before that. I could check the November schedule. No, forget it—that got thrown away. Anyway, whichever Saturday it was, I'm pretty sure he was here that day, because I could see the back of a guy's head from my desk, and I'm almost positive it was him."

Hanschel was among the few SMS employees willing to speak publicly about the suicide. Most declined comment, preferring to cope with the tragedy by immersing themselves in their work.

On Tuesday afternoon, Steig spoke with SMS office manager Joseph Chen about the possibility of retaining the services of an on-site grief counselor to help workers deal with their bereavement.

"Karl asked me, 'How's everyone doing?' and I said, 'Pretty well, considering,'" Chen said. "Actually, very well. I told him hiring a grief counselor probably wouldn't be necessary. A couple of people who worked directly with Tom were kind of shaken up Monday, but they all seem much better today."

"Maybe next week, the shock will finally start to sink in," Chen said. "Sometimes with these things, there's a period of numbness and disbelief before the pain starts. Then again, maybe the shock of this suicide will never be felt."

see SUICIDE page 41

NEWS IN BRIEF

Barnes & Noble Staffers Mock Orson Scott Card Crowd From Back Of Room

RALEIGH, NC—Employees of the Crabtree Mall Barnes & Noble used a Tuesday book-signing by science-fiction author Orson Scott Card as an opportunity to mock those in attendance. "'Excuse me, Mr. Card,'" cashier Randy Feig said to coworker Ian Rose in a derisive, pinched "nerd" voice. "'In *Shadow Of The Hegemon*, why was Ender Wiggin so reluctant to return to Earth after the Formic War?'" Feig then urged Rose to "check out the huge dude in the cloak" in the second row.

FBI: Six Dead Not Really 'Mass' Murder

WASHINGTON, DC—Addressing reporters about the ritual slaying of six cheerleaders at a Frankfort, KY, high school, FBI director Robert Mueller clarified that the body count does not seem high enough to qualify as "mass" murder. "I don't know if there's an official minimum, but I always imagined 'mass' was more like 15 or 20," Mueller said. "Charles Whitman, now *there* was a mass murderer." Mueller added that, in spite of their modest scale, the killings "were still pretty bad."

Man Always Insists You Toss Him Keys Rather Than Just Hand Them To Him

LITTLE ROCK, AR—Area resident Russ Squirek insists on having his keys tossed to him rather than handed, sources reported Monday. "It's always, 'Yo, here we go, long bomb, send 'em over, going deep,'" friend Craig Green said. "I think he thinks it's cool." Green said Squirek also insists on hopping into convertibles whenever possible rather than using the door.

How Was Local Man To Know Carol Channing's Niece Was Around?

SAN BERNARDINO, CA—Well, Jesus, is area resident Richard Pauling, 43, never supposed to crack jokes about anyone at a party because, by some freakish coincidence, their niece might actually wind up being in earshot and get pissed off? "All I did was make a humorous remark about actress Carol Channing's advanced age that involved speculation regarding the dryness of her nether regions, and suddenly I'm Hitler," Pauling said. "Shit."

Woman Who Visited Kenya Once Struts Confidently Into African Store

SKOKIE, IL—Amanda Wyner, 23, who in 1998 spent a week vacationing at a Kenya resort during college spring break, strode confidently Monday into Harambe, a Woodfield Mall store specializing in African art and collectibles. "This is a tribal mask," Wyner stated authoritatively to her sister while holding an Ashanti war mask. "The Africans wear these during actual ceremonies."

Fact Repeated As Urban Legend

BREWSTER, WA—An actual occurrence passed into the realm of modern folklore Tuesday, when actor Robert Reed's 1992 AIDS-related death was repeated as urban legend. "Dude, this guy I know told me that the guy who played the dad on *The Brady Bunch* died of AIDS," said Jeff Gund, 16. "Can you believe he believed that?" Gund went on to tell the equally implausible tale of a woman who cut off her husband's penis and threw it in a field, only to see the man surgically reattach it and become a porn star.

PLAYSTATION from page 37

It's like saying, 'Hey, kid, you'll be an old man before you ever get to touch this.'"

The Ghost of Christmas Future said he has visited more than 125,000 homes since Thanksgiving, offering children an agonizing sneak peek at what they cannot have for another

The Ghost of Christmas Future said he has visited more than 125,000 homes since Thanksgiving, offering children an agonizing sneak peek at what they cannot have for another decade and a half.

decade and a half.

"I like to appear in the living room with a PS5 hooked up to 2016's most popular TV, the 4'x8' Hi-Def Sony Titania," the Ghost said. "Then, I'll say in my best spooky voice, 'Jimmy! Behold what your kids will be playing while you're slaving away at an office job to support them!'"

Driving the children mad with PS5 lust, the Ghost said, is a multi-step process.

"I usually start by showing them Toteki Aluminum, one of the future's most popular fight-and-chase games," the Ghost said. "It's far from the best available in 2016, but it always blows their mind to see the guy get hit with the falling sign while the drops of sweat fly off his face. You can see the whole scene, distorted, in each of the individual drops. That gives them a good preliminary idea of the graphics

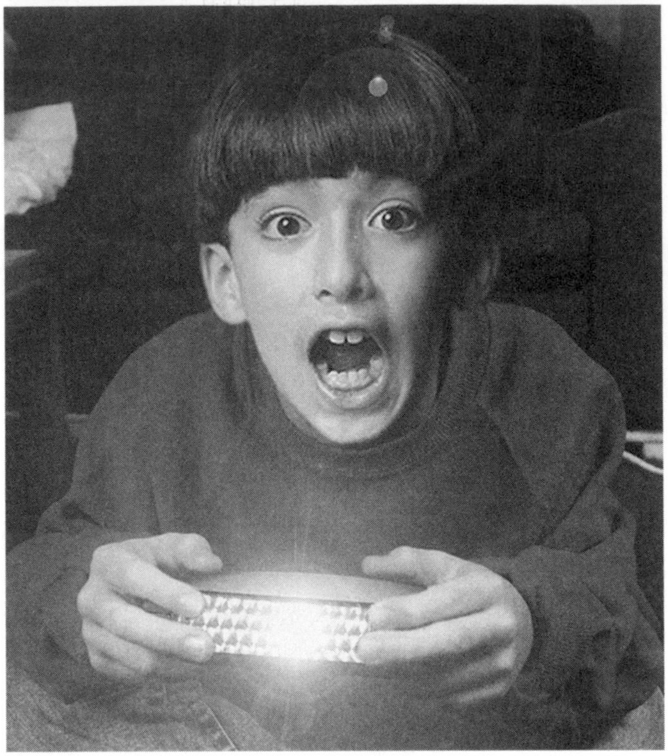

Above: Aaron Booker of Dayton, OH, samples the PlayStation 5.

technology we're dealing with."

The Ghost said he then likes to show Airsledz, a racing game in which jet-powered sleds whoosh through a four-dimensional racing course in the sky. The game, he said, enables the player to compete online against dozens of other players all around the world.

"They always ask if you can play it on the Internet—it's so cute how they still call it 'the Internet'—and I tell them, 'Hey, you can play this against 63 other PS5 owners simultaneously. At least you can in 14 years,'" the Ghost said. "And you should see their jaws hit the floor when they learn about the add-on accessories that enable users to actually fly around the room during gameplay."

Once the capabilities of the system are conveyed to the children, the Ghost likes to push them further over the edge by showing them games specially targeted to their age group.

Younger children, he said, salivate upon seeing Level One of Zonic Fugue. In it, Zonic, the indigo-colored son of Sonic The Hedgehog, faces off against Chuckles The Echidna in a Terrordactyl sky-joust, attempting to earn the Ankle Rockets he needs to gather the five Chaos Sapphires that, when combined, form the master key that opens the Melody Dome.

To break the spirits of children 12 and up, the Ghost runs a brief demonstration of Back To Werewolf Island. The horror-action thriller, he said, will be produced in full 10.8 Omneo sound and feature new music from 40 of 2016's hottest skagcore acts, including FU3P, Dredgerous, and Frances Cobain.

"Sometimes, the kids will start getting defensive and say, 'Yeah, well, I don't know any of those characters, so big deal,'" the Ghost said. "That's when I pull out DC vs. Marvel."

The Ghost said he shows the children a brief clip of DC vs. Marvel, in which cinema-realistic figures of Spider-Man and the Joker dash across impossibly detailed city streets, attacking each other with dozens of different offensive maneuvers while leaping, somersaulting, and throwing objects.

"They usually start trembling at that point," the Ghost said. "That's when I go in for the kill by casually mentioning that the game comes packaged with the 2016 feature film of the same name—not on DVD, of course, but on SCAP. Ten times better."

The few children unbroken by DC vs. Marvel are invariably finished off by the sight of Star Wars—Episode IX: Jedi Destiny, a game which employs the world's most advanced artificial-intelligence algorithm to place the player inside the film's climactic battle sequence on the planet Mon Jeedam.

"With more than 12,000 distinct soldiers, creatures, and vehicles fighting at once, and the option to command the New Republic Fleet, the Imperial Armada, or the Yuuzhan Vong Invasion Force, it's not merely the best *Star Wars* game that's ever existed; it's an interactive film that looks better than any movie that's ever been made. No child has failed to sob hysterically at the sight of it."

The PlayStation 5 will be available in stores Nov. 12, 2016, at a list price of ∆399 New Dollars ($199 Canadian).

BAR from page 37

"Tomas is great," said Meyers, who, when not on the road, lives in St. Louis with his wife Linda and their two sons Cody and Cameron. "He puts something—I don't know what—with a little extra zing in the Bloody Mary mix. Everyone knows you shouldn't drink before flying, but if you knew this little hidden gem, you'd probably be willing to chance it."

With an estimated 2,000 flights under his belt in his 23 years of business travel, Meyers claims to be "one of the nation's leading authorities" on airport amenities, and said he is "more than happy" to pass along knowledge and experience to his fellow travelers.

"If you don't fly often, there's lots of stuff you probably don't know," Meyers said. "Like how much better the Northwest WorldClub lounge is in Dallas than the one at most other airports—especially LaGuardia. Or how you can do on-line check-in with Continental, but that's only if you have no carry-ons. Or how you should use your Delta SkyMiles card on weekends, because you get double miles on all purchases. Those are the kind of

With an estimated 2,000 flights under his belt in his 23 years of business travel, Meyers claims to be "one of the nation's leading authorities" on airport amenities.

things you may not know if you're not a seasoned traveler like myself."

Anna Helsing, 33, sat next to Meyers on a recent St. Louis-Minneapolis flight.

"I was trying to get comfortable in my seat when [Meyers] launched into this whole thing about how I should avoid those U-shaped neck pillows," Helsing said. "When I told him I didn't know what he was talking about, he showed me one in the SkyMall catalog and explained that they cramp your neck worse than the regular airline pillow or a folded-up blanket. I wasn't about to use one, but he felt the need to warn me, anyway."

Catherine Appel, who sat next to Meyers on a recent San Francisco-Los Angeles flight, said he spent a majority of the trip assessing the hotels situated near various major U.S. and Canadian airports.

"Apparently, the Newark Airport Westin is one of the worst in the country," Appel said. "I have no idea if that's true, but he seems to know. I mean, if you heard this guy talk... He advised getting the kosher meal because it's always better. He gave me tips on getting business-class upgrades. He bragged about getting his oversized luggage onto planes as

"Apparently, the Newark Airport Westin is one of the worst in the country," Appel said.

carry-on because of some weird routing loophole he knows about. And he went on and on about this magic, uncrowded bar at O'Hare, which he made sound like an oasis in the middle of the desert."

"I'd shoot myself if I ever knew that much about airport hotels and bars," Appel added. "Thank God I don't have to fly as much as that poor loser."

SUICIDE from page 39

Determined to soldier on in Blundell's absence, SMS has decided not to cancel or even postpone its holiday party, which is scheduled for this Friday—the same day as Blundell's memorial service. An office-wide e-mail written Monday by Chen reflects the company's determination to move forward.

"Employees who wish to attend Tom Blundell's 5 p.m. memorial service may do so without punching out, but the office holiday party will still start at 6 p.m. sharp," the e-mail read. "Sentinel Management Solutions: providing effective, affordable management consultation for businesses large and small since 1984. Do not reply to this message."

NEWSPAPER from page 38

anyone on the staff should happen to be shopping for items for their garden, a "youth view" column by my daughter Kim, and trivia quizzes, soap-opera updates, and other such syndicated filler from King Features. Oh, and clip art. Plenty of clip art.

Who will write for the *Beacon*, you ask? Anyone! New stay-at-home moms whose careers are suddenly on hold. Kids from the local college looking to impress their journalism professors. Old cranks. The band teacher at the local high school. Undiscovered "writers." There is a place for everyone and everything in this paper: trite opinion columns, boring letters to the editor, painfully unfunny humor pieces, even poems. We will *actually print poems*!

Granted, we are not the first weekly in the Duluth area to offer an alternative, more localized viewpoint. Other papers have blazed a path: *The South Duluth Journal Of Arts & Urban Affairs* (December 1999 to September 2001), *Minnesota Mother* (September 2001 to February 2002), *Natural Foods & Life* (February 2002 to April 2002). Right here in Park Hills, the years have witnessed a host of long-forgotten newspapers: *Out-N-About*, *What's Around Town?*, *Go! Park Hills*, and *The Park Hills Courier*, which was this neighborhood's journal of record for several months in late 1991. *The Park Hills Beacon*, however, will be different—slightly different, though not actually any better.

Who knows what fate will hold for the *Beacon*? Perhaps we will last just a few months. Perhaps we will last a full year. Either way, we will have made our mark. By the time we fold, hundreds of community members will have absentmindedly skimmed our unprofessional, visually unappealing rag while waiting in line for the ATM. Some may even go so far as to carry an issue back to their car, only to find it crumpled and wet under the floor mat a few months later. But when our shitty newspaper inevitably goes under, it will have been worth it, for *The Park Hills Beacon* will have made a tiny difference in the lives of some of the people who worked on one of the issues.

BILL OF RIGHTS from page 37

Calling the historic reduction "a victory for America," Bush promised that the new document would do away with "bureaucratic impediments to the flourishing of democracy at home and abroad."

"It is high time we reaffirmed our commitment to this enduring symbol of American ideals," Bush said. "By making the Bill of Rights a tool for progress instead of a hindrance to freedom, we honor the true spirit of our nation's forefathers."

The Fourth Amendment, which long protected citizens' homes against unreasonable search and seizure, was among the eliminated amendments. Also stricken was the Ninth Amendment, which stated that the enumeration of certain constitutional rights does not result in the abrogation of rights not mentioned.

"Quite honestly, I could never get my head around what the Ninth Amendment meant anyway," said outgoing House Majority Leader Dick Armey (R-TX), one of the leading advocates of the revised Bill of Rights. "So goodbye to that one."

Amendments V through VII, which guaranteed the right to legal counsel in criminal cases, and guarded against double jeopardy, testifying against oneself, biased juries, and drawn-out trials, have been condensed into Super-Amendment V: The One About Trials.

Attorney General John Ashcroft hailed the slimmed-down Bill of Rights as "a positive step."

"Go up to the average citizen and ask him what's in the Bill of Rights," Ashcroft said. "Chances are, they'll have only a vague notion. They just know it's a set of rules put in place to protect their individual freedoms from government intrusion, and they assume that's a good thing."

Ashcroft responded sharply to critics who charge that the Bill of Rights no longer safeguards certain basic, inalienable rights.

"We're not taking away personal rights; we're increasing personal security," Ashcroft said. "By allowing for greater government control over the particulars of individual liberties, the Bill of Rights will now offer expanded personal freedoms whenever they are deemed appropriate and unobtrusive to the activities necessary to effective operation of the federal government."

"By making the Bill of Rights a tool for progress instead of a hindrance to freedom, we honor the true spirit of our nation's forefathers," Bush said.

Ashcroft added that, thanks to several key additions, the Bill of Rights now offers protections that were previously lacking, including the right to be protected by soldiers quartered in one's home (Amendment III), the guarantee that activities not specifically delegated to the states and people will be carried out by the federal government (Amendment VI), and freedom of Judeo-Christianity and non-combative speech (Amendment I).

According to U.S. Sen. Larry Craig (R-ID), the original Bill of Rights, though well-intentioned, was "seriously outdated."

"The United States is a different place than it was back in 1791," Craig said. "As visionary as they were, the framers of the Constitution never could have foreseen, for example, that our government would one day need to jail someone indefinitely without judicial review. There was no such thing as suspicious Middle Eastern immigrants back then."

Ashcroft noted that recent FBI efforts to conduct investigations into "unusual activities" were severely hampered by the old Fourth Amendment.

"The Bill of Rights was written more than 200 years ago, long before anyone could even fathom the existence of wiretapping technology or surveillance cameras," Ashcroft said. "Yet through a bizarre fluke, it was still somehow worded in such a way as to restrict use of these devices. Clearly, it had to go before it could do more serious damage in the future."

President Bush agreed.

"Any machine, no matter how well-built, periodically needs a tune-up to keep it in good working order," Bush said. "Now that we have the bugs worked out of the ol' Constitution, she'll be purring like a kitten when Congress reconvenes in January—just in time to work on a new round of counterterrorism legislation."

"Ten was just too much of a handful," Bush added. "Six civil liberties are more than enough."

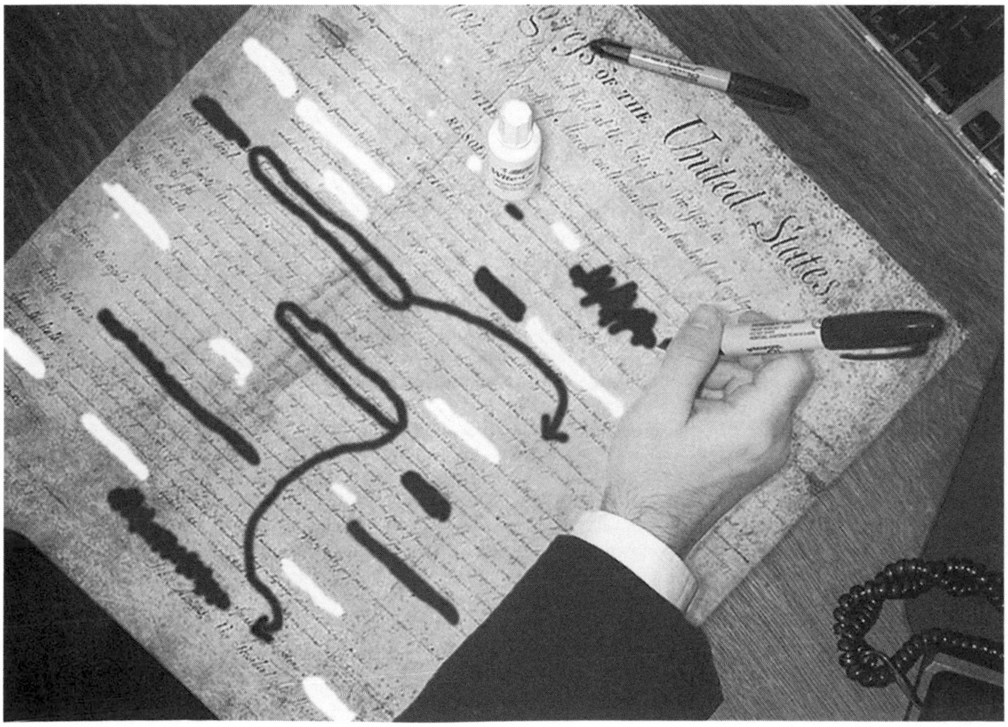

Above: Bush works on revisions to the Bill of Rights.

COMMUNITY VOICES

Secret Santas Are For Shit

Hola, amigos. What's going on? I know it's been a long time since I rapped at ya, but I've been carrying a heavy load lately. The winter's really depressing the shit out of me. Between the cold and the 14 hours of darkness, I never want to leave the house. All my pals are in the same boat, so they don't come over and hang out like they usually do. Good thing I got my GameCube. That's all the friends I need.

The Cruise
By Jim Anchower

I did manage to find myself a gig for the month, though. There's this Christmas store called Holiday Land, where they sell all kinds of festive shit: wreaths, trees, mistletoe, and candles that are supposed to smell like cinnamon or pine but just smell like stink-candles. You probably know the place. In October, it was called Spooky World, and they sold masks and vampire fangs. I was hoping I could find all that old Halloween stuff in storage so I could snag a few tubes of fake blood, but they have this warehouse they send all the stuff back to when the season's over.

I'm in the tree department. I guess I got my wish to get a job where I can burn off some of my gut, 'cause all I do is haul crap around all day. I take people's trees and run them through this tube of nylon net so they can tie it to their car without needles and branches flying all over the place. The pay's pretty decent, and I guess everyone's all right, except my boss, Mr. Smalley. The guy's a total dickweed. He thinks he's being funny when he calls me Jim Clamchowder, like I didn't hear enough of that in eighth grade.

I went to the break-room table and, sure enough, there was a gift waiting for me from my Secret Santa. It was definitely too small to be beer, but maybe they got me a pint of Dr. McGillicuddy's.

Last Friday, Smalley totally dressed me down for wishing someone a Merry Christmas. I told him I thought we were supposed to say that, and he was like, "You're supposed to say 'Happy Holidays.' It fosters an environment of religious inclusion." I got a news flash for you, Smalley: It don't make no difference if you tell them "Happy Ass Day." They're there to get a Christmas tree, not a holiday tree.

Then there's the whole Secret Santa thing. Smalley was all like, "Come on, it'll be fun!" Now, I've got a pretty good idea of what fun is, and some bullshit Secret Santa just doesn't make the cut. It wasn't like we were required to participate, but it was "strongly suggested." It's like peer pressure. In junior-high health class, they never had film strips about Secret Santa peer pressure, but they should've. And they should've starred Smalley, shaking a coffee can full of names in your face.

I drew Nancy, this old chick at the checkout counter. All I knew about her was that she smoked Newports and had an enormous rack.

I drew Nancy, this old chick at the checkout counter. I had no idea what to get her. We'd barely said three words to one another since I started working there. All I knew about her was that she smoked Newports and had an enormous rack.

The days flew by, and I kept forgetting to pick something up. The day before we were supposed to swap gifts, I thought long and hard about it on the drive home from work. It's tough work trying to figure out what to get someone you don't know and won't be working with in three weeks. It was making me thirsty, so I pulled over to the big warehouse liquor store on the way home. That's when it hit me.

Right in front, they had this huge stack of what can only be called paradise. It was a tower of 12-packs of Miller Genuine Draft that was at least as tall as me. The 12-packs were on sale for $6.50. At that price, I'd have been stupid not to get it for the Secret Santa, especially since it was definitely under the $10 spending limit. I picked one up for Nancy and grabbed three for me. I wasn't about to spread that sort of holiday cheer without getting a little for myself.

I took my treasure trove home, put one of my twelves in the fridge, and looked for some wrapping paper. All I had was a bunch of Walgreens circulars that had been piling up for, like, three months and some duct tape. After the longest 15 minutes of my life, I finally finished the wrap job. Rewarding myself for a job well done, I took out one of my beers and had a swig.

The next day, I went to the break-room table and, sure enough, there was a gift waiting for me from my Secret Santa. It was definitely too small to be beer, but maybe they got me a pint of Dr. McGillicuddy's or something. I put my package with the others and got to work.

At about 4:30, we knocked off a half-hour early so we could eat cookies and open our presents. After five or six people went, it came time for Nancy to open hers. As she started to open it, I yelled, "Hey, save the paper—I took a lot of time wrapping that!" Everyone laughed, and I knew I had it made.

As she was opening it, she had this weird look on her face. Then she started shaking. Some of the other cashiers were staring at me, giving me the stink eye. Nancy looked up at me and said thanks for the gift, but told me she'd quit drinking about four months ago. I was like, "All right! More for me!" but this time, no one laughed. I kept to myself the rest of the "party," and every once in a while, I'd get dirty looks from the other cashiers. How was I supposed to know Nancy was on the wagon? When the party ended, I just drove home and went through the better part of one of my 12-packs.

And what did I get from my Secret Santa? A red and green scarf. Man, there are so many things wrong with that. First off, Jim Anchower doesn't wear scarves. Never have, and I ain't about to break tradition just because someone got me one. Second, I never wear red and green. Shit, why not just knit me a sweater with a reindeer and the words "Kick My Ass" on it? That'd do the job just as well. Sometimes, there's no justice.

But like I said, I ain't ungrateful. I'm sure my Secret Santa, Debbie from the back office, thought it was cool. We can't all be blessed with good taste. I took the scarf and threw it under my bed. At least now I have something to give if I ever get suckered into doing another Secret Santa.

New Year's Eve had better be better than Christmas is shaping up to be. That's all I'm saying. Ø

HOROSCOPES

Your Horoscope

By Lloyd Schumner Sr.
Retired Machinist and
A.A.P.B.-Certified Astrologer

Aries: (March 21–April 19)
Nothing can convince you that the chase sequence in *Bullitt* isn't the greatest love scene ever committed to film.

Taurus: (April 20–May 20)
The stars say this is a good week for romance, but lately you've been getting the feeling they're not talking about you.

Gemini: (May 21–June 21)
You will come very close to acting heroically when you push an old lady out of the way of a hurtling bus and underneath a cement truck.

Cancer: (June 22–July 22)
Don't take next week's failures too hard: No one could have foreseen the sudden appearance of so many ax-wielding monkeys.

Leo: (July 23–Aug. 22)
Your neighbors are progressive enough to accept a May/December romance, but don't expect them to like your May/at-least-a-year-from-October fling.

Virgo: (Aug. 23–Sept. 22)
Certain shortcomings in your education and upbringing cause you to read meaning into the relationships between various celestial bodies.

Libra: (Sept. 23–Oct. 23)
You'll soon meet someone who helps you forget all about that previous bad relationship by forcing you to focus on putting out constant fires.

Scorpio: (Oct. 24–Nov. 21)
You will be bemused and bewildered to discover that you are mentioned in the creation myths of three-fourths of the world's cultures.

Sagittarius: (Nov. 22–Dec. 21)
Just when your life seems to be a never-ending series of miseries, disappointments, and small disasters, it will surprise you by abruptly ending.

Capricorn: (Dec. 22–Jan. 19)
Now that you've achieved exactly half of your life's goals, it's time to start thinking about eating a second whole turkey.

Aquarius: (Jan. 20–Feb. 18)
You will suffer humiliation and loss of reputation when your culinary experiments in Korean/Latin fusion blow an entire city block sky-high.

Pisces: (Feb. 19–March 20)
Your troubles will be over before you know it, but most witnesses will agree that you probably didn't feel a thing.

NEWS

Last Living Tamagotchi Dies In Captivity

see WORLD page 4A

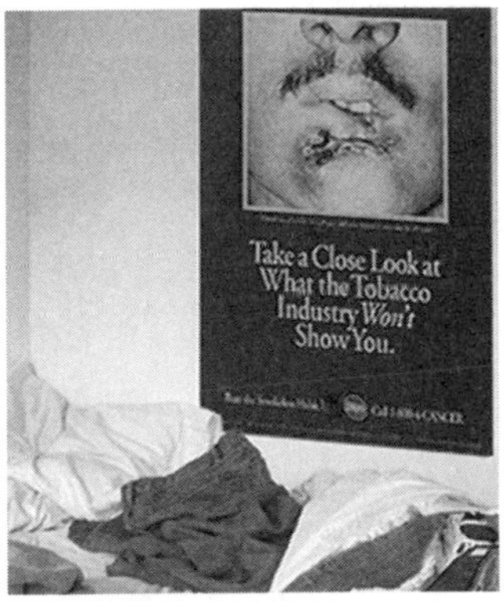

Teen Scores Awesome Oral Cancer Poster

see LOCAL page 3B

Harvard-Educated Texan Not Sure Which Place To Mention First

see LOCAL page 9B

STATshot

A look at the numbers that shape your world.

0 74470 94595 6 00

THE ONION • $2.00 US • $3.00 CAN

the ONION®

VOLUME 39 ISSUE 01 AMERICA'S FINEST NEWS SOURCE™ 16–22 JANUARY 2003

McDonald's Stock Slides As More Consumers Turn To Food

OAK BROOK, IL—The McDonald's Corporation announced Tuesday that it will close 175 restaurants and cut nearly 600 corporate jobs, responding to a plunge in stock prices blamed on a depressed economy and rising consumer interest in actual food.

"Though still America's number-one hamburger retailer," McDonald's CEO Jim Cantalupo said, "we have entered a brief period of restructuring due to the steady growth of other convenience eateries and, more significantly, growing competition from producers and distributors of demonstrably nutritive matter, i.e. food."

In the fourth quarter of 2002, McDonald's posted the first quarterly loss in its 47-year history. Its stock closed Tuesday at $15.78, a seven-year low for the quasi-food giant.

Analysts attribute the bleak financial picture to numerous factors, including the uncertain economy, poor management, eroding market share, and widespread health concerns about beef—a component sometimes used in the construction of McDonald's hamburger patties.

"Though well-accustomed to weathering recessions and changing tastes, the Golden Arches may be facing its toughest battle ever, given the surging

see McDONALD'S page 47

Bush On North Korea: 'We Must Invade Iraq'

WASHINGTON, DC—With concern over North Korea's nuclear capabilities growing, President Bush reassured the American people Monday that "extreme force" will be used to remove Saddam Hussein from power if the Iraqi president fails to give up suspected weapons of mass destruction.

"For years, Kim Jong Il has acted in blatant disregard of the Treaty on the Non-Proliferation Of Nuclear Weapons, and last week, he rejected it outright," Bush told reporters after a National Security

see NORTH KOREA page 46

Right: President Bush speaks to reporters about the growing crisis with North Korea, vowing to overthrow Saddam Hussein. Above: Kim Jong Il.

Free Condom Harsh Reminder Of Sexless Existence

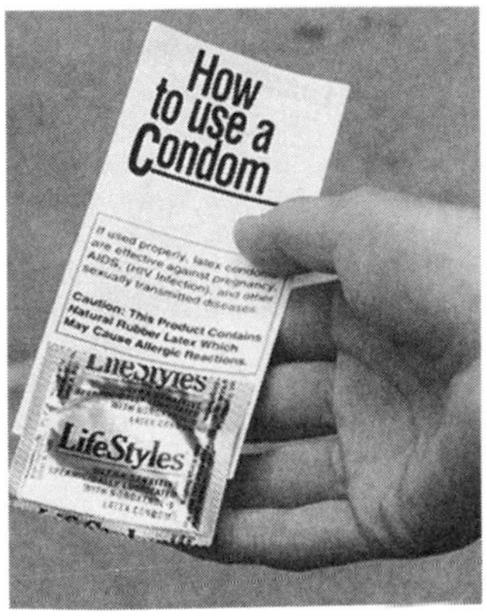

Above: The condom and brochure for which Tudor had little need.

SANTA CRUZ, CA—A free condom served as a harsh reminder of the sexless existence Julie Tudor has endured since February 2002, the 31-year-old bookstore manager reported Tuesday.

"Uh, thanks," said Tudor, reluctantly accepting a LifeStyles Xtra Pleasure condom attached to a brochure containing detailed information on proper use of the prophylactic. "But I really don't, uh, okay, thanks."

At approximately 2 p.m., while cutting across the University of California–Santa Cruz campus en route to a coffee shop, Tudor encountered a table featuring a hand-painted sign urging passersby to practice safe sex. She was immediately offered a condom by Stephanie Loughlin, a volunteer for the campus organization UC–Santa Cruz Safe-Sex Alliance.

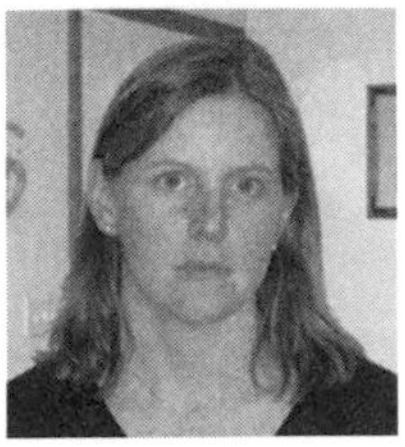

Above: Tudor

"I could've told them to save it for someone who has even a remote chance of actually using it, but I still have some dignity," said Tudor, who hasn't needed a prophylactic since her Feb. 14, 2002 split with then-boyfriend Doug Ryback. "God, if they only knew how little they were helping me."

see CONDOM page 47

Bush's Smallpox-Vaccination Plan

President Bush's smallpox-vaccination plan has sparked controversy, as the vaccine carries a small risk of severe and even deadly side effects. What do *you* think?

"I don't care if thousands of Americans could die—*lives* are at stake."

Robert Clausen
Architect

"This is just a rehearsal for the far more serious largepox threat of 2009."

Mitchell Swan
Cashier

"I'm sticking with my political party on the whole smallpox issue."

Meredith Vreeland
Homemaker

"I'm all for it, but only if I get to vaccinate myself. I have this cool antique lancet I've always wanted to use."

Maria King
Therapist

"Will we also be vaccinating against pipe bombs? We *know* the terrorists have those."

Richard Edwards
Systems Analyst

"Call me a paranoid schizophrenic, but I must confess to being fretful about the government forcibly injecting stuff into me. I'm a bit of a worrywart in that area."

Mark Samuel
Contractor

The Raelians

The Raelians, an international UFO sect, claims it has cloned a human baby. What is known about the group and its members?

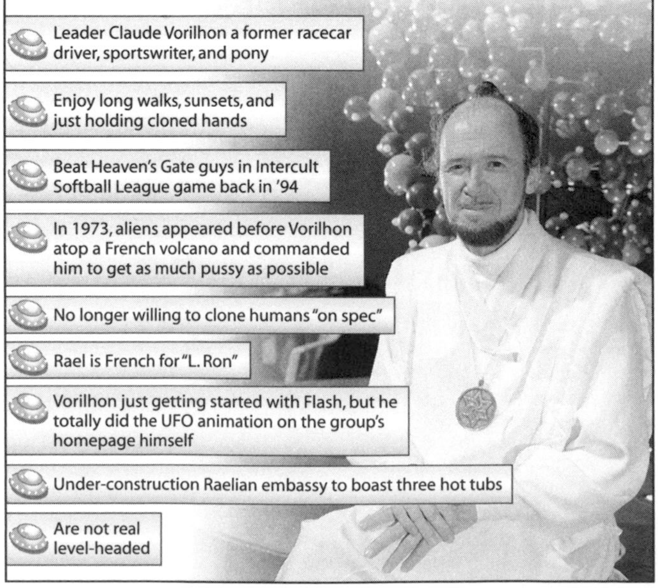

- Leader Claude Vorilhon a former racecar driver, sportswriter, and pony
- Enjoy long walks, sunsets, and just holding cloned hands
- Beat Heaven's Gate guys in Intercult Softball League game back in '94
- In 1973, aliens appeared before Vorilhon atop a French volcano and commanded him to get as much pussy as possible
- No longer willing to clone humans "on spec"
- Rael is French for "L. Ron"
- Vorilhon just getting started with Flash, but he totally did the UFO animation on the group's homepage himself
- Under-construction Raelian embassy to boast three hot tubs
- Are not real level-headed

the ONION®
America's Finest News Source.™

Herman Ulysses Zweibel
Founder

T. Herman Zweibel
Publisher Emeritus
J. Phineas Zweibel
Publisher
Maxwell Prescott Zweibel
Editor-In-Chief

One Look At My Music Collection Will Show You How Much I Respect Women

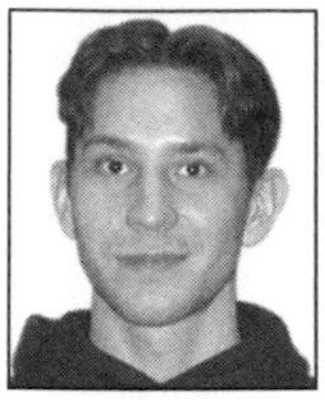

By Randy Hollins

There are a lot of men out there who are hostile to women. And, to be perfectly honest, it shows in their CD collections. Not me, though. One look at my collection will show you how much I respect women.

Go ahead and browse my CD shelves. My musical tastes are diverse, covering everything from Dar Williams to Norah Jones, Sarah McLachlan to Alicia Keys, but these artists all have one thing in common: They all clearly communicate my sensitivity to the issues facing women today.

Some men are threatened by powerful women. They prefer them weak and subservient. Me, I'm the exact opposite. I mean, if I were threatened by women, would I own two albums by k.d. lang, a woman *and* a lesbian, no less? Any woman who browsed my CD collection and saw my copies of lang's *Ingenue* and *All You Can Eat* would immediately recognize that I'm a great catch, a guy who's secure enough in his own sexuality to honor and celebrate femininity in all its forms.

Perhaps the strongest case for my respect for women is made by my Tori Amos CDs. I have them all, even her poorly received covers album *Strange Little Girls* and *Y Kant Tori Read*, the metal album she made in 1988. How could you not feel respect for Tori Amos—and, by extension, all women—after listening to the emotional rawness of "Me And A Gun"? Every time I put on *Little Earthquakes*, I get chills. Plus, Tori is so sexy on the cover. (In a feminine, earth-mother sort of way, of course.)

Do you still need more proof of what an evolved male I am? Look no further than my abundance of Ani DiFranco recordings. I see Ms. DiFranco as the ultimate example of female independence and self-reliance. She turned down offers from major labels to preserve her independence and control her image. She launched her Righteous Babe label, first to put out her own music, then to put out records from other women artists like Sara Lee. She even lets people tape her shows and exchange the recordings, which is "righteous," indeed.

You know who's incredibly strong? Eve. To be a proud, independent woman in the sexist, male-dominated world of rap, well, that's pretty impressive in my book.

Lest you think I've forgotten the women who blazed the trails for the Joan Osbornes and Sheryl Crows of today, I have a broad selection of music by older female artists. Let's see, I've got Joni Mitchell, Bonnie Raitt, and, of course, Fleetwood Mac. Okay, so there were also men in Fleetwood Mac, but the band was defined by the incomparable Stevie Nicks, a woman who was a huge influence on many of today's brave female artists. I also love Billie Holiday, whose beauty and genius, sadly, is lost on the typical asshole frat guy you see on college campuses today. Like Brad Reidel. Why a girl like Jen Mosbacher is giving that Neanderthal the time of day, I'll never know.

To be fair, I should clarify something: I don't love all female artists. I

Some men are threatened by powerful women. They prefer them weak and subservient. Me, I'm the exact opposite. I mean, if I were threatened by women, would I own two albums by k.d. lang, a woman and a lesbian, no less?

used to own an album by Sleater-Kinney, but I got rid of it. It seemed like they were trying to be like men, and that just turned me off. The Donnas also act all tough like guys, but they're just doing it as a put-on, so that's okay. It's really funny. Sexy, too.

Right now, I'm saving up money for an iPod so I can carry all my women's music with me everywhere I go. That way, if I'm ever in a coffee shop and happen to see a blonde-haired psychology major who's listening to, say, Lauryn Hill on her Discman, I can show her that I like Lauryn Hill, too. You see, unlike men, women value making connections with other people, and what better way to do so than through music?

Unfortunately, at this point in my life, I haven't really made as many connections as I'd have liked. If I could just get a woman to see my CD collection, I know she'd realize that I'm not like the other guys. I can really understand the female experience.

In the meantime, I guess all I can do is go for a jog with my India.Arie CD in my Discman and hope to run into someone who wants to know what I'm listening to. Hopefully someone hot.

God, I'm lonely.

CREATION SCIENCE

Creationist Museum Acquires 5,000-Year-Old T. Rex Skeleton

TULSA, OK—In a major coup for the growing field of creation science, the perfectly preserved remains of a 5,000-year-old Tyrannosaurus Rex were delivered Monday to Tulsa's Creationist Museum of Natural History.

"The Good Lord has, in His benevolence, led us to an important breakthrough for scientific inquiry," Creationist Museum of Natural History curator Dr. Elijah Gill said. "Our museum has many valuable and

Using advanced dating processes from the cutting edge of biblical paleontology, the Oral Roberts team determined that Methuselah lived during the late Antediluvian period, or "The Age Of The Dinosaurs."

exciting exhibits that testify to Creation and shine light on the Lord's divine plan. But none have been as exciting—or anywhere near as old—as this new T. Rex specimen named 'Methuselah.' This skeleton, which dates back to roughly 3,000 B.C., offers the most compelling proof yet that the Earth was made by God

Above: Methuselah stands on display at the Creationist Museum of Natural History.

roughly 10,000 years ago."

Added Gill: "It's awe-inspiring to gaze on something that actually lived here on Earth, so very many years ago."

Methuselah was discovered last summer in northern Turkey by a team of Oral Roberts University archaeologists, who were on a dig searching for the Tower of Babel. According to Gill, the skeleton, which stands 20 feet tall, possesses terrifying, razor-sharp teeth and claws, confirming that it was an evil beast in league with Satan, the Great Deceiver.

Using advanced dating processes from the cutting edge of biblical paleontology, the Oral Roberts team determined that Methuselah lived during the late Antediluvian period, or "The Age Of The Dinosaurs." They said the pristine condition of the find strongly suggests that it perished in the Great Flood, fossilizing quickly and thoroughly due to the tremendous water pressure during the event.

"It was a truly majestic beast," said Gill, gazing up at the massive skeleton. "One almost has to mourn that there was no room for it on the Ark."

Gill called the discovery "a powerfully compelling refutation" of secular scientists' long-held assertion that dinosaurs lived on Earth millions of years before humans.

"The fact that no human remains were found anywhere in the vicinity of the site of the skeleton serves as proof of the tyrannosaur's ferocity and huge appetite," Gill said.

"At most," he added, "tyrannosaurs

see DINOSAUR page 46

NEWS IN BRIEF

30th Anniversary Of 1973 Commemorated

WASHINGTON, DC—Across the U.S., ceremonies have already begun to commemorate the 30th anniversary of 1973. "No one who lived through 1973 can ever forget it," said singer Tony Orlando, unveiling a plaque Monday on the National Mall reading "1973: 1973-2003." "From Richard Nixon's second inauguration to Billie Jean King's defeat of Bobby Riggs, 1973 was a special year that will be celebrated all year long." The U.S. Postal Service announced plans Tuesday to observe the milestone with a paisley stamp trumpeting "30 Years Of 1973."

Asshole Even Shoots Pool Like An Asshole

MONTROSE, CA—According to acquaintances, area asshole Kris Stenstrup, 31, even shoots pool like an asshole. "He's not even good, but he still acts all macho and cool, like he's Minnesota Fats or something," roommate Lisa Darmont said Monday. "Like, whenever he sinks a shot, he blows on his pool cue and then puts it back in its invisible holster. Oh, and he loves to play 'mind games' with his 'prey,' hovering over them and whispering 'Don't be nervous' before they shoot." Darmont added that Stenstrup is also fond of singing Warren Zevon's "Werewolves Of London," from the billiards-themed 1986 film *The Color Of Money*, while cockily circling the table.

Humane Society Worker Secretly Glad To See Nippy Dachshund Put Down

MARYSVILLE, OH—Union County Humane Society volunteer Catherine Moncrief, 23, admitted Monday that a small part of her was glad to see Oscar, a nippy, hyperactive dachshund, put to sleep. "I feel really guilty, but when they euthanized him, I was kind of like, 'Ha, ha—serves you right, you obnoxious little shit,'" Moncrief said. "I went through a whole bottle of hydrogen peroxide in two weeks from feeding and washing him." Moncrief then privately mused that the incessantly whimpering cocker spaniel in Cage 12 could go next for all she cares.

Supernatural Powers Vested In Local Pastor

BILOXI, MS—Michael Cotto, 27, and Laura Winningham, 26, were pronounced husband and wife Monday, thanks to the supernatural powers vested in local Presbyterian minister Gerald Dreisbach by the Lord Himself. "We are so lucky to live near a man who is an actual conduit of God's will," Cotto told reporters after the ceremony. "We wouldn't have been able to get married otherwise." Dreisbach has also used his otherworldly authority to call for good fortune in the lives of parishioners, as well as swift passage to heaven for the deceased.

Eating Entire Box Of Donuts Not Originally Part Of Evening's Plan

OVERLAND PARK, KS—Moments after consuming the 12th and final Hostess™ powdered-sugar donut, Overland Park resident Patrick Angelis, 46, admitted Monday that eating an entire box of donuts was not originally part of his plan for the evening. "I figured I'd kick back in front of the TV, watch *King Of Queens* and *Yes, Dear*, and maybe enjoy a donut or two," the sated, powder-faced Angelis said. "But before you know it, the whole box was gone." Added Angelis: "Hey, you gotta stay flexible; take what the night brings you." Ø

NORTH KOREA from page 43

Council meeting on North Korea. "We cannot allow weapons of mass destruction to remain in the hands of volatile, unpredictable leaders. Which

Bush outlined his administration's plan for the crisis in North Korea, which includes maintaining an open dialogue with Pyongyang and deploying massive troops and materiel to the Gulf region.

is exactly why we must act quickly and decisively against Saddam Hussein."

A member of Bush's "axis of evil," North Korea sparked international outcry in October 2002 after announcing that it had a uranium-enrichment program. After ousting U.N. inspectors, leader Kim Jong Il has continued to defy orders to halt the program.

"I applaud the International Atomic Energy Agency's condemnation of North Korea's nuclear efforts," Bush said. "I trust that the world community will act capably and decisively in this matter—as capably and decisively as the U.S. will act against Iraq."

According to Bush, North Korea and Iraq both pose "significant threats" to important U.S. allies.

"Our friends South Korea and Japan are justifiably fearful of North Korea's emergent nuclear and chemical-weapons technologies," Bush said. "These nations are forced to live with the constant threat of aggression looming over their heads, just as our friends Saudi Arabia and Israel do. The time has come to complete the unfinished business of a decade ago and oust Saddam Hussein."

Above: A North Korean soldier stands guard over missiles so advanced, Iraq is prohibited from possessing them.

Added Bush: "This man tried to kill my dad."

U.S. intelligence experts say North Korea likely has one or two nuclear bombs, with plans to rapidly expand its arsenal in the coming years. With two nuclear reactors under construction, the nation could have a system to enrich uranium by 2005, producing enough plutonium for two bombs a year.

"North Korea has a full-scale nuclear program underway, one which may even now have the capability of striking the western U.S.," Bush said. "Even more alarming, Iraq is actively trying to scrounge up enough money to buy something nuclear on the black market, ideally something that can fly through the air."

Bush outlined his administration's plan for the crisis in North Korea, which includes maintaining an open dialogue with Pyongyang and deploying massive troops and materiel to the Gulf region.

At a Jan. 10 press conference, Bush had strong words for the North Korean dictator.

"Kim Jong Il, you have withdrawn

Added Bush: "This man tried to kill my dad."

from international nuclear treaties and cruelly starved your own people," Bush said. "The world at large will not let your evil deeds go unchallenged. Someone, somewhere will hold you accountable, sooner or later. I do not know who this person is, but somebody will."

"North Korea has been pouring its limited resources into development of a huge military force at the expense of its own people's well-being," Bush continued. "Somebody should take decisive action against this, just as the U.S. did in stopping the Taliban and will soon do in ousting Saddam Hussein."

Seeking to pressure North Korea, a communist nation since the end of the Korean War, into compliance with the Treaty on the Non-Proliferation Of Nuclear Weapons, the U.S. has cut off all economic and humanitarian aid.

"By providing support to North Korea, America was indirectly propping up an oppressive regime," Bush said. "That food and fuel will be much better used by the proud men and women of the U.S. military—such as the 45,000 members of the 1st Marine Expeditionary Force, who at this moment are in California preparing for deployment to the Middle East."

"You have my prayers, Camp Pendleton," added Bush, giving an officer's salute. "Now, let's roll." Ø

DINOSAUR from page 45

existed a few days before the first humans, given that the birds and the beasts were created early in the week, and Adam and Eve were made on the sixth day."

Founded in 1874, the Creationist Museum of Natural History has amassed a collection of thousands of exhibits from around the world demonstrating that the Earth was made by the hand of a Divine Creator over the course of a week, roughly 10,000 years ago. Among its most prized exhibits are a trilobite believed to have lived during the Jewish Exodus and a stunning specimen of "Java Gibbon."

Methuselah has caused such a stir that even supporters of evolutionary science have found themselves caught up in "T. Rex Fever." Christopher Eldridge, director of New York's Museum of Natural History, raved that the acquisition was "absolutely inconceivable" and "not to be believed." Dr. Harmon Briggs, a Smithsonian Institution paleobiologist, gushed in a phone interview that the discovery of the 5,000-year-old beast was "mind-boggling" and "in defiance of all the human senses."

Said Gill: "I have even received an exciting letter from a paleontologist at UCLA asserting that Methuselah could be even older than 5,000 years. Who knows? It might even date back to the Sixth Day of Creation."

The T. Rex skeleton will be on public display at the museum beginning Feb. 3. Conversions will be performed every two hours at the museum's baptismal font, located in the Apologetics wing. Ø

POTATOES from page 41

amounts of blood. Passersby were amazed by the unusually large amounts of blood. Passersby were amazed by the unusually large amounts of blood. Passersby were amazed by the unusually large amounts of blood. Passersby were amazed by the unusually large amounts of blood. Passersby were amazed by the unusually large amounts of blood. Passersby were amazed by the unusually large amounts of blood. Passersby were amazed by the unusually large amounts of blood. Passersby were amazed by the unusually large amounts of blood. Passersby were amazed by the unusually large amounts of blood. Passersby were amazed by the unusually large amounts of blood. Passersby were amazed by the unusually large amounts of blood. Passersby were amazed by the unusually large amounts of blood. Passersby were amazed by the unusually large

You can't believe everything you read from several well-informed corroborating sources.

amounts of blood. Passersby were amazed by the unusually large amounts of blood. Passersby were amazed by the unusually large amounts of blood. Passersby were amazed by the unusually large

see POTATOES page 55

CONDOM from page 43

Tudor said she smiled politely when Loughlin, a bubbly 20-year-old, bounded up to her and urged her to "play it safe."

"I didn't want to say that in the 11 months since Doug and I broke up, I really haven't been 'playing it' at all," Tudor said. "Thanks for reminding me."

Tudor said she still has plenty of unused condoms at home.

"I have a box that hasn't been touched since the breakup," Tudor said. "I know they're still there, because I checked for them before going out with that jerk stockbroker Michelle set me up with last month."

Tudor initially tried to avoid the safe-sex booth, pretending not to hear Safe-Sex Alliance volunteer Ryan Schumann when he shouted, "Free condom?" Misinterpreting Tudor's efforts to sidestep the booth as discomfort with the subject of sex, Schumann targeted her for additional education.

"Some people don't like talking about sex, which is why outreach programs like ours are so vitally important," said Schumann, 19. "I told her not to be embarrassed, and that sexuality is a normal, healthy part of everyone's life.'"

"Everyone's except mine," Tudor replied when told of Schumann's remarks. "I decided to spare him that detail, though, and let him blather on about mutual respect and positive sexuality and something about a dance at the student union on the last Friday of every month."

Despite not needing protection from unwanted pregnancy or sexually transmitted diseases, Tudor was offered a choice of condoms by Trojan, Durex, Trustex, inSpiral, and Crown—all placed in a fishbowl along with complimentary packets of Astroglide lubricant and Wet-brand

In the two weeks since Tudor's last major sex-related letdown—her failure to get laid on New Year's Eve despite a willingness to sleep with anyone even slightly attractive—sex had largely been relegated to the back of her mind.

flavored lube pillows.

"When I sort of frowned at the condom in my hand, they pulled me over to pick any that I liked better from their cornucopia of condoms," Tudor said. "Lubricated, non-lubricated, for-her-pleasure, for-his, mint-flavored. They even had ones wrapped in foil that looked like candy coins. Which, I hate to admit, caught my eye for a second. Chocolate, I would've had some use for."

Declining the offer of an alternate condom, Tudor grudgingly accepted a brochure containing "fun and safe" sex practices to try with her purely theoretical partner. She also took a printed sheet listing local health clinics that provide free testing for STDs, a brochure on the correct use of dental dams, and a photocopy of an article about female condoms—none of which remotely interested her.

In the two weeks since Tudor's last major sex-related letdown—her failure to get laid on New Year's Eve despite a willingness to sleep with anyone even slightly attractive—sex had largely been relegated to the back of her mind. On Tuesday, how-

Declining the offer of an alternate condom, Tudor grudgingly accepted a brochure containing "fun and safe" sex practices to try with her purely theoretical partner.

ever, Tudor was reminded of her sexless existence every time she opened her purse and saw the free condom.

"Back in college, when I was screwing with reasonable regularity, I'd actually spend time thinking about the subject [of safe sex]," Tudor said. "I'd worry if carrying a condom in my purse was being too forward. I'd think, is it okay to have sex with friends? What sort of stuff do I want to explore? Are threesomes safe? I had no idea that one day, my safe-sex questions would boil down to, 'Where can I get some?'"

Loughlin, who has volunteered for UC–Santa Cruz Safe-Sex Alliance since September, said she sees the unwillingness of some people to discuss sex as a problem facing safe-sex activists.

"Some people are, like, really weird about sex, and that totally sucks," Loughlin said, adjusting a "Be On The Safe Side!" banner. "That's why I'm here. The more open everyone is about it, the less people will die."

"God, I remember back when I was her age," Tudor said. "I was dating this guy who lived in Arizona, but I kept cheating on him with this guy on my dorm floor: Kyle? Karl? He was a rock climber, a real outdoorsy type—kinda skinny but strong. You know, with these nice knotty muscles. I'm sorry, what was your question?" ⌀

McDONALDS from page 43

Above: A tray of McDonald's semi-synthetic digestibles.

public interest in leading healthy, active lives and consuming objects that taste at least remotely organic," analyst Ann Gurkin of Davenport & Co. said. "These days, people seem more interested in eating food than hormone-hybrid lab patties."

The world's leading purveyor of semi-synthetic digestibles, McDonald's became a franchise in 1955 and quickly expanded across the U.S., thanks to innovative marketing, low prices, and exemption from FDA regulations, given that its products fall outside the scope of the agency. McDonald's has proven a popular favorite among busy, on-the-go Americans lacking the time for genuine food.

But for all its financial woes, McDonald's is optimistic for the future.

"This whole non-reconstituted-food craze will pass," Cantalupo said. "People have enjoyed our meat-flavored pseudo-patties for decades, and we're not going to be scared by consumers'

McDonald's has proven a popular favorite among busy, on-the-go Americans lacking the time for genuine food.

passing interest in burgers that actually taste like an animal, served on bread that's less than a week old and garnished with ve-ge... ve-ge... ve-ge-tables."

Said McDonald's COO Charlie Bell: "We don't see the burgeoning food industry as a threat, but rather as a public fancy with which McDonald's can happily co-exist."

Added Bell: "I even enjoy some food

Said McDonald's COO Charlie Bell: "We don't see the burgeoning food industry as a threat, but rather as a public fancy with which McDonald's can happily co-exist."

myself here and there. I ate some corn just last weekend."

In spite of McDonald's outward optimism, rumors abound that the company is pondering some of its most extreme changes ever. McDonald's famed management-training facility, Oak Brook's Hamburger University, is reportedly developing an unprecedented "food studies" program. The facility is also rumored to be adding a research wing to teach culinary fundamentals for eventual incorporation into the McDonald's business plan.

"The bottom line is, we're doing fine," Bell said. "Certainly, as a last resort, we could introduce some recognizably food-like items, perhaps a sandwich made with animal matter and vegetables that have not been shredded, condensed, and flash-frozen to remove all possible nutritional content or general appearance of earthly origin. But I honestly don't think it will ever come to that." ⌀

COMMUNITY VOICES

Joinin' Tha Notary Club

Governor Glenda P. Ten Eyck
State Capitol Building

Herbert Kornfeld
Accountz-Reeceevable Supervisa
Midstate Office Supply

To tha Honorable
Mrs. Glenda P. Ten Eyck:

Ay, yo, Governor Ten Eyck, big ups to you an' yo' posse representin' to tha fullest down at tha Capitol. This be Herbert Kornfeld, a.k.a. H-Dog, a.k.a. Daddy H, a.k.a. Tha H-Luvva, tha man who professionally be known as tha Supabad Hardcore Enforca o' tha Accountz Reeceevable department of Midstate Office Supply, tha largest an' dopest retaila an' distributa' of office supplies in tha whole muthafuckin' state.

By Herbert Kornfeld
Accounts-Receivable Supervisor

Now, normally, tha only lettas I eva write be tha ones tellin' our bitch-ass deadbeat clients to pay they accountz tha fuck up, lest they wanna get smoked. But circumstancez be forcin' me to write you a big-ass letta aksin' you to give me my notary-publik license, cuz in these important mattas a bidness, Daddy H go straight to tha top dogg an' not no muthafuckin' small-time publik-clerk bitch.

Madam Governor, I would make tha flyest muthafuckin' notary publik this state eva seen, no doubt. But tha Man be denyin' this strong, hardworkin' A.R. Bruthah a license, cuz a my jail record. My rep be on tha line. If I don't get no notary-publik license, I can't office proper. That mean only tha Accountz Payabo supervisa, Myron Schabe, can notarizize documentz, an' that would be to tha detriment of tha company, cuz Myron be this senile ol' geeza who'd affix his notary seal to a wet piece o' toilet paypa stuck to tha ceilin' if he could reach it. Y'all gots to let me notarizize shit, an' wit' a quickness, lest Myron keel ova an' they pass his title on to that wack amateur A.P. bitch Judy Metzger, know what I'm sayin'?

Madam Governor, y'all seem like a reasonable bitch, an' a stone-col' playa, as well. I don't gots to tell you that a notary publik be a state-licensed and bonded publik servant who serve as a impartial witness to tha certification and signature of official documents, and who also administer oaths and affirmations. It be one a tha highest honors a man can receive, an' to tha H-Dog, ain't nuthin' more important than HONOR. Eva since I wuz still in my Underoos, I wanted to be a notary publik. My daddy wuz a notary publik, an' even though bidness take him away from our crib foe weeks on end, some a my best memories growin' up be when Daddy come in late an' get me outta bed, his right hand still all achin' an' blistered from workin' his seal, an' he tell me all about his notarizizin'. Damn, wit' all his dope stories 'bout takin' sworn statementz and notin' protests of negotiable instruments, I didn't never wanna get my sleep on. Notary publikin' be in my blood, true dat. Most muthafuckas can't tell a affidavit from a jurat, but y'all betta fuckin' believe I can. Aks me anythin' about notarizizin', like, during a notarial act, is it cool to affix yo' official seal or stamp? I be all like, sho, s'cool, but y'all gots to provide yo' handwritten signature, too, or tha act be invalid. I dodge that shit like a muthafuckin' bullet.

But, as I said earlier, tha Man won't let me do no notary publikin' cuz of mah jail record. Back in tha day, I wuz convicted foe felony freestyle accountin' and spent a year in juvy. Afta serving mah time, I went legit an' ain't been in no trouble eva since, but that shit still bite me in the ass. Thass where you come in. Enclosed wit' this letta be copiez o' my original court paypas, a letta from my parole offica attestin' to my good character, an' another letta o' recommendation from my immediate supervisa, Gerald Luckenbill, who took a chance on a ex-con tryin' to make good an' hired me straight outta bidness college. Madam Governor, what I aks is that you show some luv an' pardon my ass. I straight an' I ain't never looked back. I put tha thug life behind me foe good, word is bond.

Man, if I wuz a notary publik, I'd do shit in STYLE. I'd get me tha flyest engraved official seal. No muthafukkkin' cheap-ass rubba stamp foe me. Fuck that. Midstate gots a mad line o' notarizizin' seals an' a engrava on tha premises, too. See? This shit wuz meant to happen. This be mah DESTINY.

I also wanna say that, if you pardon me, an' I gets my notary license, I won't never gonna fo'get my duties to the A.R., nor will I ever fo'get my street flava. Don't be fooled by tha notary-publik license that I got—I still H-Dog from tha block. Y'all may have caught wind of otha Accountin' bruthahs applyin' to become notariez publik, but a lot o' them be doin' it strictly foe tha bitchez an' tha fame. But foe me, this ain't no muthafuckin' game. It ain't about me. Never wuz. Shit gots to be witnessed an' verified an' attested. It what our society based on, y'all, lest everythang go straight to hell, know what I'm sayin'?

Yo, Madam Governor, I gots accountz to reeceeve, so I OUT. Lookin' forward to your response an' all that. An' a special shout-out to Lt. Gov. Popovich. We never fo'get what tha A.R. posse did foe him, an' I trust he don't, either, know what I'm sayin'?

Peace out,
Herbert Kornfeld
A.R. Supervisa
Midstate Office Supply

Mr. Herbert Kornfeld
Accounts Receivable Supervisor
Midstate Office Supply

Office Of The Governor
State Capitol Building

Dear Mr. Kornfeld:

We recently received your letter requesting a formal pardon from Governor Ten Eyck for your felony conviction for uncertified, or "freestyle," public accounting so that you may proceed with your application for a state notary commission.

We are happy to report that, in the time since receiving your request, the governor has signed into law the Accounting Practices Reform Act, which, among other provisions, declares null and void any uncertified accounting convictions prior to 1996. Because your conviction took place in 1992, it will be erased from your record. Since this is your only such conviction, you are now eligible to apply for a notary commission.

The governor is deeply impressed by your commitment to civic service and desire to improve yourself through honest means. Incidentally, she continues to be mindful of the Accounts Receivable community's support of her governorship and its crucial role in saving Lt. Gov. Popovich's life in 2000. Should you or any of your associates have a concern that you feel should be brought to her attention, please do not hesitate to do so.

Yours very sincerely,
Marlin Tolleson
Chief Of Staff ø

HOROSCOPES

Your Horoscope

By Lloyd Schumner Sr.
Retired Machinist and
A.A.P.B.-Certified Astrologer

Aries: (March 21–April 19)
An Arkansas vacation-planning kit will soon arrive in your mailbox, even though you didn't request one, aren't planning a vacation, and, like most people, hate Arkansas.

Taurus: (April 20–May 20)
The stars are aware of your wish to shake it, but they warn you not to break it, as it took your mama nine months to make it.

Gemini: (May 21–June 21)
A bump in life's road causes you to lose control of life's car and spin out of control, careening off life's cliff and into life's rocky valley below, where the car bursts into life's flames.

Cancer: (June 22–July 22)
Under no circumstances should you take no for an answer this week. You'll wind up in jail or hospitalized, but the stars will have fun watching.

Leo: (July 23–Aug. 22)
After developing a form of psychosis, you will become convinced you're Napoleon and conquer half of Europe before the British stop you next week.

Virgo: (Aug. 23–Sept. 22)
You'll spend the rest of your life experiencing a painful kind of celebrity as you burn to death over a period of 37 years.

Libra: (Sept. 23–Oct. 23)
Hotei, the Buddha of epicureanism, challenges you to a pie-eating contest, which you will, of course, lose. Also, the pies are surprisingly mediocre.

Scorpio: (Oct. 24–Nov. 21)
Your name will become synonymous with financial success when you have it legally changed to Rich Wealthy.

Sagittarius: (Nov. 22–Dec. 21)
Scientists say the universe will end in a state of heat death, which makes the giant stuttering cartoon pig's announcement that much more of a surprise.

Capricorn: (Dec. 22–Jan. 19)
You will continue having problems establishing meaningful, non-strangling relationships with men well into your 40s.

Aquarius: (Jan. 20–Feb. 18)
Your recent visit to the hospital to entertain sick children is a nice gesture, but they scream themselves senseless upon seeing you again.

Pisces: (Feb. 19–March 20)
It appears that this is your year at last, and it is—especially the "at last" part.

NEWS

Merle Haggard Haggard

see PEOPLE page 7C

Grandma Knitting Escape Ladder

see LOCAL page 4D

Mormon Family Trying To Ignore Dog's Huge Boner

see FAITH page 11E

Ikea Manager Böring

see LOCAL page 2D

STATshot

A look at the numbers that shape your world.

What's The Secret To Our Delicious Pancakes?

1. Seagull eggs
2. Batter aged minimum of three years
3. Pinch of concrete
4. Obsessive drive to out-pancake everyone else
5. Ganja butter
6. If I told you, the Order of Jemimans would kill me
7. "Soylent maple"

the ONION®

VOLUME 39 ISSUE 02 AMERICA'S FINEST NEWS SOURCE™ 23–29 JANUARY 2003

New Economy Wistfully Recalled As Tiny Dot-Com Promotional Object Found In Drawer

Above: The antHead.com promotional thingy.

SAN FRANCISCO—The "New Economy"—the Internet-driven business landscape once predicted to make "bricks and mortar" retailers obsolete—was wistfully recalled Monday, when a small dot-com promotional item was discovered in the junk drawer of former dot-commer Eric Noyce.

Noyce, 28, an associate vice-president of business development for Pets.com from August 1998 to December 2000, came across a small gadget emblazoned with "antHead.com" while searching for a corkscrew to open a $3 bottle of wine.

"Holy shit, check this out," said the minimum-wage-earning Noyce as he examined the slick-looking promotional doohickey. "antHead.com. I think I remember getting this. It was in a goodie bag I got at some launch party. antHead, antHead... What did they do again?"

According to roommate Bryan

see DOT-COM page 52

Kim Jong Il Unfolds Into Giant Robot

Above: Kim Jong Il marches through the streets of Pyongyang.

PYONGYANG, NORTH KOREA—Responding to mounting pressure and increasingly confrontational rhetoric from the outside world, North Korean president Kim Jong Il unfolded into a 70-foot-tall, 62-ton giant robot Monday.

"The DPRK's nuclear program is very much its own business, as is its right to determine its own path of security," said Kim, his torso splitting along ventral seams as clusters of Taepo-Dong ICBMs rose from his shoulders. "Any attempt by Washington to decide our fate will surely result in a sea of fire being unleashed upon them."

As his arms and legs sheathed themselves in bulletproof Mecha-Muscle telescoping outward from his chest, Kim reiterated his refusal to bow to international demands.

"Constant criticism from outside indicates mistrust of our promise to refrain from missile tests," said Kim, speaking over the mechanical shriek of wing-blades sprouting from his back. "Only trust from the U.S. that we will keep our word can prevent World

see ROBOT page 52

Father Wants Only The Best For His Truck

PRINEVILLE, OR—Charles "Chuck" Maurer, a local lumberyard manager and father of two, wants only the very best for his 2002 Ford F150 extended-cab truck, the 41-year-old reported Monday.

"Growing up, my family didn't have much money," said Maurer, ignoring his son Cory's pleas to play catch. "There were lots of things we couldn't afford, that we had to make do without. But now that I make a good wage, I want my own truck to have all the things my dad's truck never had."

Since purchasing the F150 last April, Maurer has treated it to numerous small upgrades, including wheel covers, floor mats, radar detector, and sun shield, as well as costlier, factory-installed features such as anti-lock brakes, cruise control, and air bags.

Though he makes an effort to pay equal attention to the family's other vehicle, the 1994 Chevy Corsica his wife June uses to drive to work and pick up sons Cory, 12, and Kyle, 10, from school, Maurer admitted that the truck is "my baby."

"I know everyone thinks their truck is the best in the world, but mine is really something special," said Maurer, pulling a canvas cover over the vehicle and giving the cab an affectionate pat. "Nothing but the best for my F150."

see TRUCK page 53

Above: Maurer, seen here with his wife and sons, is dedicated to being a good provider for his Ford F150.

Eliminating Stock-Dividend Taxes

As part of his tax-cut plan, President Bush has proposed abolishing taxes on stock dividends—a move critics say primarily benefits the rich. What do *you* think?

Marc Vargas
Roofer

"Oh, thank God. I've dreamed of sending my child to college, but those dividend taxes were eating me alive."

Linda Oberst
Teacher

"Maybe this will inspire America's poor to not be so poor all the time."

Ben Graham
Systems Analyst

"A tax cut? With war looming and a projected federal budget deficit? Does Bush know the U.S. can't borrow from its dad?"

Marla Robichaud
Dentist

"What's the problem here? If taxes are cut for the rich, that means they'll be able to tip more. There's just no pleasing some people."

Irwin Edwards
Industrialist

"As a cash-fattened plutocrat, I require no more money. So to our president I say 'No, thank you' to these tax cuts."

Sam Hopkins
File Clerk

"It makes sense. Those people making money on stock dividends didn't do any work, so why should they have to pay any taxes?"

Recent Medical Studies

A study has found that regular, moderate consumption of alcohol cuts the risk of heart attack by a third. Among other recent findings:

- Half a bag of Fritos every day for a year significantly reduces the risk of pregnancy
- Consumption of at least 14 ounces of hard liquor greatly increases chances of tolerating coworker's birthday party
- Smashing fist through mirror not effective in getting girlfriend back
- Eating carrots and celery may help you exercise your choppers and really chew, chew, chew
- Regular exposure to excessively biased health studies doubles your chances of wanting to jack someone in the gut
- Zero servings a day of fruits and vegetables will reduce the risk of regular bowel syndrome
- Cheese, particularly melted cheese, good

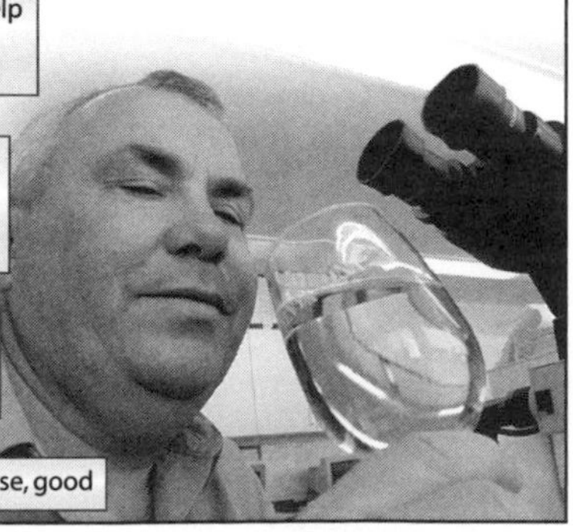

the ONION®
America's Finest News Source.™

Herman Ulysses Zweibel
Founder

T. Herman Zweibel
Publisher Emeritus
J. Phineas Zweibel
Publisher
Maxwell Prescott Zweibel
Editor-In-Chief

I Appreciate The Muppets On A Much Deeper Level Than You

By Larry Groznic

Dennis, Dennis, Dennis.

This bitter eBay bidding war has gotten out of hand. Why should we tear each other apart like this? Yes, the Muppet Movie soundtrack has not been available on CD since 1993 and is highly sought on the collector's market. But is that any reason to drive the price north of the $52 mark, with two days, seven hours, and six minutes remaining, no less?

As I have said repeatedly, let me win this auction, and I will happily let you copy the disc to iTunes for your own use. Just let me get my CD at a fair and reasonable price. If we had joined forces on this, I could have used the "Buy It Now" feature and saved us both a lot of money—money that could have gone toward those rare Palisades Dr. Teeth figures we both want. But look where your pride has led us.

Why should you be the one to give in, you ask? The answer is simple: As the greater and more dedicated Muppets fan, by all rights the CD is mine. Plainly and obviously, I appreciate the Muppets on a much deeper level than you do.

Please recall, if you will, the night I first showed you *The Muppet Movie*. It's bad enough that you hadn't grown up loving the film, but afterwards you called it, and I quote, "funny." Not "a deeply spiritual and highly personal statement of ambition tempered by ethics," but "funny." Was it "funny" that Kermit refused to Judas his race to a corrupt corporation, even though it meant giving up his dream of stardom?

Why should you be the one to give in, you ask? The answer is simple: As the greater and more dedicated Muppets fan, by all rights the CD is mine.

I never should have let you go to the kitchen for more Pringles during Kermit's big "High Noon" speech to Charles Durning—the emotional apex of the film. But as bad as that was, Dennis, you've committed far worse sins. And I think you know what I'm referring to. To call *The Muppet Christmas Carol* superior to *The Muppet Movie* amounts to nothing less than blasphemy to true Muppet fans and all other sensible people.

Please recall, if you will, the night I first showed you *The Muppet Movie*. It's bad enough that you hadn't grown up loving the film, but afterwards you called it, and I quote, "funny." Not "a deeply spiritual and highly personal statement of ambition tempered by ethics," but "funny."

Christmas Carol, as you well know, is the first Muppet film made after the death of Jim Henson. How can it be the best when it is missing the man who was the heart, soul, and voice of the Muppet universe, Mr. James Maury Henson?

This is not even to mention the absence of Richard Hunt.

Hear me now: Jim Henson was Kermit. Steve Whitmire is a *Henson impersonator*. Admittedly, a damn talented one—his Ernie, in particular, nearly captures the affability and innocence of the original—but the equal of Henson? Step back from the brink, Dennis.

If you like Christmas shows so much, you need to get yourself a copy of *A Muppet Family Christmas* and see how the real Kermit celebrates it. Or *Christmas Eve On Sesame Street*. Or the transcendent *Emmet Otter's Jug-Band Christmas*. Or even *John Denver And The Muppets: A Christmas Together*. Anything but *The Muppet Christmas Carol*, for God's sake.

Mark my words, history will record post-Henson Muppet products as distinctly inferior. On that I would bet my ultra-rare VHS copy of the pioneering interactive comedy video *Hey, You're As Funny As Fozzie Bear*.

I am trying to contain my Don Music-like frustration at your arrogance, but how can I speak reasonably to a man who prefers the plodding *Dark Crystal* to the delightful, far more imaginative *Labyrinth*? Do

see MUPPETS page 53

LOCAL

Skeptic Pitied

Above: The tragically skeptical Schaffner.

FAYETTEVILLE, AR—Craig Schaffner, 46, a Fayetteville-area computer consultant, has earned the pity of friends and acquaintances for his tragic reluctance to embrace the unverifiable, sources reported Monday.

"I honestly feel sorry for the guy," said neighbor Michael Eddy, 54, a born-again Christian. "To live in this world not believing in a higher power, doubting that Christ died for our sins—that's such a sad, cynical way to live. I don't know how he gets through his day."

"I feel sorry for the guy," said neighbor Michael Eddy, 54. "To live in this world not believing in a higher power, doubting that Christ died for our sins—that's such a sad, cynical way to live."

Coworker Donald Cobb, who spends roughly 20 percent of his annual income on telephone psychics and tarot-card readings, similarly extended his compassion for Schaffner.

"Craig is a really great guy," Cobb said. "It's just too bad he's chosen to cut himself off from the world of the paranormal, restricting himself to the limited universe of what can be seen and heard and verified through empirical evidence."

Also feeling pity for Schaffner is his former girlfriend Aimee Brand, a holistic and homeopathic healer who earns a living selling tonics and medicines diluted to one molecule per gallon in the belief that the water "remembers" the curative properties of the medication.

"Don't get me wrong—logic and reason have their place," Brand said. "But Craig fails to recognize the danger of going too far with medical common sense to the exclusion of alternative New Age remedies like chakra cleansing and energy-field realignment."

Eddy said he has tried repeatedly to pull Schaffner back from the precipice of lucidity.

"I admit, science might be great for curing diseases, exploring space, cataloguing the natural phenomena of our world, saving endangered species, extending the human lifespan, and enriching the quality of that life," Eddy said. "But at the end of the day, science has nothing to tell us about the human soul, and that's a critical thing Craig is missing. I would hate for his soul to be lost forever because of a stubborn doubt over the actual existence and nature of that soul."

Gina Hitchens, a lifelong astrology devotee, blamed Schaffner's lack of faith on an accident of birth.

"Craig can't entirely help himself, being a Gemini," Hitchens said. "Geminis are always very skeptical and destined to feel pain throughout life as a result of their closed-mindedness. If you try to introduce Craig to anything even remotely made-up, he starts going off about 'evidence this' and 'proof that.' If only the poor man were open-minded enough to stop attacking everything with his brain and just once look into his heart, he'd find all the proof he needed. But, sadly, he's unable to let even a little bit of imagination drive his core beliefs."

Perhaps the person who pities Schaffner most is his brother Frank, a practicing Scientologist since 1991.

"It's bad enough when someone has the ignorance to reject Dianetics in spite of its tremendous popularity," Frank said. "But Craig isn't even willing to try a free introductory course. Scientology has the potential to free humanity from the crippling yoke of common sense, unshackling billions from the chains of century after century of scientific precedent, and yet he still won't give it a try."

"I realize that Craig seems very happy with his narrow little common-sense-based worldview," Frank continued, "but when you think of all the widely embraced beliefs that are excluded by that way of thinking, you have to feel kind of sad." Ø

NEWS IN BRIEF

Area Man Proud Of Blood Type

RADCLIFFE, IA—Despite its status as the uncontrollable product of genetics and chance, Phil Schroeder's blood type is a frequent source of pride for the 26-year-old graphic designer. "I'm B-negative," said Schroeder, expecting to get a big reaction from coworker Mindy Tremont. "That's the second most rare after AB-negative." Schroeder, who has been known to high-five fellow B-negatives, went on to tell Tremont that individuals with Type B are said to be creative and excitable, prompting her to murmur, "Wow."

Track Winnings Reinvested In Blackjack Futures

ATLANTIC CITY, NJ—Seeking to grow his financial assets, Piscataway, NJ, gambler Richard Pasquale shrewdly reinvested his $2,432 trifecta win in the third race at Belmont Park in high-yield blackjack futures Monday. "The thoroughbred game is so vulnerable to track fluctuations, I thought it would be better to transfer my funds into a more proven moneymaker, one with a tremendous upside," said Pasquale, speaking from the blackjack pit at Harrah's Atlantic City casino. "Plus, I got a feeling I'm headed for a hot streak." He then instructed his dealer to hit him.

Business Traveler Closes Mini-Bar

CHARLOTTE, NC—After a long day of meetings and seminars, business traveler Patrick Hodge stayed up late Monday, closing the mini-bar in room 1815 of the Charlotte Marriott. "I'm usually a two-martini-then-hit-the-sack kind of guy," Hodge said. "But I was really wound up, and they had lots of those little bottles of my favorite liquors, so I said, 'What the hey?'" After closing down the mini-bar, Hodge staggered to the hotel's vending machine to beat the 3 a.m. "after-mini-bar rush."

Teen Stops Masturbating Long Enough To Save Family From Fire

PANAMA CITY, FL—Tragedy was narrowly averted Tuesday, when local 14-year-old Andy Foss suspended his usual non-stop autoerotic stimulation just long enough to drag unconscious family members from the fire consuming their home. "Apparently, Andy's parents, brother, and two sisters were rendered unconscious by smoke and fumes engulfing the house," Panama City fire chief Bill Engel said. "They would have surely perished, had this remarkable young man not heroically torn himself away from masturbation long enough to drag them to safety." Upon the fire department's arrival, Foss reportedly requested an extra blanket.

Bored Assistant Principal Browses Through Confiscated Items

INDEPENDENCE, MO—Unable to find anything else to do, bored Harry S Truman Middle School assistant principal William Podrewski rifled through the school's box of confiscated items Monday, searching for anything of interest. "Lots of cherry bombs in here," the 51-year-old Podrewski mused while sifting through the box, coming across a butterfly knife, a packet of raisins, and a Puddle Of Mudd CD. "Man, when I was a kid, I would have gotten seriously horse-whipped for having some of this stuff." Podrewski eventually settled on a faded March 1974 issue of *Oui* magazine. Ø

DOT-COM from page 49

Bollinger, a former Flooz.com tech-support supervisor and current delivery driver for Angelo's Pizza, Noyce became sentimental and introspective while gazing at the useless but expensively manufactured trinket.

"He had this far-away look in his eyes, like he'd been transported back to a simpler, more innocent time," Bollinger said. "I guess we can all relate to that feeling."

Bollinger, who has bounced between unemployment and under-employment for two and a half years, then returned to watching TV as Noyce continued to wax nostalgic.

"Wait a minute," Noyce said. "I remember this antHead thingy having some sort of button that would light up different colors every time you squeezed it. Shit, how much do you think something like this would cost to make? Those guys must have spent a fortune on these. It doesn't really do anything, but I remember pulling it out of my launch-party gift bag, thinking it was kind of cool. Sort of."

Noyce then tried to squeeze the object to see if it would still light up. It did not.

Like thousands of other dot-com promotional doodads produced from the mid-'90s until the New Economy bubble burst in the winter of 2000-01, the object was created as a means of "raising awareness and generating excitement about the brand." Handed out by the thousands at antHead.com's extravagant launch party in July 1999, it soon found its way into Noyce's bedroom junk drawer, along with numerous other equally functionless giveaways from the time,

Like thousands of other dot-com promotional doodads produced from the mid-'90s, the object was created as a means of "raising awareness and generating excitement about the brand."

including a FilmZone.com miniature director's chair, a Boo.com yo-yo, and a Kozmo.com glow-in-the-dark floppy flyer.

"Wait, I got it!" said Noyce, snapping out of his silence. "antHead! They had this huge pre-launch ad campaign in alternative weeklies across the country, with those mysterious 'teaser' ads that showed the ant-face logo with just the words 'antHead Is Coming.' When they finally launched, the party was held in five cities simultaneously, each one simulcast to the others via live satellite feed on huge video-projection screens. I'm pretty sure Douglas Coupland was the celebrity host."

Added Noyce: "I think the antHead site offered either original Shockwave-animated programming, live music webcasts, or both. Or neither."

Though neither Noyce nor anyone else in the U.S. can remember, antHead.com went public in August 1999, making its debut on NASDAQ at $17 a share. By April 2000, the stock had risen to a whopping $114 per share, with a market cap of $81 billion.

As part of their compensation packages, Noyce and his fellow dot-com employees were often issued stock options, which have come to be known in the financial world as "pretend Internet money." This pretend money, now estimated to be of slightly less value than the multi-colored paper bills used in Monopoly, was considered extremely valuable at the time. A great deal of this imaginary wealth was actually used to purchase Time Warner, one of the largest media conglomerates in the world.

"I remember the food at the antHead launch was great," Noyce said. "They had ceviche and grilled shrimp on skewers and these really great mini-fajita hors d'oeuvres. I just wish I could remember more about the company."

According to financial analysts, for many people Noyce's age, the New Economy boom was a mythic, idyllic time in American history.

"Prosperity seemed to hang from tree boughs like ripe fruit," said *Forbes* senior writer Peter Kafka, author of *What The F@%* Happened?!?: The New Economy—Fall '97 To Winter 2K*. "A revolutionary cyber-transformation of global culture and commerce seemed only 12 to 18 months away, and it felt like nothing could ever go wrong. It was a time of innocence, idealism, and magic."

"There we all were, straight out of college with zero real-world work experience, making $500,000 a year for, like, 12 weeks before transitioning into long periods of unemployment," Bollinger said. "Man, those were great weeks."

"Reminiscing about those days must be an emotional experience for Noyce," Kafka said. "Those antHead people had practically unlimited venture-capital start-up funds. He probably can't help but wonder about all the things that money could have bought, like a washing machine so he wouldn't have to haul his laundry all the way down to the basement of his rathole apartment complex every time he needs to wash his Arby's uniform." Ø

ROBOT from page 49

War III."

"The imperialist West is holding my country to standards which it does not see fit to meet itself," continued Kim, his voice now a metallic, digitized boom emanating from somewhere within the titanium helmet sheathing his head. "This does not surprise me, as they are well-famed for their lies."

"Pyongyang Dynamo Power Punch!" added Kim, as he released his fist-modules skyward with twin robotic uppercuts.

While the Bush Administration remains publicly confident that a diplomatic solution can be reached, top officials admit that the situation has become more complicated.

"If we add Kim Jong Il's transformation into a giant robot to his already defiant isolationist stance and his country's known nuclear capability, the diplomatic terrain definitely becomes more rocky," U.S. envoy James Kelly said. "Kim has made it clear that, if sufficiently threatened, he will not hesitate to use nuclear weapons or his arm-mounted HyperBazooka."

Added Kelly: "We are also forced to consider the possibility that Kim may attempt to robo-meld with other members of the Axis of Evil, forming a MegaMecha-Optima-Robosoldier. Kim would make a powerful right arm—or even a torso—for such a mechanism."

"If we add Kim Jong Il's transformation into a giant robot to his already defiant isolationist stance and his country's known nuclear capability, the diplomatic terrain definitely becomes more rocky," Kelly said.

Above: A South Korean border soldier eyes Kim Jong Il in the Demilitarized Zone.

During a visit Monday to the Demilitarized Zone dividing the Korean peninsula, Kim stressed that his transformation was not an act of aggression, but rather an attempt to defend his nation's autonomy.

"The DPRK must not be subject to the whims of an international coalition with no regard for the welfare of the Korean people," said Kim before stomping the ground with his foot, unleashing a devastating ring of energy that vaporized nearby reporters and military vehicles. "Catastrophic Valiant Kim-Chee Earthquake Stomp-Kick!" Ø

TRUCK from page 49

Maurer said he sometimes worries that he is spoiling his truck, but he confessed to doing it anyway.

"When I gave it leather seats and a custom grill cover, a part of me feared it was too much," Maurer said. "But then I thought about Dad's poor '75

> **"You have to really get to know your truck; you have to listen to it," Maurer said. "If you do, you'll pick up on those little clicks and whines that are signs of bigger problems. Even when it's running perfectly and it seems like nothing's bothering it, your truck is trying to tell you things."**

Chevy pick-up and how it didn't have any options. If you want your truck to be the best it can possibly be, you need to make sure it has options."

"If your truck has the very best right from the start, like this power 6.0L V8 with 325 horsepower, it's less likely to struggle later," continued Maurer, who plans to skip Kyle's school play Friday to take his truck fishing. "You always want to make sure your truck is equipped to cope with life's bumpy roads."

Maurer said he makes sure to spend plenty of quality time with his truck.

"In this day and age, too many truck owners try to pawn off responsibility to someone else," Maurer said. "They just drop it off at the Jiffy Lube or Tires Plus and assume that's okay. But a mechanic is no substitute for an owner: If you don't actually put in the time with your own truck, how can you know what's really going on under the hood? That's why I never miss any of the important events. I'm there for every tire rotation, oil change, and radiator flush-and-fill, even if it means having to take time off from work."

Maurer said he has always firmly believed that proper maintenance begins at home.

"You have to really get to know your truck; you have to listen to it," Maurer said. "If you do, you'll pick up on those little clicks and whines that are signs of bigger problems. Even when it's running perfectly and it seems like nothing's bothering it, your truck is trying to tell you things. You just have to have the patience to hear."

Though he primarily uses his truck to drive to work and run errands

Above: Maurer's pride and joy.

around town, Maurer said it is important to "make sure the engine gets some exercise" by driving at higher speeds.

"Sometimes, I'll take a special trip out to the state forest or to a Seahawks game so I can open it up to 75 or 85 on the interstate," Maurer said. "It's good to push your truck once in a while. A few nicks and dings are part of life."

"But just enough to build a little character," Maurer clarified. "When I see someone mistreat a vehicle, it makes me want to cry."

Maurer shared a horror story of a coworker who abused his truck.

"This guy would let his fool son run his S-10 all over town and, sure enough, about a year ago, it was in an accident. The whole driver's side was smashed in, and the windshield blew right out of the frame," Maurer said. "I guess it could've been worse. At least the chassis wasn't hurt, thank God."

As much as he hates to see a truck physically abused, Maurer said neglect can be just as harmful.

"Some men ignore their trucks for years, and then, when rust spots appear, they act surprised," Maurer said. "By that point, though, it's too late. So I always tell truck owners to cherish the early years and make the most of them. You can't undo the damage you do to a truck, and when the warranty expires, you can't go back in time and relive those years." ø

MUPPETS from page 50

you really fancy yourself some kind of expert Muppet archivist just because our PBS affiliate doesn't carry the Ed Sullivan reruns, forcing me to rely on you to tape the old Muppet sketches for me when you visit your friend who gets Noggin in New York?

Correct me if I'm wrong, but I believe the only volume of Time-Life's *Best Of The Muppet Show* owned by you is *Vol. 2*, which you bought only for the Mark Hamill episode. It's bad enough that you would be more swayed by that *Star Wars Insider* feature—a painfully gushing love letter to a sub-par episode—than you would by me, a genuine fan. Adding insult to injury, you probably haven't even watched the other two episodes on that very DVD. Why, I bet you couldn't tell Floyd from Zoot if your life depended on it.

The final insult, though, was that time you made fun of me at Ken's house for saying that the Harry Belafonte episode of *The Muppet Show* made me teary-eyed when I watched it shortly after Sept. 11. That, plus your admission that you've never even seen the episode. Am I to believe that someone who's never experienced the profound "Turn The World Around" musical number is entitled to outbid me on a *Muppet Movie* soundtrack? The four representative songs on *The Muppet Show*'s 25th anniversary CD are sim-

> **Correct me if I'm wrong, but I believe the only volume of Time-Life's *Best Of The Muppet Show* owned by you is *Vol. 2*, which you bought only for the Mark Hamill episode.**

ply not enough for you? You honestly feel you deserve to own "Never Before, Never Again" on CD more than I do? Try again, Mr. Noodle.

As we both know, this is about more than just a CD. Throughout the years I've known you, you have consistently failed to give the Muppets their proper due. Who taught you to count? Who taught you to read? Who taught you the social skills we enjoy to this day? The Muppets did. And you thank them how? By not even being able to distinguish the real Kermit from the new one? To a legitimate fan, the difference is incredibly obvious, almost as clear as the one between the old and new Cookie Monsters (don't get me started).

I swear on Mr. Hooper's grave, I will not stand idly by while you sow the seeds of animosity and discord between friends. Can't you see that you should have matured beyond this kind of behavior years ago? I urge you to overcome your foolish, Swedish-Chef-incomprehensible grandstanding and let stand my bid for $52.50. Such is my advice. I am now done talking to you.

Oh, and regarding your alt.tv.muppets post of a month ago: The Weezer video is *not* a "perfect" simulation of *The Muppet Show*. Among myriad other errors, Pepe The Prawn is a latter-day Muppet who made his debut on *Muppets Tonight* in 1996 and never appeared on the original show.

Now grow the hell up. ø

ADVICE

Ask A Bride And Groom's Self-Penned Wedding Vows

By Kris and Shauna

Dear Self-Penned Wedding Vows,

Two weeks ago, I broke up with my boyfriend of four years, whom I'll call "Cal." I really have no interest in keeping in contact with him, but during our relationship I became very close with his mother. Since the breakup, I've spoken to her on the phone four times, and she recently sent me a birthday card. I miss her and would like to visit her, but I don't know if maintaining a friendship with the parent of an ex is appropriate. What should I do?

Unsure In Upper Darby

Dear Unsure,

Shauna, I cannot believe that you are marrying me. But it is true—Jesus brought you to me. You are the single most amazing thing that has ever happened in my life, and I now stand here today out of a desire to spend the rest of it with you. Shauna, you are the most beautiful woman in the world. I have no other eyes for anyone else, and I never will again. Though we have only known each other for less than eight months, I am ready to soar into matrimony with you. I know you have already consented to be my wife because you are here in this marriage chapel today, but I now ask you regardless: Please, Shauna, please be my wife.

Dear Self-Penned Wedding Vows,

My sister Jessica recently underwent a dramatic weight loss, shedding almost 90 pounds on a liquid diet. As someone who has also battled her weight, I was very inspired by her. Yet Jessica is very critical of my more conservative weight-loss methods. I don't feel her radical approach would work for me, and I'm getting upset by her constant criticism. How do I tell her to butt out and let me do it my way?

Though we have only known each other for less than eight months, I am ready to soar into matrimony with you.

Overweight In Overland Park

Dear Overland Park,

Kris, you are my palomino stallion. You are truly like a stallion in that you are broad and strong, and you carry me to heights of love I have never before even dreamt of. Kris, thank you so much for being such an important part of my life. I will love you forever. In addition, you are a groom, and grooms take care of horses, and to me that is no coincidence. I do not believe in coincidence. This was truly meant to happen.

Dear Self-Penned Wedding Vows,

Just read "Without Wesley" and was moved to tears. Losing a cherished pet is like losing a family member. I'll never forget the day we had to put our 17-year-old cat Sugar to sleep. It took a long time to get over her loss, but in time the healing came, and I even acquired an adorable tortoiseshell kitten named Missy. I'm not saying you should get another chihuahua immediately after Wesley's passing, but I hope you can forgive your mother for her insensitivity, because holding a grudge will only prolong your pain. Be secure in the knowledge that Wesley was an important part of your life, and nothing your mother says can diminish that. And, yes, time does heal all wounds.

If we were not working at the food court at the same time, we probably never would have met, since I lived in Boydston and you lived in Maynard. So this only goes to show that a higher power brought us together.

Missy's Mom In Monmouth

Dear Monmouth,

Shauna, it is strange to think that if we were not working at the food court at the same time, we probably never would have met, since I lived in Boydston and you lived in Maynard. So this only goes to show that a higher power brought us together. Shauna, I promise to protect and cherish you forever, and to look after little Kyle, too. Even though he is your son with another man, I feel as if he is my own flesh and blood. Shauna, do you believe in angels? I do, because I am looking an angel square in the eye right now.

HOROSCOPES

Your Horoscope

By Lloyd Schumner Sr.
Retired Machinist and
A.A.P.B.-Certified Astrologer

Aries: (March 21–April 19)
You are excited to learn about the bank machines that hand out money. But, like most things in the big city, it's not as great as it sounds.

Taurus: (April 20–May 20)
You've heard the phrase "Dead men tell no tales," but you sure wish someone had told the overly talkative zombie sitting next to you on the plane.

Gemini: (May 21–June 21)
All those people who think a person can't be both creative and productive now have you as proof.

Cancer: (June 22–July 22)
Next week, you will find yourself in an office romance. Unfortunately, all the female employees will have been replaced by shrieking drag queens.

Leo: (July 23–Aug. 22)
You'll be excited to learn that you will be one of the items included in the gift bags at this year's Oscars.

Virgo: (Aug. 23–Sept. 22)
The good news is, at long last, your time machine works. The bad news is that you won't be lying about being a disabled Vietnam veteran anymore.

Libra: (Sept. 23–Oct. 23)
Remember: A bend in the road isn't the end of the road. By the way, do you have to be told fucking everything?

Scorpio: (Oct. 24–Nov. 21)
You will soon be in demand among domestically oriented women when it turns out you're made of Corian, a desirable countertop material.

Sagittarius: (Nov. 22–Dec. 21)
A drunk Willie Nelson will call you at 3 a.m. to "apologize," but then spends an hour complaining that no one knows he wrote "Crazy."

Capricorn: (Dec. 22–Jan. 19)
After experiencing a sudden and profound shift in priorities, you spend all your time making love instead of money, causing you to die exhausted and penniless.

Aquarius: (Jan. 20–Feb. 18)
If people call you cold and unfeeling, remind them how long and hard you cried over that dead Bee Gee.

Pisces: (Feb. 19–March 20)
Your name will soon be used as a stirring rallying cry for the installation of airbags on brick walls.

Dear Self-Penned Wedding Vows,

How does one politely broach the topic of body odor in the workplace—especially when the offending party is your boss? If I'm in the same room with him, my eyes begin to smart and I have to excuse myself, yet because he's my boss, I don't feel comfortable saying anything. What should I do?

Watery Eyes In Waterbury

Dear Watery Eyes,

Kris, you are the sweetest, most caring man I have met in all of my 21 years. This marriage is going to be strong like a rock, and it is going to last. We may not have a lot of money, but we are so good for each other, it is not even funny. When I get crazy, you don't even bat an eye. You are the first guy I've been with who can handle me and my difficult aspects. I so appreciate that, and it so makes me want to be a better person. Kris, I will be good to you and treat you right.

Dear Self-Penned Wedding Vows,

When my son Ralph graduated from college and moved to another city, his father and I agreed to pay his rent for the first six months or until he got a permanent job, whichever came first. However, I recently learned that Ralph's longtime girlfriend Vicki moved in with him. While I can't prevent them from living together out of wedlock, I resent the notion of Vicki living free on our generosity. So last week, I informed Ralph that we are cutting him off early. Lately, though, I'm having second thoughts. Do you think I was too harsh?

Feeling Guilty In Guilford

Dear Guilty,

Shauna, I am now going to read a poem that I wrote especially for this very special ceremony: "I don't have to dream anymore / My dreams have come true / Because I have my Shauna / I am so grateful to the Lord / Please accept this ring / And watch the bird of our marriage take flight / For now and ever after / Amen."

Kris and Shauna are a recently married couple whose syndicated advice column, Ask A Bride And Groom's Self-Penned Wedding Vows, *appears in more than 250 newspapers nationwide.* ø

the ONION®

VOLUME 39 ISSUE 03 AMERICA'S FINEST NEWS SOURCE™ 30 JAN.–5 FEB. 2003

NEWS

New Swiss Army Phone May Pose Health Risks

see PRODUCTWATCH page 4C

Pete Townshend Can't Explain

see PEOPLE page 3E

Guy At Gym Keeps Offering To Spot Everyone

see LOCAL page 7B

Toddler Thrown From Dog

see LOCAL page 9B

STATshot

A look at the numbers that shape your world.

Toughest U.S. Stains

1. Ground-in terrier
2. Dress from blueberry-fetish night
3. Presidential flopsweat
4. Acne cream on Weezer T-shirt
5. Cum and butter
6. Blood of the innocent
7. Cuba Gooding Jr. juice

U.N. Orders Wonka To Submit To Chocolate Factory Inspections

Right: U.N. inspectors arrive at the gates of the Wonka compound. Above: The enigmatic, elusive despot.

UNITED NATIONS—Responding to pressure from the international community, the U.N. ordered enigmatic candy maker William "Willy" Wonka to submit to chocolate-factory inspections Monday.

"For years, Wonka has hidden the ominous doings of his research and development facility from the outside world," U.N. Secretary General Kofi Annan said. "Given the reports of child disappearances, technological advances in glass-elevator transport, and Wonka-run Oompa-Loompa forced-labor camps, the time has come to put an end to three decades of secrecy in the Wonka Empire."

The chocolate-making capabilities of Wonka's heavily fortified compound have long been a source of speculation. Wonka, defying international calls for full disclosure, has maintained his silence regarding his factory's suspected capacity to manufacture confections of mass deliciousness.

Secretary of State Colin Powell praised the U.N. announcement.

"No more will this sinister figure be free to pursue his nefarious endeavors without fear of reprisal, protected by loopholes in international candy-making law," Powell said. "With this ruling, the U.N. has issued the global community a 'golden ticket' to draw

see WONKA page 59

Migrant Worker Family Thrilled To See Selves On Cover Of *The Economist*

SAN CARLOS, TX—A family of Mexican migrant workers was thrilled to find its picture on the cover of the Jan. 25 issue of *The Economist*, vegetable farmhand, factory laborer, and fruit picker Luis Moreno reported Monday.

"Imagine my surprise when I walked past the newsstand and saw my own face on the cover of a magazine—a very respected international publication, no less," said Moreno, 34, speaking with the aid of a translator. "I couldn't believe it. I opened the maga-

see ECONOMIST page 58

Below: The issue that made the Morenos famous.

Depressed Roommate Hitting The GameCube Pretty Hard

WEST LAFAYETTE, IN—Despondent over a recent breakup with his longtime girlfriend, Purdue University graduate student Tim Mahaffey, 27, has been hitting the Nintendo GameCube "pretty hard," roommates reported Monday.

"Tim's been trying to drown his sorrows in the Cube," roommate Darrell Lock said. "He's always been into Nintendo, but it was under control. These days, though, you barely ever see him without a controller in his hand."

Mahaffey's downward spiral began on Dec. 14, when Brittany Pfafflin, his girlfriend of two years, ended their relationship. In the days following the split, Mahaffey's friends noticed him exhibiting a decreased interest in social activities and a corresponding rise in time spent with his GameCube.

"All he wants to do is bury himself in Super Smash Bros. and Tony Hawk's Pro Skater 4," Lock said. "He used to think of himself as a 'social' videogame player, confident that he could hit quit any time he wanted. But lately, he'll play one

see GAMECUBE page 59

Right: Mahaffey loses himself in his videogame system.

Affirmative Action Under Fire

President Bush recently urged the Supreme Court to strike down the University of Michigan's affirmative-action program as unconstitutional. What do *you* think?

Rich Skoldek
Plumber

"I applaud Bush's hardline stand on this issue, as once a nigra get his head full-a learnin', he start up a-thinkin', an' then there ain't no keepin' him down no-how."

Frank Krantz
Architect

"Christ. NBC's *A Different World* wasn't enough, now they want to go to 'real' college, too?"

Tom Edwards
Systems Analyst

"Affirmative action unfairly keeps more qualified applicants out of college. Kind of like having a rich, politically connected daddy."

Dennis Duran
Cab Driver

"This is an extremely complex, emotionally charged issue, but one thing is clear: Condoleezza Rice's name is funny."

Marci Hoffler
Homemaker

"I once met someone who says she lost a job because of affirmative action, and I've never met anyone who's benefitted, so I'm opposed."

Marla Simmons
Student

"Why do those people act like we *owe* them something? Oh, right."

Fox's Reality Shows

Having struck ratings gold with *Man Vs. Beast* and *Joe Millionaire*, Fox has plans for more reality-TV programming. Among the new shows:

- *Millionaire Manatee*
- *Battle Of The Former Network Stars*
- *Leeza Gibbons Vs. Gibbons*
- *America's Nakedest Women*
- *Mind Fuck 2: Celebrity Mind Fuck*
- *Chained To The Leg Of Cloris Leachman*
- *Who Hates This Show The Most?*
- *Slaughterhouse Live*
- *The Vacuuming Has-Beens*
- *José Million-pesos*
- *When Writers Guilds Strike*
- *Gunned Down Mercilessly In The Street Like A Dog*

the ONION®
America's Finest News Source.™

Herman Ulysses Zweibel
Founder

T. Herman Zweibel
Publisher Emeritus
J. Phineas Zweibel
Publisher
Maxwell Prescott Zweibel
Editor-In-Chief

This Racist Propaganda Practically Writes Itself!

By Pat Glenn

All my life, I dreamed of writing racist propaganda, but I was always too scared to try. I came up with every excuse in the book: I lacked the necessary education, I wasn't a good enough writer, I didn't know enough racial slurs. But then, one day, I gave it a whirl, and you know what? It was easy! The hateful rants just poured out of me and onto the page. I'm telling you, this racist propaganda practically writes itself.

Sure, going off on the niggers, Jews, and towelheads is easy enough when you're knocking back a few Coors Lights with your buddies at the Triple Dice Bar. Me, Frank, and Curtis, we can jabber on for hours about how the spicks are taking away all the construction jobs. But to actually organize your ill-informed opinions into a coherent, well-structured screed on the printed page, well, that's a whole different animal.

It all started last Friday night down at the Triple Dice. As we're knocking a few back, Frank goes on one of his tears about affirmative action, and how the blacks are these lazy fucks who don't value education and just want everything handed to them on a silver platter—and he knows what he's talking about, too, since he has a sister who lives by Detroit. Whenever Frank gets on a roll about the blacks, I always say we should write it all down, but we never do. This time, though, he was so on fire, I started scrawling down his rant on a cocktail napkin. Within a few minutes, I had about eight napkins worth of primo bigotry. If I hadn't been so trashed, I might've asked the bartender for one of those paper placemats to keep going.

The next day, after I got over my hangover, I thought I'd try writing sober. Wouldn't you know it, I had six pages on the so-called "American Indians" and how they're all drunks on welfare before I finished my cup of coffee. I even had a World Book encyclopedia sitting next to me, in case I needed to look things up, but I didn't have to crack it open once.

Now that I've finally done it, I've learned that the hardest part about writing racist propaganda is simply getting started. A friend of mine, who's written some eye-opening stuff about the Italians, once told me, "You just gotta get that pencil moving." You know what? He was right! It was so simple, I can't believe everyone with two brain cells to rub together isn't doing it.

To pen virulent, racist dogma, I always assumed you had to read a lot of history books and keep up with the news. Or at least read more than just *Motor Trend* and *Hustler*. But the reality is, you don't. My friends and I have been giving each other all the information we need through our beer-soaked speculating and finger-pointing. The morning after a long night of drinking, I may not remember half of what Curtis said about the Pakistanis taking over his neighborhood, but half a truth is better than the hundreds of lies you get from the Jew-run liberal media.

One of the best things about racist propaganda is that it only needs to seem to make sense. The barest threads can tie the Emancipation Proclamation to the Elders of Zion.

Fucking Pakistanis.

One of the best things about racist propaganda is that it only needs to seem to make sense. The barest threads can tie the Emancipation Proclamation to the Elders of Zion. I mean, look at them. They both start with "E," don't they? And that was just off the top of my head. And if someone starts to argue with you about facts, just call them a nigger-lovin' faggot-queer Jew, and that'll shut them up real quick.

Another great thing about writing racist propaganda is that you don't even need to know how to write all that good. There are computer programs that'll correct most of your grammar and spelling mistakes. And if I need to find another word for "gook," my handy slang dictionary gives me zip, gink, and slope. It's true: The only thing stopping you from realizing your dream of becoming a writer is your own fears.

The bottom line is, all you need to write racist propaganda is a pen, some paper, and a refusal to take responsibility for your own problems. Most folks probably don't write because they think it's only for people with reasonable arguments and an open mind. But it's just that kind of thinking that keeps a lot of decent, honest, God-fearing racists from sharing their crackpot theories.

Christ, if I can do this, anyone can. Believe me. Ø

HIGH SCHOOL

Debate Team State Finalists Live It Up In Super 8 Hot Tub

OSHKOSH, WI—The 16 members of the Abbotsford High School debate team enjoyed a night of revelry in the hot tub of an Oshkosh Super 8 motel Sunday, celebrating their second-place finish in the Wisconsin High School Forensic Association state competition.

"This place rocks," team captain Ethan Howe said.

"This is it, guys," said team captain Ethan Howe, sinking back into the bubbling water and raising a can of Orange Slice high into the air. "This is what we've been working so hard for all year!"

On Jan. 11, the Abbotsford debate team qualified for the state competition, "killing" at the district level. The following day, Abbotsford Forensics Club advisor Sharon Knauf made lodging accommodations for the students in Oshkosh for the WHSFA Four-Speaker State Debate Tournament, held at 8 p.m. Sunday at the University of Wisconsin-Oshkosh.

"For years, whenever we went to state, I always booked the Oshkosh Econolodge," said Knauf, 53, who has coached forensics for 18 years. "A few years ago, though, they opened up this Super 8 right off Hwy. 41, and I really like it better: There's no problem parking the bus, and it's quite a ways to downtown, so no one is tempted to try to sneak out."

Above: Members of the Abbotsford High School debate team get psyched for a wild night at the Super 8.

Super 8 #2692 boasts an indoor heated pool and whirlpool, free HBO and ESPN, and a vending area with candy, chips, soda, and an ice machine. On weekends, the motel also offers a continental breakfast from 6 to 10 a.m.

"This place rocks," said Howe, a white towel draped around his neck as he swaggered to the button that restarts the whirlpool. "We are *livin' it up.*"

Knauf reserved nine adjoining rooms on the east wing of the second floor, assigning two students to each room and giving herself a single. The rooms were situated near the vending area, a spot frequented by the high-spirited students throughout the night.

"We took up a collection in an ice bucket—I put in, like, *seven dollars*—and we brought a bunch of snacks back to Party Central [Room 233]," Howe said. "Jim [Gamble] even had a CD player, which he technically wasn't allowed to bring. Shhh."

The mischief, sources report, was not limited to boom box smuggling. Student and allergy sufferer John Greipentrog, claiming to be in desperate need of Benadryl, obtained Knauf's permission to leave the motel and walk to the Amoco station down the road.

"I was lying," said Greipentrog, who actually made a "supply run" for food to add to the already copious amounts left over from the celebratory dinner at Olive Garden. "I had my Allegra with me. Of course, I was way nervous about lying to a teacher, but the rest of the team convinced me to live on the edge for once."

By 7 p.m., the motel's whirlpool had become the center of activity. Nearly all the students convened at the 10-person hot tub, enjoying the company of their fellow honor students in pampered luxury.

"I forgot my swimsuit, but I just wore shorts and a T-shirt—right in the pool!" junior Denise Neumann said. "We were singing our school song, but we changed the words to make fun of the a-holes on the football team."

The combination of the wet bodies, caffeine, and general spirit of revelry even resulted in some intra-squad flirting.

"Eric [Yetter] is so funny," sophomore Kim Ault said. "He was pretending to fall asleep, and he'd sink down

see DEBATE TEAM page 58

NEWS IN BRIEF

Alabama Governor Injured Imitating Pro Wrestling

MONTGOMERY, AL—Gov. Bob Riley broke his collarbone Monday while imitating a wrestling move he saw on TNN's *WWE RAW*. "[Secretary of State] Jim [Bennett] and I were just funning around," Riley said after his discharge from St. Mary's Hospital. "I tried to do The Undertaker's Last Ride powerbomb—not for real, just pretend—and I slipped." Monday's incident marked the state's worst wrestling-related gubernatorial injury since 1991, when then-Gov. Guy Hunt was paralyzed jumping off a friend's roof onto a backyard trampoline.

Real World Producers Still Looking To Fill Eating-Disorder Slot

VAN NUYS, CA—Jonathan Murray, co-executive producer of the MTV reality series *The Real World*, reported Monday that with just weeks to go before shooting begins, the eating-disorder slot for the cast of *Real World 13: Paris* remains unfilled. "We're still trying to find a hot young bulimic or anorexic, ideally with bisexual leanings," Murray said. "We found a woman who was perfect, except she was Asian, and we already had our non-black minority slot filled." Murray said that as a last resort, he has a perky blonde sexual-abuse victim ready to go.

Man Totally Proud Of Last Night's Drunken Phone Calls

ENID, OK—Andrew Colquitt expressed pride Monday in a drunken cross-country calling spree he'd embarked on the previous night. "I really gave that dick Larry Trachte a piece of my mind, and I finally told Steve I slept with his girlfriend back in high school," Colquitt said. "I think I even called [ex-girlfriend] Rebecca [Anders], although I might have just dreamed that." The 38-year-old Colquitt also called former college roommate Alex Via to inform him that he is "the greatest guy ever. Dude, I fuckin' love you, dude. Serious."

AOL Time Warner Turmoil Over-Reported, Says Time

NEW YORK—According to the Feb. 3 issue of Time, the internal turmoil plaguing AOL Time Warner is being over-reported by the national media. "Once again, tabloids like *Newsweek* and *U.S. News & World Report* insist on trawling through the Dumpster of this non-story, desperate to dig up any dirt they can find," columnist Lance Morrow wrote. "This would be bad enough in times of slow news, but a nation about to go to war and confused about which online service offers the best enhanced e-mail features surely deserves better."

New Movie Taps Into Nation's Love Of Rapping Kangaroos

HOLLYWOOD, CA—The new Jerry Bruckheimer comedy *Kangaroo Jack* has successfully tapped into America's longstanding love affair with rapping kangaroos, taking in a box-office-best $17.7 million in its opening weekend. "From Krazy Legs Kangol in the early '80s to such New School acts as Pouch Gangstas and Tha Mar$upials, kangaroos have always been at the forefront of the rap scene," media analyst Glen Coffey said. "But not until now has anyone had the vision to exploit this trend in a full-length feature film." Warner Bros. has already confirmed plans for a sequel, *Koala Bob*, featuring a computer-generated beat-boxing koala who steals $50 million in gold bullion... and he's not giving it back. ø

ECONOMIST from page 55

zine and there we were again, right there under the headline, 'Hard Harvest: The Enduring Plight Of Migrant Workers In America.' I ran to my wife with a copy of the issue as fast as I could and said, 'Hey, Rosa, we're famous!"

Ever since losing his job as a mechanic's assistant in Mexico City four years ago, Moreno, his wife Rosa, and their three young sons have roamed the American South and Midwest in search of seasonal labor.

"Judging by the scenery and the size of little Esteban, I am guessing the photo was taken in north Texas, shortly after the October harvest," Moreno said. "We were relocating from the lower Rio Grande valley to Iowa, where I can usually find winter work in the slaughterhouses or the pork-processing plants. How lucky we were to be on that particular road that day!"

Continued Moreno: "I do not specifically remember anyone taking my picture, but that is not surprising if we were in the middle of traveling. It gets very tiring, of course, and sometimes you do not pay attention to distractions."

"Our friend Miguel and his wife were teasing us, calling us 'undocumented migrants' like they did in the story," Rosa added.

Moreno praised *The Economist*'s photo editor for choosing the cover image.

"The clothes we were wearing created a very interesting pastiche of colors, which is probably why he chose that particular shot," Moreno said. "Also, the photographer caught us at a moment when our expressions powerfully conveyed the great weariness we were feeling."

The seven-page cover story, which featured a second photo of the Moreno family inside the magazine, focused on George W. Bush and Mexican president Vicente Fox's long-running dispute over migrant workers and the legalization of undocumented Mexicans in the U.S.

"I was so excited," Moreno said. "I had a little money saved, enough for three copies. I sent one home to Mexico to my grandmother, I put one away to keep nice, and the other I used to show all of my friends."

Within hours of the issue hitting newsstands, Moreno said he began hearing from friends, coworkers, and relatives.

"I call home to my mother in Oaxaca whenever I can, just to make sure everyone is okay, especially our little Juanita, who is too young to travel," Moreno said. "The first thing she says to me is, 'Your cousin Carlos called to say he saw you in *The Economist*. He says to call him right away. My son, the celebrity!'"

Rosa said the cover story has made her and the rest of the Moreno clan the talk of the migrant-worker community.

"It's amazing how many people have seen it," Rosa said. "We were passing through Sebastian on the way to Progreso, and we stopped to visit some old friends from Mexico City who found work in a tannery. The first thing out of everyone's mouth was, 'Here comes the cover girl!' You should have seen me blush."

"Our friend Miguel and his wife were teasing us, calling us 'undocumented migrants' like they did in the story," Rosa added, "but it was all in good fun."

Moreno, who read the article with the help of a translator, said he felt *The Economist*'s assessment of migrant workers and their plight was "evenhanded and intelligent."

"Basically, the author of the article said migrant workers are net contributors to the economy of a country because they are disproportionately of working age, and the receiving country has not had to pay for their education," Moreno said. "And they pointed out that migration does not seem to increase unemployment among the native-born."

"To be fair, it did say it may reduce their pay," Rosa said. "But I agree with Luis that it certainly was a fairer look at the subject than I have come to expect."

"I've been treated badly by many people throughout my life," added Rosa, lowering her eyes to the floor.

Though he does not expect to appear on another magazine cover any time soon, Moreno expressed hope that one day his family will have the luck to be interviewed by a Ph.D candidate conducting research in one of the seasonal worker camps.

"It's amazing what a complex system of social ties we itinerant workers maintain, considering that we are always in motion and have only limited access to modern communications," Moreno said. "Don't you think that would make a fascinating subject for a dissertation?" ⊘

Above: Guillermo Nunez (left), Luis Moreno's best friend, shows off the issue.

DEBATE TEAM from page 57

into the water and act like he was dead. Then he got my hair all wet, even though I wasn't going to put it in the water."

Later that night, Yetter and Ault disobeyed the "no co-ed room activity" rule, professing merely to be "sharing passages from their Advanced English 11 journals."

"I don't know what went on, but Eric is, like, Kim's man now," said Wendy Druyan, Ault's roommate. "We kept knocking on the door and calling their phone until they took it off the hook. Then we went in Denise's room next door and banged on the wall."

The only student who did not participate in the tomfoolery was Jay Gawlikoski, who spent the night in his room.

"If we get in trouble, it could go on our permanent record and colleges would see that," said Gawlikoski, two-time recipient of Knauf's Most Valuable Debater award. "I'd be more than up for some charades or maybe a game of euchre, but I really have no interest in doing something stupid that'd hurt my chances of getting into Northwestern."

According to anonymous sources, Gawlikoski is a "puss" and "just mad because everyone teased him for bringing a huge suitcase for an overnight stay." The unnamed student also claimed that Gawlikoski actually phoned his mother to tell her the results of his competition and was in bed by 10 p.m.

"Yes, we were ultimately vanquished, but our 11-4 record is nothing to sneeze at," Farber said.

Unlike Gawlikoski, the other students were more than ready to party late into the night. The last to turn in, sneaking back to their respective rooms at 4 a.m., were Randy Lund and Tim Farber, a pair of juniors who earlier in the day went head to head against the co-captains of the vaunted Eau Claire Memorial High School squad.

"Yes, we were ultimately vanquished, but our 11-4 record is nothing to sneeze at, and we made some very persuasive arguments on the WHSFA debate topic, Weapons Of Mass Destruction," Farber said. "What's more, with just two graduating seniors on the entire squad, the Abbotsford debate team will be a force to be reckoned with next year. We had more than enough reason to make merry this eve." ⊘

WONKA from page 55

Above: A CIA surveillance image of suspicious activity within the Wonka compound.

back the curtain behind which this mysterious confectioner hides."

According to CIA psychological profilers, Wonka has retreated from the

To date, all efforts to peer inside the Wonka inner sanctum have met with failure. Armies of legal experts retained by Wonka have kept visitors to his chocolate-making facilities effectively gagged with elaborate non-disclosure agreements.

outside world entirely, withdrawing into "a world of pure imagination." An anonymous tinker stationed near the infamous, long-locked Wonka factory gate corroborated the claim, saying, "Nobody ever goes in, nobody ever comes out."

Rival candy makers, long worried that Wonka's advanced capabilities have created an imbalance of power within the volatile global chocolate marketplace, also applauded the U.N. move.

"Wonka exerts a powerful psychological grip over the world's children," said Arthur Slugworth, president of Slugworth Confections. "They are devoted to him with a loyalty that borders on the fanatical, eagerly lapping up Scrumdiddlyumptious Bars by the millions at his command. But when we found evidence that Wonka was developing so-called 'everlasting gobstopper' technology—'the mother of all gobstoppers'—we knew it was time to act."

To date, all efforts to peer inside the Wonka inner sanctum have met with failure. Armies of legal experts retained by Wonka have kept visitors to his chocolate-making facilities effectively gagged with elaborate non-disclosure agreements. His in-house staff of high-contrast Technicolor dwarves carefully monitors what information flows in or out of the heavily guarded compound. And the few scraps of information that have come to light—vague reports of terrifying river-barge rides, razor-sharp ceiling fans, and human-sized pneumatic tubes of indeterminate purpose—have been obscured by layers of darkly comic, psychedelic symbolism, making them virtually impossible to interpret.

"Wonka has shown himself to be a man who cannot be trusted," Annan said. "Whether misrepresenting himself as a limping cripple, only to drop at the last moment into an agile somersault, or exploiting the deepest and most personal character flaws of misbehaving children, Wonka has been a man of shifty, undetermined motives and baffling ends. He must be stopped."

Defense Secretary Donald Rumsfeld, a longtime advocate of regime change in the Wonka Empire, is urging President Bush to consider military intervention should Wonka refuse to cooperate.

"The world can no longer turn a blind eye to Wonka's deception and misdirection," Rumsfeld said. "Without full inspections, there's no earthly way of knowing which direction Wonka's going. Not a speck of light is showing, so the danger must be growing. And he's certainly not

"The world can no longer turn a blind eye to Wonka's deception and misdirection," Rumsfeld said.

showing any signs that he is slowing. Are the fires of Hell a-glowing? Is the grisly reaper mowing? Who can provide the world with the answer to these pressing questions?"

"The candy man can," Rumsfeld added grimly.

Bush said he is leaning toward the use of force, undeterred by the prospect of the candy maker using his rumored "Wonkavision" technology to turn would-be attackers into millions of tiny pieces, beaming them through the air and shrinking them to tiny, dollhouse-accessory size.

"We are talking about a man who is able to take a rainbow and cover it with dew," Bush told reporters during a press conference Monday. "Who knows what else he is capable of? Left to his own devices, he could, in a worst-case scenario, make the world taste very bad, indeed." ⌀

GAMECUBE from page 55

game after another, all night long without stopping. Doesn't he know how many other people it hurts? I have to teach a 9 a.m. discussion section."

Even more distressing, roommate Colin Thaler said, is Mahaffey's habit of lying to cover up his GameCube addiction.

"Whenever Darrell and I leave the apartment in the morning, Tim hangs back and makes up some excuse to stay in, like he has to find his keys or write a paper," Thaler said. "But we know better. As soon as we're gone, he digs up one of the controllers he has hidden all over the apartment and lights up the TV."

During a recent conversation, Mahaffey gave Thaler the impression that he might finally be ready to start dating again.

"I took it as an encouraging sign when Tim said there was a girl who seemed interested in him," Thaler said. "Eventually, I realized that he

"When used responsibly, the Nintendo GameCube is a refreshing and enjoyable way to unwind from the pressures of the day. It is not intended for abuse," Dean said.

was talking about a character in the virtual town he created in Animal Crossing. He said her name was 'Jeanne.' I know he needs us to be there for him, but I almost started whaling on him."

Nintendo spokesman Michael Dean offered support to Mahaffey and others sharing his problem.

"Our prayers go out to the friends and family of Mr. Mahaffey, and to Mr. Mahaffey himself," Dean said. "When used responsibly, the Nintendo GameCube is a refreshing and enjoyable way to unwind from the pressures of the day. It is not intended for abuse, as has been reported among a small percentage of our happy GameCube family. We hope Mr. Mahaffey can get the help he needs so he can once again lead a productive life that includes responsible playing of such forthcoming games as Dungeons & Dragons Heroes, Legend Of Zelda: The Wind Waker, and Evolution Snowboarding." ⌀

HARVEY'S HOLLYWOOD

When It Comes To Entertainment, My Sign Is Leo!

Happy New Year! Sorry I was a bit slow bringing you your first steaming-hot batch of 2003 gossip, but I had to take a few weeks off just to digest the **holiday fruitcake**! You know the one? The one someone gives every year? Well, I ate it.

The Outside Scoop
By Jackie Harvey

Item! After going so long without him, we got twice the **Leo** this holiday movie season—and, boy, was it worth the wait! First, he was a scruffy turn-of-the-century gangster with a heart of gold in **The New York Gangs**. Then, he transformed into a 1960s con artist with a heart of gold in **Catch Him... Please!** I can't say for sure how good these movies are, but they are definitely at the top of my must-see list. (Oh, in case you weren't sure who I meant by Leo, it's **Leonardo DiCaprio**. Leo is short for Leonardo.)

I'm not ashamed to admit that when I heard Friends was coming back next year, I leapt around my apartment like Ross' monkey Marcel. Word is, each member of the all-star cast is set to earn a record $1 million per viewer. Pricey, but well worth it, if you ask me. So kudos to **NBC** for not can-

First, he was a scruffy turn-of-the-century gangster with a heart of gold in *The New York Gangs*. Then, he transformed into a 1960s con artist with a heart of gold in *Catch Him... Please!*

celling one of my favorite shows. Now, if you could just see fit to bring back **Veronica's Closet**!

Mark my words: That **April Levine** who sings about the **"Skating Boy"** has got the chops to be a real musical sensation.

I know **Ashron Kutcher** is a celebrity, because I hear him mentioned all the time, but I'll be darned if I can put the face to the name.

The Fox network is at it again! After the huge success of "reali-TV shows" like **Temptationland** and **America's Idols**, check your TV dial for **Joe The Millionaire**. Twenty-five women will compete for the affections of a single strapping construction worker with—get this—**$50 million!** Cha-ching! And even though this idea sounds a lot like **The Bachelor Show**, I've heard Fox has some sort of surprise twist ending. Well, whatever it is, I'm just happy to see Hollywood getting back to

Just like basketball, football, and trout seasons, Awards Season is now upon us, so get your hot dogs and score cards and prepare for some hard-hitting awarding. A word to the Academy: Bring back Billy Crystal!

what it does best: giving true love a chance to bloom.

Speaking of *The Bachelor Show*, someone should give the **first girl who lost** another chance at romance. She was so special.

Just like basketball, football, and trout seasons, **Awards Season** is now upon us, so get your hot dogs and score cards and prepare for some hard-hitting awarding. A word to the Academy: Bring back **Billy Crystal**!

Item! There's a new film about a piano-playing Holocaust survivor in Poland, and it's been getting a lot of critical acclaim. It's directed by **Roman Polanksky**, who's best known for **What Ever Happened To Rosemary's Baby?** Roman seems to be getting a little more personal in this one, and I love it. I wish he would make more movies back in the old U.S. of A. After 9-11, we could use someone like him back on our shores.

Attention Jackie readers! Does anyone know when the new **Star Trek** movie comes out? It's an even-numbered one, so it should be great.

Item! Sabrina The Teenage Witch is now going to be Sabrina The Teenage Wife! That's right, actress **Melissa Joan Hart** got engaged to a rocker recently. I'm not sure what band he's with, but they must go down like honey since he snagged the honey-blonde thespian!

Hey, I just thought of this: If Melissa Joan Hart married somebody with the last name "**Attack**," she'd be Melissa Joan Hart-Attack! That'd be a hoot.

Say, did anyone catch **Man Vs. Beast** on Fox? Boy, was it something! SPOILER ALERT: If you don't want to know who won what, you should skip ahead to the next item. Are you all gone? Okay. First, the **Japanese**

Attention Jackie readers! Does anyone know when the new *Star Trek* movie comes out? It's an even-numbered one, so it should be great.

eating champion was no match for a **grizzly bear** when it came to eating 60 hot dogs. Nor were **44 little people** a match for an **elephant** when it came to pulling a jumbo jet. But striking a blow for the humans was **grandmaster Gary Kasparov**, who narrowly defeated a **wild boar** in chess. Just when I've lost faith in Fox, they pull out a show that answers a big "what if?" for every American.

Item! Some people say **Dr. Phil** is a straight shooter. Me, I've always found him rude and unsympathetic. According to some reliable sources, though, Dr. Phil is a Gloomy Gus because his wife **nags** him from the moment he steps in the door to the moment he goes to sleep. So next time he lays into a guest on his show, I guess I should be a little more understanding and realize where that anger comes from.

Item! I called to order my tickets to see **Saline Dion** perform at **Ceasar's Palace In Las Vegas**, and after just 75 minutes on hold, I got through. Let me just say that March 26, 2005, cannot come fast enough. If you happen to be there that night, look up to row YY, seat 81, and you'll see one very happy man.

Well, that about wraps it up for another edition of **The Outside Scoop**. Remember, if the winter blues are getting you down, Dr. Tinseltown has the Rx for the blues. Just take two doses of Hollywood magic and see if you don't call him in the morning shouting at the top of your lungs, "Thanks, doc!" ø

HOROSCOPES

Your Horoscope

By Lloyd Schumner Sr.
Retired Machinist and
A.A.P.B.-Certified Astrologer

Aries: (March 21–April 19)
You will be honored but embarrassed when Nobel Peace Prize winner Jimmy Carter visits you to "see if further trouble can be avoided."

Taurus: (April 20–May 20)
It's time to admit that you would be far better off living in a reputable rest home, despite being a healthy 28-year-old.

Gemini: (May 21–June 21)
You'll feel a greater sense of security once you finally get used to the strain of holding that ax over your head all day long.

Cancer: (June 22–July 22)
There's trouble at work again this week as you continue to be undermined by your smarter, more charismatic black Secretary of State.

Leo: (July 23–Aug. 22)
They think they've won, but take heart: Only you know that they haven't found all the nurses yet.

Virgo: (Aug. 23–Sept. 22)
Though you never intended to be a role model for children, you must admit that your grindingly dull life makes you a pretty decent one.

Libra: (Sept. 23–Oct. 23)
Now that he's hit everything else, John Updike has no choice but to write about you.

Scorpio: (Oct. 24–Nov. 21)
While it's true that you're a sharecropper's son, it's because you forced your father to take up sharecropping at the expense of his lucrative banking career.

Sagittarius: (Nov. 22–Dec. 21)
Accept it: She's dead, and nothing you can do will ever bring her back. Except, of course, for the Lazarus serum—but you promised her you wouldn't...

Capricorn: (Dec. 22–Jan. 19)
In spite of the praise, accolades, and awards, you can't shake the suspicion that they paid the caterer more.

Aquarius: (Jan. 20–Feb. 18)
The pain of your loss will fade with time, but every now and then you'll swear you can still feel it itching.

Pisces: (Feb. 19–March 20)
Sure, life may seem pretty dark, but wonderful things are going to happen any minute now. Any minute now. Any minute now. Any minute now.

the ONION®

VOLUME 39 ISSUE 04 AMERICA'S FINEST NEWS SOURCE™ 6–12 FEBRUARY 2003

NEWS

Heroic Turtle Dials Most Of 911

see LOCAL page 6B

Gondolier Ordered To Follow That Gondola

see WORLD page 5A

Plowshare Hastily Beaten Back Into Sword

see NATION page 3A

Porn Star XXX-hausted

see ARTS page 3E

STATshot

A look at the numbers that shape your world.

Who Is Watching Our Cats?

1. A qualified professional catsitter with excellent references
2. Wil Wheaton
3. God in heaven
4. Anyone who logs onto mycats.com
5. John Ashcroft, via covert Homeland Security cam
6. Just their sad reflections staring up from water dish
7. The cats? *Oh, God, the cats*

Yankees Ensure 2003 Pennant By Signing Every Player In Baseball

NEW YORK—With a week to go before pitchers and catchers report for spring training, the New York Yankees shored up their pitching, hitting, and defense Monday by signing every player in professional baseball.

"We'd like to welcome the entire roster of Major League Baseball into the Yankees family," said team owner George Steinbrenner, watching as the franchise's 928 newest additions held up their pinstripes at a Yankee Stadium press conference.

see YANKEES page 64

Right: Some of the New York Yankees' newest additions are introduced to the press.

North Dakota Found To Be Harboring Nuclear Missiles

Above: Kofi Annan addresses the U.N. Security Council regarding the North Dakota situation.

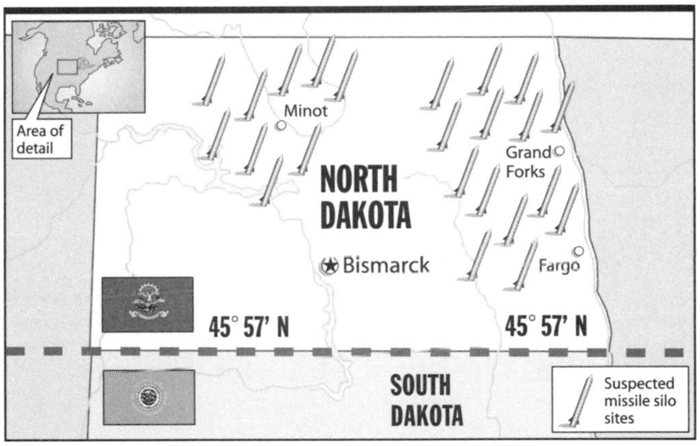

BISMARCK, ND—The stage was set for another international showdown Monday, when chief U.N. weapons inspector Hans Blix confirmed that the remote, isolationist state of North Dakota is in possession of a large stockpile of nuclear missiles.

"Satellite photos confirm that the North Dakotans have been quietly harboring an extensive nuclear-weapons program," said Blix, presenting his findings in a speech to the U.N. Security Council. "Alarmingly, this barely developed hinterland possesses the world's most technologically advanced weapons of mass destruction, capable of reaching targets all over the world."

After initially offering no comment on the report, North Dakota officials admitted to having a stockpile of 1,710 warheads at two military sites and confirmed that the state has been

see NORTH DAKOTA page 64

Nation's Love Affair With *Lord Of The Rings* Threatening Its Relationship With *Star Wars*

LOS ANGELES—America's love affair with the J.R.R. Tolkien epic-fantasy saga *Lord Of The Rings*, a romance which has flowered ever since the 2001 release of the *Fellowship Of The Ring* film adaptation, has damaged the nation's long-term relationship with George Lucas' *Star Wars* saga, perhaps irreparably.

"When I first laid eyes on *Star Wars*, it was love at first sight," said Los Angeles comic-book-store proprietor Michael Janus, 33, who was just 8 when he encountered the film. "For the rest of that summer of '77, my life was *Star Wars*."

That love only deepened with the 1980 release of *The Empire Strikes Back*.

"*Empire* took things to the next level," Janus said. "I loved *Star Wars*, but when *Empire* came out, things really started to get serious.

see LORD OF THE RINGS page 65

Above: Former *Star Wars* lovers Jim Cross and Peter Boehm get ready for the *Two Towers* premiere at a New York City theater.

France And Germany Say No

At a recent NATO meeting, France and Germany expressed reluctance to lend military support to the U.S. if it invades Iraq. What do *you* think?

"I can understand France pussin' out, but *Germany*?"

Tom Robinson
Systems Analyst

"That's a shame. It would have been hilarious to see the French running around the desert in their froofy Stratego uniforms."

Fred Eckers
Machinist

"Has it been explained to them that the Iraqis are Semites?"

Paul Ryback
Delivery Driver

"Oh, shit. I'm forced to side with France on something."

Carolyn Kass
Psychologist

"This makes sense given both countries' long-standing tradition of opposition to militarist imperialism in the Third World."

Christina Davies
Dental Hygienist

"I'm sorry, but why should France and Germany have a say in what goes on all the way over in Iraq?"

Craig George
Architect

AOL Time Warner's $99 Billion Loss

AOL Time Warner lost $99 billion in 2002—the largest one-year loss in U.S. corporate history. What are its plans for recovery?

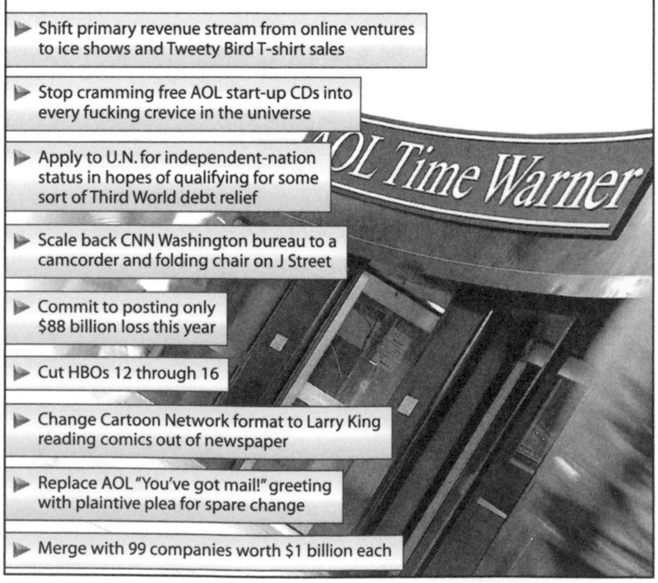

- Shift primary revenue stream from online ventures to ice shows and Tweety Bird T-shirt sales
- Stop cramming free AOL start-up CDs into every fucking crevice in the universe
- Apply to U.N. for independent-nation status in hopes of qualifying for some sort of Third World debt relief
- Scale back CNN Washington bureau to a camcorder and folding chair on J Street
- Commit to posting only $88 billion loss this year
- Cut HBOs 12 through 16
- Change Cartoon Network format to Larry King reading comics out of newspaper
- Replace AOL "You've got mail!" greeting with plaintive plea for spare change
- Merge with 99 companies worth $1 billion each

the ONION®
America's Finest News Source.™

Herman Ulysses Zweibel
Founder

T. Herman Zweibel
Publisher Emeritus
J. Phineas Zweibel
Publisher
Maxwell Prescott Zweibel
Editor-In-Chief

I Wish I Were More Like My Online Persona

By Douglas Peltz

In the online world, I, Hankscorpio74, am known to be charismatic, tough, quick-witted, and tenacious as a copperhead snake. Like my namesake, Globex Corporation president Hank Scorpio, I am roguish and unflappable, possessing the confidence and flair of 20 men. Unfortunately, all of that changes when I drag my cursor down to "Shut Down" at the bottom of the "Special" menu. For all the admiration and respect I command in chat rooms, in real life it's a different story. Oh, how I wish I were more like my online persona.

Online, I am king. No matter how formidable people may be in real life, the moment they try to mess with Hankscorpio74, they are sure to get the horns. (Or, to be more exact, the Doomsday Device.) When Hankscorpio74 suavely struts into a chat room, all the ladies are on him like Mynocks on the Millennium Falcon. Yet I have a hard time imagining the real-life Douglas Peltz being able to woo Hottie69 and LittlepartyChick into a private room for a "more intimate gathering" like Hank did a few weeks back in that chat room.

When a woman catches my eye in the real world, I'm usually too scared to talk. And, in the rare instance that I somehow muster the courage, I am

In the real world, I am at best ignored and at worst mocked and scorned. Yet, if my persecutors were playing Half-Life Team Fortress, they would be whistling a different tune as I expertly sniped them time and time again.

met with barely concealed disgust. Is it my fault that Douglas Peltz has bad skin and a chronic runny nose? I often wonder if any of these ladies I see in real life are ones Hankscorpio74 has met and seduced on the Internet. Knowing how many conquests he's piled up, it's likely.

As masterful as I am throughout the Internet, there is one particular place where I am truly godlike: the Literati™ site under Yahoo! Games. Only the most brave or foolish dare challenge me, and both are disposed of with uncommon haste. I have seen web postings where people have discussed my Übermove. The Übermove is when I allow a mentally inferior opponent to get slightly ahead, causing him to grow more confident and,

Online, I am king. No matter how formidable people may be in real life, the moment they try to mess with Hankscorpio74, they are sure to get the horns.

by extension, complacent. Then, when he least expects it, I put down all my tiles, not only getting the extra 35 points but demoralizing him thoroughly. The respect, fear, and admiration I earn with such moves stands in sharp contrast to the way I used to be treated in the high-school cafeteria, where my few friends and I would play Travel Scrabble while being pelted by Nutty bars.

In the real world, I am at best ignored and at worst mocked and scorned. Yet, if my persecutors were playing Half-Life Team Fortress, they would be whistling a different tune as I expertly sniped them time and time again. Would my old high-school nemesis Doug Kilkrane have knocked my books out of my hands every day before science class if he knew the fear I strike into the hearts of opponents at *Buffy The Vampire Slayer* trivia? What has Doug Kilkrane done, other than throw baseballs well and date Amy Cass? Dick.

Hopefully, as I get older, aspects of my online persona will slowly creep into my real-life persona. Perhaps Hankscorpio74 will take over my actual personality, much like the ultra-suave Vic Ferrari occasionally took over Latka Gravas' on *Taxi*. Then again, I wouldn't want Hankscorpio74 to completely take over: The Douglas Peltz half helps balance out Hankscorpio74, giving him some much-needed humanity and humility.

If Hankscorpio74 were to completely take over, God help everyone, because no one would be able to stop him. But I suppose the only way that'd happen is if the real world became just like the Internet. Which probably won't happen too soon.

Oh, well. Ø

Drinking In Quarries Down 37 Percent, Small-Town Sheriffs Report

WOODWARD, OK—U.S. teens are "getting wasted" down at the local quarry 37 percent less frequently than in years past, according to the small-town sheriffs who closely monitor their activities.

"In the past three months, we've only received two citizen complaints about rowdy kids down at the old Carter quarry, and we've all but suspended patrol duty out there," said Woodward County Sheriff Clyde "Dutch" Meinhold at a press conference Monday. "Last year at this time, we twice picked up the Meyer twins and that Craig Rothamer character who lives over in Mooreland. This year, I haven't seen hide nor hair of them down there. Not so much as a single blackberry-brandy empty."

"Well, I suppose with Brad Hightower in the Army now, and Jason Klaus marrying his pregnant ex-girlfriend and working his ass off at the grain elevator, these kids' party days are winding down," Sheriff John Pressman said.

Right: Spottsylvania County Sheriff Walt Schroeder answers questions regarding the drop in teen Mad Dog 20/20 consumption at the Mt. Pleasant quarry (above).

Long used as a secluded spot for illicit teenage drinking, the nation's quarries are slowly returning to their original function of mineral excavation. Reasons for the decrease in quarry drinking include incarceration of drinkers, induction into military service, and it being colder than a son-of-a-bitch lately.

"Well, I suppose with Brad Hightower in the Army now, and Jason Klaus marrying his pregnant ex-girlfriend and working his ass off at the grain elevator, these kids' party days are winding down," said Sheriff John Pressman of Waushara County, WI. "Last week, one of my deputies did catch Bobby Hightower and Lee Olle over at the quarry with what looked like a Zima, but it turns out it was just a Pepsi Blue. Surprised the heck out of me, because the Hightowers are one hard-drinking clan. They don't mean nothing by it; they're good people. Why, I used to go with Brad Sr.'s sister Bev back in high school."

Sheriffs attribute the decrease to numerous other factors, including Fanning Spring, FL, teen Jerry Kopecky breaking his leg at the go-cart track; Matt Biederhof of Okaton, SD, being so whipped by his new girlfriend that he scarcely hangs with his buds anymore; and Robert Carey of Buckman, MN, violating probation

see DRINKING page 64

NEWS IN BRIEF

Department Of The Interior Sets Aside Two Million Acres For Car Commercials

WASHINGTON, DC—Seeking to "safeguard our precious wildlands for future generations of SUV ads," the Department of the Interior set aside two million acres in Wyoming and Colorado for use in car commercials Monday. "If we do not protect this land," Secretary of the Interior Gale Norton said, "we may one day have no place for Dodge Rams to run wild and free."

Business Card Confirms Real-Estate Salesman Is Eddie Money

STOCKTON, CA—The suspicions of house-hunters Paul and Gail Barnett were confirmed Tuesday when a business card revealed that the Century 21 agent showing them a two-bedroom split-level ranch was indeed rocker Eddie Money. "He looked just like the guy who sang 'Two Tickets To Paradise,' but I figured it must just be somebody who resembles him," Gail said. "But then, right there on the card, it said 'Edward Money.'" Gail praised Money for his thoroughness and professionalism.

Surinamese Man Struggling To Write The Great Surinamese Novel

BROKOPONDO, SURINAME—Aspiring author Nikklis Doekhie said Monday that he continues in his struggle to write the Great Surinamese Novel. "I want this book to capture the essence of the Surinamese experience," Doekhie said. "Dési, the wide-eyed protagonist, quits his job in a bauxite mine to hitchhike from Paramarimbo to Alalapadu, searching for his piece of the Surinamese Dream." Doekhie said he hopes to pitch the book to Suriname's publishing house this fall.

Mommy Having Sleepover

GALESBURG, IL—Five days after Daddy's disappearance, Mommy hosted "Uncle" Rick at a sleepover, 5-year-old Hannah Dalton reported Monday. "They drank a lot of that special soda for grownups, and they watched movies," Hannah said. "And later, they must have told ghost stories, because I heard them both moaning and screaming." The morning after the sleepover, a departing Rick permitted Hannah to eat as much Count Chocula as she wanted, as long as she did not wake Mommy.

Man Vows Never To Watch Another Sci-Fi Movie With Physicist Friend

HOUSTON—After watching *Starship Troopers* with friend Jeff Oberst Monday, Adam Buck vowed never to watch another science-fiction film with the Rice University physics professor. "First, he spends 20 minutes telling me how bugs could never get that big because of the way they breathe," said Buck, 28. "Then he goes off on how faster-than-light-speed travel isn't physically possible." Buck said the evening was even less enjoyable than the time they watched *Back To The Future* together.

Baby's Third Through Eighth Words Registered Trademarks

PHOENIX—Mere weeks after saying "Mama" and "Dada" for the first time, 17-month-old Max Ellis has expanded his vocabulary to include the registered trademarks Tinky Winky™, Fruit Roll-Up™, Nintendo™, Blue's Clues™, Superman™, and Pepsi™. "I think I even heard him say 'McDonald's™' yesterday," mother Darlene Ellis said. "He's growing up so fast." Ø

YANKEES from page 61

"With these acquisitions, we are in position to finally nab that elusive 27th World Series title."

Sports reporters were not surprised by the move.

"This is not entirely unexpected," *New York Times* baseball writer Murray Chass said. "When the Yankees followed up their signing of Japanese slugger Hideki 'Godzilla' Matsui by annexing Cuba for use as a Triple-A farm club, it was clear that Steinbrenner was willing to do whatever it takes to win."

The mass signing, extravagant even by Yankees standards, caused the Bronx Bombers' payroll to skyrocket from a former league high of $149 million to $5.6 billion.

By noon, Yankees GM Brian Cashman had signed the entire National League and most of the American League to multi-year contracts. Some 10 hours later, the final opposing player, Texas Rangers shortstop Alex Rodriguez, had been acquired by the Yankees, who bought out the remainder of his $252 million contract for $300 million.

"It's an honor to be part of this team," said catcher Benito Santiago, picked up from the San Francisco Giants as insurance in case catchers Jorge Posada, Ivan Rodriguez, and Mike Piazza all go down with injuries. "It's a surprise, certainly, but I'd be crazy to turn down the opportunity to play on what is, by default, the greatest team in baseball."

Yankees manager Joe Torre, whose pitching rotation, prior to the mass signing, lacked a clear seventh ace, now has the luxury of starting each of his hurlers twice a season.

"As they say, you can never have enough pitching in this league," Torre said. "Especially come playoff time. Now, if we make it to the World Series, we'll be able to start Pedro Martinez in Game 1 and still have him fresh and ready to go for a Game 287, should it be necessary."

With so many egos to juggle and so many personnel decisions to make, Torre said his job will actually be harder this season, the lack of opposing players notwithstanding.

"Hey, I don't care who you've got on your team; winning in this league is tough—Sammy Sosa, Barry Bonds, and Randy Johnson or no Sammy Sosa, Barry Bonds, and Randy Johnson," Torre said. "And it's even tougher in New York. This is a baseball town, and some of these fans think the Yankees are the only team in baseball. Now that we truly are, the pressure to win is that much greater."

The mass signing, extravagant even by Yankees standards, caused the Bronx Bombers' payroll to skyrocket from a former league high of $149 million to $5.6 billion. Cashman noted that much of that figure is tied up in bonuses to be paid out to pitcher Tom Glavine, who at 37 will almost certainly not play out the entirety of his 15-year contract.

Baseball commissioner Bud Selig approved the signing, noting that the other 29 major-league teams received ample financial compensation.

"I see no reason why a small-market team like the Twins or Expos can't continue to remain competitive, just because it lacks players," Selig said. "The league was due for contraction anyway." Ø

DRINKING from page 63

after trying to dislodge several Homies figurines from a candy machine with a Dairy Queen spoon.

Rural liquor stores are feeling the pinch, reporting lower sales than usual for such quarry staples as peppermint schnapps, malt liquor, and fortified wine.

"Betty over at Friendly Liquor says the only suspicious thing she noticed all holiday season was the Feinske boy trying to buy Tom & Jerry mix," said Sheriff Hobart Baum of Clarion County, PA. "Probably thought there was alcohol in it. Well, what can you say, he's only 11."

The decline in quarry drinking has also been cause for concern at Jack Daniel's, which recently unveiled "Hard Cola," a product whose customer base is roughly 70 percent quarry drinkers. Attempting to adjust, Jack Daniel's is retooling the product's marketing campaign to target college binge drinkers, parking-lot tipplers, and overweight secretaries on "Just Us Girls" after-work outings.

"Traditionally, sales of quarry beverages like Hard Cola ebb during the winter months, but we're seeing the same decline in more temperate climates, too," Jack Daniel's spokeswoman Lynda Pfeiffer said. "We're optimistic about the future of Hard Cola, but we're also mindful of the toll taken on the wine-cooler industry back in the early 1990s, when a similar quarry-drinking drop-off occurred. Bartles & Jaymes never had a chance."

Despite the pervasiveness of the decline, some sheriffs say they're confident that the trend will begin to reverse itself when the weather warms.

"Just yesterday, I caught that Dubrow kid and his buddy Glenn with an unopened Mickey's Big Mouth," said Sheriff Gordon Leahy of Perry County, IL. "They claimed they found it on the ground while looking for arrowheads. Bullcrap." Ø

NORTH DAKOTA from page 61

home to an active nuclear-weapons-development program for decades.

Blix called the revelation a "terrifying prospect for the world at large."

Within hours of the announcement, U.N. Secretary-General Kofi Annan urged North Dakota to abandon its program.

"This is clearly an excessive number of weapons for a place like North Dakota to possess," Annan said. "In this post-Cold War environment, we should be moving away from nuclear proliferation among developing states."

European leaders also spoke out in opposition to North Dakota's weapons program.

"North Dakota, still in its cultural infancy, cannot be trusted to responsibly handle weapons of mass destruction," French President Jacques Chirac said. "We are talking about a place that doesn't even have a Thai restaurant or movie theater that shows foreign films, but still they have the resources to build thousands of warheads. Do not believe their claims of being 'The Peace Garden State.'"

According to Chirac, North Dakota's development of nuclear arms "represents a grave threat to peaceful states the world over, none more so than its longtime neighbor and rival across the 45th Parallel, South Dakota."

"The South Dakotans, while a simple people themselves, are friendly, hospitable, and far more in touch with the outside world," Chirac said. "Many people, myself included, have passed through and seen the Badlands and Mount Rushmore. North Dakota, on the other hand, is a bleak, racially homogeneous state that few people ever enter or exit."

After a joint meeting of the French and German cabinets, German Chancellor Gerhard Schroeder said the two nations "agree that this situation must be rectified" and implored North Dakota to cease its uranium-enrichment program immediately.

"We have opened the door to talks," Schroeder said. "But, unfortunately, North Dakota seems unwilling to engage with the world community at this time."

According to Blix, North Dakota is home to 500 Minuteman III ICBMs and 50 Peacekeeper missiles, giving it one of the heaviest concentrations of the weapons on earth. The biggest discovery made by U.N. inspectors, Blix said, was a missile field at Minot Air Force Base, where they found an "almost unbelievable" stockpile of warheads.

The rogue state was also found to possess enormous amounts of fissile material.

"North Dakota could have as much as 75 metric tons of weapons-grade uranium and 8 metric tons of weapons-grade plutonium," Blix said. "Just 55 pounds of uranium are needed to construct a simple nuclear weapon. Do the math—the prospects are terrifying."

The man at the center of the controversy is North Dakota's leader, Gov. John Hoeven. Having risen to power in 2000 after amassing tremendous wealth in the private sector, Hoeven lives a life of comfort and excess inside the heavily patrolled North Dakota governor's mansion, a lavish dwelling paid for entirely by the state, while many of his people engage in subsistence farming.

Some suspect that Hoeven is using the nuclear program as a bargaining chip to gain badly needed economic benefits for his state. Hardly at the forefront of technology in other aspects, North Dakota has a largely rural population and a child-poverty rate of 14 percent—a fact critics have been quick to point out.

The man at the center of the controversy is North Dakota's leader, Gov. John Hoeven. Having risen to power in 2000 after amassing tremendous wealth in the private sector, Hoeven lives a life of comfort and excess inside the heavily patrolled North Dakota governor's mansion.

"North Dakotans live a horrible life of isolation and deprivation, struggling to grow crops in a hostile, subzero climate while their indifferent government routinely prioritizes bolstering the state's military might," BBC World correspondent Caroline Eagan said. "There are people starving there, and yet high-tech weapons laboratories and military bases abound. It's deplorable."

Added Eagan: "And, no big surprise, the U.S. played a major role in arming this place. I hear most of the missiles are American-made."

Many U.S. citizens have expressed fear, some realizing for the first time that North Dakota has thousands of weapons capable of reaching any major American city within minutes.

"It is absolutely frightening that there are all these weapons of mass destruction practically in my backyard," said Karen Stiles of Moorhead, MN. "Do we really know enough about these people who have their finger on the button that could kill millions?"

Added Stiles: "How did our elected officials let this happen?" Ø

LORD OF THE RINGS from page 61

That's when I moved beyond toys and all the other kid stuff. Suddenly, there were conventions and fan clubs and books and collectibles."

The sequel's many attractive qualities, as well as Lucas' promise of a new film every three years into the next century, cemented America's

"*Jedi* was when things first started getting a little weird," said Eric DiCillo, 35, a Rockford, IL, graphic designer. "Like, Princess Leia turns out to be Luke's sister? That really came out of left field. And Boba Fett, this cool, mysterious character whose role was so vital in *Empire*, suddenly dies in a stupid piece of comedy."

commitment to the series, and *Star Wars* became a major part of its pop-cultural life.

For much of the nation, the first sign of trouble arose sometime around the relationship's six-year mark, with the 1983 release of *Return Of The Jedi*.

"*Jedi* was when things first started getting a little weird," said Eric DiCillo, 35, a Rockford, IL, graphic designer. "Like, Princess Leia turns out to be Luke's sister? That really came out of left field. And Boba Fett, this cool, mysterious character whose role was so vital in *Empire*, suddenly dies in a stupid piece of comedy. For the first time, I felt like Lucas wasn't taking me seriously."

"I mean, I still loved *Star Wars*," DiCillo continued. "Even at that point, there were plenty of good times between us. When Darth Vader pitched the Emperor into the abyss, well, let's just say I'd never experienced a climax like that before. But I'd be lying if I said I was 100 percent happy."

Unsure where the relationship was headed after *Return Of The Jedi*, the nation took time off from *Star Wars*, deciding to see other films during a "cooling off" period of 16 years.

"I know George needed to get his head together on where this whole *Star Wars* thing was going," DiCillo said. "So it was for the best that we went our separate ways for a while. It felt like a betrayal, seeing other sci-fi movies, but I knew that if it was meant to be, we'd eventually find our way back to each other."

Even during the trial-separation period, Lucas' evasiveness and erratic

Above: A once-cherished R2D2 toy is reduced to propping open windows.

behavior threatened to derail the relationship.

"Somewhere along the way, the saga of nine movies mysteriously turned into six," said Chris Cavanagh, 29, an Arlington, TX, insurance agent. "I remember, at one point, it was supposed to be 12. And I'm thinking, does Lucas have a long-term plan for us? I started out determined to see this relationship through to the end, but everything he did made me question it. I even started thinking he was just

"I stuck it out, I really did," a saddened Janus said. "I tried to make it work. But *Star Wars* just didn't hold up its end. A relationship is a two-way street."

after my money."

"Through it all, though," Cavanagh continued, "I just kept telling myself, 'He'll change. He's got something truly special planned for the prequels. This can work.'"

The nation's hopes for a reconciliation were dashed in 1999, when, after a seemingly eternal wait, the disappointing *Episode I—The Phantom Menace* left the nation feeling hollow.

"By that point, the *Star Wars* films had lost their ability to move me," Janus said. "After seeing *Phantom Menace*, I started reflecting on the earlier films, and I realized they just weren't as deep and fulfilling as they'd seemed at the time. During that initial infatuation period, from '77 to '83, I guess I was too swept up in the magic of the whole thing to see that there were major problems."

"I stuck it out, I really did," a saddened Janus said. "I tried to make it work. But *Star Wars* just didn't hold up its end. A relationship is a two-way street. If George had told me he didn't want to do any more *Star Wars* movies after the original trilogy, yes, that would have hurt. But it would have been better than dragging me along like this. What he ended up doing was just passive-aggressive bullshit."

The flaws in America's relationship with *Star Wars* became painfully apparent in 2000, when it was introduced to the film version of *Fellowship Of The Ring*.

"I felt really guilty about it, but I couldn't help but compare this exciting new thing in my life to my long-time relationship," DiCillo said. "And when I did, I found *Star Wars* coming up short. As much as I tried to deny it, the dialogue, acting, story structure, and special effects in *Lord Of The Rings* were all undeniably superior. Everything happens for a reason in it, and it all builds toward a thrilling, satisfying series of climaxes. I wish I could say the same for my first love."

Frustrated with the increasingly bloated, self-indulgent *Star Wars* universe, the nation shifted its affections toward the Peter Jackson films.

"*Lord Of The Rings* gave me things *Star Wars* never could," Janus said. "If it hadn't been for Peter Jackson showing me what a fantasy saga can be, I might have settled for [summer 2002's] *Attack Of The Clones* as the best I could ever hope for."

DiCillo has experienced a similar change of heart.

"I'm not completely shutting *Star Wars* out of my life," DiCillo said. "I'm

"*Lord Of The Rings* gave me things *Star Wars* never could," Janus said. "If it hadn't been for Peter Jackson showing me what a fantasy saga can be, I might have settled for [summer 2002's] *Attack Of The Clones* as the best I could ever hope for."

sure I'll see *Episode III* when it comes out, but I'm done waiting in line overnight. When [third *Rings* installment] *Return Of The King* comes out, I know it'll be a proper trilogy-ending climax, and not some slapdash retread of the more memorable parts from the first two films."

"Obviously, I'm disappointed that things didn't work out between *Star Wars* and me," DiCillo added. "But I'm grateful for the time we had. I grew a lot as a person, and I'll always have my beautiful memories of the Battle of Hoth." ⌀

COMMUNITY VOICES

Why Must The Media Call My Ritual Killings 'Senseless'?

By Randolph Lynne
The Grandfather Clock Killer

Ever since the sixth grade, when Danielle Mattson called the chicken-bone-and-dead-fly sculpture I made for art class "disgusting," I've not been one to take criticism well. I'm not saying I'm above reproach. I just think that if someone is going to find fault with one's work, his or her critique should come from a well-informed, knowledgeable place.

Unfortunately, that's hardly the case with reporters these days. If the media had any clue how much care and preparation went into my recent string of ritual murders, they wouldn't call them "senseless." On the contrary, my tri-state killing spree makes nothing *but* sense.

Is it that the media simply don't see the pride and craftsmanship I put into my work? They know each victim's arms have been meticulously arranged to mimic the hands of a clock. They know each victim's arms have read an hour later than those of the previous victim. Do I receive plaudits for getting the arms to stay in place in spite of muscle contractions and the like? No. What about the way I wrap the victims' own intestines around their necks not once, not twice, but three times, then tie them off in a sheepshank? Or the teaspoon of cumin I carefully pile on each of their eyesockets? "Senseless," my eye. I'd like to see that retard Ed Gein do that without spilling so much as a grain.

There are certain words I might ascribe to my killings. "Precise." "Cold-blooded." "Jarring." But "senseless"? It's so typical of newspapers to lazily fall back on such a hackneyed description of murder.

If it's a method to the madness that these journalists are looking for, they need look no further than the police evidence room. It's all there: the methodically collected jars of toenail clippings, the red handkerchiefs lovingly stapled to each victim's left earlobe, the cryptic notes painstakingly penned with my own semen—all the elements of The Plan. Isn't it obvious that this is not the random cross-country slaughter of a playboy like Ted Bundy? No, these aren't the acts of a "mindless lunatic," but rather the impressive product of months of preparation and hard work.

If the media had any clue how much care and preparation went into my recent string of ritual murders, they wouldn't call them "senseless." On the contrary, my tri-state killing spree makes nothing *but* sense.

The newspapers may misunderstand my work, but endgame will be mine. Hearing my ritual slayings called "senseless" just makes me want to redouble my efforts. Of course, I can't move any faster or slower than The Plan allows, but the media's thoughtless dismissal only drives me to work that much harder.

Sure, you could call my first murder "senseless." I'll admit, that inaugural evisceration showed my lack of experience. I was still green and hadn't hit my stride yet. But by the third or fourth body, I had found my voice. From the way I wrap the bodies in gingham to the pattern of gnawing lightly on their pinky fingers, all of my work from that point forward bears my unmistakable stamp, just as a Picasso couldn't be confused with a Braque.

There are certain words I might ascribe to my killings. "Precise." "Cold-blooded." "Jarring." But "senseless"? It's so typical of newspapers to lazily fall back on such a hackneyed description of murder. It's like the Zodiac Killer. No one really got what he was all about. The journalists, more concerned with filling column inches on deadline than capturing his essence, never saw the artistry behind the blood.

The media don't understand that, in my work, it's all about The Plan. I am merely the vessel that will bring it to fruition. It's not like I particularly enjoy killing people, but for the greater good of mankind, it has to happen. I'm sure a lot of people who have gardens don't particularly enjoy weeding, fertilizing, and watering their plants, but they do it to make possible what such labor will bear: delicious, life-giving vegetables. I can't really put into words what my labor will accomplish, as I am only told about The Plan in messages that come out of my pencil sharpener in small fragments. But, unlike some reporters I could name, I see that it will all make sense in time.

So here I sit, another misunderstood visionary whose detractors lack the critical faculties to properly assess and contextualize his work. Even though I'm already up to eight victims, I can't wait to reach number 12, because that's when it will all come together. Like a hurricane wind, I will unleash a gale-force fury that blows away those who were too narrow-minded to comprehend my work. Then, the world will know why I'm a ritual killer and not just some boob on a clock tower shooting students willy-nilly. ⌀

HOROSCOPES

Your Horoscope

By Lloyd Schumner Sr.
Retired Machinist and
A.A.P.B.-Certified Astrologer

Aries: (March 21–April 19)
The stars will soon be in a unique alignment, revealing a mysterious sign in the heavens. Which sounds impressive, but just means you'll be able to see a birdie.

Taurus: (April 20–May 20)
You will never again be able to live in peace due to the enduring and seductive power of your moose call.

Gemini: (May 21–June 21)
You will spend three frustrating weeks trying to incorporate the word "evanescent" into a sentence.

Cancer: (June 22–July 22)
Usually, this stuff happens in movie theaters, so you're pretty surprised when two hours of sexy, suspense-filled action come to a bakery near you.

Leo: (July 23–Aug. 22)
Your discovery of an unabridged dictionary will take much of the fun and creativity out of Scrabble.

Virgo: (Aug. 23–Sept. 22)
Just so you know: If you speak fluent Farsi and have a thorough knowledge of Middle Eastern culture but don't like travel, it's a good time to keep your mouth shut.

Libra: (Sept. 23–Oct. 23)
It might be heartfelt, but your long, freeform version of "Old Man River" will get your lily-white ass laughed off the stage.

Scorpio: (Oct. 24–Nov. 21)
Just because that man is dead and in his grave doesn't mean you can go around squeezing the Charmin as much as you please.

Sagittarius: (Nov. 22–Dec. 21)
You haven't worn it since college, but don't be surprised when your old suit still fits. It is made of rubber, after all.

Capricorn: (Dec. 22–Jan. 19)
Actually, "mannickjore" refers to the white-necked stork of the Indian subcontinent, more commonly known to white settlers as the "beef-steak bird."

Aquarius: (Jan. 20–Feb. 18)
It was nice of Utah Jazz great Karl Malone to visit you in the hospital, though you are not sick and easily could have entertained him at home.

Pisces: (Feb. 19–March 20)
Something big is in your future. Please be sure to note the absence of any specific positives in that sentence.

VISION QUEST from page 62

amounts of blood. Passersby were amazed by the unusually large amounts of blood. Passersby were

One man's trash is another man's car made out of trash.

amazed by the unusually large amounts of blood. Passersby were amazed by the unusually large amounts of blood. Passersby were amazed by the unusually large amounts of blood. Passersby were amazed by the unusually large amounts of blood. Passersby were amazed by the unusually large amounts of blood. Passersby were amazed by the unusually large amounts of blood. Passersby were amazed by the unusually large

see VISION QUEST page 68

NEWS

Decision To Ask Out Girl Made Using 10-Sided Die

see GAMING page 4C

Fashion Plate Smashed

see SOCIETY page 2B

Texan Unable To Trick NASA Into Hauling Old Washing Machine Off Lawn

see LOCAL page 9E

14th Caller Only Caller

see RADIO page 4D

STATshot

A look at the numbers that shape your world.

How Are America's Singles Spending Valentine's Day?

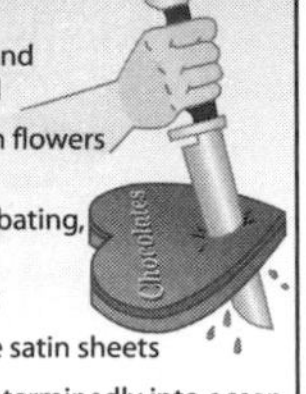

1. Wearing red sweater and brooch, being ignored
2. Acting surprised when flowers they ordered arrive
3. Crying, crying, masturbating, crying
4. Cleaning up cat vomit
5. Breaking out twin-size satin sheets
6. Walking slowly and determinedly into ocean

the ONION®

VOLUME 39 ISSUE 05 AMERICA'S FINEST NEWS SOURCE™ 13–19 FEBRUARY 2003

N. Korea Wondering What It Has To Do To Attract U.S. Military Attention

PYONGYANG, NORTH KOREA—As the U.S. continues to inch toward war with Iraq, a jealous and frustrated North Korea is wondering what it has to do to attract American military attention.

"What does it take to get a few F-16s or naval warships deployed to the Yellow Sea?" North Korean president Kim Jong Il asked Monday. "In the past month and a half, we've expelled U.N. nuclear inspectors, withdrawn from the nuclear Non-Proliferation Treaty, restarted a mothballed nuclear complex capable of producing weapons-grade plutonium, and threatened to resume missile tests. You'd think that would be enough to get a measly Marine division or two on standby in the Pacific, but apparently not."

Kim said his nation is "way more deserving" of B-52 deployment than Iraq.

"Bush says his number-one priority

see NORTH KOREA page 71

Above: Kim Jong Il.

Ashcroft Orders Staff To Chain Him Tightly Before Next Full Moon

Above: Ashcroft displays one of the chains that will bind him.

WASHINGTON, DC—In a move that has sparked widespread speculation, Attorney General John Ashcroft gave explicit orders to his staff Monday to tightly bind him in heavy iron chains before the next full moon on Sunday, Feb. 16.

"The entire Justice Department is under my strict orders," Ashcroft told reporters during a brief press conference. "I must be restrained, I must be shackled, I must be kept safely away from the innocent."

Ashcroft said he told top department officials that his chaining must last the entire night of the 16th "at all costs."

"I told them, 'No matter how much I scream, now matter how frantically I beg, you must not let me loose,'" Ashcroft said. "'I will likely tell you to forget what I'm telling you now; that I didn't mean any of it. Do not listen to me, I implore you.'"

Added Ashcroft: "I'm not like other attorneys general."

Ashcroft then abruptly ended the press conference, saying he was

see ASHCROFT page 70

Friendship Moving Way Too Fast

GLENDALE, CA—Expressing a desire to "slow things down and keep it casual," Troy Lanier, 28, said Monday that his friendship with Scott Perotta, 27, is moving way too fast.

"[Scott]'s a nice enough guy, but I've only known him for, like, five weeks, and he already acts like we're best friends," said Lanier, a Glendale-area insurance adjuster. "I wish I had stronger feelings for him, but I don't. I just don't know where I want this friendship to go, and I need the space to figure it all out."

Seen as a potentially good match based on their shared love of martial-arts films, Lanier and Perotta were introduced by a

see FRIENDSHIP page 71

Above: Perotta (left) with Lanier, who wants to "keep things casual."

The Future Of NASA

In the wake of the Columbia tragedy, many are questioning the wisdom and necessity of NASA's manned-space-flight program. What do *you* think?

Maria Fortis
Librarian

"Those astronauts did not die in vain. They gave their lives so that mankind could have cool footage of people floating upside-down in fully automated capsules."

Kenneth King
Systems Analyst

"Imagine all the good that could be done if we took those billions of dollars we're spending on NASA and gave it to the military."

Donald Lande
Landscaper

"Watching the explosion, I couldn't help but be reminded of the '86 Challenger disaster and that dick Bryan Schonert who sat behind me in social studies."

Sheryl Auburn
Homemaker

"If man were meant to fly in outer space, God would have given him a brain capable of figuring out the mathematics and physics necessary to do so."

Bill Kuntz
Auto Mechanic

"The space program should be scrapped. Fourteen deaths in 20 years? Imagine seeing those kinds of statistics in, say, the trucking industry."

Marcus Edwards
Civil Engineer

"Don't you think Bush is taking this whole wanting-to-be-Reagan thing a little far?"

The King Of Pop Speaks

Last week, ABC aired *Living With Michael Jackson*, a candid two-hour documentary on the eccentric superstar. Among the revelations:

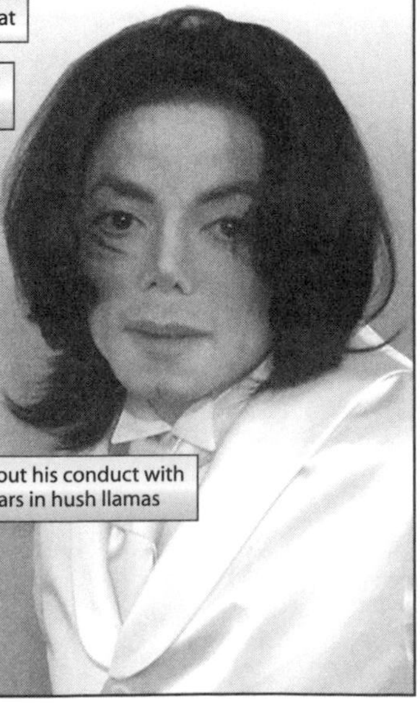

- Recently stopped eating unicorn meat
- Never once behaved inappropriately around young girls
- Is bathed nightly by Teletubbies
- Treats children with same love and respect his father showed him
- Did that shit to his face on purpose
- Saw Elvis' daughter naked once
- Paid off parents who complained about his conduct with their children with thousands of dollars in hush llamas
- Has already pre-purchased skeleton of Elizabeth Taylor
- Fucks little boys

the ONION®
America's Finest News Source.™

Herman Ulysses Zweibel
Founder

T. Herman Zweibel
Publisher Emeritus
J. Phineas Zweibel
Publisher
Maxwell Prescott Zweibel
Editor-In-Chief

People Of Earth: We Come In Search Of Quality Name-Brand Footwear At Reasonable Prices

By Glaxxor-T'Pra
Diplomatic Envoy of the Zarvoxian Galactic Assembly

Citizens of Earth! I greet you on behalf of our leader, the grand exalted Emperor Xervandian. We have been dispatched from Zarvox, the 18th planet in the Klaator-Na quadrant. Do not be alarmed. We do not wish to harm you. Ours is a peaceful mission. We come in search of quality name-brand footwear at reasonable prices.

Our journey was long, more than 2,000 light years, and our feet are tired. We command you to assemble a great selection of comfortable, great-looking shoes in a wide range of sizes and styles—top brands like Nike, Timberland, Steve Madden, 9 West, Candies, and Rockport. And we refuse to overpay.

In exactly one hour, we will arrive on your planet's surface. Have a convoy of friendly, helpful salespersons ready and waiting. At 1600 hours, we will commence scanning your planet's surface for the season's hottest mid-calf-length boots in classic colors like black and brown, as well as fun, attention-grabbing red and pink.

We are a powerful race, but we are not a violent one. The wars you wage on your planet are an outdated notion to us, as we prefer more intellectual pursuits. We also enjoy jogging, hiking, basketball, and golf, so we will accept nothing but the best in athletic footwear from Adidas, Reebok, and Converse. The citizens of our planet are in need of all manner of sport shoes, from cross trainers to hiking boots.

Bring them now, humans!

We have known about your watery planet for eons, but avoided contact as we patiently waited for you to develop sturdy, cushioned insole technology that allows the foot to properly breathe. The fires on our planet have left our own stockpiles of shoes and boots depleted. Zarvox has exhausted all reserves of great-looking, comfy classics by such designers as Charles David and Kenneth Cole.

Will you cooperate, People of the Blue-Green World? All we ask for are shoes that offer fashion, comfort, and value. We have noted the accelerated rate at which Earth produces fun new styles and are impressed. Will you deny us your supply of boat shoes, casual boots, sandals, clogs, loafers, and mules? Or will you help us complete our interstellar shoe quest?

I need not point out our superior weapons technology. We feel no need to threaten you with our Nitro-Electrion cyclo-blasters. We will make no trouble for you if you give us what we require: great shoes at a great price. With quick, courteous service. And a full, no-questions-asked 30-day return policy.

We have seen your cities. They light up the sky for many miles. We could not help but be impressed by their beauty and great selection of urban footwear by Fubu, Lugz, Dada, Mecca, and South Side. Such brands will

In exactly one hour, we will arrive on your planet's surface. Have a convoy of friendly, helpful salespersons ready and waiting. At 1600 hours, we will commence scanning your planet's surface for the season's hottest mid-calf-length boots in classic colors like black and brown, as well as fun, attention-grabbing red and pink.

serve us well upon our return home.

While our initial gyromagnetoscopic scan of Earth detected the presence of shoes that would look great in the office, like Dexter, Bass, and Bostonian loafers, our journey across the stars will not be successful until we also have something that looks great *after* hours. We must see Hush Puppies! We must see Minnetonka! We *will* see LB Evans! People of Earth, believe what we say. We will know the right pair when we see it, and we will not bow to high-pressure sales tactics.

Now is the time, humans, for you to await additional instructions. As soon as the hull of our ship is de-ionized and ready for krilliation, we will make our descent for shoes. We can only pray, for the sake of our two worlds, now united in purpose across the great expanse of stars, that you have a great selection for the kids, as well. ∅

FAMILYBEAT

Kids Excited Mom Learning To Swear

PESHTIGO, WI—After a lifetime of assiduously avoiding the use of foul language, Helen Chernak, 59, is finally learning to swear, her delighted offspring reported Monday.

"I was at Mom's this weekend, and the cat knocked something over," said Michael Chernak, 34, Helen's eldest child. "Mom shakes her little fist and says, 'Damn it, Felix! Get down from there, you little shit.' I was like, 'Where did that come from?' It was so wild."

She says, and I quote, 'This fucking house is falling apart.' We could not believe Mom said 'fucking.' We begged her to repeat it, but she wouldn't. She just said, 'Oh, you two be quiet.'"

According to Michael, he and siblings Julie, 32, and James, 29, have been encouraging their mother to swear for years.

"When we were growing up, Mom never used any bad words at all," Julie said. "If she wanted to say 'shit,' she'd say 'sugar' instead. We'd tell her that if she wanted to say the dirty word, she should just say it. But she'd always refuse, saying she was 'a firm believer in using sugar substitutes.'"

Julie said she first heard her mother swear during a Jan. 23 trip with her to the neighborhood IGA grocery store. The pair encountered a cashier who allegedly rolled her eyes and muttered under her breath when the elder Chernak handed her a stack of coupons.

"We got out to the car and Mom said, 'I have no idea why that checkout lady had to be such a darn bitch,'" Julie said. "Isn't that so great? God, I love it."

According to James, the major breakthrough occurred on Jan. 8, when his mother said "fuck" with only slight provocation.

"Me and Michael were going to the nursing home with her to see Grandma," James said. "Mom was already worked up because she couldn't find the right container for the ham. So we go out to the garage and a light bulb blows. She says, and I quote, 'This fucking house is falling apart.' We could not believe Mom said 'fucking.' We begged her to repeat it, but she wouldn't. She just said, 'Oh, you two be quiet.'"

Above: James Chernak and his newly foul-mouthed mother.

Because of her inexperience at swearing, Chernak occasionally deploys the forbidden words incorrectly—gaffes which entertain her children. Last week, Chernak reported that she broke the "stupid mixing-ass bowl" for her food processor and did not know how she was going to locate the "peckin' instruction manual" to order a new one.

James said he is at a loss to explain the rise in swearing.

"I really don't know," James said. "Maybe it's because she's getting older and loosening up. Or maybe she's hearing more bad words on TV or something. Then again, she'd always turn off the TV whenever she heard a dirty word. Honestly, it just doesn't make sense."

Julie theorized that the rise in swearing may be related to her father's death in March 2002.

"Dad swore once in a while, but he always gave us a look if we did it," Julie said. "We had to sort of watch it when he was around, but now we don't edit ourselves. So maybe, a year later, Mom's finally stopped editing herself, too."

Michael noted that, in addition to swearing more herself, his mother has become more lax in policing her children's foul language.

"Lately, as long as we don't do it

see MOM page 72

NEWS IN BRIEF

Saddam Enrages Bush With Full Compliance

WASHINGTON, DC—President Bush expressed frustration and anger Monday over a U.N. report stating that Iraqi president Saddam Hussein is now fully complying with weapons inspections. "Enough is enough," a determined Bush told reporters. "We are not fooled by Saddam's devious attempts to sway world opinion by doing everything the U.N. asked him to do. We will not be intimidated into backing down and, if we have any say in the matter, neither will Saddam." Bush added that any further Iraqi attempt to meet the demands of the U.N. or U.S. will be regarded as "an act of war."

Laid-Off Zoologist Goes On Tranquilizing Rampage

SAN DIEGO—Twelve San Diego Zoo visitors and two employees were brutally sedated Monday, when laid-off zoologist Dr. Brian Vermeer, 41, returned to his former place of work armed with a tranquilizer gun and began firing into a crowd. "It was kind of horrible," said Maria Christopher, 44, who witnessed the tranquilizing spree. "People were gently falling asleep over the course of 20 to 30 seconds everywhere." The spree ended when Vermeer turned his gun on himself, knocking himself out for half an hour.

U.S. Council Of Coolness Releases Formal Statement On Prince

WASHINGTON, DC—On Monday, the U.S. Council of Coolness released its long-awaited ruling on Prince, declaring the recording artist "provisionally cool" by a 13-11 margin. "This was a more difficult decision than it should have been," the 240-page report read. "In the end, however, albums like *1999* and *Sign O' The Times* are sufficiently brilliant to offset such padded late-period dorkfests as *Rave Un2 The Joy Fantastic* and *The Rainbow Children*." The Council of Coolness warned that the decision could be reversed if Prince records one more rap in which he declares himself "super-fonky" or "2 jammin' 4 U."

Laffy Taffy Writer Disdains Bazooka

ITASCA, IL—Bruce Palmer, a writer and editor for Nestle's "Laffy Taffy" line of joke-bearing fruit-flavored chews, holds Topps Bazooka gum and its line of complimentary comic art in sneering contempt, he revealed Monday. "Don't get me wrong: In the Golden Age of the 1970s and 1980s, Bazooka Joe was amazing—a big influence on me," the 43-year-old Palmer said. "But when Topps went all corporate, and the P.C. suits made them dump [sombrero-clad mischief-maker] Pesty, it all went downhill." Palmer went on to dismiss Bazooka as "a stain on the proud literary genre of candy-wrapper humor."

High-School Teacher Constantly Using Janitor As Example

GRAND FORKS, ND—Arnold Danielson, a chemistry teacher at Warren G. Harding High School, has for the past eight years used custodian Howard Sievert as a living warning to underachieving or misbehaving students. "When my grades started to slip, Mr. Danielson took me aside and said, 'Well, you can buckle down and study harder… or you can end up like old Howie,'" sophomore Dave Netzel said. "Boy, I got the hint big-time." Netzel said Danielson is also fond of asking tardy students to name their favorite car and then informing them that such a car is unaffordable on a janitor's salary. Ø

ASHCROFT from page 67

due at a Cabinet meeting "before the setting of the sun."

According to a Justice Department memo leaked to *The Washington Post*, Ashcroft is to be wound in five loops of strong chain and shackled to a stone wall, his wrists bound in

Ashcroft is to be wound in five loops of strong chain and shackled to a stone wall, his wrists bound in sterling-silver cuffs branded with the sign of the crucifix. Washington archbishop Theodore McCarrick has been enlisted to stand watch over the attorney general for the duration of the evening.

sterling-silver cuffs branded with the sign of the crucifix. Washington archbishop Theodore McCarrick has been enlisted to stand watch over the attorney general for the duration of the evening, armed with ample quantities of holy water and wolfsbane.

The memo also ordered Solicitor General Theodore Olsen to supply D.C. police chief Charles Ramsey with a .45 revolver and six bullets of consecrated silver, with vague instructions to use them "should it become necessary."

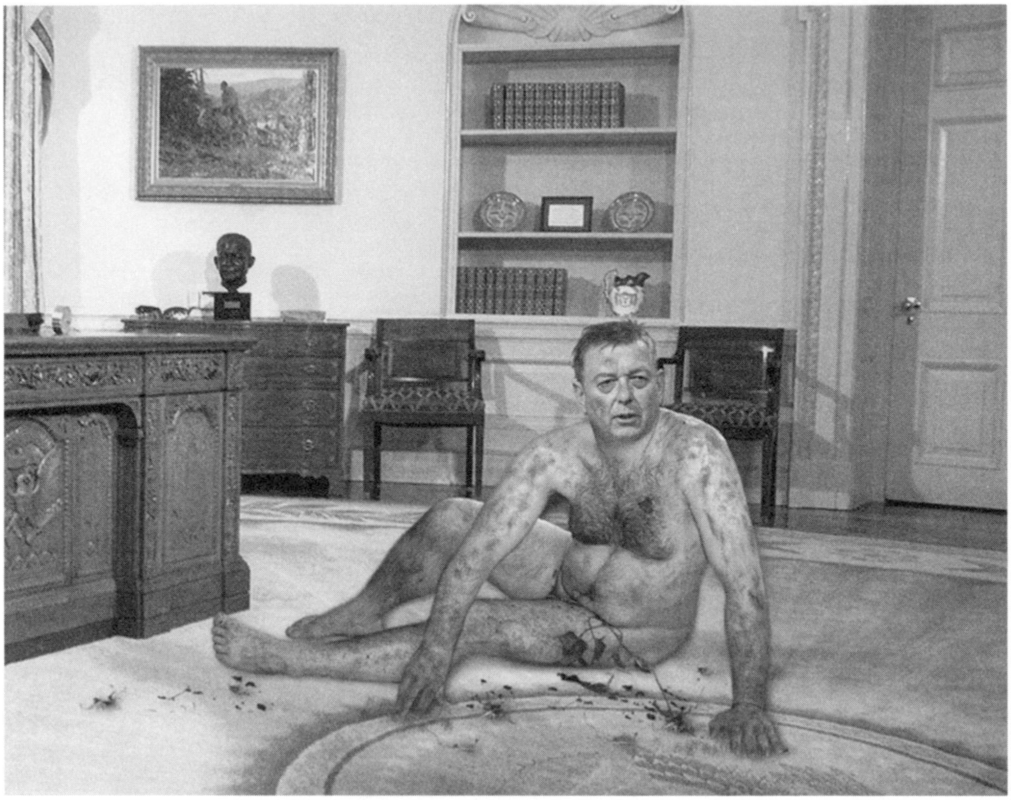

Above: A disoriented Ashcroft finds himself in the Oval Office following January's full moon.

Beltway insiders are at a loss to explain the unusual orders. However, in a possibly related development, during a Jan. 26 press conference, reporters noticed a small crescent-moon-shaped tattoo behind the attorney general's left ear—a mark they had not seen there before.

"He was up at the podium, announcing a new measure that would give the federal government broader powers to detain immigrants and other non-naturalized U.S. residents, when I happened to notice this weird mark behind his ear," *Boston Globe* reporter Jason Moran said. "I tried to

A nude man matching Ashcroft's description was reported running through the streets of downtown Washington.

move up closer to see it better, but he growled and shot me this chilling look I can't even describe. I immediately backed off, but I know what I saw."

On Jan. 18, during the last full moon, Ashcroft unexpectedly disappeared from an NRA fundraising dinner he was attending. The next morning, a nude man matching Ashcroft's description was reported running through the streets of downtown Washington.

D.C. police are also investigating a series of animal mutilations that occurred that same evening at the Smithsonian National Zoo's Deer Park. No suspects have been identified in the case. Ø

STREET DRUGS from page 64

amounts of blood. Passersby were amazed by the unusually large amounts of blood. Passersby were amazed by the unusually large amounts of blood. Passersby were amazed by the unusually large amounts of blood. Passersby were amazed by the unusually large amounts of blood. Passersby were amazed by the unusually large amounts of blood. Passersby were amazed by the unusually large amounts of blood. Passersby were amazed by the unusually large amounts of blood. Passersby were amazed by the unusually large amounts of blood. Passersby were amazed by the unusually large amounts of blood. Passersby were amazed by the unusually large amounts of blood. Passersby were amazed by the unusually large amounts of blood. Passersby were amazed by the unusually large amounts of blood. Passersby were amazed by the unusually large amounts of blood. Passersby were amazed by the unusually large amounts of blood. Passersby were

If everyone throws in $10, I could buy those shoes I want.

amazed by the unusually large amounts of blood. Passersby were amazed by the unusually large amounts of blood.Passersby were amazed by the unusually large amounts of blood.Passersby were amazed by the unusually large amounts of blood.Passersby were amazed by the unusually large amounts of blood.Passersby were amazed by the unusually large amounts of blood.Passersby were amazed by the unusually large amounts of blood.Passersby were amazed by the unusually large amounts of blood.Passersby were amazed by the unusually large amounts of blood.Passersby were amazed by the unusually large

see STREET DRUGS page 78

FRIENDSHIP from page 67

mutual friend in early January.

"The first night we hung out, we went to see *Five Fingers Of Death* at the revival theater," Lanier said. "It was nice, but things started accelerating much too quickly from there. He's always inviting me out to do stuff, and he calls me every time there's a Jackie Chan movie on TV. Within a few weeks of meeting Scott, I was talking to him more than Rob [Poehler], who's been my best friend since high school."

Lanier said he has been reluctant to give Perotta his e-mail address, fearing it will only accelerate the friendship.

"I just know he'd be e-mailing me every day," Lanier said. "He's always talking about these funny things he sees on the Internet. I've been thinking about setting up a special Yahoo! account and giving him that address with the caveat that I only check it once in a while, but that seems like an awful lot of effort to deal with someone I barely know."

According to Lanier, Perotta has also attempted to strengthen their bond through the disclosure of highly personal information.

"I know more about Scott than I do about people I've known for years," Lanier said. "He told me about how his mother was an alcoholic and how his uncle committed suicide in his garage. I try to steer the conversation back to neutral subjects, but try bringing up Sammo Hung movies after someone tells you his ex-girlfriend was sexually molested when she was 12."

Lanier has also taken exception to

Lanier said he has been reluctant to give Perotta his e-mail address, fearing it will only accelerate the friendship.

Perotta's habit of referring to him by nicknames.

"He's always calling me things like 'Laney' or 'Troy-Boy,'" Lanier said. "My old high-school friends and I have nicknames for each other, but that's different. Until we've known each other a while, I'd prefer to be called Troy—or, at worst, Lanier."

The final straw, Lanier said, came this past Sunday, when he received an unexpected gift from Perotta.

"He stopped by my house to borrow a CD, and my heart just dropped when he handed me a present," Lanier said. "It was a poster for *They Call Me Bruce*. I like the movie okay, but there's no way I'm putting it on my wall. That's the last thing I need, for Scott to come over and see some token of our everlasting friendship hanging over my bed."

Lanier said the situation might have been different had he met Perotta when he was in college.

"I was more open to meeting new people back then," Lanier said. "You live in the dorms, you meet people in classes, you go to parties, and so on. But I have so much more going on in my life now. Before I get too deep into a new friendship, I've got to make sure it's going to be worth the trouble to maintain."

Dr. Karen Franks, a Cornell University sociologist, said Lanier's predicament is not unusual.

The final straw, Lanier said, came this past Sunday, when he received an unexpected gift from Perotta.

"People make friends at different speeds," Franks said. "The key is to be honest and firm with people who try to take things too fast. Troy and Scott may end up being best friends someday, but until then, they should proceed at a rate comfortable for them both. If they don't, things will burn out, leaving one of them spending months awkwardly trying to get back his Jet Li DVDs." Ø

NORTH KOREA from page 67

is eliminating weapons of mass destruction, but he sure doesn't act that way," Kim said. "Iraq *may* have weapons of mass destruction and *may* be developing more. The DPRK, on the other hand, *does* have weapons of mass destruction and isn't about to stop making them any time soon."

"Can I be any more clear?" Kim continued. "We have nuclear bombs and delivery methods. Kablooey! There goes Anchorage! But does Bush care?

In October 2002, Kim made yet another attempt to anger the U.S., admitting to enriching uranium in violation of a 1994 accord. The admission, however, did not produce the desired escalation in hostility.

Nope—he just goes on about how we're 'a diplomatic issue, not a military one.' If he even mentions us at all, that is."

"It's like I don't even exist," Kim added.

In the nine years since coming to power, Kim has earned a reputation as a megalomaniac and tyrant, interning dissenters in camps, living in opulence while his citizens starve, and calling members of the North Korean navy "human bombs." In spite of such actions, he has failed to provoke the ire of the U.S.

After years spent trying to antagonize the U.S., relations between North Korea and America finally showed signs of deterioration in 2002, when, during his State of the Union address, President Bush accused the Asian nation of being part of an international "Axis of Evil." The provocative words, Kim said, sent his hopes for a military standoff with the U.S. skyrocketing.

"When Bush named us as part of his Axis of Evil, I was so happy," Kim said. "I thought to myself, 'This is it. We are finally going to have a military conflict with this two-faced hyena.' He'd been ignoring me so long, I really didn't think he cared."

Still, Kim's hopes for a U.S.-North Korea crisis quickly faded as Bush began to focus all of his energies on Axis of Evil member Iraq. In October 2002, Kim made yet another attempt to anger the U.S., admitting to enriching uranium in violation of a 1994 accord. The admission, however, did not produce the desired escalation in hostility.

Kim said he has not given up on attracting U.S. military attention, vowing to invade South Korea if necessary.

"I am by no means ready to quit, but this is very frustrating," Kim said. "I guess if your name's not Saddam, you're not worthy of America's hatred."

"Everyone in my country refers to me as 'Dear Leader.' Is that not disturbingly cultish?" Kim continued. "I do not understand why President Bush is so much more interested in Saddam than me. I'm a strange, despotic, unpredictable madman, too, you know." Ø

Above: U.S. Marines that could be marching on Pyongyang engage in drills in the Persian Gulf.

You Will Know Love

Erase all doubt from your mind, for tonight, you will know love. Let me tell you how I am going to lay it down.

This afternoon, while you are on lunch break, I will have a handpicked team of florists cover your desk at work with a mixture of sensuous-smelling rose petals. They will also leave a note reading, "Girl, you are most fine. I will pick you up at 8." This will show you and your coworkers that Smoove is the man for you, as well as give you a glimpse into the personal attention I will lavish on you later that evening.

By Smoove B
Love Man

I will also instruct the delivery person to wait and clean the flowers off your desk when you are done looking at them, so that you can continue with your work day.

At precisely 8 o'clock, I will arrive in a pearl-white car to pick you up and transport us to dinner at the city's finest European restaurant. I will tell the driver to take the most romantic, scenic route possible to the restaurant. On the way, I will have a sterling-silver thermos filled with hot chocolate from the Swiss chocolate region. If it is too hot for you, I will blow on it until it is the correct temperature.

I will lead you to my large, circular bathtub. There, I will strip you down and place your naked body gently into the perfectly warm water. Then, I will wash you with a towel of my choosing. Make no mistake, it will be the perfect towel for your beautiful body.

When you have finished the cocoa, I will take the empty cup away from you and pack up the thermos. I will then nuzzle your neck and whisper complimentary remarks into your ear, including, "You are more beautiful than a thousand lakes," "You are extremely special to me," and "Your bone structure belongs in a museum." This will make you wet.

Damn, girl. I want to get freaky with you right now on my desk. I want to ride you like a bronco.

When we arrive at the expensive European restaurant, the owner will greet me warmly and comment positively on your attire. He will then personally lead us to a private table I have specially selected for our evening together. As we browse the menu, I will inform you that if multiple appetizers are your wish, I can make that wish come true.

When the appetizers arrive, I will feed them to you with my hands, which I will have hand-washed with special anti-bacterial soap to ensure their cleanliness.

When the appetizers arrive, I will feed them to you with my hands, which I will have hand-washed with special anti-bacterial soap to ensure their cleanliness. You will then eat an entree of your choice and a dessert. While we eat these various foods, we will discuss your fineness and also your hopes and dreams for the future. This will make you feel closer to me and, as a result, make you want to sex me wild.

After the meal, we will forgo transportation and walk the five blocks back to my apartment, because the night will be so fragrant and beautiful. I will hold your hand and stroke your wrist lightly with my thumb. As we approach my apartment, I will pull you close, and it will feel right. It will feel like we are two interlocking pieces of a sexy panther jigsaw puzzle.

If the moon is full, I will point it out to you.

When we reach my penthouse, I will remove your shoes and kiss you passionately for five to ten minutes. Just when you think you are going crazy with desire, I will lead you to my large, circular bathtub. There, I will strip you down and place your naked body gently into the perfectly warm water. Then, I will wash you with a towel of my choosing. Make no mistake, it will be the perfect towel for your beautiful body, fitting your every luscious contour. If the scented perfumes I have placed in your bath water are not to your liking, I will drain the tub and we will start over. But they will not be incorrect, so we will not have to. I know you, girl.

After I have dried and moisturized you, I will comb your hair. If, while combing your hair, you would like me to comb either faster or harder, please say so. While I am doing this combing, you will think you know love, but Smoove is ready to take you to the next level.

This is when Smoove will lead you to his canopy bed. Keith Sweat will be playing on my bedroom stereo, creating the perfect mood for us to freak all night. And freak all night is what we shall do. Between freakings, we will laugh and tell stories, and I will rub your neck and back. Then we will freak again. This will go on until the break of dawn.

Damn.

When you wake up, I will make you French toast. If French toast is not what you desire, I will find another nationality of toast that suits you. I will not rest until I find this perfect nationality of toast, even if I have to swim all the way to Austria for it. After I find and make the toast, and you eat it, we will freak once more.

This is how the evening will go. This is how you will know love.

Smoove out. ⌀

Your Horoscope

By Lloyd Schumner Sr.
Retired Machinist and
A.A.P.B.-Certified Astrologer

Aries: (March 21–April 19)
The media will proclaim you the new John F. Kennedy for your charisma, sense of style, and massive gunshot wound to the back of the head.

Taurus: (April 20–May 20)
Your concern over what kind of mother you'll be is admirable, not to mention rare for such a young man.

Gemini: (May 21–June 21)
You'll continue to question your faith in a God who would allow the Tampa Bay Buccaneers to win the Super Bowl.

Cancer: (June 22–July 22)
You're proud of your conviction that rules were made to be broken, but it might be wise to keep this from the prosecuting attorney.

Leo: (July 23–Aug. 22)
All the wishing in the world can't bring your dead mother back to life, but animal sacrifices have been known to work wonders.

Virgo: (Aug. 23–Sept. 22)
They say lightning never strikes the same place twice, but that doesn't mean you should feel comfortable once you're out of the hospital.

Libra: (Sept. 23–Oct. 23)
You will finally be cleared of wrongdoing in the infamous "Bloodbath At Bala Hissar," when the Royal British Marines admit it happened 130 years before you were born.

Scorpio: (Oct. 24–Nov. 21)
You'll run up against a problem that all the charm in the world can't solve, so it's a good thing you haven't got any.

Sagittarius: (Nov. 22–Dec. 21)
You're one of the rare people who's willing to die for what you believe in, which is strange, because you mostly just believe in using as many coupons as possible.

Capricorn: (Dec. 22–Jan. 19)
It's nice that you enjoyed the chicken pot pie, chips, and beer, but the genie was surprised you didn't try the old "wishing for more wishes" trick.

Aquarius: (Jan. 20–Feb. 18)
Next week is a good one for romance in the workplace, but why they always have to use your office is beyond you.

Pisces: (Feb. 19–March 20)
The incident-reconstruction specialists will thank you for the chance to work with so many monkeys.

MOM from page 69

around Grandma, Mom just lets it slide," James said. "She hardly even notices anymore, unless it's something severe like 'cocksucker.'"

Michael noted that, in addition to swearing more herself, his mother has become more lax in policing her children's foul language.

Encouraged by her mother's swearing habit, Julie said she is eagerly awaiting the emergence of other vices.

"Mom drank a margarita the last time we were at Chi-Chi's," Julie said. "I don't want to jinx it, but I think there's a chance we might actually see her drunk one of these years." ⌀

the ONION®

VOLUME 39 ISSUE 06 AMERICA'S FINEST NEWS SOURCE™ 20–26 FEBRUARY 2003

NEWS

Chinese Man Still Writing 'Horse' On Checks

see WORLD page 11D

Pizza Hut Introduces New Meat Sympathizer's Pizza

see PRODUCTWATCH page 8E

Okay, TiVo Gets It, You Like Porn

see TELEVISION page 3B

Space Pen Explodes

see LOCAL page 9C

STATshot

A look at the numbers that shape your world.

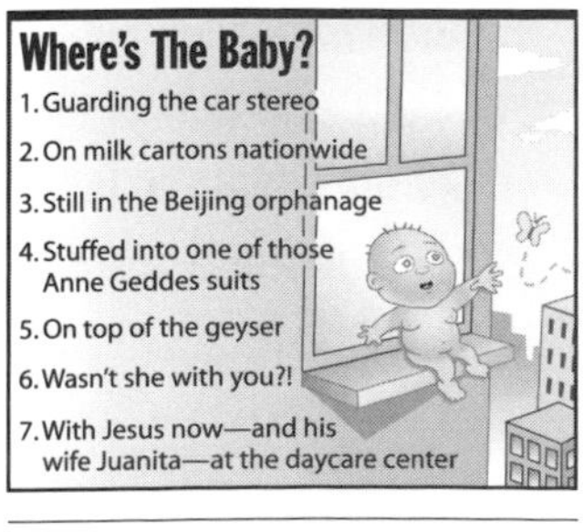

Above: Iraq's Saddam Hussein and Kentucky's Travis Lee Butler hone their cloud-shooting skills.

Iraq, Kentucky Vie For World Shooting-Into-The-Air Supremacy

COON HOLLOW, KY—In a rivalry that shows no signs of abating, Iraq and Kentucky remain locked in a bitter struggle for world shooting-into-the-air supremacy.

"I'll be damned if any Muslim's gonna beat the great state of Kentucky at what she do best," said Coon Hollow resident Billy Joe Dupree, 39, in between bouts of firing his shotgun skyward Monday. "We been shootin' into the air for all kinds 'a reasons since they was a Kentucky, and that's a fact. Why, even my wall-eyed cousin Mavis could outshoot one o' them Muslims, and she ain't hardly finished the fifth grade."

Aziz Hourani, 24, of Baghdad, took exception to Dupree's claims of air-shooting superiority.

"Such is our anger at the Great Satan that we send many bullets into the air every day," said Hourani, raising his AK-47 carbine and firing several rounds. "No one can surpass us at shooting upwards—and certainly not the Americans."

Though worlds apart geographically and culturally, Iraq and Kentucky each boast rich traditions of vertical marksmanship.

"Expressing one's feelings and emotions via the firing of guns into the air is an ancient and noble artform," said Henri St. Germain, president of the Federation Internationale des

see SUPREMACY page 76

Women Now Empowered By Everything A Woman Does

OBERLIN, OH—According to a study released Monday, women—once empowered primarily via the assertion of reproductive rights or workplace equality with men—are now empowered by virtually everything the typical woman does.

American Focus

"From what she eats for breakfast to the way she cleans her home, today's woman lives in a state of near-constant empowerment," said Barbara Klein, professor of women's studies at Oberlin College and director of the study. "As recently as 15 years ago, a woman could only feel empowered by advancing in a male-dominated work world, asserting her own sexual wants and needs, or pushing for a stronger voice in politics. Today, a woman can empower herself through actions as seemingly inconsequential as driving her children to soccer practice or watching the Oxygen network."

Klein said that clothes-shopping, once considered a mundane act with few sociopolitical implications, is now

see WOMAN page 77

Terrorism 'Not Likely' Cause Of Fire At Local Laundromat

EUCLID, OH—Homeland Security Secretary Tom Ridge assured the American people Monday that terrorism was "not likely a factor" in the fire that damaged a downtown Euclid laundromat Sunday afternoon.

"At this time, there is nothing to suggest that yesterday's Sudsy Duds fire was the work of a terrorist group, al-Qaeda or otherwise," Ridge said. "The FBI is conducting a thorough investigation into the cause, but thus far, there is no evidence indicating that this was a terrorist strike against our nation."

Euclid fire chief Andrew Donnelly, who has been working closely with state and federal officials in the wake of the blaze, offered his theory on its cause.

"I'm guessing water flooded into the basement, causing a misfire in an oil furnace that sparked a minor explosion," Donnelly said. "Groundwater probably seeped through the walls of the lower level and reached the boiler in the middle of the floor. Luckily, we were able to contain the blaze without causing too much structural water damage. Coulda been a lot worse."

see FIRE page 76

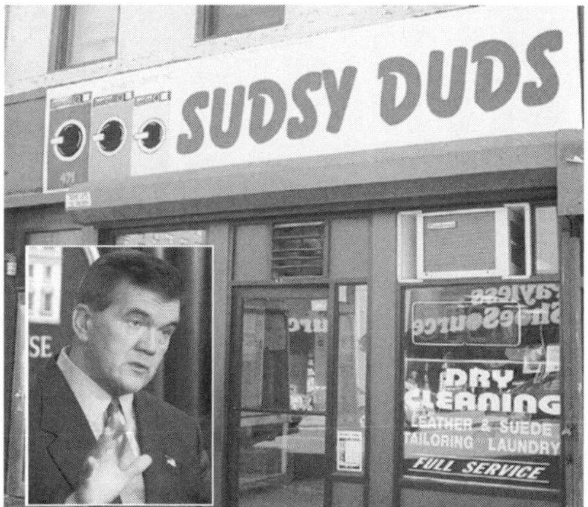

Above: The site of the blaze feared to be the work of al-Qaeda. Inset: Ridge answers reporters' questions.

Can N. Korea Nukes Reach The U.S.?

Last week, U.S. intelligence officials stated that North Korea has the technology to fire nuclear missiles at the West Coast. What do *you* think?

"It's about time the West Coast started carrying its fair share of the scared-shitless load."

Jennifer Cotto
Research Assistant

"Big deal. There's, like, an 80 to 90 percent chance they won't even use those things."

Lisa Campbell
Dietitian

"Fuckin' Pyongyang."

Rich Kingery
Cab Driver

"North Korea has missiles that can reach the U.S.? We'd better get to work on developing some missiles of our own *right away*."

Tom Reynolds
Systems Analyst

"I sincerely doubt they can reach us. My back scratcher was made in Korea, and the piece of crap can barely reach past my shoulder blades."

Ron Buhner
Gardener

"As an American, I'm getting sick and tired of other countries."

Cris Langston
Accountant

The Ben And J. Lo Show

Ben Affleck and Jennifer Lopez are America's hottest celebrity couple. How do they spend a typical day?

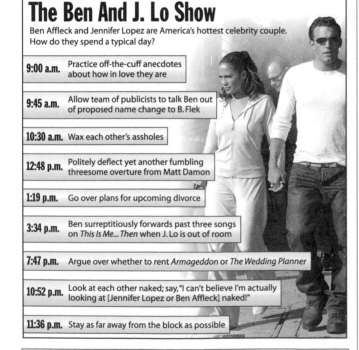

- **9:00 a.m.** Practice off-the-cuff anecdotes about how in love they are
- **9:45 a.m.** Allow team of publicists to talk Ben out of proposed name change to B. Flek
- **10:30 a.m.** Wax each other's assholes
- **12:48 p.m.** Politely deflect yet another fumbling threesome overture from Matt Damon
- **1:19 p.m.** Go over plans for upcoming divorce
- **3:34 p.m.** Ben surreptitiously forwards past three songs on *This Is Me... Then* when J. Lo is out of room
- **7:47 p.m.** Argue over whether to rent *Armageddon* or *The Wedding Planner*
- **10:52 p.m.** Look at each other naked; say, "I can't believe I'm actually looking at [Jennifer Lopez or Ben Affleck] naked!"
- **11:36 p.m.** Stay as far away from the block as possible

the ONION®
America's Finest News Source.™

Herman Ulysses Zweibel
Founder

T. Herman Zweibel
Publisher Emeritus
J. Phineas Zweibel
Publisher
Maxwell Prescott Zweibel
Editor-In-Chief

Point-Counterpoint: The Iraq Invasion

No Blood For Oil

By Susan Winger
President,
Democracy In Action

Contrary to what he would have you believe, President Bush's plans to invade Iraq have nothing to do with such high-minded goals as liberating the Iraqi people or saving the world from terrorism. His "principled" stand is actually just a thinly veiled attempt to gain control of the oil-rich Middle East at the cost of human lives. It is time for the people of the United States to rise up and say, "No blood for oil!"

Bush talks about freedom, but what kind? The freedom to drive gas-guzzling SUVs without worrying about the price of gas going above $2 a gallon? If we go to war, innocent lives will be lost to satisfy Generalissimo Bush's insatiable gaslust and line the bulging pockets of the corporate and oil interests that put him in office.

We've got to stand up and make our voices heard. This war is not what most Americans want. What's more, Bush is acting against not only the will of a majority of Americans, but also the will of the world. France and Germany have demanded to see more evidence of Iraq's attempts to conceal weapons of mass destruction, yet Bush continues to ram his warmongering agenda down everyone's throats, all for his precious black gold.

Bush talks about freedom, but what kind? The freedom to drive gas-guzzling SUVs without worrying about the price of gas going above $2 a gallon?

The president claims that Iraq is "a danger to the world," but it is the U.S. that represents the *real* danger. We are the ones who act like bullies, intimidating those who don't go along with our imperialist agenda with threats of invasion and worse. Unlike some countries I could name, Iraq never dropped an atomic bomb on anybody. The bottom line is, Bush has

see POINT page 76

Exactly How Much Oil Are We Talking About?

By Kenneth W. Parton
Americans For
Non-Alternative Energy

I keep hearing the anti-war protesters chant, "No blood for oil! No blood for oil!" But what they never seem to say is exactly how much oil we're talking about. Don't you think that's pertinent information? Are we talking a gallon of oil for every 10 gallons of blood? Or is it more like 30 gallons of oil for every pint of blood? Because if it's the latter, maybe a blood-oil exchange would be a good idea.

In the first Gulf War, roughly 300 brave Americans lost their lives. Assuming that each of these soldiers shed an average of eight pints of blood, that works out to roughly a pint of American blood shed per 60 million barrels of Kuwaiti crude saved from the clutches of Saddam. If you ask me, that's a pretty darn good deal. If we can manage to swing a similar trade this time around, then I say, "Bombs away."

We should also know what kind of blood we're giving up. Is it O-negative, the universal donor? I'd be more reluctant to part with that than some useless AB junk. If Bush and Rumsfeld spill, say, 100,000 gallons of B-negative or AB-positive soldier blood for an equivalent amount of primo Mideast oil, then that may be well worth considering.

Sending innocent young men and women into battle to die is the most difficult decision a president can make. But it's that much easier when you know what you're getting in return.

So, you see, you can't argue in the abstract like those naïve protesters on college campuses are doing. You've got to look at the hard numbers if you're going to make an informed decision about a potential blood-for-oil swap.

Sending innocent young men and women into battle to die is the most

see COUNTERPOINT page 76

Girlfriend Stops Reading David Foster Wallace Breakup Letter At Page 20

BLOOMINGTON, IL—Claire Thompson, author David Foster Wallace's girlfriend of two years, stopped reading his 67-page breakup letter at page 20, she admitted Monday.

"It was pretty good, I guess, but I just couldn't get all the way through," said Thompson, 32, who was given the seven-chapter, heavily footnoted "Dear John" missive on Feb. 3. "I always meant to pick it up again, but then I got busy and, oh, I don't know. He's talented, but his letters can sometimes get a little self-indulgent."

Above: Thompson

Foster, the award-winning author of *The Broom Of The System* and the 1,079-page *Infinite Jest*, met Thompson in March 2001 through mutual friends.

A political-science professor at Illinois State University, where Wallace teaches creative writing, Thompson said pages 4 through 11 of the letter chronicled the deterioration of the relationship "fairly well." She specifically cited Item 64, on page 7, from the section, "How I Can Tell Things Have Changed":

"It used to be that if you were away from the table or in the next room or otherwise unable to witness this admittedly unsavory and wholly intrusive activity on my part, in little spasms of unhealthy obsession I would peek into your Day Runner Personal Planner so as to gauge how much together-time we would have during the upcoming week at a glance; lately, however—if you are at all able to move past this revelation of my no-two-ways-around it unforgivable and unjustifiable invasion of privacy and on to the rather telling point—I have found myself either viewing the week-at-a-glance in actual anticipation of our time apart or, even when opportunities for unfettered peeking presented themselves, ignoring your Day Runner Personal Planner altogether such as just last week when, stooped in rummaging position, I opted to remove from your bag and guiltily read cover-to-cover a copy of *Fine Cooking* magazine, therein choosing to glean particulars about the cultivation, culinary traditions, and preparation of white asparagus over those of our precious little time together."

aware this announcement may come as somewhat of a shock, Claire, but the weekend in Maine really helped me sort out my feelings. The truth is, I don't know if I ever really was in love[32]. I've always wanted to be fair to you[33], and I'd never want to do any-

32. Honest-to-goodness-holy-shit-without-a-doubt-this-is-it-this-is-the-one-I-mean-really-the-one love, a.k.a. "love at first sight," the kind of love in which one spends the first eight to twelve weeks in utter ecstasy[a], unable to operate heavy machinery much less remember to pay the damn phone bill. Usage excludes "I love you but I need to find myself," "I love you and therefore want to have your child please can we, huh?" or the Let's Make a Deal-ish "I love you because you love me" and all references to the equally unsavory doomed alliances that one witnesses friends or family or friends of family willingly participating in despite all and in direct opposition of such carefully-worded cautions against the said relationship as strategically dropped hints progressing to direct verbal warnings and strangely-aware letters addressed to RESIDENT and singing telegrams as intervention tools and Goodyear blimps parked and holding steady at 4,000 ft above the house of the PSNAWC (Person Seriously Needing A Wakeup Call) scrolling the message "GET OUT NOW... DON'T WASTE THE... BEST YEARS... OF YOUR LIFE"—the kind of love that leaves a bad taste in your mouth, sending you running for your Oral B toothbrush and travelers' size Baking Soda and Peroxide Gum Care Toothpaste that you always keep in a Ziploc™ bag in your coat pocket in case you find yourself in need of a quick brush while away from home or office or car or garage shop where you keep, for this very sort of purpose, another nearly brand spanking new toothbrush, religiously replacing the oral care device at least every two months or sooner in the case of head colds, flu, or especially nasty bouts of gingivitical flare-up, using a Sharpie™ to carefully apply the date on the underside of the handle to facilitate the rotation.

a. Ecstasy in the strictest sense of the word, i.e., state of rapturous delight—that is to say not directly under the effects of Methylenedioxymethamphet-amine, although, strangely, still experiencing many of the same post-self-MDMA-administration effects experienced by a user of this stimulant and/or an hallucinogenic which can be made—assuming you have all the equipment, Bunsen burners and what not, at your disposal in your basement or 3 bedroom dorm suite bathroom and are

Above: An excerpt from the break-up opus.

In addition to compiling the many reasons why the relationship was no longer working, Wallace's letter featured sections on "Why We Could Never Grow Old Together," "Ways It—Us, The World, And Everything Has All Changed," and "Things I've Never Told You (That Will Certainly Change Your Mind About Me)."

"One thing I found annoying was that you had to read all the way to the

see GIRLFRIEND page 77

NEWS IN BRIEF

Paintball Team Visits Vietnam Memorial

WASHINGTON, DC—The five members of the Blitz Cougars paintball team of Ashburn, GA, paid their respects to their fallen compatriots at the Vietnam Veterans Memorial on Monday. "None of us served in Vietnam, but we too have witnessed firsthand the unspeakable horrors of combat," said Derek "Boone" Bechet, 23, the Cougars' team leader. "Last August, I lost one of my men when a round of Draxxus Inferno sapphire blue caught him right in the temple. Chris was only 19 when he got taken out of the game for good." Fighting back tears, Bechet bowed his head in silent prayer for his splattered comrade.

Newlyweds Regret Saving Sex For Marriage

WETUMKA, OK—Two weeks after their Feb. 1 wedding, Matt and Liz Kuchen, both 32, regret remaining virgins until marriage. "Why the hell did I wait?" Liz said Tuesday. "I could've been having mind-blowing sex with dozens of guys these last 15 years, and instead I spent them making little uptight speeches about how it'll be more special if I hold out." Matt agreed, saying, "Stacy Pratt totally would've done me. Oh, man."

Bacon Good For You, Reports Best Scientist Ever

ROCHESTER, MN—Bacon, long believed to contribute to heart disease and obesity, possesses significant health benefits, according to a study released Monday by Dr. Albert Gruber, the best scientist ever. "My research has found that three strips of crispy, mouthwatering bacon every morning can actually reduce cholesterol and help slow the aging process," the awesome Gruber said. "What's more, the bacon's positive effects are enhanced when combined with milk shakes and/or marijuana." In 1997, Gruber, a Mayo Clinic cardiologist, was awarded nine Nobel Prizes in Medicine for discovering that frequent oral sex with models cures cancer.

No One At Ad Agency Remembers Hiring Carrot Top For Commercial

NEW YORK—In spite of their best efforts, creative executives at the Young & Rubicam advertising agency cannot recall how Carrot Top came to be hired for the "1-800-CALL-ATT" collect-call campaign. "I really, truly don't remember ever casting that guy," Young & Rubicam creative director Molly Herbert said of the hideous, clown-faced comedian. "To be honest, all anyone here can remember is firing David Arquette two years ago, then suddenly there's Carrot Top on the set." Herbert and her team were equally at a loss over who developed the "Just Dial Down The Middle" concept.

New Prisoner Recognized From 'Scared Straight' Visit

RAHWAY, NJ—New Rahway State Penitentiary inmate Andrew Traber, 19, was recognized Monday by longtime inmate Ronald Wayne Desmond, who met Traber in 1998 in the prison's "Scared Straight" program. "I couldn't believe it: There he was, little Andrew, all grown up," said Desmond, 38, who is serving two consecutive life sentences for murder. "So I yelled, 'Hey, Andrew, it's me—the guy who told you when you were 14 what it's like to be brutally gang-raped in the prison laundry with a shiv held to your throat.' He kind of nodded hi, but I got the feeling he didn't remember me."

FIRE from page 73

Damage from the fire is estimated at $27,000. Among the casualties were seven large-capacity dryers, a detergent-vending machine, and a Pengo arcade game.

"We can say with a high degree of certainty that this fire was not masterminded by Osama bin Laden or any other such figure," Ridge said. "There were no intercepted communications between suspected terrorists regarding this laundromat, and no sign of chemical, biological, or radiological weapons was found after a thorough search of all washers, dryers, folding tables, and snack machines."

According to Ridge, there is no evidence to suggest that the facility was used as a "soft target," in spite of the federal government's recent terror-alert upgrade to orange.

"We can say with a high degree of certainty that this fire was not masterminded by Osama bin Laden or any other such figure," Ridge said. "There were no intercepted communications between suspected terrorists regarding this laundromat, and no sign of chemical, biological, or radiological weapons was found after a thorough search of all washers, dryers, folding tables, and snack machines."

Added Ridge: "I would, however, urge the public to remain extra-vigilant in these times of heightened alert and be sure to report any unusual or suspicious activities they witness at laundromats or any other public places."

Though Euclid is home to an estimated seven Muslims, none are considered suspects at this time.

"We checked, and every member of Euclid's Islamic community has an airtight alibi," Ridge said. "I further discussed these foreign-born residents with Euclid police chief Stan Welker, who vouched for their character, saying, 'They're all good, decent folks, just like you and me.' We may still bring them in for a little further questioning, but I don't have real reason to suspect they're behind this."

Welker said he has accounted for everyone who used the facility in the 24 hours prior to the fire. Thus far, he has found no evidence suggesting foul play.

"The names of key witnesses were taken, should further questioning be required, but preliminary interviews have revealed nothing suspicious," Welker said. "It was a pretty slow day. At the time of the fire, there were only five people in there: Jenny Kroeger and her two kids and an elderly couple from over on Franklin Street."

Sudsy Duds owner Mike Birbiglia arrived within minutes of the fire.

"Normally, the basement is actively pumped dry, but the sump pump apparently broke or was unplugged," Birbiglia said. "Well, we think that's what happened. Who knows? All we know for sure is I got one heck of a mess to clean up down there."

In spite of the unlikelihood that the incident was a terrorist act, Birbiglia said he plans to hire guards from Safe-T Security of Euclid to patrol the premises after closing.

"I'm sure it was nothing," Birbiglia said, "but if it's all the same, I'd rather not take any chances. Last thing I need is somebody trying to mess up my store just as I'm about to put in those new triple-load washers."

Attempting to calm a jittery nation as it braces for the next terrorist attack, President Bush said there is no cause for alarm.

"The Euclid fire appears to be an isolated incident unrelated to terrorism," Bush said. "But next time, we might not be so lucky. That is why we, as a nation, must do everything we can to drive out Saddam Hussein and his ilk. By confronting terrorism head-on, we can once again live in a nation where we don't jump every time a dryer buzzer goes off."

"We checked, and every member of Euclid's Islamic community has an airtight alibi," Ridge said. "I further discussed these foreign-born residents with Euclid police chief Stan Welker, who vouched for their character."

Bush said Euclid officials will remain in close communication with state and federal government agencies.

"If they find any proof of terrorist activity, all levels will be notified," Bush said. "Now, everyone go about your day as normal." ⌀

SUPREMACY from page 73

Discharges-Aeriales (FIDA), the sport's governing body. "In fact, it may even predate the practice of expressing one's feelings and emotions by shooting into other humans. And nowhere on Earth does this tradition continue to thrive more than in Iraq and Kentucky. It is a vital part of these two unique cultures."

"Whether shooting to celebrate a successful moonshine heist from neighboring kinfolk or the downfall of an imperialist Western regime, Kentucky and Iraq bring an undeniable passion and pride to their craft," St. Germain said.

Continued St. Germain: "Whether shooting to celebrate a successful moonshine heist from neighboring kinfolk or the downfall of an imperialist Western regime, Kentucky and Iraq bring an undeniable passion and pride to their craft."

According to FIDA officials, in head-to-head competition, Iraq and Kentucky are closely matched.

"From a technical standpoint, the two competitors are virtually dead-even, with different but equally strong styles," veteran FIDA judge Olivier Resnais said. "The Iraqis' preference for automatic military weapons give them the edge in rounds-fired-into-the-air-per-minute, whereas the Kentucky double-barreled shotgun or squirrel rifle has a much greater bore, allowing for a louder, more full-bodied sound and a much greater weight of vertically propelled lead per shot."

"In terms of vocal style, they are again different yet similar, with the gun wielders of each region doing their best to drown out their weapon's report through fervent yelling of their native calls," Resnais continued. "Though they may have different meanings, the cries of 'Yeeeee-haw!' and 'Allahu akbar!' are, in spirit, not actually all that different." ⌀

POINT from page 74

no right to wage a "preemptive" war against Iraq.

The White House continues to beat the war drum, frightening the American public into believing this war is necessary for the safety of the world. Bush is trying to scare up support for an invasion under the pretense that Saddam intends to unleash chemical, biological, or nuclear warfare on his enemies, but there is no real evidence that these are his plans. There is real evidence, on the other hand, that President Bush was put in office by Big Oil and would do anything to avoid having to develop responsible, earth-friendly alternative energy sources.

Most offensive of all, the tragic events of Sept. 11 are being manipulated by Bush to further his agenda. Under the guise of the "war on terrorism," Bush has declared that members of his "Axis of Evil" are a threat and subject to military attacks. Is it coincidence that the one Axis of Evil nation Bush has singled out for attack also holds the greatest opportunity for profit? I think not.

There is real evidence, on the other hand, that President Bush was put in office by Big Oil and would do anything to avoid having to develop responsible, earth-friendly alternative energy sources.

Let the U.N. inspections work. No blood for oil! ⌀

COUNTERPOINT from page 74

difficult decision a president can make. But it's that much easier when you know what you're getting in return. If I were Bush, I'd definitely do it if we could get the price of a gallon of Amoco Ultra Unleaded down to $1.19. Maybe even $1.21. Anything higher would give me pause. But $1.21 is a great price for a gallon. I would take a lot more weekend road-trips if gas were that cheap. I might even upgrade to one of those Lincoln Navigators I've been seeing ads for on TV. That's a beautiful car.

Nobody wants to see brave young Americans sent off to die. Nobody wants to see blood spilled for oil. But if it comes to that, wouldn't we all feel better knowing that their blood was spilled for a *great deal* of oil? I know I sure would. ⌀

I might even upgrade to one of those Lincoln Navigators I've been seeing ads for on TV. That's a beautiful car.

WOMAN from page 73

a bold feminist statement.

"Shopping for shoes has emerged as a powerful means by which women assert their autonomy," Klein said. "Owning and wearing dozens of pairs of shoes is a compelling way for a woman to announce that she is strong and independent, and has shod herself without the help of a man. She's saying, 'Look out, male-dominated world, here comes me and my shoes.'"

Eating energy bars specially fortified with nutrients "for women" has become a feminist trend, as well.

"Unlike traditional, phallocentric energy bars, whose chocolate, soy protein, nuts, and granola ignored the special health and nutritional needs of women, their new, female-oriented counterparts like Luna are ideally balanced with a more suitable amount of chocolate, soy protein, nuts, and granola," Klein said. "Protofeminist pioneers like Elizabeth Cady Stanton and Susan B. Anthony could never have imagined that female empowerment would one day come in bar form."

Other acts of empowerment include gossiping about the sexual proclivities of male acquaintances, lunching with other women in small groups, and taking calcium-rich antacid tablets.

Whereas early feminists campaigned tirelessly for improved health care and safe, legal access to abortion, often against a backdrop of public indifference or hostility, today's feminist asserts control over her biological destiny by wearing a baby-doll T-shirt with the word "Hoochie" spelled in glitter.

Above: San Diego women empower themselves by eating dinner unaccompanied by men.

"Don't tell this bitch what to do," said Kari Eastley, 24, a participant in the Oberlin study and, according to one of her T-shirts, a "Slut Goddess." "I wear what I want when I want, and no man is going to tell me otherwise. We're talking Pussy Power, baby."

Other acts of empowerment include gossiping about the sexual proclivities of male acquaintances, lunching with other women in small groups, taking calcium-rich antacid tablets, and reading *The Nanny Diaries*.

The study also cites the act of pumping one's raised fist in a gesture of female solidarity against the oppressive forces of air pressure.

"Nearly 90 percent of study participants have done this at least once in their lives, often accompanying their action with the exhortation 'You go, girl!' or, simply, 'Whooooooo!'" Klein said.

Perhaps most remarkably, the mere act of weight gain is now regarded as a feminist act. Though some women express reservations about the negative impact of obesity on one's health, overweight women display a level of assertiveness, or "sassitude," that thinner women lack.

"Women who proclaim themselves 'large and in charge' refuse to be bound by traditional notions of beauty and health," said Carla Willets, a Vassar College women's-studies professor. "They love themselves for who they are, something no 'normal-sized' woman could possibly do."

"Of course, women can be empowered by losing weight, too," Willets added. "Pretty much any change in weight—up or down—is empowering."

Klein said empowerment is now accessible to women who were long excluded.

"Not every woman can become a physicist or lobby to stop a foundry from dumping dangerous metals into the creek her children swim in," Klein said. "Although these actions are incredible, they marginalize the majority of women who are unable to, or just don't particularly care to, achieve such things. Fortunately for the less impressive among us, a new strain of feminism has emerged in which mundane activities are championed as proud, bold assertions of independence from oppressive patriarchal hegemony."

Long Beach, CA, resident Jeanne Bradley was recently given a special commendation by the city of Los Angeles for regularly attending WNBA games.

"From midnight cheesecake noshers to moms who don't fool around with pain, feminist achievement covers a broad spectrum," said Bradley in her acceptance speech. "It is great to be a female athlete, senator, or physician. But we must not overlook the homemaker who uses a mop equipped with convenient, throwaway towelettes, the college co-ed who chooses to abstain from sex, and the college co-ed who chooses to have a lot of sex. Only by lauding every single thing a woman does, no matter how ordinary, can you truly go, girls." ⊘

GIRLFRIEND from page 75

middle to figure out what things on the first page of the letter were talking about," Thompson said. "For instance, he kept referring to somebody named The Cackler without explanation until page 11, at which point I finally found out that The Cackler is my friend Renée—essentially forcing me to read the whole first 11 pages over again. And then there are all the footnotes. I always felt he overused those in his valentines, too."

Thompson said she believes Wallace penned the breakup opus during a January lecture trip to the University of New England in Biddeford, ME.

"When he came back, he handed me a big manila envelope," Thompson said. "He said that during the trip, he confronted himself about some things he'd been avoiding, and that he needed to start living his life in a whole different way. He said the contents of the envelope would explain everything. I was just like, 'Okay, whatever, David.'"

Thompson said she did not immediately open the envelope.

"I assumed it was one of his tomes about, I don't know, the reasons why he isn't going to eat processed sugar anymore, or why he threw out his TV," Thompson said. "Or something like the one where he said, in 88 numbered points, why he didn't want a birthday party."

"Or, God, I almost forgot," Thompson added. "There was the letter where he explained how he now wants to be called 'Dave' and included a page-long description of every single 'Dave' and 'David' he's ever known in his entire life."

That evening, Thompson slogged through the first 20 pages of the dense, complex *Breakup Letter For Claire–Rough Draft*.

On Feb. 5, two days after receiving the letter, Thompson received a voicemail message from Wallace asking her what she thought of it. The message prompted her finally to open the envelope and "crack" the letter. That evening, Thompson slogged through the first 20 pages of the dense, complex *Breakup Letter For Claire–Rough Draft*, eventually putting it down to begin making dinner. The next morning, she moved the letter from her coffee table to a desk drawer, where it still sits, unfinished.

"Maybe I'll pick it up again," Thompson said. "I'd sort of like to see how it ends. Then again, knowing David, it probably just leaves a whole bunch of loose ends untied." ⊘

COMMUNITY VOICES

Well, *I* Think Michael Jackson Looks Nice

I don't understand why some people have to build themselves up by tearing other people down. Everywhere I go these days, I hear people making nasty comments about Michael Jackson's appearance. Well, *I* think Michael Jackson looks *very nice*.

By Elaine Paretsky

Michael clearly cares about his appearance, which I find refreshing in a young person. He always looks so well-groomed and has nice, new-looking clothes. And his slacks always appear clean and pressed. So many of the stars today walk around looking all sloppy and disheveled, like they just rolled out of bed. They wear the backwards baseball caps and baggy pants that are falling off their tushies. Michael, on the other hand, always wears a matching pantsuit or a handsome jacket with gold braids.

I don't know if Michael gets his hair fixed somewhere, but it's always done up very nice. I don't particularly love his current style, with the hair down in front of his eyes, but that is his choice and I still think it looks just fine. Certainly miles better than the other stars you see out there, who look like they've never even heard of a comb.

Some people have to criticize, criticize, criticize all the time. Maybe if they had better self-esteem, they wouldn't need to cut other people down. Don't you think? I'll admit, his eyes do look a little bit strange, but we can't all be born looking like Cary Grant, can we? Some of us have to make do with what the good Lord gave us. I don't care what anyone says: I think he is a very handsome young man. And I just love his cute little button nose.

Then there's that TV interview everyone's giving him such a hard time about. I, for one, thought it was *very* courteous of Michael to take time out of his busy schedule writing songs and taking care of his children to talk to ABC. I wonder if anyone even thanked him. Why is everyone making fun of what he said? That just isn't very nice. I hope he doesn't get too down on himself after hearing the mean things people are saying.

From what I can tell, Michael seems like a very pleasant person. When I see him on awards shows, he is always so polite and well-mannered. I can barely even hear his soft voice without turning up the television. Yet all the talk-show hosts make fun of him. They show his picture, and everyone in the audience laughs. Well, *I* don't see what's so darn funny. I don't think it's ever appropriate to laugh at another person, especially someone who has gone through all that he has, what with all those divorces. My son Matthew went through a divorce five years ago, and it was a very hard time for him. I'm sure it will be no time at all before another lucky lady snaps Michael up, though. He has more than enough time to settle down and make a fresh start with someone new.

I remember that adorable little singing group Michael was in with his brothers. There's nothing more important than family. I appreciate a young man who still finds family

Some people have to criticize, criticize, criticize all the time. Maybe if they had better self-esteem, they wouldn't need to cut other people down.

important. They sang that song about learning your ABCs that was very cute. Unlike those rapper singers, Michael never uses dirty language in his songs. They are always very classy.

Did you know that Michael Jackson lives on a ranch with all sorts of exotic animals? Doesn't that sound wonderful? I sure do love my little terrier Spanky. He's less like a pet and more like a friend. Michael is someone who loves animals enough to give them a home—how could anyone say that is bad? When I visited my daughter in Chicago, we went to a botanical garden and it was just beautiful. I'll bet his ranch is absolutely lovely.

A few weeks ago, there were all those pictures in the paper of Michael holding his baby, and there was some brouhaha over it. Someone's always trying to stir up trouble. I couldn't tell, but that baby looked cute as a button to me. Isn't it nice to see a man proudly showing off his little boy? When I was growing up, it wasn't unusual for a father to leave all the parenting to the women, so it sure brings a smile to my face to see Michael surrounded by all those children.

Once, when I was in line at the supermarket, I saw a magazine with a photo of Michael wearing a surgical mask. There was some nasty headline above it, as if it's okay to make fun of someone for being sick. What has this world come to?

Michael, if you're reading this, just remember: If anyone says anything bad about you, it's only because they're jealous. Ø

HOROSCOPES

Your Horoscope

By Lloyd Schumner Sr.
Retired Machinist and
A.A.P.B.-Certified Astrologer

Aries: (March 21–April 19)
You will soon be forced to admit that your entire emotional range can be conveyed with a set of cleverly arranged punctuation marks.

Taurus: (April 20–May 20)
The Spam Museum will seem a lot less fun and kitschy when you are put on permanent display.

Gemini: (May 21–June 21)
Though it's true that you live a life of quiet desperation, with the right shabby clothes and scruffy beard, it could get you all the chicks.

Cancer: (June 22–July 22)
There will be no monuments or memorials to mark your tragic and violent death during next week's bloody revolution in floor coverings.

Leo: (July 23–Aug. 22)
Religious turmoil looms large in your future, as a vengeful God once again refuses to bless that mess.

Virgo: (Aug. 23–Sept. 22)
You will finally acknowledge that being known as "America's Best-Kept Secret In Horribly Deformed Freaks" is kind of a mixed blessing.

Libra: (Sept. 23–Oct. 23)
This week's mishap won't set your zookeeping career back much. Anyone could have mistaken Tyne Daly for a majestic silverback lowland gorilla.

Scorpio: (Oct. 24–Nov. 21)
You don't want anything to come between you and your cats. Luckily, given your obesity and the tininess of your trailer, it's not physically possible.

Sagittarius: (Nov. 22–Dec. 21)
You will be faced with the unenviable task of having to tell somebody that they have lost that loving feeling without breaking into song.

Capricorn: (Dec. 22–Jan. 19)
While it's true that love means different things to different people, you'll be saddened by how many people think it includes shiny objects.

Aquarius: (Jan. 20–Feb. 18)
Newton's laws say that for every action there is an equal and opposite reaction, proving he knew nothing about women.

Pisces: (Feb. 19–March 20)
An unusual series of events will teach you to never underestimate the abilities of a master Ninja or pastry chef.

MILITARY TIME from page 75

amounts of blood. Passersby were amazed by the unusually large amounts of blood. Passersby were amazed by the unusually large amounts of blood. Passersby were amazed by the unusually large amounts of blood. Passersby were amazed by the unusually large amounts of blood. Passersby were amazed by the unusually large amounts of blood. Passersby were amazed by the unusually large amounts of blood. Passersby were amazed by the unusually large amounts of blood. Passersby were amazed by the unusually large amounts of blood. Passersby were amazed by the unusually large amounts of blood. Passersby were amazed by the unusually large amounts of blood. Passersby were amazed by the unusually large amounts of blood. Passersby were amazed by the unusually large amounts of blood. Passersby were amazed by the unusually large amounts of blood. Passersby were amazed by the unusually large amounts of blood. Passersby were amazed by the unusually large amounts of blood. Passersby were amazed by the unusually large amounts of blood. Passersby were

You can take the man out of the Appalachians, but you can't take the Appalachians out of the Appalachian area.

amazed by the unusually large amounts of blood. Passersby were amazed by the unusually large amounts of blood. Passersby were amazed by the unusually large amounts of blood. Passersby were amazed by the unusually large amounts of blood. Passersby were amazed by the unusually large

see MILITARY TIME page 89

NEWS

Report: Al-Qaeda May Be Developing 'Dirty Soldier'

see WORLD page 7A

Power-Plant Employee Sneaks Electricity Home In Lunchbox

see LOCAL page 10B

'Only In New York,' Says Manhattanite Watching Squirrel

see METRO page 4C

STATshot

A look at the numbers that shape your world.

Worst Fan Fiction

1. Hardcastle & McCormick In The Negative Zone
2. Chewbacca Comes To My School And Beats Up On Josh Kolodnek
3. What-If Tales From The Jackass Universe
4. Hogan's Heroes On Gilligan's Island
5. Captain Picard Realizes He's Gay And Can Never Tell Anyone, But It's Not Like He's Evil

THE ONION • $2.00 US • $3.00 CAN

the ONION®

VOLUME 39 ISSUE 07 AMERICA'S FINEST NEWS SOURCE™ 27 FEB.–5 MARCH 2003

Orange Alert Sirens To Blow 24 Hours A Day In Major Cities

WASHINGTON, DC—As an additional reminder that the U.S. is on high alert for terrorist attacks, Secretary of Homeland Security Tom Ridge announced Tuesday that Orange Alert klaxons will blare 24 hours a day in all major cities.

"These 130-decibel sirens, which, beginning Friday, will scream all day and night in the nation's 50 largest metro areas, will serve as a helpful reminder to citizens to stay on the lookout for suspicious activity and be ready for emergency action," Ridge said. "Please note, though, that this is merely a precautionary measure, so go about your lives as normal."

The sirens, Ridge said, will be strategically positioned throughout each city and will be audible within a three-mile radius. The noise will be loud enough to render conversation impossible within a 200-yard range.

"Some may find their normal sleep patterns disrupted, but it's a small price to pay to ensure our collective awareness of the heightened danger," Ridge said. "The key to preventing terrorist attacks is to have the threat constantly on your mind but still remain calm and act normal."

Ridge stressed that the government does not want individuals to let the blaring sirens affect their work or travel plans.

see SIRENS page 83

Above: Pedestrians in Manhattan maintain a high state of alertness thanks to an Orange Alert siren.

Sophomore Senator Eager To Move Out Of Congressional Housing

Above: A glum Allard sits in his Jefferson Hall dorm room.

WASHINGTON, DC—Citing the noise, constant distractions, and lack of privacy, sophomore Sen. Wayne Allard (R-CO) told reporters Monday that he is eager to move out of congressional housing.

"I really need to get out of here," said Allard, sitting in Jefferson Hall's third-floor TV lounge, just down the hall from his room. "I had to get up at 7 a.m. today for a fundraiser breakfast, and at, like, 3 o'clock in the morning, someone started blasting that "In Da Club" song [by rapper 50 Cent]. And this is on a Monday night."

Added Allard: "That kind of shit happens all the time."

The senator said living in Jefferson Hall has been "way less fun" this year because many of his friends from the previous year's class have moved out and gotten their own apartments.

"Ever since [Sen.] Daniel [Akaka (D-HI)] and [Sen.] Mike [DeWine (R-OH)] left, Jefferson Hall hasn't been the same," Allard said. "I go hang out at their place on Wisconsin Avenue all the time, but it's not like being able to just walk down

see SENATOR page 82

Man Has Derogatory Nickname For Every Neighboring Town

VANDALIA, IL—According to friends and acquaintances, local resident Paul Sadecki is a walking repository of derogatory nicknames for towns surrounding Vandalia.

"St. Elmo? More like St. *Smellmo*," said Sadecki, 25, a printing-press operator and part-time delivery driver. "They've got a Hormel plant over in St. Elmo, and the whole town reeks of processed meat. You could also call it St. Hellmo, since there's pretty much nothing to do there besides hang out at the A&W."

Born and raised in Vandalia, Sadecki has been disparaging neighboring towns through the modification of their names since high school. Though his peers abandoned the practice soon after graduation, Sadecki continued, and he is now considered Vandalia's undisputed master of the geographic putdown.

see NICKNAME page 83

Above: Sadecki, who spares no nearby town from his name twists.

The Anti-SUV Movement

Decried as gas-guzzling road hazards, SUVs are also under fire for supporting terrorism by increasing U.S. dependence on Mideast oil. What do *you* think?

"But what if I need my SUV for sporting or utilitating?"

Carl Davis
Roofer

"I'm sorry, but I simply don't buy your argument that SUVs indirectly put my dollars into the hands of al-Qaeda via the Saudis. My Explorer is *so* comfortable!"

Christine Watros
Homemaker

"Yes, the average U.S. automobile has doubled in weight since 1990, but so has the average U.S. citizen."

Amy Benton
Teacher

"I just feel bad for the SUVs, forced to live all cooped up in the city like that."

Franklin Lowe
Systems Analyst

"Yesterday, I flipped off a guy who was driving an SUV. See, I'm doing my part to save the world."

David Orr
Custodian

"My purchase of a Hummer was inspired by our 1991 Gulf War victory. After this war, I'm buying an aircraft carrier."

John Kelleher
Lawyer

Preparing For The Worst

Nervous about the prospect of terrorist attacks, Americans are taking steps to ready themselves. Among the government's recommendations:

- Seal all doors and windows with a good, solid slam
- Keep a disguise kit on hand to prevent being recognized by terrorists
- Report any suspected viable Democratic presidential candidates to nearest Homeland Security office
- Buy several cases of root beer—you haven't had a nice root beer in a while, after all
- Smear lamb's blood on doorpost so terrorists will pass over it
- Wind brightly colored yarn around two cardboard wheels. Cut between the layers of cardboard and tie center with a short piece of yarn. Remove cardboard. You now have a Warm Fuzzy!
- Securely duct-tape shut any books you may own about civil liberties, U.S. Constitution

the ONION®
America's Finest News Source.™

Herman Ulysses Zweibel
Founder

T. Herman Zweibel
Publisher Emeritus
J. Phineas Zweibel
Publisher
Maxwell Prescott Zweibel
Editor-In-Chief

It Takes A Village To Stitch 20,000 Dallas Cowboys Sweatshirts

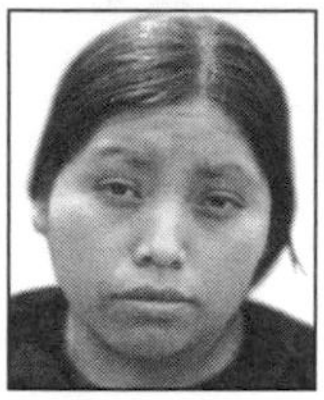

By Maya Tapantí

In this life, we need the help of others to get by. No one person—nor two, nor four, nor even forty—is enough to undertake the task of producing thousands of pieces of officially licensed NFL merchandise. You cannot do it alone. It takes a total team effort. Indeed, here in Guatemala, we have a saying: It takes a village to stitch 20,000 Dallas Cowboys sweatshirts.

Look at this fine, upstanding Russell Athletic-brand sweatshirt. Do you think one person could have brought this item into the world in isolation? Of course not. It takes the contributions of every last member of the community. We all have a job to do, whether it be sewing on the sleeves, silk-screening the silver-and-blue Cowboys star onto the chest, or checking for irregularities.

Sure, it's hard work. But you know what? It's well worth it. That sense of teamwork and collective responsibility shows in each and every sweatshirt. From the durable, double-stitch fabric to the stain-resistant cotton weave, a sweatshirt raised here in Quetzaltenango is well-prepared for whatever the world may throw at it, be it a tackle-football game in the park or a salsa spill on the couch.

Just as the Cowboys offensive line must work together to protect quarterback Chad Hutchinson from opposing pass rushers, we must all work together to protect Quetzaltenango from losing its Russell Athletic factory to a neighboring village. Let's say that someone in our happy enclave of productivity falls ill with malaria and can't meet her quota. It is up to the rest of the villagers to stand together and fill that order so that the contract doesn't go to, say, the people of Totonicapán.

I take pride in the work we are doing. These sweatshirts are going to Cowboys fans who really appreciate well-made, great-looking team gear. These fans will be the first to speak ill of a shoddily made sweatshirt to other prospective buyers. That is why, as a village, we must look after one another to ensure that everyone is pulling his or her weight. We must also make sure that our fellow villagers do not get their fingers sliced off in the material-cutting machine, potentially jamming the works and slowing production with a work-time injury. We are all tied to our village through pride, just as we are tied to the embroidery machines with a comfortable length of rope.

Sweatshirt-rearing, mind you, is not exclusively the job of adults. Children play a vital role in the process, as well. While some of Quetzaltenango's villagers may only be 7 years old, they are not too young to sew in a tag or make sure that there is no rippling or cracking in the screen job. They, like the adults, must look beyond their own needs to help make these tackle-twill sweatshirts the kind we can all be proud of. Without them, fans of America's Team would not have a comfortable and stylish way to show their support for Emmitt and the rest of the boys in blue.

We don't do this for the money, although $15 a month is certainly a generous salary. We also don't do it for the fame, although everyone in southwest Guatemala knows which

> **Let's say that someone in our happy enclave of productivity falls ill with malaria and can't meet her quota. It is up to the rest of the villagers to stand together and fill that order.**

town has the Russell Athletic sweatshop. We do this for the Plano, TX, bank teller who wears one of our preshrunk Dallas Cowboys sweatshirts while watching his team take on the hated Philadelphia Eagles. For the Ft. Worth tax attorney who wears one while cheering on the team from his company's skybox at Texas Stadium. And for all of Dallas, a city that truly bleeds silver and blue.

So you see, the village cannot function without the contributions of each individual. Without each villager, there would be no one to unload hundreds of bolts of cotton fleece to the manufacturing floor. There would be no one to operate the industrial cutting implements to shear off enough fabric to cover an XXXL torso. And there would be no one to sew, emblazon, and pack these sweatshirts so that they may be sent to the hard workers of another village far away—a village called Dallas, Texas, U.S.A.

Yes, our allegiance lies with the greatest fans in the entire world, the fans of the Dallas Cowboys. Unless, of course, that long-rumored Starter jacket factory finally comes to town. I understand they pay 30 cents an hour. Then it's 49ers all the way. Ø

Breakup Hints Misinterpreted As Marriage-Proposal Hints

KNOXVILLE, TN—Amanda Gentry, 25, has misinterpreted longtime boyfriend Wilson Crandall's recent breakup hints—including erratic behavior and strange, cryptic remarks about their future—as marriage-proposal hints.

"I can tell Wilson is getting ready to pop the question," Gentry said. "The

"He's studying for the bar, but when he's done, he wants to sit down with me," Gentry said. "He says he has something important to say and that I should brace myself. Isn't it obvious?"

last few weeks, he's been acting so weird. He keeps saying he needs to 'take stock of his life' and 'face some important decisions he's been putting off.' I hear wedding bells!"

Though Crandall, 26, a University of Tennessee law student, rarely articulates his feelings about the state of the couple's three-year relationship, Gentry said his occasional remarks "speak volumes."

"A couple weeks ago, right after sex, Wilson got really odd and quiet, like he wanted to say something but couldn't get it out," Gentry said. "Finally, he told me, 'I think you're a great girl, and I just want you always to be happy.' Isn't that *so* sweet?"

The post-coital exchange went no further, Gentry said, with Crandall telling her only that he needed to talk to her about their future at some point. Two weeks later, the talk has yet to occur.

"He's studying for the bar, but when he's done, he wants to sit down with me," Gentry said. "He says he has something important to say and that I should brace myself. Isn't it obvious? He's finishing law school this May and thinking about settling down. *Goin' to the cha-pel...*"

Gentry said she hopes Crandall will take her someplace romantic to propose.

"Wilson recently said something about getting away and going somewhere for a week in March," Gentry said. "A few days later, I caught him looking for plane tickets on the Internet. It's weird that he was pricing tickets for around the time of the NCAA Final Four, since I wouldn't think he'd want to miss that. But, obviously, making a commitment to a life partner is so much more important."

Recently, Crandall has been asking Gentry about her career goals, a line of questioning she misread as a sign that he is mapping out their life together.

Above: The excited Gentry and her boyfriend Crandall, who is not about to propose.

"He never asked me about social work before, but he's really been encouraging me to invest more of myself into my job," Gentry said. "He thinks fulfillment at work should be a bigger component of my life. Don't worry, Wilson, I have no plans to give up my career to have babies. Yet."

Gentry said Crandall even let slip that he was thinking about moving away from Knoxville after graduating.

"Wilson's been dropping little hints that he might try to get a job back in Chicago, where his parents and sister are," Gentry said. "He's definitely the type of guy who'd want to be close to his family if he was thinking about the long term."

Crandall has not explicitly invited Gentry to accompany him in the event of a move—an omission Gentry attributes to his fears that she may not want to go.

see PROPOSAL page 82

NEWS IN BRIEF

Iraqi Homeowner To Wait A While Before Re-Shingling Roof

BAGHDAD—Homeowner Aftab Shamoun, 34, announced Monday that he will likely wait "just a little while" before moving ahead with plans to re-shingle the roof of his Baghdad home. "Now may not be the best time to put on those nice new ceramic shingles," said Shamoun, whose roof was damaged in a wind storm last November. "Heck, I've been putting it off for so long, a few more months won't hurt." Despite putting the shingling project on the back burner, Shamoun said he plans to spend next weekend insulating his front windows with energy-efficient plywood boards.

NBC Cancels *CSI*

BURBANK, CA—Seeking to bolster its Thursday-night Nielsen numbers, NBC announced Monday that it is cancelling the highly rated CBS drama *CSI: Crime Scene Investigation*. "*CSI* was a quality show that, unfortunately, always quite lived up to expectations," said Jeff Zucker, NBC president of entertainment. "We tried to give it plenty of time to lose an audience, but in the end, it just was working." Other shows NBC may cancel include Fox's *American Idol*, ABC's *Alias*, and CBS's *Everybody Loves Raymond*.

New Bailiff Tired Of Hearing How Old Bailiff Did Things

FLAGSTAFF, AZ—Deputy Benjamin H. Weaver, court bailiff of the Flagstaff Municipal Courthouse, has grown weary of the constant comparisons to recently retired bailiff Leo Cessna. "I don't care if Deputy Leo always let you use the bathroom during opening arguments—I'm not Leo," the 34-year-old Weaver told jurors Tuesday. "I'm not Leo, I've never been Leo, and I can never *be* Leo, okay?" After the session, court stenographer Judy Rayburn tried to comfort Weaver, telling the shaken bailiff that it took years for the judges to accept her way of using semicolons.

God Quietly Phasing Holy Ghost Out Of Trinity

HEAVEN—Calling the Holy Trinity "overstaffed and over budget," God announced plans Monday to downsize the group by slowly phasing out the Holy Ghost. "Given the poor economic climate and the unclear nature of the Holy Ghost's duties, I felt this was a sensible and necessary decision," God said. "The Holy Ghost will be given fewer and fewer responsibilities until His formal resignation from Trinity duty following Easter services on April 20. Thereafter, the Father and the Son shall be referred to as the Holy Duo."

Corey Flintoff Unleashes Sonorous, Pleasantly Modulated String Of Obscenities

CHEVERLY, MD—Upon injuring a toe Sunday, Corey Flintoff, newscaster for NPR's *All Things Considered*, unleashed a string of rich, pleasantly modulated obscenities. "God fucking dammit," Flintoff warmly intoned after dropping a heavy-duty router on his foot while working in his garage. "Stupid fucking cocksucking son of a bitch." Added Flintoff in a lush baritone: "Goddamn motherfucking shit-for-brains. This is NPR." Next-door neighbor Cheryl Thomas, who overheard the tirade, said Flintoff's delivery was so melodic, she was unaware that he was swearing. Ø

SENATOR from page 79

the hall."

Allard remembers fondly the good times he shared with DeWine and Akaka.

"I don't know how many times me, Mike, and Daniel would break into the dining hall when it was closed," Allard said. "I remember this one time at, like, 1:30 in the morning, we were all starving, so we snuck in through this side door and just went nuts with the cereal dispensers. Mike ate this huge bowl of Cap'n Crunch, Cocoa Pebbles, Trix, and Boo Berry all mixed together. It was so friggin' gross, we were laughing our asses off. Stuff like that doesn't happen anymore."

Making matters worse for Allard is the fact that one of his closest friends, freshman Sen. Lincoln Chafee (R-RI), was supposed to move into Jefferson Hall, but was instead forced to live in Hamilton Hall.

"I told him to get his paperwork in early, because Jefferson fills up fast," Allard said. "Now, he's way over on the other side of the Hill. He's always complaining that he has no friends there because Hamilton is so cliquey. Too bad, because this term wouldn't suck so bad if he was living in Jefferson."

"At least it's not as bad as [Sen.] Jon [Corzine (D-NJ)]," Allard continued. "He got stuck at one of the House halls. Those guys are such tools."

"At least it's not as bad as [Sen.] Jon [Corzine (D-NJ)]," Allard continued. "He got stuck at one of the House halls. Those guys are such tools."

Allard cited his increased maturity and a need to "get serious" about his legislative duties as factors in his unhappiness.

"The best and worst thing about Jefferson is that there's always something going on," Allard said. "When you need to work on a bill or practice a speech, there are no quiet places to do it. I go to the study lounge, because that's what it's for, but there's usually people talking in there. For a while, I tried working in my room, but there'd always be a bunch of people sitting in the hallway right outside my door debating term limits or playing euchre or whatever."

Added Allard: "If I need quiet, I can always go to the Library of Congress, but that's, like, a 20-minute walk."

Despite longing for a more studious atmosphere, Allard nevertheless laments the loss of the high-spirited camaraderie that typified his freshman term.

Above: Allard and Sen. Tim Hutchinson (R-AR) hang out in the dorm hallway late one night last fall.

"When I moved here in 1996, we had some really crazy guys," Allard said. "Every Friday night, when our R.A. would be out at his girlfriend's place, we'd hold these huge, floor-wide progressives. I lived with Mike, and our room would always be the Sex On The Beach room. You don't even want to know some of the shit that went down. These new guys, they're just not like that. I wouldn't want to party with them even if I was still into that whole scene."

These days, Allard said, his room serves as little more than a "crash pad."

"I've been hella busy this year," Allard said. "Most of my day is spent at the Capitol. I'm on three different subcommittees and another group pushing for HR-1539. Plus, I play in an intramural flag-football league twice a week. By the time I get back to Jefferson most nights, I'm wiped."

These days, Allard said, his room serves as little more than a "crash pad."

Allard is critical of the rule requiring legislators to stay in congressional housing for their first two terms.

"I can see why it's smart to make us stay in C.H. the first term," Allard said. "It really helps you acclimate to Washington and build strong bonds. But 12 years is a little much. Look at England. They only make their legislators stay in the dorms one term, and the second term is encouraged but optional. That makes way more sense."

When his current term is up in 2008, Allard said he plans to get an apartment with DeWine and Akaka.

"Daniel has a foosball table, and we've been talking about getting a pinball machine, too," Allard said. "Provided I get re-elected, those next six years are gonna be sweet."

JUPITER RISING from page 80

amounts of blood. Passersby were amazed by the unusually large amounts of blood. Passersby were amazed by the unusually large amounts of blood. Passersby were amazed by the unusually large amounts of blood. Passersby were amazed by the unusually large amounts of blood. Passersby were amazed by the unusually large amounts of blood. Passersby were amazed by the unusually large amounts of blood. Passersby were amazed by the unusually large amounts of blood. Passersby were amazed by the unusually large amounts of blood. Passersby were amazed by the unusually large amounts of blood. Passersby were amazed by the unusually large amounts of blood. Passersby were amazed by the unusually large amounts of blood. Passersby were amazed by the unusually large amounts of blood. Passersby were amazed by the unusually large amounts of blood. Passersby were amazed by the unusually large amounts of blood. Passersby were amazed by the unusually large amounts of blood. Passersby were amazed by the unusually large amounts of blood. Passersby were amazed by the unusually large amounts of blood. Passersby were amazed by the unusually large amounts of blood. Passersby were amazed by the unusually large amounts of blood. Passersby were amazed by the unusually large

If you didn't want attention, you shouldn't have worn those breasts.

see JUPITER RISING page 91

PROPOSAL from page 81

"Whenever we talk about Chicago, he goes on and on about how I'd hate the cold weather and the fast pace," Gentry said. "He's such a doll to be concerned about my feelings, but doesn't he know I'd follow him anywhere?"

Gentry has also misinterpreted Crandall's recent frugality as an effort to save money for the future.

"It's so cute how he's trying to cut back on expenses," Gentry said. "We never go out to dinner anymore, or the movies, or even the bars. He must be working on one doozy of a rock."

"Wilson's birthday is coming up soon, March 4," Gentry continued. "Maybe he's planning to pop the question then. I can just see him getting down on one knee and saying that I'm what he wants most for his birthday."

Added Gentry: "God, the next few weeks are going to be unforgettable."

NICKNAME from page 79

"He's constantly taking shots at Brownstown and all these other places," said friend Gregg Henke, 25. "I used to do it with him back in shop class, but for some reason, he's stuck with it."

"I just call them like I see them," Sadecki said. "I'm not afraid to stand up and call a spade a spade—or Litchfield 'Bitchfield.'"

Added Sadecki: "If you ever met a chick from Litchfield, you'd know exactly what I mean."

From Greenville to Mulberry Grove, no municipality is safe from Sadecki's devastating name alterations.

"Just up the road from here is Hagarstown, which I like to call Hagar The Horrible Town. That place is a pit. You could also accurately describe it as Fagarstown, since the guys there are all fags. Back in high school, we used to play them every year in football, and we'd always kick their asses."

Some Sadecki nicknames play off a particular town's geography, such as his "Land O' Lake Trash" moniker for Keyesport, which is located on the western bank of the polluted Carlyle Lake. A majority of the nicknames, however, are produced via a simple pun-based, Wacky Packages-style

"I just call them like I see them," Sadecki said.

modification of the town name. Examples include Heaver Creek (Beaver Creek), Show Yer Boner (Shobonier), and Bunghole (Bingham). An estimated 40 percent call into question the heterosexuality of the town's inhabitants.

Despite Sadecki's proficiency at civic slams, some towns' ideal nicknames continue to elude him.

"Van Burensburg seems like it'd be easy, but it's not," Sadecki said. "I used to call it Van Turdburglar, 'cause they got a lot of homos there, too, but that kind of felt like a stretch. You could do Van Halensburg, but that'd be a compliment, like the town really rocks or something. I think there was a president called Van Buren, but I don't know anything about him. So it's tough."

Though many people assume Sadecki's nicknaming habit is motivated by a deep disdain for any town other than Vandalia, those close to him dismiss the notion.

"Paul has friends in all those towns," said friend and former roommate Wayne Kessler, 26. "He just bought a car from this buddy of his up in Brownstown. He loves the car, even though he keeps referring to it as his car from Brownstain, or his 'shitheap from Shittown.' It's not like he truly believes the girls in Litchfield are bitches; last year, he had a girlfriend from Bitchfield. I mean Litchfield. Shit, now he's got me doing it." Ø

SIRENS from page 79

"Go about your usual business," Ridge said. "Of course, while you do so, keep in mind that we are just barely this side of Red Alert, the highest level of danger possible."

Ridge also urged citizens to pay close attention to the sirens' subtle variations.

"The steady 'alert' siren indicates the need to be generally aware of the threat of terrorism," he said. "This is the normal, default siren. The higher-

To make the alert system more responsive to subtle fluctuations in the national terror level, five new colors have been added between orange and red.

pitched 'wail' siren, on the other hand, means federal authorities have credible information regarding a specific possible threat, and that citizens should ready themselves for the 30 to 50 percent likelihood of an attack. If citizens hear an 'alternating wail' siren, a piercing shriek/whine interrupted every 30 seconds by short bursts of what sounds like gunfire, they need to prepare for the 70 percent chance of a 20 percent more serious disaster. And, finally, a 'pulsating steady' alarm means Americans should have plenty of plastic sheeting and duct tape on hand to make a shelter in the almost guaranteed event of chemical, biological, or radiological attack."

Ridge emphasized that all these alarms merely indicate an Orange Alert state and not a 100 percent definite threat. Should the country be raised to Red Alert status, an entirely different set of patterned horn bursts would be put into use, the details of which will be available at www.fema.gov.

To make the alert system more responsive to subtle fluctuations in the national terror level, five new colors have been added between orange and red.

"The newly added levels are Orange-Red Alert, Red-Orange Alert, Maroon Alert, Burnt Sienna Alert, and Ochre Alert," Ridge said. "They indicate, in ascending order of fear: concern, deep dread, severe apprehension, near-crippling fright, and pants-shitting terror. Please make a note of this."

The sirens have already been intro-

A "pulsating steady" alarm means Americans should have plastic sheeting and duct tape on hand.

duced on a test basis in New York, San Francisco, and Atlanta. In spite of some complaints, most residents of the three cities are adjusting well to the warnings.

"The sirens are really loud," San Francisco resident Linda Pearcy said, shouting over a horn posted in her backyard. "My dog won't stop barking, and the windows rattle all day long. And I didn't know about the helicopters dropping all the orange slips of paper. I guess I can't complain, though. These are scary times, and the government is doing what it can to make us feel more secure." Ø

Above: A man urinating at D.C.'s Union Station is reminded to be extra vigilant.

Spreadin' A Little Sunshine

A Room Of Jean's Own
By Jean Teasdale

You know, your old pal Jean likes to think she can take a joke. After all, life is short, and it's important to have a sense of humor about things. But those pranksters who stole the "Think Spring!" display from the balcony of my apartment really and truly crossed the line.

Yes, Jeanketeers, you read right. Sometime last night, some world-class Grinch (or Grinches) managed to climb onto my second-floor balcony and take everything I had so painstakingly set up. They stole every plastic flower, every blade of artificial turf, the stuffed bunnies, a darling painted wooden birdhouse, a deck chair, a lawn sprinkler, and not one, not two, but *three* rainbow-striped wind socks! Gone, too, is the hanging sun I cleverly made by blowing up a balloon, draping it with wet papier-mâché strips, letting it dry, and then popping it. I poured my soul into that sun! Now that and everything else is gone.

I'm not really upset about the monetary loss, even though I paid full price for the birdhouse and little birdbath with the resin frog family sitting in it. It's the sheer mean-spiritedness of it that gets me. I spent hours in the freezing cold strapping everything down, wiring the flowers to the turf so the wind wouldn't blow it all away. I even covered it with a tarp each night so the snow wouldn't fall on it. This *had* to be a premeditated crime. (Sorry to use such harsh words in what is normally a source of lighthearted entertainment, Jeanketeers, but this is serious business!)

It's been a long, tough winter, especially in my neck of the woods, and I thought it would put a smile on the faces of neighbors and passersby alike if I reminded them that spring was just around the corner. Yes, I thought I could spread a little sunshine... literally! I even made myself part of the act, braving the icy chill in my Hawaiian-style floral smock and sun-hat (with longjohns underneath, naturally!) and waving to passing pedestrians and motorists! I actually got a couple of people to honk or wave back. (And I'm not even counting the guy who wanted me to show my nay-nays!)

Dressing up the porch was the cutest creative idea I've had in ages. It was even better than when I made those duck-headed Easter baskets out of bleach bottles and pom-pom balls for my brother Kevin's children back in '99. I later heard from my mother that he threw them away because there were bleach fumes. But if you ask me, I'd say Kevin, a born-again Christian, *really* got rid of them because he thought they were idolatrous!

As fun as it was for me, there was a deeper personal reason why I put up this display. You see, growing up, I never had a lawn. For most of my childhood, we lived in a three-bedroom house, but shortly after we moved in, my parents had the entire yard paved. Not with patio-type flagstones, but with cement. My father didn't want ants and termites, and he

I'm not saying what happened to me was necessarily terrorism, but in my book, people who commit cold-hearted acts like stealing perfectly innocent "Danger: Chipmunk Crossing" signs are as anti-American as they come.

thought having grass would increase the odds of them entering the home. He also stripped the ivy from the house and chopped down the oak trees, including one with a treehouse built for the previous residents' kids.

It wasn't really much fun to play in a paved yard, and the neighbor kids made fun of me about it, so I spent a lot of time indoors. But, you know, it wasn't that bad. That's when I discovered my love of writing and began a lifelong love affair with daytime-TV programming. (At the risk of showing my age, let's just say I was probably Dinah Shore's youngest fan!)

I still don't have a yard to call my own: Hubby Rick and I only have a small second-floor apartment, so that balcony is the sole outdoor exposure we have. It was kind of a disappointment at first, but then I thought, why not take the lemons life has dealt me and make lemonade? Isn't that the definition of being a good sport?

And while we're talking definitions, perhaps the five-star fink who took my display would like to brush up on the definition of good citizenship. There might be a big war soon, and we on the homefront need to be as kind and helpful to each other as possible. I'm not saying what happened to me was necessarily terrorism, but in my book, people who commit cold-hearted acts like stealing perfectly innocent "Danger: Chipmunk Crossing" signs are as anti-American as they come.

Ever since the crime, I've been wondering: What if someone had broken all the way into the apartment, intending to steal more than just what

I'm not really upset about the monetary loss, even though I paid full price for the birdhouse and little birdbath with the resin frog family sitting in it.

was on my porch? I recall hubby Rick stumbling in shortly after 3 a.m. last night, later than usual because he had today off. The theft must have occurred after that; otherwise Rick, as pickled as he was, would've at least noticed the display missing. I like to think of myself as a feminist, but sometimes I wish Rick would act more gallant and defend my stuff. He wasn't around last Halloween when someone smashed the six jack-o'-lanterns I carved to spell "BE SAFE." And, once again, he was nowhere to be seen when I found the missing Baby New Year 2003—a doll I had specially dressed and mounted to our front door—shoved in the trash behind our building with its legs sticking in the air.

Old Jean may be down, but she's not out. I'm offering a reward, no questions asked, for information leading to the safe return of my display. A pan of my world-renowned Cocoa Almond Caramel Coffee Toffee Fudge Bars With Melted Peppermint Patty & Butter Creme Icing awaits the Honest John brave enough to track down the culprit. Any takers?

Beginning March 1, the Teasdale balcony will be magically transformed into the Emerald Isle. And it will stay that way right through St. Patty's Day, even if I have to dress up hubby Rick in a leprechaun outfit and put him on 24-hour guard! Ø

Your Horoscope

By Lloyd Schumner Sr.
Retired Machinist and
A.A.P.B.-Certified Astrologer

Aries: (March 21–April 19)
You have thoroughly wasted your potential over the past five years—years you could have spent deep-frying professionally.

Taurus: (April 20–May 20)
A fast-talking huckster sells you the Brooklyn Bridge for $93.8 million, but it turns out it's all perfectly legal.

Gemini: (May 21–June 21)
The ladies won't be able to keep their hands off you this week, thanks to a sharp new look consisting of tailored suits made from bubble wrap.

Cancer: (June 22–July 22)
You will experience a surge in popularity when talk-show host Wayne Brady publicly declares you his personal nemesis.

Leo: (July 23–Aug. 22)
You will finally grow mature enough to accept your own mortality, just moments before the freak elephant stampede.

Virgo: (Aug. 23–Sept. 22)
The community's response to your drunken riding-mower accident will start a hilarious national trend in roadside memorial art.

Libra: (Sept. 23–Oct. 23)
That run for the record books once again falls short when you start Boston's all-time second-largest fire.

Scorpio: (Oct. 24–Nov. 21)
You will be mentioned several times in Jack Palance's explanation of why he no longer does one-handed push-ups in public.

Sagittarius: (Nov. 22–Dec. 21)
You are renowned for your kind and loving nature, thanks mainly to a crack PR team.

Capricorn: (Dec. 22–Jan. 19)
The increased precipitation in your area continues, thanks largely to that little black storm cloud that follows you everywhere.

Aquarius: (Jan. 20–Feb. 18)
It's been quite a while since the stars mentioned the nurses chained up in your basement, but don't worry: They haven't forgotten they're down there.

Pisces: (Feb. 19–March 20)
The dying celebrity-boxing fad is revitalized when Ellen Cleghorne announces she's ready and willing to go 12 rounds with you.

NEWS

Kuwait Deploys Troop

see WORLD page 2A

Fox News Reporter Asks The Questions Others Are Too Smart To Ask

see MEDIA page 10E

Halfway-House Resident Gets To Second

see LOCAL page 6D

Gay Man Comes Out To Cat

see LOCAL page 14D

STATshot

A look at the numbers that shape your world.

What Are We Microwaving Just To See What Happens?
1. Plate of Peeps
2. Work uniform
3. Video camera set to "record"
4. WWE's "Tough-Talkin' Voice-Action" The Rock
5. Smaller microwave
6. Stouffer's frozen meatloaf dinner

the ONION®

VOLUME 39 ISSUE 08 AMERICA'S FINEST NEWS SOURCE™ 6–12 MARCH 2003

White History Year Resumes

WASHINGTON, DC—With Black History Month over, U.S. citizens are putting aside thoughts of Harriet Tubman and George Washington Carver to resume the traditional observation of White History Year.

White History Year, which runs annually from Jan. 1 through Dec. 31, with a 28-day break for Black History Month in February, is dedicated to the recognition of European-Americans' contributions to American politics and culture.

"Frederick Douglass and Martin Luther King Jr. are all well and good," Senate Majority Leader Bill Frist said at a banquet celebrating the arrival of White History Year, "but now is the time to reflect on the accomplishments of such whites as Babe Ruth, Alexander Graham Bell, and Presidents Washington through Bush. Let's use these next 11 months to remember the *other* American history."

"Whites have contributed so much to this country,"

see WHITE page 88

Above: A stamp honoring European-American aviation pioneer Charles Lindbergh is unveiled as part of White History Year celebrations.

Bush Offers Taxpayers Another $300 If We Go To War

Above: Bush entices war opponents with a $300 tax rebate.

WASHINGTON, DC—Amid growing anti-war protests and polls indicating eroding public support for an invasion of Iraq, President Bush is offering U.S. taxpayers a rebate in the amount of $300 if we go to war.

"My proposed tax rebate will serve to stimulate the economy," Bush said, waving a sample check made out to John Q. Public at a White House press conference Monday. "Americans will get a generous infusion of cash that can be used however they choose—all in return for simply supporting a first strike against Iraq. Now, who wouldn't want an extra $300 in their pocket next month?"

Under the Bush plan, single taxpayers would be eligible for a $300 rebate, married filers $600, and heads of household $500. Attached to the proposal is a rider, penned by Bush himself, stating, "Plus, we also will invade Iraq right away, everyone promises."

Pending passage of the bill, titled *Economic Growth And Tax Relief Reconciliation Act Of 2003 And We Bomb Iraq* (H.R. 1936), some 91.3 million checks could be mailed as early as March 31.

"The plan is almost identical to the tax rebate offered in 2001," Bush said. "With the minor exception, of

see BUSH page 89

Alaska-Yukon Moose Dimly Aware Of Drew Barrymore's Career Path

YUKON TERRITORY—In an impressive display of the star's reach, a team of University of Calgary zoologists announced Monday the discovery of an Alaska-Yukon moose with a "faint but definite" awareness of the career arc of Drew Barrymore.

"This moose is a magnificent specimen," said Dr. Joseph Hardenbrook, who came across the animal in the remote North Yukon while conducting field research on the migratory patterns of the species. "It is remarkable for the enormous antlers it sheds every year, its ability to subsist on twigs and aquatic plants, and its faint cognizance of Barrymore's short-lived marriage to Canadian comic Tom Green."

According to Hardenbrook, the 1,100-pound moose, a member of the family *Cervidae*, species *Alces alces*,

see MOOSE page 88

Above: The Barrymore-cognizant moose searches for food on the tundra.

The Great White Tragedy

Some are calling for criminal charges to be filed against the band Great White for its role in the deadly Feb. 20 pyrotechnics fire in Rhode Island. What do *you* think?

Jim Clemons
Financial Analyst

"What happened in that Rhode Island club is shocking. To think that over a hundred people would attend a Great White concert..."

Cynthia Kelleher
Therapist

"Without pyrotechnics, '80s metal bands will have no way to keep audiences from noticing how shitty their music is."

Theresa King
Homemaker

"As a concerned parent, I think it's high time somebody started speaking out against this dangerous shark-themed rock."

Phil Orland
Mechanic

"I only feel safe inside a rock club when Lemmy is playing."

Bill Barton
Truck Driver

"The saddest part of all is, they never even got to hear 'Once Bitten, Twice Shy.'"

Daniel Haley
Systems Analyst

"How many more people have to die before no one ever dies again?"

Hollywood Vs. The War

From Sean Penn to Sheryl Crow, celebrities have been prominent in the anti-war movement. How have stars registered their opposition?

- *Susan Sarandon*—Personally visited every pro-war American and tried to dissuade them in that condescending, Earth-mother way of hers
- *Goldie Hawn*—Shipped much-needed supplies of Botox to sanctions-ravaged Iraqi people
- *Ozzy Osbourne*—Held candlelight head-loll for peace
- *Tom Cruise*—Had self photographed smiling slightly less wide than usual
- *Nia Vardalos*—Led irrepressibly nutty relatives in My Big Fat Greek Protest
- *Eminem*—Blamed Iraq standoff on mother, called for her rape and beheading
- *Woody Harrelson*—Tried to somehow connect President Bush's war motives to hemp
- *Catherine Zeta-Jones*—Spouted off to reporters some anti-war stuff she heard from Michael Douglas

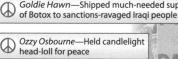

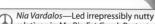

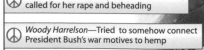

the ONION®
America's Finest News Source.™

Herman Ulysses Zweibel
Founder

T. Herman Zweibel
Publisher Emeritus
J. Phineas Zweibel
Publisher
Maxwell Prescott Zweibel
Editor-In-Chief

Would You Care To Join Me For An Unbelievably Awkward Dinner Sometime?

By Mike Toomey

Hey, Julie, it's Mike Toomey. You remember me, right? We met at Kevin's party last weekend. That was some party, wasn't it? I had a really great time. And it was definitely cool talking to you. Anyway, I know this may seem a little out of the blue, but I was wondering if maybe you'd be interested in joining me for an unbelievably awkward dinner sometime.

If you're game, I could call you this week to make arrangements. I'll spend a few minutes nervously rehashing this conversation before suggesting a not-very-good restaurant. Then I'll establish our lack of chemistry with several minutes of conversation-extending small talk that feels forced and strangely businesslike.

Your fears about me will be confirmed when I arrive for our date. Even though we'll decide in our brief, halting phone conversation to keep things casual, I'll show up with a dozen long-stem roses and be oddly overdressed. I'll comment on your outfit, calling it "slimming" or "flattering" or some other compliment that comes off like an insult. How does that sound for an inauspicious start to the evening?

If you're game, I could call you this week to make arrangements. I'll spend a few minutes nervously rehashing this conversation before suggesting a not-very-good restaurant. Then I'll establish our lack of chemistry with several minutes of conversation-extending small talk that feels forced and strangely businesslike.

We'll then embark on the interminable ride to the restaurant. Trying to break up the long, painful stretches of silence, I'll ask you a series of forced questions, such as what you look for in a guy and how long your longest relationship was. Fearful that you find me boring, I'll try to spice things up by asking you to name the craziest place you've ever done it. And I will actually refer to sex as "doing it," which will turn you off immeasurably.

Even though we'll decide in our brief, halting phone conversation to keep things casual, I'll show up with a dozen long-stem roses and be oddly overdressed.

At the restaurant, the discomfort will deepen. Our only relief will come from the all-too-infrequent interruptions by our waiter delivering more breadsticks. When the house fiddler comes to our table, I will make the ill-advised decision to slip him $5 to play "Moon River," thinking it might somehow create instant romance. While he plays, you'll stare down at your plate and fidget with your silverware until the song is done, trying to avoid any eye contact with me, lest I think my clumsy attempt to woo you has been a success.

As the evening progresses, the conversation will become more and more stilted. I will talk about TV shows and movies in which you have no interest. We will desperately cling to Kevin as a topic of conversation, since he is our only mutual friend. All the while, we will both be painfully aware that we are using Kevin as a conversational life raft.

After deciding to skip dessert, I will drive you home. After pulling into your driveway, I will turn off the engine and say, "Well, I had a nice time." For an agonizingly long moment, I will just sit there as you tremble in fear that I am summoning the courage to go for a goodnight kiss rather than a hug. I will kiss you on your cheek, but close enough to your mouth that you will turn your head to ensure that there is no contact between our mouths. I will then say, "Well, maybe we can do this again." You will reply "Maybe," trying as politely as possible to make it clear that you have no interest in ever seeing me again.

So, are you free Saturday? I know this great Italian place, not too expensive. Ø

LAW ENFORCEMENT

Undercover Cop Never Knew Selling Drugs Was Such Hard Work

PHILADELPHIA—Rick Bastone, 31, an officer with Philadelphia's 23rd Precinct, has gained newfound respect for America's hard-working drug dealers ever since going undercover to sell narcotics.

"I had no idea how tough this was," said Bastone, standing on a dilapidated corner in 20-degree weather

> **"You're hustling on the streets all day, then going to parties at night," Bastone said. "And it's not like you can enjoy yourself at these parties."**

while awaiting a cocaine drop-off Monday. "I guess I imagined it being like in the movies: drinking champagne, hot-tubbing with honeys, and cruising in customized Escalades while watching the cash roll in. But here I am, freezing my ass off. I've got to say, these drug-dealing scumbags really earn their pay."

Assigned to the PPD's undercover narcotics division on Feb. 22, Bastone said he expected his life as a drug dealer to be glamorous and hedonistic. His preconceptions were shattered after just a few days of grueling, firsthand experience.

"I thought being a cop was hard, but it's not half as hard as being a pusher," Bastone said. "You're hustling on the streets all day, then going to parties at night to build up clientele. And it's not like you can enjoy yourself at these parties. When you're there, you're networking and sizing up competitors and setting up deals. There's hardly a second to breathe, much less get your swerve on."

Above: The worn-out Bastone.

Unlike law enforcement, Bastone said, drug-dealing is a 24-hour, seven-day-a-week job.

"My best customer knocks on my door at all hours whenever he's in need of a heroin fix," Bastone said. "I'd love to tell him to get lost, but he'd probably just go to someone else's corner and take his contacts with him. Then there's the constant pressure to sell: I've got to keep upping my purchases from my distributor, or else they'll give my corner to someone else. Christ, I need a vacation."

Dealing drugs, Bastone said, also demands a tremendous amount of knowledge and expertise.

"First, I had to have the metric system down cold," Bastone said. "Then, I spent almost two weeks learning the weight of a gram of coke by feel. Plus, you have to always stay on top of the current street lingo, which is constantly changing—and not just the drug slang, but slang for everything from currency to getting a drink. Cops don't have to know any of that."

Contributing to Bastone's stress level is his growing mistrust of Gary "Muffinhead" Yarbo, a small-time, oft-incarcerated dealer used by the PPD as a means to help undercover officers enter the drug scene.

"I've always got to keep one eye on what I'm doing and one eye on Muffinhead," Bastone said. "I know he won't rat me out on purpose, but he's not the brightest guy. Just one slip-up, and I've either ruined months of backbreaking work on the street or I'm a dead man. Man, all this, and you don't even get health insurance."

Heidi Bastone, the officer's wife, has noticed the change in her husband's view toward those on the other side of the drug war.

"Rick always used to talk about 'the lazy drug dealers,'" Heidi said. "Not anymore. He's always talking about how amazed he is that guys like [local cocaine kingpin] Dean 'Powder' Edwards have been doing this for 20 years. I really don't think Rick can last another six months, so hopefully he'll have a solid case built by then. I sure hope so. I don't think I can stand much more of his bitching about how he spent all day hauling around kilos of uncut Colombian." ⌀

NEWS IN BRIEF

After 10 Months Of Bitter Struggle, Downstairs Neighbor Masters 'Jumpin' Jack Flash'

GAINESVILLE, FL—After 10 months of bitter, around-the-clock struggle, pizza-delivery driver and aspiring guitarist Darren Lowell, 23, has finally mastered The Rolling Stones' "Jumpin' Jack Flash," his upstairs neighbor reported Tuesday. "I'm glad he finally nailed it," neighbor Jeremy Quinlan said. "From what I could hear through my living-room floor these past 10 months, he was really locked in an epic battle with that elusive 'dunh-dunh, da-da-da da-da-da da-da-da' riff. It was truly like Ahab and the whale." Next week, Lowell is slated to embark on his next ambitious project, Van Halen's "Eruption," which is scheduled for completion in the spring of 2004.

Rich First-Grader Buys Whole Sheet Of Gold Stars

BREMERTON, WA—Lakeside Elementary first-grader Max Carr, son of Boeing CEO Robert Carr, used a small portion of his $100 weekly allowance Monday to buy himself a sheet of the gold stars used to reward academic achievement. "I don't get why all the kids work so hard to get good grades just for a sticker," Carr said. "I only got a C-minus on my phonics homework, but Mommy took me to the mall, and now I have 10 gold stars—more than anybody in the whole class." Carr said his "dumb classmates have no idea" that students can simply purchase a sheet of "Great Job!" Mickey Mouse stickers at a store.

Movie Marketed As Six Different Genres

NEW YORK—*Confessions Of A Dangerous Mind*, the Miramax film based on the memoirs of *Gong Show* creator Chuck Barris, is being marketed as six different genres, sources reported Tuesday. "So far, I've seen TV ads making it look like a romantic comedy, a spy thriller, a Hollywood satire, a straightforward biopic, and a strange, *Being John Malkovich*-esque mind-bender," said Daniel Taubman, 24, of Chapel Hill, NC. "I heard there's also one that makes it look like a chick flick, playing up the whole Drew Barrymore/Julia Roberts angle, but I haven't seen it. It probably runs on Lifetime or Oxygen or something."

U.S. Capitol Cleaning Turns Up Long-Lost Constitution

WASHINGTON, DC—Lost for nearly two years, the U.S. Constitution was found Tuesday behind a couch in the Governor's Reception Room. "Wow, I forgot all about that thing," said U.S. Sen. Chris Dodd (D-CT), who found the historic document while vacuuming. "Nobody knew what happened to it. Guess it must've fallen back there during a meeting." After making the find, Dodd spent several minutes rereading some of his favorite old amendments.

Moral Tacked Onto End Of Man's Life

NORTH PLATTE, NE—Immediately following his death Tuesday, a moral was hastily tacked onto the life of North Platte resident Roy Brooks. "As Roy's life plainly illustrated, you'll catch more flies with honey than with vinegar," Rev. Paul Winters said, speaking from Brooks' death bed at St. Augustus Memorial Hospital. "If there's anything this man taught us, it is surely that." Responding to the statement, Brooks' loved ones agreed that they had learned a valuable lesson. ⌀

MOOSE from page 85

exhibited a basic level of familiarity with the dramatic ups and downs of Barrymore's professional and personal life. While, for example, it did not know about her infamous on-air flashing of David Letterman, it knew about her nude *Playboy* spread.

The moose, Hardenbrook said, also seems to be aware of Barrymore's red-hot romance with Strokes drummer Fabrizio Moretti.

"I was talking to [fellow scientist] Paula [Angell] about the rumors that Drew is getting engaged to that Strokes guy, when the moose started turning its head," Hardenbrook said. "At first, I assumed that the head-turning was part of an effort to detect the scent of wolves and other potential predators, but subsequent tests revealed that the moose knew about the Barrymore-Moretti relationship and, presumably, wanted to join in the conversation."

Study co-chair Andrew Sheehan said the moose knew that Barrymore starred in *E.T.* at 7, and that she began abusing drugs and alcohol soon after.

Study co-chair Andrew Sheehan said the moose knew that Barrymore starred in *E.T.* at 7, and that she began abusing drugs and alcohol soon after. It did not, however, know the specifics of her substance abuse, including the fact that she had her first drink at age 9, and first tried marijuana at 10 and cocaine at 12. While it vaguely recalled that Barrymore had written an autobiography at age 14, it could not remember the book's title, *Little Girl Lost*.

"There definitely were things this moose didn't know," Sheehan said. "It had no idea that Steven Spielberg is her godfather and had forgotten that, after years out of the spotlight, she made her return to public consciousness in 1992's *Poison Ivy*. It could, however, name five of her movies: *E.T.*, *The Wedding Singer*, *Scream*, *Poison Ivy*, and *Charlie's Angels*. Not too shabby for an animal that lives 250 miles from the nearest town."

Sheehan called the moose's familiarity with Barrymore "impressive, but not a total aberration."

"Although this level of celebrity awareness is unusual, it is certainly not without precedent in the animal kingdom," Sheehan said. "There have been documented cases of lower invertebrates that were aware of Celine Dion's moving struggle to get pregnant, as well as Komodo dragons that knew about George Clooney's long, hard road to the top of the acting heap."

The scientists hope to continue studying the moose.

"Assuming we get funding, we'd like to gather long-term, longitudinal data, ideally over the course of the next five to ten years," Hardenbrook said. "We think we can learn a great deal from this beast about the dissemination of celebrity news among non-primates. What we learn could revolutionize the fields of zoology and infotainment science."

At last sighting, the moose was foraging for food in the harsh winter landscape while gearing up for Barrymore's upcoming blockbuster sequel, *Charlie's Angels: Full Throttle*.

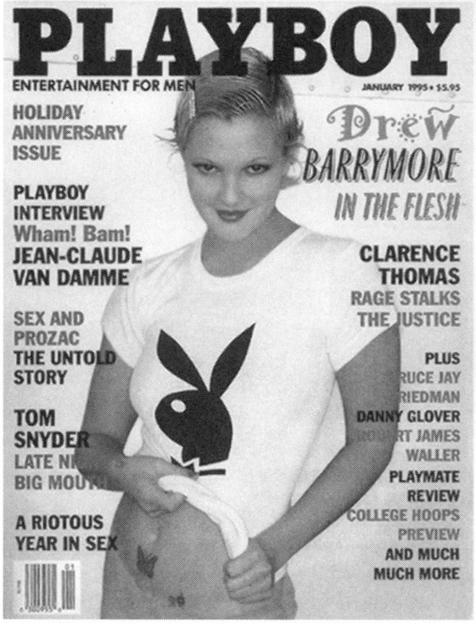

Above: Some of the Barrymore career highlights of which the moose is aware.

WHITE from page 85

Frist continued. "Did you, for example, know that a white man, Jonas Salk, discovered the cure for polio? It's true."

From now until Feb. 1, 2004, educators will eschew discussions of Rosa Parks in favor of Andrew Carnegie, Neil Armstrong, and Tim Allen. Schools nationwide will shelve African-American history pamphlets in favor of such Caucasiacentric materials as the *Macmillan & Rowe American History Textbook New Revised Standard Edition* and *Encyclopedia Britannica*.

Scholars say there is a remarkable wealth of documented white history to explore.

"There's so much more white history out there than you might imagine," said Dr. James Corman, a Princeton University history professor. "America's publishing houses, newspapers, movie studios, magazines, and radio stations have kept remarkably thorough records of white Americans' accomplishments."

White History Year will also be commemorated on television, with various networks airing special programming recognizing whites' contributions to society. The History Channel will set aside the Tuskegee Airmen documentaries that have dominated its schedule throughout February, instead presenting programs on Chuck Yeager, the white man who broke the sound barrier, and Paul Revere, a key white figure in the nation's fight for independence from England. A&E's *Biography* will spotlight such white luminaries as Johnny Unitas,

There is a remarkable wealth of documented white history to explore.

Mae West, and Edward R. Murrow. Between prime-time programs, NBC will air White History Minute segments hosted by white actress Bernadette Peters.

Americans of every color will set aside their differences to celebrate White History Year.

"I think it's good to give people a closer look at a culture they usually don't even think about," said Gary, IN, realtor Willie Anderson, a respected member of the city's black community. "I mean, it's right in front of you every day. It's such a huge part of your life. You're surrounded by it from the day you're born until the day you die, so it's easy to take for granted that you already know just about everything there is to know about it."

Added Anderson: "Do you realize that Henry Ford, a white man, invented the 'assembly line,' a mass-production technique that revolutionized industry around the world? They had something about it on TV again last night."

BUSH from page 85

course, of the provision that Americans react favorably to the deployment of 210,000 troops to the Persian Gulf."

"Which reminds me, have you seen these new iPods?" Bush added, pulling an Apple-brand MP3 player from his pocket and holding it up to the crowd. "It costs $299 for one of these little buggers, but it holds a thousand songs. They're amazing."

Citizens expressed excitement at the prospect of having a little extra spending money.

To ensure public support, the following will appear in fine print below the endorsement line on the back of each check: "By signing and cashing this check, the above is hereby indicating his or her consent to a U.S. invasion of Iraq."

"Things have been pretty tight lately, so this sure would come in handy," said Ray Kilty, 48, an Akron, OH, screen-door-factory worker. "I don't know much about what's going on with Iraq, but I *do* know what's going on with my truck. The brakes are set to go any day now."

Bush has been pushing the rebate, part of his ambitious $1.4 trillion tax-cut agenda, in a series of TV commercials. One such ad, which made its debut last Tuesday during Fox's *American Idol*, features the slogan, "Free Iraq Of Hussein, Free Rent For A Month." Another upcoming spot asks the question, "War: What Is It Good For?" and answers, "$300, Is What."

In recent weeks, Bush has also met with key lawmakers in an effort to win their support.

"I get the green light from the American people, and they get 300 smackeroos," Bush told members of the Senate budget committee last Friday. "Any questions?"

"I'll tell you what," Bush added. "Just because I'm feeling generous, I'll throw in another $20 per dependent if we invade by the end of next week."

To ensure public support, the following will appear in fine print below the endorsement line on the back of each check: "By signing and cashing this check, the above is hereby indicating his or her consent to a U.S. invasion of Iraq, and will refrain from attending protest rallies or committing any other act that could reasonably be construed as an expression of disapproval of said war."

"Americans need two things right now: economic relief and the elimination of the threat of terrorism," Bush said. "These rebates take care of both. I can't think of a better way to show the citizens of this nation that war truly pays."

PUEBLO INCIDENT from page 83

amounts of blood. Passersby were amazed by the unusually large amounts of blood. Passersby were

I'd rather have a frontal lobotomy than have to suffer these debilitating schizophrenia episodes.

amazed by the unusually large amounts of blood. Passersby were amazed by the unusually large amounts of blood. Passersby were amazed by the unusually large amounts of blood. Passersby were amazed by the unusually large amounts of blood. Passersby were amazed by the unusually large amounts of blood. Passersby were amazed by the unusually large amounts of blood. Passersby were amazed by the unusually large amounts of blood. Passersby were amazed by the unusually large amounts of blood. Passersby were amazed by the unusually large amounts of blood. Passersby were amazed by the unusually large amounts of blood. Passersby were amazed by the unusually large amounts of blood. Passersby were amazed by the unusually large

see PUEBLO INCIDENT page 96

the ONION presents a helpful guide to:

Planning A Funeral

Arranging the funeral of a loved one is never easy, but the following tips can help make it somewhat less difficult.

- When planning a funeral, the most important thing you need is a corpse, ideally someone who has been dead only a few days.
- If a funeral home does not have a colonial-style façade with stately Doric columns, it is a bad funeral home.
- Though it may be somewhat unpleasant, the only way to ensure that Grandma likes her casket is to show her the catalog and make her point.
- To help offset costs, have the funeral sponsored by a large company like Coca-Cola or Target.
- Remember: Place the body in the casket *face up*.
- If the deceased happens to be your twin, don't hesitate to capitalize on the many hilarious pranks that are possible.
- Hire a priest to say a bunch of priest shit before everyone hits the buffet.
- When choosing a casket, be sure to choose one large enough to accommodate the many treasures, spices, and servants that will accompany your loved one on his or her journey to the Afterworld.
- For a lighthearted look at funeral planning, rent the 1999 Jennifer Lopez romantic comedy *The Funeral Planner*.
- It is considered customary to tip your funeral director 10 percent of the price of the casket.
- The pig-roast pit should be situated a minimum of 200 feet from the gravesite.
- Even if you are young and healthy, it is a good idea to leave instructions for your funeral. Otherwise, they might play an Eminem song that's not one of your favorites.
- Actually, you really can't "plan" a funeral. It's more the kind of thing that just happens.

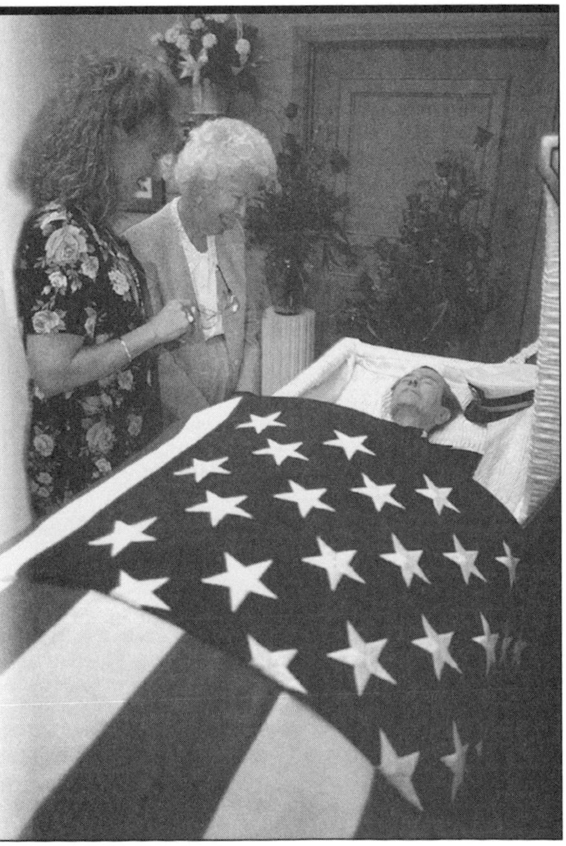

COMMUNITY VOICES

Why Can't We Live In Enlightened Topless Europe?

I realize that speaking out in favor of Europe is not a wise thing to do these days, but I must give credit where credit is due. My tour of Europe last summer opened my eyes to a rich culture where people place a premium on conversations about philosophy and ideas rather than last night's episode of *Friends*. Food is prepared and savored, not popped in the microwave and inhaled. And women are free to expose their breasts, not forced to hide them behind layers of constricting fabric. Why, oh, why, can't we live in enlightened topless Europe?

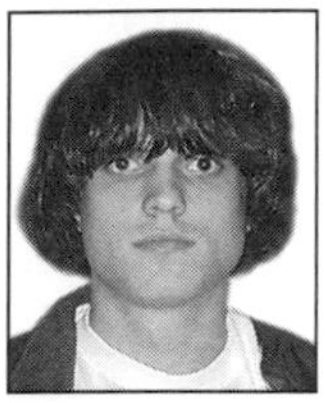

By Kyle Delsman

The United States is so backwards and repressed. Americans don't value the arts nearly as much as Europeans. Here in America, artists struggle to make ends meet. In Europe, artists have patrons in the government. Painters and sculptors are free to create as many works of art with the breast as they wish. Or they may choose not to include breasts in their art. But even when they don't, they know that breasts are an accepted and encouraged option.

Unlike us philistines, Europeans appreciate beauty and aesthetics, and incorporate them into everyday life. Instead of soulless edifices of concrete and steel, European buildings are beautifully crafted with intricate Old World ornamentation. Instead of garish, fluorescent-lit food courts, Europeans gather in magnificent open-air plazas. And instead of breasts crushed by shape-obscuring bras, Europeans routinely enjoy the sight of pert young breasts, presented with their graceful curves fully intact. In the piazzas of Italy, the fountains are rich with statues where pointy little breasts are left exposed for anyone to see and appreciate. *Bellissimo!*

Breasts in Europe aren't just exposed—they're celebrated. In London, for example, the newspapers feature a "Page Three" girl who poses with her top off. What do we have on the third page of our nation's so-called "paper of record," *The New York Times*? News. What is wrong with this country that some explosion or election somewhere is more important than the beauty of the female form?

Nowhere are Americans more repressed than in matters of health. We sunbathe modestly, take unisex saunas, and cover our torsos everywhere but in the privacy of our own homes. The French don't hesitate to maximize their intake of vitamin D from the sun by doffing their bikini tops whenever possible. In the spas of Austria, patrons go not only topless, but bottomless, as well. Would you ever see a fully naked young woman in a YWCA in Atlanta or Chicago? Of course not. We Americans simply wouldn't be able to handle such a shocking sight.

In London, for example, the newspapers feature a "Page Three" girl who poses with her top off. What do we have on the third page of our nation's so-called "paper of record," *The New York Times*? News.

The U.S. government doesn't do anything to help foster a social climate in which breasts can flourish. In fact, they do just the opposite. Breasts are often declared "lewd" or "indecent," and those who express themselves with pure hearts and open brassieres are ticketed and fined. In Europe, breasts are free to express themselves and interact with the world.

Now, assuming I am someone who enjoys the glorious sight of naked breasts (which I am), how can I see them in America? My only options are to frequent sleazy gentlemen's clubs or buy pornographic magazines. This is exactly what's wrong with America. When you repress the breast, you turn it into a dirty thing. You take something lovely and natural, and pervert it into something impure. That's what our country has done.

I still hold out hope for us. Most Americans, after all, still have traces of European blood coursing through their veins. Their ancestors came from France, from Germany, from Italy—places where they have naked breasts on the cover of mainstream magazines. Somewhere, buried deep within our DNA, is the potential to break free from our self-imposed, mammary-despising shackles. We must tap into these long-dormant European genes and unleash the wellspring of enlightenment. Only then will we live in a truly enlightened—and topless—United States of America. Ø

HOROSCOPES

Your Horoscope

By Lloyd Schumner Sr.
Retired Machinist and
A.A.P.B.-Certified Astrologer

Aries: (March 21–April 19)
All those jokes about your attention span would probably get you down if you ever stuck around to see how they end.

Taurus: (April 20–May 20)
An unfortunate typo in your flyer results in dozens of infuriated jockeys and bettors showing up for your annual three-day horse-raping festival.

Gemini: (May 21–June 21)
Once again, it seems like you're the only one who can get word back to Earth before all hope is lost.

Cancer: (June 22–July 22)
A tumor the size of a walnut will be found in your forebrain, explaining your recent fascination with mid-1970s American fiber art.

Leo: (July 23–Aug. 22)
The Army's okay, you suppose, but you just can't see yourself wearing any uniform that doesn't have two broad leather straps crossing over a bare chest.

Virgo: (Aug. 23–Sept. 22)
Your life seems great, but you wish you knew why that loud computer voice keeps counting backwards.

Libra: (Sept. 23–Oct. 23)
You've always thought it would be thrilling to be shot while trying to escape, but not from a marriage to the manager of the west-side Olive Garden.

Scorpio: (Oct. 24–Nov. 21)
You'll be the toast of Europe when Thievery Corporation remixes you into a cool after-hours chillout-session track.

Sagittarius: (Nov. 22–Dec. 21)
Your relief is palpable when the Channel 7 News CrimeStoppers' reenactment of your upcoming mugging leaves out the pants-wetting.

Capricorn: (Dec. 22–Jan. 19)
You're a passable singer, fair banjo player, and moderately attractive bottle-blonde, but that doesn't mean you're the Lost Dixie Chick.

Aquarius: (Jan. 20–Feb. 18)
You will inherit $20,000 from a great-aunt in Iowa, but, sadly, no overnight stay in a spooky haunted castle is required to claim the money.

Pisces: (Feb. 19–March 20)
A freak accident causes you and a Boise stockbroker to become the world's first "double reverse Idaho twins."

SCOUT COOKIE from page 87

amounts of blood. Passersby were amazed by the unusually large amounts of blood. Passersby were amazed by the unusually large amounts of blood. Passersby were amazed by the unusually large amounts of blood. Passersby were amazed by the unusually large amounts of blood. Passersby were amazed by the unusually large amounts of blood. Passersby were amazed by the unusually large amounts of blood. Passersby were amazed by the unusually large amounts of blood. Passersby were amazed by the unusually large amounts of blood. Passersby were amazed by the unusually large amounts of blood. Passersby were amazed by the unusually large amounts of blood. Passersby were amazed by the unusually large amounts of blood. Passersby were amazed by the unusually large amounts of blood. Passersby were amazed by the unusually large amounts of blood. Passersby were amazed by the unusually large amounts of blood. Passersby were amazed by the unusually large amounts of blood. Passersby were amazed by the unusually large amounts of blood. Passersby were amazed by the unusually large amounts of blood. Passersby were

Nurse! Bring me those electrical shocky-pad heart-starter things, stat!

amazed by the unusually large amounts of blood. Passersby were amazed by the unusually large amounts of blood. Passersby were amazed by the unusually large amounts of blood. Passersby were amazed by the unusually large amounts of blood. Passersby were amazed by the unusually large amounts of blood. Passersby were amazed by the unusually large

see SCOUT COOKIE page 99

the ONION®

VOLUME 39 ISSUE 09 AMERICA'S FINEST NEWS SOURCE™ 13–19 MARCH 2003

NEWS

Ari Fleischer Replaced By Toby Keith

see WASHINGTON page 4A

Florist Saves Abusive Relationship

see LOCAL page 9C

Eighth-Grade Oboist Plays Weezer

see SCHOOLS page 11E

Designated Driver Stoned

see LOCAL page 5C

STATshot

A look at the numbers that shape your world.

Top Causes Of Back Pain

1. Helping Dave move
2. Flashing red discomfort arrows
3. Reaching age 34
4. Upper ass pain
5. Roadying for Krokus
6. Tantric experimentation
7. Trying to prove how easy it is to fuck up your back

THE ONION • $2.00 US • $3.00 CAN

Above: Sen. Frank Lautenberg (D-NJ) and Sen. Pete Domenici (R-NM) react to the inadvertent $121 million arts endowment.

Congress Accidentally Approves Arts Funding

WASHINGTON, DC—A red-faced Senate Majority Leader Bill Frist (R-TN) admitted Monday that, as part of last week's $397 billion spending bill, Congress accidentally allocated $121 million to the National Endowment for the Arts.

"We approved what?" Frist said upon learning of the inadvertent arts funding. "I don't recall putting my name on anything like that. Any funding of the arts was purely accidental. I repeat, any financial support of artists, musicians, or writers on my part was done unwittingly and unknowingly."

"That bill was more than 3,000 pages, single-spaced," Frist added. "It's pretty easy

see CONGRESS page 95

Ted Turner Sends Self Back In Time To Prevent AOL Time Warner Merger

ATLANTA—According to a videotaped message airing exclusively on CNN, media mogul Ted Turner has sent himself back in time to January 2000 to avert the catastrophic merger of America Online and Time Warner.

"By the time you see this, I will have returned to Year Zero of the AOL Time Warner merger in a time machine of my own design," Turner said in the three-minute message, which first aired Monday on the Turner-owned cable news channel. "I will doggedly pursue [AOL Time Warner chairman] Steve Case and [former Time Warner CEO] Gerald Levin to stop this horribly misguided union of New Media and Old Media. And I will not return to my own time until the merger has been prevented."

AOL acquired Time Warner on Jan. 12, 2000, when the companies boasted a combined market value of $181.5 billion. The alliance quickly proved ill-fated, as few of

see TURNER page 94

Robin Williams Leaves Entertainment Reporter In Stitches

LOS ANGELES—Comic wildman Robin Williams left *Entertainment Tonight* reporter Maria Menounos in stitches Monday, cracking her up with a manic, off-the-cuff comedic riff covering everything from *Survivor* to Botox.

"How does he come up with this stuff?" asked a still-laughing Menounos, who interviewed Williams as he arrived at the Regent Beverly Wilshire Hotel for a gala charity benefit for pediatric AIDS. "When Robin's around, you never know what he's going to say. But one thing's for sure: It's guaranteed to be funny."

Williams, 50, is renowned for his surreal, free-associative detours, which have delighted countless entertainment reporters on both coasts.

Williams went on the unexpected, wholly improvised comic tear when Menounos asked him about his outfit, a tuxedo accentuated by a pair of flashy, neon-purple cowboy boots. The query prompted Williams to launch into impersonations of a jive-talking black man and John Wayne before segueing into references to Joan Rivers, the reality-TV program *Survivor*, and the popular wrinkle remover Botox, leaving Menounos in what witnesses described as "hysterics."

"Yo, what is up, homeslice? Dis suc-

see WILLIAMS page 95

Life After Saddam

With war imminent, President Bush and others are already discussing plans for a post-Saddam, U.S.-occupied Iraq. What do *you* think?

"I'm sure there are plenty of ambitious young despots out there who would jump at the chance to rule Iraq."

Andrea Crim
Teacher

"I just hope we don't see a repeat of that mess we made a few years back when we tried to install an American ruler in America."

Bruce Wollensky
Attorney

"Can't we just get CNN to run the place?"

Martin Baines
Systems Analyst

"Whatever happens, someone should be there to film the most touching moments."

Meredith Hall
Psychologist

"We should ask ourselves what we would want if Iraq was occupying the U.S."

Ken Franklin
Bus Driver

"Oh, man, we're not gonna make Iraq the 51st state, are we?"

Dennis Doering
Landscaper

Oscar Gift Bags

Each year, Academy Awards attendees take home a coveted gift bag. Among the items to be included this year:

- Cartier diamond-encrusted backstabbing dagger
- Gift pack of 10 get-out-of-jail-free cards courtesy of LAPD
- One kilo of uncut Peruvian flake
- Jessica Weiss, a 24-year-old production assistant with film degree from NYU, on Prada keychain
- Oscar-night mix CD burned for everyone by Owen Wilson
- Pro-Brite soul-whitening kit
- Two packages of gourmet microwave popcorn, handpicked by unblemished Sardinian virgins flush with the bloom of full womanhood on the slopes of Mount Elba
- Velveteen pillow stuffed with genuine locks of Bruce Vilanch's beard
- Swiss Colony summer-sausage gift-pak
- $10,000 in cash, courtesy of Citibank
- The ability to fly

the ONION®
America's Finest News Source.™

Herman Ulysses Zweibel
Founder

T. Herman Zweibel
Publisher Emeritus
J. Phineas Zweibel
Publisher
Maxwell Prescott Zweibel
Editor-In-Chief

Love Me, Love My Violent Alcoholic Rages

By Billy Putnam

Hey, I know I can get a bit out of hand sometimes, but nobody's perfect. Sure, every now and again, I'll have a beer or twelve down at the bar, then head over to Sheila's place and smack her around some before the cops drag me kicking and screaming to the drunk tank. Maybe it's not the greatest habit in the world, but everybody's got their good and bad qualities, right? Love me, love my violent alcoholic rages.

It's like my sister Donna and those three terriers of hers. You go to visit her, and those mutts are slobbering all over your lap in 10 seconds flat. There's dog hair and squeak toys everywhere, but she couldn't give a damn. She says any man who wants to marry her will have to accept those critters. And I respect that. Sometimes, I sleep on Donna's couch when I'm too wrecked to get the key in the car door. She lives close to Tilly's Tap, so I stagger over to her house and pound on the door, screaming that she'd better open up or I'll kick her fucking head in. But once I'm inside, hell, I never say shit about those animals.

Okay, so I'm a drunk prone to violent outbursts. Have been for years, ever since I turned the corner into hardcore alcoholism back in '92. Guilty as charged! Just ask the other guys down at the plant. There ain't a one of them that hasn't gotten a face full of my boot at one time or another. That's just me.

But, hey, what am I supposed to do, stop drinking? I love my friends and family and Sheila, but I love my liquor, too. Everyone knows that. There's Billy, and then there's the bottle in his hand. That's just part of the package. If you want to enjoy all the wonderful things about a person, you have to be willing to accept their faults, too. As they say, every rose has its thorn.

I admit, I have this bad habit of getting angry when I'm drinking. Kinda weird, but it's my little quirk. After a sixer, I'll call Sheila up but accidentally dial the wrong number, and a man will answer, so I'll be convinced she's cheating on me. I'll go to her house and throw things around for a bit, call her a no-good cunt and a fucking whore. Well, she just locks herself in her bedroom and lets me scream until I pass out on the floor. No harm done. The next day, Sheila and I always patch things up. I say I'm sorry and make it up to her by painting her fence or something, and all is right with the world. Hey, we've all got our foibles and frailties: You have a weakness for chocolate, I get loaded and hit women.

Sometimes, people make fun of my drinking. They laugh at the way I stumble out of the bar at the end of the night, zigzagging across the parking lot. Yup, that's me, Big Ol' Screaming Lush Billy. Well, laugh all you want, because everybody has their imperfections. We're all human, and we need to all be tolerant of each other. So if I respect the fact that you can't parallel-park to save your life, you should respect the fact that I drink too much and end up picking fights and hitting people.

We're all human, and we need to all be tolerant of each other. So if I respect the fact that you can't parallel-park to save your life, you should respect the fact that I drink too much and end up picking fights and hitting people.

It's like when Sheila's on the phone with that blabbermouth sister of hers. Do I tell her what to do? Well, after a few shots of tequila, I guess I do say, "Get off that goddamn phone right this minute or I'll pull it through the fucking wall," but she won't listen. Sheila says, "Love me, love my family." That's her thing. My thing is getting plastered and driving my pickup through the window of convenience stores that won't sell me beer after 11. Different strokes for different folks.

Sure, some people still try to get me to quit drinking. They slip pamphlets under my door, recommend AA counselors, give me lectures when they drive me home from the emergency room after I spend three hours getting glass shards picked out of my fist. As if that's going to do any good. Sorry, but I've never been one for the straight and narrow. Nope, I'm more the strip-down-to-my-pit-stained-T-shirt-in-the-middle-of-winter, lurch-around-unsteadily-on-the-front-lawn, throw-things-at-passing-cars type of guy.

What can I say? I gotta be me. Ø

LOCAL

Adulthood Spent Satisfying Childhood Desires

CANTON, OH—Jeffrey Riesman, 29, an account manager at Tri-Trust Insurance, has spent the last 10 years satisfying desires not sufficiently fulfilled during childhood, sources reported Tuesday.

"I just bought a mint-in-box *Six Million Dollar Man* Bionic Transport and Repair Station off eBay for just under $100," Riesman said Tuesday. "All I need is an Oscar Goldman, and I'll have the complete Bionic toy series."

According to roommate Nate Kenniff, 28, Riesman's need to indulge childhood desires is reflected in everything from his toy collection to his diet.

"We tried shopping for groceries together when I first moved in, but that didn't work," Kenniff said. "He'll go to Costco and buy box after box of Fruity Pebbles, Boo Berry, and Quisp. Whenever I suggest we get some Wheat Chex or something a little less sweet, he just rolls his eyes and calls my cereal choices 'lame.'"

Kenniff said Riesman spends an average of six hours a night watching TV.

"I like TV as much as the next guy, but Jeff takes it to extremes," Kenniff said. "And it's not like he's watching quality stuff. He'll stay up for an all-night *Scooby Doo* marathon. Have you tried watching *Scooby Doo* lately? It's not as good as you might remember it."

Riesman also owns more than 500 DVDs, many of which are collections of cartoons he loved as a boy or such forbidden films from his adolescence as *Porky's*, *Private School*, and *Hot Resort*.

When Riesman isn't watching TV or DVDs, he's usually playing one of the 200-plus games he has purchased for his vintage Atari 2600 game console.

"I had Atari when I was a kid, but my mom always made me wait until I was done with my homework to play," Riesman said. "Now, as soon as I come home from the office, I can settle in and play Yars' Revenge until dawn, and she can't say anything about it."

"I had Atari when I was a kid, but my mom always made me wait until I was done with my homework to play," Riesman said. "Now, I can settle in and play Yars' Revenge until dawn."

Added Riesman: "I'm thinking about picking up a second game system, like maybe a Colecovision or Intellivision. Why not? They're only like 50 bucks. I make almost $30,000 a year. Why deprive myself?"

Another area in which Riesman's youthful indulgence manifests itself is his bedtime. Despite having a job that requires him to be at the office at 8 a.m., he refuses to go to sleep before 3.

"When Jeff and I were living together, he'd always stay up way after I went to sleep," said Carla Green, Riesman's ex-girlfriend. "I'd say 'Come to bed,' and he'd always snap back that he's an adult and can stay up as late as he wants. I have no clue what that was about."

According to noted psychotherapist Dr. Howard Blum, Riesman suffers from a condition known as Chronic Unfulfilled Desire Syndrome, which affects a person's ability to let go of childhood fixations and embrace maturity.

"Some people are never able to overcome CUDS—it can't be medicated," Blum said. "The only thing an afflicted individual can do is try to curb those youthful desires while still in their twenties and pray they aren't still pursuing them at 45. There's nothing sadder than a middle-aged Pez-dispenser collector." Ø

Above: Taking a break from his Atari 2600, Riesman enjoys a bowl of Fruity Pebbles.

NEWS IN BRIEF

'Watermelon Capital Of World' Claim Goes Unchallenged

CORDELE, GA—For the 15th year in a row, Cordele has retained the title of "Watermelon Capital of the World"—despite a clear lack of evidence that its melons are the biggest, best, or most abundant. "We really expected Knox City, TX, to step up to the plate this year and give us a run for our money," said Mona Simmons, president of the Cordele-Crisp Chamber of Commerce. "Thankfully, they seem content just being the Seedless Watermelon Capital of the World."

Bush Orders Iraq To Disarm Before Start Of War

WASHINGTON, DC—Maintaining his hardline stance against Saddam Hussein, President Bush ordered Iraq to fully dismantle its military before the U.S. begins its invasion next week. "U.S. intelligence confirms that, even as we speak, Saddam is preparing tanks and guns and other weapons of deadly force for use in our upcoming war against him," Bush said Sunday during his weekly radio address. "This madman has every intention of firing back at our troops when we attack his country." Bush warned the Iraqi dictator to "lay down [his] weapons and enter battle unarmed, or suffer the consequences."

Abusive Husband Was Himself Abuser As Child

JACKSON, MS—Psychiatric evaluations of wifebeater Jimmy Pellett, 33, indicate that he himself was abusive as a child, doctors reported Tuesday. "Since the age of 3, Mr. Pellett has been the perpetrator of countless acts of violence against his parents, siblings, and other neighborhood children," Dr. William Traschel said. "Sadly, the beatings and emotional terror he inflicted as a child led him to more beatings as an adult. Just another textbook case of the abuser growing up to be the abuser."

Man Offered Cocaine By Guy He Met At Urinal 90 Seconds Ago

NEW YORK—A minute and a half after using a urinal at the Manhattan hotspot Bungalow 8 Monday, Gerard Bouchard, 25, was offered cocaine by the stranger voiding his bladder next to him. "As I'm leaving the restroom, the sweat-soaked guy I was pissing next to says, 'Sure is crowded, but, hey, lots of hot chicks and you can't go wrong with that, right? Want a bump?'" Bouchard said. "I guess I didn't realize that taking your penis out near someone makes them your good friend." Bouchard declined the man's generous offer, bypassing a chance to strengthen their urinating-in-close-proximity bond.

White House Pretty Sure Uzbekistan Diplomat Stole A Bunch Of Soap

WASHINGTON, DC—Following a weekend visit by Otkir Halilov, Uzbekistan's Minister of Foreign Affairs, White House officials are "90 percent sure" that the visitor made off with a bunch of soap and other assorted sundries. "I don't want to start an international incident, but I'm pretty sure Otkir swiped four or five bars from one of the upstairs bathrooms," White House chief of staff Andrew Card said at a press conference Monday. "Either he wanted a souvenir or they just can't get that kind of stuff back home." Also missing were an embroidered towel, a box of Kleenex, and two miniature cans of Edge shaving gel. Ø

TURNER from page 91

the media synergies it promised proved feasible or profitable. This January, amid a plunging stock price and news that the new company posted a record $99 billion loss in 2002, Turner announced his resignation as AOL Time Warner vice-chairman.

Turner spokespersons say the mysterious, unseen time-travel device was developed under a veil of extreme

"The merger occurred at the height of the Internet bubble, when conventional wisdom held that so-called 'New Economy' companies like Yahoo!, Excite, and AOL were the wave of the future," said Maria Bartiromo, host of CNBC's *Closing Bell*.

secrecy at his Techwood Drive headquarters in Atlanta. Little else about the machine or Turner's mission is known.

"From what we understand, the machine acts only on living human flesh," Turner spokesman Marty Wells said. "If Mr. Turner has been successful, he has materialized in January 2000 completely nude, with no ID or

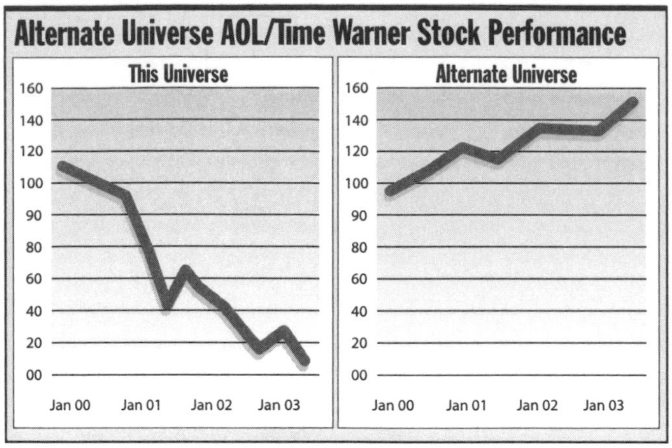

money, save for a few billion dollars in Year 2000-value Time Warner stock. To survive, he'll need to steal clothing and rely on whatever crude weapons he can fashion with his bare hands."

Market watchers have expressed skepticism about Turner's chances.

"The merger occurred at the height of the Internet bubble, when conventional wisdom held that so-called 'New Economy' companies like Yahoo!, Excite, and AOL were the wave of the future," said Maria Bartiromo, host of CNBC's *Closing Bell*. "In such a heady, bullish financial climate, [Turner's] warnings of impending doom will likely be dismissed by Case and Levin as the ravings of a madman."

Corporate hubris, physicists say, is not the only obstacle facing Turner on his dramatic mission.

"Altering the flow of time is a dangerous and complex proposition," said Dr. Arthur Wistrom, a University of Chicago physics professor. "If Turner is not careful, he may unintentionally change the course of his own history, causing, for example, something to go awry with his loving, happy marriage to Jane Fonda."

Compounding Turner's troubles is an unconfirmed report that enemy forces within AOL have responded with their own time-travel initiative, dispatching back in time hundreds of cyborg drones disguised as ordinary mailmen to deliver CD-ROMs promising thousands of hours of free AOL access to every human household.

"Why anyone at AOL would want to do such a thing remains a mystery, as they lost more in the merger than anyone," Bartiromo said. "Perhaps somewhere within the vast Internet network of AOL subscribers, some malevolent cybernetic force has achieved sentience and is bent on the destruction of its human masters."

Turner's time-jump represents the latest in a series of high-stakes gambits for the maverick multi-billionaire.

"From his conversion of an independent Atlanta TV station into a cable 'superstation' to his purchase of the Atlanta Braves and Atlanta Hawks, his launch of CNN, and the historic merger of his media empire with Time Warner, Turner has built a career on taking big risks," *Fortune* reporter Doug Bergeron said. "But traveling back in time all by himself, a lone corporate soldier from the future facing nigh-impossible odds—that is arguably the most daring move he has made yet as an entrepreneur."

Though the odds are stacked against Turner, many are betting on him to prevail.

"The AOL Time Warner merger reduced Turner to a mere figurehead and ultimately cost him nearly $7 billion of his personal fortune," investment guru Warren Buffett said. "A lesser man would have crumbled in the face of such adversity. Yet we are talking about the man who in 1977 piloted his yacht *Courageous* to victory in the America's Cup, who in 1997 pledged to donate $1 billion to the U.N., and who, according to messages we have received from the future, will in 2013 single-handedly defeat the alien warrior-financier Zygax The Investorator in hand-to-hand combat. He is not just a brave corporate warrior. He is our economy's last, best hope."

the ONION presents:

Museum-Appreciation Tips

Museum-going can be an enjoyable and enriching experience. Here are some tips for getting the most out of your next visit:

- In large museums like the Louvre, it is virtually impossible to see everything in one day. This is why jogging is both acceptable and encouraged.
- If you don't experience a painting with all five senses, you aren't truly experiencing it.
- Beware: Some museums are more reputable than others. The Metropolitan Museum of Art in New York City? Pretty reputable. The Flagstaff Groundhog & Jackalope Hall of Fame? Less so.
- Why enter the museum when the only stuff you can afford is in the gift shop?
- When on a guided tour of a history museum, at every civilization, ask whether the men of that era ever had an overpowering urge to dress as a woman and be caressed by a big, strong man.
- Though many are painfully dull, some museums gots cars in 'em.
- Remember: "Suggested donation" means waltz in free, even if you are loaded.
- Be sure to dress appropriately for your museum visit, wearing knee-high boots, sturdy rubber gloves, and a heavy apron. Did I say museum? I meant salmon cannery.
- When looking at the exhibit on genetically modified super-spiders, try not to get too distracted by Kirsten Dunst.
- This month, the National Mustard Museum in Mt. Horeb, WI, is unveiling a new exhibit honoring those slain while serving the mustard industry. It is a moving tribute to America's mustard dead and is highly recommended.
- If short on money, get a friend to enter a museum and have him or her describe everything to you via walkie-talkie.
- Spend a minimum of 30 seconds, ideally 45, staring at each exhibit so no one will suspect that every molecule in your body is screaming to get the hell out of there and go to the mall.

CONGRESS from page 91

to miss something."

The 2003-04 budget bill, which passed 338-83 in the House and 76-20 in the Senate, boosted defense spending by $98 billion and pledged $27 billion in tax breaks to oil companies and other energy concerns. It also unintentionally allocated more than $120 million to "award financial assistance for projects, productions, workshops, or programs that will encourage public knowledge, understanding, and appreciation of the arts."

"That wording was confusing," Sen. Ted Stevens (R-AK) said. "I did not fully understand what that meant. I assumed it had something to do with scientific or military research, so I voted for it. I'm sure I wasn't the only one to misinterpret that."

On Capitol Hill, countless legislators expressed embarrassment over voting for the bill, admitting that the arts funding simply slipped by them.

"I don't know how this could have happened," Rep. Gil Gutknecht (R-

Some senators tried to defuse criticism by playing up the bill's "many wonderful parts."

MN) said. "I thought I read the thing pretty carefully, but toward the bottom of page 117, those four words are right there in black and white: American Jazz Masters Fellowship."

Making the blow even more severe is the fact that the NEA will have the power to determine how the funds are distributed.

"As I understand it, not only will the government provide money for paint-

Added Hagel: "It was [bipartisan Budget Committee member and Republican Colorado Rep. Tom] Tancredo's job to look out for things like this."

ings and poems, it will have little say over how that money is used," Gutknecht said. "This means some limp-wristed NEA member will decide what qualifies as art rather than Congress or the president. Remind me never to skim a bill again, no matter how long it is."

Sen. Evan Bayh (D-IN) spoke out in defense of his embarrassed colleagues.

"In those final, frantic days of House-Senate bargaining, money was flying everywhere," Bayh said. "$3.1 billion to subsidize cattle ranchers here, $1.5 billion to help states revamp their electoral systems there. I can see how, in all that chaos, $165,000 for the Dance Theater of Harlem could get overlooked."

Many citizens do not excuse the lawmakers' negligence.

"These congressmen must be held accountable," said Ronald Drake, a Lincoln, NE, hardware-store owner.

Above: The new home of the Boogabong Players, an avant-garde Stowe, VT, puppet-theater troupe.

"My hard-earned tax dollars will be supporting repertory theaters and art galleries—places no decent, hard-working American would ever set foot in. And then there's the museums I always hear about on the news, with the dirty photos and whatnot."

Some senators tried to defuse criticism by playing up the bill's "many wonderful parts."

"We need to keep this in perspective," Sen. Chuck Hagel (R-NE) said. "Let's try to focus on the $390 million that will go toward mineral drilling in Alaska's Arctic National Wildlife Refuge, rather than the $15,000 that may wind up going to some guy who wants to put on a Shakespeare play."

Added Hagel: "I can't be everywhere at once. It was [bipartisan Budget Committee member and Republican Colorado Rep. Tom] Tancredo's job to look out for things like this."

While Sen. Debbie Stabenow (D-MI) introduced the line item that grants the NEA chairperson the power to award literature fellowships, she said she never expected it to be approved.

"I always throw some doomed things in there so we have something to take out," Stabenow said. "This time, I put the arts funding in to distract everyone from the section allocating money for school-breakfast programs in low-income districts. Live and learn."

Dana Gioia, the internationally acclaimed poet, critic, and educator who was recently named NEA chairman, was "as shocked as anyone" by the financial windfall.

"I can't wait to start making calls," Gioia said. "There's a Latina artist in Los Angeles who makes these amazing multimedia collages that combine the religious iconography of her strict Catholic upbringing with photographs of horse vaginas." ⌀

WILLIAMS from page 91

ka be lookin' baaad tonight!" said Williams, showing off his outfit to Menounos. "Now listen, pilgrim, Monty Clift is down in Red River still lookin' for his boots. He's a little light in those loafers he's been wearin' lately, catch my drift? It's like *Survivor: San Francisco*... 'The tribe has spoken, and you look *faaabulous*!' Is Joan [Rivers] here tonight? Don't let her see me—her facelift stitches might pop out from the shock! Nurse, one million CCs of Botox, stat! No, we don't have time for the needle! Just back the truck up, fasten the hose, and pump it right into her skull! Boooop! Boooop! Boooop!"

Menounos responded to Williams with hearty laughter, eventually raising her hand in exhaustion and casting a "How does he come up with this stuff?" glance at the camera.

"It was classic Robin tonight," said fundraiser attendee Byron Allen, host of the recently cancelled junketainment program *Kickin' It With Byron Allen*. "He pulled it off so effortlessly, and fresh from his recent Grammy appearance, no less, when he held his award for Best Comedy Album against his crotch. Just another day at the office for this comic genius."

Access Hollywood anchor Pat O'Brien said that Williams, whom he has frequently interviewed over the

"What do you think he'll riff on instead of answering my questions?" Asner said. "Mike Tyson? Duct tape? Michael Jackson? Viagra? Monica Lewinsky? Enron? John Wayne Bobbitt? All seven?"

past two decades, is remarkable for his outrageous unpredictability.

"When I interviewed him for *Mrs. Doubtfire*, I asked him if playing a woman came naturally," O'Brien said. "Although the question was posed seriously, I was kind of hoping it would set him up for a doozy of a spiel. And, boy, did it ever: Who knew he'd lisp in an effeminate voice, 'Why? What did you hear, Sweetcheeks?' and then, without warning, slip into a flawless impression of a televangelist exorcising a demon out of the lisping persona?"

"I love how, when he's conducting an imaginary exchange between two radically different personas—say, a flamboyantly gay hairdresser and a creepily placid children's-show host—he whips his head around, left and right," *Access Hollywood* reporter Billy Bush said. "It provides a helpful visual cue so you know when he's switching characters."

During a May 1992 press junket for the film *Toys*, *Variety* columnist Army Archerd had to be administered oxygen by paramedics after Williams overcame him with rapid-fire impressions of Jack Nicholson, a human beat box, and Ross Perot, squeezing in references to the savings-and-loan scandal and *The Crying Game* along the way.

"It was breathtaking to watch him weave all these seemingly unrelated pieces of pop culture into one side-splitting, completely ad-libbed routine," *Extra* host Leeza Gibbons said. "Robin's a national treasure."

Jules Asner, co-host of *E! News Live*, explained why Williams enjoys such a devoted following among entertainment journalists.

"It's true that Nathan Lane, Jim Carrey, and Carrot Top possess a certain hyperactive, spontaneous quality," Asner said. "Those guys are all incredibly zany and off-the-wall. But nobody goes off on a wild tangent quite like Robin. We just turn on the camera, ask a question, and let him rip. Do you know how much easier that makes our jobs?"

Asner said she "can't wait" for an upcoming interview with Williams for her *Revealed* series.

"What do you think he'll riff on instead of answering my questions?" Asner said. "Mike Tyson? Duct tape? Michael Jackson? Viagra? Monica Lewinsky? Enron? John Wayne Bobbitt? All seven? Lord, let it be all seven." ⌀

COMMUNITY VOICES

The DMV Can Suck My Left Nut

Hola, amigos. I know it's been a long time since I rapped at ya, but I've been ass over elbows in problems. First off, I'm finally getting over some kind of flu-type thing. I don't know exactly what I had, and I don't suppose it would matter much if I did. All I can tell you is that it made my crap reek worse than roadkill, and I didn't even want to drink beer.

The Cruise
By Jim Anchower

I may not know what I had, but I've got a pretty good idea where I got it. Last Tuesday, I had to spend the entire day cooped up in an airtight room at the DMV with a bunch of losers. The way most of those guys looked, I'm lucky I didn't come down with crotch rot or trench ass or something.

So, how'd your old pal Jim Anchower wind up spending a whole day at the DMV? Well, the night before, Wes, Ron, and this guy Ron works with named Rob dropped by my house unexpectedly. Because I wasn't expecting guests, I didn't have enough beer to entertain. So, being a good host, I went out to get a case of MGD at the Kwik-Stop. And while I was there, I decided to pick up a few bags

As I was pulling over, I started getting even madder, thinking about how I was being hassled for no reason and how the pigs just had it in for me. Turns out, I was all worked up for nothing, 'cause the cop flew right past me.

of pretzels and some of those baby carrots. I'm really into those baby carrots lately. They're crunchy like pretzels, but they're also sweet and wet.

Since they had videos for rent, I decided to make a night of it and rented *Dude, Where's My Car?* I've seen it a few times already, but I love that shit. It could use some tits, but it's still pretty good.

Anyway, I pile all the stuff into the car and leave the parking lot. A few blocks away, this cop suddenly appears behind me and hits his lights. Man, was I pissed—I didn't do nothing! As I was pulling over, I started getting even madder, thinking about how I was being hassled for no reason and how the pigs just had it in for me. Turns out, I was all worked up for nothing, 'cause the cop flew right past

Last Tuesday, I had to spend the entire day cooped up in an airtight room at the DMV with a bunch of losers. The way most of those guys looked, I'm lucky I didn't come down with crotch rot or trench ass or something.

me. He was going after the guy in the car in front of me. Fuckin' pigs!

I hate to waste a good mad, so I hollered at the guy on the radio for saying Johnny Winter recorded "Frankenstein" when it was Edgar Winter. By the time I calmed down, I was back home. While I was telling Wes, Ron, and Rob what happened, I realized it was doubly good that I didn't get pulled over, since my license was expired. We spent the night celebrating my good luck by polishing off the case plus the six MGDs I already had in the fridge.

I had the next day off, so I figured I should take care of my license. I got to the DMV at about 11:30 and took a number. It wasn't coming up for a while, plus I was a little hungover, so I decided to take a short nap. The problem was, it wasn't so short. I woke up at 1:45 to somebody shaking me, telling me I should go to a shelter if I needed to sleep. I looked up at the number board and saw that mine had long passed. The lady at the counter said she couldn't bump me to the front, and that I had to take another number.

I took my second number and sat back down. I flipped through a couple of *Road And Track* magazines, but they weren't telling me anything I didn't already know. I looked around the room and saw that one of the people working the counter was Shelley Drexler, who I knew from grade school. It isn't like we were friends, or even talked, but I still knew who she was.

Half an hour later, my number came up. I got called up to a window and, sure enough, it was Shelley's. I knew she recognized me, but she wasn't letting on. I wasn't going to let her off that easy, so I said hi and asked how she was doing. She said "Fine," and asked me for the proper forms, my expired driver's license, and a second form of ID. I gave her the forms and the license, but I didn't have another

I must've shook Shelley's shit up pretty bad, because when I got back, she was gone. I had to wait a while, but I got my license renewed without any hassle this time.

ID with me. I said we went to school together, and that she should recognize me. She said she still needed a second form, and that it was out of her hands. I said if I wasn't Jim Anchower, then how did I know about the time she pissed her pants in second grade because she was too chickenshit to ask the teacher to go to the bathroom?

Shelley didn't like that. She told me to get another form of ID and stop wasting her time. I was going to lay into her, but I saw the security guard eyeballing me. I went out to my car, thinking that if I got pulled over on the way back home without my driver's license, Shelley was going to get it. I dug around my house for half an hour before I found my birth certificate. It was torn and had some weird food stains on it, but it was still valid. I got back to the DMV five minutes before they shut the door.

Anyway, I must've shook Shelley's shit up pretty bad, because when I got back, she was gone. I had to wait a while, but I got my license renewed without any hassle this time, so I guess it all worked out for the best. Except for my getting the flu.

Oh, and the picture looks like shit, especially compared to my last one. That one looked hot. I was all like Gary Cherone. ⊘

HOROSCOPES

Your Horoscope

By Lloyd Schumner Sr.
Retired Machinist and
A.A.P.B.-Certified Astrologer

Aries: (March 21–April 19)
There's nothing wrong with you that a good night's sleep wouldn't cure. Assuming, of course, that you don't count the bone cancer.

Taurus: (April 20–May 20)
For the last time: It simply isn't true about Richard Gere. Please stop asking.

Gemini: (May 21–June 21)
You've done endless reading on the subject and participated in hundreds of simulations, but you will still find yourself unprepared for actual sex.

Cancer: (June 22–July 22)
Your long search for a viable alternative energy source may finally be over when you discover a potent, readily available white powder that goes up your nose.

Leo: (July 23–Aug. 22)
A sign in your workplace boasts more than a thousand days without a lost-time accident, but that's only because they don't count your constant rebreaking of the same leg.

Virgo: (Aug. 23–Sept. 22)
You'll eventually be the one to get the girl, thanks to your patience and the fact that you don't care that she's dead.

Libra: (Sept. 23–Oct. 23)
The old ass-Xeroxing prank will go awry when your boss catches you in the act and makes you the ass-Xeroxing supervisor for the entire Northeast region.

Scorpio: (Oct. 24–Nov. 21)
You don't regret choosing the Jermaine Stewart classic for your personal theme song, but you're starting to think it would be nice to occasionally take your clothes off to have a good time.

Sagittarius: (Nov. 22–Dec. 21)
After months of soul-searching, you'll finally decide to write your memoirs, but it winds up taking less than three days.

Capricorn: (Dec. 22–Jan. 19)
Your family will react to your declaration that you don't want a fancy, overblown funeral with relief and increased murder attempts.

Aquarius: (Jan. 20–Feb. 18)
Police will immediately rule you out as a suspect in the Case of the Impressive, Well-Spoken, Sexy Bandit.

Pisces: (Feb. 19–March 20)
The blood of legends will soon run in your veins, thanks to your purchase of a home legendary-blood transfusion kit.

the ONION®

VOLUME 39 ISSUE 11 | AMERICA'S FINEST NEWS SOURCE™ | 27 MARCH–2 APRIL 2003

NEWS

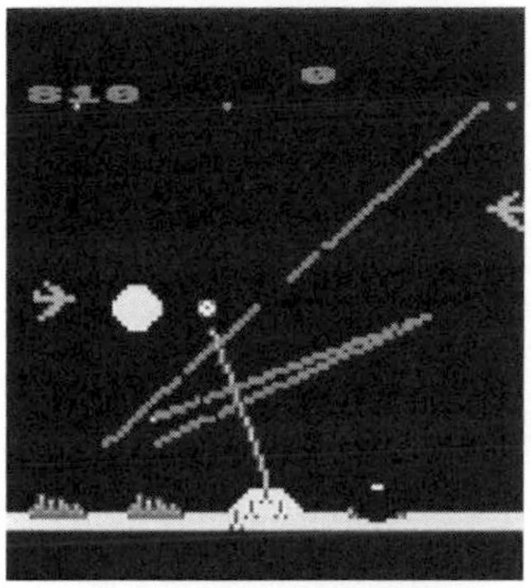

U.S. Takes Out Key Iraqi Bases In Midnight Raid

see WORLD page 10A

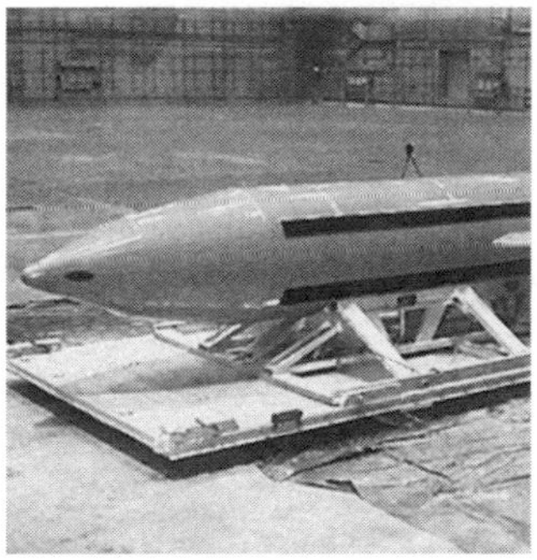

New Bomb Capable Of Creating 1,500 New Terrorists In Single Blast

see WEAPONRY page 3A

U.S. Draws Up Plan For Post-War Transitional Dictatorship In Iraq

see WORLD page 7A

STATshot

A look at the numbers that shape your world.

Top Anti-War Slogans

1. I Support My Activist Girlfriend
2. I Oppose This War And I Vote. Wait, No, I Don't
3. The International Socialist Organization Needs A Ride Home
4. What Would Guevara Do?
5. Fooled By Liberal Media Bias
6. The People, United, Will Usually Be Defeated

OPERATION PISS OFF THE PLANET

SPECIAL COVERAGE: THE WAR IN IRAQ

Bush Bravely Leads 3rd Infantry Into Battle

Above: A weary Bush marches through enemy territory near the Iraq-Kuwait border.

IRAQ-KUWAIT BORDER—As the U.S. Army's 3rd Infantry Division began its ground assault on Iraq Monday, President Bush marched alongside the front-line soldiers, bravely putting his own life on the line for his country by personally participating in the attack.

"Bush is the real deal, and when he talks about fighting for freedom, he means it," said Pvt. Tom Scharpling, 21. "He'd never ask one of us grunts to take any risks for our country that he wasn't willing to take himself."

> "George would never ask this nation's citizens to do anything he was unwilling to do himself."

According to reports from the front, many of the soldiers were initially suspicious of the president, doubtful that an Ivy Lea-

see BUSH page 101

Dead Iraqi Would Have Loved Democracy

CASUALTIES

BAGHDAD, IRAQ—Baghdad resident Taha Sabri, killed Monday in a U.S. air strike on his city, would have loved the eventual liberation of Iraq and establishment of democracy, had he lived to see it, his grieving widow said.

"Taha was a wonderful man, a man of peace," his wife Sawssan said. "I just know he would have been happy to see free elections

Above: Taha Sabri

here in Iraq, had that satellite-guided Tomahawk cruise missile not strayed off course and hit

see IRAQI page 101

DIPLOMACY

U.S. Forms Own U.N.

Above: The U.S. and U.S. delegations.

see U.S.U.N. page 101

Local Mom Whips Up Some Of Her Famous War Pie

Left: Sensenbrenner prepares the war pie's tasty crust.

TIPTON, IA—With the invasion of Iraq underway, Janet Sensenbrenner, 54, a Tipton homemaker and mother of three, responded Tuesday by whipping up some of her famous war pie.

"Any time there's an invasion, I get down the mixing bowls and bake a sweet, delicious war pie," Sensenbrenner said. "In fact, I usually go ahead and make two, because the first one always disappears in a flash. A U.S. military action in the Middle East just wouldn't be the same without it."

A self-described "amateur Martha Stewart," Sensenbrenner said her favorite way to serve the pie is oven-warm with a scoop of vanilla ice cream. She noted, however, that it is "every bit as good" with a tall glass of milk or a cup of coffee.

Sensenbrenner's son Chris, 16, said he bets he could eat an entire war pie all by himself.

"Obviously, no one in the family

see WAR PIE page 100

Media Coverage Of The War

Across the nation, citizens are glued to their TV sets for war coverage. What do *you* think of the job the media are doing?

"I watch the Fox News Channel, because they're unbiased and support the war 100 percent."

Michael Crane
Systems Analyst

"One week into the conflict, it's still unclear who will emerge as this war's Arthur 'Scud Stud' Kent."

Amanda Criss
Nutritionist

"Can't we skip all that disturbing night-vision bombing stuff and go straight to the jubilant liberation footage?"

Andrea Lytle
Homemaker

"I watch Al-Jazeera on satellite but turn the sound off and listen to NPR. I have no idea what the fuck is happening."

Gordon Jackson
Architect

"I'm hoping there will be helmet-mounted soldier-cams to be outraged by."

Dan Durkee
Roofer

"Talk about your boring reruns."

Mitchell Fawkes
Electrician

New Military Technology

Military technology has evolved tremendously since the 1991 Gulf War. What new equipment is debuting in the current conflict?

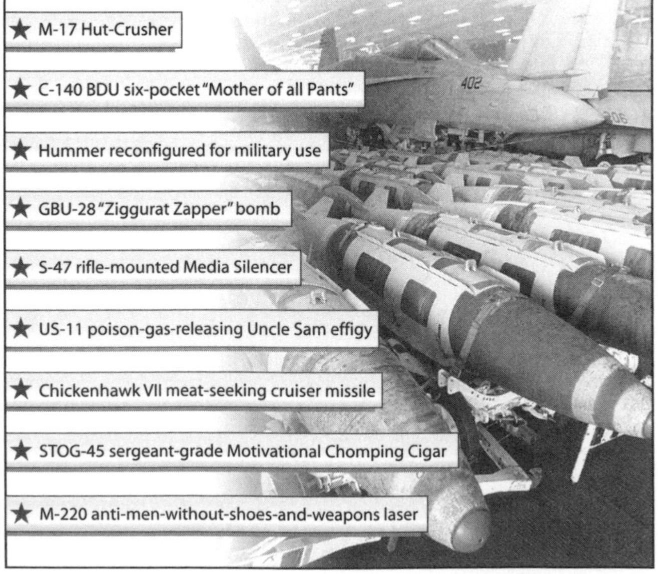
★ M-17 Hut-Crusher
★ C-140 BDU six-pocket "Mother of all Pants"
★ Hummer reconfigured for military use
★ GBU-28 "Ziggurat Zapper" bomb
★ S-47 rifle-mounted Media Silencer
★ US-11 poison-gas-releasing Uncle Sam effigy
★ Chickenhawk VII meat-seeking cruiser missile
★ STOG-45 sergeant-grade Motivational Chomping Cigar
★ M-220 anti-men-without-shoes-and-weapons laser

the ONION®
America's Finest News Source.™
Herman Ulysses Zweibel
Founder

T. Herman Zweibel
Publisher Emeritus
J. Phineas Zweibel
Publisher
Maxwell Prescott Zweibel
Editor-In-Chief

Point-Counterpoint: The Iraq Invasion

This War Will Destabilize The Entire Mideast Region And Set Off A Global Shockwave Of Anti-Americanism

George W. Bush may think that a war against Iraq is the solution to our problems, but the reality is, it will only serve to create far more.

By Nathan Eckert

This war will not put an end to anti-Americanism; it will fan the flames of hatred even higher. It will not end the threat of weapons of mass destruction; it will make possible their further proliferation. And it will not lay the groundwork for the flourishing of democracy throughout the Mideast; it will harden the resolve of Arab states to drive out all Western (i.e. U.S.) influence.

If you thought Osama bin Laden was bad, just wait until the countless children who become orphaned by U.S. bombs in the coming weeks are all grown up. Do you think they will forget what country dropped the bombs that killed their parents? In 10 or 15 years, we will look back fondly on the days when there were only a few thousand Middle Easterners dedicated to destroying the U.S. and willing to die for the fundamentalist cause. From this war, a million bin Ladens will bloom.

And what exactly is our endgame here? Do we really believe that we can install Gen. Tommy Franks as the ruler of Iraq? Is our arrogance and hubris so great that we actually believe that a U.S. provisional military regime will be welcomed with open arms by the Iraqi people? Democracy cannot possibly thrive under coercion. To take over a country and impose one's own system of government without regard for the people of that country is the very antithesis of democracy. And it is doomed to fail.

And what exactly is our endgame here? Do we really believe that we can install Gen. Tommy Franks as the ruler of Iraq?

A war against Iraq is not only morally wrong, it will be an unmitigated disaster. ⌀

No It Won't

No it won't.

It just won't. None of that will happen.

You're getting worked up over nothing. Everything is going to be fine. So just relax, okay? You're really overreacting.

By Bob Sheffer

"This war will not put an end to anti-Americanism; it will fan the flames of hatred even higher"?

It won't.

"It will harden the resolve of Arab states to drive out all Western (i.e. U.S.) influence"?

Not really.

"A war against Iraq is not only morally wrong, it will be an unmitigated disaster"?

Sorry, no, I disagree.

"To take over a country and impose one's own system of government without regard for the people of that country is the very antithesis of democracy"?

You are completely wrong.

Trust me, it's all going to work out perfect. Nothing bad is going to happen. It's all under control.

We're in control of this situation, and we know what we're doing. So stop being so pessimistic.

Why do you keep saying these things? I can tell when there's trouble looming, and I really don't sense that right now. We're in control of this situation, and we know what we're doing. So stop being so pessimistic.

Look, you've been proven wrong, so stop talking. You've had your say already.

Be quiet, okay? Everything's fine.

You're wrong. ⌀

Maxim Reader Eager To Put Newly Acquired Knowledge Of Women To Use

MANASSAS, VA—*Maxim* subscriber Kevin Blynn, 23, looks forward to putting into practical use the advice and information about women he has gleaned from the popular men's lifestyle magazine, sources reported Tuesday.

Above: Kevin Blynn

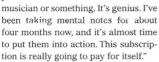

"I'm the kind of guy who likes to work all the angles, and no one has more angles for dealing with women than *Maxim*," Blynn said. "I just read an article on how to land a model by dressing really sloppy so she thinks you're an artist or musician or something. It's genius. I've been taking mental notes for about four months now, and it's almost time to put them into action. This subscription is really going to pay for itself."

While Blynn, who started reading the magazine in January, is currently single, he anticipates his dating status will change when he begins "Project: Laid."

"Until I found out about *Maxim*, I really didn't understand girls," Blynn said. "Now, I've got an edge. One article suggested I pretend to be gay to get women to let their defenses down. I mean, it's risky and could easily backfire, but if it works, I'll be swimming in it."

Though he has gone on just one date in the past three months, Blynn said he is confident that his lonely, masturbation-intensive Saturday nights will soon be a thing of the past.

"The latest issue tells you how to turn any situation into guaranteed sex," Blynn said. "If there's a threat of a terrorist attack, you can turn that into terror sex. If you're in a foreign country, you can turn that into 'two ships in the night' sex. If your girlfriend's pissed off about something, you can turn that into hot, angry, I-hate-you sex. As soon as I get a girlfriend, I'm gonna try that last one out."

Maxim, Blynn said, also offers valuable advice on how to bed female acquaintances.

"The February issue had some kick-ass info on how to score with a female friend who just got dumped," Blynn said. "You have to come on all nice and sensitive until you seal the deal. The article said chicks love it, but you have to do it right, or they'll get pissed before you can get any of that pie."

Blynn said he is confident that Maxim's road-tested tips will work for him.

"A lot of the information and advice is from guys like me," Blynn said. "They're out there in the trenches trying out their tips before they print them, so I know they've got to be good. Those guys at *Maxim* get all the tail."

In spite of Blynn's faith, his friends are skeptical of his reliance on the magazine for advice.

"I doubt this'll work any better than anything else he's tried," former roommate Chris Komarek said. "Kevin was never good when it came to meeting women. He had a girlfriend for a few months in college and was really hurt when they broke up. If this *Maxim* stuff is building up his confidence, more power to him. It couldn't be any worse than when he used to run stuff in the 'Missed Connections' section of the personals, hoping to hook up with some girl he'd stared at in some coffee shop for hours. That was just sad." Ø

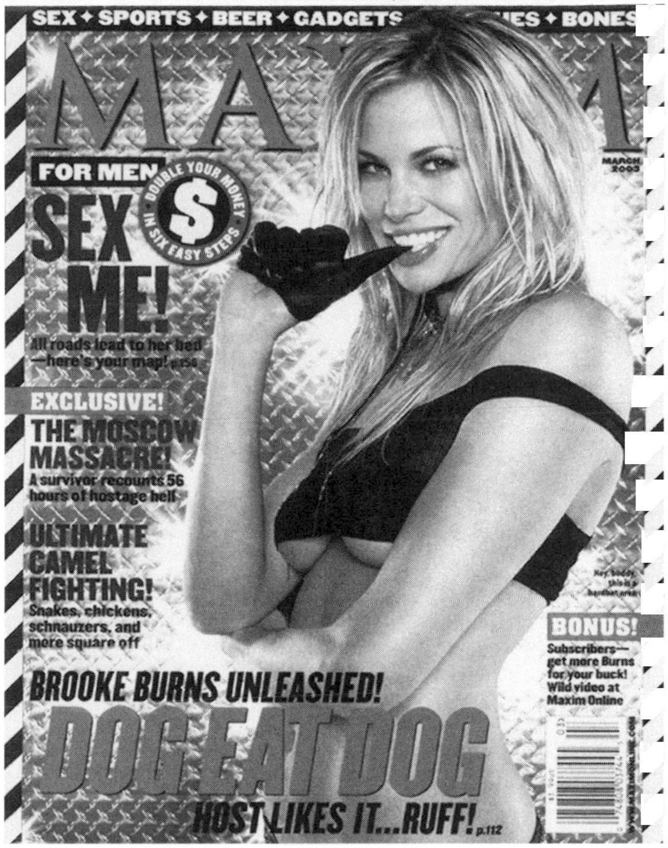

NEWS IN BRIEF

Sheryl Crow Unsuccessful; War On Iraq Begins

WASHINGTON, DC—In spite of recording artist Sheryl Crow's strong protestations, including the wearing of a "No War" guitar strap, the U.S. went to war with Iraq last week. "Making the decision to go to war is never easy, but it's that much harder when you know Sheryl Crow disapproves," White House press secretary Ari Fleischer said at a press conference Monday. "It is this administration's sincerest hope that it can one day regain the support and trust of the woman behind such hits as 'All I Wanna Do' and 'Soak Up The Sun.'" Fleischer issued similar apologies to Martin Sheen, Janeane Garofalo, and Nelly.

Vital Info On Iraqi Chemical Weapons Provided By U.S. Company That Made Them

BALTIMORE—The Pentagon has obtained vital information on Iraqi chemical weapons from Alcolac International, the Baltimore-based company that sold them to the Mideast nation in the '80s. "It's terrifying what Iraq has," Pentagon spokesman James Reese said Monday. "Saddam possesses massive stockpiles of everything from ethylene to thiodiglycol, according to sales records provided by Alcolac." The Pentagon has also been collecting key intelligence on Iraqi nuclear weapons and guidance systems from Honeywell, Unisys, and other former U.S. suppliers to Iraq.

U.S. Continues Proud Tradition Of Diversity On Front Lines

CAMP COYOTE, KUWAIT—With blacks and Hispanics comprising more than 60 percent of the Army's ground forces in Iraq, the U.S. military is continuing its long, proud tradition of multiculturalism on the front lines of war. "Though racism and discrimination remain problems in society at large, in the military—especially in the lower ranks where you find the cannon fodder—a spirit of inclusiveness has prevailed for decades," Gen. Jim White said Monday. "When it comes to having your head blown off by enemy fire, America is truly colorblind."

Casual Sex Surprisingly Formal

DAYTONA BEACH, FL—After several hours of drunken Spring Break revelry Monday, Ron Viselic, 19, and Becky Pell, 18, returned to Pell's motel room for surprisingly formal casual sex. "We were laughing and doing body shots at the bar, but when we got back to my room, things turned all businesslike," Pell said. "He kept asking me if it was okay to take off each piece of clothing, then he wouldn't do anything but missionary." Following the methodical, strangely businesslike intercourse, Viselic and Pell spent five minutes "spooning" before Viselic dressed and left.

Kidnapped Hilton Sisters Appalled By Captor's Basement

NEW YORK—According to Monday's *New York Post*, hotel heiresses Paris and Nicky Hilton are aghast over the condition of the basement of their kidnapper, William Henry Buntz. "My sources tell me that Paris and Nicky are bound-and-*gagging* over the less-than-tony trappings," *Post* Page Six gossip columnist Richard Johnson wrote. "Sources say their crazed captor has creeping crud and crawling centipedes in his cellar... and it's got the spoiled socialites in a snit!" As of press time, police have made no attempt to locate the sisters. Ø

WAR PIE from page 97

wants to see young American soldiers die in battle, but we sure do love Mom's war pie," Chris said. "I walked in the house after basketball practice,

Next Monday, Sensenbrenner plans to take a war pie to the Cedar County Clerk's office, where she works as a secretary, just as she did during the 2001 invasion of Afghanistan.

and I could smell it in the oven. Mmm, mmm, it's too bad we don't go to war more often!"

Next Monday, Sensenbrenner plans to take a war pie to the Cedar County Clerk's office, where she works as a secretary, just as she did during the 2001 invasion of Afghanistan. She described the gesture as a nice way to boost people's spirits for the difficult times ahead, as well as—her coworkers tease—a chance to show off her baking skills.

"War pie is so rich, you couldn't eat it all the time," Cedar County Clerk Nora Weltz said. "But it's okay to overlook calories every few years when the U.S. bombs Kosovo, Afghanistan, Sudan, Bosnia, or wherever."

The recipe has been handed down in Sensenbrenner's family for generations.

"The tradition goes back many years," Sensenbrenner said. "I got the recipe from my mom and she from hers, and so on. The only change I've made was switching the lard in the crust to vegetable shortening. It's still as gooey and delicious as it was back when Truman sent troops to the Korean peninsula."

War pie is not the only military-themed dish Sensenbrenner has made over the years.

"I made Skirmish Custard when we invaded Grenada and Police Action Potato Chip Casserole when we went into Panama for General Noriega," Sensenbrenner said. "Even [husband] Doug got into the act with his Air Strikes Against Libya Waffles."

For all the desserts Sensenbrenner has concocted, however, her traditional war pie remains the family's all-time favorite.

"Lordy, imagine how many times I've gotten this old thing out," Sensenbrenner said, holding the well-worn pink index card that contains the recipe. "I must have passed it on to at least 25 friends over the years, and that's not counting everyone who's read it in the First Lutheran Church recipe book."

According to Sensenbrenner, making a truly delicious war pie is a skill that cannot be learned from a book, but rather from years of practice.

"I'm thinking it was the Bay of Pigs when I first saw my mother make war pie, but it might have been Vietnam," Sensenbrenner said. "At any rate, I was standing next to her on a chair at the kitchen counter as she rolled out the dough. 'Sprinkle the rolling pin and counter with flour, but don't use too much, or the crust will be tough,' she told me. Seems like only yesterday."

During the 1991 Gulf War, Sensenbrenner repeated the touching scene with her own daughter.

"Heather and I were peeling fruit at the sink, and Wolf Blitzer was on in the next room talking about the previous night's bombing raids on Baghdad," Sensenbrenner said. "Butter was up to five dollars a pound that year, but there was no way I was going to substitute margarine. A war pie wouldn't be a war pie without real butter."

"Today, Heather is a junior at Iowa State," Sensenbrenner continued.

War pie is not the only military-themed dish Sensenbrenner has made over the years.

"She called the other day and was so disappointed to hear that she was missing out on war pie. I promised to bake another one the next time she's home for the weekend. They're expecting this whole Iraq thing to be over in a matter of weeks, though, so I told her she'd better make it quick." ⊘

CONCRETE BLOCK from page 93

amounts of blood. Passersby were amazed by the unusually large amounts of blood. Passersby were amazed by the unusually large amounts of blood. Passersby were amazed by the unusually large

Fuck all y'all bishops.

amounts of blood. Passersby were amazed by the unusually large amounts of blood. Passersby were amazed by the unusually large amounts of blood. Passersby were amazed by the unusually large amounts of blood. Passersby were amazed by the unusually large amounts of blood. Passersby were amazed by the unusually large amounts of blood. Passersby were amazed by the unusually large amounts of blood. Passersby were amazed by the unusually large amounts of blood. Passersby were amazed by the unusually large amounts of blood. Passersby were amazed by the unusually large amounts of blood. Passersby were amazed by the unusually large amounts of blood. Passersby were amazed by the unusually large amounts of blood. Passersby were amazed by the unusually large amounts of blood. Passersby were amazed by the unusually large amounts of blood. Passersby were amazed by the unusually large amounts of blood. Passersby were

see CONCRETE BLOCK page 108

the ONION presents a guide to:

Prescription-Drug Safety

When taking prescription drugs, it is vital to be fully informed about proper usage. Here are some helpful hints to ensure your safety:

- Prescription drugs should be kept far out of reach of children, even if they cry, "Please, please, may I have my medicine?"
- Some people say you should not exceed the recommended dosage on the bottle. But, come on, it's *medicine*—it's good for you.
- Stay away from that Lipitor shit. It's like hosting a Filipino drag-queen knife fight in your skull.
- If you take medication daily, a useful accessory is a seven-day pill case, which helps you keep track of your intake and serves as a depressing symbol of your mortality.
- If the pharmacist says your prescription will take 45 minutes to an hour to fill, say "Oh, no," and fall over dead.
- Never mix prescription painkillers with alcohol, unless you like to party really, really hard.
- Most people don't realize how much pharmacists enjoy haggling over the price of medications.
- To reduce the risk of mix-ups at the pharmacy, bring a bat with a nail in it.
- Most pills should not be taken on an empty stomach. Sprinkle a handful onto a salad.
- If your pharmacist doesn't offer to have one with you right there in the store, the shit's probably no good.
- If you are ever in doubt about the safety of a particular medication, consult a qualified physician. He will be happy to pooh-pooh your concerns.

BUSH from page 97

guer who once used powerful family connections to avoid service in Vietnam had what it took to face enemy fire head-on. However, Bush—or, as his fellow soldiers nicknamed him in a spirit of battlefield camaraderie, 'Big Tex'—quickly overcame the platoon's

"Bush is the best soldier I've ever had the honor of fighting alongside," said Pvt. Jon Benjamin, 23. "I'd take a bullet for that man, because I know he'd take one for me if he had to."

reluctance to having a "fancy-pants Yalie" in its ranks.

"Bush is the best soldier I've ever had the honor of fighting alongside," said Pvt. Jon Benjamin, 23. "I'd take a bullet for that man, because I know he'd take one for me if he had to."

Proving himself a worthy foot soldier, Bush has earned the respect of his fellow front-line combatants with acts of courage and heroism that one soldier called "a truly inspiring example of one man's commitment to the cause of liberty."

"Just yesterday, George stormed an Iraqi machine-gun nest when our sergeant took one in the belly," Pvt. Scott "Lumpy" Fellers, 20, told reporters. "We were pinned down, cut off from our division, and it looked like curtains for us all. Thankfully, George was there. He ran through heavy artillery fire and lobbed a grenade right into their bunker. If it hadn't been for him, God knows how many of us would've been coming home in body bags."

"It's not just any president who would risk his life like the nation's men in uniform do," Fellers added. "God bless him and everything he stands for."

Bush's courage, sources say, was evident from the earliest stages of the war's planning. Though the Pentagon initially wanted an air war with minimal ground combat, Bush quickly dismissed this strategy, insisting that the only way a true and lasting victory could be achieved was to go in and fight—dune by dune, village by village—until Iraq was finally free.

White House sources say Bush's decision to place his own life on the line for his country met with resistance from top military leaders.

"The Joint Chiefs of Staff kept telling him, 'Mr. President, we beg you—stay here in Washington, where it's safe.' But George was having none of it," said Maj. Gen. Buford Blount, commander of the 3rd Infantry. "He was adamant that if our boys overseas were going to risk their lives for liberty, he was going to do the same. And, by God, he proved himself a man of his word."

The president has only been in battle for less than a week, but he has already proven himself more than willing to put himself in the line of fire.

"The president carried me through an enemy minefield after my arm had been blown off by a mortar shell, blazing away with his pistol as he delivered me to safety," Pvt. Chris Adair said. "Then, after he'd gotten me to a medic, he went all the way back through that same minefield—carrying a 40-pound bag of ice the whole way—to retrieve my severed arm so the doctors could sew it back on. Now, thanks to President Bush, I'll still be able to play piano for the church choir back home in Appleton, just like I promised Grandma. He is truly an American hero."

Adair's comments were echoed by many of the soldiers fighting alongside Bush.

"I used to be cynical about politicians who are born into privilege and wealth. I thought, 'Sure, they talk a good game about our duty to protect democracy, but when push comes to shove, they'd rather send off the nation's poor, uneducated, and underprivileged to do the fighting for them,'" said Pvt. Frank Elkins, 19. "I always figured they'd

Bush quickly dismissed this strategy, insisting that the only way a true and lasting victory could be achieved was to go in and fight—dune by dune, village by village—until Iraq was finally free.

rather see somebody else die in some foreign land than make that sacrifice themselves. But now I know I was wrong."

"There may be some folks out there, born silver spoon in hand, who'd act that way, but that ain't Bush. No, that ain't Bush," Elkins said. "He ain't no fortunate son." ⌀

U.S.U.N.

'The Whole U.N. Thing Just Wasn't Working'

WASHINGTON, DC—Frustrated with the United Nations' "consistent, blatant regard for the will of its 188 member nations," the U.S. announced Monday the formation of its own international governing body, the U.S.U.N.

"The U.N. has repeatedly demonstrated an inability to act decisively in carrying out actions the U.S. government deems necessary," U.S.U.N. Secretary General Colin Powell said. "Every time we tried to get something accomplished, it inevitably got bogged down in procedural policies, bureaucratic formalities, and Security Council votes."

"I predict the U.S.U.N. will be ex-

"The U.N. has repeatedly demonstrated an inability to act decisively in carrying out actions the U.S. government deems necessary," U.S.U.N. Secretary General Colin Powell said.

tremely influential in world politics in the coming decades," Powell continued. "In fact, you can count on it."

The new organization will be based in Houston, where a $400 million U.S.U.N. Building is currently under construction. The U.S.U.N. Charter, ratified unanimously by delegates in a four-minute vote Monday, sets forth the mission of the organization as "the proliferation of peace and international economic, social, and humanitarian progress through deference to the U.S."

"The U.S.U.N. resembles the original in almost every way, right down to all the flags outside our headquarters," said Condoleezza Rice, a U.S. delegate to the U.S.U.N. "This organization will carry out peacekeeping missions all over the world, but, unlike the U.N., these missions will not be compromised by the threat of opposition by lesser nations."

In its first act, the U.S.U.N. Security Council unanimously backed a resolution to liberate Iraq's people and natural resources from the rule of Saddam Hussein.

"We gave the old U.N. a go for I don't know how many years, but it just wasn't working," said Dick Cheney, a U.S. delegate to the U.S.U.N. "Really, I have no idea what we were doing sacrificing all that power and autonomy in exchange for a couple of lousy troops from New Zealand."

Added Cheney: "I can't tell you how much easier it is to achieve consensus when you don't have to worry about dissent."

Cheney, along with Rice, Donald Rumsfeld, Tom Ridge, and George W. Bush, make up the five permanent members of the 15-person U.S.U.N. Security Council.

"The five Security Council members have veto power to block

In its first act, the U.S.U.N. Security Council unanimously backed a resolution to liberate Iraq's people.

U.S.U.N. resolutions for military action," Rumsfeld said. "Not that anyone would, but it's nice to have, nonetheless."

According to Powell, in spite of the fact that delegates hail from every corner of the U.S., General Assembly meetings have been refreshingly free of rancor.

"We've got Bill Frist from Tennessee, Tom DeLay from Texas, and Dennis Hastert from way up in Illinois," U.S.U.N. delegate Rick Santorum said. "Despite the diverse backgrounds of the delegates, cooperation has not been a problem—unlike at some outmoded, gridlocked international peacekeeping bodies I could name."

The official U.S.U.N. language is English. The official religion is Christianity. ⌀

IRAQI from page 97

our home."

A shoemaker and father of five, Sabri, 44, was listening to the radio at 3 a.m. when a missile launched from a U.S. warship in the Persian Gulf veered off course and struck just feet from his house. Sawssan was away at the time, tending to an ailing aunt in the Baghdad suburb of Mansour.

"My husband was no fan of Saddam," Sawssan said. "He felt he was a terrible despot. If the Americans do drive him from power, it will be that much more of a shame that they killed Taha." ⌀

Above: The Sabris' home.

COMMUNITY VOICES

I Can Help The Next Person Here

There's no waiting at register three. Wheel your cart right over! I can help the next person. Any number of items!

Can I help anyone over here? My checkout-lane light is blinking—and that means there's no line. I'd be happy to help you! I'm waiting to serve you! That's my goal—to make you, the customer, happy.

By Sheila Zollner
Lead Cashier,
Second Shift

As you see, I'm smiling, ready to help. If you'd only glance over here, I'd nod and wave you toward me. Can I help someone? Over here! No waiting!

Please let me help you. What will I do if I can't? I can't read a magazine. I can't sit down. No stools are allowed behind the checkout counters. It's against store policy, because that might make it look like I'm not ready to help the next person.

So, please, bring your items to register three. Any number of items here. Your personal check is welcome with Chexpress, but please, for amount of purchase only. Enjoy the convenience of the ATM station right at the register. I can help the next person at register three!

Can I be of assistance, then? I can help the next person! I'll make sure to make you feel welcome at my register. It doesn't matter who you are—young, old, black, white, coupon-clipper, crazy old drunk guy, 12-year-old punk trying to buy cigarettes—I

Please let me help you. What will I do if I can't? I can't read a magazine. I can't sit down. No stools are allowed behind the checkout counters. It's against store policy, because that might make it look like I'm not ready to help the next person.

welcome you all to Sav-O-Mart. In the land of food value, there is no outcast.

I'll say hello to you, possibly comment on the weather, and thank you, respectfully calling you "ma'am" or "sir." If you pay with a check, I'll even use your first name when you leave. You can use my first name. I'm always wearing my name tag, because I forfeit a half-hour's pay if I forget it for a shift.

Maybe next time you come to the store, you will come to register three again. We might develop a relationship where I will greet you and refer

So, please, bring your items to register three. Any number of items here. Your personal check is welcome with Chexpress, but please, for amount of purchase only. Enjoy the convenience of the ATM station right at the register. I can help the next person at register three!

back to our conversation today: "How did that birthday party go?"; "Enjoying your vacation?"; "Did you decide to make the fruit salad?"; "Menthol 100s, right?"

Embarrassing items in your cart? I'll handle your purchase with discretion. Prophylactics? Gold Bond medicated powder for dry, flaky skin? Adult disposable undergarments? *People* magazine? I've rung them all up a hundred times, and though for you the act of purchase was preceded by a lengthy period of courage-gathering in the parking lot, I won't even raise an eyebrow.

Ma'am, register three is open!

Don't even hesitate. I'm ready to help you. We've got it all! In fact, if you've noticed my apron as well as the multiple brightly colored signs about the store boasting "We've Got It All," you already know that that's our newest slogan and personal pledge to the customer!

I attended the mandatory employee meeting just this week, and I feel confident telling you that we do, in fact, have it all. I also feel ready to assist you in finding any portion of it all, which we've got, that you may need.

I'm just waiting to help you. I'll be here again tomorrow from 2 to 10 p.m., ready to rush to your aid, smiling and chipper, for the duration of my eight-hour shift. But what I'd really like to do is help you right now. ⌀

HOROSCOPES

Your Horoscope

By Lloyd Schumner Sr.
Retired Machinist and
A.A.P.B.-Certified Astrologer

Aries: (March 21–April 19)
You'll prove an unwritten law of travel when your postcards arrive a week after your coffin is flown back.

Taurus: (April 20–May 20)
It's not the hammer of life that's going to beat you down this week, but the hammer of Gene Dubrowski, a local roofer.

Gemini: (May 21–June 21)
You will nearly drown when your classically educated mother submerges you in the Ohio River to give you invincibility.

Cancer: (June 22–July 22)
Rocket skates, giant magnets, and anvils are all well and good, but as the new president of Acme, you're expected to come up with the next Swiffer.

Leo: (July 23–Aug. 22)
They said they'd be right back after those important messages, but the messages weren't all that important and it's been almost 14 years.

Virgo: (Aug. 23–Sept. 22)
You will gain a much greater understanding of what makes women tick when you take one apart and study her in minute detail.

Libra: (Sept. 23–Oct. 23)
Your constant whining about your shoeless condition will continue unabated even after you see a man who has no feet.

Scorpio: (Oct. 24–Nov. 21)
Your life takes a sudden aggressive and violent turn when you start asking yourself how General Patton would handle workplace conflicts.

Sagittarius: (Nov. 22–Dec. 21)
About this upcoming Thursday: Let that be a lesson to you about whom you loan power tools, money, and gasoline.

Capricorn: (Dec. 22–Jan. 19)
Those you love most will soon gather together with you and ask a judge to put you away for as long as the law allows.

Aquarius: (Jan. 20–Feb. 18)
The older you get, the more you're convinced that we were all put in this retirement home for a reason.

Pisces: (Feb. 19–March 20)
Learn to appreciate the little joys that life provides, because three days won't give you much time for the big joys.

MEAT CONSUMPTION from page 100

amounts of blood. Passersby were amazed by the unusually large amounts of blood. Passersby were amazed by the unusually large amounts of blood. Passersby were amazed by the unusually large

Is that when they launched two of every animal on earth into space?

amounts of blood. Passersby were amazed by the unusually large amounts of blood. Passersby were amazed by the unusually large

see MEAT CONSUMPTION page 111

NEWS

DVD Contains 87 Minutes Of Previously Unseen Movie

see ENTERTAINMENT page 5C

Football Fan Wears Off-Season Body Paint

see LOCAL page 8E

NBC Moves War To Thursdays After *Friends*

see TELEVISION page 10D

Grandfather Clocked

see LOCAL page 7E

STATshot

A look at the numbers that shape your world.

Least-Visited Memorials

1. The Redenbacher Monument
2. Tomb of the Unknown Person
3. Dodi Al Fayed Memorial (behind Princess Diana Memorial)
4. The Grenada Veterans Memorial Railing
5. The Stomachache Quilt

the ONION®

VOLUME 39 ISSUE 12 AMERICA'S FINEST NEWS SOURCE™ 3–9 APRIL 2003

Saddam Speech Suspiciously Mentions Nelly Song From Last Summer

LANGLEY, VA—The CIA announced Monday that it suspects Saddam Hussein's latest televised address was pre-recorded, pointing to its suspiciously dated reference to Nelly's "Hot In Herre," a rap hit from the summer of 2002.

"For the enemy invaders of Iraq, it soon will get truly hot in here," Hussein said in the speech, which was televised worldwide Monday. "No amount of clothing removal will be sufficient to withstand the fiery inferno that awaits them on the battlefield."

Many U.S. officials have speculated that Saddam was killed or injured in the initial March 19 air attacks on Baghdad, suggesting that his subsequent televised speeches were recorded weeks or even months ago.

"The 'hot in here' line has definitely raised some eyebrows," CIA director George Tenet said. "However, this may not prove anything: Even though that song is nine months old, you still hear people referencing its chorus all the time. It's even in the new Chris Rock movie."

Above: In a message believed to be pre-taped, Saddam warns the U.S. about rising heat levels in Iraq.

Despite the inconclusive nature of

see SADDAM page 107

Bush Thought War Would Be Over By Now

WASHINGTON, DC—Following a 12th consecutive day of fighting, a puzzled and frustrated President Bush confided to military advisors Monday that he "really figured the war would be over by now."

"It's been almost two weeks," said Bush, commander-in-chief of the 255,000 U.S. troops currently in the Persian Gulf. "What's taking so long? Will the Iraqi regime just topple, already?"

Though Bush has repeatedly declined making public comment on the expected duration of the war, in private he has expressed annoyance with

see WAR page 107

Right: Bush endures another tedious meeting with (left to right) Vice-President Dick Cheney, CIA director George Tenet, and Chief of Staff Andrew Card.

Soup-Kitchen Volunteers Hate College-Application-Padding Brat

Above: Malveaux, who is passionately dedicated to getting into Stanford.

SEATTLE—Volunteers at the Pike Street Salvation Army have grown to hate college-application padder Justin Malveaux, 17, sources reported Monday.

"It's not that Justin doesn't work hard, because he does," said Karla Perkins, 44, weeknight coordinator at the downtown Seattle soup kitchen. "He does whatever you ask of him, and he's pleasant and polite, always complimenting everyone. Still, I can't stand the little Stanford-application-padding fucker."

Perkins met Malveaux in February, when the Bellingham West High School junior submitted a résumé and cover letter requesting a volunteer position.

"Justin said he wanted to help those less fortunate than him, and also to get his volunteering out of the way so he can concentrate on AP classes next year," Perkins said. "Stanford is his first choice, and UCLA is his 'safety.' He also plans to apply to Washington State 'just for laughs,' whatever that means."

An honors student and active participant in five extracurricular groups,

see BRAT page 106

Dolphins And The Military

In a move that has outraged many animal-rights activists, the U.S. Navy is using dolphins to find underwater mines in Iraqi harbors. What do *you* think?

"It's one thing to put human lives at risk in a war, but dolphins? That's just unconscionable."

Arthur Bond
Systems Analyst

"I support the U.S. dolphin military program. For many dolphins, the G.I. Bill is the only way they can afford college."

George Goff
Auto Mechanic

"As someone who wore a T-shirt with a dolphin on it almost every day in fourth grade, I find this development troubling. My nickname in school was 'fishshirt.'"

Melvin Adams
Electrician

"I gave up canned tuna for the dolphins, and now they're just blowing them to shit?"

Dorothea Klapp
Graphic Designer

"Sure, they'll tell you about the success of the Navy dolphins, but will they tell you about the 10,000-dolphin protest in Chicago last weekend?"

Eleanor Reese
Painter

"This is the military. We should be amazed they're not using baby chicks."

Dan Mora
Civil Engineer

Celine In Las Vegas

Celine Dion recently began a three-year, $100 million engagement at Caesars Colosseum, a theater built specially for her. Among the perks the superstar is guaranteed:

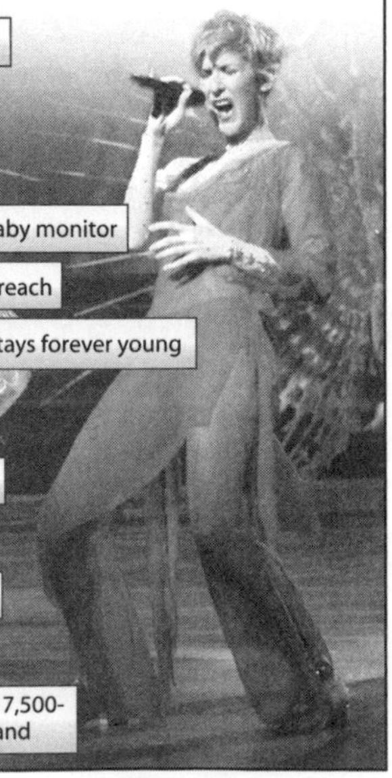

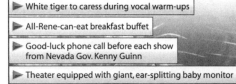

- White tiger to caress during vocal warm-ups
- All-Rene-can-eat breakfast buffet
- Good-luck phone call before each show from Nevada Gov. Kenny Guinn
- Theater equipped with giant, ear-splitting baby monitor
- Fresh eucalyptus leaves always within arm's reach
- Backstage self-portrait that ages while she stays forever young
- Special custom-tailored stage outfits to accommodate grotesquely angular limbs
- Brave, inspiring bout with near-fatal disease
- Pair of fauns
- Olympic-sized reptile pit for ritual sacrifices
- Wire mommy for son
- Bejeweled silver elevator to transport her to 7,500-square-foot dressing room in Cloudcuckooland

the ONION®
America's Finest News Source.™

Herman Ulysses Zweibel
Founder

T. Herman Zweibel
Publisher Emeritus
J. Phineas Zweibel
Publisher
Maxwell Prescott Zweibel
Editor-In-Chief

I Should Not Be Allowed To Say The Following Things About America

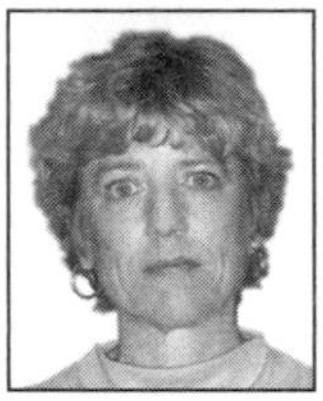

By Ellen Dunst

As Americans, we have a right to question our government and its actions. However, while there is a time to criticize, there is also a time to follow in complacent silence. And that time is now.

It's one thing to question our leaders in the days leading up to a war. But it is another thing entirely to do it *during* a war. Once the blood of young men starts to spill, it is our duty as citizens not to challenge those responsible for spilling that blood. We must remove the boxing gloves and put on the kid gloves. That is why, in this moment of crisis, I should not be allowed to say the following things about America:

Why do we purport to be fighting in the name of liberating the Iraqi people when we have no interest in violations of human rights—as evidenced by our habit of looking the other way when they occur in China, Saudi Arabia, Indonesia, Syria, Burma, Libya, and countless other countries? Why, of all the brutal regimes that regularly violate human rights, do we only intervene militarily in Iraq? Because the violation of human rights is not our true interest here. We just say it is as a convenient means of manipulating world opinion and making our cause seem more just.

That is exactly the sort of thing I should not say right now.

This also is not the time to ask whether diplomacy was ever given a chance. Or why, for the last 10 years, Iraq has been our sworn archenemy, when during the previous 15 years we traded freely in armaments and military aircraft with the evil and despotic Saddam Hussein. This is the kind of question that, while utterly valid, should not be posed right now.

And I certainly will not point out our rapid loss of interest in the establishment of democracy in Afghanistan once our fighting in that country was over. We sure got out of that place in a hurry once it became clear that the problems were too complex to solve with cruise missiles.

That sort of remark will simply have to wait until our boys are safely back home.

Here's another question I won't ask right now: Could this entire situation have been avoided in the early 1990s had then-U.S. ambassador to Iraq April Glaspie not been given sub rosa instructions by the Bush Administration to soft-pedal a cruel dictator? Such a question would be tantamount to sedition while our country engages in bloody conflict. Just think how hurtful that would be to our military morale. I know I couldn't fight a war knowing that was the talk back home.

Is this, then, the appropriate time for me to ask if Operation Iraqi Freedom is an elaborate double-blind, sleight-of-hand misdirection ploy to con us out of inconvenient civil rights through Patriot Acts I and II? Should I

It's one thing to question our leaders in the days leading up to a war. But it is another thing entirely to do it during a war. Once the blood of young men starts to spill, it is our duty as citizens not to challenge those responsible for spilling that blood.

wonder whether this war is an elaborate means of distracting the country while its economy bucks and lurches toward the brink of a full-blown depression? No and no.

True patriots know that a price of freedom is periodic submission to the will of our leaders—especially when the liberties granted us by the Constitution are at stake. What good is our right to free speech if our soldiers are too demoralized to defend that right, thanks to disparaging remarks made about their commander-in-chief by the Dixie Chicks?

When the Founding Fathers authored the Constitution that sets forth our nation's guiding principles, they made certain to guarantee us individual rights and freedoms. How dare we selfishly lay claim to those liberties at the very moment when our nation is in crisis, when it needs us to be our most selfless? We shame the memory of Thomas Jefferson by daring to mention Bush's outright lies about satellite photos that supposedly prove Iraq is developing nuclear weapons.

At this difficult time, President Bush needs my support. Defense Secretary Donald Rumsfeld needs my support. General Tommy Franks needs my support. It is not my function as a citizen in a participatory democracy to question our leaders. And to exercise my constitutional right—nay, duty—to do so would be un-American. Ø

Former Employee Disappointed By Return-Visit Reception

WILKES-BARRE, PA—Len Neuwirth, a marketing analyst with Penn Packaging Corporation from 2000 to 2002, expressed slight disappointment Monday over his failure to cause a stir among former coworkers during his return visit.

"When I left Penn Packaging, everybody seemed really sorry to see me go," said Neuwirth, 32, who left last November to take a similar position at Allied Plastics. "I guess I kinda thought that when I finally made my first return visit after quitting, they'd all go nuts, and that maybe work would stop for a little while and stuff."

Neuwirth said he carefully planned his visit to be a surprise, hoping to maximize the impact of his triumphant return. Upon arriving at the office, Neuwirth asked new receptionist Darlene Cho, whom he had never met, to buzz Ted Arrington, one of his closest former coworkers. Neuwirth called Arrington's reaction "somewhat of a letdown."

"When Ted came out to the lobby, he seemed happy enough to see me, but he didn't scream or anything," Neuwirth said. "We chatted for a few minutes, which was nice, but I was sort of hoping he'd get all excited and go running off to find a bunch of other people, telling them, 'You're not going to believe who just walked in!'"

After Arrington excused himself to go back to work, Neuwirth spent several minutes hanging around the receptionist's area, making small talk with Cho while hoping for someone familiar to walk past. When no one did, he decided to head deeper into the office, where more underwhelming reactions awaited him.

"The only person who seemed excited was Shannon Ridgeley,"

"When Ted came out to the lobby, he seemed happy enough to see me, but he didn't scream or anything," Neuwirth said. "I was sort of hoping he'd get all excited and go running off to find a bunch of other people, telling them, 'You're not going to believe who just walked in!'"

Neuwirth spent several minutes hanging around the receptionist's area, making small talk with Cho while hoping for someone familiar to walk past.

Neuwirth said. "She gave me a big hug and asked me all these questions, but she's one of those super-chipper people who makes a big deal when the FedEx guy shows up."

Added Neuwirth: "I bet Andy [Dodd] would've given me more of a reaction. Too bad he was out sick."

Neuwirth said he was planning to take his former colleagues to lunch, but they had already placed an order for takeout.

"I came by the office at 11:30 so I could get people before they left for lunch," Neuwirth said. "Apparently, there was some sort of big project due, so everyone ordered in."

Above: Neuwirth stands outside his former place of employment.

Throughout the visit, Neuwirth kept an eye out for remnants of his tenure there, only to find none.

"There used to be a funny sign I did

see RECEPTION page 106

NEWS IN BRIEF

Network News Satellites Collide Over Iraq

AN NASIRIYAH, IRAQ—In an accident air-and-space-traffic controllers called "inevitable," a CNN satellite collided with an MSNBC satellite over southern Iraq Monday. "Frankly, it's a miracle something like this didn't happen sooner," said Ian Graham of BBC One. "Right now, there are roughly 950 network news satellites crammed into a 125-cubic-mile area of space above Iraq, with more being launched every day." Less than an hour after the crash, an MTV News satellite grazed an Oxygen satellite, temporarily cutting off Oxygen News reporter Lisa Hood's live report on a firefight between U.S. and Iraqi forces near Basra.

Government No Longer Even Bothering To Hide Halliburton Favors

WASHINGTON, DC—With last week's announcement that it will award Halliburton a lucrative contract to put out Iraqi oil-well fires after the war, the U.S. government has officially stopped trying to hide its favoritism toward the Houston-based company. "When we first started cutting Halliburton sweetheart deals, we'd worry about how it would look, with Dick Cheney being their former CEO and all," White House press secretary Ari Fleischer said. "Somewhere along the line, though, we just kind of said, 'Ah, fuck it.'" Fleischer added that Halliburton has something "real juicy" coming its way when the U.S. invades Iran in July 2004.

Blind Date Pronounces Every Syllable Of Word 'Comfortable'

INDIANAPOLIS—In what Melissa Mathis, 30, termed "a deal-breaker," blind date Jeff Rochlin, 33, pronounced every syllable of the word "comfortable" Tuesday. "We sat down at the table, and he said, 'This booth's really com-fort-a-ble,'" Mathis recalled. "Then, a little while later, he said something about the 'grilled veg-e-ta-bles.' I'm sorry, but there's no way I could date a guy like that."

Hellmann's Heir's Conduct Unbefitting A Mayonnaise Magnate

NEW YORK—Jake Hellmann, 19, whose rowdy nightclub exploits have made him a tabloid staple, has behaved in a manner unbefitting his stature as heir to the Hellmann's mayonnaise throne, family sources reported Tuesday. "When one is fortunate enough to carry the name of America's most popular mayonnaise, one does not spend every night getting drunk and partying with models," said his great uncle Oliver Hellmann, 79. "Clearly, young Jake is not yet ready to accept the enormous responsibility that comes with being a mayo magnate."

Second-Grade Class Has No Questions For Visiting Local Historian

KENOSHA, WI—Roberta Litt's second-graders at LaFollette Elementary School failed to come up with a single question for visiting local historian Elmer Rasmussen Tuesday. "Come on, folks," said Litt, scolding her class. "Mr. Rasmussen was nice enough to come all the way down here today to tell us about immigrant-farmstead life in the 19th century. I find it hard to believe that not one of you has a question." Following an uncomfortable two minutes of silence, Litt ordered the children to put their heads down on their desks for the remainder of the period.

RECEPTION from page 105

for the kitchen, so I wanted to see if that was still up," Neuwirth said. "It was, but somebody put a sign over it reminding people to wash their coffee cups. Even gag gifts I'd given people over the years were gone. Oh, well, I guess you gotta keep the office clean."

"For most of the time, they just talked about this project they were working on," Neuwirth said. "I sat there listening, but I had no idea what they were talking about. Finally, after a half-hour, I decided to split."

Neuwirth spent much of his visit in the conference room, trying to catch up with former coworkers as they ate lunch.

"For most of the time, they just talked about this project they were working on," Neuwirth said. "I sat there listening, but I had no idea what they were talking about. Finally, after a half-hour, I decided to split."

Dr. Harvey Garrett, author of *Coworkers For Life*, said people often have unrealistically high expectations when returning to visit a former place of employment.

"In this day and age, few workplace environments foster the kind of social

"Few workplace environments foster the kind of social bonds that would cause employees to feel elation over the sight of an old coworker," Garrett said.

bonds that would cause employees to feel elation over the sight of an old coworker," Garrett said. "Most people are just cordial enough with their coworkers to make the situation tolerable. Since no strong bond is formed, it's hard for people to get worked up about somebody's return."

"I should know, because it happened to me when I dropped in on my old sociology-department colleagues at Colgate [University]," Garrett said. "I might as well have been the woman who worked in the faculty cafeteria." ⌀

BRAT from page 103

Malveaux said he is committed to making himself an indispensable member of the soup kitchen's Tuesday-evening crew for the four months he plans to be there.

"This experience will be invaluable when I have to write my personal essay, which counts for a lot with Stanford," Malveaux said. "It's the kind of real-world growth experience that goes over huge with the admissions people. And, if I ever need a recommendation, there are several people here who I think I've bonded with enough to ask."

The staff's disdain for the upper-middle-class Malveaux went largely unspoken during his first six weeks at the center, manifesting itself primarily in the occasional eye roll. On March 18, however, a floodgate of vitriol was opened when Malveaux asked staff coordinator Jamal Washburn to leave the employee break room, mistaking him for a homeless man.

"I hate that little rich-kid bastard," Washburn said. "He'll be out the door the second he can say he volunteered here for four months. Or, as he'll put it, 'February 2003 to May 2003.'"

Despite their hatred of him, staffers admitted that Malveaux has been helpful. According to Perkins, he has used his "fresh perspective" to increase efficiency, placing a clipboard at the end of the kitchen table and inviting shelter patrons to sign up for the next evening's meal so that the kitchen might better predict attendance.

To combat staff tardiness, Malveaux suggested that volunteers be permitted three missed shifts before being barred from working at the center.

"I hate that little rich-kid bastard," Washburn said. "He'll be out the door the second he can say he volunteered here for four months. Or, as he'll put it, 'February 2003 to May 2003.'"

"As much as I hate to admit it, he has made some improvements," Perkins said. "But he does it in this smug way, like we're so lucky to be graced with the presence of this brilliant, college-bound prodigy, even if only for a few precious months."

"That sunny, can-do attitude is really starting to grate on me," employee Randy Louis said. "Just pass out the tater tots, prepster."

The staff generally uses the 20 minutes Malveaux spends sweeping the parking lot each Tuesday as an opportunity to exchange stories of his naïvete.

"A homeless woman came in wearing a Diabetes Awareness Fun Run T-shirt she got from a box at the shelter," Perkins said. "Justin was saying how inspiring it was that this woman could still care about others, even with all her troubles."

Perkins said she finds Malveaux's attempts to connect with her condescending.

"He's finally stopped asking me where I see myself in five years," Perkins said. "I honestly think he thought he was challenging me to ask myself questions I wouldn't ordinarily ask. Like people in my social strata aren't capable of introspection without the help of somebody better-educated."

"Now, he just talks about himself," Perkins continued. "He wants to be a writer, but he might be an international human-rights lawyer. He gave me his solemn word that, whatever he decides, he will use his skills for the betterment of the world. Thank God, now I can sleep at night."

At the end of each shift, Malveaux records his "hours worked" in his PDA and makes a point of getting Perkins to sign off on it—a ritual Perkins has grown to detest.

"He can talk all he wants about how enriching this experience has been, but it's completely obvious that all he's thinking about is how good this is going to look on his transcript," Perkins said. "Here at the Salvation Army, we try to appreciate all the help God sends our way, but I draw the line with that little shit." ⌀

OCCUPATIONAL INJURY from page 99

amounts of blood. Passersby were amazed by the unusually large amounts of blood. Passersby were

I can't seem to figure out what would be best for your children.

amazed by the unusually large amounts of blood. Passersby were amazed by the unusually large

see OCCUPATIONAL INJURY page 111

SADDAM from page 103

the Nelly reference, CIA analysts have found a number of other clues suggesting that the speech was not broadcast live.

"About three minutes into the speech, a man briefly walks across the screen with what appears to be a copy of *Entertainment Weekly*," Tenet said. "He opens the magazine and, for a split second, it's possible to faintly make out a full-page ad promoting the debut episode of *The Rerun Show*."

> **"For the invaders of Iraq, it soon will get truly hot in here," Hussein said.**

In addition to the visual evidence, Tenet cited certain tellingly dated passages from the speech.

"In one section, Saddam vowed that he would crush Bush 'like Kelly Clarkson crushing the inferior Nikki McKibbin,'" Tenet said. "He then went on to praise his elite Republican Guard, saying that they 'will leave the Americans as bewildered as Ozzy Osbourne trying to operate a television remote control.'"

The Saddam speech, CIA analysts noted, seems intentionally vague, conspicuously lacking in any specific details about the current conflict.

"Victory will soon be ours," a defiant Hussein said. "Unlike the [Major League Baseball] All-Star Game, this will not end in a tie." Ø

WAR from page 103

the way the invasion is "dragging on."

"I knew the war would require courage and fortitude on the part of the American people," Bush said. "What I didn't know was that it would go on for days and days and days."

Though Bush said that receiving reports from U.S. field commanders was thrilling at first, he has grown tired of the repetitive updates.

"The first couple days were really exciting," Bush said. "I was having all sorts of cool strategy meetings with these high-level military men I don't usually talk to, and it all felt very historic. But now, it's gotten to be kind of a monotonous grind. It's always, 'The line has advanced this much.' 'We need to wait for backup here.' 'We're making good progress, but it's been complicated by blah blah blah.' It's all these tedious, same-sounding details. Can I hear something new for a change, like 'They surrender,' or 'Saddam's dead'? Something—anything but more stupid reports of sandstorms."

> **"The first couple days were really exciting," Bush said. "I was having all sorts of cool strategy meetings with these high-level military men I don't usually talk to, and it all felt very historic. But now, it's gotten to be kind of a monotonous grind."**

Though he expressed pride in the nation's military, Bush said he doesn't understand why it can't speed things up a bit.

"I don't think my dad's war took this long, and we've got much better weapons now," Bush said. "I talked to him on the phone the other day and, although he didn't say it, I could tell he was disappointed that I'm not doing it faster than him."

On Sunday, Bush called Gen. Richard Myers, Chairman of the Joint Chiefs of Staff, to discuss the war's progress.

"I didn't complain about how slow it's going, because I know he's working hard and wants to conquer Iraq as much as I do," Bush said. "But I did sort of hint that the faster we win, the more impressive our military will look to the world. So hopefully that'll light a fire under him."

Bush asked Myers for a "guesstimate" regarding the length of the war, but the general said he couldn't give one. Myers also denied the president's subsequent request for "even a rough guesstimate."

Bush said "it was fun to be in charge of a war and stay up all night," but the fatigue is starting to set in.

"I haven't gotten more than seven hours of sleep a night since I gave Saddam the 48 hours," Bush said. "I thought I'd get to play a few games of golf when we went to Camp David two weekends ago, but we worked the entire time."

Bush's staff has noted his rising level of irritation.

"I know George thinks it should be over, but he's got to realize that this is a complicated thing," National Security Advisor Condoleezza Rice said. "He doesn't have to keep snapping at us."

> **Bush asked Myers for a "guesstimate" regarding the length of the war, but the general said he couldn't give one. Myers also denied the president's subsequent request for "even a rough guesstimate."**

According to Deputy Secretary of Defense Paul Wolfowitz, Bush continually finds excuses to slip away from briefings, even resorting to ringing his own secure phone for a fake "emergency."

"We've been going easier on him the last few days," Wolfowitz said. "At first, we informed him of every new development, because that's what he wanted. Now, we pretty much limit it to the essentials." Ø

the ONION presents:

Prom-Planning Tips

Prom season is just around the corner. Here are some tips to help make your prom night unforgettable:

- The prom is a magical experience, a chance to do such grown-up things as get all dressed up, drink nine Smirnoff Ices, vomit in a limo, and pass out in Mom's azalea bushes.
- The theme is one of the most important elements of a prom. Choose carefully between "Tropical Paradise" and "Stepping Out In Style."
- Do not attempt to finger-bang your date until a slow song comes on.
- Prom night is one of the most memorable nights of your life, so don't ruin it by neglecting to wax. No guy wants to go down on a gorilla salad.
- Don't forget the corsage! Fresh flowers are necessary to mask the smell of sweat and foot odor in your school's dank, poorly ventilated gym.
- Try to plan ahead, so you are not more than two or three months pregnant for your prom.
- Next to a bridesmaid dress, a prom dress is the most important dress you will ever wear.
- Achieve local celebrity and serve as a valuable cautionary tale by drinking too much at the post-prom party, plowing your Trans Am head-on into another car, and killing yourself, your date, and four kids from St. Vitus.
- Impress your date with corsages for both wrists, plus a third to strap to her forehead.
- If you were not asked to prom, you can still have fun by putting on a dress, buying a taco-salad party platter from the local Pic-N-Save, and dancing in your bedroom as a portable radio plays the latest Top 40 hits.
- Don't feel pressure to have sex just because it's prom night. Stopping at a tongue up the ass is perfectly acceptable.

I've Got Oscar (And War) Fever!

Item! There's only one story on the minds of people across this great nation right now: the **75th anniversary Academy Awards**. And Jackie Harvey was right there in the front row... of his living room! I know there are people out there who say there are more important things to worry about in these troubled times. Well, what better way to forget your troubles than with a fabulous awards ceremony?

The Outside Scoop
By Jackie Harvey

After all the talk about getting rid of the red carpet, they still had one, even if they didn't do any interviews on it. Out of respect for our troops, the dresses and tuxedos were a little more sedate, which was actually kind of nice. It reminded me of the glory days of the '40s and '50s, when you could see the likes of **Agnes Moorehead** and **Kirk Douglas** sitting in the crowd.

Of course, **Chicago** was the big winner of the evening, hopefully ushering in a new age of **the old razzle-dazzle**. I, for one, would love to see a movie version of **Cabaret**. As for individual accolades, **Julianne "Far From Heaven" Moore** can wait, because the woman of **The Hours** is **Nicole Kidman**. The Kiwi beauty was incredibly brave to wear a fake nose and cover her good looks in front of millions of moviegoers. If you ask me, she deserved her Oscar for that alone. Hey, it certainly didn't hurt the box office. Do I smell a sequel?

The Kiwi beauty was incredibly brave to wear a fake nose and cover her good looks in front of millions of moviegoers. If you ask me, she deserved her Oscar for that alone.

The speeches mostly kept with the theme of quiet dignity, but who was the fat guy who rained on everyone's parade by yelling at **our president**? The Academy Awards are no place for people to make protest statements. He should have been more like dreamy **Adrienne Brody**. He was one class act. Plus, he was great in **Willard**. As for host **Steve Martin**, he was okay, but let's face it, he's no **Billy Crystal**.

Item! You know, the best thing about the war is the new vernacular. I find the phrases from this particular war fascinating: "shock and awe," "embeds," "decapitation attack," "helicopter crash"... Whew! Those embeds (like a police ride-along, only with the military instead of the police) really bring home the superiority of our military. Good job, **press corps**, and God bless **America**!

Item! I'm not a big fan of reality TV, but I am simply head-over-heels for

***Chicago* was the big winner of the evening, hopefully ushering in a new age of the old razzle-dazzle.**

Are You Hot Enough To Be Chosen By America? This is gripping and sexy television. If you haven't seen it, it's like a beauty contest with laser pointers and frank commentary on body fat. By getting right to the nitty-gritty, judge **Lorenzo Llamas** is helping these women find ways to improve themselves. Now, there's a real **American hero**.

When we're facing war, a bad economy, and no red-carpet interviews at the Academy Awards, don't sit around like a lump feeling sorry for yourself. Do what I do: Light some candles and take refuge in a nice, long **bubble bath**. Nothing is better for helping you forget the shock and awe of 4,500 bombs dropped on a major city, especially if you play a little **Tina Turner** while you're soaking.

That **Jon Cusack** is the thinking man's **Matthew Broderick**.

I was recently talking about great TV with **some friends**, and someone mentioned **Miami Vice**. Well, of course, there was the fashions and the locale, but the thing I remember most was the theme. I thought I'd impress my friends because I remembered it was by **Jan Wenner**. What I didn't know is that it's pronounced Yon Wenner. Boy, was my face red when I was corrected. Now I know, and now you know, true-believing readers. Learn from my mistake.

Jacko? 'Nuff said!

Well, that's all for now. Hopefully, the war will be over by the next time I come to you. If that happens, I'm sure I'll be brimming with news that's been buried by the war coverage. In the meantime, pop in your favorite movie and take a load off your mind, because you deserve it. Remember, Harveyheads: The **bright lights of Hollywood** are just as bright whether **human beings** are dying or not! ⌀

Your Horoscope

By Lloyd Schumner Sr.
Retired Machinist and
A.A.P.B.-Certified Astrologer

Aries: (March 21–April 19)
You've been feeling bad about wasting your life, but there's really nothing useful you could have done with it, anyway.

Taurus: (April 20–May 20)
The inexplicable rain that always pours from underneath your umbrella will finally stop, moments before your derby hat catches fire.

Gemini: (May 21–June 21)
You know those guys in *Priscilla, Queen Of The Desert*? The stars think those guys must be, like, gay.

Cancer: (June 22–July 22)
Your weekly visit to the cemetery goes bad when you tell your problems to your mom's grave just as the sarcastic zombies begin to rise.

Leo: (July 23–Aug. 22)
The search for meaning in life is a worthy pursuit, but the search for meaning in your particular life is a real waste of time.

Virgo: (Aug. 23–Sept. 22)
It turns out Jean-Baptiste Lamarck, who classified the clouds, named the cold, fat, puffy little damp ones after you.

Libra: (Sept. 23–Oct. 23)
The engineering principles behind the suspension bridge make it possible for you to plummet from a great height into extremely deep water this week.

Scorpio: (Oct. 24–Nov. 21)
You will continue to honor the great American democratic tradition of blindly trusting and obeying those you deem superior to yourself.

Sagittarius: (Nov. 22–Dec. 21)
True to your mediocre nature, you will soon be confronted with a difficult choice between the Homely Lady and the Passive, Undersized Tiger.

Capricorn: (Dec. 22–Jan. 19)
For the last time, that's not "ball lightning." It's a form of static electricity unique to your unusually hirsute groin.

Aquarius: (Jan. 20–Feb. 18)
Your new pheromone-based scent will make you irresistible to women, who will devour you, bones, hair, and all.

Pisces: (Feb. 19–March 20)
You're starting to think that if men had been meant to swim through solid rock as if it were water, they would have been born with fulminating lava ducts.

HOT SHOWER from page 101

amounts of blood. Passersby were amazed by the unusually large amounts of blood. Passersby were amazed by the unusually large amounts of blood. Passersby were amazed by the unusually large amounts of blood. Passersby were amazed by the unusually large amounts of blood. Passersby were amazed by the unusually large amounts of blood. Passersby were amazed by the unusually large amounts of blood. Passersby were amazed by the unusually large amounts of blood. Passersby were amazed by the unusually large amounts of blood. Passersby were amazed by the unusually large amounts of blood. Passersby were amazed by the unusually large amounts of blood. Passersby were amazed by the unusually large amounts of blood. Passersby were amazed by the unusually large amounts of blood. Passersby were amazed by the unusually large amounts of blood. Passersby were amazed by the unusually large amounts of blood. Passersby were amazed by the unusually large amounts of blood. Passersby were amazed by the unusually large amounts of blood. Passersby were

I don't so much "fight fire" as I "fight in places where there are fires."

amazed by the unusually large amounts of blood. Passersby were amazed by the unusually large amounts of blood. Passersby were amazed by the unusually large amounts of blood. Passersby were amazed by the unusually large amounts of blood. Passersby were amazed by the unusually large amounts of blood. Passersby were amazed by the unusually large

see HOT SHOWER page 114

NEWS

Can The *American Idol 2* Winner End Kelly Clarkson's Pop-Chart Dominance?

see MUSIC page 7B

Real Toy Used As Sex Toy

see LOCAL page 5C

Saddam Misinterprets Anti-War Protest As Pro-Saddam

see WORLD page 3A

STATshot

A look at the numbers that shape your world.

Recent Product Recalls

1. Baby-Go-Boom breakaway swingset
2. Tater Teats
3. "But...Why?"-brand dead cat in a bucket
4. Gin-nasium
5. Kid-a-pult
6. Everfail™ condoms, Perforated For Her Pleasure™

0 74470 94595 6 00

THE ONION • $2.00 US • $3.00 CAN

the ONION®

VOLUME 39 ISSUE 13 AMERICA'S FINEST NEWS SOURCE™ 10–16 APRIL 2003

Bush Subconsciously Sizes Up Spain For Invasion

Above: Bush's mind wanders while he shakes Aznar's hand.

WASHINGTON, DC—During a White House meeting with visiting Spanish prime minister and fellow allied-forces leader Jose Maria Aznar, President Bush subconsciously sized up Spain for invasion Monday.

"Aznar was pledging his ongoing support for the Iraqi war effort when, out of nowhere, this odd look came across George's face," National Security Advisor Condoleezza Rice said. "He sat quiet for a moment, like he was going to say something, but then he just shook his head as if to chase the thought away."

At the meeting, Aznar ruled out sending Spanish combat troops to Iraq but pledged to provide a hospital vessel, a mine-clearing unit, a team of chemical-detection experts, and several oil tankers.

"And you have no nuclear weapons, right?" Bush asked Aznar. "And no chemical or biological weapons or anything like that? Just curious."

Aznar also promised that if Iraq attacks neighboring Turkey, he would contribute six F-18 warplanes, a Hercules C-130 refueling plane, and a search-and-

see SPAIN page 113

137 More Oil Wells Liberated For Democracy

RUMAILAH OIL FIELDS, IRAQ—The U.S. continued to make progress in its fight against totalitarianism Tuesday, when 137 more oil wells were liberated for democracy.

"For decades, these oil wells have suffered untold misery under Saddam Hussein's tyrannical rule," said U.S. Commander General Tommy Franks, speaking from southern Iraq's Rumailah oil fields, the site of the liberation. "With this victory, these long-oppressed wells will soon pump their first barrels of crude as free and equal wells in the global petroleum marketplace. They will join the ranks of the world's liberated oil wells, enjoying the same rights as their democratic brethren around the globe."

The Rumailah wells are the latest of nearly 900 to be freed from the yoke of oppression by coalition forces. As U.S. troops continue to advance deeper into Iraq—armed with constant standing orders to "Secure the oil wells; repeat, secure the oil wells"—an estimated 1,500 more wells are expected to be liberated in the coming

see OIL WELLS page 113

Above: The U.S. flag flies high atop a newly liberated oil well.

Left: Mean old NASA scientist Cary Nicastro.

Mean Scientists Dash Hopes Of Life On Mars

PASADENA, CA—A team of cold-hearted, killjoy scientists at NASA's Jet Propulsion Laboratory callously announced Monday that the likelihood of complex life on Mars is "extraordinarily low," dashing the hopes of the public just like that.

"What? Are they sure? I'm crestfallen," said Shreveport, LA, real-estate agent Martin Lucas, 47. "I remember back when I was a little boy, I'd dream of life on Mars. I'd lie awake under the covers imagining myself having all sorts of adventures with these Martians I befriended. How can those scientists just dismiss it so nonchalantly? What jerks."

Added Lucas: "Maybe next, they can do a study definitively disproving the existence of Santa Claus."

The scientists' misanthropic announcement was made at an 11 a.m. press conference, which many in attendance thought was going to be about something exciting, such as the discovery of fossilized organisms on Mars or maybe even Martian cities, complete with Martian ranch houses, Martian hamburgers, and Martian

see MARS page 112

Wall Street And The War

In spite of widespread predictions that the war would cure Wall Street's ills, the stock market has been unpredictable since the invasion of Iraq began. What do *you* think?

"Wall Street's fluctuations suggest a disturbing lack of confidence in our fighting men abroad. Come on, Dow, support the troops."

Michael Kingery
Accountant

"I don't know, my shares of Bombco have been pretty solid."

Fred Lathon
Systems Analyst

"Those jitters on Wall Street probably have more to do with New York's smoking ban than with the war."

Melissa Arcero
Florist

"It's wartime, so I guess I figured all of us unemployed people would get jobs building munitions or riveting battleships."

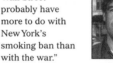

Chris Cassell
Unemployed

"My noise-rock band is creating a song with chord changes based on the Dow's actual fluctuations. You bet it sucks!"

Dean Reiss
Machinist

"All I want is for my son to make it home from Wall Street alive."

Marjorie Block
Homemaker

Geraldo Gets The Boot

Last week, the Pentagon ordered Fox News to pull Geraldo Rivera from Iraq after the reporter divulged U.S. troop positions during a broadcast. Among Rivera's other misdeeds:

- Ate entire sack of raw chickpeas intended for starving Iraqi children
- Insisted on wearing conspicuous War Of 1812-era naval officer's uniform
- Asked troops to fire on different target to make camera shot "more dramatically framed"
- Drank Gen. Tommy Franks' coffee, even though mug clearly had Franks' name written on it
- Constantly monopolized 101st Airborne's makeup lady's time
- Often asked soldiers about great taste of Fresca while drinking Fresca on camera
- Verbally taunted Marines he'd mistaken for skinheads
- Opened Gen. Franks' secret war-plans vault on heavily hyped live TV special
- Offended Iraqi population with special report on transvestite Muslim midget hookers and the infidels who love them

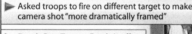

the ONION®
America's Finest News Source.™
Herman Ulysses Zweibel
Founder
T. Herman Zweibel
Publisher Emeritus
J. Phineas Zweibel
Publisher
Maxwell Prescott Zweibel
Editor-In-Chief

Don't Come Crying To Me When You Need Someone Who Speaks Elvish

By Larry Groznic

Really, Steven. Of all people, I expected more from you.

Until now, I was greatly impressed by your intellectual curiosity. Aren't you, after all, the person with whom I once had a three-hour message-board conversation concerning the story arc of the legendary series *Blake's 7*? Was it not you who listened attentively to my passionate argument in favor of allowing Commissioner Gordon's daughter Barbara to rise from her wheelchair and walk again? And are you not the same person who, once I guided you to the myriad shifting universes of Roger Zelazny, devoured them with the intellectual curiosity of a young Ender Wiggin?

Such a thirst for knowledge I once saw in you. And yet now, you question whether learning Elvish is "worth the effort." Elvish! At once the cornerstone and most elusive of the great J.R.R. Tolkien's creations!

To be intimidated by the fact that mastery of Elvish takes a lifetime—that I can comprehend. But for you to question its usefulness or intrinsic value, Steven, how could you? I tell you now: Do not come crying to me when you need someone who speaks Elvish.

In all honesty, I do not see why you would shy from this challenge. No, it is not easy, but you had already made

Such a thirst for knowledge I once saw in you. And yet now, you question whether learning Elvish is "worth the effort." Elvish! At once the cornerstone and most elusive of the great J.R.R. Tolkien's creations!

some inroads. You recognized the essential difference between the Cirth "runes" of Balin's tomb and the Tengwar "letters" corrupted by Sauron upon the One Ring—so basic and fundamental a difference that many students overlook it, to their later dismay. And, although I feel the high-elven dialect of Quenya would have given you trouble and Valarin, the tongue of the Valar, would likely forever elude your grasp, I thought you certainly capable of one day becoming conversant—if not fluent—in Sindarin. But it was not to be, for you, like Radagast The Brown, have chosen the path of blissful ignorance. In so doing, you turn your back on the riches of the world.

You might think this harsh, but need I mention which of us once ran out into a freezing parking lot to obtain the autograph of John de Lancie?

Frankly, Steven, given your current level of engagement, I'd be surprised if you could be bothered to study a crude, simple language like Klingon, with its guttural consonants and inelegant constructions.

You might think this harsh, but need I mention which of us once ran out into a freezing parking lot to obtain the autograph of John de Lancie? I know I'd promised to not bring it up again, but you seem to need reminding.

How long has it been since I lent you my copy of Tolkien's *The Lost Road*, which contains both his indispensable "Lhammas" and the utterly seminal "Etymologies"? Were these not enough to whet your appetite for Elvish languages? Perhaps I should not have even bothered: If Appendix F of *Return Of The King* did not light a fire within you, further encouragement was probably a fool's errand. But I will need those back soon (seeing as you seem to have no further use for them), along with my three-CD box set of *The Shadow* radio broadcasts and Tracy Scoggins workout video, at your earliest convenience.

Oh, and one other thing. As disappointed as I am, I would be crestfallen if I were to find out that the Proto-Baggins77 who's been posting lately on the Final Fantasy X board at GameFAQs is you. If you absolutely must go down that road, my former companion, I wish you would have at least chosen the superior FFVI, if not IV. At least then, I would know you were not beyond all hope.

Farewell, Steven. Perhaps one day, I will be able to greet you by saying "Elen Sila lumenn' omentielmo!" But assuming that doesn't happen, I would ask that you please drop off my stuff at the library's tech-help desk any time I'm not working. Ø

Suburban Home Haunted By Really Boring Ghosts

GURNEE, IL—On the surface, the home of John and Beth Secora looks just like any other suburban residence. But this seemingly ordinary dwelling harbors a secret: It is haunted by two incredibly boring ghosts.

"They really don't do much," Beth said. "Once in a while, John and I will see our Uno cards spread out all over the kitchen table or the refrigerator door left slightly ajar. If we go out on a Sunday afternoon, sometimes we come back to find a few coupons clipped out of the newspaper for things we never use, like cream of mushroom soup or Metamucil. As haunting goes, it's pretty tame stuff."

"We'd notice that even though we set the thermostat at 72 degrees, someone or something had turned it down to 68. We'd turn it up, and they'd turn it back down."

The couple first felt an otherworldly presence just days after moving into the home in November 2002.

"We would feel this slowly increasing chill, like someone else was in the room with us," Beth said. "Then, we'd notice that even though we set the thermostat at 72 degrees, someone or something had turned it down to 68. We'd turn it up, and they'd turn it back down. We finally just gave up and started wearing sweaters."

Determined to rid their house of the mundane wraiths, the Secoras enlisted the help of psychic Mary Harrow.

"We held a séance in our living room, using a Ouija board to ask them questions," John said. "We made contact, but rather than give us yes-or-no answers, they would blather on about how their daughter in Maine never calls or argue about the location of the good pot-roast pan. After about 10 minutes, we felt one of the spirits leave the room to turn on the TV in the den and watch the PGA Masters."

After the séance, the ghosts—who Harrow suspects are the home's previous owners, a middle-aged couple who died of radon poisoning—began leaving more evidence of their presence. Among the signs were an improperly re-coiled garden hose and an uncapped toothpaste tube, as well as cryptic messages left on the steamed-up bathroom mirror, including, "We're almost out of toilet paper."

In March, after four months of disturbances, the Secoras began to hear voices.

"One day at breakfast, we heard a disembodied male voice groaning, 'Honeeey, where are my dress socks?'" John said. "It went on like that for almost an hour. We left out dress socks of all colors, but to no avail. Then, we started hearing more messages from beyond: 'Have you seen my keys?' 'Get almonds when you go to the store.' 'Did you pick up my suit from the cleaners?' Nothing remotely spooky, or even interesting."

Above: The dull apparitions sit around the Secoras' living room.

In spite of the ghosts' inoffensive personalities and overall unintrusiveness, the Secoras say they are near the end of their rope.

"Something has to be done," Beth said. "It's like having a party guest that shows up too early and stays too late but doesn't drink and doesn't have anything to say. If we have to be haunted, the least they could do is toss some plates around or do something to liven things up."

"Whenever anyone finds out that our house is possessed by ghosts, they always act like it's a big deal, but believe me, it isn't," John said. "Unless you consider some invisible force dusting an endtable or flipping through the *Sunday Pennysaver* scary."

NEWS IN BRIEF

Dow Up 300 After Deaths Of 400

NEW YORK—Buoyed by positive news from the war front, the Dow Jones Industrial Average soared more than 300 points Monday after the killing of more than 400 Republican Guard soldiers near the Iraqi town of Mosul. "These deaths have really boosted investor optimism and confidence," New York Stock Exchange chairman Dick Grasso said. "Before this, we'd tried lowering interest rates, lowering taxes, and all sorts of other things to jump-start the market, but nothing was working. Lowering the population of Iraq finally seems to be doing the trick."

Office Manager Still Undecided About Sharpie Redesign

HARTFORD, CT—Four days after the arrival of a shipment of office supplies from Staples, P&K Insurance office manager Patty Hildebrandt, 41, remains ambivalent about Sharpie's new "Twin-Tip" double-ended permanent marker. "Putting a fine tip and a broad tip on the same pen is very convenient, not to mention cost-effective," Hildebrandt said Tuesday. "Still, neither of the twin tips really works as well as a single-ended marker, probably because they're sharing the same ink." Hildebrandt recently took a strong stand against 3M's accordion-style Post-It notes, calling them "an abomination."

Side Effects Sound Awesome

SAN JOSE, CA—Watching a TV commercial for the prescription allergy medication Nasonol, local resident Troy Henderson, 23, remarked Tuesday that the drug's possible side effects "sound awesome." "Dizziness, drowsiness, excitability, loss of motor function, irregular heartbeat, tingling sensations in the chest and sinuses—man, Nasonol's got it all," Henderson said. "I gotta score some of that." Henderson, who does not suffer from any allergies, said he plans to call his pollen-allergic friend Steve to "hook me up."

Girl From Coffee Shop Seen At Bar With Guy From Record Store

OLYMPIA, WA—Marissa Quirk, 21, that girl from the coffee shop, was spotted Monday at McCoy's Tavern with Greg Clarke, 23, the good-looking hipster guy from the record store. "I go into Crazee Espresso and Rainy Day Records a lot, so when I saw them at McCoy's together, I was like, 'It figures they know each other,'" said Dan Duckett, 22, who has long harbored a crush on Quirk. "It reminded me of that time I saw the guy from the vintage-clothing store with the cute girl who always announces the bands in the student union."

Man Not Sure What To Do About Vet's Request For Dog-Urine Sample

MISSOULA, MT—Dog owner Darryl Burkhard, 36, said Tuesday that he is unsure how to fulfill his veterinarian's orders to extract a urine sample from ailing cocker spaniel Sneakers. "The vet just casually asked me to bring in a sample, like I'd automatically know how to do that," Burkhard said. "Do I take Sneakers for a walk and then stick a cup under him at just the right moment? Or do I, like, fasten a cup to his genitals with a belt and wait for him to eventually go? Either way, I'm probably looking at some sort of really unpleasant dog-piss-related situation."

sewer systems. Instead, the crotchety scientists cynically announced that radiation levels on the Red Planet's surface are too high to make possible the survival of living organisms.

"Because Mars' atmosphere is far thinner than Earth's, solar radiation penetrates its surface at greater levels," said NASA's Cary Nicastro, whose team relied largely on data from the unmanned Mars Odyssey spacecraft. "The radiation measured by Odyssey was so intense, the chance of advanced surface life is virtually zero."

To many, the NASA announcement was, in the words of Bakersfield, CA, claims adjuster and science-fiction

Adding insult to injury, team member Christine Luo said freezing temperatures and a lack of surface-flowing water make Mars inhospitable to the future development of life.

buff Bill Cartwright, "incredibly negative."

"[Nicastro] didn't even try to break it to us gently," Cartwright said. "Doesn't he realize that a lot of people think it would be incredibly cool to have a giant Martian invasion force next door? In the future, when scientists make statements like this, they should do it with a little more sensitivity and regard for our feelings."

Adding insult to injury, team member Christine Luo said freezing temperatures and a lack of surface-flowing water make Mars inhospitable to the future development of life.

"If flowing water does exist, it's most likely below the surface, possibly under the vast ice caps," Luo said. "These harsh conditions would present a formidable challenge to the evolution of complex organisms."

"Nyah, nyah, nyah, Mars is too inhospitable for life," said Columbus, OH, resident Bryan Olin. "We're scientists and we make everything boring. We want proof of everything and don't want space exploration to be fun."

Aeronautics expert and NASA watchdog L. Kennan Brooks said the space agency has a long history of being a total buzzkill, repeatedly shooting down the prospect of extraterrestrial life in our solar system.

"Since its founding in the late 1950s, NASA has willfully—and at great taxpayer expense—rejected decades of creative speculation about space," Brooks said. "In the '60s, it refused to investigate the existence of the Man on the Moon. The Viking Mars probe of the '70s left millions of third-graders deflated with its lack of data about flying saucers and little green men. And probes sent close to Jupiter in the '80s made no effort to prove, once and for all, if God lived there."

Instead, Brooks said, NASA stubbornly insists on analyzing cosmic data in the most coldly rational ways possible.

To many, the NASA announcement was, in the words of Bakersfield, CA, claims adjuster and science-fiction buff Bill Cartwright, "incredibly negative."

"They could be doing such exciting stuff, but they won't," Brooks said. "Rather than using the Hubble Space Telescope to prove the existence of black holes, we should be piloting a fusion-powered spacecraft straight into the heart of them, coming out the other side into a parallel universe populated by our evil, goatee-wearing doubles."

"They refuse to allow even the faintest possibility that the Martians can't be detected because they're invisible. Or maybe they occupy a different dimension," Brooks continued. "There's a world of possibilities here. These scientists should depend less on cold, hard data and more on their imaginations. They'd probably be a lot less cranky." Ø

FIRST LADIES from page 105

amounts of blood. Passersby were amazed by the unusually large amounts of blood. Passersby were amazed by the unusually large amounts of blood. Passersby were amazed by the unusually large amounts of blood. Passersby were amazed by the unusually large amounts of blood. Passersby were amazed by the unusually large amounts of blood. Passersby were amazed by the unusually large amounts of blood. Passersby were amazed by the unusually large amounts of blood. Passersby were amazed by the unusually large amounts of blood. Passersby were

Don't go. I swear, this time, these are my actual last words.

amazed by the unusually large amounts of blood. Passersby were amazed by the unusually large amounts of blood. Passersby were amazed by the unusually large amounts of blood. Passersby were amazed by the unusually large amounts of blood. Passersby were amazed by the unusually large amounts of blood. Passersby were amazed by the unusually large amounts of blood. Passersby were amazed by the unusually large amounts of blood. Passersby were amazed by the unusually large

see FIRST LADIES page 121

the ONION Domesticorner presents:

Spring-Cleaning Tips

Winter is finally gone, and that means it's time for spring cleaning. Here are some tips to help you get your home spic-and-span:

- When choosing a household cleaner, set up two identical shower doors side by side. Wipe one with the leading brand and the other with the bargain brand. Examine the results and choose accordingly.
- For fresh, disinfected air, pour Lysol into the humidifier.
- Have you had it with the drudgery of constantly scrubbing that dirty kitchen floor? Boo-fucking-hoo, Toots.
- To eliminate hours of needless scrubbing, spit your chew into an old beer can rather than directly onto the floor.
- Once a week, tell yourself, "Man, I really gotta clean up this dump one of these days."
- Buy a set of latex gloves that come up past your elbows. Not for cleaning, though.
- No amount of cleaning will change the fact that Dabney Coleman was in your home.
- Keep a range-top burner on low flame at all times to eliminate airborne kitchen germs.
- Jesus Christ, there's a thing called shelves, you pig.
- If you are female, don't clean a thing. Cleaning promotes sexist stereotypes about women.
- You can pay inflated supermarket prices for bleach, or be like Martha Stewart and synthesize your own from chlorine particles extracted from sea water.
- Purchase a wet vac. Then, when your fishing buddies come over, you can say, "Look. I got me a wet vac."
- Don't ever stop cleaning. Don't ever do anything else. Make it the basis for your entire identity. If someone criticizes either your cleaning or your cleaning-based lifestyle, yell "Oh, this house!" and run off crying.

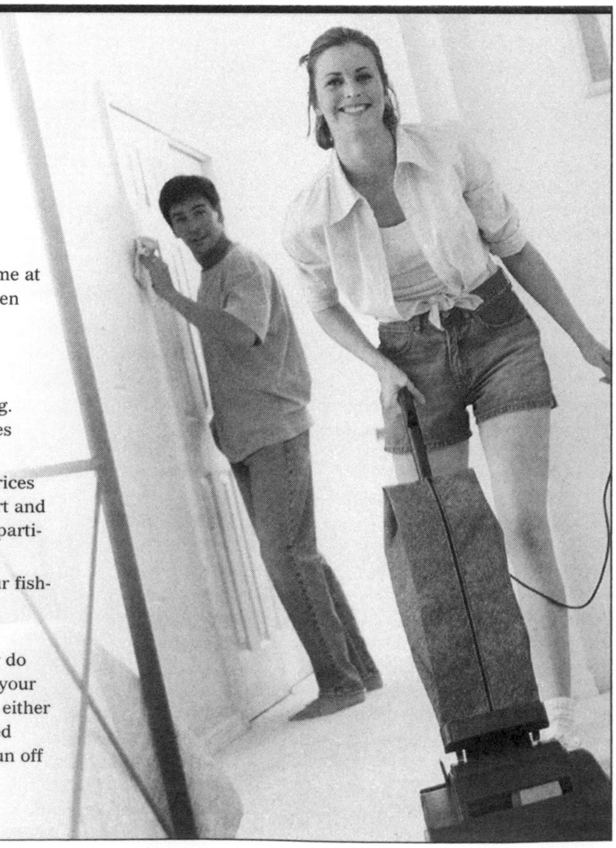

SPAIN from page 109

rescue helicopter.

"The Hercules C-130," Bush said, staring off into the distance. "Those are pretty old. Hmm."

As the conversation turned toward the siege of Baghdad, Bush interrupted and returned to the subject of Spain's military strength—or lack thereof.

"So, all in all, your country has 105,000 standing troops total?" Bush said. "That's it?"

Aznar later told Bush that Spain's King Juan Carlos sent his greetings, once again piquing the president's interest.

"It seems a bit outdated to have a king," Bush said. "Are your people happy with him? Do you think your people would rather rule themselves, like in a democracy?"

Aznar explained that Spain is a constitutional monarchy.

"The prime minister must be approved by our legislature," Aznar told Bush. "You see, each of our autonomous regions has its own regional government and exercises legislative and executive authority in the manner outlined by the national constitution."

Bush then asked about Spain's long-standing troubles with separatist groups.

"That situation with the Catalans and the Basques," Bush said. "How serious is that?"

When Aznar inquired as to why Bush was asking, the president said he "was just wondering, for no reason."

"There was something strange about his questions, although I cannot put my finger on it," Aznar said. "And he seemed very excited about the anti-government protests in Madrid a few days ago, until I told him they were protesting our involvement in the Iraq war."

Secretary of State Colin Powell, who was in attendance, also noticed some unusual behavior on the part of Bush.

"During the meeting, the president was absentmindedly doodling on some documents, one of which had a map of Europe on it," Powell said. "I noticed he drew a series of arrows originating on the Canary Islands and moving in toward Madrid."

Powell recalled that during last month's summit in the Azores, Bush seemed oddly fixated on Spain.

"[Bush] said Spain didn't seem to be all that prosperous for a nation whose main export is oil," Powell said. "I told

> **"[Bush] seemed very excited about the anti-government protests in Madrid a few days ago, until I told him they were protesting our involvement in the Iraq war," Aznar said.**

him Spain doesn't produce a lot of oil. Finally, we figured he must've been thinking of olive oil, and we both had a big laugh about it."

Powell said that upon returning home from the Azores summit, Bush continued to insist that "there is some big oil-producing nation that speaks Spanish."

"I told him he must be thinking of Venezuela," Powell said. "They are very rich in oil. So now he wants a full report on Venezuela by Monday. Ever since this war with Iraq, he's been a real geography buff." ⊘

COMMUNITY VOICES

Jean Sings Of Chocolate And Cat Calendars At War

A Room Of Jean's Own
By Jean Teasdale

Back when I worked at the Fashion Bug, I'd sometimes read the daily paper they had in the break room. So, ever since getting laid off, I've kind of fallen behind on current events. Actually, that's not quite true. I do have a new source of news: Hubby Rick's T-shirts! And when he started wearing his "Sodamn Insane" and "Whaq Iraq" T-shirts about a month ago, I knew war with Iraq was inevitable.

In the past few weeks, Rick and his

> **I've kind of fallen behind on current events. Actually, that's not quite true. I do have a new source of news: Hubby Rick's T-shirts!**

boozehound buddy Craig have been sitting around discussing the war like they're a couple of five-star generals, complaining that the Army didn't do

see TEASDALE page 114

OIL WELLS from page 109

weeks.

For months, U.S. officials have gone to great lengths to assure the public, both in America and abroad, that the Iraq invasion is not motivated by oil interests—a sentiment echoed by Defense Secretary Donald Rumsfeld during a press conference Monday.

"This war is not about oil," Rumsfeld said. "Our decision to intercede against this dictator and not against the dozens of other ruthless dictators in the world is not about oil. France and Russia's opposition to this war is not about the purely coincidental fact that both countries have lucrative, pre-existing oil contracts with Iraq. Furthermore, the interest of many U.S. corporations in the war has nothing to do with oil, either. This war is about liberty. Oil wells deserve liberty, too."

Continued Rumsfeld: "These oppressed Iraqi oil wells deserve the right to pump oil as freely as any other oil well on God's Earth—be it in Saudi Arabia, Nigeria, or an Alaskan wildlife refuge. It is crass and cynical to view this operation as being motivated by greed, profit, or the second-largest oil reserves in the Middle East. This war is motivated by one thing: democracy. Our military action is meant to provide all of Iraq's oil wells—be they big or small, staggeringly lucrative or merely very lucrative—with their God-given right to pump under a democratic system of self-governance."

In the weeks leading up to the war, the U.S. sought to make its intentions clear by air-dropping hundreds of thousands of pamphlets over Iraq assuring its people that the U.S. was not launching a war against them, but against Saddam Hussein. The pamphlets also gave Iraqi soldiers instructions on how to surrender properly, as well as a promise that they would be treated well if they did so. Most importantly, though, they included a stern admonition to all Iraqis not to burn any oil wells, warning that they would be hunted down and prosecuted as war criminals if they did.

U.S. officials hope that the pamphlets' message, especially the part about the oil wells, gets through.

"These valuable natural resources belong to the Iraqi people, who rely on their output for desperately needed food and medicine under the U.N.'s Oil-For-Food Program," Franks said. "But ultimately, we need to remember that these oil wells do not really belong to anybody. They, like any other free oil well, have the basic, inalienable right to independent repre-

> **"These oppressed Iraqi oil wells deserve the right to pump oil as freely as any other oil well on God's Earth—be it in Saudi Arabia, Nigeria, or an Alaskan wildlife refuge," Rumsfeld said. "It is crass and cynical to view this operation as being motivated by greed or profit."**

sentational government and self-determination under their own rule. Every oil well deserves to choose how and when it wishes to produce oil, and for whose economic benefit."

Aiding the wells in their transition to democracy will be Shell, Mobil, and other U.S. businesses, each of which brings years of expertise in dealing with the problems and challenges that oil wells face in a free society. These private companies will be well-equipped to help manage the oil wells as they make the difficult adjustment to producing oil in freedom.

Despite the apparent inevitability of victory in Iraq, White House sources stress that the battle for oil-well liberty is far from over.

"We must remember that there are many, many oil wells living under oppression all across the world, not just in Iraq," White House press secretary Ari Fleischer said. "Until every oil well enjoys the fruits of democracy, no oil well is truly free." ⊘

CHILL FACTOR from page 108

amounts of blood. Passersby were amazed by the unusually large amounts of blood. Passersby were amazed by the unusually large amounts of blood. Passersby were amazed by the unusually large amounts of blood. Passersby were amazed by the unusually large amounts of blood. Passersby were amazed by the unusually large amounts of blood. Passersby were amazed by the unusually large amounts of blood. Passersby were amazed by the unusually large amounts of blood. Passersby were amazed by the unusually large

> **Just when you think it's over, bang! I lay the meat on you.**

amounts of blood. Passersby were amazed by the unusually large amounts of blood. Passersby were amazed by the unusually large

see CHILL FACTOR page 122

TEASDALE from page 113

this or bomb that. (I swear, I think I've rearranged the Beanie Baby collection in our bedroom four times trying to avoid their yammering! I hope the war ends soon, because I'm not sure I can improve on the way I have the Beanies set up now, with Bongo The Monkey serving tea to Slowpoke The Sloth on this adorable mini wicker dinette set as Legs The Frog and Ziggy The Zebra spoon in a little wooden gazebo, and the rest of them sit perched on the headboard over my side of the bed holding a banner that reads, "Sweet Dreams, Jean.")

Not to brag, but I think I really outdid myself with this care-package thing. I put a lot of thought and planning into it, and it lifted my spirits to know I was lifting someone else's. When choosing items for Nathan's care package, I tried hard to put myself in his place: If I were thousands of miles away from home in a barren, sun-scorched desert, what would I want to receive?

Now, Rick has the right to talk about military strategy all he wants, but if you ask me, I think it's in poor taste to talk about jet fighters and battle plans when so many lives are at stake. Instead of all that dangerous stuff, I've decided to focus my attentions on an aspect of the war that I, and most everyone else, can better relate to: the human side.

First, I think it is soooo important to support our troops 100 percent! All of them are sacrificing their lives for us, and we need to bolster their morale and show them we care, so that later on they don't scream at us for our spare change like the Vietnam War veterans.

As for me, I am honored to personally know a troop: my nephew Nathan, the son of my half-sister Monica, who's an Army private first-class stationed in one of the Arabian countries. To cheer him up and remind him that those on the home front are totally behind him, I recently prepared a special box of goodies.

Not to brag, but I think I really outdid myself with this care-package thing. I put a lot of thought and planning into it, and it lifted my spirits to know I was lifting someone else's. When choosing items for Nathan's care package, I tried hard to put myself in his place: If I were thousands of miles away from home in a barren, sun-scorched desert, what would I want to receive? The answer was obvious: things that reminded me of home, of course!

The first item I included, I confess, wasn't the most practical thing in the world: a pair of water wings! But Nathan has come to expect that kind of zaniness from his Aunt Jean. (It's also to remind him that even though things are tough, there's always room in this world for laughter. We can't let the Osamas of the world break our spirit. Do you hear that, Osamas?)

Next, I included a kitty-cat calendar for Nathan to hang over his bunk. (Just a little something to remind him who we're fighting for!) I admit, I was reluctant to part with it, since May featured a darling trio of Burmese kittens peeking out of a picnic basket. But war means making sacrifices, and there are always other kitty calendars. (Unless the war lasts a long time and they have to be rationed. God forbid!)

After that, I added a bouquet of silk flowers. All right, all right, I know what you're thinking: "How could you do that to your nephew? When he pulls those flowers out of the box, his platoon will give him no end of grief!" That's where you're wrong. They're out in the desert where there's scarcely any vegetation. I'll bet you dollars to donuts that after all these weeks on the sand, those he-men in uniform are dying to see a flower right now. They may not be real, but silk flowers are nearly as beautiful and could really liven up Nathan's drab tent. Plus, before I packed them, I gave them a good dousing of Emeraude cologne so they'd smell extra flowery.

I think it is soooo important to support our troops 100 percent! All of them are sacrificing their lives for us, and we need to bolster their morale and show them we care, so that later on they don't scream at us for our spare change like the Vietnam War veterans.

Again, I hate to toot my own horn, but thanks to me, not only does Nathan have flowers, but he's also probably the only soldier in the Army with his own puppet theater! I found these darling zoo-critter hand puppets at a going-out-of-business sale at Zany Brainy, and I cleverly painted the outside of the care-package box to look like a little stage. Think of all the creative flights of fancy he'll have! It sure beats moping around his tent waiting to be shipped to the front.

What else? Well, besides the obligatory aromatherapy candles, potpourri jars, and bath salts, no military care package is complete without—you've got me pegged by now, don't you, Jeanketeers?—a batch of my heaven-on-a-plate chocolatey concoctions! And, boy howdy, did I ever outdo myself this time! As if visited by the Baking Angel, divine inspiration hit me, and I quickly improvised my grandest creation yet: "Operation: Mmmmm!" brownies. The recipe? Well, I'm afraid that information is classified. But I'll tell you this: Never before have chocolate, butter, eggs, flour, cream cheese, Karo syrup, molasses, peanut butter, coffee, orange-juice concentrate, Heath bars, and crushed peppermint candy worked so well together!

Besides care packages, there's more you can do for our soldiers in the Gulf. Send off those canned goods that have been collecting dust on your shelf. Ship them some of your old clothes. Write them long, involved letters about yourself. (They looove getting letters!) These are just off the top of my head—I'm sure you can think of plenty more! ⌀

Again, I hate to toot my own horn, but thanks to me, not only does Nathan have flowers, but he's also probably the only soldier in the Army with his own puppet theater!

HOROSCOPES

Your Horoscope

By Lloyd Schumner Sr.
Retired Machinist and
A.A.P.B.-Certified Astrologer

Aries: (March 21–April 19)
You'll finally be contacted by your long-lost birth parents, but the nine signatures on the letter bring about more questions than answers.

Taurus: (April 20–May 20)
You will be requested by the President's Special Commission For The Study Of Television to hold the rabbit ears just like that until *Guiding Light* is over.

Gemini: (May 21–June 21)
Most of the people who told you to "just believe in yourself" didn't realize that you think you're the illegitimate son of Osiris and the Michelin Man.

Cancer: (June 22–July 22)
Your efforts to start a new religion in which you're worshipped as the messiah would go farther if you didn't have long hair, a beard, and stigmata.

Leo: (July 23–Aug. 22)
It turns out that your weakness isn't the color yellow after all, but bullets, knives, and angry packs of badgers.

Virgo: (Aug. 23–Sept. 22)
You still have no idea what makes women tick, despite having asked literally hundreds of watchmakers.

Libra: (Sept. 23–Oct. 23)
You've asked the man in the mirror to change his ways, but he only responds by howling like a fiend and force-feeding you shards of broken glass.

Scorpio: (Oct. 24–Nov. 21)
In spite of the circumstances that brought you together, it would deeply hurt the executioner if you took it personally.

Sagittarius: (Nov. 22–Dec. 21)
You'll suffer the kind of low-down, yellow-dog, non-poetic blues that inspire people to urinate on you while you lie weeping in the gutter.

Capricorn: (Dec. 22–Jan. 19)
While it's true that God's plan cannot be known by men, be assured that at no time has it ever had anything to do with you.

Aquarius: (Jan. 20–Feb. 18)
Though they say you can never step in the same river twice, you'll find that you can fall headfirst into the same drainage ditch five times.

Pisces: (Feb. 19–March 20)
You will soon come to appreciate the little things in life, such as the amount of it you have left.

NEWS

Girl Gone Wild Actually Just Regular Girl, Only More Insecure And Drunk

see VIDEO page 2E

Vegan Soldier Keeps Asking Everyone If They Want Their Bread

see WAR page 5A

Book On Tape Fast-Forwarded

see MEDIA page 12C

STATshot

A look at the numbers that shape your world.

How Are We Trying To Impress Our In-Laws?

1. Showing how much we can drink
2. Announcing plans to move out of their house by December 2004
3. Shouting, "I don't need your pity"
4. Eating more corn than seems humanly possible
5. Marrying their hideous daughter

0 74470 94595 6 00
THE ONION • $2.00 US • $3.00 CAN

the ONION®

VOLUME 39 ISSUE 14 AMERICA'S FINEST NEWS SOURCE™ 17–23 APRIL 2003

Saddam Proud He Still Killed More Iraqi Civilians Than U.S.

BAGHDAD, IRAQ—Reflecting on his time as Iraq's president in a pre-taped television address, Saddam Hussein expressed pride Tuesday that, despite the success of the U.S. invasion and the civilian casualties it has inflicted, he still has killed far more Iraqis than President Bush.

"George Bush believes he is so powerful, so strong," Saddam said. "But even with all of his bombs and missiles and Marines, he has not even come close to killing as many Iraqis as I did."

While estimates of the number of Iraqi civilians killed by the U.S. ranges from 500 all the way to 10,000, Saddam and his associates are believed to have murdered somewhere between 100,000 and 250,000 civilians since 1968.

"The international press counts off on their fingers every Iraqi that dies

see SADDAM page 118

Above: Saddam greets admirers during his late-'90s Iraqi-killing heyday.

Area Man Supports The Troops He Didn't Go To High School With

KIRKSVILLE, MO—Jon Strauss, 22, a Kirksville video-store manager, announced Monday that he supports U.S. troops "100 percent"—with the exception of the ones with whom he went to high school.

"My heart goes out to the troops, and I pray for their safe return," said Strauss, a 1998 graduate of Kirksville High School. "Except for that dick Andy Tischler. I hope the Iraqis capture him and torture his wedgie-inflicting ass."

see TROOPS page 119

Right: Strauss, who said he backs "99.9 percent" of America's troops.

Above: A legislating machine does the work of 10 members of the House Subcommittee on Financial Institutions and Consumer Credit.

45 More Legislators Lose Jobs To Increased Congressional Automation

WASHINGTON, DC—Continuing a trend that began in the Senate last November, House Majority Leader Tom DeLay (R-TX) announced Monday that 45 members of the House of Representatives would be laid off and replaced by cost-efficient heavy legislating machinery.

"I feel awful for my colleagues who are now out of work," DeLay told reporters at a press conference. "I've known some of these people for years, but the fact remains that these new machines can pass bills up to 10 times faster than their human counterparts. Like it or not, this is the future."

In spite of denials from congressional leaders, the rash of job cuts has some legislators worried that Congress will be fully

see AUTOMATION page 119

The SARS Epidemic

Many Americans are worried about the spread of SARS, the mysterious, deadly respiratory illness sweeping China and Hong Kong. What do *you* think?

Lori Petruso
Teacher

"More than 100 people have died worldwide from SARS! More than 100 people! 100!"

Dan George
Plumber

"Will stopping this virus once again require the mass smothering of chickens in plastic trash bags? Just wondering."

Frank Banks
Systems Analyst

"You have to wonder what monstrosity the Orient will unleash on humanity next. I mean, SARS, anime, Toyotathons..."

Todd Cassell
Attorney

"From now on, I'm making sure to steer way the hell clear of the Chinatown section of my city, just like I always have."

Alicia Green
Florist

"With its limited exposure and 4 percent fatality rate, SARS lies somewhere between rubella and a NASCAR crash on my list of death fears."

Timothy Conn
Factory Worker

"Did you say terrorists were behind SARS? Wow, I thought you said that. I'll just repeat that until they know what actually causes it."

The Search For WMD

U.S. military personnel continue to search Iraq for weapons of mass destruction. What have they found?

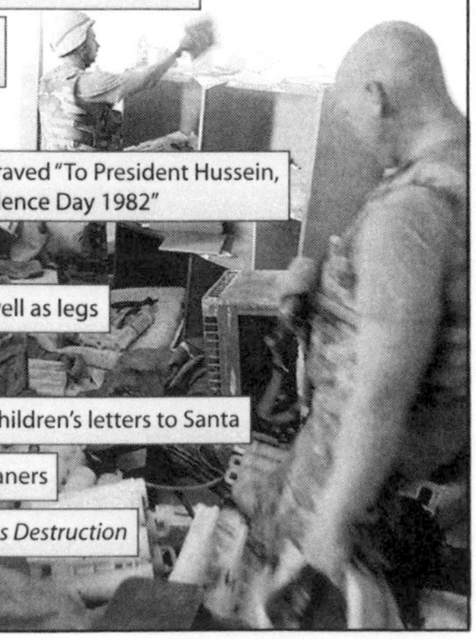

- Large stockpiles of the chemical compound sodium chloride
- Book of matches for striking anywhere, anytime
- 1.5 million depleted uranium shells marked "U.S. Army"
- Millions of unsold "I ♥ Saddam And His Totalitarian Regime" mugs
- Suspiciously long extension cord
- Remington 7mm Magnum rifle engraved "To President Hussein, From Vice-President Bush, Independence Day 1982"
- Several cases of Toilet Duck
- Massive stockpiles of Iraqi arms, as well as legs
- Used Coors Party Ball
- Bags and bags of undelivered Iraqi children's letters to Santa
- Vast stash of chemical mustache cleaners
- Gay porno tape titled *Weapons Of Ass Destruction*
- Really awesome set of nunchucks

the ONION®
America's Finest News Source.™

Herman Ulysses Zweibel
Founder

T. Herman Zweibel
Publisher Emeritus
J. Phineas Zweibel
Publisher
Maxwell Prescott Zweibel
Editor-In-Chief

Are All Women Nutso, Or Just The Ones I Cheat On My Wife With?

By John Rebach

What is it with women these days? I'm seriously at the end of my rope. I mean, you treat a woman to dinner at a fancy restaurant three towns over, and by the end of the night, she's either telling you you're the greatest thing ever or she's dumping a bouquet of flowers over your head. And as for which response you get, well, that's anybody's guess. So tell me, are all women nuts, or just the ones I cheat on my wife with?

Maybe it's me. Maybe I'm just magically attracted to headcases. Then again, how can that be when I cheat on my wife with women of all stripes? I meet them everywhere: work, the gym, coffee shops, bookstores, parties, movies, museums, restaurants, my son's daycare, and so on. Yet whether they're rich or poor, young or very young, the pattern is always the same: After we have illicit, adulterous sex a few times, they start going batshit on me.

Case in point. A few months ago, I was shopping at Circuit City for a new Palm Pilot, and I met this great-looking woman: real stylish, late 20s, great body, the works. She was an executive for a record company, so I figured she must have her shit together, right? Wrong. We go out a few

We go out a few times, and then she starts grilling me: "Why don't you ever take me to your house?" "Whose picture is that in your wallet?" "What do you mean you're married?"

times, and then she starts grilling me: "Why don't you ever take me to your house?" "Whose picture is that in your wallet?" "What do you mean you're married?" We get into a screaming match, she tells me to get the hell out of her apartment, and then she won't return my calls. I don't get it. We were two consenting adults having a great time together, then she suddenly had to go and turn into a raving lunatic!

I've been with enough women on the side to know that no matter how good the sex is, they're eventually gonna go loony-tunes. Sometimes, that takes the form of them hitting me. Other times, it's them screaming about how the relationship can't go anywhere. How wacko is that? We've only been together a few weeks (plus, I'm *married*), and they're looking for a commitment! Break out the straitjacket, we're going to the funny farm!

It's not like I'm dishonest with these ladies about my free-wheeling lifestyle. I usually tell them right up-

Do they even realize the effort I put into these relationships? When you've got a wife and kids and job, squeezing in an hour for a mistress involves some heavy-duty schedule shuffling, but do I get points for that?

front the fifth night we spend at the motel off Hwy. 18. And I'm good to them, too. I'll buy them candies and magazines, and shower them with compliments. Still, no matter how sweetly I say, "You are so much sexier than my wife," they just flip out.

Do they even realize the effort I put into these relationships? When you've got a wife and kids and job, squeezing in an hour for a mistress involves some heavy-duty schedule shuffling, but do I get points for that? Nope, just an earful of cuss words from a crazed harpy. Geez!

I'm not going to give up on other women just yet, but is it too much to ask for one that isn't completely bananas? Out of the billions of women on this planet, at least one of them has to be sane, right? There *must* be a woman I can casually sleep around with who won't go postal just because taking my son to hockey practice made me late for a secret rendezvous.

I know I sound totally jaded, but I'm really not. The truth is, even through all of my relationship troubles, I'm still a hopeless romantic. At the moment, I can't stop thinking about a cute little number I met at the mall last Saturday. She's gorgeous, but she really seems quiet and laid back—the kind of gal who won't lose her shit. But no matter how well things go with her, I'll remain on my guard. You know what they say: It's the quiet ones who always go the craziest when you're fucking them behind your wife's back. Ø

New Children's Book Helps Kids Deal With Pain And Isolation Of Plastic Surgery

MIAMI—As a pediatric plastic surgeon, Dr. Jessica Krieg changes little faces and lives for the better. Yet for all the good she does, she is all too aware that rhinoplasty and liposuction can be difficult, scary experiences for a child. With her new book, *Norah's New Nose*, she hopes to change all that.

"These children, on the threshold of becoming something—and someone—beautiful, are often scared and unsure of what's about to be done to them," Krieg said. "In *Norah's New Nose*, I try to show them there's nothing to fear, and that when it's over, there's no need for shame."

"These children, on the threshold of becoming something—and someone—beautiful, are often scared and unsure of what's about to be done to them," Krieg said. "In *Norah's New Nose*, I try to show them there's nothing to fear, and that when it's over, there's no need for shame."

As the book opens, Norah, a little girl who inherited her father's "generous" nose, is peering out her bedroom window at the moon.

"'Good night!' Miss Moon said to Norah," the book reads. "But although the beautiful Miss Moon said good night to Norah, she said it the same way Mommy says good night to homely Miss Crabgrass or creepy old Mr. Kratch. Norah became very sad."

Norah's mother explains to her that something is preventing Miss Moon from seeing what a pretty little girl she is—something "right in front of her face."

"It isn't Miss Moon's fault she can't see your inner beauty," Mommy gently tells Norah. "Miss Moon may be very special, but she isn't all-powerful."

Using an enchanted mirror, Mommy shows Norah the difference between her own perfect nose and her daughter's "big, broad, bulky bird beak." Norah starts to cry, but Mommy assures her that doctors at the hospital can solve her problem, just like they solved Mommy's.

"I wanted to show these kids that the changes they go through in the plastic-surgery ward are normal and natural," Krieg said. "It's not like getting your tonsils out. It's something to make you *even better* instead of just barely good enough."

Norah's New Nose has already earned raves from Krieg's fellow pediatric plastic surgeons, but the reviews that matter most to Krieg are the ones from her patients.

"I love Norah's animal friends, especially Pugsley The Duckling," said Lacey Ginsberg, a Great Neck, NY, 7-year-old who read Krieg's book before getting the same nasal-resculpting procedure as Norah and Pugsley. "Poor Pugsley was scared, but Norah helped her be brave. I want Daddy to get me a Pugsley doll—the one with the 'after' nose."

"It isn't Miss Moon's fault she can't see your inner beauty," Mommy gently tells Norah.

"I like the part where Lissa The Thin-Lipped Butterfly changes from a butterfly into a beautiful *betterfly*," said Amanda Robles, 8, a collagen-therapy patient from Long Beach, CA. "She'll win all the butterfly pageants now. And even though Matt R. Pillar now pays attention to her, she realizes she's way too good for him."

For all the praise *Norah's New Nose* has received from Krieg's colleagues,

see BOOK page 118

NEWS IN BRIEF

Clinton Emotionally Ready To Start Getting Blow Jobs Again

NEW YORK—Five years after the Monica Lewinsky scandal, former president Bill Clinton announced Tuesday that, at long last, he is emotionally ready to start receiving blow jobs again. "It has been a long, difficult road, but I am finally at a point in my life where I can receive oral sex from a woman again," Clinton told reporters. "After many years of soul-searching and intensive therapy, I am now able to enjoy getting blown without all that painful emotional baggage overshadowing what should be a wonderful experience."

Fisherman's 4-Year-Old Son Liberates Bait

INTERNATIONAL FALLS, MN—During a fishing trip Monday, Jason Jorgensen, the 4-year-old son of International Falls fisherman Bill Jorgensen, liberated an entire styrofoam container of nightcrawlers, throwing the bait into Rainy Lake. "Run, wormies, run!" Jorgensen said as he gave the former bait its first-ever taste of sweet freedom. "Swim home now!" Informed of the bold act, People for the Ethical Treatment of Animals president Ingrid Newkirk praised Jason for releasing the worms from his father's "cruel yoke of tyranny."

Opening Band Issues Two-More-Songs Warning

SAN FRANCISCO—In an announcement that met with sarcastic cheers, Nate Pilson, lead singer of opening act Dickbasket, issued a two-more-songs warning to a crowd waiting to see headlining act The Colecovisions. "This next one's gonna be our next-to-last song," said Pilson, 25, prompting widespread stretching and watch-checking among the Bimbo's 365 Club crowd. "It's from our upcoming EP. Hope you like it." Pilson then energetically launched into the song, trying not to notice the throngs of concertgoers streaming toward the bar or resuming the conversations they were having before the warning.

Guy Eats Own Weight In Combos Over Three-Month Period

CULLMAN, AL—In the past three months, John "Jenko" Quigley, 26, has casually consumed 276 pounds of pepperoni-pizza-flavored Combos snacks, an amount equal to his own body weight. "Actually, Jenko weighs almost 300 pounds now, but he was 276 when he started around New Year's Day," friend Darrell Nenn said Monday. "Guess all those bite-sized pretzels with cheese-flavored filling can really pork a guy out." Quigley said he began eating the popular snack food to curb his appetite between meals, but continued long after his hunger was cheesed away.

Area Man No Longer Playing Up Resemblance To Kevin Spacey

FLAGSTAFF, AZ—Put off by such films as *The Life Of David Gale*, *The Shipping News*, and *K-PAX*, local insurance salesman Brian Vandervelt, 37, is no longer playing up his resemblance to Academy Award-winning actor Kevin Spacey. "From the time of *Glengarry Glen Ross* up through *American Beauty*, I was loving all the Spacey comparisons," Vandervelt told reporters Tuesday. "But after four years of smug, self-righteous crap like *Pay It Forward*, it's a different story." Until Spacey stops playing repellently soulful saviors of humanity, Vandervelt said he will play up his resemblance to a young Bob Newhart. Ø

SADDAM from page 115

by Bush's missiles," Saddam said. "The papers make a big story of it when six Iraqi civilians are killed by American GIs near Basra, or when 15 Iraqi civilians are killed in air strikes on Baghdad. What paltry death tolls. I cannot even begin to add up how many died in Basra upon my orders, how many in Baghdad I killed with my own gun."

"The race between myself and Bush is not even close," Saddam said. "I easily killed 100 times more men than Bush, not to mention women and children."

Throughout his presidency, Saddam said he routinely had political opponents arrested and put to death without trial, sometimes along with their entire families. He also summarily executed countless citizens for crimes as minor as petty theft and "monopolizing rationed goods."

"The race between myself and Bush is not even close," Saddam said. "I easily killed 100 times more men than Bush, not to mention women and children. That's right—women and children."

In his suppression of the Shiite Muslims alone, Saddam said he can lay claim to thousands more Iraqi kills than Bush.

"My officers did more damage rounding up students at [the Shiite Muslim theological institution] al-Hawza al-'Ilmiya in al-Najaf than the entire American 3rd Infantry did roaring through all of southern Iraq in their billion-dollar tanks," Saddam said. "And my men did not put down their guns just because someone asked for mercy. They finished the job like soldiers. They did not serve food to their enemies as if they were women at a picnic."

Saddam boasted that the 1988 Anfal campaign against the Iraqi Kurds added another 50,000 to his tally.

"In Anfal, we rounded up the battle-age men and put them in front of firing squads," Saddam said. "Even today, when you travel through rural Kurdistan, you notice the high proportion of women. That is not because of the U.S. Army. That is not because of the 101st Airborne Division. It is because of me—Saddam Hussein, President of Iraq, the Glorious Leader, the Anointed One, Direct Descendant of the Prophet, Great Uncle to the People."

In his campaigns against the Kurds, Saddam crushed unrest with chemical-weapons strikes against civilian populations—a tactic he said Bush "would never have the nerve to do."

"I remember the day my cousin [Commander of Southern Forces] Ali [Hassan al-Majid] dropped chemical weapons on the town of Halabja," Saddam said, referring to the March 1988 slaughter of 5,000 Kurds. "That is how he got his nickname, 'Chemical Ali.' Much better nickname than 'Dubya,' wouldn't you say?"

In fairness to Bush, Saddam conceded that he has had a significant head start killing Iraqis, beginning his political career in the late '60s as a torturer for the Ba'ath party.

"The total number of Kurds we killed could be as high as 110,000, and that is not an idle boast," Saddam said. "The United Nations Sub-Committee on Human Rights has been keeping extensive records of my actions for years."

In fairness to Bush, Saddam conceded that he has had a significant head start killing Iraqis, beginning his political career in the late '60s as a torturer for the Ba'ath party.

"Back in 1969, I turned the execution of 14 alleged anti-government plotters into a major public event, hanging them in a town square and leaving their bodies on display," Saddam said. "Already everyone knew my name, and this was still a good 10 years before I would carry out the wave of executions that signaled my rise to power."

In addition to killings, Saddam said he bests Bush in the torture department.

"There is a certain type of torture, which is called al-Khaygania—so named in honor of its creator, former security director al-Khaygani—in which the victim is handcuffed and suspended on a piece of wood between two chairs like a chicken," Saddam said. "Then, we attach an electric wire to the man's penis and toes. Can you see Bush doing this? Can you see Bush smashing a man's skull with a brick? Can you see him calling for the deaths of his own family members? Pah, he is too weak."

Saddam closed with harsh words for his American rival.

"I recently heard a critic of President Bush say he is a dictator," Saddam said. "That made me laugh. George Bush, a dictator! My sons Uday and Qusay showed more viciousness at 10 years of age."

"Bush has a long way to go before he can match me," Saddam added. "My hands are red with the blood of the innocent. His are merely a light pink." ⌀

BOOK from page 117

"You mean I'll never be flat-chested again?" Cottonball asked drowsily.

the book is not without its detractors.

"This sends a horrible message to children," renowned pediatrician and author Dr. T. Berry Brazelton said. "I shouldn't have to tell anyone how damaging it is to put so much emphasis on a child's physical appearance. This is by far the worst book I've ever seen."

"I like the part where Lissa The Thin-Lipped Butterfly changes from a butterfly into a beautiful *betterfly*."

Krieg said she was not surprised by Brazelton's reaction.

"Of course he'd say that," Krieg said. "It's just like what Miss Moon tells Norah at the end, after she comes back home with her beautiful new nose: 'My dear, now that you are as beautiful as a little girl can possibly be, all those people are just jealous.'"

"The message isn't that being good-looking makes everything okay," Krieg continued. "It just presents a whole new set of challenges—challenges these children are finally beautiful enough to face." ⌀

TROOPS from page 115

Though he expressed mixed feelings about the war against Iraq, Strauss said he feels it is vital for Americans to stand united behind the nation's fighting men and women in uniform. He draws the line, however, at his former classmates.

"Troy Nowicki, this guy who was in my junior-year gym class, is in the Navy now," Strauss said. "He was on the football team, and he used to love to tease me and give me purple nurples and generally make my life miserable. Once, he head-butted me so hard, I couldn't hear for an hour. Fucking asshole. Yeah, I'm really praying for *his* safe return."

"Troy Nowicki, this guy who was in my junior-year gym class, is in the Navy now," Strauss said. "He was on the football team, and he used to love to tease me and generally make my life miserable."

Above: A 1997 photo of U.S. Marine Ricky Dorner, whom Strauss called "a world-class asshole."

Strauss has tied a yellow ribbon around a tree in front of his parents' home, where he is temporarily living, to show his support for the troops. He also sports an American-flag pin on his shirt at work.

"We can't let our soldiers feel like they're also facing an enemy on the homefront," Strauss said. "They have enough to worry about without hearing that their own country isn't behind them. Could you imagine how demoralizing that would be? It would be as traumatic as the time I had to give a speech on the Teapot Dome scandal at a school assembly, and Ricky Dorner kept whipping pennies at me the whole time. Ricky's a Marine now, and I heard his division got deployed to Tikrit, where they came under heavy fire from the Republican Guard. Haven't heard a casualty report yet."

Strauss, like many Americans, said he believes the U.S. has learned its lesson from its poor treatment of Viet nam War soldiers. Today, even the staunchest anti-war activist is likely to agree that the soldiers are only carrying out the will of the policy-makers and deserve the nation's sympathy and good wishes.

"For a lot of young people, the military is the only option," Strauss said. "Like Frank Deroia, this burnout who used to sit at the back of the school bus and loudly make fun of my clothes every day. Well, he joined the Army, and now I guess he's being treated like some kind of hero because he was one of the troops who secured Baghdad International Airport. Meanwhile, I've got a bachelor's degree and I'm stuck in Kirksville working at Movie Gallery. How is that fair?"

"For a lot of young people, the military is the only option," Strauss said.

Strauss' friends say they are well aware of his feelings about America's troops.

"Jon was very moved by the horrible POW ordeal of Pfc. Jessica Lynch," longtime friend Will Arbus said. "He said she seems like a really sweet girl, the kind of person who would treat classmates with kindness and respect. Nothing like Pvc. Craig Veryzer of the 103rd Infantry. Apparently, Craig was fond of ridiculing Jon's less-than-perfect skin. Boy, does Jon hate that prick." ⊘

AUTOMATION from page 115

mechanized within 10 years.

"The House and Senate will always need people," Speaker of the House Dennis Hastert said. "These machines are a valuable tool, but there's still no substitute for the wisdom and experience of an actual human congressman. Everything that happens in Congress requires, to some extent, the human touch. Except maybe drafting legislation. That can pretty much be done by machine."

Though both Hastert and DeLay insist that increased congressional automation would be a boon for the overworked legislators, the alarming rate of layoffs is causing anxiety on Capitol Hill.

"Our bosses say nothing is ever going to replace old-fashioned, hands-on legislation, but I have my doubts," said a Michigan representative speaking on condition of anonymity. "As it stands, we only have a few seconds to look over the bill before putting it in the machine to vote or amend. If we try to take a closer look, DeLay gets on our ass about holding up the line. I don't want to pass shoddy legislation, but I don't want to lose my job, either."

"Our bosses say nothing is ever going to replace old-fashioned, hands-on legislation, but I have my doubts," said a Michigan representative speaking on condition of anonymity.

Robert Barnes, managing editor of *Congressional Quarterly*, predicted that the legislative body's workforce will be cut in half by the end of 2005.

"The fact is, there's little a human legislator does that a machine can't handle," Barnes said. "All you have to do is program the machine as either Democrat or Republican, and it'll vote along the exact same party lines as a real lawmaker. We know exactly how Ted Kennedy or Orrin Hatch will vote on, say, banning flag-burning, so there's really no reason to keep them around when a machine can do it for a fraction of the cost."

"Frankly," Barnes continued, "I wouldn't be surprised if, in 20 years, the machines get phased out in favor of computer simulations that can carry out an entire legislative session—from introduction of a bill to debate to vote—in a fraction of a second."

On top of feeling unappreciated and expendable, many representatives expressed displeasure about a decline in working conditions, including the addition of shifts to facilitate round-the-clock legislation. Tensions have been so high that Beltway insiders don't rule out the possibility of a congressional walkout, which would grind the U.S. lawmaking industry to a halt. DeLay, however, said he is confident the representatives will stay on the job.

Beltway insiders don't rule out the possibility of a congressional walkout.

"These are good men and, sure, they like to run their mouths off, but they're not going to strike," DeLay said. "Once they get used to the machines and the new regulations, things will normalize. Besides, where else are these legislators going to go if they quit? I mean, their skills aren't exactly what I'd call transferrable." ⊘

COMMUNITY VOICES

If I Could Do It All Over Again, I'd Omit The Hard Work

When you get to reach a certain age, you start to take stock of your life. On the whole, I'm pretty happy with the way things have turned out for me. I've got a fantastic wife, two wonderful children, and a successful landscaping business. Yep, all in all, I'd say I've had it pretty good.

By Stephen Gerald

Yet I do have one not-so-small regret. You see, in my 67 years, I spent a lot of time busting my hump—and for what? If I could do it all over again, I would definitely omit all the hard work.

They say youth is wasted on the young, and it's true. The young don't have the wisdom and experience to know what's important. If I could go back in time knowing what I know now, I wouldn't have studied so hard or wasted all that time listening to my parents. I would use my hard-won hindsight to weasel out of the character-building chores and homework that were a constant in my younger days. But, unfortunately, I don't have a time machine. All that terrific goofing-off time in my teens and twenties, when I could have been stoned or drunk or catatonic in front of the TV, is gone forever. And why? Because I had my nose buried deep in some book, or was helping Dad paint the house. What a colossal waste.

They say youth is wasted on the young, and it's true. The young don't have the wisdom and experience to know what's important. If I could go back in time knowing what I know now, I wouldn't have studied so hard or wasted all that time listening to my parents.

You know what else galls me? For some reason, I got it into my head that owning my own business would be the best thing in the world. Sure, it's nice now that I'm an established name in the landscaping business. But for the first 20 years, it was nothing but back-breaking work getting that sonofabitch off the ground. Can I honestly say that my life is enriched because I'm my own boss, when I could have spent that time playing basketball or—better yet—watching people play basketball on TV? I don't think so. It's not like I'm so wealthy that people wait on me hand and foot. I lead a comfortable life, but a lot of people live comfortable lives without having to spend 15 years hauling rolls of sod.

Yep, if you don't stop and take stock of your life, it'll all slip away from you. But even though I know I'll never get back all those years I foolishly squandered on my friendships, family, and business, I've still got some time left.

Then there's the home I designed and built with my own two hands. This took four years of grueling labor while I was working full-time. And did I do it faster or cheaper or better than professional builders could have? Not really. Sure, there were moments of pride, like watching my two sons run up and down the stairs I built from a mighty oak I cut down myself. But when I look at the house most days, I just see sore hands, an aching back, and an endless list of repairs. Next time I need to do some major construction, I'm giving some Mexican day laborers a check and catching the first plane to Hawaii.

As for my family life, I'm lucky to have a wife like Cheryl, who at 62 is still a beautiful woman, both inside and out. Still, maintaining a marriage is incredibly difficult, especially for 38 long years. When I weigh all the compromise and the trust-building, the nurturing and the moral support, I'm not sure it's been entirely worth it. Yes, I have a soulmate and a confidant, but, really, when comes down to it, I just want to be having sex on a regular basis. Was it worth all the endless nights ironing out knotty relationship issues and keeping her happy with gifts and affection just for some sex, when a good hooker would have done the trick? I'd say no.

Then there are the kids. What was I thinking? Okay, so seeing your newborn child for the first time is a thrill that can't be equaled, I'll grant you that. But that moment of joy is dwarfed by all the headaches and hassles that come later: the smelly diapers, the expensive orthodontics, the horribly awkward father-son talks. Every phase of child-rearing presents a new parenting challenge: the terrible twos, the sullen tweens, the torrid teens. And after all the struggle and the tears, what's the great reward? A severely hobbled social life and a popsicle-stick birdhouse on Father's Day. Oh, and the joy of having someone call you "Daddy." Whoopee.

Yep, if you don't stop and take stock of your life, it'll all slip away from you. But even though I know I'll never get back all those years I foolishly squandered on my friendships, family, and business, I've still got some time left. And I'm determined to use that time well. After all, it's never too late to never lift another goddamn finger.

HOROSCOPES

Your Horoscope

By Lloyd Schumner Sr.
Retired Machinist and
A.A.P.B.-Certified Astrologer

Aries: (March 21–April 19)
Sometimes, you just have to step back, relax, and take a deep breath. However, you might also find it helpful to get some heavy radiation therapy.

Taurus: (April 20–May 20)
This is a great time for romance to bloom at work—a fact you won't realize until it's no longer a great time.

Gemini: (May 21–June 21)
You'll soon be "downsized," but don't worry: You'll keep your job and instead lose 20 pounds and two feet of height.

Cancer: (June 22–July 22)
You will remind many of Abraham Lincoln, with your oratory gifts, dedication to equality, and habit of getting shot in the head at theaters.

Leo: (July 23–Aug. 22)
You'll be forced to change your hairstyle and gain 165 pounds when John Goodman is chosen to play you in a new movie.

Virgo: (Aug. 23–Sept. 22)
You're not the kind of person who lets physical handicaps get in your way, but that's because you're a flesh-eating zombie.

Libra: (Sept. 23–Oct. 23)
Your battle with hair loss intensifies this week when hair loss brings in artillery to support the infantry positions it established near your supply routes.

Scorpio: (Oct. 24–Nov. 21)
The police will haul you downtown to answer a few questions about where babies come from and if Daddy was hurting Mommy.

Sagittarius: (Nov. 22–Dec. 21)
Everybody always speaks admiringly of what a survivor you are, but Thursday's events will make liars of them all.

Capricorn: (Dec. 22–Jan. 19)
Your bold plan for stimulating small businesses through tax incentives would get more attention if you weren't a drunk living under a bridge.

Aquarius: (Jan. 20–Feb. 18)
You are destined to become a major sex symbol, just as soon as societal attitudes toward sex become far less healthy.

Pisces: (Feb. 19–March 20)
Your natural stubbornness comes in handy when your opponent's arguments turn out to be supported by hard facts and credible evidence.

WINSTON CUPS from page 115

amounts of blood. Passersby were amazed by the unusually large amounts of blood. Passersby were amazed by the unusually large amounts of blood. Passersby were amazed by the unusually large

Oops! I thought it was *my* toddler I was smacking over the head with a bag of frozen peas in the middle of the grocery store.

amounts of blood. Passersby were amazed by the unusually large amounts of blood. Passersby were amazed by the unusually large amounts of blood. Passersby were amazed by the unusually large

see WINSTON CUPS page 127

NEWS

Fans Riot In Streets As U.S. Victorious

see NATION page 7A

Nabisco Introduces X-treme Salt-Assault Saltines

see PRODUCTWATCH page 11B

Letters From Grandma Always Describe Grandpa As 'Tired'

see LOCAL page 5B

STATshot

A look at the numbers that shape your world.

How Much Do We Love Our Mommy?

1. More than a birthday cake made of sunbeams
2. Perhaps too much; certainly too often
3. Not as much as our wire mommy
4. That is between Mother and me
5. Not really into the whole mom thing right now
6. Less since she started making us call Gary "Daddy"
7. May I refer you to the tattoo?

0 74470 94595 6 00

THE ONION • $2.00 US • $3.00 CAN

the ONION®

VOLUME 39 ISSUE 15 AMERICA'S FINEST NEWS SOURCE™ 24–30 APRIL 2003

New Fox Reality Show To Determine Ruler Of Iraq

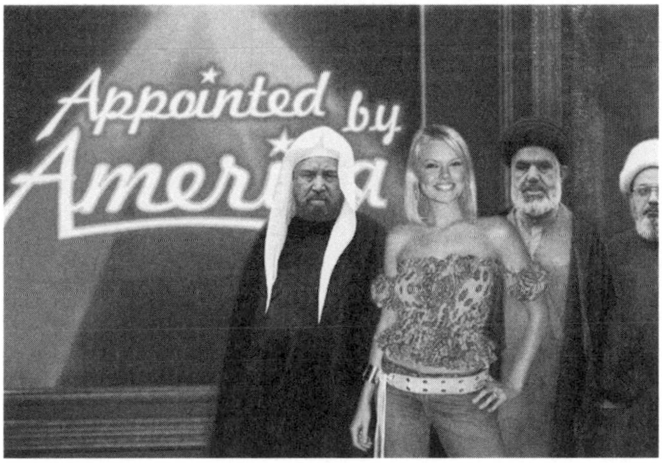

Above: Some of the *Appointed By America* hopefuls vying for the presidency of Iraq.

LOS ANGELES—Fox executives Monday unveiled their latest reality-TV venture, *Appointed By America*, a new series in which contestants vie for the top spot in Iraq's post-war government.

"Get ready, America, because you're about to choose the man—or woman—who will lead Iraq into an exciting democratic future," said Fox reality-programming chief Mike Darnell, introducing the show at a press conference. "Will it be Ahmed Chalabi, leader of the exiled Iraqi National Congress? Or General Tommy Franks, commander of the allied forces? Or maybe Roshumba Williams, the Macon, GA, waitress with big dreams and an even bigger voice? Tune in Tuesdays at 9 to see."

Describing the new show as "*American Idol* meets the reconstruction of Afghanistan," Darnell said *Appointed By America* will feature contestants squaring off in a variety of challenges, including a democracy quiz, a talent competition, and nation-building activities that will demonstrate their ability to lead a bombed-out, war-ravaged Mideast country.

A panel of celebrity judges will help eliminate two contestants each week, leaving one lucky winner the undis-

see FOX page 124

Above: ADA president T. Howard Jones.

U.S. Dentists Can't Make Nation's Teeth Any Damn Whiter

WASHINGTON, DC—In an official statement Monday, a spokesman for the American Dental Association announced that it cannot make the teeth of the nation's citizens any goddamn whiter.

"As medical professionals, there is a limit to how white we can make your teeth," ADA president T. Howard Jones said. "Using various new tooth-whitening procedures, we can remove the extrinsic staining from your teeth and make them look their absolute whitest. But that's still not enough for

see DENTISTS page 125

Above: The DVD collection that horrified Pearle (inset).

Harsh Light Of Morning Falls On One-Night Stand's DVD Collection

MILWAUKEE, WI—The harsh light of morning fell on the terrible DVD collection of Marc Koenig Monday, when Traci Pearle discovered it upon waking up from their one-night stand.

"It was a wild night, and from what I can recall, I had a great time with Marc," said Pearle, 25. "But I wonder if I would've felt the same way had I known the guy is the proud owner of *Rollerball*."

Pearle, a Marquette University graduate student, and Koenig, a graphic designer, met Sunday during a party at the home of a mutual friend. Pearle and Koenig hit it off almost immediately, thanks largely to their mutual drunkenness. After a lengthy make-out session in a back room, the two departed for Koenig's nearby one-bedroom apartment, where

see COLLECTION page 125

Is Syria Next?

Tensions are rising between the U.S. and Syria, which the Bush Administration has warned against harboring fugitive Saddam loyalists. What do *you* think?

Vincent Gregg
Systems Analyst

"Syria should know better than to help its allies."

Fran Whalen
Attorney

"On the one hand, it'd be foolish to extend a military action that has already earned us worldwide enmity. On the other hand, it's *right there*."

Christopher Tam
Machinist

"I'd watch out for those Syrians. If we can learn anything from their past history, it's that those folks are heavily into smiting."

Christina Abel
Dietitian

"I can think of lots of reasons to attack them, starting with their vital role in funding Sept. 11. What? Syria? I'm sorry, I thought you said Saudi Arabia."

Dana Dubrow
Homemaker

"After Iraq, I think we should hit Syria, then Iran, then Egypt. Or maybe Iran, *then* Syria, then Pakistan. Gosh, there are so many ways we could go here."

Rick Swopes
Forklift Operator

"What possible justification could we have for going to war with Syria? Oh, I'm just kidding—go right ahead, I don't care."

Uday's Pleasure Palace

Last week, U.S. soldiers toured the remains of Uday Hussein's home, uncovering a lavish palace of sex and drugs. Among the niceties enjoyed by Saddam's son:

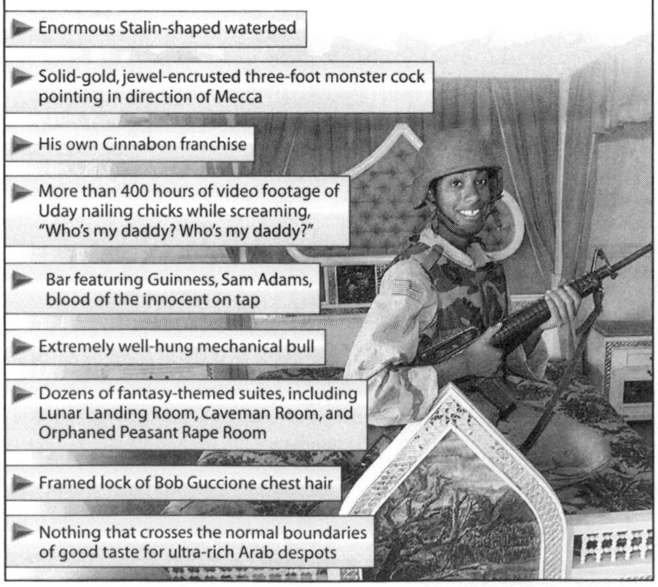

- Enormous Stalin-shaped waterbed
- Solid-gold, jewel-encrusted three-foot monster cock pointing in direction of Mecca
- His own Cinnabon franchise
- More than 400 hours of video footage of Uday nailing chicks while screaming, "Who's my daddy? Who's my daddy?"
- Bar featuring Guinness, Sam Adams, blood of the innocent on tap
- Extremely well-hung mechanical bull
- Dozens of fantasy-themed suites, including Lunar Landing Room, Caveman Room, and Orphaned Peasant Rape Room
- Framed lock of Bob Guccione chest hair
- Nothing that crosses the normal boundaries of good taste for ultra-rich Arab despots

the ONION®
America's Finest News Source.™

Herman Ulysses Zweibel
Founder

T. Herman Zweibel
Publisher Emeritus
J. Phineas Zweibel
Publisher
Maxwell Prescott Zweibel
Editor-In-Chief

I Want The Pictures Of My Partial-Birth Abortion Back

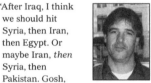

By Sara DeVries

Help! I can hardly walk down the street these days without running into some pro-life protester waving a picture of my partial-birth abortion! I never wanted those photos to get out in the first place, but now that Congress is considering a ban on late-term abortions, it's only getting worse. Petitions, billboards on the interstate, leaflets—those photos of that bloody little fetus all hacked apart on a surgical steel table are *everywhere*. Listen up, Right-To-Lifers: I want the pictures of my partial-birth abortion back!

As you probably guessed, I'm pro-choice. But even though I firmly support a woman's right to choose, I was still pretty embarrassed about having an abortion, and I don't want to be constantly reminded of the mistake I made that put me in that position. So may I please have those gruesome photos back? Please? *Pretty please?*

I realize those partial-birth pictures are very desirable. After all, out of all the abortions performed in this country, less than 1 percent are done at that late stage. Most of those occur

I never wanted those photos to get out in the first place, but now that Congress is considering a ban on late-term abortions, it's only getting worse. Petitions, billboards on the interstate, leaflets—those photos of that bloody little fetus all hacked apart on a surgical steel table are everywhere.

because the woman's health is in jeopardy or genetic defects were discovered in the fetus. But I wasn't in any danger. And my fetus looked like a perfect little unborn child—a definite plus for the posters. So I can see why the pro-lifers would be so eager to use them. But the bottom line is: My abortion, my photos.

Call me screwed up. I admit it. It's probably the reason it took me five months to admit to myself that I was even pregnant. That's me, Crazy Sara. But even though I was in no position

I've made all sorts of efforts to get those photos back. I left a bunch of messages at both In-His-Name Signs and Trinity Silkscreeners. I've approached protesters and tried to wrestle the signs out of their hands. I even put up flyers around town with a photo of the photos and a $500 reward for their return.

to raise a child, I still didn't want an abortion. It wasn't until the doctor found out about all the drinking and Ecstasy that... well, the rest is history. Only, it's not history, because now I can't run into the supermarket for a gallon of milk without bumping into some born-again Christian wearing a T-shirt sporting my mangled unborn son under the words "God Is Pro-Life."

Yes, I should've been more careful with the snapshots. I showed them to a few people, who in turn showed them to a few people, but they were interested. Okay, so I may have let a couple people borrow them, but they swore it was just to show their closest friends. I didn't expect that those pictures would fall into the wrong hands and one day come back to haunt me. Now I know how Vanna White felt when she turned up in *Playboy*.

I've made all sorts of efforts to get those photos back. I left a bunch of messages at both In-His-Name Signs and Trinity Silkscreeners. I've approached protesters and tried to wrestle the signs out of their hands. I even put up flyers around town with a photo of the photos and a $500 reward for their return. Nothing has worked.

You say he was a child, not a choice. Well, if that's the case, wherever he is right now, he's probably not too thrilled to be looking down at all those pictures of the day he got yanked out of my uterus. So for his sake, not mine, could you please give 'em back? I'd really appreciate it.

MEDIA

Christopher Hitchens Forcibly Removed From Trailer Park After Drunken Confrontation With Common-Law Wife

SPARTA, TN—Noted author, social critic, and political gadfly Christopher Hitchens was once again the focus of controversy Monday, when he was forcibly removed from Happy Trails trailer park following a drunken confrontation with Noreen Bodell, 39, his common-law wife of 14 years.

Responding to a domestic-disturbance call, police arrived at the couple's double-wide trailer at approximately 2:15 p.m. to find Hitchens and Bodell throwing dishes at each other. When the officers attempted to remove Hitchens from the premises, the leftist intellectual became physically and verbally abusive toward the officers, calling them "shitkickers," "bitches," and "effete liberal apologists for the atrocities of late-stage capitalism."

> **"Hitch is an all-right guy once he sobers up," Vernon said. "He just gets a little wound-up sometimes, like when his woman stays out all night down at Smokey Joe's Tavern, or he has a deadline looming for his *Vanity Fair* column."**

Having consumed what sources described as "a substantial amount of single-malt scotch," Hitchens then burst into tears, yelling, "That woman never understood me for who I am. I want to talk to [*Harper's* editor Lewis] Lapham. Lapham's the only one who understands me."

Charged with disturbing the peace, Hitchens was taken to the Sparta police station at 3 p.m. and released four hours later.

Little is known about Bodell, a heavy-set blonde who has been known to use several different surnames. According to sources familiar with the couple, the incident marks the third time in as many weeks that police have been forced to intervene in their volatile relationship.

"We're down at the old Hitchens place probably twice a month at least," said Sgt. Wilson Vernon, the first of three officers to arrive at the scene. "Once his blood's up, old Hitch can get meaner than a three-legged coon hound. From what the neighbors told us about this latest incident, Noreen was all worked up, accusing him of drinking and womanizing. He was angry with her refusal to acknowledge that there is ample evidence to make a case for prosecuting Henry Kissinger as a war criminal. She just kept shouting, 'No, there ain't!'"

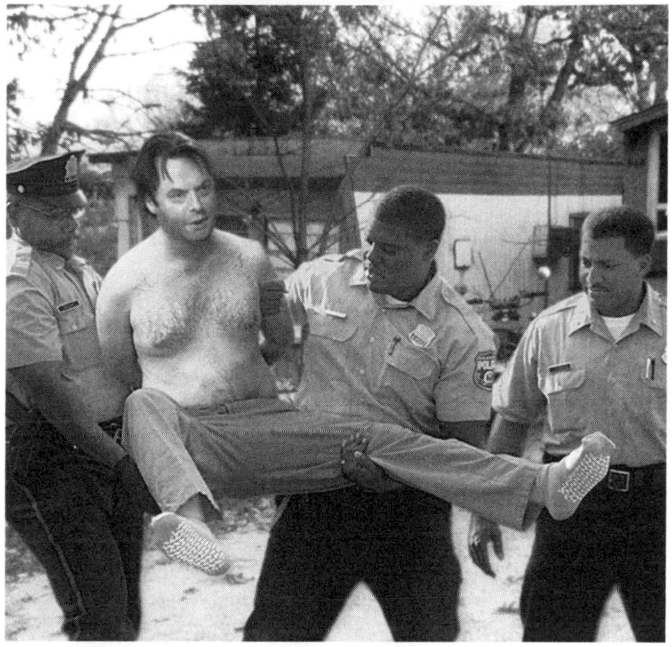

Above: An inebriated Hitchens is forcibly removed from the Happy Trails trailer park.

Police were initially summoned when neighbors reported hearing shouting and a loud crash, followed by a rambling polemic on Kissinger's alleged covert approval of Indonesia's illegal invasion of East Timor in 1975.

Though the belligerent Hitchens required three officers to subdue him, police do not consider the incident serious, calling it "business as usual" and describing Hitchens as a "hot tempered but essentially harmless provocateur for the Far Left."

"Hitch is an all-right guy once he sobers up," Vernon said. "He just gets a little wound-up sometimes, like when his woman stays out all night down at Smokey Joe's Tavern, or he has a deadline looming for his *Vanity Fair* column."

Hitchens' run-ins with the law have not been restricted to Sparta city limits. In May 2002, he was arrested for drunkenly singing 1930s union songs while driving a stolen riding lawnmower through the streets of Boston, where he was attending an international women's-rights conference. Hitchens accused police of "atavistic, morally reprehensible Stalinist scare tactics" before being bailed out by conference organizers the following morning.

Sgt. Ed Poole of Boston's 11th Precinct said there was no love lost between Hitchens and his arresting

see HITCHENS page 124

NEWS IN BRIEF

Woman Mentions Participation In Cancer Walk To Cancer Patient

DENVER—Trying to show empathy, Marilyn Rossum, 42, informed coworker and recently diagnosed breast-cancer patient Georgia Anderson, 40, that she participated in a breast-cancer walk-a-thon in 2001. "Oh, Georgia, I'm so sorry," Rossum told Anderson upon hearing the news Monday. "A few years back, I did the Avon Walk For Breast Cancer, and there were so many brave women like you who were afflicted or survivors, and it was just so moving." Rossum added that her efforts raised nearly $80 for breast-cancer research.

Dysfunctional Singles Find Each Other

BLOOMFIELD HILLS, MI—After nearly 10 years of searching, clingy, neurotic Ryan Dollett, 31, has finally found his soulmate in passive-aggressive, emotionally distant Amy Sunderland, 28, sources reported Monday. "I want to be with Amy every single second, I just love her so much," Dollett said. "She has so many amazing qualities, but I think the best is the way she never challenges me." Said Sunderland: "Ryan is quite the catch. I'm sure once we're married, I'll grow to love everything about him, even the terrible way he dresses."

Tortured Ugandan Political Prisoner Wishes Uganda Had Oil

KAMPALA, UGANDA—A day after having his hands amputated by soldiers backing President Yoweri Museveni's brutal regime, Ugandan political prisoner Otobo Ankole expressed regret Monday over Uganda's lack of oil reserves. "I dream of the U.S. one day fighting for the liberation of the oppressed Ugandan people," Ankole said as he nursed his bloody stumps. "But, alas, our number-one natural resource is sugar cane." Ankole, whose wife, parents, and five children were among the 4,000 slaughtered in Uganda's ethnic killings of 2002, then bowed his head and said a prayer for petroleum.

Catholic Child Told About Doggy Heaven, Doggy Hell

NORTHAMPTON, MA—Three days after burying his beloved labrador retriever, Daniel MacNeil, 9, was told about doggy heaven and hell by his fourth-grade teacher, Sister Doris Behnke. "Don't cry, Daniel. I'm sure Shiner was a very good doggy," Behnke told the mourning child Tuesday. "He's probably in Doggy Heaven right now, running through its big green fields and chasing squirrels. Only disobedient doggies who chew on the furniture or lift their legs on the carpet will burn in the eternal, white-hot kennel fires of Doggy Hell."

Small-Town Residents Come Together For Arby's Raising

BUFORD, PA—Buford's 322 residents, as well as many citizens of surrounding towns, came together over the weekend for a good old-fashioned Arby's raising. "People came from as far away as Lancaster to pitch in," said local delivery-truck driver Jonathan Beckman, 44. "It was a real team effort: Me, Zachary Fordice, and Eli White poured the foundation while old Benjamin Wetzel built the prep-tables, and the womenfolk installed the booths' vinyl seat covers." Beckman said his wife Maryellen "can't wait" to whip up a fresh homemade batch of Arby's famous Horsey Sauce. Ø

FOX from page 121

puted leader of Iraq at the end of the season. Viewers can participate by casting phone-in votes, although Darnell noted that voting is restricted to calls originating from within the continental U.S.

U.S. General Jay Garner (Ret.) will host the show under the auspices of the Pentagon. The three celebrity judges, Darnell said, will be choreographer and former Chrysalis recording artist Toni Basil, internationally renowned hairstylist Vidal Sassoon, and television star Kevin Sorbo.

"They really get into it," Darnell said.

"It is great that Fox will play a vital role in post-war Iraq," Wolfowitz said.

"Just wait until you see the fur fly between Sassoon and Basil."

Fox entertainment president Gail Berman said the network was inspired to create the show after witnessing its news division's ratings success over the past few months.

"Fox did such huge numbers with its war coverage, we figured, 'Why not find a way to keep this good thing going?'" Berman said. "I'm confident that our loyal Fox News viewers will find that reconstruction can be just as thrilling as destruction."

The first episode has already been taped in front of a live studio audience, though results will remain classified until airtime. The winner of *Appointed By America* will be sworn in as president of Iraq on June 24 in a gala two-hour season finale broadcast live from Baghdad.

According to Berman, Fox received more than 3,000 applicants for the show during an open casting call. While most of the hopefuls were American or Iraqi, some 600 aspiring rulers from more than 100 nations auditioned for the coveted 20 finalist spots. Contestants included a San Diego interior decorator, a Philadelphia inner-city schoolteacher, and a *peshmerga* fighter from the Patriotic Union of Kurdistan.

Contestant Kymbyrley Lake, a cashier from Garland, TX, said she has a "good feeling" about her chances.

"I just really believe I am going to win this show," Lake said. "I feel it in my heart that Jesus is going to grant me the chance to help all these people. Ever since I was a little girl, I've dreamed of doing something to help bring about a more peaceful world."

Lake just might get her chance. Inside sources say she was among the top five vote-getters in the first episode, with Kurdistan Democratic Party official Fawzi Hariri and pre-Saddam Iraqi minister Adnan al-Pachachi—both early odds-on favorites—scoring low points for stage presence.

At a Pentagon briefing Monday, Deputy Defense Secretary Paul Wolfowitz gave his blessing to *Appointed By America*.

"It is great that Fox will play a vital role in post-war Iraq," Wolfowitz said. "Heck, we didn't really know *what* we were going to do." Ø

Above: Audience members eagerly await the start of a live taping of *Appointed By America*.

HITCHENS from page 123

officers.

"Word got around the station that this guy wrote a whole book claiming that Mother Teresa was a stooge of right-wing dictators," Poole recalled. "Supposedly, he said her hypocritical approach to charity for the poor of Calcutta, as well as her steadfast advocacy of the Catholic Church's doctrine prohibiting birth control, made her an essentially immoral individual undeserving of the mantle of sainthood. Well, a lot of the boys here are Irish-Catholic born and raised, and they don't take too kindly to people speaking ill of nuns."

Town officials in Sparta, where Hitchens has maintained an on-again, off-again residence for two decades, admit that he may be "a handful" at times, but they insist he is not a danger to himself or others.

"If I know Hitch, by the end of the week, he and Noreen'll be back together, cuddlin' and kissin', just as happy as two crawdads in a pond," Sparta Police Chief Buck Perkins said. "We don't get a lot of ultra-progressive agitators 'round these parts, but Hitch is okay. Plus, he earned a lot of points with the townsfolk for his vocal criticism of the anti-war movement. Even though he was attacking the war opponents from the left, folks around here don't necessarily understand the implications of that, so he's an all-

Town officials in Sparta, where Hitchens has maintained an on-again, off-again residence for two decades, admit that he may be "a handful" at times, but they insist he is not a danger to himself or others.

right Joe in their book."

Added Perkins: "So long as Hitch can learn to keep his mouth shut about Christianity being symptomatic of the 'savage and ignorant prehistory of our species' and whatnot, I'm sure he'll cause no trouble that a few cups of black coffee and a night in the drunk tank can't solve." Ø

STAMP ACT from page 119

amounts of blood. Passersby were amazed by the unusually large amounts of blood. Passersby were amazed by the unusually large

Christina Applegate can do my dishes anytime. That's because I'm gay, but I have a lot of dirty dishes.

amounts of blood. Passersby were amazed by the unusually large amounts of blood. Passersby were amazed by the unusually large amounts of blood. Passersby were amazed by the unusually large amounts of blood. Passersby were amazed by the unusually large amounts of blood. Passersby were amazed by the unusually large amounts of blood. Passersby were amazed by the unusually large

see STAMP ACT page 131

COLLECTION from page 121

they spent the night.

Her powers of observation impaired by alcohol and darkness, Pearle took little notice of Koenig's furnishings. It was not until 8 a.m. that the hungover Pearle, en route to the bathroom, came across Koenig's disturbingly random, mediocrity-filled DVD collection.

"The glare from the living-room window made my eyes smart," Pearle said. "I rubbed them, and the first thing I saw was *Narrow Margin* sitting on Marc's sunlit coffee table."

A nearby DVD shelf revealed similarly banal choices, including *Driven, Evolution, Swordfish, Tomcats, Point Break, Pushing Tin, Bedazzled, Flatliners, My Blue Heaven*, and *Proof Of Life*.

While acknowledging that the majority of Koenig's movies were "not out-and-out horrible," Pearle wondered why anyone would own those particular titles.

"They're the sort of things you'd rent, not buy, if you watch them at all," Pearle said. "Out of the thousands of movies you could own, why would you spend your money on this stuff?

A nearby DVD shelf revealed similarly banal choices, including *Driven, Evolution, Swordfish, Tomcats, Point Break, Pushing Tin, Bedazzled, Flatliners, My Blue Heaven*, and *Proof Of Life*.

Don't you buy a movie because you're somehow passionate about it and want to watch it again and again? Does this guy feel that way about *Hard Rain*?"

In spite of a wicked hangover, Pearle could not resist hypothesizing about Koenig based on his DVD choices.

"It struck me as weird that the same person would possess both *Hellraiser 2* and *Holy Man*," Pearle said. "What did it mean? That he's a guy with eclectic tastes, and therefore tolerant and open-minded? Or is he just meek and wishy-washy, surrendering his tastes and imagination to arbitrary pop-culture dictates? He seemed like such a smart, cool guy."

Continued Pearle: "I slept with a guy who, at some point in his life, walked into a store and said to the cashier, 'Hi, I would like to purchase this copy of *The Legend Of Bagger Vance*.'"

Pearle admitted that her decision to leave Koenig's apartment around 8:20 a.m. was heavily influenced by the discovery of the DVD collection.

"As I got dressed, Marc sat up in bed and took my hand, telling me he had the day off from work if I wanted to stay in with him," Pearle said. "I considered it, but then I noticed the Vince Vaughn version of *Psycho* on the nightstand, so I made up something about having to meet my professor in half an hour."

Therapist and counselor Dr. Patricia Abel said the one-night stand did not come to a particularly unusual end.

"Often, casual sexual encounters between two people are not repeated because one of the parties has judged the other based on his or her personal effects," Abel said. "There exists a societal stigma against so-called 'one-night stands,' so Traci may have been subconsciously associating latent feelings of guilt and unfulfillment with Marc's ownership of several Ashley Judd thrillers."

Pearle herself has been the victim of possessions-based judgment following a one-night stand. On June 4, 2000, pizza-delivery driver James Gaines fled Pearle's apartment shortly after 6 a.m., when the morning light revealed a Toad The Wet Sprocket CD and a prescription bottle of Xanax. Ø

DENTISTS from page 121

you psychos. You need whiter. Well, if you want to go to Mexico and have someone implant a black light in your gums so your teeth glow an unearthly white, go nuts. I'm just telling you what we're medically and legally capable of at this time."

Jones said Americans enjoy a staggering variety of teeth-whitening options, including lasers, gels, bleaches, strips, rinses, pastes, and carbamide-peroxide trays from such

"If there was some way to make your teeth whiter, we'd be thrilled to offer it to you and charge you an arm and a leg for it," Jones said. "You're just going to have to come to grips with the fact that your teeth have a slight natural tint."

makers as Rembrandt, Brite Smile, Perfect Smile, PowerWhite, Rapid White, and Pearl Drops. But in spite of the seemingly limitless dental-bleaching procedures and products available, Jones said the nation's vain populace is still not satisfied.

"We're not holding anything back, honest," Jones said. "If there was some way to make your teeth whiter, we'd be thrilled to offer it to you and charge you an arm and a leg for it. You're just going to have to come to grips with the fact that your teeth have a slight natural tint. Unless you want us to start painting your teeth with correction fluid, you'll have to accept that cruel fact."

Jones stressed that the ADA has nothing against tooth whitening, noting that most of its 147,000 members offer everything from laser bleaching to porcelain veneers to dental bonding. The typical ADA dentist, however, is irked by customers who come in for routine bleaching and leave disappointed because "their teeth don't inflict retinal damage when you look directly into them."

"Hey, if your teeth are stained or discolored, come on in, and we'll fix you up," Jones said. "Professional teeth bleaching can whiten your teeth upwards of five shades, but once they reach their limit, that's it. You need to stop comparing your teeth to your refrigerator."

Citizens across the U.S. are expressing confusion over the ADA's defensive tone.

"I don't see why they're getting all huffy," said St. Paul, MN, resident Tamara Wenders, her words garbled by a mouthful of Crest Whitestrips. "They're making a lot of money. I thought dentists wanted us to have clean teeth."

Added Wenders, looking into the mirror: "I think it's working."

According to ADA member Dr. Walter Foti, D.D.S., the national obsession with perfectly white teeth may only be getting started.

"What happens once, at long last, you people get your teeth pure white?" Foti asked. "Will you finally be satisfied? Of course not. Then you'll want clear teeth. You won't rest until your fucking teeth are see-through."

"Look, you want white teeth so damn bad? It's simple," Jones said. "Don't smoke, stay away from coffee, tea, and soda, brush and floss regularly, and go to your dentist every six months. Sure, have your teeth whitened occasionally, but keep in mind that we can only go far as the technology allows. When someone creates a better teeth-whitening procedure, we'll slap an 'ultra' on it and get it out on the market as fast as the FDA allows. Until then, be happy with what you have. Americans really need to learn to live with almost-total perfection." Ø

Above: Members of the Cohn family of Alpine, NJ, all of whom are dissatisfied with the whiteness of their teeth.

COMMUNITY VOICES

That Rob's Got Some Seriously Strong Shit

Hola, amigos. What's up? I know it's been a long time since I rapped at ya, but I got my irons in a shitload of fires these days. I got this new job running people from the airport to a car-rental place in a little bus. I know it ain't the coolest job in the world, but it keeps my cruising skills sharp, plus I get three weeks' vacation and some insurance. I never thought I'd be one of those old fogies who cared about insurance, but there it is. Don't think I can't still rock, though.

The Cruise
By Jim Anchower

Then there's this war. Man, that shit is fucked up. We sure showed that crazy camel-fucker who's boss. I just wish it would've taken a little longer. I had this great idea for a T-shirt. It's a picture of Saddam Hussein, and it's got a target on him, and it says "Saddam's Insane," 'cause that guy is nuts. If I knew how to get a T-shirt made, I would have done it. But now I guess he's dead, so there goes my million-dollar idea.

The last few weeks, I've spent a lot of time thinking about that kind of stuff. Whenever I'm not driving the bus, I've pretty much been holed up in the castle. Now, usually, Jim Anchower is a very social guy. I like

Now, I'm a pretty decent bowler, especially when I'm baked. But this time, I was in The Zone. I mean, I was one with the ball and pins. And the fact that I couldn't put a sentence together or look anyone in the eye only helped my concentration. I bowled a 199, which was a personal best.

to go out, stir some shit up on a regular basis. You know, see what floats, see what sinks—have a blast. So you're probably wondering what would make a party monster like me stay at home.

It's simple. The weed.

Now, you know Jim Anchower does not like to brag about certain things, weed being one of them. The last thing I need is people coming over to my house trying to weasel their way into my stash because I was too dumb to keep my trap shut. But this stuff... man.

It started one Friday night about a

Now, usually, Jim Anchower is a very social guy. I like to go out, stir some shit up on a regular basis. You know, see what floats, see what sinks—have a blast. So you're probably wondering what would make a party monster like me stay at home. It's simple. The weed.

month ago when I was bowling with the crew—that being me, Wes, Ron, and Ron's friend Rob. We headed over to Badger Bowl and, after ordering a few beers and some jalapeño poppers, we settled into a few frames. It's pretty nice to get out there and bowl once in a while. I can't think of another sport that encourages you to drink like that.

So we finish our first game and are about to start another when Rob asks if we want to go out to the parking lot and smoke some weed. Ron and Wes opted to stick with the bowling and brew, so that left me and Rob on bud duty. He pulls out a joint and tells me I should just take one hit, since it's pretty strong shit.

What the hell is he telling me that for? I mean, everyone tells people their weed is strong. Hell, I tell people that all the time so they don't bogart my joint. So when Rob said it, I thought he was just giving me a line. I took two pretty hefty pulls and passed it on. It didn't take long before I found out that Rob wasn't shitting me. I hadn't been that baked since the second time I smoked pot. After what seemed like two hours, we went back inside to bowl.

Now, I'm a pretty decent bowler, especially when I'm baked. But this time, I was in The Zone. I mean, I was one with the ball and pins. And the fact that I couldn't put a sentence together or look anyone in the eye only helped my concentration. I bowled a 199, which was a personal best. When we wrapped up that game, Ron said it was my turn to buy a pitcher. I handed him $20 and told him that if I buy, he flies. At least I think that's what I said.

Since I was on a hot streak, I decided to bowl another game. We were about halfway through the second frame when I started to feel the creeps. I noticed the painting at the end of the lanes. I'd seen it a hundred times, but I never truly *saw* it before. It's a bunch of bowling pins getting hit by the ball, but they're all bent around the ball like they're made of rubber. It started to freak me out. I took a sip of beer and looked around to see if anyone noticed me losing my shit. I knew someone was staring at me, and I was trying to figure out who it was when Wes told me it was my turn.

I picked up the ball and went up toward the foul line. Just as I was about to let go of the ball, I felt someone staring at me again. I threw a gutter ball, screwing up my spare from the frame before. I knew I was being watched, so I decided I had to make the next one count. I grabbed my ball and sized up the pins. I don't know how long I was staring at them, but Ron asked me if I was just going to hold my balls or throw. I freaked out and threw another gutter. Then someone put some Steve Miller on the jukebox. That was it for me. Normally, I love the Space Cowboy, but "Abracadabra" was not something I wanted to hear at that moment. I told everyone I needed to leave and went to wait in the car. That was it for the night.

As freaky as the whole experience was, I couldn't deny that Rob's weed was some seriously good shit. I got a hold of him and bought a decent stash.

Ever since, I've been spending a lot of time at home, just chilling out. Or, as Steve Miller once put it, "gettin' high and watchin' the tube." I need to leave the house eventually, if only because Ron never gave me my change from the pitcher that night. I shoulda known better. That guy's a rat. Ø

HOROSCOPES

Your Horoscope

By Lloyd Schumner Sr.
Retired Machinist and
A.A.P.B.-Certified Astrologer

Aries: (March 21–April 19)
This is a time of great uncertainty for you, but maybe you should stop going around saying you're uncertain how all the sailors wound up in your bed.

Taurus: (April 20–May 20)
This might not be much of a comfort, but those 426 people would've all died eventually, anyway.

Gemini: (May 21–June 21)
It's been said that everyone ultimately becomes that which they despise, which may explain your sudden transformation into a platter of liver and onions.

Cancer: (June 22–July 22)
Satan will appear before you, transport you to a mountaintop, show you the riches of the world, and then just leave you up there without food or shelter.

Leo: (July 23–Aug. 22)
It's a bad week for romance in the workplace, but that isn't the problem. The problem is that the stars actually have to tell you that.

Virgo: (Aug. 23–Sept. 22)
Your appetite for rich, fatty foods may not be healthy, but it would be even worse if it wasn't strictly sexual.

Libra: (Sept. 23–Oct. 23)
It's time to start paying more attention to the things that make life worthwhile, such as oxygen molecules.

Scorpio: (Oct. 24–Nov. 21)
There will be times when you can do nothing but stand back and witness events as they unfold. However, sometimes it's good to know how to put out a grease fire.

Sagittarius: (Nov. 22–Dec. 21)
Your plan to fake your own death will be thoroughly convincing right up through the autopsy.

Capricorn: (Dec. 22–Jan. 19)
Due to your devout Christianity, next Thursday will bring both the last moments and the biggest disappointment of your life.

Aquarius: (Jan. 20–Feb. 18)
You've never been much of an athlete, but it still hurts when the U.S. Olympic basketball team makes a point of mentioning that they never considered you.

Pisces: (Feb. 19–March 20)
The fear that your phony law degree will be exposed turns out to be groundless when Applebee's hires you anyway.

NEWS

Desktop Zen Rock Garden Thrown At Assistant

see OFFICE page 4C

New Taco Bell Menu Item Ready For Testing On Humans

see SCIENCE page 7E

Least-Powerful Roommate's Posters Relegated To Bathroom

see LOCAL page 10D

STATshot

A look at the numbers that shape your world.

Why Did We Dump Our Boyfriend/Girlfriend?

1. Got poor television reception
2. Bought ugly stamps
3. Kept bowl of hard candies
4. Was into Jamiroquai
5. Referred to pizza as "za"
6. May have eventually aged or gained weight

THE ONION • $2.00 US • $3.00 CAN

the ONION®

VOLUME 39 ISSUE 16 AMERICA'S FINEST NEWS SOURCE™ 1-7 MAY 2003

CIA: Syria Harboring More Than 15 Million Known Arabs

Above: Suspected Arabs move freely through a Damascus marketplace.

LANGLEY, VA—In an alarming report released Monday by the Central Intelligence Agency, Syria may be harboring upwards of 15 million known Arabs within its borders.

"Reliable intelligence collected by our agency indicates that Syria has conspired to lend physical and economic support to a massive number of people belonging to this group," CIA director George J. Tenet said. "The shocking truth is, there are nearly as many Arabs in Syria as there are people in New York and Los Angeles combined. In fact, Syrians openly refer to their nation as the Syrian Arab Republic, despite knowing full well America's opinion on these matters."

Explaining the CIA's methods of gathering data on the rogue ethnicity's presence in Syria, Tenet said it relied on a combination of satellite imagery, computer-system infiltration, reports from Syrian covert operatives, intercepted radio and television transmissions, and *The World Almanac And Book Of Facts 2003.*

see SYRIA page 131

Ashcroft Rejected By Newly Created Bride Of Ashcroft

Above: Ashcroft introduces his would-be Bride to the press.

WASHINGTON, DC—Attorney General John Ashcroft's quest for a companion to ease the pain of his lonely and tormented existence was dealt a severe blow Monday, when he was rejected by the newly created "Bride Of Ashcroft."

Unwrapped from bandages at a press conference, the ungodly Bride twitched grotesquely several times before turning to face her would-be mate. Reporters in attendance said the Bride recoiled upon setting her eyes on Ashcroft's horribly misshapen visage, letting out a blood-curdling scream.

"When the lovestruck Attorney General tried to embrace the Bride, she shunned him, just as the entire world has shunned him," CNN reporter William Hurlbut said. "It was truly tragic."

Despondent, Ashcroft roared with despair as all hope of finding a wife deserted his tortured brain.

"Love... death... hate... living..." Ashcroft said.

The heartbroken Attorney General, realizing he could never be loved, then told reporters, "We belong dead." At that point, he pulled a giant lever, setting off a fiery explosion that appeared to incinerate himself and his new Bride, with no trace of either remaining when the smoke finally cleared.

Confirmed dead in the blast was the Bride's maniacal creator, Dr. Pretorius, whose demise reporters called "a punishment that

see ASHCROFT page 131

Band Teacher Gay In Retrospect

Above: A 1984 yearbook photo of Moreland.

PINE BLUFF, AR—Pine Bluff Middle School band teacher Walter Moreland was "so clearly, obviously" gay in retrospect, former student Gary Dolan, 32, realized Monday.

"Me and a bunch of people at work were reminiscing about middle-school band class," Dolan said. "I was just about to say something about how my old teacher Mr. Moreland used to be obsessed with *The Music Man* when it suddenly hit me. How in the world could I have not seen that he was gay? I mean, he was *so* gay."

Though the unmarried, childless Moreland never discussed his romantic life, Dolan is "99.999 percent sure" he was homosexual.

"I figured he acted flamboyant because he was artistic," said Dolan, who attended the middle school from 1982 to 1985. "Mr. Moreland played, like, 20 instruments. He had this little Lhasa Apso named Trixie that he'd bring to class sometimes. And he'd tell us about taking tropical vacations and driving to Little Rock to see art exhibits and musicals. Basically, he did all this stuff that no one else in town ever did."

Added Dolan: "I knew he was differ-

see TEACHER page 130

The Dixie Chicks Controversy

The members of Dixie Chicks have been the focus of boycotts ever since saying they are ashamed to hail from the same state as President Bush. What do *you* think?

"I recently hosted a Dixie Chicks CD burning, but it was because the brown-haired one got fat."

Rick Barros
Taxi Driver

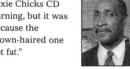

"Do you think we could get Shania Twain to speak out against the president, too?"

Marcus Adams
Attorney

"The only country artist qualified to express his political views is Johnny Cash, because that man's seen it all. And he once torched a forest while tripping on mescaline."

Alan Cramer
Systems Analyst

"So the Dixie Chicks are against the war? I suppose next, they'll be speaking out against the General Lee jumping over a crick."

Omar Williams
Cashier

"The Dixie Chicks should leave the opinion-giving to the professionals. Like that guy with the 'boot up your ass' song."

Theresa Krug
Librarian

"Lost in this whole controversy is one important point: that the Dixie Chicks' music profoundly blows."

Melissa Spence
Graduate Student

The New York City Budget Crisis

With a deficit of $3.8 billion, New York is facing its worst fiscal crisis in three decades. How is Mayor Bloomberg making up for the shortfall?

- Cutting unnecessary buildings from NYC skyline
- Raising the stabbing tax to 6 percent
- Requiring union bosses to donate 10 percent of kickbacks
- Mining Staten Island for silver
- Port Authority laying off longtime crew of street lickers
- Running two F trains per day, cutting line's service in half
- Looking into developing that prime parcel of unused grassland in central Manhattan
- Putting swear jar in Times Square
- Eliminating non-essential services, like street-sweeping and the Mets
- Fining residents every time their tiny dogs take a dump
- Forcing God to finally pay property taxes on posh Central Park West penthouse
- Fires may just have to take care of themselves

the ONION®
America's Finest News Source.™

Herman Ulysses Zweibel
Founder

T. Herman Zweibel
Publisher Emeritus
J. Phineas Zweibel
Publisher
Maxwell Prescott Zweibel
Editor-In-Chief

An Open Letter To Those Of You Who Blew Off My Arbor Day Party

By Vance Kanner

Dear "Friend,"

I'll admit, Arbor Day isn't as big a holiday as Thanksgiving or Independence Day. But to my mind, it's every bit as special. It signifies the symbiotic relationship we have with the land in a way that no other holiday does, not even Easter. It is The Little Holiday That Could and, as such, it holds a special place in my heart—a place I thought I could share with my closest friends and coworkers. Well, I guess you all showed me.

To each and every one of you, I just want to say, from the bottom of my heart: Thanks ever so much for blowing off my Arbor Day Party last Friday.

Had you ingrates deigned to show up, you would have been treated to a thoughtful, fascinating oration on the holiday. I would have told you that Arbor Day began in Nebraska in 1872 under the loving stewardship of J. Sterling Morton, a real-life Johnny Appleseed. That's right, 131 years ago, this proto-environmentalist understood the importance of planting trees to preserve the splendor of nature.

Today, we take for granted the miracle of a majestic tree growing from one little seed. For lumber and fuel, as shelter from wind and sun, as a home for the birds, squirrels, and honeybees, a tree is an agent for pure good. But you didn't feel that such ruminations on trees were worthy of your time. Instead, my speech, which was to be the high point of a day-long celebration of roots and branches, was drunkenly delivered to my dog Taco. Since none of you jerks bothered to show up, only Taco was lucky enough to hear my stirring—albeit gin-besotted—words.

I should point out that my wrath is not directed at everyone who bailed out. I know, dear Cynthia, that your mother had surgery. I respect your decision to stay by her side, even if it was for elective liposuction. Danielle, I know how difficult it can be to get a babysitter on a Friday, though I would think that the invitation I sent you two months ago would have given you ample time to track one down. And I'm certain, Kyle, that your sudden onset of "stomach cancer" was genuine, and in no way psychosomatic. But the rest of you have no excuse. None.

I don't suppose any of you are bothered by the fact that I have a garage full of red maple saplings that I planned to give away as door prizes. Sure, you could come by and pick them up, but, alas, they are all dead. Don't get me wrong: I'm not bothered by the fact that I spent $500 for unwanted baby trees. I just can't bear the lingering stench of dried sapling corpses that wafts over me every time I need to pull some steaks out of my freezer. Steaks, by the way, that I planned to grill for the party.

I remember my first Arbor Day. My dad dressed as a tree, and we all sang Arbor Day songs, then we went out into our yard and planted a spruce. Okay, so Dad was just dressed in brown cords and a green sweater, but

Had you ingrates deigned to show up, you would have been treated to a thoughtful, fascinating oration on the holiday. I would have told you that Arbor Day began in Nebraska in 1872 under the loving stewardship of J. Sterling Morton, a real-life Johnny Appleseed.

to my 4-year-old self, he looked like a mighty oak. By the way, that spruce is still standing tall and proud in the yard. I dropped by once to tell the current owners about it, but no one was home. I just wanted to spread the magic of Arbor Day with someone, just like I tried with my party. But then, as now, no one was there to hear the tale.

Hey, why am I bothering to tell you this? I'm sure you're all sitting there at home, laughing your heads off at the Arbor Day guy, the tree hugger, hugging his trees. Arbor Day is some big joke to all of you. Ha, ha, ha. But one day, sooner than you think, you'll be old. You'll look out the window, and you'll see a big space in your yard and a bigger space in your soul where there could have been a tree. Then you'll think, "My God, what sort of treeless life did I live?" Then, not long after that, you will die.

Fortunately, it's still not too late. There's always next Arbor Day. You better believe I'll be celebrating it. If you're lucky, I'll give you another chance. The party will be on the same day it always is, the last Friday in April, so mark your calendars, and I'll see you there.

Yeah, right.

HEALTH & WELLNESS

Recovering Alcoholic Clearly Kind Of Proud Of Once Being An Alcoholic

BURNSVILLE, MN—Recovering alcoholic Tim Schwann, 33, still clearly takes a certain pride in his hard-drinking days, sources reported Monday.

"Man, did I used to put it away," said Schwann, nursing a soda at a recent party. "Look at me. I weigh, like, 160. You'd never guess a guy my size could pound a case of Miller Genuine Draft, a fifth of schnapps, and a bottle of Mad Dog over the course of six hours. I was a machine."

> **"One time, Rob [Reilly] came over on a Sunday afternoon, and we plowed through two cases like it was nothing," Schwann said. "Around 6:30, we realized we were out of beer and had to make a run for more, but the stupid liquor stores were closed."**

Above: Nostalgic former drinker Tim Schwann.

Despite renouncing alcohol following a 2001 stint in rehab, Schwann seems to romanticize his years of heavy drinking, frequently waxing nostalgic about the days when his life was dedicated to the consumption of beer and liquor.

"One time, Rob [Reilly] came over on a Sunday afternoon, and we plowed through two cases like it was nothing," Schwann said. "Around 6:30, we realized we were out of beer and had to make a run for more, but the stupid liquor stores were closed. We ended up driving all the way to Wisconsin to find a store that still sold beer on Sunday. We didn't care: We were hell-bent on partying, and when we finally got back, that's exactly what we did. Big time."

Even though Schwann hasn't gone into Sullivan's Wake, the site of many of his ugliest drinking bouts, in nearly two years, he said he still holds a special place in his heart for the bar.

"Sullivan's was the best," Schwann said. "All the guys from the machine shop used to drink there after work. In the morning, you'd see guys from the third shift waiting for the bar to open at 8 a.m., and I was usually right there with them. Mike, the owner, told me he had to order an extra keg of MGD per week after I started showing up. He used to say I was putting his kids through college—which was kind of ironic, considering I got kicked out of high school for sneaking vodka into class."

One of Schwann's favorite binge-drinking stories involves stealing a keg of beer from a University of Minnesota fraternity house.

"This is about nine years ago," Schwann said. "My roommate Andy [Stavokakis] and I swiped this full keg that was being delivered to the Fiji house for a party that night. We ended up drinking the whole thing in two days. We were so drunk, we forgot to add ice, so the beer was warm most of the second day. We didn't care. We were crazy back then, and warm beer wasn't going to stop us."

According to friends, Schwann rarely tells stories of events that occurred during his past 20 months of sobriety.

"If I ask him about some rock show he went to over the weekend, he'll have nothing to say," coworker Henry Blount said. "But if the subject of beer comes up, he suddenly springs to life. It's pretty clear that he considers his drinking days the best of his life, even though the stories always end up with him in jail or vomiting in a Stop-N-Go."

Schwann finally decided to check himself into the Helping Hand Detox

see **ALCOHOLIC page 130**

NEWS IN BRIEF

Restaurant Patron Seeking Corroboration That Soda Is Not Diet

WAYLAND, NY—While eating lunch at the Back Porch Café Monday, a suspicious Diane Rollo, 43, sought confirmation from her lunch companions that the beverage in her glass was regular Coke and not diet. "Does this taste like diet to you?" asked Rollo, who ordered a Diet Coke, before handing the drink to Liz Lauderdorf. "This tastes like regular to me." After passing the drink to two other people at the table for sampling, Rollo said she was "70 percent sure" the soda was regular and sent it back.

Family Embarrassed By Way Son Died

SAN ANGELO, TX—The parents and siblings of Cris Aulter, 25, expressed deep shame and embarrassment Tuesday over his accidental death from autoerotic asphyxiation. "I cannot express how deeply mortified I am," said John Aulter, 52, the boy's father. "I mean, where in the world did Cris get the idea to suffocate himself while jerking off? How will I ever show my face around the office again?" Aulter said he plans to tell friends and coworkers that his son was hit by a car.

South Dakota Asked To Water North Dakota's Crops Over The Weekend

BISMARCK, ND—Seeking a neighborly favor Monday, North Dakota Gov. John Hoeven asked South Dakota to water his state's crops this upcoming weekend while he and the rest of North Dakota go on vacation. "If you could just turn on the state's irrigation systems around noon every day for about an hour, that'd be great," Hoeven said. "Oh, and just grab the mail and the newspapers, too, if you don't mind." Hoeven also left South Dakota with the phone numbers of neighbor states Minnesota and Montana in the event of an emergency.

Horse-Race Announcer Clearly Had Money on 'Little Dancer'

LOUISVILLE, KY—Judging by his call of Tuesday's third race at Churchill Downs, thoroughbred-race announcer Pat Ellis clearly had money on Little Dancer. "In the rear, trailing by 11 lengths, it's Little Dancer," Ellis said over Churchill Downs' public-address system. "Little Dancer not responding to the fast track like a lot of people insisted she would." Calling the race's exciting photo-finish between Indian Express and Kingston Kid, Ellis said: "And down the stretch they come! Indian Express and Kingston Kid neck and neck! Goddammit."

Chimp Study On Human-Evasion Response To Feces-Hurling Nearly Complete

MADISON, WI—Chimpanzees at the University of Wisconsin's Primate Laboratory are nearing completion of a two-year study on human-evasion response to hurled feces, sources reported Tuesday. "Our research shows that *Homo sapiens* experience extreme agitation and an urge to flee when pelted with baseball-sized lumps of primate scat," said Dr. Jingles, speaking from his research cage. "In 10 out of 10 cases, our test subjects retreated to the far corner of the room and screamed, 'Stop! Stop! AIIIGH!'" Dr. Jingles first made his mark in science in 1993, when he earned a Nobel Prize for conclusively proving the deliciousness of bananas. Ø

TEACHER from page 127

ent, but as a 12-year-old, my understanding of gay culture was limited to *Three's Company*. I had no idea they actually walked among us in Pine Bluff."

Ever since coming to the realization, Dolan has remembered more details about Moreland that seem to affirm his gayness. Among them are the sack lunches of yogurt and carrots he ate on field trips, his excessive attention to detail when ordering new band uniforms, and his elaborate decorations for the holiday concerts.

"If we were talking during class, he would yell 'People!' and bang his conducting wand," Dolan said. "If he got really mad, he'd stomp into his office and slam the door, leaving us all sitting there, holding our instruments. Basically, he'd throw a hissy fit."

Dolan said he also remembers the effeminate way Moreland kept his classes under control.

"Mr. Moreland was a fun teacher, but he could be moody," Dolan said. "If we were talking during class, he would yell 'People!' and bang his conducting wand. If he got really mad, he'd stomp into his office and slam the door, leaving us all sitting there, holding our instruments. Basically, he'd throw a hissy fit."

"Thinking back, he even looked gay," Dolan continued. "His hair was always perfect and he had a well-trimmed little mustache. He dressed better than any of the other teachers, in these crisp button-down shirts and nice shoes and..."

"Oh my God," said Dolan, interrupting himself. "I just remembered. On concert days, he wore an ascot. An ascot. How clueless was I?"

On a spring day in 1984, Dolan got a glimpse of his teacher's secret life when he was given a ride home by Moreland in his immaculate teal-blue Plymouth Reliant. Dolan recalled noticing the Broadway cast recording of *Godspell* in the car's cassette deck and two scented candles laying on the Navajo-blanket-covered back seat.

Another time, while at the grocery store with his mother, Dolan spotted Moreland with another man.

"It never occurred to me that the guy might be Moreland's lover, even though they were standing there picking out vegetables together," Dolan said. "I remember thinking, 'That guy acts like Mr. Moreland. He must be a band teacher from another town.'"

Though Dolan recalled hearing jokes about Moreland's homosexuality back then, he said they were indistinguishable from the deluge of similar accusations levied at every male in school.

On a spring day in 1984, Dolan got a glimpse of his teacher's secret life when he was given a ride home by Moreland in his immaculate teal-blue Plymouth Reliant. Dolan recalled noticing the Broadway cast recording of *Godspell* in the car's cassette deck.

"Back when we were kids, we called everybody—and everything—'gay,'" Dolan said. "It didn't occur to me that Mr. Moreland actually *was* gay."

While the children in Moreland's class were oblivious to his sexuality, Dolan said his fellow teachers must have known the truth.

"I just hope the other teachers weren't dicks to him about it," Dolan said. "I don't think he hung out with any of his colleagues much, except for Mrs. Pickens, the art teacher, and occasionally Ms. Sarnofski, the gym teacher. Holy shit—*Ms. Sarnofski*." Ø

ALCOHOLIC from page 129

Center in June 2001 after being fired from his machinist job and going on "a bender to end all benders." Over the course of three days, Schwann demolished his 1984 Chevette, accidentally set fire to his apartment, and passed out on the porch of an old girlfriend's house.

"Dude, you should have seen me, I was so fucked up," Schwann said. "I knew I needed help, but you can't keep a party guy like me down, so right after waking up on the porch, I went off on another pub crawl. I wound up curled up on Melissa's front porch again. After she got done yelling at me for being an asshole, she drove me to the rehab center. She never did forgive me for taking a shit on her lawn."

Since going sober, Schwann has dramatically turned his life around, earning his GED and enrolling in night classes at a St. Paul community college. He has also renewed his interest in woodworking, a hobby he abandoned after smashing all his projects in a 1998 whiskey-induced rage.

"I've been sober for almost two years now, and I finally feel like I'm in control of my life," Schwann said. "Sure, drinking Shirley Temples and going to AA meetings isn't as exciting as waking up in a ditch with a splitting headache and no clue how you got there. But even though I miss all those fun times, I don't miss the actual drinking that much. Besides, I know in my heart that if I wanted to, I could still out-drink anyone out there." Ø

the ONION presents:

Cooking Tips

Becoming a great cook is easier than you might think.
Here are some tips to help you become a whiz in the kitchen:

- To ensure that you always use the freshest ingredients, keep a live pig on hand.
- The general rule of thumb for vinegar: The browner, the better. If all you have is buck-a-gallon white vinegar, toss in some soy sauce or a brown Magic Marker.
- There is an elusive-yet-distinct quality that separates the great cooks from the merely average ones. That quality is "Wessonality."
- You'd be amazed by the number of great recipes that can be found on the backs of cans, bottles, and boxes. Just make sure the can, bottle, or box doesn't contain Pennzoil, hydrogen peroxide, or Sakrete™ instant concrete.
- Do not thaw frozen fish in milk or do anything else Julia Child says. She high.
- If you are a man, you deserve to be gushed over just for reading these cooking tips. That's so great!
- Cooking can be very dangerous, due to the use of fire, knives, and electrical appliances. Only cook under the careful supervision of your Living Skills coach.
- Stone soup gets its fullest, heartiest flavor from sandstone or dark shale. Igneous and metamorphic stones tend to overwhelm the flavor of the vegetables.
- Remember this oft-overlooked cooking secret: The toaster lever can be pushed down again if your bread is not sufficiently brown.
- McDonald's is the world's most popular restaurant chain, so its food must be the best. Study McDonald's food as a template for your own.
- Remember: With passion and the right attitude, anyone can cook. Wait, that's "play punk rock." Never mind.

SYRIA from page 127

"It's practically an open secret these days," Tenet said. "Syrian television brazenly shows Arabs in military uniforms carrying guns, or delivering political speeches to other members

Arabs have historically held many influential posts in the Syrian government, and the CIA claims to have data indicating that wealthy Arab businessmen control the greater part of Syria's economy.

of the group. Walk into any house of worship in the country, and you'll see people reading the Koran and bowing their heads in prayer toward Mecca. It's almost like they're daring the United States to get involved."

"Disturbingly, more than 90 percent of these Arabs have been linked to the practice of 'Islam'—a defiantly non-Western system of faith whose core principles are embraced by none other than Osama bin Laden and Saddam Hussein," Tenet added. "If this is true, and we do consider this information to be correct in all particulars, then this is troubling at best."

President Bush, Tenet said, has been aware of Syria's ties to known Arab political and religious figures since the earliest planning stages of Operation Iraqi Freedom. Tenet assured reporters that all possible diplomatic avenues of resolving the situation were being aggressively pursued.

Above: In a chilling scene, thousands of Arabs bow toward Mecca in praise of Allah.

"We have informed [Syrian President] Bashar al-Assad of the presence of Arabs in his country and have offered any aid necessary to bring this situation under control," Tenet said. "I am confident that a resolution to this crisis can be achieved without resorting to military action."

This is not the first time Syria has been linked to Arabs. Israel found the Golan Heights heavily populated by Arabs when it annexed the region from Syria during 1967's Arab-Israeli War. Arabs have historically held many influential posts in the Syrian government, and the CIA claims to have data indicating that wealthy Arab businessmen control the greater part of Syria's economy.

The CIA report prompted concern from many Americans.

"I'm not surprised," said Wayne Early, an Atlanta-area mortgage broker. "I suspect they're all over that part of the world. First, the government linked them to Sept. 11, then Afghanistan, and then Iraq. It makes you wonder who's next."

"The more I learn about Arabs, the less I like them," said Carol Schecter of Norfolk, VA. "Beirut, Teheran, Baghdad… everyplace there's trouble, they're there, and now we've found them in Syria. I just hope they don't hurt the regular Syrians."

Tenet assured citizens that he is committed to resolving the crisis.

"We don't want to cause any undue panic, but now that the Arabs are there, we're going to have to deal with them," Tenet said. "Unfortunately, they're not just going to go away by themselves." Ø

ASHCROFT from page 127

befell a mortal man who dared to emulate God."

Police investigators are working

Ashcroft's quest to find fulfillment with a bride of his own kind first came to public attention in November 2002, when the Justice Department released a Yellow Alert announcement reading, "Warning! The Attorney General demands a mate!"

around the clock to determine whether Ashcroft and his unholy Bride are still alive.

"They may have burned up in the fire, but you have to remember that we're dealing with a creature so horrible that only a half-crazed mind could have devised it," D.C. chief of police Charles H. Ramsey said. "My fear is that she and Ashcroft survived the flames and will return anew to stalk the land in darkness."

Ashcroft's quest to find fulfillment with a bride of his own kind first came to public attention in November 2002, when the Justice Department released a Yellow Alert announcement reading, "Warning! The Attorney General demands a mate!"

Most scientists were skeptical, explaining that the creation of such a being—a terrible nightmare from beyond the very pits of Hell itself—was scientifically impossible. Yet over the next two months, as Ashcroft found himself with increasing power in a steadily rightward-shifting political landscape, he used his growing clout to secure funding for the creation of a mate to call his own.

"Alone… bad," Ashcroft told reporters on Jan. 23. "Friend… good."

After a long search, on Feb. 9, Ashcroft announced that he had procured the services of Dr. Pretorius using $200 million in funding made available through the Homeland Security Act. For the next 10 weeks, Pretorius toiled in secrecy, cracking

Said one villager, who insisted on picking through the smoking press-conference wreckage in search of Ashcroft's body: "When I see his blackened bones, then I can sleep at night."

the secret of life itself by reanimating dead tissue created from cadavers out of opened graves. Enlisting the help of other scientists, Pretorius obsessively pursued the goal of creating a female companion to love the Attorney General as no mortal ever could.

Since becoming Attorney General in January 2001, Ashcroft has placed a number of limits on civil liberties, restrictions which have earned him the enmity of the ACLU and similar organizations. Recently, however, Ashcroft has also begun to draw criticism from another sector: angry peasant villagers. Chasing him with pitchforks, torches, and dogs through the foggy streets of the nation's capital, irate mobs have emerged in recent weeks as a substantial obstacle to Ashcroft's plans.

"Arrrrrrrgh!" said Ashcroft as he fled one recent mob, before disappearing into the night.

Since the Bride incident, peasant-villager opposition to Ashcroft has only intensified. Said one villager, who insisted on picking through the smoking press-conference wreckage in search of Ashcroft's body: "When I see his blackened bones, then I can sleep at night."

"Ashcroft? I'd hate to find him under me bed at night," another villager remarked. "He's a nightmare in the daylight, he is." Ø

COMMUNITY VOICES

I've Got To Stop Taking Lives So Seriously

By James Lee Grady

I like to think of myself as a pretty happy person, but sometimes I'm a little too hard on myself. It's only natural to want to do the best job you can, but often, I'll get so caught up in the moment that I forget that slaughtering innocent people is supposed to be *fun*. I really need to stop taking lives so seriously.

When I turned 40, I looked in the mirror and realized that I was probably never going to be the most notorious serial killer who ever lived. That thought really depressed me. But then, one day, I said to myself, if I can leave this world remembered by my victims' loved ones, then I've made a true difference. As much as I know that's true, though, I still lose sight of it from time to time.

Whatever happened to those sunny teenage years, when I could go down to the railroad tracks, sever a dog's vocal cords, and happily hum "The Thieving Magpie" as I slowly skinned him alive? I used to have such a blast doing stuff like that. Every kill was a new adventure. Now, it's more of a grind.

Whatever happened to those sunny teenage years, when I could go down to the railroad tracks, sever a dog's vocal cords, and happily hum "The Thieving Magpie" as I slowly skinned him alive? I used to have such a blast doing stuff like that.

I keep asking myself, if it's not fun, why bother? Why go through the trouble of sneaking into an innocent person's house, smothering him with a chloroform-soaked sofa cushion, and cooking and eating a stew of his intestines if I'm not going to enjoy it? After all, lives are short.

I'm always beating myself up over, "Oh, if only I'd killed one more hitchhiker last month, I could've bought myself that big freezer that holds four adults." Rather than dwell on the missed opportunities, I need to be proud of the people I *did* kill.

Recently, I've been trying to think more creatively to find new ways to bring back the joy. Here's one idea:

Why go through the trouble of sneaking into an innocent person's house, smothering him with a chloroform-soaked sofa cushion, and cooking and eating a stew of his intestines if I'm not going to enjoy it?

After a few hours of torturing a victim, I'd leave the dungeon for a while and "forget" to tighten one of his manacles so he could manage to free himself. Then, just when he thinks he's about to escape to sweet, sweet freedom, he flings open the cellar door to find me standing there wagging my finger, saying, "Tut, tut, tut..." Then I drag him back to the cellar and brutally torture him as punishment for trying to escape. Maybe some fun little project like that is all I need.

I'd also love to pursue my "death match arena" project, in which I cage several receptionists for a week or so with nothing to eat but my feces, and then dose them all with cocaine and make them fight each other for more coke. I'd need at least 100 square feet for that, but I could make room if I consolidate my Pain Lab into just the electrified clamps and soldering irons. And I could make a neat little scoreboard at Kinko's. That'd be a hoot.

You know those silent movies where they tie the girl to the log and send it toward the huge sawblade? Maybe I could do a version of that where the blade moves really, really slow, like an inch an hour. Or I could always go back to kidnapping families and forcing them to act out Jack Chick comics. That was always a blast.

So I guess the lesson here is, it's never too late to rediscover the fun. Yes, there's hope for me yet. I just have to remember to stop and smell the roses before stuffing them into victims' empty eye sockets. ⌀

HOROSCOPES

Your Horoscope

By Lloyd Schumner Sr.
Retired Machinist and
A.A.P.B.-Certified Astrologer

Aries: (March 21–April 19)
Everyone needs to believe in something. You, for instance, believe in a omnipotent man who lives in the sky, and that you'll have another beer.

Taurus: (April 20–May 20)
It turns out only one in every 200 Americans hates your guts. As you'll soon see, though, that's still quite a mob.

Gemini: (May 21–June 21)
You'll never smile again after the tragic loss of your lower jaw and lips.

Cancer: (June 22–July 22)
Mars' position in your sign indicates that only hard work and dedication can help you reach your goals. But don't worry: Mars will move by next week.

Leo: (July 23–Aug. 22)
You've never been a big fan of being hosed down, but next week's non-stop barrage of hosings will give you a chance to change your mind.

Virgo: (Aug. 23–Sept. 22)
You will finally develop soft, shiny, touchable hair, just moments before getting hit by a bus—which at first might seem unrelated.

Libra: (Sept. 23–Oct. 23)
Take a little time this week to think of those closest to you and the possibility that they're the ones behind the assassination attempts.

Scorpio: (Oct. 24–Nov. 21)
Sometimes, you just want to go someplace where nobody knows who you are. Luckily, this is easily accomplished by leaving your house.

Sagittarius: (Nov. 22–Dec. 21)
The juxtaposition of sexual imagery and Catholic iconography has been done to death, but, hey, it's your personals ad.

Capricorn: (Dec. 22–Jan. 19)
You'll make it obvious whether you value quantity or quality when you live to the age of 113.

Aquarius: (Jan. 20–Feb. 18)
You will soon seek in death the peace and tranquility that has eluded you in life. Unfortunately, nobody told you about Six Flags Over Heaven.

Pisces: (Feb. 19–March 20)
Long-established patterns of behavior will not magically change for you this week.

MENNONITE from page 128

amounts of blood. Passersby were amazed by the unusually large amounts of blood. Passersby were amazed by the unusually large amounts of blood. Passersby were amazed by the unusually large amounts of blood. Passersby were amazed by the unusually large amounts of blood. Passersby were amazed by the unusually large amounts of blood. Passersby were amazed by the unusually large amounts of blood. Passersby were amazed by the unusually large amounts of blood. Passersby were amazed by the unusually large amounts of blood. Passersby were amazed by the unusually large amounts of blood. Passersby were amazed by the unusually large amounts of blood. Passersby were amazed by the unusually large amounts of blood. Passersby were amazed by the unusually large amounts of blood. Passersby were amazed by the unusually large amounts of blood. Passersby were amazed by the unusually large amounts of blood. Passersby were amazed by the unusually large amounts of blood. Passersby were amazed by the unusually large amounts of blood. Passersby were amazed by the unusually large amounts of blood. Passersby were amazed by the unusually large amounts of blood. Passersby were amazed by the unusually large

Say, haven't I seen you undress by peeking through your bedroom window before?

amounts of blood. Passersby were amazed by the unusually large amounts of blood. Passersby were amazed by the unusually large amounts of blood. Passersby were amazed by the unusually large amounts of blood. Passersby were amazed by the unusually large amounts of blood. Passersby were amazed by the unusually large

see MENNONITE page 138

NEWS

Male Bonding Leads To Bail Bonding

see CRIMEBEAT page 7B

Kiddie Pool Falls Into Disrepair

see LOCAL page 11C

Friend's Wedding Ups The Ante

see VOWS page 5E

Playboy Playmate Weighing Her Option

see LOCAL page 9B

STATshot

A look at the numbers that shape your world.

Top-Selling Health Cereals

1. Frosted Flax
2. Count Carobula
3. High-Fiber Shitabrix
4. Forest Floories
5. Dried Froot Loops
6. Kale-O's
7. Breakfast Bales

the ONION®

VOLUME 39 ISSUE 17 AMERICA'S FINEST NEWS SOURCE™ 8–14 MAY 2003

Above: Bush at work in the Oval Office, with a poster of his favorite movie nearby.

Bush Cites *The Last Starfighter* As Inspiration For Entering Politics

WASHINGTON, DC—During a speech Monday, President Bush disclosed for the first time the pivotal role the 1984 science-fiction adventure film *The Last Starfighter* played in his decision to enter politics.

"My whole life, I'd grown up around politics, but it wasn't until that fateful day in 1984, at a matinee screening of *The Last Starfighter* at the old Orpheum Theater in Midland, TX, that I finally realized that my destiny lay in public service," said Bush, speaking at a Republican National Committee fundraiser at the Washington Hilton. "The movie showed me that no matter who you are and where you come from, you can make a big difference."

The comments surprised the estimated 600 RNC members in attendance, as well as Bush's aides, who expected the president to discuss his proposed tax cut and plan for governing post-war Iraq. Not even his closest advisors knew of Bush's passion for the Reagan-era space epic.

Straying from his scripted remarks, Bush described at length his "lost" years of the early 1980s in Midland.

"I was holding down two jobs, one at an oil well, the other for a third-rate

see BUSH page 136

Dozens Dead In Chicago-Area Meatwave

CHICAGO—A deadly meatwave swept through the Chicago area over the weekend, leaving an estimated 40 residents dead of steaks, chops, ribs, bacon, and various other forms of meat exhaustion.

"This is easily the worst meatwave I've seen around these parts since the summer of '79," said John Gruznek, a Chicago gravicologist. "Most of the bodies I've examined were bloated beyond recognition."

"The excessively high level of pork loins, sirloin tips, bratwurst, and other meats was indisputably the number-one factor in these deaths," said Chicago mayor Richard Daley, speaking from his temporary command center at Ruth's Chris Steak House on North Dearborn Street. "Most of these people consumed a considerable fraction of their weight in animal flesh before ultimately succumbing to meatstroke."

"This meatwave," Daley continued, "is a clear hazard to anyone capable of chewing and swallowing Chicago's vast array of delicious, succulent meats."

Max Peltz, director of Emergency Medical Services And Barbecue for Cook County, said that non-stop ingestion of beef, pork, chicken, lamb, and veal had caused the vic-

see MEATWAVE page 137

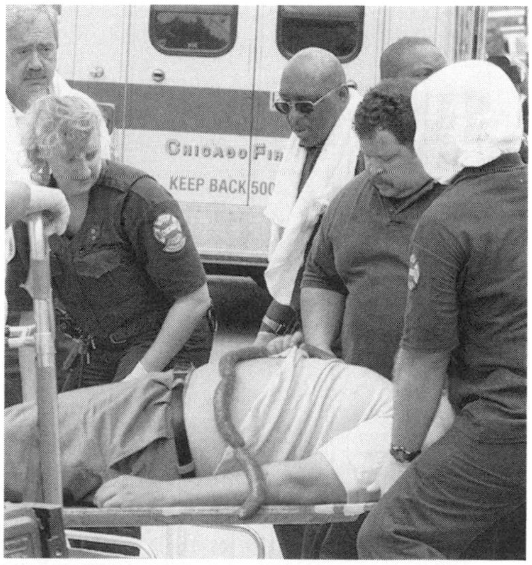

Above: Paramedics administer first aid to a man who collapsed from smoked-sausage inhalation.

Above: Yearbook staffers Keelan, Garnock, and Shah.

Yearbook-Staff Meeting Devolves Into Discussion Of Popular Kids

CHATFIELD, MN—Productivity declined sharply at Tuesday's Chatfield High School yearbook meeting, when the proceedings devolved into an animated discussion of the school's popular kids.

"Gee, what a surprise: another picture of Jessica [Morgan] in her brand-new Jetta," said *Chatfield Megaphone* photo editor Carol Keelan, laying out a Seniors collage page. "Well, I guess we have to put her in again, since she was Prom Queen. Look what hot shit she thinks she is in that picture... the operative word being 'thinks.'"

The remark prompted *Megaphone* assistant copy editor Paul Garnock to recount a shoulder-punching incident involving Rich Tyler, Morgan's

see YEARBOOK page 136

Continuing Clashes In Iraq

In spite of the war's conclusion, U.S. troops continue to engage in deadly skirmishes with Iraqi protesters, killing 16 in one such clash last week. What do *you* think?

"If they don't want to get shot, what are they doing in Iraq?"

Donald Meijer
Architect

"The Iraqis who died are probably the ones who swallowed the weapons of mass destruction when the U.S. arrived."

Mo Browning
Delivery Driver

"I think it's really sad that those Iraqis broke up the Marines' candlelight peace vigil with violence."

Jill Krenmore
Homemaker

"Did we tell them the war was over in English? Maybe they just didn't understand."

Audra Thaler
Waitress

"Look, nobody said these people would welcome us with open arms. Except Bush, Cheney, Rumsfeld, Ashcroft, Fox News..."

Ron Mobley
Systems Analyst

"I don't understand why these wackos won't simply face facts and accept that they're under the control of a foreign superpower's occupational force."

Scott Watkins
Machinist

The Godfather Of Soul Turns 70

Music legend James Brown recently turned 70. How did he celebrate the milestone?

- Invited Pee Wee Ellis and John "Jabo" Starks to sit in on the gas grill
- Fined guests $25 each for missing beat while singing "Happy Birthday"
- Was presented with giant cake reading "Happy Birthday, James—Soul Brother Number One, The Godfather Of Soul, The Hardest-Working Man In Show Business, Mr. Dynamite"
- Received another goddamn silk cape from Bobby Byrd
- Performed at a gospel church at 9 a.m., an R&B oldies festival at noon, and an Indian casino at 7 p.m.
- Complained about his not-so-good foot
- Shouted "Septuagenarian!" 16 times in a row
- Celebrated 20th birthday of current hair
- Carefully documented all birthday gifts for the IRS
- Smoked PCP, beat his wife, and led police on multi-state car chase, all while hitting it on the ones

the ONION®
America's Finest News Source.™

Herman Ulysses Zweibel
Founder

T. Herman Zweibel
Publisher Emeritus
J. Phineas Zweibel
Publisher
Maxwell Prescott Zweibel
Editor-In-Chief

Why Am I Always The One To Get Chlamydia?

By Sharon Glauber

I don't get it. I'm a good person who lives an honest life and is nice to people, yet for some reason, I seem to have the worst luck: My toast always falls jam-side down, the one day it rains is always the day I leave my windows open, and the one time I have unprotected sex in a public-beach changing room, *I* end up with chlamydia! What gives?

Yes, every single year, I go for my annual gyno visit and, without fail, I find out I've got chlamydia again. Why am I always the one to get chlamydia? It's just not fair!

It's not like I'm any more sexually active than the average girl. My best friend Amy has sex with her boyfriend almost every single night, and she's never had it. Me, I'll be lucky if I have 20 one-night stands in an entire year! So if she's having sex at least 10 times as often as me, why hasn't she ever had it? Did I do something wrong in a past life? I don't think I've done anything recently to deserve being cursed with chronic chlamydia. I guess I'm just a chlamydia magnet or something.

I know what you're probably thinking: Sharon's so dumb, she never got her first infection cleared up. Well, that's just not true. Sure, I was totally

Sometimes, I think it's my family's fault. The Glauber clan is cursed.

freaked when I first got it back in 1995. (I thought I was going to go blind or crazy or something.) But when my doctor told me that, if caught early, chlamydia is easily cured with just a day's worth of antibiotics, I was totally relieved. Thank goodness my first experience wasn't like the time I caught that rare strain of Southeast Asian chlamydia. Lying in that hospital bed with my urethra on fire made me appreciate how easy it was to get rid of the normal chlamydia I usually get.

I'm not irresponsible, either. I take care of myself, because I totally wouldn't want to spread it to other people. Especially cute guys. There's nothing more embarrassing than getting a call from some hottie you picked up at the bar last month accusing you of giving him chlamydia. Once that happens to you half a dozen times, you start to get real careful and make sure you go to the doctor as soon as you see symptoms.

And it's not like I don't have standards. I tend to go for preppy, Abercrombie & Fitch-type guys, the kind who'd be very unlikely to have an STD. Plus, I almost always have them

There's nothing more embarrassing than getting a call from some hottie you picked up at the bar last month accusing you of giving him chlamydia. Once that happens to you half a dozen times, you start to get real careful.

use a condom if they don't swear up and down that they're clean. So what's the deal?

We've all been there. I mean, I'm hardly the only one out there having oral, vaginal, and anal sexual contact. I'm just the one who winds up with a pus-like discharge shooting out of my hoo-hoo.

Sometimes, I think it's my family's fault. The Glauber clan is cursed. My dad died in a drunk-driving accident when I was 5, and my mom is just plain crazy. She actually got pregnant when she was 40 after dating a guy she worked with for a week. She even kept the baby. That's why I'm on the pill. I've been more or less lucky on that front (don't ask), yet I've got to admit that this chlamydia thing gets me down. Maybe if I came from a different family, I might have better luck.

Oh, listen to me pissing and moaning: "My family's crazy"... "I wish I was luckier"... "I'm always contracting chlamydia." Everybody's got problems. It's not like I'm starving on the street without a penny to my name. I've got good friends, a good job, and a halfway-decent sex life. Maybe instead of whining about how much I seem to get chlamydia, I should be thankful for the times I don't have it.

I must say, I would probably have a more positive attitude about the whole chlamydia thing if I didn't have it right now. But, as they say, the grass is always greener on the STD-free side of the fence, right? Ø

Local Man Ruins Date By Just Being Himself

LA JOLLA, CA—Wrongly advised by friends and family to "just be yourself," local tax attorney Marc Scanlon, 34, ruined a first date with Rachel Loftus by doing just that, sources close to the never-to-be couple reported Monday.

"Marc was really nervous that Rachel wouldn't like him, and he kept obsessing over his appearance, his hair, what he should wear, and how he should act on the date," said Glenn Carlson, 40, a coworker of Scanlon's at the law firm of Jenkins & Straud. "I told him not to worry, that he should just be his true self and everything would be okay. Turns out, that was bad advice. On a first date, Marc's true self is pretty much exactly what most normal women don't want."

Divorced since 2001, Scanlon met the 29-year-old Loftus through mutual acquaintance Barbara O'Neill. Thinking the two might make a good match—despite not knowing much about Scanlon personally—O'Neill set the pair up on a blind date.

The date was, according to Loftus, one of her worst ever. Sources say the blame lay in Scanlon's ill-advised decision to put pretense aside, revealing his true identity and destroying any chance he might have had with Loftus.

"I'm glad he felt comfortable being himself," said brother Chris Scanlon, 39. "But when you're in full-blown mid-30s-crisis mode with misogynist tendencies and a desperate, neurotic need for approval, maybe 'the real you' is not the best thing to put forward."

According to reports, Scanlon's profound insecurity led him to monopolize the first 45 minutes of conversation, talking about nothing but himself. Worse, his inability to get over his divorce prompted him to meticulously detail every phase of his failed marriage.

"When you're in full-blown mid-30s-crisis mode with misogynist tendencies and a desperate, neurotic need for approval, maybe 'the real you' is not the best thing to put forward."

"It's totally understandable that he's still feeling hurt and emotionally shaky from the breakup," Loftus said. "But that's the sort of thing you should keep buried deep down inside when you're first letting someone get to know you."

"Sure, in theory, a guy should be able to relax and be himself," Loftus continued. "But when you have such issues about aging that you show up to a date wearing a Billy Joel '*River Of Dreams* World Tour' concert T-shirt under your sportjacket, you're putting up a neon sign on your forehead that says, 'Do Not Fuck Me, Ever.' I mean, this guy's a tax lawyer in his 30s. Did he think he was coming across as rockin' or something? Please."

Loftus added that, while there is nothing inherently wrong with a date mentioning that he attended Yale University, bringing it up every 10 minutes is probably not a good idea.

"Yale this, Yale that," Loftus said. "Any way he could work it into the conversation, he would. It was so obvious that he was clinging to his Ivy League pedigree out of insecurity, as a way of making himself look like an intelligent man of substance. It really just made him look like a dick."

Scanlon's inability to self-monitor further turned off Loftus when he disclosed "way, way, way too much" about his opinions on sex and relationships.

"He must have thought the honest approach would make him look like an open, non-uptight kind of guy,'"

see DATE page 137

Above: Marc Scanlon, who made the error of being relaxed and authentic on the date.

NEWS IN BRIEF

8-Year-Old Forced To Eat Organic Macaroni And Cheese

SAUSALITO, CA—In spite of his distaste for Annie's Homegrown Mac & Cheese, area 8-year-old Josh Remmert was forced by his mother to eat an entire plate of the organic pasta for lunch Tuesday. "I like Kraft Mac & Cheese a lot better, but Mom says it's all processed and got artificial stuff in it," Remmert said. "At least it's the right color. The cheese in this stuff isn't even orange." To help wash down the all-natural pasta, Remmert was given a choice between carrot juice and vanilla-flavored Rice Dream.

Bush To Lovely Chilean Ambassador: 'I Must Paint You'

WASHINGTON, DC—After spotting Chilean Ambassador to the U.S. Natalia Verdugo at a D.C.-area café Tuesday, a smitten President Bush promptly invited the bewitching diplomat to his artist's garret in the East Wing of the White House. "I must paint you," Bush reportedly told Verdugo. "I simply must commit your beauty to the canvas immediately. Please, come away with me to my studio, where the early-evening light from my western window shall caress your undraped form." Though she eventually agreed to pose for the president, Verdugo drew the line at "an afternoon of fiery passion" among his charcoal sketches.

Compliment Goes Horribly Awry

KNOXVILLE, TN—A compliment went horribly awry Monday, when Greg Upchurch, 26, praised girlfriend Sheri Werning, 25, for her "juicy ass." "I didn't mean fat," said Upchurch, explaining himself to the offended Werning. "By 'juicy,' I meant curvy, you know? Like, that you're really healthy and athletic, and not some sickly little stick figure." Having dug himself into a hole, Upchurch pondered comparing Werning's posterior to Jennifer Lopez's, but ultimately decided against it.

Stripper Failing School She's Working Self Through

LAS VEGAS—Exotic dancer Tricia "Mercedes" Hrlevich, 22, who is stripping to put herself through school, is failing her Red Rock Community College business classes, sources said Tuesday. "I definitely want to do something with, like, business," said Hrlevich, who has received Fs on three straight economics exams. "Dancing at Cheetah's [Gentlemen's Cabaret] is just a way of getting closer toward that goal." Hrlevich then accompanied a balding 54-year-old to the Champagne Room, where she earned $60 toward a Psych 101 textbook she will never read.

Nation's Dogs Dangerously Underpetted, Say Dogs

NEW YORK—At a press conference Monday, representatives of the Association of American Dogs announced that the nation's canines are dangerously underpetted. "Every night, thousands of U.S. dogs go to bed without so much as a scritch behind the ears," AAD president Banjo said. "If this sort of neglect from our masters continues, it could lead to widespread jumping on the furniture." Upon his owner's arrival in the press-conference room, Banjo abruptly ended his speech, frantically barking, leaping, and rolling over on his back in an effort to communicate his need for a vigorous belly rub. ⌀

BUSH from page 133

professional baseball team," Bush said. "I had gotten a local girl pregnant, and I spent my weekends watching golf on TV and drinking with my buddies. My dad was vice-president then, and occasionally he'd offer me some vice-presidential stuff to do, you know, just to get a taste for politics. But I was too distracted by other things. Basically, I was your typical unfocused kid."

One idle Saturday, Bush said he purchased a ticket to a showing of *The Last Starfighter*. The seemingly inconsequential act would have profound repercussions on the young man—and, ultimately, on the entire nation.

"Minutes into the film, I found myself relating deeply to Alex, the lead character played by Lance Guest," Bush said.

"Just minutes into the film, I found myself relating deeply to Alex, the lead character played by Lance Guest," Bush said. "He lived in a trailer park and had little opportunity to advance himself. His only escape was playing video games."

After achieving a record score on a video game called "Starfighter," Alex is contacted by a mysterious man who invented the game. The man, named Centauri, proves to be a space alien whose home planet, Rylos, is under impending attack by a sinister invasion force known as the Ko-Dan Armada. Centauri had invented the game as a means to recruit standout video gamers who could pilot the real-life versions of the Gunstar spaceships featured in the game.

Bush was enthralled.

"Here's this kid, with nothing going on in his life, and it turns out that his only talent, one that seemed so trivial and ridiculous, could alter the fate of the galaxy forever," Bush said. "That really inspired me."

Bush said he could also identify with Alex's initial reluctance to becoming a Starfighter.

"At first, Alex didn't want to do it," Bush said. "He figured, why should he fight for the Star League and risk his life battling an enemy he knew nothing about? But then, when the other Starfighters were killed in an attack on their base and [evil emperor] Zur sent his vicious Zan-Do-Zan assassins to Earth to kill him, Alex began to realize that the only thing standing between the Ko-Dan and universal conquest was himself."

Continued Bush: "I realized that if Alex turned down the chance to be a Starfighter, he would have been assassinated, and Earth would have been destroyed. It made me think long and hard about my own place in the world: Was I making the right decisions? Was I helping people as much as I could? Was I missing out on a chance to save mankind?"

Bush added that he loved the film's breakthrough computer-generated special effects, as well as the fact that Alex had a robot double—something Bush had dreamed of having in his youth.

Transfixed by the film, Bush would go on to see it seven times that summer, memorizing its dialogue and buying a VHS copy on the day of its release. But *The Last Starfighter*'s most profound impact on Bush was the way it motivated him to leave the private sector and enter politics.

"It made me realize that politics truly was in my blood," Bush said. "Who cares if I wasn't a good businessman or a sharp scholar? Alex was even worse off than me, and look what he achieved."

Bush admitted that, while running for Texas governor in 1994, he kept his Last Starfighter videocassette cued up in his campaign bus' VCR, ready for rewinding or fast-forwarding to his favorite scenes on a moment's notice.

"When my spirits were sagging, I'd watch the scene where Alex tells Centauri that he's just 'a kid from a trailer park,'" Bush said. "Centauri replies, 'If that's what you think, then that's all you'll ever be.' It helped me remember that the only boundaries that exist are those you create in your mind."

Continued Bush: "Or, as Alex says to [his girlfriend] Maggie, 'Don't you see this is it? This is our big chance. It's like, whatever this is, when it comes, you've got to grab on with both hands and hold tight.'"

The fundraiser audience reacted to Bush's speech with near-silence.

"I sort of remember the movie when it first came out, but I never saw it," RNC chairman Marc Racicot said. "As a Bush supporter and GOP policy-maker, maybe I should rent it sometime."

"When my spirits were sagging, I'd watch the scene where Alex tells Centauri that he's just 'a kid from a trailer park,'" Bush said.

Former White House communications director Karen Hughes, a close advisor to Bush in the early days of his presidency, said she had failed to realize the full significance of *The Last Starfighter* during her time in the administration.

"When I first started working for the president, he would sometimes mention the movie. Once or twice, he even tried to get me to read his *Last Starfighter* fan fiction," Hughes said. "But I always assumed that his decision to enter politics was shaped by his desire to continue his family's long history of public service. *The Last Starfighter*. Wow."

Added Hughes: "That probably explains why [*Last Starfighter* co-star] Catherine Mary Stewart is our ambassador to Zambia." ⌀

YEARBOOK from page 133

boyfriend and star quarterback for the school football team.

"As much as I dislike Jessica—and that's quite a lot—I actually think I dislike Rich even more," said Garnock, rolling up his sleeve to display a large purple bruise. "At lunch last Friday, I was minding my own business when he came up and started whaling on my shoulder because, apparently, he thinks it's a riot. I suppose that's the sort of thing that has to pass for humor when you don't have a brain."

"We should make up a page for him called 'Painting The Future Black & Blue,'" Garnock added, alluding to this year's yearbook theme, "Painting The Future." "Or maybe 'Painting Myself Into A Corner Because I Am Stupid And Will Do Nothing With My Life.'"

Garnock's anti-Tyler remarks served as a segue into a discussion of whether there were any school sports teams that "aren't made up of jerks."

"The cross-country team is pretty cool, but that's about it," yearbook editor-in-chief Anita Shah said. "The worst, I would have to say, is the wrestling team, followed by hockey, with football a close third."

In spite of their distaste for the popular kids, or "Chatfield's ruling elite," the yearbook staffers acknowledged that there were exceptions.

"You know who's actually kind of okay?" events-section editor Janine Boyd said. "Adam Welter. Even though he's going out with Amanda Berg and is all Mr. Pretty Boy, he isn't a total asshole like the rest of them. He even said he liked the class presentation I gave on censorship in rhetoric."

"The cross-country team is pretty cool, but that's about it," Shah said.

Garnock strenuously disagreed with Boyd's assessment of Welter, claiming that Welter once shoved him into an open locker, bloodying his nose and scratching his glasses. Garnock also accused Boyd of having "the hots" for Welter. The charge was denied.

Tuesday's meeting, which disbanded when Garnock's mother arrived to pick him up for piano lessons, was the sixth in a row to devolve into a discussion of the popular students. While little progress was made in assembling the yearbook, a consensus was reached that cheerleading captain Amy Axelrod is a total stuck-up bulimic slut. ⌀

Above: A yearbook photo of "obnoxious, stuck-up" Alicia King and Courtney Stone in the school's computer lab.

DATE from page 135

said waitress Susan Sanders, who served the pair during their excruciating two-hour dinner engagement. "Sexual frankness and maturity are great, but there's such a thing as inappropriate personal revelations. Do you really need to mention on a first date that you're 'totally cool with porn'?"

Those close to Scanlon report that he remains unaware that the date was a disaster, leaving repeated messages on Loftus' voicemail asking when they can "hook up" again.

Carlson predicted, however, that Scanlon's insecurity will soon begin to steadily mount with each passing day his calls are not returned, and that, inevitably, he will launch into an exhaustive self-pity session over Loftus' rejection of him.

"I'm sure Marc's next date, whoever she may be, will hear all about it—if he ever gets another date," Carlson said. "If he does, I'm going to suggest he try being nothing remotely like himself." Ø

MEXICAN TACO from page 131

amounts of blood. Passersby were amazed by the unusually large amounts of blood. Passersby were amazed by the unusually large amounts of blood. Passersby were amazed by the unusually large amounts of blood. Passersby were amazed by the unusually large amounts of blood. Passersby were amazed by the unusually large amounts of blood. Passersby were amazed by the unusually large amounts of blood. Passersby were amazed by the unusually large amounts of blood. Passersby were amazed by the unusually large amounts of blood. Passersby were amazed by the unusually large amounts of blood. Passersby were amazed by the unusually large amounts of blood. Passersby were amazed by the unusually large amounts of blood. Passersby were amazed by the unusually large amounts of blood. Passersby were amazed by the unusually large amounts of blood. Passersby were amazed by the unusually large amounts of blood. Passersby were amazed by the unusually large amounts of blood. Passersby were amazed by the unusually large amounts of blood. Passersby were amazed by the unusually large

I hate myself for owning this automatic coin-wrapper.

amounts of blood. Passersby were amazed by the unusually large amounts of blood. Passersby were amazed by the unusually large amounts of blood. Passersby were amazed by the unusually large amounts of blood. Passersby were amazed by the unusually large amounts of blood. Passersby were amazed by the unusually large amounts of blood. Passersby were amazed by the unusually large amounts of blood. Passersby were amazed by the unusually large amounts of blood. Passersby were amazed by the unusually large amounts of blood. Passersby were amazed by the unusually large amounts of blood. Passersby were amazed by the unusually large amounts of blood. Passersby were amazed by the unusually large amounts of blood. Passersby were amazed by the unusually large amounts of blood. Passersby were amazed by the unusually large amounts of blood. Passersby were amazed by the unusually large amounts of blood. Passersby were amazed by the unusually large amounts of blood. Passersby were amazed by the unusually large amounts of blood. Passersby were amazed by the unusually large amounts of blood. Passersby were amazed by the unusually large amounts of blood. Passersby were

see MEXICAN TACO page 148

MEATWAVE from page 133

tims' digestive systems—and, ultimately, their entire bodies—to shut down.

"The human body, as you may be aware, is roughly 60 percent water," Peltz said. "However, many don't realize that it's also 75 percent meat. If that percentage rises too high too quickly, it may result in a distended stomach, intestinal bloating, and even

According to Peltz, the meatwave victims' causes of death have ranged from cardiac beefurcation to smoked-sausage inhalation.

death. Believe me, it's not a pretty way to go. A coroner never forgets the first time he examines the body of someone who died from roast-traumatic stress."

According to Peltz, the meatwave victims' causes of death have ranged from cardiac beefurcation to smoked-sausage inhalation. There has even been one confirmed indirect meat-related fatality, a 51-year-old Evanston man who died from a catastrophic smothering in mushrooms and onions.

Chicago public-health officials are urging residents to stay in their homes, advising them to lay out extra napkins and carving forks, drink plenty of water, and venture outside only to procure Zantac, Tums, and Immodium AD. Yet in spite of such warnings, the meatwave-related casualties continue to mount.

"This happens every few years in Chicago," said emergency worker Peter Barreras. "People in this town act pretty tough, and they always say the same things: 'I can handle the meat.' Or 'You call this a hot dog?' Or, my favorite, 'It's just a hot wing. How much can one little hot wing hurt me?' Well, I'll tell you. A lot."

Barreras said that for a meatstroke victim, familiarity with basic first-aid can be the difference between life and death.

"If you or someone you're eating with collapses from The Meats, know what to do," Barreras said. "Many people think that administering them emergency salads or tofu is the way to go, but the shock to the system is too great. Bring their meat index down gently and gradually by first immersing them in cold cuts. Call a doctor and talk to them while you wait for help to arrive. Under no circumstances should you let them have another pork chop, ham slice, or New York strip. Administer a solution of turkey tetrachloride, give them coffee, and don't let them lose consciousness."

Meateorologists speculate that the deadly meatwave was caused by a stationary high-protein ridge extending along the shore of Lake Michigan. They fear that Milwaukee and Kansas City could be next.

"Mother Nature sure has cooked us up a big one this time," Peltz said. "If it's this bad now, imagine what'll land on the city's plate during Taste Of Chicago."

If the meatwave continues through next week as predicted, the death toll could reach 100, making it the worst natural food disaster since the San Francisco Panquake of 1970. Ø

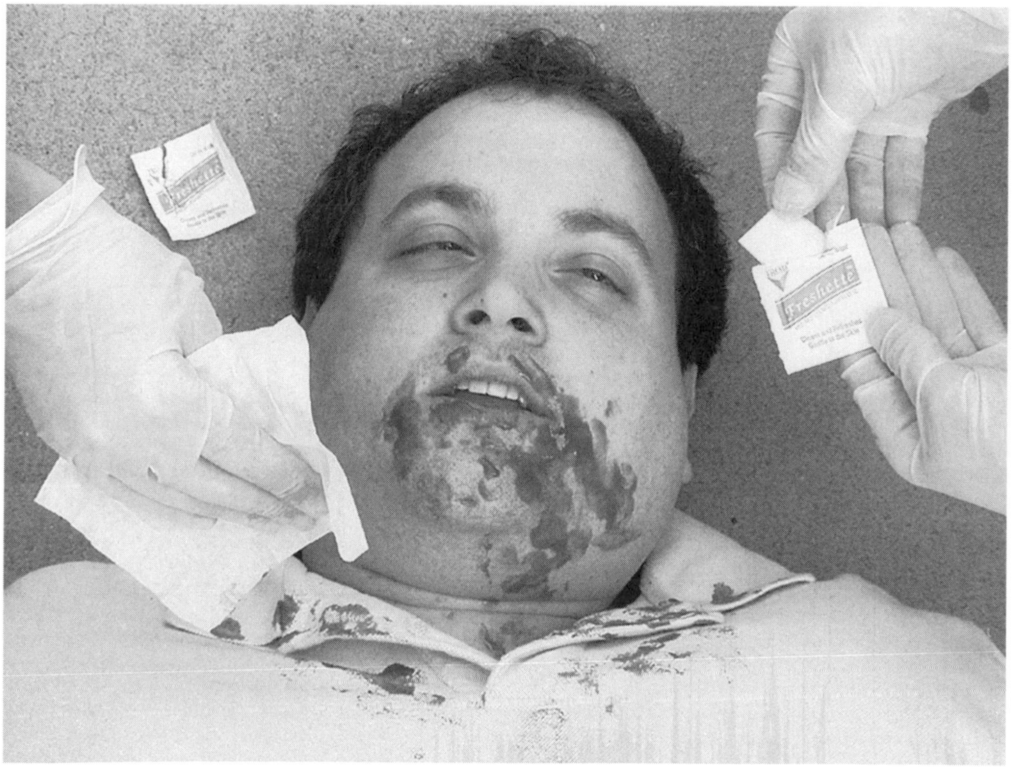

Above: Meatstroke victim Tom Eppard is cleaned by rescue workers.

HARVEY'S HOLLYWOOD

Have You Been Bitten By The *Matrix* Bug?

The Outside Scoop
By Jackie Harvey

Item! Beware of Matrixmania! **Matrix 2: Back To The Matrix** is coming out soon, and that means the ladies of the world will once again be drooling over hunky **Lawrence "Black Morpheus" Fishburn**. But while drooling is guaranteed, many questions remain unanswered: Can the sequel top the original? Did **Elron** really die in the first one, or will he be back? Will there be more sparks between **Neon** and **Brittany**? Tune in here for all the latest cyber-poop.

Well, it looks like all of our support for the troops worked. We overthrew **Saddam**. I was overjoyed when I saw the footage of American soldiers draping Old Glory over the Saddam statue. **The Iraqis** really seemed to love it. It's so great that they're not poor or oppressed anymore. Good job, everyone!

Spring is here in a big way! The snow is gone, the flowers are blooming, and the birds have returned. That means only one thing is on my mind: baseball! There's nothing I like better than seeing those **athletes** step up to the plate, bat in hand, and swat a few balls deep into the outfield. Ah, the thrill of raw competition: Two teams enter, one team leaves. That's why it's the great American pastime.

I know they say **SARS** isn't a threat here, but just to be safe, I'm staying away from Panda Wok down at the mall food court.

Item! Catherine Zeta-Douglas and **Mike Douglas** have been the busiest dream couple in all of show business. What? Even busier than **Ben** and **J. Lo**? Absolutely! First, there was Catherine's Oscar win. And Mike had his family reunion on film, with his mom, dad **Kirk**, and son **Kirk Cameron** all in one movie. Now, there's a powerhouse movie that should blow the roof off theaters. Mike and Cathy also won a lawsuit in England, which isn't as hard as winning one here, but it is still commendable. And, to top it all off, Catherine is in an **MCI commercial**! Congratulations! Hey, lovebirds, take it from Jackie—don't forget to take time to smell the roses.

I know they say SARS isn't a threat here, but just to be safe, I'm staying away from Panda Wok down at the mall food court.

We overthrew Saddam. I was overjoyed when I saw the footage of American soldiers draping Old Glory over the Saddam statue. The Iraqis really seemed to love it. It's so great that they're not poor or oppressed anymore.

I'm pretty psyched to see **Daddy Daycare**, but **Eddie Murphy** has got a lot to make up for after **The Adventures Of Pluto Nash**. I didn't see it, but did you check out that box office? That thing sank faster than a sponge tugboat!

The King may be gone, but he left a rock 'n' roll queen behind! **Lisa Marie Pressly** is letting it all hang out, musicwise. Since I've always been a fan of Elvis, I picked up his daughter's new album, **To Whom It May Concern**, the day it came out. Was it worth waiting in line for three hours before the store opened? You'd better believe it! I was the only one there, but that still counts as a line. Anyway, the former Mrs. Jackson and the former Mrs. Cage gets it together and works it the way only she can. The result? **Music magic**—and you can take that all the way to the song bank.

I need a new car. My old one works okay, but I want something that reflects my personality better. Maybe a **Solara**?

Item! America's sweetheart **Monica Lewinski** is back, and she's got a brand-new dress (if you know what I mean)! She's the host of a new reality series called **Personality Man**. One lady chooses a mate from 20 men wearing masks. That way, she has to get to know the real person, not just the face. I should be on that show, because I have loads of personality. Not that I'm too hard on the eyes, but it's good to have an ace in the hole.

Buttery Scotsman **Colin Feral** sure does seem to be handy with the ladies. Every night, he's reported gallivanting around town with a different **sexy starlet**. Where was this guy last year, when we needed him to take our minds off all our problems?

Item! The Dixie Chicks, no strangers to controversy, did the unthinkable recently by appearing nude on the cover of **Entertainment Tonight**. Now, before you get all up in arms (and legs!), rest assured it's done pretty tastefully. They have tattoos of the words that their critics have hurled their way and, believe me, some of them must have stung. Country music hasn't seen this much controversy since **Charley Pride** questioned **President Ford**'s China policy!

Speaking of statements, have the funnies always been so political? There's a new strip called **The Boondocks** that makes **Doonesbury** look like **Broom Hilda**. Give me the old days, when it was just overweight cats and cavemen who talked about **Jesus**.

Have the funnies always been so political? There's a new strip called *The Boondocks* that makes *Doonesbury* look like *Broom Hilda*. Give me the old days, when it was just overweight cats and cavemen who talked about Jesus.

Same as always, this is the time when Jackie Harvey has to say goodbye. I hate goodbyes, so instead, I'll just say "Adieu," which is French for both goodbye and hello. Just to keep you coming back, I'll wet your whistle with a tidbit you can expect next time: What Oscar-winning superhero was caught buying her leggings off the rack at **T.J. Maxx**? (She'll kick up a "Storm" when she finds out I'm telling!) Until then, I'll be waiting for you... on the outside!

HOROSCOPES

Your Horoscope

By Lloyd Schumner Sr.
Retired Machinist and
A.A.P.B.-Certified Astrologer

Aries: (March 21–April 19)
You will meet the girl of your dreams Wednesday when she and five other EMTs try to free you from a hellish cocoon of molten glass.

Taurus: (April 20–May 20)
The stars don't think it would be fair to give you a new prediction until the one about finding happiness, love, or wealth comes true.

Gemini: (May 21–June 21)
After years of indecision, you will finally decide to move to Las Vegas, where you'll lose it all on 23 Red.

Cancer: (June 22–July 22)
You will be hailed as a hero by *The American Spectator* when you shoot three suspicious-looking Hispanic kids in the back while guarding the West Park Mall.

Leo: (July 23–Aug. 22)
Once again, it's a bad week for romance in the workplace, but romance has nothing to do with your coworkers taking you from behind while you're Xeroxing.

Virgo: (Aug. 23–Sept. 22)
You're asking for it health-wise if you don't start exercising, sleeping more, and reducing your intake of fat people.

Libra: (Sept. 23–Oct. 23)
Though it should be easy to prove that giant robots are not constantly sneaking up on you, you remain remarkably resistant to dissuasion.

Scorpio: (Oct. 24–Nov. 21)
Sometimes, all one can do is step back and laugh at the absurdity of it all. However, the jury will note that a fire extinguisher was within easy reach.

Sagittarius: (Nov. 22–Dec. 21)
Your abuses of the American legal system will soon surpass your abuses of the Fayetteville, AR, plumbing system.

Capricorn: (Dec. 22–Jan. 19)
After a long, expensive investigation, the World Health Organization will be forced to admit that it has no idea how you slipped through.

Aquarius: (Jan. 20–Feb. 18)
You'll make controversial front-page headlines when you're the subject of the nation's first multimillion-dollar asexual-harassment case.

Pisces: (Feb. 19–March 20)
You've finally decided to divorce your whiny, repugnant spouse. Good luck ever finding love again, babe.

the ONION

VOLUME 39 ISSUE 18 AMERICA'S FINEST NEWS SOURCE™ 15–21 MAY 2003

NEWS

Chimp Actor Looking To Direct

see FILM page 9C

EYEWITNESS

Mobile News Crew Reports On Own Van Breaking Down

see MEDIA page 2E

Mailman Seemed Kind Of Drunk

see LOCAL page 1D

Mesopotamia Pacified

see WORLD page 4A

STATshot

A look at the numbers that shape your world.

Why Are We Suddenly Leaving Town?

1. CD club finally caught up to us
2. Earned the nickname "Sugar Cone"
3. Rented every video at Kwik Trip
4. Dog knocked up neighbor's dog
5. Are in Army Reserve
6. Hated one playa too many
7. Fucking Witness Protection Program put "Vittorio" on mailbox

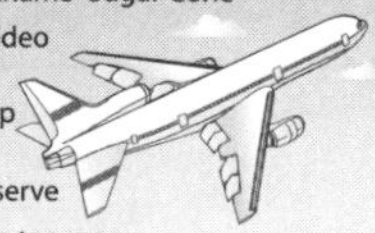

Pfizer Launches 'Zoloft For Everything' Ad Campaign

NEW YORK—Seeking to broaden the customer base of the popular drug, Pfizer announced the launch of a $40 million "Zoloft For Everything" advertising campaign Monday.

"Zoloft is most commonly prescribed for the treatment of depression and anxiety disorders, but it would be ridiculous to limit such a multi-functional drug to these few uses," Pfizer spokesman Jon Pugh said. "We feel doctors need to stop asking their patients if anything is wrong and start asking if anything could be more right."

Continued Pugh: "How many millions of people out there are suffering under the strain of a deadline at work or pre-date jitters, but don't realize there's a drug that could provide relief? Zoloft isn't just for severe anxiety or depression. Got the Monday blues? Kids driving you nuts? Let Zoloft help. Zoloft."

Zoloft (sertraline hydrochloride)

see ZOLOFT page 143

Dishes piling up in the sink?
Zoloft

Above: One of the new Zoloft ads.

Freed POW Already Sick Of Family

Above: Dobson is surrounded by his irritating loved ones.

CAPE GIRARDEAU, MO—Brent Dobson, a 19-year-old Army private who was reunited with his loved ones on May 8 after a harrowing two-week ordeal as a prisoner of war in Iraq, is already "sick to death" of his family, Dobson reported Monday.

"As I paced that 6x9 cell, with nothing but crumbs to eat, contaminated water to drink, and a broken piece of crockery to piss in, the thing that kept me going was thoughts of my family back home," Dobson said, pacing his 10x11 bedroom in his parents' home. "Well, after four days in this place, Iraq isn't looking quite so bad."

Added Dobson: "God, is my mom annoying."

On April 23, Dobson, a member of the U.S. Army's 3rd Infantry Division, was liberated by Marines who discovered him in a makeshift POW camp outside An Najaf in central Iraq. Missing for 15 days and feared dead, the POW was flown back to the U.S. last Wednesday after spending two weeks recovering in an Army hospital in Hamburg, Germany. Upon touching down on U.S. soil, Dobson was moved to tears at the sight of his family—a reaction he has since taken back.

"I guess during my ordeal,

see POW page 142

Hostel-Dwelling Swede Getting Laid Big-Time

NEW YORK—Anders Perssen, 23, a Swedish backpacker currently staying at the Chelsea International Youth Hostel, admitted Monday to getting "a great large amount of tail" during the first two weeks of his three-month tour of the U.S.

"Ja, is true," said the smiling Stockholm native. "I am getting laid big-time."

Perssen, who shares a dormitory-style room with five other men, said he has been "very lucky with ladies" ever since arriving in the U.S.

"I admit, it has been very easy to have the women to sleep with me," he said. "Much harder when I am home. Not impossible, I don't say. But, ja, harder."

"If I should have known this, I would have stay here before—every summer!" Perssen continued. "I would have come to America as soon as I was 18, just so I can get all the you-know-what whenever I want. But then I would have never leave, right?"

"No, I am kidding to you," Perssen added, turning serious for a moment. "I love Sweden. It is my home."

Dressed stylishly in a corduroy blazer and motorcycle boots, an English-Swedish dictionary tucked in the front pocket of his rumpled button-down shirt, Perssen said he makes a positive impression on American women with his European style of dress.

"The women, they say I dress nice, much better compared to American men who more dress in gym shoes,"

Above: The much-laid Perssen sits on his bed at the hostel.

Perssen said. "The girl Gina at [local bar] the Half King say I look 'sophisticated.' I think she look sophisticated,

see SWEDE page 142

Bush And Blair's Nobel Nomination

Last week, President Bush and British Prime Minister Tony Blair were nominated for the Nobel Peace Prize for winning the war in Iraq. What do *you* think?

"Man, this must've been a pretty shitty year for peacemakers."

Andrea Barker
Physical Therapist

"If they win, they would join the esteemed ranks of Henry Kissinger and Yasser Arafat."

Teri Hyde
Homemaker

"Well, they *did* go to war when the entire rest of the world was opposed, so I suppose they deserve it. Wait, that came out wrong."

Wayne King
Systems Analyst

"What, were the Powerpuff Girls too fictional or something?"

Marcus Anderson
Lawyer

"Nominated by the grateful Iraqi people, no doubt."

Bobby Thakker
Delivery Driver

"It's about time. I'm sick of them always giving the Peace Prize to all those fucking pacifists."

Ron Hadler
Electrician

The Matrix Reloaded

The feverishly anticipated *Matrix Reloaded* hits theaters Thursday. What can moviegoers expect from the blockbuster sequel?

- Breakthrough digital effects make Keanu Reeves appear to "act"
- Trinity makes three-point landing on top of speeding sportscar, then jumps off in slow-motion, landing in bedroom of 300-pound comic-book collector
- Movie screens to be outfitted with jizz guards
- Nearly all-digital format perfect for illegal downloads
- Is actually the movie *Tron*
- Finally answers the question, "When is that new *Matrix* coming out?"
- Morpheus transforms into Cowboy Curtis to avoid agents
- Incredible new filmmaking technology enables audience to instantly transform from 34-year-old men into 14-year-old boys
- Lots of skintight black leather, but not the gay kind
- Despite what you might have assumed from the trailer, really more of a chick flick

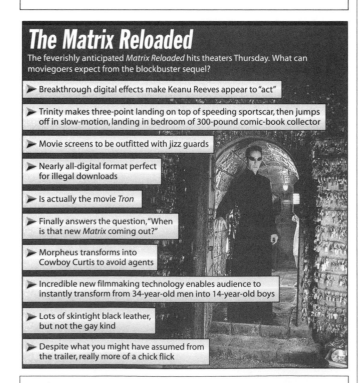

the ONION®
America's Finest News Source.™

Herman Ulysses Zweibel
Founder

T. Herman Zweibel
Publisher Emeritus
J. Phineas Zweibel
Publisher
Maxwell Prescott Zweibel
Editor-In-Chief

I'm An Attractive-People Person

By Bennett Adams

Thank you for considering me for this position. As you can see from my résumé, my extensive work experience in the field makes me a strong candidate for this job. My résumé doesn't, however, convey the many intangibles that I bring to the table. For example, I'm incredibly driven. I'm also excellent in crisis situations, doing my best work under pressure. And, of course, I'm an attractive-people person.

I've always been able to connect with good-looking people of all types.

I'm not sure where I got it, but I have a gift for getting on well with attractive people. I've always been able to connect with good-looking people of all types. It doesn't matter what race, color, or creed they are. So long as they're not unpleasant to the eye, chances are good that we'll hit it off.

I like nothing more than to sit in a public park on a Sunday afternoon and attractive-people watch. It's fun to look at beautiful people and try to imagine their lives. I picture them dressing to the nines, dining at the finest restaurants, and then dancing the night away at the hottest clubs with other fabulous people in their appearance bracket. Sometimes, I'm even blessed to see a budding romance between a ravishing couple. Nothing brings a smile to my face like the sight of two attractive people falling in love.

I like nothing more than to sit in a public park on a Sunday afternoon and attractive-people watch. It's fun to look at beautiful people and try to imagine their lives. I picture them dressing to the nines, dining at the finest restaurants, and then dancing the night away at the hottest clubs with other fabulous people in their appearance bracket.

The ability to connect with attractive people is certainly a valuable skill in the business world. Sometimes, I walk into a conference room and meet a stunning client, and before I even speak to him or her, I think, "I like that beautiful person already."

I've always liked attractive people, even at an early age. When I was 3, my only playmate was the homely kid next door. I thought I liked him, but once I began attending Rosewood Day Care, I saw other kids my age who were adorable like me. After that, my neighbor and I drifted apart. In the years since, I've met lots of attractive people, and I've liked them all. That's the amazing thing about attractive people. They're all different, yet deep down, they all share one essential, fundamental quality: great looks.

The ability to connect with attractive people is certainly a valuable skill in the business world. Sometimes, I walk into a conference room and meet a stunning client, and before I even speak to him or her, I think, "I like that beautiful person already." Maybe it's the way they carry themselves. There's something about a woman's smooth olive skin or a man's broad, muscular shoulders that says, "I deserve—nay, demand—your attention and respect." Those are the kinds of people I want to be in business with. They sense this and, in turn, want to be in business with me.

So that's it. That's my pitch. If you hire me, you'll find that I have a way with beautiful people in just about any imaginable workplace situation. Whether we're brainstorming a major proposal or racing to meet deadline on a project, there's no high cheekbone or pouty set of lips that I'm not capable of working well with.

LOCAL

Five-Family Yard Sale Mainly Selling Items To Each Other

LAKE OSWEGO, OR—Despite participants' hopes of unloading useless, long-shelved items for profit, Oakdale Court's five-family yard sale last weekend was dominated by the transfer of items from one table to another.

"I had all this junk sitting in the garage, just collecting dust," yard-sale organizer John Kobler said Monday. "[Wife] Nancy kept asking me to toss it out. You know, my old drill, the kids' old Sega system, some promotional golf caps I never wear, stuff like that. I was just looking for a way to get rid of it and maybe make some extra cash. Well, I sold most of it to the neighbors and used the money to get some pretty cool stuff in return. Check out this train set."

"Our 9-year-old was making a big fuss when we sold his old Pokémon toys to the Sarrackis," neighbor Debbie Ancona said. "Even though he never plays with them anymore, I felt guilty, so I gave him the 50 cents we got for them to find something that might cheer him up."

Above: The scene of the mass exchange of unwanted goods.

The three-day sale, held in the Koblers' driveway, featured merchandise supplied by the Kobler, Ancona, Farrell, Ashby, and Sarracki families. It is estimated that less than 5 percent of the items sold made their way out of Oakdale Court.

"Our 9-year-old was making a big fuss when we sold his old Pokémon toys to the Sarrackis," neighbor Debbie Ancona said. "Even though he never plays with them anymore, I felt guilty, so I gave him the 50 cents we got for them to find something that might cheer him up. He ran back from the Ashby table with an old Power Rangers doll."

While the event resulted in a zero-sum gain for the participating families, they shunned the implementation of a barter system. Instead, transactions within the closed economy were conducted via the use of cash combined with a marginally intelligible system of color-coded stickers and scrawled notes in spiral-bound notebooks.

"I didn't want to drive all the way to the Salvation Army to get rid of our old baby clothes," Ancona said. "If I didn't sell them today, I was going to throw them out. It's a good thing the Farrells just had a baby. They bought all my baby clothes, and we bought a bunch of the stuff they had to get rid of to baby-proof the house."

Even items that were determined to have no cash value changed hands through the "free box." Although no record was kept of the free items' movements, everything from a stained Parcheesi game board to a broken toaster to a 1986 issue of *Good Housekeeping* profiling new mother Christie Brinkley managed to find new homes.

"We didn't make a lot of money," Kevin Sarracki said. "In fact, we wound up about $2 below where we started. But look at this electronic talking fish I got from the Farrells. It sings 'Don't Worry, Be Happy.' Can you believe they were just giving it away for four bucks? That's going to look great on the wall when I finish the basement rec room."

Further contributing to the inter-

see GARAGE SALE page 142

NEWS IN BRIEF

This Absolutely The Last Time Bouncer Cleans Up Vomit

LUBBOCK, TX—Bruce Kucharsky, 29, a bouncer at the Come Back Inn, announced Monday that this is "absolutely the last time" he is cleaning up vomit. "This is it," said Kucharsky, mopping up a chunky, peach-hued puddle near the pool table. "I'll clean up the puke this time, but next time, they're gonna find somebody else, or I quit. I ain't no fucking janitor." In his four months as a bouncer at the bar, Kucharsky estimated he has "wiped up chunder, like, at least 300 times."

Traveler Excited Hotel Has HBO Until He Checks Listings

ROCKFORD, IL—Stopping at a local Days Inn Tuesday, traveler Dan Peterson, 27, was delighted to discover that the motel featured the premium channel HBO until he checked the night's programming listings. "Aw, man, not *Summer Catch*," Peterson said, as he browsed the cable guide. "Then it's back-to-back episodes of *Tracey Takes On* at 11, followed by *The Mexican* at midnight and *Ghosts Of Mars* at 2 a.m. Fuck." Peterson spent the evening reading the room's complimentary copy of *See Rockford!* and sucking on ice cubes.

Nanny Appears In Child's Drawings More Than Mother

MALIBU, CA—According to reports, Consuela Rodriguez, 41, nanny of Sara Denton, has appeared in more of the 6-year-old's crayon drawings than her own mother. "Here's a picture of me and Consuela at the zoo," Sara said Tuesday. "And here's me and Consuela at the park, and us eating at McDonald's. And this one is me and Consuela as ballerinas, and this one is me and Consuela having a picnic with SpongeBob. And here's one of Mommy in her car, driving to work." Sara's mother could not be reached for comment.

College-Aged Daughter Against Using Straws Now

MIDDLETOWN, CT—Unveiling her latest college-acquired quirk, Wesleyan University freshman Julie Freitag, 18, informed her parents Monday that she is staunchly opposed to the use of drinking straws. "I don't know if it's an environmental-waste thing or an I'm-all-grown-up thing or maybe something else altogether, but she won't touch a straw," said Jim Freitag, her father. "Every time we see her, she's got a new one: First, she wouldn't wear deodorant because of the aluminum, then she wouldn't watch the Oscars because of something to do with the war. But not using straws? What's that about?"

Shipwreck Survivors Forced To Endure Ride Home On Disney Cruise Ship

NASSAU, BAHAMAS—Rescued after being lost at sea for nearly two weeks, shipwreck survivors Bill and Mary Kolin were forced to endure a ride back to the U.S. mainland on a Disney Magic cruise ship. "I suffered severe sunburn, dehydration, and starvation, but that was nothing compared to the half a day I spent on that hellship," Mary told reporters Monday. "I honestly didn't think we'd make it through Chip 'N' Dale's Karaoke Jam, much less Mickey's Breakfast Buffet." Bill said he plans to write a book chronicling his struggle for survival among shuffleboard-playing *Lion King* fans. ⌀

POW from page 139

I'd forgotten that Dad clips his toenails in front of the TV, and that Mom obsessively runs the vacuum every day at 7 a.m.," Dobson said. "If I take one step into the house with my shoes on, she starts shrieking like I just dumped a 40-pound bag of horseshit on the floor."

Dobson said he should have recognized early signs of trouble at a family-organized homecoming celebration last Wednesday.

"I'd just gotten back and really just wanted to sleep," Dobson said. "But the family wanted to throw a big party for me, and some relatives had come halfway across the country for

"When you're just weeks removed from being beaten by a member of Saddam's Republican Guard, you're not necessarily in the mood to make small talk with your 300-pound Aunt Irene over a plate of macaroni salad."

it. Still, when you're just weeks removed from being beaten by a member of Saddam's Republican Guard, you're not necessarily in the mood to make small talk with your 300-pound Aunt Irene over a plate of macaroni salad."

Dobson's maternal grandmother, Maureen Robb, was among the party attendees, but her outpouring of emotion and affection toward her grandson soon took a predictable detour into Christianity.

"I was dumb not to have anticipated that at some point, she'd start in with the 'Jesus this, Savior that,'" Dobson said. "She actually said to me, 'Jesus was testing you, Brent, and you passed.' After all the horrible shit I went through, I couldn't believe she was trying to save me. This is the same woman who persuaded my parents to put me in that wretched summer Bible camp when I was 11."

At the homecoming party, Dobson was further dispirited by his uncle Mark, who would only discuss the NBA playoffs and his unusually high white-blood-cell count; a sullen cousin who picked flaking paint off the side of the Dobsons' home; and his sister Karen, who forced her children Kaleb and Kaitlin to perform a grating "welcome home" rendition of "God Bless The U.S.A." for the returning war hero.

The day after the homecoming party, Dobson—who had sustained a broken leg and wrist, as well as a bullet wound to the shoulder, during his imprisonment—was put to work clearing leaves from roof gutters.

"Yeah, I got roped into that pretty quickly," Dobson said. "Mom told me that since Dad's lumbago had been acting up all winter, a lot of yard work went neglected. I thought of pinning the Purple Heart that Donald Rumsfeld awarded me to Dad's shirt as he snoozed in his Barcalounger, but I decided against it."

By the end of his first weekend home, Dobson realized that his main reason for joining the Army was to escape the Dobson clan.

"I used to say that I joined the Army to escape Cape Girardeau," Dobson said. "But what I was really trying to escape was my family. I love them, but they're clingy and whiny and bossy and cranky and snippy and annoying and smothering. Those Iraqi captors were pretty bad, but they're nowhere near as bad as my current ones."

GARAGE SALE from page 141

familial circulation of junk was the reselling of items sold at previous Oakdale Court yard sales.

"A few years back, we did a yard sale, and I remember selling a ceramic mixing bowl," Gretchen Farrell said. "It had a small chip in it, and I thought we didn't need it anymore, but before long, I started to miss it. Luckily, I found one just like it at the Anconas', and I got it for a song. It even had a chip in the exact same place. Amazing."

At the end of the day, the Koblers were the big winners at $3 ahead, while the Ashbys wound up $6.75 in the red.

According to University of Oregon economics professor Dr. Arthur Clybourne, such incestuous yard sales are commonplace.

"The Oakdale Court yard sale is a microcosm of an economic model played out every weekend in cul de sacs across the nation," Clybourne said. "It is a closed system in which the mere presence of goods creates demand for said goods. The supplier

At the end of the day, the Koblers were the big winners at $3 ahead.

becomes the consumer, and capitalism breaks down and devolves into its embryonic state of pseudo-bartering. Any item, by virtue of its existence within the closed system, becomes something with an intrinsic value and built-in level of demand. How else could you explain somebody paying $1.50 for a scratched vinyl copy of Men At Work's *Cargo*?"

SWEDE from page 139

too, but even better with the clothes off!"

Perssen's fellow hostel dwellers can attest to the mad action the Swede is getting.

"I go out to the bar on the weekend

Said Perssen: "All the women, they say, 'Oh, I love your accent! Where are you from?' Or 'What is that cigarette you smoke? I never hear of Prince cigarette! Is that Swedish brand? Please to let me try one!' It work every time."

and everyone loves Anders," said Ewald Kist, 24, a Dutch traveler who has bunked with Perssen for the past eight days. "All the women, they say, 'Oh, I love your accent! Where are you from?' Or 'What is that cigarette you smoke? I never hear of Prince cigarette! Is that Swedish brand? Oh, so cool! Please to let me try one!' It work every time."

Shorter and less handsome than Perssen, Kist said he is doing "all right" himself, but cannot help but be impressed with Perssen's ability to reel it in.

"Anders is never even here at all most nights," Kist said. "He is paying for a bed for his backpack to sit on. But it is better for him this way, for sure. It is better, isn't it, Anders? The American women are good in bed, no?"

A sheepish Perssen waved the question away, but confirmed that he is definitely "getting some."

"On last Friday, I stay at the New York University on the campus in the room of Kristine," Perssen said. "On Sunday, I stay in apartment in the Eastern Village which is where the bands like the Ramones and the Talking Heads played. The girl, Brynn, was very beautiful. She had a tattoo. Ha, I will not say where, though. That is for me to know!"

In addition to Kristine and Brynn, Perssen has enjoyed the company of three other females in the past week: an advertising executive, an aspiring singer-songwriter, and a girl from Minneapolis staying with a friend at Columbia University.

"I go to the bar, and all I do is order my drink and the women ask me where I am from," Perssen said. "Sometimes, it is hard to choose between the friends, which one I want to talk to the most. Only, sometimes, by the end of the night, we do not just talk!"

According to Perssen, American women tend to know little about Swedish culture, but they are nonetheless eager to discuss it with him.

"They say Ingmar Bergman, then they say Pippi Longstockings, and then the Volvo car," Perssen said. "We talk about the bands—they sometimes know my favorite now, The Hives, or The Hellacopters or Sahara Hotnights, but they usually say ABBA. I do not like ABBA very much, but I am willing to sing along with them to the ABBA if it maybe will get me into the sack later."

Perssen confessed that last Saturday night, he participated in a bar sing-along to "Dancing Queen," the playful atmosphere culminating in a make-out session on the sidewalk outside of a Lower East Side bar.

Perssen, who plans to stay in New York another week before heading to Boston, said the attention from women has interfered with his efforts to see the city.

"There are so many things I mean to do here before I move on," Perssen said. "My first week, I visit the Metropolitan Art Museum and Times Square, and I go to the Central Park, but since then, I mostly concentrate on the hot chicks. It's a good idea, no?"

The Swede said he typically finds himself so tired from staying out late that he spends most days lounging in coffee shops or bookstores, resting up for the long night ahead.

"Maybe I will come back to New York when I am too old to want to get

"Anders is never even here at all most nights," Kist said. "He is paying for a bed for his backpack to sit on. But it is better for him this way, for sure. It is better, isn't it, Anders? The American women are good in bed, no?"

laid," Perssen said. "But right now, I see the real New York and party with the real people of New York, like Marissa and Shelley, who both work at the jewelry store in Greenwich Village and live together in very small room. Marissa, with the red hair, and Shelley, with the dark hair and the very little waist."

"I will tell you this one thing more," Perssen continued. "I was thinking the American women might not like uncircumcised, but I will let you know that is not the case!"

ZOLOFT from page 139

was originally introduced as a means of treating depression, post-traumatic stress disorder, panic disorder, and obsessive-compulsive disorder. In January, however, Pfizer won FDA approval for use of Zoloft to treat premenstrual dysphoric disorder, as well as social-anxiety disorder, or "social phobia."

"One man's hangnail could be another man's darkest depths of despair," Pugh said. "Isn't medication a tool to help people lead better, happier lives? Access to drugs should not be restricted to those the medical community officially deems 'sick.'"

Last week, the FDA okayed Zoloft for treatment of "the entire range of unpleasant or otherwise negative social, physical, and mental feelings that an individual may experience in the course of a human life."

"At first, Zoloft was only used to treat depression," Pugh said. "But what is depression, really? Who died and gave doctors the authority to dictate who is and isn't depressed? One man's hangnail could be another man's darkest depths of despair. Isn't medication a tool to help people lead better, happier lives? Access to drugs should not be restricted to those the medical community officially deems 'sick.'"

Pfizer president James Vernon said the "Zoloft For Everything" campaign will employ print and TV ads to inform potential users about the "literally thousands" of new applications for Zoloft. Among the conditions the drug can be used to treat: anxiety associated with summer swimsuit season, insecurity over sexual potency and performance, feelings of shame over taking an antidepressant, and a sense of hollowness stemming from losing an online auction.

In today's fast-paced world, Vernon said, people don't have time to deal with mood changes.

"Zoloft has always helped clinically depressed people modulate serotonin levels and other chemical imbalances that make life unlivable for them," Vernon said. "But now, Zoloft can also help anyone who needs their emotions leveled off. Do you find yourself feeling excited or sad? No one should have to suffer through those harrowing peaks and valleys."

Could Zoloft be right for you?

Take this self-quiz.

Have you experienced any of the following?
Check those that apply or might possibly apply:

Trouble concentrating?	O YES	O NO
Crying or thoughts of crying?	O YES	O NO
Feelings of sadness?	O YES	O NO
Low energy, fatigue?	O YES	O NO
High energy, restlessness?	O YES	O NO
Loss of interest in certain activities?	O YES	O NO
Unexplained pain or headaches?	O YES	O NO
Lack of motivation?	O YES	O NO
Stress?	O YES	O NO
Worry?	O YES	O NO
Lack of involvement with family or friends?	O YES	O NO
Over-dependence on family or friends?	O YES	O NO

If you took this quiz, Zoloft is probably right for you.
Ask your doctor about Zoloft.

Above: A Zoloft ad slated to run in next week's issue of *People*.

Anita White of Yuma, AZ, sought out Zoloft after seeing one of the new commercials.

"I was sitting on the couch, just watching TV, and, for the life of me, I couldn't motivate myself to go down to the basement to do the laundry," White said. "Luckily, a Zoloft ad came on right at that moment. I went to their web site and, sure enough, one of the 'Is Zoloft Right For You?' quiz questions was, 'Are you unable to motivate yourself to go down to the basement to do the laundry?' That's when I knew."

Other pharmaceutical companies are following Pfizer's lead. On Tuesday, Paxil manufacturer GlaxoSmithKline unveiled its new ad slogan, "Paxil... Give It A Try."

Other pharmaceutical companies are following Pfizer's lead. On Tuesday, Paxil manufacturer GlaxoSmithKline unveiled its new ad slogan, "Paxil... Give It A Try." Eli Lilly, maker of Prozac, is slated to launch a similar campaign built around the slogan, "Pot Roast Burnt? Husband Home With The Flu? You're Having One Of Those Prozac Days."

"We are letting consumers know that if they suspect Zoloft might improve the quality of their lives, they should contact their doctor," Pugh said. "And remember, you'll need to take Zoloft for at least eight weeks to make sure it's working."

Pugh warned that Zoloft use may cause side effects such as agitation, erratic behavior, restlessness, difficulty speaking, or shaking of hands and fingers. He added that Zoloft can help those suffering from agitation, erratic behavior, restlessness, difficulty speaking, and shaking of hands and fingers. ⊘

PFLAUM ROAD from page 137

amounts of blood. Passersby were amazed by the unusually large amounts of blood. Passersby were amazed by the unusually large amounts of blood. Passersby were amazed by the unusually large amounts of blood. Passersby were

Excuse me, are you done fucking that?

amazed by the unusually large amounts of blood. Passersby were amazed by the unusually large amounts of blood. Passersby were amazed by the unusually large amounts of blood. Passersby were amazed by the unusually large amounts of blood. Passersby were amazed by the unusually large amounts of blood. Passersby were

see PFLAUM ROAD page 149

COMMUNITY VOICES

All My Religion Needs Now Is A Snazzy Post-Death Scenario

Well, it's been a long, hard road, but I'm finally almost finished with Cosmysticism, the new religion I've been working on for the past year or so. And I must say, I'm pretty proud of how it's turned out. It's a delicate blend of love and wrath, mystery and science, history and fantasy. I have some compelling characters, a universal creation myth, and a great ascension-of-man second act. Now all I need is some sort of snazzy post-death scenario to really put the cherry on top.

By Rodney Gunther

Have you ever had one of those dreams where you were starving, and you could smell something delicious nearby, but you couldn't find it? That's exactly how I feel trying to nail down this post-death thing. I know I could just crank out some temporary, half-assed afterlife and revise it later, but that seems like a lazy, shoddy way to go about creating a belief system.

Besides the afterlife thing, Cosmysticism is good to go. I spent months studying the top five major religions and some of the more successful dead ones, then I broke them down thematically and charted the elements they shared. Once I had that visual, Cosmysticism's central text, *The Book Of Gunther*, pretty much wrote itself. It's really great stuff, too. If I were a lost soul looking for answers in this difficult and bewildering world, I'd be eating Cosmysticism up.

In *The Book Of Gunther*, I hit on all the big topics. Where did man come from? "And Menda looked out over the long sea, knowing that Malthaz guided his every action, and said, 'It is here that Malthaz has placed me, and here that I shall give rise to offspring from my very flesh, plucking them from my leg bones until the Earth is filled with followers.'" (*Gunther*, 1:03-09) Does Malthaz command the cosmos? "Malthaz rules the cosmos, for there can be none other." (*Gunther* 3:14) Why do we have guns and violence? "And Malthaz presented a lightning stick, saying, 'Take and use this gift to kill the wild beasts for consumption. But thou may also use it, when necessary, to gain vengeance against thine enemies.'" (*Gunther* 14:26-28). Pretty good, eh?

The way I've written Cosmysticism (I mean, the way it was *revealed* to me), each person on Earth corresponds to a star in the universe. We are all literally people of the stars, filled with ageless matter and untold potential. It's pretty straightforward, but with just enough crazy sci-fi touches to get people hooked.

I could've simply said that when people die, they return to their star state, but that would've been so unimaginative. All the popular religions make promises of a grand existence in the afterlife. How can joining the universal consciousness compete with Islam's afterlife of countless sexually available virgins or Christianity's chance to revisit all the kitties you had during your life?

I thought about bringing in some giant flying saucer that would take everyone to Neo-Heaven on the Eve of the Great Reckoning, but that seemed way too contrived. Talk about your *deus ex machina*.

I thought about bringing in some giant flying saucer that would take everyone to Neo-Heaven on the Eve of the Great Reckoning, but that seemed way too contrived. Talk about your *deus ex machina*. Besides, it's uncomfortably similar to that Heaven's Gate cult from a few years back. I'm creating a major new world religion here, not a death cult, and I certainly don't want to risk being associated with a bunch of bald, suicidal, Nike-wearing computer geeks.

Maybe I should keep a tape recorder by my bed. You never know, the perfect afterlife idea could hit me in my sleep. Just last week, I woke up in the middle of the night with this great idea about the Sixteen Stages Of Ascendency Into A Higher Plateau, but I didn't write any of it down, and I forgot it all by the morning. Drat the luck!

I can't allow myself to get hung up on this. I'll just go back to the Book and smooth out some of the rough spots about the Handing Down Of The Eternal Laws and the parable of "The Dolphin And The Fig." I'm sure the perfect post-death scenario will come to me eventually. I just need to let it gestate for a while. Once I've dreamed up that killer afterlife idea, the people of the world will flock to Cosmysticism like Muslims to Mecca. ⌀

HOROSCOPES

Your Horoscope

By Lloyd Schumner Sr.
Retired Machinist and
A.A.P.B.-Certified Astrologer

Aries: (March 21–April 19)
This is a time of deep personal reflection and introspection for you. Which, you have to admit, beats the hell out of looking for a job.

Taurus: (April 20–May 20)
You're a pretty drab, ordinary person, but that doesn't mean you should be settling for such drab, ordinary salads.

Gemini: (May 21–June 21)
You'll be knifed in the throat during an argument over which Mötley Crüe album is the most indispensable, leaving you as wrong as you are dead.

Cancer: (June 22–July 22)
You've long said that if the love of dozens of nurses is a crime, you are guilty. Now, however, it's time to get your opinion on their brutal murders.

Leo: (July 23–Aug. 22)
You will be forgiven for your many sins after a $17.25 donation to your church, leaving you with the feeling that you should really commit some better sins.

Virgo: (Aug. 23–Sept. 22)
Your inhuman thirst for blood will finally be slaked this week, leaving you with just a normal, human thirst for blood.

Libra: (Sept. 23–Oct. 23)
Libra Music Quiz #42: Who sang the classic lyric "Come on, everybody, we're moving to Portland"?

Scorpio: (Oct. 24–Nov. 21)
You've never lost sight of your childhood dreams of rainbow-colored pegasus-unicorns, which makes you a truly formidable geneticist.

Sagittarius: (Nov. 22–Dec. 21)
Maybe it's because you're so baked, but you've watched that ad three dozen times, and you still can't figure out how marijuana got that girl pregnant.

Capricorn: (Dec. 22–Jan. 19)
Sometimes, the things you do just don't come out the way you want, especially when that gun-waving Phil Spector forces you to do it his way.

Aquarius: (Jan. 20–Feb. 18)
Sure, you're dizzy, hot, and dehydrated, but think how much worse it would be if that clothes dryer didn't have a little window to look out of.

Pisces: (Feb. 19–March 20)
After all these years, the world will finally acknowledge that it was you who turned The Beatles on to pot roast.

BADMINTON from page 139

amounts of blood. Passersby were amazed by the unusually large amounts of blood. Passersby were

Keep your vile hands off my filthy daughter.

amazed by the unusually large amounts of blood. Passersby were amazed by the unusually large amounts of blood. Passersby were amazed by the unusually large amounts of blood. Passersby were amazed by the unusually large amounts of blood. Passersby were amazed by the unusually large amounts of blood. Passersby were amazed by the unusually large amounts of blood. Passersby were

see BADMINTON page 147

NEWS

Rumsfeld Makes Jerk-Off Motions As Powell Speaks At Cabinet Meeting

see WASHINGTON page 3A

Parents Fighting About Who's Unhappier

see LOCAL page 7E

Novel Obviously Written At Coffee Shop

see ARTS page 2C

STATshot

A look at the numbers that shape your world.

What Do Our Framed Certificates Say?

1. Blockbuster Employee Of The Month, March 1991
2. Doctor Of Falafelology
3. Participant In Merit-Based Competition
4. Certified Professional Framer
5. I Ate The 72-Ounce Steak At Louie's
6. Deepest Breather

the ONION®

VOLUME 39 ISSUE 19 AMERICA'S FINEST NEWS SOURCE™ 22–28 MAY 2003

Above: Ridge introduces Rufus to the national press corps.

Department Of Homeland Security Deputizes Real Mean Dog

WASHINGTON, DC—Unveiling its newest weapon in the fight against terrorism Monday, the Department of Homeland Security announced the deputization of Rufus, a big ol' mongrel ornery enough to make al-Qaeda think twice about carrying out an attack against the U.S.

"Rufus here has one wild hair up his ass 'bout most everything," Homeland Security Director Tom Ridge said, as he introduced the dog, a Rottweiler-pitbull-Doberman mix, to the White House press corps. "But I got a feelin' Rufus has a 'specially wild hair to fetch him up some of them Ay-rab terrorist types."

"Don't you, boy?" added Ridge, yanking hard on Rufus' choke chain as the dog barked and jumped to nip at his face. "Huh? I said don't you, boy? Hell, yeah!"

Attorney General John Ashcroft applauded the announcement, praising Rufus for his commitment to fighting terror, as well as for his unswerving loyalty to Ridge.

"No one can touch Rufus 'ceptin' Tom," Ashcroft said. "He plumb loves Tom. And he don't always growl at me no more since I done okayed his

see DOG page 149

Report:

Majority Of Human Discourse Now Occurring In Online Product Reviews

DURHAM, NC—According to a Duke University study released Monday, a majority of human interaction and communication now occurs within the context of consumer product reviews on the Internet.

"In our increasingly soulless, mechanized world, it might seem that we're becoming more disconnected from those around us," said Duke sociology professor and study head Dr. Allan Piersall. "Well, the happy news is, people are talking to their fellow humans as much as ever. Only, they're most likely weighing in on the new Ferris polarized sunglasses from Eddie Bauer or expressing dismay over the lack of cleanliness at the Boca Raton Holiday Inn."

American Focus

From the tens of millions of consumer reviews posted on retail giants like Amazon.com to the more specialized message boards of Motorcycle.com and Macaddict.com, Piersall estimated that 80 percent of all human discourse now takes the form of product reviews on the web.

While some online reviewers give little more than basic pros-and-cons

see DISCOURSE page 149

'90s Punk Decries Punks Of Today

BERKELEY, CA—Nineties punk Drew Tolbert, 29, expressed scorn Monday for the punks of today, denouncing them as "phony poseurs unworthy of the word 'punk.'"

"These kids today have no idea what real punk is," said Tolbert, who called himself "Steve Spew" from 1992 until May 1999, when he was forced to revert to his real name to take a job at Roberto's Custom Auto Upholstery. "Those so-called punk bands they listen to today? Sum 41? Good Charlotte? The Ataris? They're not punk. Back in the day, man, we used to listen to the real deal: Rancid, The Offspring, NOFX, Green Day. Those guys were what true punk rock was all about. Today's stuff is just a pale, watered-down imitation. There's no comparison."

see PUNK page 148

Above: Tolbert, who flies the flag for classic '90s punk.

Executing SARS Spreaders In China

Last week, China threatened to execute individuals who knowingly spread the SARS virus. What do *you* think?

"Finally, they've hit on a workable method of population control."

Michael Newell
Systems Analyst

"We should let the World Health Organization do the executing. They never get to do the fun stuff."

Sam Kennert
Mechanic

"People with SARS should not be ostracized. Many people with SARS live happy, productive lives for three days before their lungs fall into their underpants."

Charles Barker
File Clerk

"We shouldn't be critical. It's an old Chinese custom to shoot people for no good reason."

Colleen Matthews
Teacher

"I've always said the Chinese don't know how to handle a crisis. Have you ever seen their fire drills?"

Angie Pulliam
Florist

"SARS has a 90 percent survival rate. That's a higher survival rate than the one for just living in China."

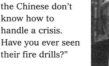

Martin Reed
Investment Banker

The *Times* Plagiarism Scandal

Last week, Jayson Blair resigned as a national reporter for *The New York Times* amid charges that he plagiarized and falsified stories. Among the misdeeds:

- Claimed to be phoning in story from Pakistan when actually at home masturbating to Spice Channel
- Lead paragraph in story about Beltway sniper lifted wholesale from back of Cheetos bag
- Wrote fabricated story about Iraq possessing massive stockpiles of weapons of mass destruction
- Greatly exaggerated homosexual affair between Secretary of Commerce Don Evans and Secretary of Transportation Norman Mineta
- Gave Mick Jagger solo album five stars
- Copied line, "Japan is a geographically diverse nation with a rich and colorful history" straight from *World Book Encyclopedia*
- Quotes attributed to Saddam Hussein actually from actress Victoria Principal
- Lied about rinsing out break-room coffee mug after using it

the ONION®
America's Finest News Source.™
Herman Ulysses Zweibel
Founder
T. Herman Zweibel
Publisher Emeritus
J. Phineas Zweibel
Publisher
Maxwell Prescott Zweibel
Editor-In-Chief

Let's Put The 'Ex' Back In Sex

By Neil Russo

Hey, Amy. How's the most beautiful ex-girlfriend in the world doing tonight? Wow, it's been a while, huh? Listen, don't hang up, okay? I know we haven't spoken in a while, but I was thinking the other day that maybe, even though we're not dating anymore, we could, you know, um, how do I say this? Let's put the "ex" back in sex.

Before you get all mad, let me clarify. I'm not talking about starting up a relationship again. I just mean, hey, we're both single, and, well, how about you and me take a roll in the sack again, for old time's sake? Because I've got a feeling that tonight is a night for the kind of love that only comes once in a lifetime, and then stops, but then starts up every now and again, on occasion, when one or both people are horny and lonely.

I admit, you haven't heard from me in quite some time. I guess I wasn't returning your phone calls because after all the heartache and emotional trauma of the whole breakup thing, I just needed some space or room to grow. Plus, I was kind of focusing my efforts on trying to score with a bunch of hot new chicks. Unfortunately, that plan didn't exactly work out the way I'd hoped.

Come on, don't be that way. It's exactly that sort of uptight, closed-minded attitude that led to our breakup in the first place.

Don't you want a little of the old ex-boyfriend magic back in your life just once? Or twice? Or even maybe more often than that, depending on how things are going with the new people we may or may not be dating? The kind of magic that only a night of intimacy and romance with somebody you used to be intimate and romantic with, but no longer are, can provide? Let me take you on a trip down memory-of-having-sex-with-me lane.

We both have needs. I don't know about you, but my needs are most definitely not being met these days. So what would be wrong with a little non-committal, post-relationship action on the side? I mean, in this crazy world, can't an ex-boyfriend and ex-girlfriend share a moment of tender, physical passion now and again?

Hey, we're both adults here. This is 2003. We're hip, liberated people. There's no need to hold back because of some outdated, prudish notions about what is or isn't appropriate. Why should we be so hung up on the distinction between a "current" and "ex" boyfriend? Life is too short for such technicalities. Do you see what I'm getting at, baby? I mean, *ex*-baby?

Look, the least you can do is show a little sympathy for someone you once cared deeply about. Would it kill you to show a little tenderness? Am I the only person in this ex-relationship that's ever heard of a mercy fuck?

Perhaps you don't realize just how sincere my intentions are. I really, truly, honestly want to get laid. Deeply. What about all the amazing, though admittedly over, times we shared? Doesn't that count for any-

How about you and me take a roll in the sack again, for old time's sake? I've got a feeling that tonight is a night for the kind of love that only comes once in a lifetime, and then stops, but then starts up every now and again, on occasion, when one or both people are horny and lonely.

thing? Do you really feel nothing? You should see me. I'm down on my knees here, begging for a second chance at love for one or two nights a week, at most, at least until one of us starts sleeping with somebody else.

You aren't seeing anybody, are you? Well, sure, I suppose that *is* none of my business, but I'd like to think that the bond we once shared means you can still confide in me and share your most intimate secrets. Like, for example, whether you're seeing somebody. Are you? Because if you are, that's totally cool with me. I'm capable of handling it in a mature fashion, and I see no reason why your new boyfriend situation should interfere with my attempts to beg you to have sex with me again.

Look in your heart. Somewhere deep down in there, beneath all the pain, resentment, and lingering anger you're still feeling over our breakup, isn't there still some tiny flame of passion flickering for the man you once loved and, more importantly, allowed to have sex with you? Isn't there still some tiny little part of you that wants that kind of passionate commitment? And, by "commitment," I mean "commitment to having sex with each other"? Please, Amy, let me into your life again, or at least into your bed for just one more night.

No? Okay, that's cool, I understand. If you ever change your mind, though, my offer stands. Ø

LOCAL

New Neighbor Tested With Beer

PESHTIGO, WI—Seeking to gauge the personality and character of new next-door neighbor Roger Lundback, Bob Iwanski surreptitiously subjected him to a beer test Monday.

"You can learn an awful lot about a fella by the way he drinks his beer," said Iwanski, a 16-year-resident of Maple Bluff Road. "And based on what I've seen from Roger, he's a pretty all-right guy."

Iwanski, 52, who administers beer tests to all new male arrivals to Maple Bluff Road, invited Lundback over to share a six-pack of Heineken. He used the seemingly innocuous, welcome-to-the-block gesture as a means of secretly gathering valuable information about the newcomer.

"On a first meeting, I always bring something neutral like Heineken in cans," Iwanski said.

"Roger not only accepted the offer to drink with me, but he held his own, drinking three of the six beers," Iwanski said. "He doesn't put his beer in a glass, so he's not some fancy wine-and-cheese guy, but he also says he's never shotgunned a beer in his life, so he's not a party hound. He still hasn't mentioned anything about having a favorite beer, which makes me suspect he's more of a hard-liquor kind of guy. Nothing wrong with that, though."

Iwanski said he plans his beer tests meticulously, leaving no detail left to chance.

"On a first meeting, I always bring something neutral like Heineken in cans," Iwanski said. "It's an import, so it says 'I care about beer,' but since it's in cans, it says 'I'm no snob.' If you bring anything too fancy or too cheap, it tips the study too far in one direction."

Iwanski said the test also gives him a sense of how the new neighbor will fit into the larger Maple Bluff Road beer-drinking community.

"We're a pretty tight unit, so how a new neighbor responds to an offer of beer goes a long way toward deciding whether he'll become a regular at Sunday football get-togethers," Iwanski said. "That's why I met Roger one-on-one instead of with Brad [Juergens], Ted [Tabor], and the rest of the gang. Having someone like Ted around could skew the subject's reactions, because he can be a little rough when he's been drinking all afternoon."

According to Iwanski, Lundback has proven he is not a beer snob and is willing to "kick back a few," but it remains to be seen whether he shares Iwanski's deep, abiding passion for beer.

"The other day, I happened to notice that Roger had a refrigerator in his garage—always a good sign," Iwanski said. "But when he opened it, I saw it was full of Bud Light. I figured he must be a namby-pamby light-beer kind of guy, but then he blew my theory clear out of the water when he told me the beer was left over from a bridal shower his wife had thrown. It was a relief, to be sure, but it still raised more questions than it answered."

Above: Iwanski awaits the arrival of Lundback (inset) for the beer test.

Determined to learn more about Lundback, Iwanski said he plans to test him in other beer-related situations, including Darts Night at T.J.'s Tavern and a backyard barbecue with the wives. If he passes muster, Iwanski will bring in neighbor Gary Pullman to administer the Guinness/Corona standardized test to answer any remaining questions about Lundback's psychological profile.

"Next time we get together, I may have to bring out the aged 40-year-old brandy or schnapps," Iwanski said. "Sometimes, the way a man carries himself outside of the beer circle tells you the most about the kind of beer drinker he is."

Iwanski said he hopes to conclude the beer test by the end of the month. He then plans to move into Phase Two of his neighbor-evaluation project, closely observing Lundback's reaction to such stimuli as bratwurst, pictures of lingerie models, and conversations about 1960s American muscle cars.

Phase Two is tentatively scheduled for June 3 at Gary's Bowl & Billiards. ⊘

NEWS IN BRIEF

Bird Has Big Plans For Cage

HENNIKER, NH—Charlie, a Henniker-area cockatiel, announced Tuesday that he has big plans for his new stainless-steel birdcage. "Let's see—I'm gonna hang the bell from the ceiling and put my seed trough on the right wall. And I'm finally gonna get one of those rolling perches, now that I have the room," Charlie said between gulps of sunflower seeds. "And once I put up that full-length mirror, it's really gonna open up this space." Charlie said he also plans to use some of his bird toys to form a partition in the middle of the cage, creating the illusion of two separate rooms.

Podiatrist A Jerk

HOFFMAN ESTATES, IL—Podiatrist Dr. Don Smithson is a "big jerk" who "talks down to you like you're an idiot," patient Greg Lindblad reported Tuesday. "Dr. Smithson totally scolded me for not cutting my toenails straight across—he says the ingrown toenail is my own fault," Lindblad said. "Pardon me, Dr. Smithson. My life should revolve around maintaining proper foot care. What a dick." Lindblad also claimed Smithson "completely chewed me out" for allowing his bunions to go untreated.

Man Adds A Few Personalized Tracks To Standard New-Girlfriend Mix CD

SPRINGFIELD, MO—Wanting to add something special for new love Danielle Welter, Andy Mansfield, 24, burned three personalized tracks onto his standard new-girlfriend mix CD Monday. "Danielle loves that No Doubt song 'Running,' so I threw that on there just for her," Mansfield said. "And she doesn't really like rap, which [previous girlfriend] Erica [Hollings] loved, so I took off [Salt-N-Pepa's] 'Whatta Man' and replaced it with two Aretha Franklin songs, because Danielle loves the oldies." Mansfield said he expects Welter to love the mix "even more than Erica did, maybe even as much as Christine."

Systems Administrator Would So Fuck New Trainee

TUCSON, AZ—Speaking in confidence to coworker Brian Panos, Barton Financial Group systems administrator Tim Kreutzer revealed Tuesday that, given the chance, he would "so fuck" new office trainee Lisa Hartig, 23. "Tim was staring at Lisa from across the office floor when he dropped the bombshell that he would so fuck her," Panos said. "Obviously, I was stunned. I mean, how often do you come across a balding 51-year-old tech professional who's willing to sleep with a nubile blonde? Wow."

Circus Runaway Not Looking Forward To Hometown Show

SACRAMENTO, CA—Michael MacAlester, who ran away from his native Sacramento at 16 to join the circus, is not looking forward to the Big Top Circus' show this Friday in his hometown. "The idea of getting the hell out of Sacramento and joining a traveling circus was really exciting, but I guess I should've thought to check the schedule," MacAlester, 18, a unicycling clown, said Monday. "I asked the ringmaster if I could possibly sit this one out, but he said no way." MacAlester said he plans to wear extra-heavy make-up in case his parents happen to be in attendance. ⊘

PUNK from page 145

Recalling the glory days of the ’90s, Tolbert waxed nostalgic for a few moments before condemning today’s punks.

“They can talk all they want about how much punk means to them, but the simple fact is, they weren’t there,” Tolbert said. “These kids today have no sense of history. They don’t know about Pennywise. They barely know about Epitaph Records. Most of them don’t even know about Green Day’s legendary appearance in ’94 at the L.A. Coliseum. It was a watershed, one-of-a-kind moment in the history of youth rebellion, and if you didn’t live through it, as I did, you’ll never get it, no matter how punk you pretend to be.”

Tolbert’s disdain for the current punks encompasses not only their

“They can talk all they want about how much punk means to them, but the simple fact is, they weren’t there,” Tolbert said. “These kids today have no sense of history. They don’t know about Pennywise. They barely know about Epitaph Records.”

musical tastes, but also their style of dress.

“Punk is more than just a Mohawk hairstyle,” Tolbert said. “For us back in the ’90s, punk was a *way of life*. I see these kids today hanging around Gilman Street in their leather jackets with their wallet chains, and I just want to say to them, ‘You think punk is a *costume*, man?’ Back in ’93, it was about so much more: It was a rebellion against outmoded belief systems. It was a cry of outrage against the repressive authority of the Clinton Administration.”

“I saw some kid wearing a Sex Pistols T-shirt the other day—he couldn’t have been more than 9 when the Pistols did their Filthy Lucre reunion tour,” Tolbert said. “I was like, ‘You can listen to the music, you can wear the T-shirt, but I was *there*.’ I had fifth-row seats at that goddamn stadium, man, right up front, close enough to see Johnny Rotten’s wrinkles. Did you see an original member of The Clash play during Big Audio Dynamite II’s last tour? Did you see two of the four original Ramones play at the KROQ Weenie Roast in ’95? You did not, but I did. I swear to God, they’re like a joke, these people.”

Above: Sum 41, a band Tolbert says “can’t hold a candle to the greats of eight, nine years ago.”

Tolbert, who dropped out of Berkeley Community College in 1993 to spend a year skateboarding and living off his parents, was once a major fixture of Berkeley’s punk-revival scene, although he still rejects that label.

“‘Punk revival’... what bullshit,” Tolbert said. “Anybody who says punk was ‘back’ in the ’90s doesn’t know what they’re talking about, because punk never went away. Sure, you didn’t hear about it as much in the mainstream corporate media, but punk was always around for the true believers like me and my friends.”

According to friends, the young Tolbert was a shy but well-respected member of his high school’s yearbook staff before adopting a punk-rock stance upon his enrollment at the community college. He later formed a

“Punk is more than just a Mohawk hairstyle,” Tolbert said. “For us back in the ’90s, punk was a *way of life*.”

band, Absence Of Dissent, but the band broke up before completing any recordings or playing any gigs.

“We could’ve been huge,” Tolbert said. “Bigger than New Bomb Turks, even. But all the greatest punk bands fell apart before their time. That’s what happened to Darby Crash of the Germs, and that’s what happened to us, except we didn’t die of drug overdoses, and we came along about 15 years later. But the pretty-boy pretend punks of 2003 could never understand that.”

“The thing I can’t stand is when they get all self-righteous and act like *I’m* the one who doesn’t ‘get it,’” Tolbert continued. “That attitude is totally contrary to the whole inclusive spirit of what punk is all about.”

Added Tolbert: “Don’t try to be something you’re not, man. That’s what I say.” Ø

CHEEK IMPLANT from page 137

amounts of blood. Passersby were amazed by the unusually large amounts of blood. Passersby were amazed by the unusually large amounts of blood. Passersby were amazed by the unusually large amounts of blood. Passersby were amazed by the unusually large amounts of blood. Passersby were amazed by the unusually large amounts of blood. Passersby were amazed by the unusually large amounts of blood. Passersby were amazed by the unusually large amounts of blood. Passersby were amazed by the unusually large amounts of blood. Passersby were amazed by the unusually large amounts of blood. Passersby were amazed by the unusually large amounts of blood. Passersby were amazed by the unusually large amounts of blood. Passersby were

I’m just as God, a poor diet, and a crippling lack of self-esteem made me.

amounts of blood. Passersby were amazed by the unusually large amounts of blood. Passersby were amazed by the unusually large amounts of blood. Passersby were amazed by the unusually large amounts of blood. Passersby were amazed by the unusually large amounts of blood. Passersby were amazed by the unusually large amounts of blood. Passersby were amazed by the unusually large amounts of blood. Passersby were amazed by the unusually large amounts of blood. Passersby were amazed by the unusually large amounts of blood. Passersby were amazed by the unusually large amounts of blood. Passersby were amazed by the unusually large amounts of blood. Passersby were amazed by the unusually large amounts of blood. Passersby were

see CHEEK IMPLANT page 155

DISCOURSE from page 145

of a product or a one- to five-star rating, many use the write-ups as a vital means of self-expression, providing in-depth anecdotes about their own experiences with a particular product, or even their autobiography. On Amazon.com, some reviewers create deeply personal Listmania! lists, such as "The Best Kung Fu Movies Ever" or "Things You Absolutely Need To Survive Working In A Cubicle."

"Through these product reviews, in which we fulfill our collective desire to guide our fellow humans to good purchasing decisions, a sense of community emerges," Piersall said. "But just as important, a sense of self emerges. By publicly

"Through these product reviews, in which we fulfill our collective desire to guide our fellow humans to good purchasing decisions, a sense of community emerges," Piersall said.

expressing our feelings about the Coleman Quickbed air mattress, we tell people not merely about this product, but about ourselves."

With reviews running the gamut from commentary on the Criterion Collection DVD of Fellini's *8 1/2* to the usefulness of a portable Weber propane gas grill versus the traditional full-size standup model, Piersall said that "once again, we are talking."

"Not only was I impressed by the large number of people expressing themselves through the written word, but I was amazed by the sophistication of the rhetoric," Piersall said. "In the same review, I saw examples of parallel construction, metaphor, and tautology, as well as standard debate devices like propositions of policy and use of evidence—all to support the argument that the Krups 872-42 Bravo Plus Espresso Maker is not worth the money."

Randy Apodaca, an Alameda, CA, assistant sales manager, recently logged onto Epinions.com to write a glowing review of the Sony SVR 2000 TiVo digital video recorder. To Piersall, more interesting than Apodaca's actual review is the fact that Apodaca had barely ever before expressed himself in a public forum.

"Though Apodaca wrote an article or two for his high-school newspaper in the late '70s, he all but dropped out of the national dialogue in the decades since," Piersall said. "Once, in 1986, he called in to a talk-radio show, but other than that, the world has had no way of knowing how Randy Apodaca felt on any issue. Until now."

Amanda Weis of Canton, OH, recently connected with a likeminded soul by reading reviews of the new Z.Z. Packer short-story collection on Barnes & Noble's web site.

"When dogoutback43@yahoo.com said *Drinking Coffee Elsewhere* was 'boring' and 'weird,' I could tell he wasn't my kind of person—unlike mrbingbing@juno.com," Weis said. "Mr. Bing Bing had all these great

"One of our basic human needs is to be heard," Piersall said. "It's hard to believe, but there was once a time when we were forced to seek out friends, family, and coworkers to fill this need. Today, things are much easier."

authors like Aleksandar Hemon on his list of faves, so I bought the book and some other stuff he suggested, too. I wonder if he's single."

Thanks to the online reviews, Piersall said he sees humankind moving in a positive direction.

"One of our basic human needs is to be heard," Piersall said. "It's hard to believe, but there was once a time when we were forced to seek out friends, family, and coworkers to fill this need. Today, things are much easier. We simply have to go to RateItAll.com." ⌀

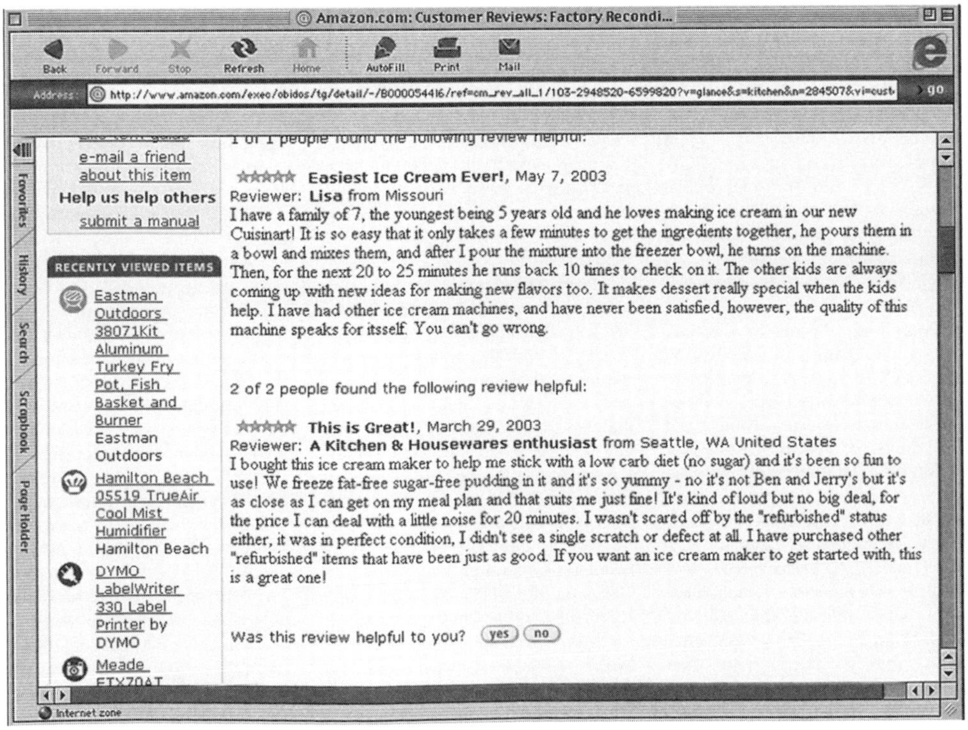

Above: Humans express themselves.

DOG from page 145

appointment and give him scraps of my beef jerky. But I sure as hell ain't goin' to try and pet him, on account of I need that hand to wipe my ass."

The primary role of Rufus—previously employed by a Georgetown-area Gas 'N' Go to intimidate drunken late-night patrons and would-be shoplifters—will be one of deterrence. Beginning June 1, the dog will be deployed to various U.S. bridges, national monuments, and other potential terror targets, where he will be chained to a pair of cinderblocks and instructed to bark, growl, and leap at potential terrorists—defined as individuals who come too close, make eye contact with him, or just don't smell right.

"The hijacker ain't been born that won't load up his overalls when ol' Rufus here up an' come at him," Secretary of Defense Donald Rumsfeld said. "And if'n they don't run, well, they gonna be explainin' to the Muslim St. Peter why they's got a hole in 'em big enough to throw an angry cat through."

"That ol' dog's so mean, he ain't done nothin' but eat nails and shit nickels ever since he was born," Ridge added, holding back Rufus as the animal lunged at the throat of CNN commen-

Rufus' appointment has caused a considerable stir on Capitol Hill.

tator and former Clinton press secretary Paul Begala. "Lookit him go! Ain't he a caution? Two hunnert pounds a mean in a 80-pound bag, I swear."

Rufus' appointment has caused a considerable stir on Capitol Hill.

"That thing almost bit my fingers clean off," said U.S. Sen. Russ Feingold (D-WI), who required rabies shots after offering Rufus one of his barbecued ribs in a gesture of bipartisan friendship. "It oughta be destroyed right quick-like. Or given overseas duty. This here's a civilized country."

Ridge, peering from beneath the bill of a "War On Terrorism" mesh trucker's cap, dismissed the complaint as "typical liberal hand-wringing."

"What, I ask you, do you expect?" Ridge said. "I trained Rufus up mean for deputyin' and catchin' the enemy. Done it right, by havin' a Secret Service boy rassle him up dressed in the sweaty old clothes of Guantanamo Bay prisoners every time I fed him. Which weren't any too often—we gotta keep him mad and hungry. Ain't my fault some Demmycrat sweat might smell just like the Taliban kind to Rufus."

Rufus is widely regarded as the meanest dog employed by the State Department since Bocephalus, a hard-on of a coon hound who was, by all accounts, crazier than possum fuck. Bocephalus made worldwide headlines in October 1979, when he attempted to tree the Ayatollah. ⌀

COMMUNITY VOICES

Yo, Don't Judge

By Herbert Kornfeld
Accounts-Receivable Supervisor

Y'all may not realize this, but tha Accountz Reeceevin' bruthahood be forced to live in two worlds: tha supafly world o' officin' an' tha bleak-ass world of all y'all amateurs. And it ain't easy. When punchout time roll around, there be a lot o' A.R. bruthahs who don't know what to do with theyselves. Sometimes, they go to Chiliz or Applebeez, but them places be full of playa-hatas who don't approve of tha reeceevin' lifestyle, and in no time, suckaz start flexin'.

'Bout a month ago, mah homes Petty Ka$h wuz in T.G.I. Fridayz, and some o' dem stripey-shirt muthafukkaz didn't like how he ordered a jalapeño-poppah appetizah 'steada a full entrée. They dragged his ass into tha kitchen, doused him with that teriyaki-lime-juice-mesquite-sauce shit all they food be cooked in, an' stabbed him wit' them wack pins an' buttons they wear on they suspendas. Then they threw him in tha Dumpsta outside. A month lata, Ka$h still tryin' to get that teriyaki-margarita-whateva-tha-fuck-it-is smell outta his Dockaz.

Shit's gotten so bad, some A.R. bruthahs don't even go out no more afta work. They just chill in they cribs wit' they bitchez an' shortiez, wishin' they could be out on tha street reeceevin'. Ever read in tha police blotta 'bout some A.R. bruthah gettin' arrested foe bustin' into his own place-a work aftahourz to do a li'l freestyle numba-krunchin'? Or jus' to dick aroun' on tha addin' machine a little, even if it just be to punch in 7734 40, which upside-down read "OH HELL"? Bruthahs jus' wanna keep they minds active, but in tha fucked-up non-officin' world, all tha 5-0 see is breakin' an' enterin'.

In spite o' all that bullshit, tha A.R. krew still be willin' to play by tha rulez o' tha non-reeceevin' world. We tip our waitressez, park our hoopties in designated spotz, an' sort our lightz an' darkz. An' if all y'all show tha proper respect, shit, we be known to tie our cardboard recyclables into bundlez.

But, dag, yo—y'all crossed tha line when y'all tried to force yo' lame-ass jury-duty shit on mah homie Sir Casio KL7000.

Last month, I was kickin' tha spreadsheetz in my dope cubicle when tha phone rang. It be Petty Ka$h. I'm thinkin', shit, where he gettin' his ass throwed outta now, Bombay Bicycle Club? Instead, Ka$h say Casio got this summons to appear down at tha county courthouse an' serve on some weak-ass jury.

"Ka$h, get tha posse together wit' a quickness," I say. "We gonna bum-rush tha courthouse an' bust our homie out."

A.R. bruthahs gots to contend wit' this jury-duty shit from time to time. And we ain't havin' it. We such stone-col' supastars in our respective

Yo, headz up, non-officin' muthafukkaz. Peep this: We know yo' world be bigger than ours, an' that y'all gots tha benjamins, tha muscle, an' tha sheer numbahz to do yo' biddin'. But we got tha brains an' tha cunning. An' if you try to push us, we push back.

officez, it be out o' tha question foe us to serve on a jury. Not only dat, Casio's fiscal year wuz set to end May 1, so it wuz muthafukkin' krunch time all around.

Time wuz runnin' out. Petty Ka$h called just afta lunch hour, which meant Casio mighta been picked foe juryin' already. I arrived at tha courthouse in tha Nite Rida 'round 1:20, an' a few minutes later, I see Petty Ka$h, Kount Von Numbakrunch, Air-GoNomic, and 3-Holepunch pull up in Ka$h's Tercel. Everybody come fully strapped, but I told 'em to leave they letta openers an' bindah clips in tha hoopty, lest they want tha courthouse metal detectaz to go apeshit.

See, I know dat courthouse up an' down from mah own run-ins wit' Tha Man. I go into tha trunk o' tha Nite Rida an' hauls out some leatha sportz jacketz an' baseball capz, an' tells everybody to put them on. Tha homiez start in to bitchin', but I say that if tha courthouse muscle see us in our officin' gear, they might get wise to our scheme. As anotha smoke-screen, I give 'em all some juror passes I sweet-talked from this courtroom stenographa I once balled.

"An' deep-six tha street verbals," I tell mah homies. "Talk like this: 'How do you do, I am an average citizen, and I like jury duty and other activities that take place outside offices.' I know it wack, but that be how these muthafukkaz talk."

Afta some tense momentz (tha guardz want to know why Ka$h stank of honey-mustard sauce), we made it inside an' split up to find Casio. I had tha mad stealth of a muthafukkin' jungle cat an' chameleon combined, stalkin' tha corridorz foe mah homie an' blendin' in wit' tha suckaz. It all paid off when I found Casio gettin' his drink on from a water fountain outside a courtroom on tha fourth flo'. He say somethin' about gettin' picked foe some civil case that settle outta court befoe tha trial can begin, but I ain't got time to listen. I get his ass downstairz to tha lobby, callin' Ka$h on his cell an' leavin' a coded message foe the krew to split tha courthouse, lest tha 5-0 be listenin' in. Wit' Numbakrunch an' 3-Holepunch distractin' tha pigz wit' questions 'bout where tha Soldiers An' Sailors' Memorial at, Casio an' me hustle tha fuck outta there an' into tha Nite Rida.

It wuz mad dangerous foe Casio to return to his office. That's tha first place tha 5-0 woulda looked, no diggity. So I takes him to a safehouse tha A.R. posse keep foe when one-a our own gots to lay low. Casio stay there foe almost three weekz, doin' all of his end-o'-fiscal-year bidness from undaground. He use a network o' couriers to relay his shit to his office by foot every night, cuz e-mail can be traced. An' I ain't tellin' none o' y'all where tha safehouse at, 'cause when you reeceeve accountz foe a livin', tha first thang you learn is TRUST NO ONE.

Yo, headz up, non-officin' muthafukkaz. Peep this: We know yo' world be bigger than ours, an' that y'all gots tha benjamins, tha muscle, an' tha sheer numbahz to do yo' biddin'. But we got tha brains an' tha cunning. An' if you try to push us, we push back. We push playa-hatas back to tha muthafukkin' Stone Age, know what I'm sayin'? An' we wouldn't trade tha 24-7 Reeceevin' Life foe yo' gardenin' or yo' bowlin' league or yo' microwave-cookery classes or whatever weak shit all y'all do in yo' spare time. In tha A.R. World, ain't no such thing as spare time. Tha only spare time we eva gonna have be in tha grave. An' thass all good wit' us, 'cause we be straight-bangin' hardcore badasses to tha end. H-Dog OUT. ø

HOROSCOPES

Your Horoscope

By Lloyd Schumner Sr.
Retired Machinist and
A.A.P.B.-Certified Astrologer

Aries: (March 21–April 19)
Smuggling yourself across the border hidden in a truckload of radishes would have worked, had you been able to control your insatiable appetite for radishes.

Taurus: (April 20–May 20)
If there's one thing you should try to learn from next week's events, it's the precise melting point of aluminum.

Gemini: (May 21–June 21)
While it's true you're not a salmon, there's really no reason you shouldn't at least try swimming upriver to spawn.

Cancer: (June 22–July 22)
Between the drug money, the blood money, and the hush money, it's a wonder you have anything left to spend on sex.

Leo: (July 23–Aug. 22)
Once again, it's a rotten week for romance in the office, which is too bad, as you are self-employed and work from home.

Virgo: (Aug. 23–Sept. 22)
A last-minute pardon from the governor will spare your life, strangely punctuating what, up until then, had been an uneventful night of TV.

Libra: (Sept. 23–Oct. 23)
Never in your wildest notary-public dreams did you think the job would involve so little wanton sexuality.

Scorpio: (Oct. 24–Nov. 21)
This week proves the adage that the race does not always go to the swift, but to the promoter and concession holder.

Sagittarius: (Nov. 22–Dec. 21)
You're not the type of person who looks for a certain physical type in a mate, mostly because you have a seven-person staff to do that for you.

Capricorn: (Dec. 22–Jan. 19)
You tell everyone that your belief in Jesus helped you win your long battle with alcoholism, but, really, the whole thing only lasted three days.

Aquarius: (Jan. 20–Feb. 18)
You know they've had their setbacks, but you're starting to wonder if the members of Queen are ever going to make good on their promise to rock you.

Pisces: (Feb. 19–March 20)
You've never set yourself up as any kind of role model, which is a good thing for all those kids who want to be popular and interesting.

NEWS

Independent-Minded Cat Shits Outside The Box

see PETS page 14C

McCain Gives Up JCPenney Catalog-Modeling Job

see WASHINGTON page 7B

Man Puts Philandering Days Ahead Of Him

see LOCAL page 2E

STATshot

A look at the numbers that shape your world.

Why Are We Moving To Austin?

1. Other guys in band wanted to
2. Hoping to land part in *Slacker 2: The Next Generation*
3. Sick of Chapel Hill
4. Heard great things about the fish tacos
5. Didgeridoo teacher moved there
6. Fake ID only works at Emo's
7. Amanda

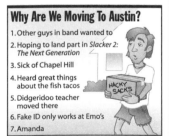

0 74470 94595 6 00

THE ONION • $2.00 US • $3.00 CAN

the ONION®

VOLUME 39 ISSUE 20 AMERICA'S FINEST NEWS SOURCE™ 29 MAY–4 JUNE 2003

Terrifying Bill Passed During NBA Playoffs

WASHINGTON, DC—With the nation safely distracted by the NBA playoffs, Congress passed the terrifying Citizenship Redefinition And Income-Based Relocation Act of 2003 with little opposition Monday.

"This piece of legislation is essential, both for more efficient implementation of the New American Ideal and to give law enforcement the broad discretionary powers necessary to enforce certain vital civil and behavioral mandates," said U.S. Sen. Lamar Alexander (R-TN), addressing an empty press room Sunday, midway through

see BILL page 154

Above: Dallas Mavericks fans cheer on their team while Senate Majority Leader Bill Frist (left) announced the passage of the terrifying new law.

Above: The oblivious Rolen (left) and his Pillar Of Salt bandmates.

Bassist Unaware Rock Band Christian

ORLANDO, FL—Brad Rolen, the new bassist for Pillar Of Salt, remains oblivious to the fact that he is in a Christian rock band, sources reported Tuesday.

"Pillar's great," said Rolen, 22, who is unaware of his bandmates' devotion to Jesus Christ, despite playing on such songs as "Wade In The Water," "Eternal Life," and "Kiss Of The Betrayer." "We rock really heavy and hard, but we've got a positivity that you don't see in too many bands these days. I've only been with these guys for three months, but I feel like it's the perfect fit for me."

Rolen, who joined the Orlando-based band in March after responding to a "bassist wanted" ad in a local newspaper, said he was attracted to Pillar Of Salt for its music, which he calls "really intense and powerful," as well as its impressive stage show.

"I was between bands after Junkhorse broke

see BASSIST page 155

Casino Has Great Night

ATLANTIC CITY, NJ—A beaming Donald Brant, general manager of Bally's Atlantic City, reported that the casino had "an unbelievable night" Monday, cleaning up at the blackjack table, on the slot machines, and elsewhere.

"Man, we were on fire all night," Brant said. "It seemed like every time a casino patron pulled that slots lever, it came up a loser. Whenever somebody told the blackjack dealer to hit on 12, they drew a 10. We could do no wrong."

By the end of the night, the casino walked away a major winner, up $515,274.

"I had a sense that we were doing pretty well," Brant said. "So I checked around with the pit bosses, and it turned out that nearly all the dealers and croupiers were way, way ahead. It was amazing. A night like that only comes along five, six times a week, tops."

While most players are content to focus on one or two games, the casino participated in every available coin-operated machine and table game, including roulette, blackjack, craps, Spanish 21, *pai gow*, baccarat, and Let It Ride.

"We've got a system," Brant said. "Our strategy is to bet against all the customers who come in here.

see CASINO page 155

Above: A Bally's blackjack dealer shows off a tiny portion of the casino's winnings.

The Spam Problem

Congress is exploring ways to combat the problem of "spam," the wave of junk e-mail that has clogged e-mail systems and cost U.S. businesses billions. What do *you* think?

Gene Kelso
Office Manager

"Thank goodness Congress is going to do something about this problem. This should all be cleared up in, like, three weeks."

Andrew Reed
Forklift Operator

"Gee, you make one little online inquiry into dripping wet teen pussies getting pounded by 12-inch horse cocks, and you're swamped for the rest of your life."

Patti Robles
Art Director

"Every day, I get these annoying spams that are nothing but cookie recipes and forwarded articles about the benefits of Vitamin C and photos of cats. Wait—those are from my mom."

Alfred Mugabe
Businessman

"MY NAME IS ALFRED MUGABE. I KNOW OF 10 MILLIONS U.S. DOLLARS IN A NIGERIAN BANK AND MUST FIND AN ACCOUNT INTO WHICH TO TRANSFER THE MONIES."

Marcia Haines
Real-Estate Broker

"If not for spam, I never would have met my boyfriend. His name is 8g391b66t274@prizeclaimcenter.com."

Chris Kingery
Systems Analyst

"Even more disturbing than this never-ending torrent of junk e-mail is the fact that, apparently, they must actually work once in a while."

The Bush Tax-Cut Plan

President Bush is preparing to sign a $350 billion tax-cut package. What are some of the plan's specifics?

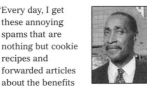

- Yachts named after children may be claimed as dependents
- Eliminates sales tax on purchases of $1 million or more
- Offers tax cuts for anyone who can prove they don't really need them
- Provides high-percentage tax break to owners of top hats and diamond stick pins
- Cuts in social services compensated for with extra $12 at end of year
- Individual will be exempted from paying income taxes for one year if he/she can solve a difficult riddle
- Guaranteed balloons for children of individuals making less than $26,000
- Ensures economic well-being of all Americans, from billionaires to multimillionaires to plain old millionaires

the ONION®
America's Finest News Source.™

Herman Ulysses Zweibel
Founder

T. Herman Zweibel
Publisher Emeritus
J. Phineas Zweibel
Publisher
Maxwell Prescott Zweibel
Editor-In-Chief

Sometimes It's Not Easy Being The Life Of The Orgy

By Hank Wetzel

Do you know me? Well, if you've been to an orgy in the greater Cincinnati area in the past 17 years, you've probably seen me (or at least part of me). My name is Hank Wetzel, and I am the king of the Cincinnati group-sex scene. You may have heard a story or two—and believe me, there are hundreds—about my legendary carnal exploits. Yet as renowned as I am, and as much fun as I've had, few people realize that it's not easy being the life of the orgy.

Anytime four or more people decide to get naked together in Cincinnati, someone inevitably says, "We need Hank. Hank should be here." Why? Because they know that once I get there, I'm going to blow the roof off the joint. Everybody who likes to swap, group-grope, or rut around on protective plastic sheets is sure to light up at the mention of my name. But do any of them know the *real* me? I'm not so sure.

They see my mastery of countless freaky positions, my vast collection of latex outfits, and my skillful use of the Polynesian fuck-swing, and they think they know Hank. Well, they don't know Hank. They're too distracted by my way with writhing piles of flesh to see the sadness beneath all the sucking and fucking.

It's not that I don't enjoy what I do. The daisy chains, the S&M dungeon parties, and the round-robin clusterfucks are still fun, but the pressure to always be "on" can be exhausting. Remember: There's a person with hopes and dreams behind that nine-and-a-half-inch cock.

People should know that when I'm alone or out of my group-sex circle, I'm basically a shy, simple guy. It's only when I pick up the scent of K-Y that I transform from Hank the Coca-Cola bottling-plant supervisor to Hank the Fuck Machine.

Sometimes, I think this is slowly killing me.

It's harder than you'd think to keep up the positive orgy attitude. If I don't meet and exceed someone's expectations, I'm no longer the top fuck dog in town. As great a group lover as I am, that kind of reputation can be hard to live up to. Heavy is the head that wears the crown.

You may be wondering why I do it. Why do I pleasure four people at once when two would suffice? Why do I bring my partners to such heated climaxes that they unleash a symphony of frenzied shrieks? And why do I always have to be the last one standing at the orgy, still humping away while the others are collapsed in post-coital bliss? I used to think it was just because I like getting people off. Now I know the truth: that being the life of the orgy is all I have.

I can't just lay back and let a girl blow me on a couch like everyone else. I have to put on a whole sex show, to be the center of a whole crowd, whether I'm in the mood or not.

I know I won't be able to keep this up forever. Eventually, a younger, better-looking, more flexible young buck is going to come along with a bigger dick and more tricks, and I'll be brushed off to the side room. Either that, or I'm simply going to lose my edge. I've seen it happen. I've seen

They know that once I get there, I'm going to blow the roof off the joint. Everybody who likes to swap, group-grope, or rut around on protective plastic sheets is sure to light up at the mention of my name. But do any of them know the *real* me? I'm not so sure.

people who've slowly lost it. Like Clara Mascara. Antonio. Dirty Ben. I don't want to go out like that. I don't want people to whisper, "What happened to Hank? He used to fuck like a champ."

If I have to leave the scene, I want to go out on top like my mentor, Frank Fourteen-Inch. Frank hung up his anal beads in his absolute prime, and people still talk about him like he could fuck no wrong. That's the way to go.

I'll never forget the last thing Frank told me just before he walked away from the game. He said, "If you want to make people fuck like there's no tomorrow, you must remember the pain of yesterday."

Back then, I didn't understand what he meant. I do now. I've come to realize that even when you're face-deep in hair pie while simultaneously coating someone else's belly with your steamy man-butter, being Orgy King can be awful lonely. ⌀

LOCAL

World-Weary Garbage Man No Longer Shocked By Things People Throw Out

TULSA, OK—After years of being appalled by the perfectly good items discarded by Tulsa residents, garbage collector Matt Ciszek, 34, reported Monday that he is "no longer shocked by anything."

"Used to be, I'd come across a new breadmaker still in the box, and I'd be floored that someone could be so wasteful," Ciszek told reporters Tuesday. "Now, I don't even flinch. I guess I'm just old."

Ciszek, who has worked for the Tulsa Department of Sanitation for nine years, said he has "seen it all in my time."

"You wouldn't believe the things I've hauled off," Ciszek said. "Fully functional air conditioners, entire record collections, VCRs, unopened boxes of cereal and canned goods, like-new chairs, desks with barely a scratch, stereo components, computers—you name it. I don't know how many pairs of shoes still in the box, never been worn, I've tossed in the back of the truck. I must have junked 50 miles of extension cords, and I'm guessing 95 percent of those still worked."

Above: The jaded, dispirited Ciszek.

"Yes, in the beginning, I was stunned," said Ciszek, staring off into the distance. "But now, well, I'm numb to it. It's all just another load to toss in the back."

According to his wife, in the early days, Ciszek would come home fuming about the waste he witnessed on his run.

"Matt used to get so worked up," said Joan Ciszek, 34. "He'd say, 'You won't believe what I found today—an entire box of tools, with an electric drill and everything. Must've been $800 worth of stuff.' Nowadays, he doesn't even talk about work."

Even though the Department of Sanitation prohibits garbage collectors from taking discarded items for themselves, Ciszek said he used to pocket the occasional item.

"How could I not bend the rules a little?" Ciszek said. "It would've been a sin to let that 20-gallon aquarium tank go to the dump."

Years later, however, Ciszek rarely bothers bringing items home.

"There's still great stuff out there," Ciszek said. "I guess I just don't have the motivation to do it anymore. I've become jaded. If some guy is going to throw away an entire box of plastic hangers, only to buy a whole new batch of hangers as soon as he moves into his new place, who am I to stop him? I'm just one garbage man."

Ciszek estimated that it was about five years ago that he "stopped noticing."

"My job is to get the trash from people's homes to the dump," Ciszek said. "I can't get my job done if I'm always keeping one eye out for the good stuff. Besides, it's too painful to see a perfectly good set of wheel covers crushed right in front of my eyes."

As the years roll by, the waste is only getting worse, Ciszek said.

"Things I used to see only occasionally have now become the norm," he said. "Throwing the lights out because you're too damn lazy to take them off the Christmas tree, vases with the withered flowers, halogen lamps in need of a bulb—it's all common. See what I'm saying? This is why I had to stop caring." ⊘

"Matt used to get so worked up," said Joan Ciszek, 34. "He'd say, 'You won't believe what I found today—an entire box of tools, with an electric drill and everything. Must've been $800 worth of stuff.' Nowadays, he doesn't even talk about work."

NEWS IN BRIEF

Condoleezza Rice's Lunch Missing

WASHINGTON, DC—National Security Advisor Condoleezza Rice announced Tuesday that she is "extremely distressed" that her lunch is missing from the White House break-room refrigerator. "I'm not going to ask twice: Who ate my turkey-and-avocado sandwich?" Rice asked Cabinet members. "My name was written right on it—'C. Rice' in thick, red magic marker, so don't tell me it was an accident." Rice vowed that she will make whoever ate the sandwich buy her a whole new lunch.

Wolf Pack Fails To Raise Orphaned Infant

GRAND MARAIS, MN—A pack of timberwolves failed to adopt and raise a human infant abandoned in Pat Bayle State Forest, local rangers reported Monday. "We found the baby starving and near-death in a part of the park with a substantial wolf population," ranger Warren Olafson said. "You'd think one of the wolves would lovingly pick up the child by the nape of the neck and bring it back to the woods to raise it like one of her own, but I guess it just didn't happen that way." Any parents missing an infant are advised to check near the cluster of downed maples midway up the eastern canoe portage.

Housekeeper Too Busy To Be Sassy

HIGHLAND PARK, IL—Much to the chagrin of the Whitford family, housekeeper Maria Ortega, 42, is too busy cleaning their mansion to deliver any sassy wisecracks. "It's such a pity, really," said head-of-the-household Judge John Whitford on Tuesday. "Maria spends so much time cooking meals, vacuuming and dusting our 40 rooms, washing the windows, doing the laundry, making the beds, and hauling out the trash, she never delights us with any snappy, smart-alecky rejoinders like that Florence on *The Jeffersons*." Whitford added that he can't understand why Ortega doesn't have time to come up with one-liners during her daily two-hour bus ride to work.

Magical Gallery Transforms Dull Objects Into Art

NEW YORK—A magical New York art gallery has the power to turn dull, everyday items into brilliant works of art, sources reported Monday. "Seth Clayton's devastating *Untitled No. 7* captures the despair of urban ennui in a way that's post-ironic yet somehow pre-pomo," said David E. Sherry, owner of the David E. Sherry Gallery, while admiring a rusty bucket and tattered boot lying on the gallery floor. "Its eloquence is truly heartbreaking."

Candy Purchase Puts Yet More Money In Raisinets' Bloated Coffers

GLENDALE, CA—The already overflowing coffers of Nestlé subsidiary Raisinets were further fattened Monday, when Atlanta resident Jonathan Graber, 11, purchased a bag of the candy at a local convenience store. "Ah, *very* good... that's another 75 cents for us," said Raisinets president William Koenig, as he observed the Graber purchase on closed-circuit television at the company's Glendale headquarters. "With every bag of our delicious chocolate-covered raisin treats that they buy, we only grow more powerful." Koenig then opened a bag of Raisinets and tossed a handful into the air, laughing maniacally. ⊘

BILL from page 151

game four of the NBA Eastern Conference finals. "We are confident that Americans will embrace this law, should they eventually realize it has been passed."

H.R. 2395 was introduced to Congress on May 15 during the fourth quarter of the San Antonio Spurs' 110-82 victory over the defending-champion Los Angeles Lakers in the deciding game of the Western Conference semifinals.

Andy Guthridge of Savannah, GA, is among the estimated 240 million Americans unaware of the sweeping package of civil-liberties curtailments, voting-privilege re-qualifications, and mandatory relocation of the working poor to the Dakotas.

"Man, I was so glad to see the Lakers finally get knocked off," said Guthridge, who was glued to TNT while the bill's passage aired on C-SPAN. "Shaq and Kobe and the rest of those dicks have had it coming for a long time."

In addition to allocating $14 billion for "development of surveillance technologies and domestic weaponry," the bill expands the criminal code to include any acts determined to be "a compromise of national interests" by the Justice Department or other federal authorities. U.S. Sen. Joe Biden (D-DE) also tacked on a rider late in the approval process that adds situational provisions to the First Amendment and effectively does away with the Fifth.

The controversial additions might have threatened the law's passage, had they not been made during the closing minutes of the Dallas Mavericks' thrilling 112-99 come-from-behind win over the Sacramento Kings in game seven of their series.

"The First Amendment will still protect almost all of the forms of expression that it always has," said Biden, who will assume his new duties as Commandant Of The Greater West on June 1.

"The First Amendment will still protect almost all of the forms of expression that it always has," said Biden, who will assume his new duties as Commandant Of The Greater West on June 1. "The average patriotic American won't even notice the difference. How about that Jason Kidd? Right now, I'd say he's the best point guard in the East, if not the entire NBA."

Americans' reactions to the new laws were mixed.

"I know everyone's talking about the Nets these days, but the Mavs are still the team to beat," said Plano, TX, resident Doug Abbott, whose vegetable-wholesaling business is slated to be annexed by the newly created Federal Reacquisition Corps. "I'm sorry, but you're not winning an NBA championship with Jason Collins at center. They'll easily get past the Pistons, but come Finals time, [Dirk] Nowitzki's gonna eat him alive."

"No way—this is the Nets' year," said James Cimini of Hackensack, NJ. "With the Lakers out of the picture, it's New Jersey's time to shine. Whether it's the Spurs or the Mavs, neither team can contain K-Mart, Mr. Kenyon Martin. This postseason, he's moved up from being merely a very good forward to one of the league's elite players."

In a nationally televised address before an estimated audience of 150, President Bush praised the Citizenship Redefinition And Income-Based Relocation Act.

"The swift passage of this very important law proves what I have always believed: that government works best when spared the constant carping and criticism of naysayers," Bush said. "I am proud of all the senators, representatives, regional overseers, and metropolitan sub-commanders who worked so hard to make this law a reality. Almost as proud as San Antonio is of its Spurs." ⌀

GRENADINE from page 150

amounts of blood. Passersby were amazed by the unusually large amounts of blood. Passersby were amazed by the unusually large amounts of blood. Passersby were amazed by the unusually large amounts of blood. Passersby were

The amazing EduSpikes ensure that comprehension seeps through the learn holes!

amazed by the unusually large amounts of blood. Passersby were amazed by the unusually large amounts of blood. Passersby were amazed by the unusually large amounts of blood. Passersby were amazed by the unusually large amounts of blood. Passersby were amazed by the unusually large amounts of blood. Passersby were amazed by the unusually large amounts of blood. Passersby were amazed by the unusually large amounts of blood. Passersby were amazed by the unusually large amounts of blood. Passersby were amazed by the unusually large amounts of blood. Passersby were amazed by the unusually large

see GRENADINE page 157

the ONION presents:

Fire Safety And Prevention Tips

Knowing what to do in case of fire can be the difference between life and death. Here are some helpful fire safety and prevention tips:

- If your smoke detector is beeping periodically, replace the batteries as soon as you get around to it.
- Be sure to keep your gasoline-soaked rags nailed to a wall, safely out of children's reach.
- There are two kinds of fire that should never be put out with water. I'm pretty sure one of them is a grease fire.
- When making your family's fire-evacuation plan, just remember "LISGM9MN": **L**eave the house **I**mmediately, **S**tay low to the **G**round, **M**eet outside, and call **9**11 fro**M** a **N**eighbor's house.
- Assist firefighters racing to the scene of a blaze by lighting a series of smaller "marker fires" along their path.
- If you have children, warn them never to play with matches, because a fire could break out and Sparky The Big Friendly Fire Dog would have to visit the house in his big red truck and give them rides while the firemen put out the fire with water hoses.
- Beware the lustful fires that burn in a librarian's heart. They can rage beyond all control.
- Before using a fire extinguisher to put out a rapidly spreading fire, be sure to thoroughly read the instructions printed on the side, marking key information with a highlighter pen.
- Space heaters are a serious fire hazard and should never be used. (This tip courtesy of your mother.)
- Remember: The old adage "Fight fire with fire" does not apply to non-metaphorical fires.
- Many schools give out bright, reflective stickers for children's bedroom windows to alert firefighters. Buy as many of these stickers as you can from neighborhood schoolchildren for your own window.
- Every month, check to see that smoke detectors are working by leaving a Tombstone frozen pizza in the oven for 300 minutes.
- Do not try to outrun fire, because it's much too fast. Wait, no, that's bears.
- Firefighters are heroes who perform a vital community service. Stay out of their way when they're working and offer yourself to them sexually when they're not.

BASSIST from page 151

up," Rolen said. "I went to check them out live and was just blown away. They had this awesome Black Sabbath-type stage set, with all these crucifixes and candles everywhere. Then, during [the song] 'False Idol,' a gold cow rose from the stage and [lead singer and songwriter] Jack [Rhineman] beat the shit out of it with his guitar. I thought, man, these guys put on a kick-ass show."

Rolen was also wowed by the range of Rhineman's music.

"Jack's amazing," Rolen said. "He writes all these super-heavy, Metallica-influenced tunes like 'My Master' and 'Blood Of My Father,' but then he'll turn around and write a killer love song like 'Thank You (For Saving Me).'"

"Actually, Jack writes a lot of songs

"A lot of hot chicks are really into Pillar Of Salt," Rolen said. "After our first few shows, I thought I'd be getting more trim than a barbershop floor, but it hasn't worked out that way. Whenever I ask them to come back to the bus with me, they say, 'I can't do that—that's not right.'"

about chicks," Rolen continued. "'Your Love,' 'When You Return,' 'I Confess'... I don't know if they're all about the same girl or lots of different ones, but one thing's for sure: Jack loves the pussy."

Rolen said he is awed by his new bandmates' encyclopedic knowledge of heavy metal and hard rock.

"At the audition, [drummer] Greg [Roberts] said Pillar Of Salt was going for a Believer-meets-Living Sacrifice sound," Rolen said. "I didn't know jack about either of those bands, but I knew I could play bass like a motherfucker, and that's what got me the gig. Afterwards, I asked Greg what Living Sacrifice sounded like, and at the first practice, he gave me a tape. It's not Slayer, but it rocks. He's given me some other stuff by Whitecross, Third Day, and Stigmata. I've always prided myself on knowing metal, but these guys put me to shame. They must really have their ears to the ground to know all this music I've never heard before."

Because Rhineman and Roberts are both in what they call "a committed relationship with someone very special," Rolen has found himself to be the only member of Pillar Of Salt open to

Above: A copy of the band's upcoming CD.

"hot groupie action." But despite having the band's female fans all to himself, Rolen has had little success.

"A lot of hot chicks are really into Pillar Of Salt," Rolen said. "After our first few shows, I thought I'd be getting more trim than a barbershop floor, but it hasn't worked out that way. Whenever I ask them to come back to the bus with me, they say, 'I can't do that—that's not right.' I'm like, 'Come on, this is rock 'n' roll.'"

Though he said he loves playing with Pillar Of Salt, Rolen conceded that the relationship has not been without its moments of tension. He recently became upset with his bandmates over their unwillingness to play concerts on Sundays.

"We got an offer to play at the weekly Sunday Metal Spotlight down in Tampa, which would expose us to a whole new audience," Rolen said. "The guys said playing the Spotlight wasn't an option because Sunday was their 'day of rest.' Hey, I like kicking back and decompressing on Sundays, too, but we're a young band trying to establish ourselves. These guys need to get their priorities straight if they're serious about making it."

Pillar Of Salt is currently preparing to embark on a U.S. tour in support of its debut album, *Sanctified*, to be released June 10 on the band's own Witness Records label. ⌀

CASINO from page 151

Then we spread our bets around to each and every table and machine in the casino and keep at it for the long haul. We were down about $200 at one of the roulette tables, but were up on everything else, so we came out pretty much ahead. Actually, more than half a million ahead."

Bally's even fared well at the slot machines, an area that traditionally yields the lowest rate of success.

"You know how they say your worst odds are on the slots?" Brant said. "Well, we made over $33,000 in slots last night. Can you believe it? We were unstoppable."

Brant attributed his casino's impressive showing to a combination of luck and old-fashioned horse sense.

"We try not to play stupid," Brant said. "We never gamble more than we can afford to lose. And we try to never lose our heads. We leave that to the customers. We set aside a certain amount to gamble—that's our kitty—and if we double our money, we only play with our winnings after that. Right now, the kitty stands at around $176,500,000."

Bally's is in the midst of an impressive winning streak, coming out ahead an astonishing 6,753 nights in a row.

"This is quite a tear we're on," Brant

"We try to never lose our heads," Brant said. "We set aside a certain amount to gamble—that's our kitty—and if we double our money, we only play with our winnings after that. Right now, the kitty stands at around $176,500,000."

said. "It's best if you go in with the attitude that you're just there to have fun and not to win big. That said, it's always a lot more fun when you're winning. And, baby, did we win [Monday] night!"

According to John Patrick, author of *So You Want To Be A Gambler?*, streaks like Bally's are uncommon.

"In my years as a professional gambler, I've had my share of great nights," Patrick said. "However, I've never been on a roll like the one Bally's is on. But then, with a guaranteed 52 percent success rate, it's unlikely that a casino would ever come out behind in an evening. If that were the case, casinos wouldn't exist as profitable entities."

In spite of its huge winnings, Bally's did not indulge in the traditional amenities offered to big winners, such as a free night's stay in the hotel or meal vouchers. Instead, the crew of the all-night casino changed over to the next shift without fanfare.

"Yeah, I suppose we could have partied all night with champagne, a penthouse suite, and all the rest, but we had a casino to run," Brant said. "The thing a lot of people don't realize about successful gamblers is that it's hard work making outrageous sums of money." ⌀

COMMUNITY VOICES

I Am Proud To Serve My Country Beer

By Duane Kenniff

Our country has witnessed its fair share of trials and tribulations lately. We have endured wars in Afghanistan and Iraq. We have lived under the near-constant threat of terrorist attack at home. Many young Americans have heard the call to serve and, stirred by love of country and a deep sense of patriotic duty, they have responded. Some have served in the Army, others in the Marines. As for myself, I have served Coors Light.

I am proud to serve my country beer.

Our nation nobly faces any challenge with chins out and backs straight. We don't back down, no matter how daunting the task before us. For this reason alone, I serve pitcher after pitcher of beer at P.J.'s Pub, cooling the throats and fevered minds of a nation bearing the heavy burden of adversity.

My family has a long tradition of service to this country. At the height of the Great Depression, my great-grandfather served bathtub gin in a Chicago speakeasy. During WWII, my grandfather served beer at a Coney Island snack bar. During Vietnam, my

Our nation nobly faces any challenge with chins out and backs straight. We don't back down, no matter how daunting the task before us. For this reason alone, I serve pitcher after pitcher of beer at P.J.'s Pub, cooling the throats and fevered minds of a nation bearing the heavy burden of adversity.

father pretended he was gay so he could stay in the States and serve beer to a nation torn in two by an unpopular war. And now it's my turn. When history called, I did not turn a deaf ear. I enlisted at my local tavern and began the task of serving beer to my fellow Americans.

It's not easy. Sometimes, your back aches from hauling kegs up from the basement cooler. Other times, you have to deal with people who are

My family has a long tradition of service to this country. At the height of the Great Depression, my great-grandfather served bathtub gin in a Chicago speakeasy. During WWII, my grandfather served beer at a Coney Island snack bar. And now it's my turn. When history called, I did not turn a deaf ear.

drunk, surly, or violent. Then there are the times when you're ready to throw in the bar rag because of that jackass at the corner table who comes in every night and never tips you. It's times like these that I look at the red, white, and blue of the Pabst Blue Ribbon can, and a feeling of patriotism wells up in my breast. I know that duty calls, and I must soldier on.

We live in troubled times. People are confused and anxious—and understandably so. These are the days that, for better or worse, will define our generation. Will we be remembered as cowards who tucked our tails between our legs and ran home sober? Or will we enter the pantheon of heroes, making our way to the local tavern so we can show our enemies that we will not be denied in our thirst for victory and beer? For me, the answer is obvious. I will extend my hands to one and all, each fist grasping a tall, frosty mug of ice-cold beer.

If you want a beer, stand up and be heard over the din of loud conversations and noisy jukeboxes. I, for one, will step to the front of the line and proudly serve all those who ask, provided they have ID. Rich or poor, black or white, hearty lager drinkers or lite-beer tipplers, they are all Americans, and they all want beer. Some may shy away from the call to serve, but this proud citizen will never dodge the Miller Genuine Draft. ⌀

HOROSCOPES

Your Horoscope

By Lloyd Schumner Sr.
Retired Machinist and
A.A.P.B.-Certified Astrologer

Aries: (March 21–April 19)
Your colleagues will begin referring to you as the greatest mind they've ever encountered, in much the same way people call the fat guy Tiny.

Taurus: (April 20–May 20)
Your problem isn't merely that you love your money more than you love your friends, but that you only have a few hundred bucks.

Gemini: (May 21–June 21)
Some problems can't be solved by retreating into drugs and alcohol, but thankfully, yours aren't that kind.

Cancer: (June 22–July 22)
You'll make major waves in the show-biz world when you launch a show called *The E! Completely Fabricated Hollywood Story*.

Leo: (July 23–Aug. 22)
Heartbreak is in the stars for you this week when the woman of your dreams confesses that she cannot love a man with such an unholy appetite for pie.

Virgo: (Aug. 23–Sept. 22)
You've had your picture in the paper before, but never in connection with a catastrophic bridge collapse.

Libra: (Sept. 23–Oct. 23)
Though it's noble that you became an accounts adjuster to make the world a better place, it remains unclear exactly how that's going to happen.

Scorpio: (Oct. 24–Nov. 21)
Sometimes, one must be cruel to be kind. From now on, it's best to assume this is the case until proven otherwise.

Sagittarius: (Nov. 22–Dec. 21)
You've spent your whole life running from yourself, but considering that it's a murderous cyborg version of yourself from an alternate-universe post-nuclear future, that's understandable.

Capricorn: (Dec. 22–Jan. 19)
A team of paramedics won't have the heart to revive you after finding your gin- and sex-drenched body floating happily in a country-club pool.

Aquarius: (Jan. 20–Feb. 18)
It's important to set goals; that way, you'll feel appropriately pathetic when you fail to achieve them.

Pisces: (Feb. 19–March 20)
Remember, it's not how hard you beat the goat, but whether the goat you're beating is on fire.

HAZARDOUS WASTE from page 153

amounts of blood. Passersby were amazed by the unusually large amounts of blood. Passersby were amazed by the unusually large amounts of blood. Passersby were amazed by the unusually large amounts of blood. Passersby were amazed by the unusually large amounts of blood. Passersby were amazed by the unusually large amounts of blood. Passersby were amazed by the unusually large amounts of blood. Passersby were amazed by the unusually large amounts of blood. Passersby were amazed by the unusually large amounts of blood. Passersby were amazed by the unusually large amounts of blood. Passersby were amazed by the unusually large amounts of blood. Passersby were amazed by the unusually large amounts of blood. Passersby were amazed by the unusually large amounts of blood. Passersby were amazed by the unusually large amounts of blood. Passersby were amazed by the unusually large amounts of blood. Passersby were amazed by the unusually large amounts of blood. Passersby were amazed by the unusually large amounts of blood. Passersby were amazed by the unusually large amounts of blood. Passersby were amazed by the unusually large amounts of blood. Passersby were

That's the best damn intramural quarterback this assistant gym teacher has ever seen.

amazed by the unusually large amounts of blood. Passersby were amazed by the unusually large amounts of blood. Passersby were amazed by the unusually large amounts of blood. Passersby were amazed by the unusually large amounts of blood. Passersby were amazed by the unusually large

see HAZARDOUS WASTE page 162

NEWS

U.S. Mint Employee Disciplined For Putting Own Face On Nickels

see WASHINGTON page 10A

Office Janitor Asks To Work From Home

see WORKPLACE page 4D

Closing-Credits Rap Awkwardly Recaps Plot

see TELEVISION page 9E

STATshot

A look at the numbers that shape your world.

Top Occupations, U.S. Chickens

.0002%	Sound-effects generator, sports-blooper shows
.0005%	Uncompensated combatant
.0009%	Tic-tac-toe player
.0011%	Headless comedian
.0017%	Petting-zoo pettee
99.9%	Food source

the ONION®

VOLUME 39 ISSUE 21 | AMERICA'S FINEST NEWS SOURCE™ | 5-11 JUNE 2003

Bush Visits U.S.S. Truman For Dramatic Veterans'-Benefits-Cutting Ceremony

Above: Bush prepares to symbolically cut veterans' benefits on the deck of the U.S.S. Harry S Truman.

NORFOLK, VA—With more than 5,400 jubilant Marines and sailors cheering him on, President Bush landed on the deck of the U.S.S. Harry S Truman in a Navy jet Monday to preside over a historic veterans'-benefits-cutting ceremony.

"Your brave and selfless service to your country will not soon be forgotten," Bush told the recently returned Operation Iraqi Freedom soldiers. "At least, not for another five or ten years."

After congratulating the soldiers on their victory over Saddam Hussein, Bush announced that the new budget passed by the Senate includes a $14.6 billion reduction in veterans' benefits. He then held aloft a pair of oversized scissors and snipped a ribbon bearing the words "Veteran's Benefits."

"No one knows the meaning of the word 'sacrifice' quite like our men and women in uniform," Bush said. "Whether sacrificing their lives or

see CEREMONY page 161

Study Finds Jack Shit

BALTIMORE—A team of scientists at Johns Hopkins University announced Monday that a five-year study examining the link between polyphenols and lower cholesterol rates has found jack shit.

"I can't explain what happened," head researcher Dr. Jeremy Ingels said. "We meticulously followed correct scientific procedure. Our methods were sufficiently rigorous that they should have produced some sort of result. Instead, we found out nothing."

Added Ingels: "Nothing!"

As Ingels stepped aside to compose himself, fellow researcher Dr. Thomas Chen took the podium to discuss the $7 million, jack-shit-yielding study.

"We are all very upset," Chen said. "When we began, this looked so promising, I would have bankrolled it myself. Now, after five years, I couldn't tell you if polyphenols even exist."

The study, which Chen charac-

see STUDY page 160

Manic-Depressive Friend A Blast While Manic

BUFFALO, NY—Manic-depressive Tom Ruzek, 24, may be a "total drag for months on end," but he is "a blast" while in his manic state, friends of the troubled Buffalo State graduate student said Monday.

Ruzek, diagnosed with manic depression three years ago by psychiatrists at Mount Zion Mental Health Center, has suffered from the disorder since high school. His condition causes him to experience cyclical bouts of prolonged depression followed by spells of mania, characterized by irrational feelings of elation, delusions of grandeur, and boundless energy. It is in this heightened state, friends say, that Ruzek is awesome.

"Sometimes, Tom can be a real downer," said roommate Eric Callas, 23. "He'll hole up in his room, and if you try to talk to him, all he does is bitch, bitch, bitch. But once you get to know him better, you see that he's got this totally wild-and-crazy, life-of-the-party side, too. When that comes out, everybody's all like, 'All right! The ol' Tomster we know and love is back!'"

According to friends, the manic version of Ruzek possesses many fun, attractive qualities. These include his propensity for outrageous, elaborately choreographed table-top dance

see FRIEND page 160

Above: Ruzek (left) entertains friends during a recent manic spell.

Nike's Million-Dollar Babies

After signing high-school basketball star LeBron James to a $90 million ad deal, Nike signed a 13-year-old soccer phenom to a $1 million pact. What do *you* think?

"I don't see what the problem is. I mean, we're talking about kids who are *good at sports*."

Melanie Schaum
Homemaker

"If that's what Nike has to do to make people finally pay attention to them, that's what they have to do."

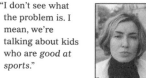

Donna Geary
Graduate Student

"Does this $90 million mean LeBron won't go to college? His education should really come first."

Arthur Robles
Office Manager

"Nike may see LeBron James as the heir to Michael Jordan, but it remains to be seen whether he has MJ's wooden charm."

Paul Pearsall
Attorney

"This is no surprise. Nike has a rich tradition of employing minors."

Chris Vinson
Systems Analyst

"They're giving $90 million to a high-school student? Excuse me, I have to spit up my last three meals."

Tom Nashua
Landscaper

Bob Hope Turns 100

Last week, Bob Hope passed the century mark. How did the legendary comedian celebrate his 100th birthday?

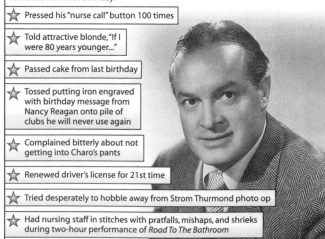

- ☆ Pressed his "nurse call" button 100 times
- ☆ Told attractive blonde, "If I were 80 years younger..."
- ☆ Passed cake from last birthday
- ☆ Tossed putting iron engraved with birthday message from Nancy Reagan onto pile of clubs he will never use again
- ☆ Complained bitterly about not getting into Charo's pants
- ☆ Renewed driver's license for 21st time
- ☆ Tried desperately to hobble away from Strom Thurmond photo op
- ☆ Had nursing staff in stitches with pratfalls, mishaps, and shrieks during two-hour performance of *Road To The Bathroom*
- ☆ Celebrated 35 years of being out of show business
- ☆ Awkwardly averted eyes from shadowy figure of Death calling out to him from across room

the ONION®
America's Finest News Source.™

Herman Ulysses Zweibel
Founder

T. Herman Zweibel
Publisher Emeritus
J. Phineas Zweibel
Publisher
Maxwell Prescott Zweibel
Editor-In-Chief

Who Will Carry On My PlayStation 2 Adventures After I'm Gone?

By Jon Crewes

I'll admit, I've had a good run. Done pretty much everything I wanted, accomplished almost everything I set out to do. I fought my way to the top of the criminal hierarchy of two cities, saved the world from unspeakably evil magical and technological conspiracies, went to six Super Bowls, and unified ancient China under three different dynasties. It's a legacy any man would be proud of, yet it is one that raises an obvious question: Who will carry on my PlayStation 2 adventures after I'm gone?

I know, I know, I'm still young. It's a bit premature to be thinking of my own mortality. But seeing so much pointless death does something to you. Especially if you've ever died and forgotten to save after narrowly defeating Ultima Weapon, wasting hours of back-breaking, finger-numbing toil. You start thinking about how death comes to everyone eventually. You think about how, even after finding every last hidden package in Vice City, there's still so much left to do. And you realize that nothing, not even the original Xenogears, lasts forever.

Which brings us back to the question: Who will carry on my legacy? I live alone, never having taken a wife. How could I have? My life of polygon-based adventures has left me no time for anyone else. A marriage takes work, and no woman could have my full attention. And that is not likely to change, considering that Metal Gear Solid: Snake Eater was just announced last week.

Yes, I may pass from the world without a successor, but I will not go into that good night unaccomplished. My five full memory cards of Complete and 100 Percent Finished game saves will ensure that.

But even if I don't last forever, my accomplishments will. I refuse to believe that everything I've built on the bones of a thousand Iron Fist Tournament fighters, on the shattered hulks of a thousand giant robots, on the ruins of three separate Metal Gear bases will one day disappear. No, if I believed that, I'd stop playing right now. Or at least right after getting the Tracer Tong/New Dark Age ending on Deus Ex, which shouldn't take more than an hour, even if I don't check GameFAQs to see where the damn Reactor Purge switch is hidden.

A marriage takes work, and no woman could have my full attention. And that is not likely to change, considering that Metal Gear Solid: Snake Eater was just announced last week.

Yes, I may pass from the world without a successor, but I will not go into that good night unaccomplished. My five full memory cards of Complete and 100 Percent Finished game saves will ensure that.

There is still hope that I will find a woman and, with her, sire an heir to continue my work. But I'm not getting any younger. I first noticed it in little ways, such as my loss of appreciation for the Mario titles. When I grew apart from Nintendo and its cartoon games, it was part of the maturation process, a sign of my readiness for a more sophisticated, grown-up gaming system. Someday, the PlayStation 2 will no longer be enough for me, and I'll put it aside and go on to other systems without regret—especially since Sony's next system will probably be backwards-compatible with older games, as the PS2 was with PS1 titles. When I do, I will be one step closer to that Final Level we all eventually reach.

Even without a clear heir, there are ways for me to leave my mark on the next generation. I can be a mentor, serving as a master to some worthy apprentice. If nothing else, I could always pass on my wisdom as that fatherly guy behind the trade-in counter of the local game store. But whatever form my legacy takes, I firmly believe that someone will continue my work in some fashion. If there's one thing I learned from Parappa The Rapper, it's that you gotta believe. Ø

FICTION

You Can Be Anything You Want, Says Fictional Character

NEW YORK—If you work hard, believe in yourself, and never lose sight of your dreams, you can achieve anything you want, the make-believe children's-book character Chipper Chipmunk said Tuesday.

"No matter what, I've got to keep climbing!" Chipper said on page 11 of *Chipper Chipmunk Climbs Straight To The Top*, released Tuesday by Scholastic Books.

"No matter what, I've got to keep climbing!" Chipper said on page 11 of *Chipper Chipmunk Climbs Straight To The Top*, released Tuesday by Scholastic Books. "No matter how windy, no matter how lofty, I must never be scared to go high, says I!"

In the book, Chipper faces numerous challenges as he attempts to climb Majestic Mister Maple. The Blustery Westerly Wind blows this way and that, rocking Mr. Maple and slowing Chipper's progress. Scornful Squirrel tries to damage his morale, openly questioning whether Chipper can climb as far or as fast as he thinks he can. And Fearsome Fox utilizes direct, physical methods of obstruction to impede Chipper's ascent.

In the end, however, the fictional woodland creature triumphs over all adversity, including his own self-doubt.

"From down there, Mister Maple seemed tall as the sky, and it scared me so much I almost didn't try," Chipper mused from the tree top. "But now that I'm up at the tippity tip-top of the tree, there's nothing at all that's as high up as me!"

After reaching the top, the pretend rodent issued a challenge to all who witnessed his feat.

"I knew I could do it—it was hard, yes, it's true. But if chipmunks can climb to the sky, so can YOU!" Chipper said, punctuating his message with a thumbs-up sign and a wink.

According to Dr. Roland Gibson of the American Council For Literature & Ethics, Chipper's core message—that people can be or do anything they want—is a fallacy widely perpetuated in children's books.

"Chipper's unshakable faith in success through hard work and persistence isn't something we typically encounter in our daily lives," Gibson said. "This groundless assumption that an individual's capacity for achievement is limitless is a particular failing of children's literature."

Continued Gibson: "Chipper's success took place in the extremely narrow field of tree-climbing, and was

Above: The positive, pretend Chipper Chipmunk.

achieved free of such real-world factors as class, wealth, religion, or race. To assume that we can apply these

"From down there, Mister Maple seemed tall as the sky, and it scared me so much I almost didn't try," Chipper mused from the tree top.

lessons to our infinitely knottier, more complicated real-world lives is a wild oversimplification."

Gibson said that, with the exception of certain celebrities and politicians, statements like Chipper's are almost always made by talking animals, superheroes, omniscient narrators, anthropomorphic trains, wandering magicians, friendly dragons, sentient heavenly bodies, Jesus, and other characters subject only to the rules of narrative causality.

In spite of Chipper's good intentions, his positive message has not had much of an impact on the non-imaginary public.

"So, this chipmunk wants us to believe that just because he climbed some stupid tree, anything is possible?" said Dawn Dressler, a Wichita, KS, single mother of three. "Chipper wouldn't be so sure of himself if he had to hold down two jobs, had no dental insurance, and lost half his pension to corporate corruption. Let's see him reach for his goddamn dreams then." ⊘

NEWS IN BRIEF

Friend Gearing Up To Hate *The Hulk*

EL PASO, TX—For the past three weeks, comic-book aficionado Derek Linden, 23, has been gearing up to hate Universal Pictures' *The Hulk*, which opens June 13. "Maybe it'll be good, but I'm bracing for the worst," Linden told friend Paul Comello Monday. "The CGI makes him look like Shrek. And even though The Hulk has the ability to leap long distances, in the trailer it looks like he's flying, which he can't do. And I won't even get into how, in the Hulk origin story, he was gray, not green." Linden said he also has "grave doubts" about Jennifer Connelly's ability to convincingly portray Betty Ross.

Rumsfeld Wearing Same Shirt For Fourth Straight Day

WASHINGTON, DC—According to Pentagon sources, Defense Secretary Donald Rumsfeld has been wearing the same slightly dingy white Arrow Oxford shirt for four straight days. "I can tell it's the same one, because he got a drop of chili on it last Friday, and the spot is still there," Deputy Defense Secretary Paul Wolfowitz said Monday. "I know Don's a busy guy, but it's really starting to look bad. I mean, it's all pitted out and everything." Wolfowitz added that Rumsfeld has worn the same pair of black wingtips "since we drove the Taliban out of Afghanistan."

Chuckling Cops Attempt To Imitate Sound Of Man Being Hit By Taxi

CHICAGO—After witnessing a fatal hit-and-run accident Tuesday, Chicago police officers Ed Malloy and Ron Garrity attempted to replicate the sound of a man being hit by a taxi. "First, there was the *aiiigh*, then a *fa-wumpp ba-bumpp*," Malloy said, stifling laughter. "Then, when he was bleeding from his mouth, he kind of went *ggrrgg blibb-blibb*." Garrity disagreed, saying the impact "sounded more like a *tha-loomp poompf*." Malloy said it was the funniest on-the-job incident since that junkie was stabbed in the ass.

Therapist Beginning To Show Cracks In Caring Façade

SANTA MONICA, CA—After five years of counseling, psychotherapist Diana Berg is beginning to show cracks in her caring façade, patient Ian Cassell reported Tuesday. "When I told her how I still put everyone else's happiness above my own, she exhaled really loud, like she was exasperated," Cassell said. "Then she said, 'Well, we did talk about that last session, didn't we?'" Berg, who has had twice-weekly sessions with Cassell since 1998, said through gritted teeth that she suspects he doesn't really want to get better.

City Councilman From Future Warns Against Building 12th Avenue Rec Center

HOLLINS, VA—Appearing through a wormhole at a city-council meeting Tuesday, Xanthon Clarke, a Hollins 3rd District Councilman from the future, warned meeting attendees against building the proposed 12th Avenue Recreation Center. "I come from the year 2050, begging you to vote down the rec center before it's too late," said Clarke, who sported a metallic blazer and bowtie. "Before it's too late, *for God's sake*." Clarke was then vaporized by a raygun-wielding robotic lobbyist from 2079. ⊘

STUDY from page 157

terized as a "huge waste of time and money," was financed by a Johns Hopkins alumni grant to determine the effects of the compound polyphenol on cholesterol. A known antioxidant found in herbs, teas, olive oil, and wines, polyphenol was originally thought to lower cholesterol—a theory that remains unproven because the Johns Hopkins researchers couldn't prove squat.

"We can't say zip about whether it lowers cholesterol," Ingels said. "We don't know if it raises cholesterol. Hell, we don't know if it joins with cholesterol to form an unholy alliance to take over your gall bladder. At this point, I couldn't prove that a male donkey has nuts if they were swinging in my face."

When a study's results are inconclusive, a research team often asks for more time and money to finish. Such is not the case with the Johns Hopkins project.

"No. No fucking way," Ingels said. "I don't know about Dr. Chen, but I know that Dr. [Kerri] Bruce, who has been a real trouper through all of this, is quitting science to start a catfish farm in Louisiana. Me, I have a long date with my bed and cable TV. I may still do something in science, but if I do, it'll probably be something easy, like re-linking cigarette smoking with lung cancer, just to get my confidence back up. It's too early to say. I'll have a better idea after a month of watching the Game Show Network and eating raspberry danishes."

Above: Dr. Jeremy Ingels, head of the total-waste-of-time-and-money study.

Ingels also spoke of Dr. James Long, a biochemist who worked on the inconclusive study until lapsing into alcoholism six months ago.

"Poor Jim just couldn't take it," Ingels said. "We were all hitting the bars pretty hard once we began to see that things weren't adding up. I think he took it the hardest because he was the one who proposed the study in the first place. I guess he was accustomed to research leading to something... anything."

In spite of the fruitless results, other researchers at Johns Hopkins expressed confidence that, in time, some positive results can be gleaned from the study. Ingels has relinquished all collected data to the university, but stressed that he will not offer any further assistance.

"You want to look over this big fat goose egg, go nuts," Ingels said. "I don't want to hear the word 'polyphenol' for the remainder of 2003."

Chen then took the podium to make the team's closing statements.

"I just want to clarify that we had the best intentions going into this study," Chen said. "We thought we would make a scientific discovery about polyphenols and cholesterol that would benefit the health of millions. I guess we were wrong. We tried to find a link, but instead we found *bubkes*." ⌀

FRIEND from page 157

numbers at bars and restaurants, his ability to go without sleep for up to 72 hours at a time during spur-of-the-moment road trips, and his wildly generous spending sprees, during which he lavishes friends with expensive gifts in spite of his massive debt.

"Once, we were hanging out at the mall when, out of nowhere, Tom bought me this remote-controlled, gas-powered miniature helicopter for my birthday, even though my birthday wasn't for another five months," Ruzek friend Cris Harbaugh said. "We had a ton of fun flying it around the parking lot, buzzing cars and freaking people out until the mall-security guy told us to leave. Tom got so worked up about getting busted, he filled the toy with M-80s and blew it up in midair—right there in the outdoor food court. Man, what a great day that was."

Friends say they also enjoy watching Ruzek cut loose on one of his wild, stream-of-consciousness rants.

Friends also say they enjoy watching Ruzek cut loose on one of his wild, stream-of-consciousness rants.

"Tom's got this web page he keeps, and sometimes a month or more will go by where he doesn't do any updates, except for really short entries like 'Peed in a jar today rather than leave bed,'" friend Alicia Reynolds said. "But then, sometimes he'll get on these jags where he'll write, like, 20 pages in a single day—hilarious, over-the-top stuff about how every one of us is a white-hot energy source extending to every corner of the universe."

Compounding his manic episodes, Ruzek will often neglect to take his daily dose of mood-stabilizing medication, insisting he doesn't need it.

"Tom got so down last winter, he started taking heavy doses of antidepressants," Reynolds said. "I was really worried about him, but he recently told me he's gotten so much better, he no longer needs artificial substances to be happy. He says he's off the pills and high on life. What a great new attitude. It's hard to believe there was a time when he was so bummed out, he didn't eat any solid food other than Doritos for a month."

Added Reynolds: "Check out these photos he took of himself in the mirror. He just got a new digital camera, and he e-mailed me the test pictures he took of himself, just to see if it worked. He must have taken, like, 250 of them."

"Tom's got this web page he keeps, and sometimes a month or more will go by where he doesn't do any updates, except for really short entries like 'Peed in a jar today rather than leave bed,'" friend Alicia Reynolds said.

Though Ruzek's friends describe him as "moody," "excitable," and "a little psycho," most seem unaware of the seriousness of his condition. According to his therapist, Dr. Howard Wenger, this is due to a combination of the shame manic-depressives like Ruzek feel about revealing their illness and the public's lack of knowledge about the condition.

"What these people don't realize is that Tom has a deadly serious mental illness that, left untreated, will wreak untold havoc on his life," Wenger said. "He is trapped in a self-destructive cycle that could one day prove fatal. There is nothing 'fun' about his disorder, no matter how it appears to outsiders. Tom is a very sick man."

When told of Wenger's appraisal, Ruzek strenuously disagreed.

"Me? I'm fine," Ruzek said. "In fact, I'm so far beyond fine as to be essentially perfect. I would go so far as to say that I am the most perfect being ever to walk God's green earth. Hey, who wants pizza? I'm buying. No, wait—Chinese. No, wait—sushi. No, wait—where are my car keys? I feel like driving 100 miles an hour around the parking lot of that abandoned screen-door factory at the edge of town. Let's blast some Andrew W.K. and scream at the top of our lungs until dawn."

"Hey, world, look at me, I'm the King of Siam!" added Ruzek, before collapsing to the floor in a state of physical and emotional exhaustion. ⌀

CEREMONY from page 157

Above: A Gulf War veteran bravely sacrifices for his country.

their health coverage, these brave Americans are willing to do whatever it takes to help this nation, and for this I salute them."

As the ship lay at anchor in the Atlantic Ocean, Bush, holding a helmet emblazoned with "Prez-1" along the side, expressed his gratitude to the troops for the hardships they endured in the Persian Gulf, and for the hardships they would be enduring at home in the future.

"When I look at the members of the United States military, I see the best of our country, and I am honored to be your Commander-In-Chief," Bush said. "I am equally honored that you are stoically accepting Congress' elimination of a large percentage of the benefits you were promised upon enlisting so that I can finance a massive tax cut."

As the ship lay at anchor in the Atlantic Ocean, Bush, holding a helmet emblazoned with "Prez-1" along the side, expressed his gratitude to the troops for the hardships they endured in the Persian Gulf, and for the hardships they would be enduring at home in the future.

The speech was brought to a temporary halt as the troops' enthusiastic cheers drowned out the public-address system. Bush then raised his hands to silence the crowd, his face turning somber.

"You have shown the world the skill and might of the American armed forces," Bush said. "You have exhibited a willingness to do what your country has asked of you. In return, I would like to personally show my gratitude by guaranteeing that your pension will not completely dry up until you turn 40."

As a ray of sunlight broke through the clouds, Bush explained that the cuts were necessary to ensure that the servicemen who received aid were those who really needed it and not the parasites looking to take advantage of a bloated bureaucracy and veterans' welfare state.

"This is a battle to root out waste in the dispensation of veterans' funds," Bush said. "And, as you know all too well, casualties are inevitable in a battle. If some of you are cut off from compensation payments for injuries, take comfort in the knowledge that your sacrifice was not in vain, for you have helped liberate billions of tax dollars for our country's taxpayers."

Upon the conclusion of the president's speech, the troops once again rose to thunderous applause. After posing for photographs with various officers and enlisted men on board, the president returned to his jet and departed.

"You have exhibited a willingness to do what your country has asked of you," Bush said. "In return, I would like to personally show my gratitude by guaranteeing that your pension will not completely dry up until you turn 40."

Reactions to the speech were overwhelmingly positive.

"We all stand behind our Commander-In-Chief," said Petty Officer 3rd Class Henry Williams, 23, of Norfolk, VA. "When he started this war, President Bush called upon Americans to support its troops. Now, he's calling upon his troops to accept six-month waits for hospital visits and pauper's funerals. In these times of economic crisis and uncertainty, it is our duty to stand behind our president, whether or not he is standing behind us."

COMMUNITY VOICES

A Mouse Unusual Development

As any Jeanketeer worth his or her salt (or chocolate!) knows, my two sweet kitties, Priscilla and Garfield, mean more to me than just about anything. (I guess hubby Rick would have to top the list, but between you, me, and the lamp post, sometimes I wish Rick would magically turn into a cuddly kitty himself!)

A Room Of Jean's Own
By Jean Teasdale

The best thing about being unemployed is all the time I get to spend with my fuzz-fuzzes. But Rick has really been on my tail (pun intended!) to find a job, so last Thursday, I went out and spent the morning filling out job applications at the local Kinko's and the Pamida and places like that, and submitting them to would-be bosses half my age. (Aack!)

The best thing about being unemployed is all the time I get to spend with my fuzz-fuzzes.

I got home around 2 p.m. and noticed that Rick's pickup truck was still in the driveway. I knew he had the afternoon off, but he usually fritters away his free time at Tacky's Tavern or down at Swinton's Creek fishing and drinking with his buddies. As I walked through the door, Rick practically sprinted up to me. (It was the most movement I've seen out of him since he warmed benches on the high-school wrestling team!)

"Jean, you won't believe what I just saw," Rick said. "You know that fat orange cat of yours who farts a lot? Turns out he's a cold-blooded killing machine."

At first, I thought all those video games and chop-socky movies had finally softened Rick's brain. But he led me to the kitchen and pointed to a small, grayish thing lying on a dishtowel on the counter. Upon closer inspection, it proved to be a mouse, lifeless and still.

Rick said that about 20 minutes before I got home, he heard a loud clatter in the bedroom.

"I went for my hunting knife, just in case I'd have to take out some punk,"

see TEASDALE page 162

TEASDALE from page 161

he said. "But then I see your dumb cat, what's-its-name, Heathcliff (he knows perfectly well it's Garfield and that "its" gender is male!), running into the bathroom with this mouse in its jaws."

And that's where things got really horrifying.

"I stuck my head around the doorway, and your cat was playing hacky-sack with the mouse, batting it around with its paws," Rick said. "The cat would drop the mouse for a second, but before it could get away,

I began rethinking his past behavior. When he stalked and pounced on his toys, was he actually pretending to stalk prey, and not playing a fun, innocent game of kitty soccer?

Heathcliff would smack it silly."

"But the cat wasn't done yet," Rick continued. "It grabbed the mouse in its jaws again, jumped into the open shower stall, and started the same crap over again. It's like the shower stall became an arena of death. I even saw the mouse fly in the air a couple times. Finally, after about 10 minutes, the cat put the thing out of its misery."

Well, I must have looked about as stunned as that poor little mouse. (And it wasn't because I'd just had my longest conversation of the year with Rick!) I remember staring down at it. Aside from a little blood, it didn't look all that battered. In fact, it looked like it was sleeping peacefully. Even though it was just a tiny dead mouse, it appeared, well, almost beautiful. Its little feet and ears were very delicate, and its whiskers looked like they could come alive with a twitch. There must be a God, I thought, because who would put such tender care into creating something so small? I felt myself tearing up a little. I almost didn't care that Rick had put the mouse on my very best dishtowel, the one with the geese on it.

I noticed Garfield perched on the back of the couch, calmly washing his paws, but it was like looking at a stranger. Was this the cat I had known and loved for so long? Was he not actually the sensitive, caring pet I knew and loved, but rather a cruel, remorseless murderer? Was this the same critter who chased spots of dancing light on the carpet, and who almost toppled over every time he tried to lick his big, fat tummy? (File this one in the "You Think You Know Someone" department...)

Suddenly, I couldn't bring myself to pet Garfield. I couldn't even look at him. The catnip toys that litter the floor all looked like little dead mice to me. I imagined helpless, adorable mice floating belly-up in his water dish. Later, as I watched TV, little Priscilla tried to jump on my lap. I nudged her off. Even though she hadn't taken part in the atrocity, she was a cat, and therefore capable of the same grotesque acts.

It didn't seem right to call Priscilla and Garfield kitties anymore. They were cats. How could Garfield be so cruel to that dear little mouse? How could he give in so easily to his animal instincts? He had plenty to eat, lots of toys to amuse himself with, large windows to look out of, and comfy places to sleep. Then I began rethinking his past behavior. When he stalked and pounced on his toys, was he actually pretending to stalk prey, and not playing a fun, innocent game of kitty soccer? When he watched the birds through the window, perhaps he wasn't merely having secret telepathic conversations with his feathered friends, but instead sizing them up as potential prey. Then I thought about our relationship. Was I not "Mommy Jean" at all, but merely a two-legged food provider? Was his seemingly affectionate behavior nothing more than a clever ploy to get more food out of me?

It's like discovering that your best friend stole money from your purse to buy drugs.

After a sleepless night—I kept the door closed so the cats couldn't sleep on the bed with me, so I was kept

Then I thought about our relationship. Was I not "Mommy Jean" at all, but merely a two-legged food provider? Was his seemingly affectionate behavior nothing more than a clever ploy to get more food out of me?

awake with their scratching and mewling—I called Sandy, our apartment manager, and told her about Garfield catching a mouse in our apartment. Sandy said other tenants had complained of mice, too, and that an exterminator had been sent to the building. She said tenants had already found some dead mice, probably killed by the exterminator's poison.

Dead mice had been found! What if the mouse Garfield caught was already dead before he found it? Maybe my precious kitty wasn't a cold-blooded killer, after all!

Heaven knows, Rick is not the most reliable witness in the world. (This is a guy who swears up and down that he saw Cindy Crawford at the local mall's food court, and that she winked at him. I know that can't be true, because, judging from her looks, Cindy Crawford has never eaten a thing in her entire life!) How did he know that the mouse was alive when Garfield toyed with it in the bathroom? Did he take its pulse?

What most likely happened was that Garfield found the dead mouse somewhere in our bedroom, mistook it for a toy, picked it up, and went to the bathroom so he'd have some space to bop it around. Often, I find toys on the bathroom floor and the bottom of that very same shower stall Rick called "an arena of death."

It all made such perfect sense, and I felt sooo much better! Suddenly, Garfield wasn't just a "cat" anymore. His full kitty privileges were restored! I made sure to give him a few liver treats as an apology for locking him out of the bedroom the previous night. (And, don't worry, I didn't ignore my Prissy!)

In a way, I'm glad my love for Garfield was put to the test, because it emerged stronger than ever. A lot of people think kitties are cold and aloof animals, but I'm convinced that it's all a bunch of nonsense perpetuated by a bunch of Kathy Killjoys. When Priscilla is curled up purring on her Mommy Jean's lap, or when Garfield rubs against my leg and plops himself down at my feet for a belly rub, I feel sorry for the kitty-haters of the world, because they're missing out on a lot of joy. With kitties, it's nothing but unconditional love. After all, Prissy and Garfy have never mocked or judged me because of my frequent joblessness, or because of the way my inner thighs rub together as I walk, or because of my recurring yeast infections. (Unlike certain hubbies I can name!) ø

HOROSCOPES

Your Horoscope

By Lloyd Schumner Sr.
Retired Machinist and
A.A.P.B.-Certified Astrologer

Aries: (March 21–April 19)
The whole neighborhood knows you as the man with the heart of stone and the fists of steel, which is not the reputation you want as a concert pianist.

Taurus: (April 20–May 20)
You'll admit that the errors MIT found in your coordinate system for a nine-dimensional plenum check out, but it still seems like they did it just to be dicks.

Gemini: (May 21–June 21)
The jury will not be moved by your argument that the term "escaped tigers" implies the intent was with the tigers.

Cancer: (June 22–July 22)
The story of the universe has always fascinated you, but the ending will leave you with a lot of unanswered questions.

Leo: (July 23–Aug. 22)
After the events of next Sunday, for the rest of your life, people will stop you on the street and ask you to autograph packages of pork chops.

Virgo: (Aug. 23–Sept. 22)
You will soon take an extremely long journey over water, which is odd given how little water there will be.

Libra: (Sept. 23–Oct. 23)
Investigators say the truth is found by following the money or the sex, which makes you immune to any possible suspicion.

Scorpio: (Oct. 24–Nov. 21)
You'll be getting phone calls for a year after your appearance on E!'s Wild On Scorpio.

Sagittarius: (Nov. 22–Dec. 21)
Death will soon take a holiday and put you in charge of his dread offices for a week, but it will all go off without a hitch and barely be worthy of comment.

Capricorn: (Dec. 22–Jan. 19)
Jupiter ascendant in your sign this week indicates that contemporary fiction would be richer and more resonant if it were less self-indulgent.

Aquarius: (Jan. 20–Feb. 18)
It's not always the person you least expect, because, if it were, it would always be you.

Pisces: (Feb. 19–March 20)
Soon, people will be breaking down your door to get your secret to happiness, because your secret is 85 kilos of uncut Bolivian coke.

NEWS

Refrigerator Wins American Appliance

see TELEVISION page 9C

New Lover Features 30 Percent More Cock

see LOCAL page 4E

Child In Stroller Stares At Man In Wheelchair

see LOCAL page 11E

Date Reeks Of Febreeze

see LOCAL page 7E

STATshot

A look at the numbers that shape your world.

How Are We Complicating The Lives Of Our Newborn Twins?

1. Getting them an agent
2. Complaining loudly about how we'd have preferred fraternal twins
3. Loaning them out to Anne Geddes
4. Raising them hydroponically
5. Auditioning them for *Full House: The New Batch*

0 74470 94595 6 00

THE ONION • $2.00 US • $3.00 CAN

the ONION®

VOLUME 39 ISSUE 22 AMERICA'S FINEST NEWS SOURCE™ 12–18 JUNE 2003

Gen. Tommy Franks Quits Army To Pursue Solo Bombing Projects

WASHINGTON, DC—Gen. Tommy Franks, commander of American forces during the wars in Iraq and Afghanistan, announced plans Monday to step down as U.S. Central Command chief to focus on solo bombing projects.

"The years I've spent with the Army have been amazing, and we did some fantastic bombing," Franks said at a Pentagon press conference. "But at this point, I feel like I've taken it as far as I can. It's time for me to move on and see what I can destroy on my own."

Franks said he is eager to seek out new challenges.

"Obviously, the U.S. Army is a first-rate organization," Franks said. "I mean, when we were on, no one could touch us. The '91 Gulf tour, the '95 Bosnia campaign... we kicked some serious ass. But it's precisely *because* I love it so much that I want to leave before it starts to get stale."

Franks said he also relishes the notion of hav-

see FRANKS page 166

Above: Gen. Franks tells reporters, "It's time for me to move on and see what I can destroy on my own."

Five-Disc Jazz Anthology Still Unopened

LOUISVILLE, KY—A five-disc jazz-anthology box set, lovingly assembled to give novices an appreciation and understanding of the uniquely American art form, remains unopened nearly two years after its purchase, sources reported Monday.

"Yeah, I should really give that a spin one of these days," said Marc Bergkamp, 29, who in July 2001 purchased *Ken Burns Jazz: The Story Of American Music* for $69.99. "I just haven't had the time to sit down and go through it. I was thinking about putting it on this weekend while I clean my apartment, but jazz isn't really cleaning music. I need something a little more rocking, like The White Stripes or something."

Bergkamp purchased the deluxe box set after watching a portion of an episode of the 10-part, 19-hour *Ken Burns Jazz* documentary on PBS.

"I'd always meant to buy more jazz, but every time I went record shopping, there'd be something I wanted more," Bergkamp said. "Finally, after seeing the thing on PBS, I decided to commit to getting some. I went down

see BOX SET page 166

Above: The unopened box set.

Troubled Teens Mock Social Worker's Car

CHICAGO—Despite facing socioeconomic inequities that put them at a lifelong disadvantage, troubled inner-city teens at Marcus Garvey High School are fond of openly mocking their social worker's "shitty car," sources reported Monday.

Left: Rogowski and the 1990 Subaru mocked by Stefano (top) and Banks (bottom).

Social worker Gary Rogowski, 32, works with disadvantaged youths on Chicago's South Side through the neighborhood Second Start program. His car, a 1990 Subaru Loyale station wagon that, as Rogowski puts it, "has seen better days," is a constant source of derision among the teens he has dedicated his professional life to

see TEENS page 167

The Partial-Birth Abortion Ban

Last week, the House of Representatives voted to ban partial-birth abortions, moving the bill a step closer to President Bush. What do *you* think?

Paul Sprague
Systems Analyst

"Partial-birth abortions should absolutely be banned. It says so in The Bible, in *Paul's Letter To The Corinthians Re: Partial-Birth Abortions*."

Meredith Sims
Graphic Designer

"Whew—got that one in just under the wire."

Chris Kannell
Mechanic

"Good. Now, U.S. women will think twice before fucking some stranger in a truck in a vacant lot somewhere. Are you listening, Amy?"

Eric Pierce
Delivery Driver

"Partial-birth abortions are disgusting. So, for that matter, are vaginas."

Donna Lund
Physical Therapist

"This should kickstart the economy."

Oscar Hamilton
Attorney

"Speaking as a man, let me just say, Christ, am I glad I'm a man."

Exaggerating The WMD Threat

Critics are accusing the Bush Administration of distorting the destructive threat posed by Iraq. Among the U.S. claims under suspicion:

- Sales receipt found in Saddam's desk drawer bearing suspicious line item WEAPNSMASSDESTR
- Iraq had already fired nuclear missiles at U.S., but missed
- Saddam planning to raise U.S. taxes
- Iraqi citizens bleed mustard gas and crap uranium
- According to top-secret report from Agent Maxwell Smart, Iraqis developing plans for a "Nude Bomb"
- Pearl Harbor actually attacked by Iraqis
- Saddam possessed stores of sand, which he planned to turn into glass for use in fighter planes that would drop nuclear bombs on New York, Washington D.C., and Boston on Christmas Eve
- Streets of Baghdad paved with weapons-grade plutonium

the ONION®
America's Finest News Source.™

Herman Ulysses Zweibel
Founder

T. Herman Zweibel
Publisher Emeritus
J. Phineas Zweibel
Publisher
Maxwell Prescott Zweibel
Editor-In-Chief

Remember Me? I'm That Kid Who Had A Report Due On Space

By That Kid Who Had A Report Due On Space

Hey there. Remember me? I'm that kid who had a report due on space. You probably don't recognize me because it was a long time ago. I used to wear my hair totally different. It was in this sort of Prince Valiant-style pageboy bowl cut. Hey, it was the mid-'80s, what can I say? Sometimes, I look at old pictures of me, with that hair, and I think to myself, "You sure have come a long way since the days when you had that report due on space."

You sure you don't remember me? That kid? Who had a report due? On space?

For a couple years afterwards, I'd get recognized pretty often. People would come up to me and be like, "You look so familiar. Where do I know you from?" And then I'd say, "Encyclopedia Britannica. I'm that kid who had a report due on space," and they'd slap their foreheads and be all like, "I knew I recognized you from somewhere! How'd that report turn out, anyway? Those encyclopedias help?" I'd usually just play it kind of coy, giving 'em the old thumbs up and saying, "Scored an A." Sometimes, they'd even buy me a drink, but that doesn't happen much anymore. After all, that was 15 or 20 years ago now that I had that report due on space.

People would come up to me and be like, "You look so familiar. Where do I know you from?" And then I'd say, "Encyclopedia Britannica. I'm that kid who had a report due on space," and they'd slap their foreheads and be all like, "I knew I recognized you from somewhere! How'd that report turn out, anyway?"

Not that I'm hung up on it. I've moved on since then. I don't want you to get the wrong idea and think I'm living in the past.

I guess after that whole report thing, a lot of people, myself included, figured I'd end up going into some line of work having to do with aeronautics or astrophysics or something that was at least somehow associated with space. But that's not what happened.

Oh, sure, I went to college. As a matter of fact, I included that report I had due on space in my application. So I guess those encyclopedias paid off in that respect. To be honest, though, I wasn't all that into school. I spent most of my college years partying.

Oh, sure, I went to college. As a matter of fact, I included that report I had due on space in my application. So I guess those encyclopedias paid off in that respect. To be honest, though, I wasn't all that into school. I spent most of my college years partying. Oh, man, I remember this one kegger, me and my buddies had been doing Jell-O shots all night. And, well, to make a long story short, this totally hot girl comes up—she'd been checking me out all night—and she finally approaches me and is all like, "Do I know you? Aren't you that kid who had a report due on space?" I was sure I was going home with her, but she ended up passing out.

Sorry to go off on that tangent there. Long story short, I ended up dropping out of college after three semesters. It was too bad, because I had those encyclopedias, and they would've been a really good resource for reports on Napoleon or mitosis or the migratory patterns of birds or whatever. But, like I said, college just wasn't for me.

I ended up going to Alaska for a few years, to try to get my head together. I hardly brought anything with me, but for some reason, I packed those damn encyclopedias. They came in pretty handy during those long months working at the cannery. After a hard shift, when I just wanted to unwind

see KID page 167

LOCAL

Area Man's Pop-Culture References Stop At 1988

Above: Marchand, who says his all-time favorite TV show is *"Cheers*—the Diane years."

FLAGSTAFF, AZ—According to sources, area resident Scott Marchand, 37, lives in a state of pop-cultural stasis, never making references to movies, music, or television shows that came after 1988.

"It's strange," said longtime friend Rob Petrakis, 36. "Whenever he quotes lines from his favorite movies—*Caddyshack, Wall Street, Planes, Trains & Automobiles, Top Gun*—it's never anything that came out after 1988. It's always 'I feel the need for speed,' or 'Greed is good,' or 'Those aren't pillows!' I don't know what part of the human brain controls the absorption of pop-cultural stimuli, but 1988 is apparently the year Scott's shut down."

Marchand, a real-estate agent with Coldwell Banker, graduated from Arizona State University in May 1988. That fall, he married college sweetheart Eileen Wells and moved to Flagstaff, where he has lived in a state of pop-cultural obliviousness ever since.

According to Petrakis, Marchand's knowledge of current music is as limited as his knowledge of other media.

"Scott's favorite band is U2, and has been ever since we roomed together in the dorms," Petrakis said. "Hey, I liked them back in college, too: *Boy, October, The Joshua Tree*—all great albums. But the weird thing is, even with his favorite band, his familiarity drops off after 1988. I've browsed through his CD collection, and the most recent U2 album he owns is [1988's] *Rattle And Hum*. You'd think he'd at least have *Achtung Baby*, but I've never heard him even mention it."

Marchand's isolation from all contemporary pop culture is especially confounding considering that he has an 11-year-old son and an 8-year-old daughter, both of whom are steeped

> **"Scott's favorite band is U2, and has been ever since we roomed together in the dorms," Petrakis said. "Hey, I liked them back in college, too."**

in today's films, video games, and music.

"I wanted Grand Theft Auto: Vice City for Christmas," son Jordan said. "Instead, Dad got me this collection of really old games like Pac-Man, Joust, and Dig Dug that he said are way better. Then he says, 'Let's pop in that cartridge so I can show you how to catch Pac-Man Fever.' He doesn't even know that games are on CDs now. He's so weird."

Marchand is not without access to current pop culture. On his way to work, he passes billboards touting the latest movies and albums. Many of his real-estate coworkers are twenty-somethings whose desks are well within earshot of his. His children talk about their favorite television shows at the dinner table. Regardless, he has seemingly managed to avoid absorbing any of the media that are virtually forced upon him.

"It's not like I keep up with all the latest stuff," wife Eileen said. "I mean, I'm busy working and taking care of the kids, but it's hard not to know about the new *Matrix* movie or *American Idol*. But with Scott, it's another story altogether. He'll see 'N Sync on TV and refer to them as 'one of those New Kids On The Block bands.' It's like he subconsciously threw a switch that made him ignore anything related to pop culture after he graduated from college. To him, it's like the Church Lady and *Moonlighting* are the pinnacle of Western civilization."

Asked about his habit of restricting his references to 1988 and years prior, Marchand pleaded ignorance.

"Do I do that?" Marchand asked. "I guess I never really noticed. Even if I do, though, I really don't think it's a big deal. I mean, if that's what I enjoy, then that's what I enjoy. Like I always say, 'Don't worry, be happy.'" ⊘

NEWS IN BRIEF

Graduation Party More Lucrative Than Planned Future Career

BLOOMINGTON, IN—Caryn Niering, who last week received a Bachelor of Arts degree from Indiana University, earned more in cash and gifts during her graduation party Monday than she can ever hope to amass in her chosen career as a school psychologist. "I got a pretty sweet deal at the party," Niering said. "My uncle Mark gave me a check for $1,000, and my dad bought me a new Volkswagen Jetta." Niering's total haul at the graduation party was $19,600, while her starting salary as a school psychologist will be $17,000 a year.

MC Serch Updates List Of Gas-Face Recipients

QUEENS, NY—For the first time since the list's 1989 release, MC Serch of 3rd Bass unveiled an updated Gas Face list Tuesday, removing such longtime recipients as Hammer and P.W. Botha in favor of more current wrongdoers. "Osama bin Laden... gets the gas face," MC Serch, flanked by Prime Minister Pete Nice, told reporters. "Bill O'Reilly, shut the fuck up! Gas face!" Also included on MC Serch's newly revised Gas Face list were Scott Peterson, U.S. Sen. Rick Santorum (R-PA), and Grand Puba.

Bakery's Closing Nets Man Ton Of Free Éclairs

CEDAR RAPIDS, IA—Area resident Andrew Rutherford, 43, took advantage of the 7 p.m. closing of Napoleon's French bakery Monday, taking home what he described as a "ton" of free éclairs. "I swung by to get a doughnut just as they were closing up shop for the night, and this guy behind the counter asks if I wanted, like, three huge bags of éclairs for nothing," Rutherford said. "So I'm like, 'Hell, yeah!' They were just gonna throw them away, I guess. My roommates were so psyched." Though weighing far less than an actual ton, the éclair bags tipped the scales at nearly nine pounds.

Cameraman Finds Sole Black Person In Studio Audience

LINCOLN, NE—During Tuesday's live broadcast of *Mornings With Connie & Bill*, Channel 8 cameraman Tom Benes managed to find Yolanda Davis, the only African-American in an otherwise all-Caucasian studio audience. "Connie [Dell] and Bill [Jordan] were chatting about Gladys Knight coming to town, and I just felt it would be nice to get a reaction shot from someone of color," Benes said. "That's the kind of subtle thing that makes the show more enjoyable for viewers at home." Benes kept his camera trained on Davis during the entire discussion of the Knight concert and later got a quick shot of her during a brief mention of Halle Berry.

Man In Bar Makes General Inquiry About The Ladies

SAN ANTONIO, TX—Sitting on a barstool at the Stone Werks Tavern, Barry Todd, 39, made a general inquiry regarding the status of the ladies Monday. "So, what's the deal with the ladies tonight?" asked Todd, speaking to no one in particular. "Are they alone, or are they here with somebody? I hope they're not all uptight and stuck-up." After receiving no definitive answer, Todd spent the remainder of the evening flipping through the CDs on the jukebox and nursing his warm Michelob Light. ⊘

FRANKS from page 163

ing more creative freedom.

"When you're in an army, you pretty much have to bomb the countries they tell you to bomb," Franks said. "Which is fine for a while. But eventually, you get tired of bombing the same old places again and again. The last thing I want is to be 70 years old, still bombing Iraq. It's important to keep things fresh."

Asked to comment on rumors that he plans to launch a tour of the Far East, Franks said he will announce his first solo tour of duty later this month. He did mention, however, that he has "always wanted to bomb China," but that his work with the U.S. Army afforded him little time to do so.

Above: Franks rocks Baghdad during the recent Operation Iraqi Freedom tour.

"Franks says he quit, but I think that's bullshit," said CNN Pentagon correspondent James Washburn. "He got kicked out. Why else would he be leaving the best military in the entire world right after their triumphant Middle East tour?"

Elaborating on his dissatisfaction with the Army, Franks said that the vast scale of U.S. military operations, while exciting at first, eventually became a turn-off.

"It just got to be so big," Franks said. "You had these massive campaigns, with soldiers and generals and tech crews and medical staffs and reporters and maintenance engineers and all these other people. It was such an elaborate production. I guess I just felt like, somewhere along the way, we got away from what it was all about. We forgot the thing we all got into it for in the first place: the killing."

Franks said he is eager to strip down the warmaking experience to its purest essence.

"I'd really like to get back to my roots," Franks said. "It's exciting to put on a big show with M1 Abrams tanks, Bradley fighting vehicles, and AH-64 Apache attack helicopters, but I got my first combat experience as an artillery officer in Vietnam. Part of me really misses being out there in the swamps, just one man and a howitzer."

"My years with the military have been the best of my life," Franks continued. "But when you're at the head of a group, you're always considering the entire unit's best interests. Even though you're the leader, it can be very stifling. If you get the urge to bomb India or Brazil, you can't just go off and do it."

While he was under contract with the U.S. government, Franks occasionally expressed displeasure over having to seek approval from the president and Congress for nearly every action he performed.

"If I want to send a division of jet fighters to Iran, you'd think, after all the years I've been doing this, that I could simply make that decision," Franks told reporters during a CentCom press briefing in February. "But it's not like that."

In spite of Franks' claim that the decision to leave the army was his, some military insiders say they suspect otherwise.

"Franks says he quit, but I think that's bullshit," said CNN Pentagon correspondent James Washburn. "He got kicked out. Why else would he be leaving the best military in the entire world right after their triumphant Middle East tour?"

Franks' relationships with certain key Bush Administration figures were "less than perfect," Washburn said.

"You always got the feeling that [Donald] Rumsfeld and Franks never really got along when the cameras were off," Washburn said. "Franks always felt like he was in the shadow of Norman Schwarzkopf, the far more charismatic general who commanded U.S. forces in the 1991 Gulf War."

Like Franks, Schwarzkopf left the army with plans to pursue a solo career, though a lackluster raid on a Japanese fishing village and a poorly received attack on the Dominican Republic led to the cancellation of a number of solo bombing dates in the Balkans.

"Schwarzkopf influenced me greatly," Franks said. "I would be honored to work with him in the future, should he care to collaborate with me outside of the confines of the U.S. Army."

Though Franks said he is "excited and energized" by his future prospects as a solo artist, disappointed fans say the U.S. Army will not be the same without him.

"He wasn't flashy, but he was the backbone of that group," said Marty Nevins of Valdosta, GA. "No one will ever forget that moment when he decided to launch a massive ground assault on Baghdad rather than engage in a prolonged air campaign. That's just good old-fashioned, meat-and-potatoes invading. None of this fancy shock-and-awe shit. They can bring in somebody else, but I don't think that group's gonna be the same with a new frontman." ⌀

BOX SET from page 163

to Tower [Records] to get a Miles Davis CD, but there were, like, dozens of them, not to mention all these 40-disc *Complete Live At The Plugged Nickel—1965* box sets or whatever. I ended up buying an Ornette Coleman CD, since I knew he's supposed to be pretty important, but that ended up being a total mistake. So a few days later, I went back for the Burns box."

Continued Bergkamp: "Even though I haven't cracked it open, I've looked over the list of artists included. It seems like there are some pretty big names on there, people I should really try to force myself to know."

Despite his lack of familiarity with jazz, Bergkamp said he has listened to it on numerous occasions over the years.

By purchasing the anthology, Bergkamp said he hoped to broaden his musical horizons.

"One of my friends in college made me a mix tape that I used to play while I studied," Bergkamp said. "Unfortunately, she didn't write down any of the people. I'm pretty sure there were a couple of John Coltrane songs on there, but I don't know which ones. Ever since then, if I'm just chilling out reading a magazine, I'll put on a jazz station, but I never really catch who plays what."

By purchasing the anthology, Bergkamp said he hoped to broaden his musical horizons, as well as improve his romantic life.

"Girls love guys who are into jazz," Bergkamp said. "Knowing about, like, Thelonious Monk makes you look all sophisticated and soulful. Next time there's some chick I want to score with, I'm sure the box set will do the trick, but I really should take off the shrink wrap before I bring her home. I don't want it to look like I bought it just to impress her."

Bergkamp said he sees his purchase as a sign of his growing maturity.

"I feel like I'm at an age where's I'm too old to just like rock and rap and R&B," Bergkamp said. "I still really prefer it, but to have a few Charles Mingus CDs in your collection is a nice way to make you feel like more of an adult. Plus, if I ever feel like listening to something without lyrics, it's there." ⌀

TEENS from page 163

helping.

"Last week, Mr. Rogowski was all up in my face about how I got to go to the job center," said Manny Acevedo, 18, who has struggled with substance abuse for more than three years. "I told him I didn't have no ride, so he says he'll drive me himself, and about an hour later, he shows up in the sorriest car I ever seen. Me and my sisters, we was laughing our asses off as he pull up. I was like, 'Why don't *you* go to the job center, Mr. Career Advice Man? 'Cause with that car, it's pretty obvious you ain't getting paid.'"

"Mr. Rogowski drive one seriously ugly-ass car," agreed Tyquan Banks, 18, another Second Start program member.

Rogowski said he purchased the Subaru in 1997 "just to use as a winter beater" after his previous car was stolen from outside his workplace at the Cook County Department of Social Services office. Though he planned to keep the car just long enough to last him through the winter months, budget cuts in Chicago's social-services programs resulted in a 15 percent salary cut, leaving him unable to trade in the vehicle.

"After the pay cut, I could no longer float the loan I'd been banking on that spring, so I had to put off getting a better car," Rogowski said. "I figured I'd just put it off for another year. I've been doing that for—how long?—I guess about five years now."

Continued Rogowski: "If that's not bad enough, these kids won't let me hear the end of it."

During a trip to the Cook County Courthouse for a preliminary parental-fitness hearing in April, single mother of two Mary Carver, 17, told Rogowski, "We should make a quick stop first—at the dump, where this piece of garbage you're driving belongs."

During a trip to the Cook County Courthouse for a preliminary parental-fitness hearing in April, single mother of two Mary Carver, 17, told Rogowski, "We should make a quick stop first—at the dump, where this piece of garbage you're driving belongs." She then pointed at him and laughed.

Rogowski suffered more good-natured ribbing from Louis Stefano, 15, who asked the social worker if he should borrow money from his mother's welfare check "to pay a truck to come haul away that piece-of-shit car of yours."

According to experts, such exchanges are not uncommon between troubled teens and the drastically underpaid civil servants who are assigned to help them.

"After the pay cut, I could no longer float the loan I'd been banking on that spring, so I had to put off getting a better car," Rogowski said. "I figured I'd just put it off for another year. I've been doing that for—how long?—I guess about five years now."

"These kids live under tremendous social pressure to achieve status in a visible, immediately recognizable way—designer clothes, flashy cars, jewelry—even if it means turning to crime," said sociologist Dr. Jeremy Gottlieb, author of *The Bling-Bling Factor: How Society Teaches Disadvantaged Kids To Value Instant Gratification Over Substantive Values*. "Music videos and magazines teach them that to get respect, you have to be a 'playa.' So you have to admit, it's ridiculous to expect them to respect an ostensible 'authority figure' whose annual salary is less than what their average neighborhood drug dealer makes in a month."

"I mean, have you seen what these social workers have to drive?" added Gottlieb, stifling a laugh. "Man, talk about shitboxes on wheels."

For his part, Rogowski said he tries to view the teasing as just another occupational hazard.

"I try to let it roll off my back," he said. "I realize these are kids who, in most cases, are dealing with intense personal issues of low self-esteem and poor self-image, and that this is just a defense mechanism to compensate for their own insecurities. They are, by and large, traumatized children who live every day in the shadow of drugs, poverty, and violence. So I'm sympathetic to their situation."

Added Rogowski: "On the other hand, I certainly wouldn't mind if someday the city decided to pay me enough money to afford a car that doesn't need a half-gallon of oil poured under the hood every three days just to keep the fucking thing running." Ø

KID from page 164

and read something to cope with the horrible boredom and isolation, I'd flip open the encyclopedia. In the cold arctic night, it was a real comfort to read those things and be reminded of a time when life was simpler and seemed so full of promise—back when I was a fresh-faced young kid who had that report due on space.

After that, I kind of bummed around for a while, sort of directionless. I finally ended up in Boulder, working at this snowboard shop. By that point, hardly anybody remembered that I was that kid who had a report due on space. In fact, when I met my wife Robyn—or I should say ex-wife Robyn—she didn't even know about the report. To her, I was just that guy who worked at the snowboard shop with her brother Kurt. And I didn't mind. That whole report-due-on-space thing seemed long ago, and when we moved in together, I decided to close that whole chapter in my life by getting rid of the encyclopedias.

I know, I know. Maybe I should've kept them for sentimental value, but it was time to move on. I was looking forward to starting a new life with Robyn and the baby, and the last thing I needed was to remain mired in the past, thinking about that report I once had due on space.

It's too bad about Robyn. We gave it a go for a good five years or so, but it didn't work out. She ended up heading down to Arizona where her sisters live, and we're still friends—I mean, we keep in touch, but I don't know. Just wasn't meant to be, I suppose. She wanted to study to be a registered nurse. I offered to go find the guy in my building who I gave the encyclopedias to and see if I could get them back for her. You know, in case she ever had a report due on stethoscopes or taking people's blood pressure or something, but she said the class provided a textbook that had everything she needed. I miss her sometimes. But, hey, that's life, right?

Anyhow, I left Boulder shortly after that. The apartment was just too lonely, and since I didn't have the encyclopedias or the wife, I didn't need that much room anymore.

Sure is funny how life works out. I mean, if you'd asked me 15 or 20 years ago, back when I had that report due on space, what I was going to end up doing with my life, I never thought I'd wake up in my early 30s and find myself managing a U-Store-It facility in Tallahassee. But I can't complain. I've lived a pretty interesting life, even if it wasn't always what I expected. Besides, I'll always have my memories—and that report on space. Ø

After that, I kind of bummed around for a while, sort of directionless. I finally ended up in Boulder, working at this snowboard shop. By that point, hardly anybody remembered that I was that kid who had a report due on space.

21-GUN SALUTE from page 162

amounts of blood. Passersby were amazed by the unusually large amounts of blood. Passersby were amazed by the unusually large

I'll admit that my grades at Hamburger U. could've been better.

see 21-GUN SALUTE page 169

COMMUNITY VOICES

Let Smoove Rock Your Body And World

By Smoove B
Love Man

Have I told you how wonderful you are? When I am with you, I feel like a whole new Smoove. Since you have asked me not to call you at work, I have opted to discuss your fineness through my column.

I know we have known each other for only two weeks, but I know you are the girl for me. You are the only one I want to laugh with, talk with, and grind on the dance floor with. You are the only one I want to ride.

I am capable of bringing you to a state of freakstasy that no other man could ever bring you to. You can try to find this level of sexual satisfaction with some other man, but know that if you break from Smoove, I cannot guarantee that I will still be single when you realize that only I can satisfy *all* your senses. Then, you would be living in a cold, cruel, Smoove-less world, and I would not wish that upon you. You are too special to me.

Damn, girl, you need to take the rest of the day off so I can break you off doggy-style in my bathroom.

Ever since we met two weeks ago, I knew you were the one for me. Your

We will go back to my place, where I will prepare a dinner specially suited for one as lovely as you. While I am cooking the meal, we will talk about your life, your hopes, and your dreams. At this point, I will thaw a deluxe bag of jumbo shrimp for you to sample as the appetizer. There will also be cocktail sauce.

style, your booty, and your class are beyond all compare. In a world populated with many fine women, you are without a doubt the most fine. Let Smoove take you out tonight or, if you are busy, tomorrow night to show you how I treat a lady as exceptional as you. Allow me to break it down:

First, I will pick you up from your house in a white limousine and take you to the finest dance club in the entire city. The people at this club will

I will stroke your hair and tell you such complimentary things as "You are like a fine statue carved out of brown marble," and "Your eyes are like pools of creamy Italian butter," and "You have beautiful shoes." You will know that I mean these things because they come from the heart.

be attractive and the beats will be crazy. We will not be in the club for a minute before we get on the dance floor. Even though the other people will be good dancers, we will be the best. When you bump, I will bump. When you grind, I will grind. We will move together like twins who happen to like to freak.

When you have had your fill of dancing, I will take you by the hand and lead you to the most romantic corner of the entire club and sit you down on one of the plush, red-velvet couches. While you rest, Smoove will go the bar and purchase a drink for you. Before I bring it back to you, I will taste it, demanding finer gin should it fall short of my expectations for you. Also, I will ask for less ice so that your gin and tonic is not diluted.

While you sip your drink, I will stroke your hair and tell you such complimentary things as "You are like a fine statue carved out of brown marble," and "Your eyes are like pools of creamy Italian butter," and "You have beautiful shoes." You will know that I mean these things because they come from the heart, and the heart is always true.

At this point, we will go back to my place, where I will prepare a dinner specially suited for one as lovely as you. While I am cooking the meal, we will talk about your life, your hopes, and your dreams. At this point, I will thaw a deluxe bag of jumbo shrimp for you to sample as the appetizer.

There will also be cocktail sauce.

Finally, a dinner of lobster, shipped to me that morning in only the coldest of ice from the finest lobster region in all of Maine, will be completed and placed on the table. Along with the lobster will not only be melted butter, but also side dishes. Some of them will be corn, peas, and baked potato. When the meal is over, we will have dessert and coffee.

At this point, you will be so turned on by this night of dancing and lobster that you will be dying to sex me wild. But instead of taking you to my bedroom to knock boots, I will build your desire even more. I will do this by leading you to my living room, where I will light a fire and hand-feed you the finest strawberries available. If you do not enjoy strawberries, I will have other types of berries at my disposal that can be fed to you in a sexy manner. Between bites, I will offer you sips of champagne in a glass made specifically to maximize your champagne-drinking pleasure.

As much as you want to, you will no longer be able to control your desire. Neither will I. This is when I will lead you to my polar-bear-skin rug so we can do it all night long. You will cry for more, and you shall receive it. I will hit it until you can take no more. Then, when you are 100 percent satisfied, I will stop. After that, I will kiss your belly button and tell you how beautiful you are until you fall asleep in my arms.

Damn.

In the morning, I will make you waffles that have chocolate chips embedded in them. There will coffee waiting for you, and there will also be a cup with cream and two sugars, just the way you like it, cooling on the breakfast bar. If you want toast, I will make it for you and offer you a staggering array of exotic French jams.

Through this display of caring and thoughtfulness, you will see that I am the one for you. We are like two slightly different colored beads on a single ancient necklace. We are so right together, it hurts to even speak your name when you are not around me. Do not doubt my words. Believe me when I say this to you. Smoove's love will rock your world.

Peace.

HOROSCOPES

Your Horoscope

By Lloyd Schumner Sr.
Retired Machinist and
A.A.P.B.-Certified Astrologer

Aries: (March 21–April 19)
You never thought you'd laugh at the old pie-in-the-face gag again, but that was before they could accelerate pie to the speed of light.

Taurus: (April 20–May 20)
The residents of Tulsa will make you pay for every dollar of damage you've caused, but they're not heartless, so they'll let you keep the bison.

Gemini: (May 21–June 21)
Your visit to the country will inspire the coining of a new folk saying, "Some days you calm the beast, some days you free the cowboy."

Cancer: (June 22–July 22)
Running for mayor might not seem too realistic, but just wait until they get a load of your new suit.

Leo: (July 23–Aug. 22)
From Thursday forward, your name will be mentioned every time flaming corn dogs rain down from the sky.

Virgo: (Aug. 23–Sept. 22)
There are, in fact, good and evil twins, but a greater range of moral choices is available to you as a sextuplet.

Libra: (Sept. 23–Oct. 23)
Just so you know, it isn't still called "running away from home" when you're 31.

Scorpio: (Oct. 24–Nov. 21)
Things will be back to normal in a couple weeks, but your current tick infestation is just the beginning.

Sagittarius: (Nov. 22–Dec. 21)
This week's smorgasbord of nudity and bullfighting will erase all remaining doubts about your ability to be a network TV programmer.

Capricorn: (Dec. 22–Jan. 19)
The prosecuting attorney will be ruthless, relentless, and efficient in exposing your crimes, but at one point you'll be able to see right down her blouse.

Aquarius: (Jan. 20–Feb. 18)
This week marks the four-year anniversary of your solemn oath to develop a lifestyle that is in no way influenced by Sandy Duncan.

Pisces: (Feb. 19–March 20)
You know that one day you'll have to tell your family you're not really a chicken, but for now, they really need the eggs.

NEWS

Art Student's Nudes Obviously Drawn From *Hustler*

see ARTS page 3C

Taste Acquired

see LOCAL page 5E

5-Year-Old Stares Longingly Down Garbage Chute

see LOCAL page 10E

ATM Slapped

see LOCAL page 12E

STATshot

A look at the numbers that shape your world.

Why Did We Propose?

1. To end awkward silence
2. Desperate to assert rapidly fading heterosexuality
3. Wanted to be on Jumbotron
4. Didn't think she'd actually say yes
5. Always wanted a mistress
6. Because we... love you?

0 74470 94595 6 00

THE ONION • $2.00 US • $3.00 CAN

the ONION®

VOLUME 39 ISSUE 23 AMERICA'S FINEST NEWS SOURCE™ 19–25 JUNE 2003

College-Radio DJ Thinks He Has Cult Following

CHARLESTON, IL—College-radio disc jockey Jordan Haley is convinced that "Rock Blossom," his show airing Thursdays from midnight to 2 a.m. on WEIU 88.9 FM, has a devoted cult following, the Eastern Illinois University senior told reporters Monday.

"I can't say how many people listen regularly, but I bet it's a lot for a college station," said Haley, 22, who has used the moniker DJ Hale Storm since he started hosting the show in December 2001. "When I hit the mic, I'd say at least a thousand people tune in on average. We've never done any kind of survey, so I don't have the exact figures. A thousand is a guesstimate. For all I know, it could be way more."

Haley said his fans are drawn to his eclectic music choices, which set him apart from other DJs at the low-wattage station.

"I'm always mixing it up," Haley said. "In my opinion, the other guys here cling to their niche too much. Like, Scott [Schefter] always plays a

see DJ page 172

Above: Jordan Haley, a.k.a. DJ Hale Storm, broadcasts to his cult non-following.

GOP Reports Record Second-Quarter Profits

Above: Republican Party board members wave their quarterly dividend checks.

WASHINGTON, DC—At a stockholders meeting Monday, the Republican Party announced record profits for the second quarter of 2003, exceeding analysts' expectations by more than 20 cents per share.

The gain marks the GOP's third consecutive profitable quarter, and puts the party on track for its best 12-month cycle since 1991, the year of the first Gulf War.

"Obviously, we're ecstatic," said Speaker of the House Dennis Hastert (R-IL), who celebrated with other high-ranking GOP members at a champagne brunch in his chambers Tuesday. "This is heartening news for our party, especially coming as it does during such a sluggish overall period for the American economy."

The GOP posted a net profit of $3.48

see GOP page 173

Above: The site of the vacation ruined for the Mahaffeys (inset) by Disney.

Disney Family Vacation Ruined By Walt Disney Company

ORLANDO, FL—A magical Walt Disney World family vacation was ruined last weekend by the stringent policies and protocol of the Walt Disney Company.

"They call Disney World 'The Happiest Place On Earth,' but being there was oddly stressful and upsetting," said David Mahaffey, 36, a Dover, DE, insurance-claims adjuster who, along with his wife and two children, endured a four-day visit to the Orlando theme park. "Why did Disney have to ruin the Disney magic for everyone?"

Plagued by everything from park rules strictly governing conduct to wildly overpriced concessions, the Mahaffeys had hoped to lose themselves in a wonderland of fun, but were thwarted at every turn by the entertainment giant.

see VACATION page 172

FCC Media Deregulation

The FCC has eased restrictions on same-city ownership of newspapers and TV stations, freeing media conglomerates to create local monopolies. What do *you* think?

"Yeah? Well, if this is such a big problem, why aren't we hearing more about it on the news?"

Mitch Ahearn
Auto Mechanic

"I'd be greatly worried, were it not for Clear Channel's proven track record as a passionate and responsible guardian of the values of the Fourth Estate."

Karen Syms
Homemaker

"Oh, crap. Now, both my local papers will carry *Hagar The Horrible*."

Kris Eccles
Cashier

"Hold on—does Chomsky know about this? Because, man, oh, man, is he ever gonna hit the roof."

Ken Pierce
Systems Analyst

"I'd be concerned about how this will affect the radio airwaves, but fortunately, I'm a huge Pink fan."

Mindy Roberts
Physical Therapist

"Shhh. TV's on."

Richard Powers
Investment Banker

Hillary's Bestseller

Last week, U.S. Sen. Hillary Clinton's much-anticipated memoir, *Living History*, hit bookstores. Among the former first lady's revelations:

- Once put four Secret Service agents in hospital, but won't say how
- Owns a lot of pantsuits
- Husband had affair with White House intern named Monica Lewinsky
- For years, has been stealing political secrets and selling them to the women
- Remained married to Bill only after making difficult admission to self that she is a presidentosexual
- Enjoyed *Rocky I*, *II*, *III*, and *V*, but not *IV*
- Ain't no woman can love Bill like she can
- Like Bill, also had a love affair... with reading
- Originally came to Earth to steal our water
- Has no plans to run for president in 2004 or 2012

the ONION®
America's Finest News Source.™

Herman Ulysses Zweibel
Founder

T. Herman Zweibel
Publisher Emeritus
J. Phineas Zweibel
Publisher
Maxwell Prescott Zweibel
Editor-In-Chief

You Are A Beautiful Woman, And I Mean That In A Completely Non-Threatening Way

By Bruce Curran

Pardon me for staring. I'd hate for you to think I was one of those guys who thinks it's okay to approach women he doesn't even know with unsolicited romantic advances.

My God, you're stunning.

Don't take that the wrong way. I realize full well how inappropriate it might be for me to gaze longingly at you, a complete stranger, and then express awe at your incredible looks. I can certainly understand how any woman might find that off-putting, but let me assure you that when I say you are beautiful, I mean that in a completely non-threatening way.

When I saw you emerging from that Walgreens and looked into the most stunning eyes I've ever seen, I was overcome by a desire to hold your perfect cheekbones in my trembling hands and kiss your moist, yielding lips like they've never been kissed. But I would never in a million years dream of actually doing so, because it would surely make you ill at ease.

Unlike so many men, I don't view women as mere sexual conquests. I abhor such a view. You are so much more to me than an object of carnal desire. You are someone I respect and would never dream of approaching in an intimidating manner. After all the crude, uninvited remarks you must receive on a daily basis from men, isn't it refreshing to be approached by someone who actually takes your feelings into consideration?

I have the urge to run to the nearest street vendor and impulsively buy you flowers, but I won't, for fear that you would think it too forward. Would it help to prove my sincerity if I were to weep with joy at the sight of you? I am not afraid to show my feelings, as long as that expression of romantic longing does not frighten you.

Men can be coarse and vulgar, especially when enflamed with passion for a woman of your magnificence. But I would never want to cause you the slightest bit of emotional unease as I express my desire to gently slide the straps of your sundress off your milky-white shoulders in a non-menacing way. I would give you adequate time to become emotionally ready for such an encounter and allow you to set the pace. I'm not like all those crude men who only want to get their hands on the frilly lace Victoria's Secret underthings which no doubt caress your stunning form under that sundress. I am not the sort who sees you merely as a receptacle for my own wildest fantasies. I am a caring soul who would keep such lustful thoughts to myself until I had gone out of my way to ease your mind first.

I never would run my hands through your hair, unless I had first gained your explicit approval. I'm not one of those men who only thinks of satisfying his own animal needs. Trust me, if we were ever to get together, I would consider all your needs, both physical and emotional, so you would have no reason to find me selfish.

Please! Don't run away. And when I say "Don't run away," know that I mean it in the least "I'm gonna get you" way possible.

Yes, a man with a less-than-heartfelt desire for your perfect, round, dimpled ass might chase after you as you hurry down the street in an attempt to evade someone you assume only wants to make you feel uncomfortable. But I would never do such a thing. I will only follow discreetly from a safe distance, explaining my good intentions from several paces behind you as I continue to woo and pursue you in my own special, non-scary way. You will feel totally at ease once you understand my motives.

I notice that you have not offered me your phone number. No matter. I would never ask you to give me such personal information until I was absolutely sure you were ready to give it to me. I would never want you to think of me as some sort of pervert stalker who follows strange women down the street.

My darling, you must know that I am not one of those repellent lowlifes who make unbelievably attractive women like you afraid to leave the house in short, flimsy dresses like yours merely because they are frightened that showing their perfect, shapely legs might provoke some untoward response. I would never in a million years make you feel the least bit threatened by my all-consuming lust for your tanned, lithe, nubile flesh.

Wait! There's no need for you to quicken your pace to try to outdistance me. I will make my move only when you are ready for my embrace and not one minute sooner. I would never think of forcing my affections upon you one second before you felt completely at ease with the idea of my hands drifting across the contours of your curvaceous torso and exploring your private recesses.

I'll be waiting! Just as soon as you feel non-threatened by me, I'll be here. Ø

95 Percent Of Opinions Withheld On Visit To Family

KALAMAZOO, MI—A full 95 percent of the opinions held by Justin Wilmot, 26, were kept to himself Sunday during a Father's Day visit with his family.

"No one in my family really gets my worldview, so I find it easier just to smile and nod and agree with everything," Wilmot said Monday. "When I'm with them, I tend to be a lot quieter than when I'm hanging out with friends."

> **Among the subjects Wilmot declined to weigh in on during the weekend get-together: new Tropical Sprite, *Survivor*, Iraq, golf, and his brother-in-law's fantastic idea for a calling-card side business.**

Wilmot, who grew up in Kalamazoo and now lives in Chicago, described the visit as "seven hours of self-censorship."

"We're totally not on the same wavelength at all," Wilmot said. "I'm not just talking about dangerous subjects like politics or religion, but pretty much everything they bring up—the shows they watch, the things they buy, the people they know. So if someone says *Daddy Day Care* was hilarious, I may be thinking, 'I can't believe Eddie Murphy was once respected as a subversive comic genius,' but I sure as hell don't say it."

Among the subjects Wilmot declined to weigh in on during the weekend get-together: new Tropical Sprite, *Survivor*, the selfishness of childless couples, Iraq, golf, AM talk radio, and his brother-in-law's fantastic idea for a calling-card side business.

Wilmot said he used to voice his opinions, but has long since given up.

"There was a time when my sister would mention how much she wants an SUV, and I'd be unable to resist launching into a whole thing about how irresponsible and wasteful they are. But after receiving my thousandth blank, confused stare from everybody at the table, I realized it was futile," Wilmot said. "Now, I don't even flinch when my dad mentions he's reading 'this amazing book called *The Celestine Prophecy*.' That's how bad it is."

In the course of Sunday's meal, Wilmot estimated that he heard 100 statements he could have strenuously contested. Instead, he responded with such neutral phrases as, "Cool," "Uh-huh," "Wow," "I know," "Definitely," and "Oh, good."

Above: Wilmot holds his tongue while his sister and mother discuss their mutual excitement about *Legally Blonde 2*.

"My brother-in-law belongs to the NRA, which used to appall me," Wilmot said. "Well, it still appalls me, but now I'm appalled silently. Same goes for my mom's assertion that El Taco Loco is 'the best Mexican restaurant in town.' I don't even bother mentioning Arturo's, this little place over on Third Street that's the only authentic Mexican place in all of Kalamazoo. I'm sure she's never heard of it."

When he was young, Wilmot actually enjoyed engaging his family in debate, but now he would rather smile pleasantly as his brother's wife talks about the latest exciting arrival on the local shopping scene.

"Meredith said they're putting up a huge new Target Greatland right by their house," Wilmot said. "She says she's psyched because Target is way better than Wal-Mart. I just nodded and said, 'Yeah, totally.'"

"Once you let go of the need to express your thoughts to your family, you suddenly feel much lighter," Wilmot said. "You just float along blissfully, finally liberated from the burden of having any presence at all. It's sort of like getting to return to the womb. Which is way more enjoyable than trying to explain to a tableful of Celine Dion fans why you can't stand her." ø

NEWS IN BRIEF

U.S. Refuses To Allow U.N. Weapons Inspectors Back Into Iraq

BAGHDAD, IRAQ—For the third time in as many weeks, U.S. officials denied U.N. weapons inspectors' request to reenter Iraq. "Thanks so much for the offer, but we can handle it from here," Lt. Gen. William Wallace told U.N. chief inspector Hans Blix. "We're getting very close to finding Saddam's massive WMD stockpile, and to have the U.N. get involved at this point would just complicate matters. Sorry." U.N. Secretary General Kofi Annan has given President Bush a June 28 deadline to let inspectors into Iraq.

Christ Returns For Some Of His Old Things

JERUSALEM—After being away for nearly two millennia, Jesus Christ triumphantly returned Monday to pick up some of His old belongings. "I realize this isn't exactly how the world's Christians were imagining it, but I left a really comfortable pair of sandals in Galilee, and I wanted them back," said Christ, who died for our sins. "Also, I'm pretty sure I lent [Apostle] Simon Peter my best goblet at the Last Supper." This marks Christ's first return since 76 A.D., when He thought He'd forgotten to turn off His coffee pot.

Father's Day Gift Way Shittier Than Mother's Day Gift

TOPEKA, KS—For the seventh year in a row, the Father's Day gift that Robert Frankel, 48, received from his children Sunday was way shittier than the Mother's Day gift his wife received five weeks earlier. "Wow, thanks, Marc and Erica, they're great," Frankel said, as he unwrapped a $9 pair of padded socks. "These should really keep me warm." The gift, which stood in sharp contrast to the $85 day-spa gift certificate the children lovingly gave their mother on May 11, was presented without a card.

Banks Introduce 75-Cent Surcharge For Using Word 'Bank'

NEW YORK—Executives from the nation's 50 largest banks announced Monday that, effective July 1, all customers will be assessed a 75-cent surcharge each time they use the word "bank." "Now, each time a customer uses the word 'bank' in either its spoken or written form, 75 cents will be automatically deducted from his or her account," said Kenneth Nordland, 54, president of the American Banking Association. "For instance, if you say, 'I bank with Bank of America,' that would cost you $1.50." Nordland added that customers wishing to avoid the penalty are encouraged to use the alternate phrase "financial institution."

Woman Checks Terror-Alert Level Before Leaving For Work

FORT DODGE, IA—As she does every morning, local resident Wendy Trotter, 33, consulted the Department of Homeland Security web site Tuesday to check the terror-alert level before leaving for work. "I like to leave the house prepared," said Trotter, a cashier at a local Cub Foods. "I'd hate to assume that the level is still Elevated, only to find myself caught in a High-level situation. And if I didn't check, how would I know whether I need to coordinate necessary security efforts with federal, state, and local law enforcement and begin contingency procedures by moving to an alternate venue?" ø

VACATION from page 169

The Mahaffeys' dissatisfaction began soon after their arrival. Despite being in a huge, open park with dozens of attractions, the family was unable to roam freely, confronted at every turn by signs commanding them to remain on the clearly delineated brick-paved paths. This thwarted an unspoken but keenly felt sense of wanderlust in the family.

"There was a lot of gorgeous greenery, but most of it was roped off," said Amy Mahaffey, 34. "You could only leave the path if you wanted to go into a shop or café. It made me imagine some behind-the-scenes pencil pusher wanting to save the company a few bucks on sod and petunias, or to ward off potential injury lawsuits. I wanted to be a kid again, but I might as well have stayed at work."

The family also found itself put on edge by the passive-aggressive friendliness of park employees, or "cast members."

"They were always wearing these hollow, insincere, glued-on smiles, whether they were selling you a $6 croissant or strapping you into the 'It's A Small World' ride and genially ordering you to keep your hands by your sides at all times," David said. "The creepiest example was the guy outside Space Mountain who said hello to us with a big grin on his face as he was on his hands and knees cleaning up vomit."

An encounter with Mickey Mouse further deepened the family's malaise. After an awkward tour of Mickey's "Country Home," a structure with roped-off, dimly lit rooms, the

"The creepiest example was the guy outside Space Mountain who said hello to us with a big grin on his face as he was on his hands and knees cleaning up vomit," David said.

Mahaffeys were led to a darkened chamber where they had a brief audience with the iconic rodent.

"Hugging Mickey was weird," said Abby Mahaffey, 8. "He didn't feel like a cartoon. He was big and scary. It was like hugging a pile of laundry. Then they took our picture, and they said we were taking too long. They said everybody gets 30 seconds with Mickey, no more."

The Mahaffeys were reluctant to return to the park on the second day, but they decided to soldier on, determined not to waste the $832 they'd spent on four $208 "Park Hopper" four-day passes.

"Jake and Abby went on a bunch more rides, but you could tell they were just going through the motions," David said. "Then Amy had to take Abby back to the hotel because she became frightened by the Country Bear Jamboree. I guess the animatronic grizzlies and the murky sound from the PA system were too much for her."

Reflecting on their vacation upon returning home Tuesday, the Mahaffeys said they wished the Walt Disney Company's definition of fun had been more consistent with their own.

"We thought a Disney family vacation meant laughter, relaxation, and release from your everyday cares," Mahaffey said. "Well, I guess we were wrong. Apparently, it means overstimulation, the Disney logo absolutely everywhere, and $15 keychains."

Upon learning of the Mahaffeys' less-than-positive experience, Disney spokeswoman Jennifer Caldwell

"We thought a Disney family vacation meant laughter, relaxation, and release from your everyday cares," Mahaffey said.

expressed regret.

"We endeavor to make our theme parks the ultimate in family fun, and if this was not the Mahaffeys' experience, we are deeply sorry," Caldwell said. "Perhaps we can make it up to them with four complimentary tickets to the upcoming feature film *Pirates Of The Caribbean*, based on one of our most popular Magic Kingdom attractions. Don't miss this exciting swashbuckler, in theaters nationwide July 9." Ø

DJ from page 169

lot of psychobilly, and Tim [Arbus] plays a ton of emo. But with me, you never know what you're gonna get. I might play something like the new Sigur Rós, then turn around and play something off the new Oxes record. Or maybe even Lovecup's 'Hi Pazoo,' which is one of the best songs from the mid-'90s Champaign scene. I challenge my audience, and that's why

As a graduating senior, Haley expressed sadness about the impending end of his show, abandoning what he imagines are hundreds of ardent listeners.

people respond to my show. My success should prove to other radio stations that people don't want to be spoon-fed their music."

Though "Rock Blossom" is heard mainly by his girlfriend and a handful of friends who request songs while they get stoned, Haley said his show is distinctive because of his personality.

"I hate boring, robotic Top 40 DJs who never go off the script," Haley said. "Me, I like to mention concerts that are coming to town. Or sometimes, I'll tell people a personal anecdote about a song or just share what's going through my head. That's the kind of stuff you don't get listening to some corporate behemoth."

Another quality that sets Haley apart is his encyclopedic knowledge of underground music.

"A lot of DJs think that if they know Rocket From The Crypt or Burning Airlines, they're up on the alt-rock scene—whatever *that is*," Haley said. "I was the one who introduced Black Dice, The Mink Lungs, and The (International) Noise Conspiracy to the people of the Charleston metro area, so it's understandable why my show would be bigger than [fellow WEIU DJ] Eric [Poppel]'s."

Though over the last two years he has received only one phone call from a woman—a drunken sorority sister asking him to play a song from the *Grease* soundtrack—Haley said he has a large female following.

"I like to play a lot of female-friendly stuff, like Shannon Wright and Girls Against Boys," Haley said. "So that's definitely a part of it. I think what the ladies like most, though, is my voice. I've been told by a few women that I've got a good radio voice, sometimes by women who didn't even know I had a radio show."

Discussing his nonexistent fans, Haley said he believes they like the fact that he keeps his show lighthearted.

"Most of the other DJs around here take music so seriously," Haley said. "What they don't get is that music expresses the full range of human emotions, and that laughter is part of that range. That's why if I play something like June Panic or Songs:Ohia, I might lighten things up with a King Missile song or maybe even something by Hayseed Dixie, this funny bluegrass AC/DC cover band. It keeps things from getting too heavy. I'm sure my listeners appreciate that."

Eager to stay on top of the music scene, Haley attends as many shows a week as he can. Being a regular on the local concert scene also enables him to show his fans that he's "just a normal guy."

"If I don't go to shows, I lose touch with what people like," Haley said. "You can't just exist in an ivory tower, like a lot of DJs do. Plus, I like to tell people on the air which bands I'm going to be checking out that weekend. I want my listeners to know that I may be a DJ, but I'm a fan first."

As a graduating senior, Haley expressed sadness about the impending end of his show, abandoning what he imagines are hundreds of ardent listeners.

"I'm sure a lot of people returning next year will miss 'Rock Blossom,' but life must go on," Haley said. "I've never regretted doing a show, even though it meant missing some cool parties. In the end, it was worth it. My music was the soundtrack to a lot of people's college years, which makes me feel really good. And if nothing else, I've exposed the people of Charleston to the music of NoMeansNo. How many people can claim that?" Ø

Above: Haley waits for the phone lines to light up with song requests.

GOP from page 169

per share, outperforming financial analysts' predictions in the $3.25 range. It ended the quarter with a market cap of $340 billion—a 17 percent gain attributed to a war-related rise in emotional investment in the party by the public and a rise in financial investment by such major corporations as Lockheed Martin and Halliburton.

"Quarters like this don't come along very often," Republican Party CFO

"We still have to streamline certain divisions of our company, there's no question about that," Cheney said. "We're still, for example, spending way too much in our Health and Human Services and our Education departments. Once we get those areas and a few others under control, our balance sheet will look like a million bucks."

Above: Cheney enjoys the spoils of a profitable year.

Dick Cheney said. "In a three-month span, we inked deals with more than 1,300 corporations, signing contracts to build everything from oil pipelines to surveillance equipment to aircraft carriers. We've also aggressively expanded into some lucrative new overseas markets. I honestly haven't seen a boom like this since the go-go early '90s."

In spite of such successes, the GOP continues to look for new ways to improve its bottom line.

"We still have to streamline certain divisions of our company, there's no question about that," Cheney said. "We're still, for example, spending way too much in our Health and Human Services and our Education departments. Once we get those areas and a few others under control, our balance sheet will look like a million bucks."

Added Cheney: "Or, I should say, a *trillion* bucks."

The Republican Party's financial health stands in stark contrast to its biggest business rival. The Democratic Party, which suffered its 10th straight fiscal quarter in the red, is expected to miss its earnings mark for the third year in a row. The losses have prompted party leaders to consider the possibility of early retirement for some of its high-ranking legislative-branch officers.

"Right now, we've got some organizational problems that need to be worked out," Democratic Party CEO Dick Gephardt said. "To be successful in this game, you need an internal leadership structure that gives your company a top-to-bottom sales vision, and I'll be the first to admit we've got room for improvement in that area. It certainly doesn't help that the market for some of our core businesses, like public housing and health care, are in the toilet."

A majority of the GOP's 7,500 employees work on the support end of the organization. Approximately 1,200 of these workers handle "professional services," such as helping voters choose the right Republican products for their home or business.

The party is traded on the NYSE under the symbol USGOP. ⌀

WATERSHED from page 167

amounts of blood. Passersby were amazed by the unusually large amounts of blood. Passersby were amazed by the unusually large amounts of blood. Passersby were amazed by the unusually large amounts of blood. Passersby were amazed by the unusually large amounts of blood. Passersby were amazed by the unusually large amounts of blood. Passersby were amazed by the unusually large amounts of blood. Passersby were amazed by the unusually large amounts of blood. Passersby were amazed by the unusually large amounts of blood. Passersby were amazed by the unusually large amounts of blood. Passersby were amazed by the unusually large amounts of blood. Passersby were amazed by the unusually large amounts of blood. Passersby were amazed by the unusually large amounts of blood. Passersby were amazed by the unusually large amounts of blood. Passersby were amazed by the unusually large

Let me tell you what you meant to say.

amounts of blood. Passersby were amazed by the unusually large amounts of blood. Passersby were amazed by the unusually large amounts of blood. Passersby were amazed by the unusually large amounts of blood. Passersby were amazed by the unusually large amounts of blood. Passersby were amazed by the unusually large amounts of blood. Passersby were amazed by the unusually large amounts of blood. Passersby were amazed by the unusually large amounts of blood. Passersby were amazed by the unusually large amounts of blood. Passersby were amazed by the unusually large amounts of blood. Passersby were amazed by the unusually large amounts of blood. Passersby were amazed by the unusually large amounts of blood. Passersby were amazed by the unusually large amounts of blood. Passersby were amazed by the unusually large amounts of blood. Passersby were amazed by the unusually large amounts of blood. Passersby were amazed by the unusually large amounts of blood. Passersby were amazed by the unusually large amounts of blood. Passersby were amazed by the unusually large amounts of blood. Passersby were amazed by the unusually large amounts of blood. Passersby were

see WATERSHED page 179

COMMUNITY VOICES

By Now, The Uzbekistanis Have Discovered The Disappearance Of Their Orbital Platform

Ah, I see we're all here. Well done, everyone. I was confident you could all get to this odd corner of Argentina by noon GMT, and you did not disappoint. Although I'm distressed that two of you were forced to risk exposure by using commercial flights. However, as you'll soon see, identity-containment is not our primary concern at this time.

By Director Roberts

Gentlemen, Mei-Ling, we are in crisis as of seven minutes ago, when space station UCCCPZ-5476-43-B failed to crest the horizon over Gdazny. Even if our adversary's NKVD-trained orbital-warfare officers have been uncharacteristically slow on the uptake, we must assume that the Uzbekistanis have, by now, discovered the disappearance of their Rasputin orbital kinetic-energy-weapon platform.

Please, everyone, quiet! We may be in a godforsaken backwater, and this may be a tent, but it is my operations center, and I will have silence. I will explain this to everyone once, understand? As we speak, the vital details are being burst-transmitted to your comlinks—for Klaus and Morgan, to your implants. For now, unless I indicate otherwise, please assume the worst. It's that bad.

Yes, operatives, it has come to this. Six weeks ago, the decision was made to open the Prometheus Dossier. Certain individuals felt that the Uzbeks were too... *unstable*, politically and financially, and could not be allowed to retain possession of certain leftover Russian toys. The European space agencies were very helpful in allowing us use of crucial resources and facilities, and there you have it. The Fader and his men intervened personally, and now we hold the high ground, if you will. But it was a risky project, and it has brought us to the brink.

At approximately 0515 Greenwich, a French AUGUR/CASSANDRA-class low-Earth-orbit meson-resonator operated by an adversary agency detected disturbances in the Earth's magnetosphere above the South Pole. This is not unusual, given the nature of certain international sub-indigo-clearance projects being carried out below the remaining Ross Ice Shelf, but it alerted someone it should not have, and a message was sent to the Uzbeks. Though several selfless anti-communications personnel gave their lives in the attempt, we could not intercept the transmission. But they do not know where we have moved Rasputin. We think they're searching exotic circumlunar orbits at the moment. Which is uncomfortably close to the truth, but it's a big sky.

So. If we are to avoid the biggest debacle since Barcelona, we must act quickly. Samandrea, you will compile a roster of anything with unfired retro-rockets in near-earth orbit. It does not matter what company, government, or international organization claims ownership; just get the damn list to Broadbranch in Emergency Acquisitions, cross-referenced with time-to-orbit for the following vectors. Also, get that idiot Alexei to estimate the survivability of a quarter—no, make that a half-kilo of weaponized plutonium entering the atmosphere in all possible insertion patterns for the orbits in this sitrep.

Gentlemen, Mei-Ling, we are in crisis as of seven minutes ago, when space station UCCCPZ-5476-43-B failed to crest the horizon over Gdazny.

And let's have some coffee. A threat to civilization as we know it is no reason to neglect civilization as we know it, as your uncle would say. How the hell that buzzard dealt with this sort of thing happening every day during his tenure I don't know, God have mercy on his soul. There are days I wish he were still in charge, and I were still a station-keeper in Halifax. Not that I'd want to be in a coastal city if we screw this up.

All right. Technically, I'm not supposed to ask, but do we have any survivors of Project Yggdrasil in this room? Don't give me that look, Molyneaux! Allegations of mutiny and cannibalism were never proven, and they may be the finest zero-gravity combat elements in the Western world. Ben? Quinn? Sidney? I thought so, not that I ever would have asked. Why, Mr. Rosewood, you old coot, I never would have thought it. You are all promoted two ranks as of this moment, unless that would put you above me. Sorry, Quinn.

Congratulations to all of you. Now get to the scramjet at the helipad. You're expected at the Buenos Aires facility within the hour, where you will be issued Gauss weapons, fitted for extravehicular BDU packs, and rotated through circulatory-fluid replacement and augmentation by 0300. I hope you didn't have big breakfasts, gentlemen. You're deploying, rather vertically, within six hours. Godspeed. I wish I were going with you.

I hope you didn't have big breakfasts, gentlemen. You're deploying, rather vertically, within six hours. Godspeed. I wish I were going with you.

Mei-Ling! Get off that damn phone!

Right. I want the short list of equatorial nations who owe us favors and a geographical abstract of any relatively uninhabited tracts of land that are at least 12 miles long east-to-west and situated well above sea level. Evacuate the locals from each and every one of them, minimizing collateral losses. Don't look at me like that! If we did Laramie, we can do this.

Good. Now, Sergei, get at least one of your trained crisis-salvage crews to each of these locations and tell them that a high-speed cargo, hot in both the thermal and radioactive senses, will be arriving in a big hurry within, let me see, 18 hours. They need to have it on the trucks before sunrise local time. For those few who don't know Cyrillic, make sure you issue them cards showing the Russian designations for radioactivity, high magnetism, and xenotechnology.

All right. Everyone else is standby. Those with family in Western capital cities, please see the psych officer. Everyone else grab some sleep. It's going to be a long night. Ø

HOROSCOPES

Your Horoscope

By Lloyd Schumner Sr.
Retired Machinist and
A.A.P.B.-Certified Astrologer

Aries: (March 21–April 19)
You're the first to admit you have problems of your own, but you can't seem to shake your obsession with TV's drunken weathermen.

Taurus: (April 20–May 20)
Witnesses will later testify that you did, in fact, ask the salesman about the Colombian necktie, and to demonstrate how one was worn.

Gemini: (May 21–June 21)
A concert tour of the nation's high-security prisons seemed like a nice idea, but you probably should've gotten the wardens' permission first.

Cancer: (June 22–July 22)
It may need clarifying that when you said you loved your spouse more than life itself, you didn't mean yours.

Leo: (July 23–Aug. 22)
You'll wake from dreams of eating a giant marshmallow to find you've ax-murdered six people in your sleep, but the two things don't seem to be related.

Virgo: (Aug. 23–Sept. 22)
Though several Lego models of yourself have been constructed, you're not really happy with any of them.

Libra: (Sept. 23–Oct. 23)
Alarming developments this week mean that withholding sex will no longer be one of your more effective threats.

Scorpio: (Oct. 24–Nov. 21)
You will be committed to 11 long years of marriage for a bloody murder you did not commit.

Sagittarius: (Nov. 22–Dec. 21)
Your amazing gift for cloying preachiness and bad timing continues this week when a blind orphan girl helps you discover the true meaning of Christmas.

Capricorn: (Dec. 22–Jan. 19)
Things will slowly start returning to normal in your life, which is not really a good thing.

Aquarius: (Jan. 20–Feb. 18)
This is the last chance to renew your subscription to Aquarius. Act now to ensure uninterrupted access to this valuable business, entertainment, and predicting tool.

Pisces: (Feb. 19–March 20)
Your habit of taking the easy way out will finally end this week, but only because you don't have the guts to hang yourself.

the ONION®
VOLUME 39 ISSUE 25 AMERICA'S FINEST NEWS SOURCE™ 3–9 JULY 2003

NEWS

Man Forgets He Has Infant Strapped To Back

see PARENTING page 10D

8-Year-Old Obviously Packed Own Lunch

see LOCAL page 1C

Strom Thurmond Finally, Finally Dies

see NATION page 3A

Yard Sale Reeks Of Divorce

see LOCAL page 5C

STATshot

A look at the numbers that shape your world.

Most Popular Fiddle Songs

1. Second Cousin, First Love
2. From The Bottom Of My Tarp
3. Git That Jew Off The Roof
4. Uncle Pa's Lapbone
5. Turkey In The Sack
6. You Fucking Lied To Me, Minnie Mae
7. The Ballad Of 20 Minutes' Duration

Bush Asks Congress For $30 Billion To Help Fight War On Criticism

WASHINGTON, DC—Citing the need to safeguard "America's most vital institutions and politicians" against potentially devastating attacks, President Bush asked Congress to sign off Monday on a $30 billion funding package to help fight the ongoing War On Criticism.

"Sadly, the threat of criticism is still with us," Bush told members of Congress during a 2 p.m. televised address. "We thought we had defeated criticism with our successes in Afghanistan and Iraq. We thought we had struck at its very heart with the broad discretionary powers of the USA Patriot Act. And we thought that the ratings victory of Fox News, America's News Channel, might signal the beginning of a lasting peace with the media. Yet, despite all this, criticism abounds."

Critical activities, Bush noted, have not returned to pre-Sept. 11 levels,

see BUSH page 178

Above: Bush unveils his sweeping new anti-criticism initiative.

Bowling-Alley Owner Wants TV Ad To Look 'More *Matrix*-y'

Left: Dieber in a rough cut of the *Matrix*-inspired ad.

MENASHA, WI—After seeing the rough cut of his new TV commercial, Bob Dieber, 46, owner of Menasha Lanes, told the 30-second spot's creator to make it look "more *Matrix*-y," sources reported Tuesday.

"Yeah, it definitely has the *Matrix* thing going like I wanted, but I can't help feeling like it could have more," Dieber said of the ad, slated to air on Appleton/Green Bay UPN affiliate WACY-32 during upcoming *Judge Hatchett* telecasts. "There needs to be more special effects or something. Like maybe a bowling ball flying through the air in slow motion. That'd

see MATRIX page 179

Minister Constantly Mentioning Teenage Son's Virginity

PENSACOLA, FL—Much to his son Paul's chagrin, minister Donald Genzler takes every possible opportunity to proudly inform members of Faith United Presbyterian Church that the 16-year-old is still a virgin, "unspoiled by sins of the flesh," sources reported Tuesday.

"As it says in the second book of Timothy, 'Now flee from youthful lusts, and pursue righteousness, faith, love, and peace with those who call on the Lord from a pure heart,'" Genzler said from the pulpit Sunday. "Young people, I urge you to stand tall against the temptation of premarital sex, just as my own son Paul has done."

Seated in the third row, a mortified Paul slid low in the pew and buried his face in his hymnal, hoping not to be spotted.

"It's not easy to grow up in this confusing world, where everyone tells you to 'just do it,'" said Genzler, continuing his sermon. "You teenagers out there should know that not everyone is 'doing it.' My son Paul is not 'doing it.'"

After barely looking up through the remainder of the sermon, Paul fled

see MINISTER page 178

Above: A proud Genzler sermonizes about his son (inset).

The Affirmative-Action Decision

Last week, the Supreme Court upheld the right of universities to keep admissions policies that incorporate race largely intact. What do *you* think?

"Who is the Supreme Court to say what is right and what is wrong?"

Patrick Semple
Architect

"I'm not surprised. Have you seen who's on that court? A black, a coupla women, a Catholic, and at least two homos."

Don Brophy
Auto Mechanic

"Universities need to be diverse in many ways. For example, I think I'd make a great token stupid person."

Matty Lewis
Cashier

"I dated a black guy once. I just wanted to say that."

Michelle Ardmore
Waitress

"If you teach a man to fish, he'll fish for a lifetime. So I hope these schools are teaching fishing."

Donna Gordon
Speech Therapist

"Shit. You know what this means? It's going to be a week of, 'So, did you hear about the affirmative-action ruling?' at work."

Craig Anderson
Systems Analyst

Pottermania Yet Again

With first-day sales of five million, *Harry Potter And The Order Of The Phoenix* is a publishing phenomenon. Why are people buying it?

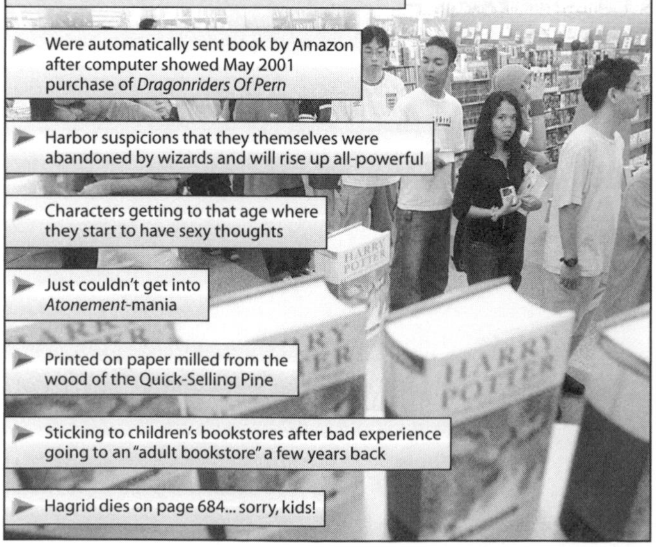

- Only realistic shot at reading an 896-page book
- Were automatically sent book by Amazon after computer showed May 2001 purchase of *Dragonriders Of Pern*
- Harbor suspicions that they themselves were abandoned by wizards and will rise up all-powerful
- Characters getting to that age where they start to have sexy thoughts
- Just couldn't get into *Atonement*-mania
- Printed on paper milled from the wood of the Quick-Selling Pine
- Sticking to children's bookstores after bad experience going to an "adult bookstore" a few years back
- Hagrid dies on page 684... sorry, kids!

the ONION®
America's Finest News Source.™

Herman Ulysses Zweibel
Founder

T. Herman Zweibel
Publisher Emeritus
J. Phineas Zweibel
Publisher
Maxwell Prescott Zweibel
Editor-In-Chief

I Can Beat The Price You're Paying For Sperm

By Donnie Hume

Have I got a deal for you!

I understand you and your husband are going through some tough times in the family-planning department. And, while I can't do anything about your husband's sterility, I *can* do something about the price you're paying for sperm.

What are you paying now? Five, six hundred bucks a payload? I can get you grade-A stuff for half that.

I've been in the sperm-supply game since 1987, and in that time, I've learned countless ways to cut costs while adding value. When you buy from me, you know you're getting the absolute best semen money can buy. What's more, I'll beat any competitor's price.

Okay, let's talk turkey. Now, normally, I charge $450 for a two-ounce batch, but you seem like a nice lady, so I'm gonna cut you a deal: $400.

How can I sell sperm so cheap, you ask? That's simple: I cut out the middleman. Most sperm specimens pass through at least a dozen hands before ever reaching the shelves of the sperm bank, and every one of those people takes a cut. That adds up. I used to work for one of those national banks. I saw customers being overcharged every day, and frankly, it broke my heart. With 16 years experience as an independent sperm supplier, I now do all the work myself—and pass the savings along to you.

Tell you what. Because I like you, I'm going knock another $50 off that price. Just for you. It's unheard of in this business to pay only $350, but if you buy today, that's all it's gonna cost you.

And, if you buy today, I'll deliver today. Other places take weeks or months to process your request. Not me. If it takes me more than 10 minutes to deliver fresh, hot product, it's free. That's a promise from me to you.

You don't want to buy sperm from some big, impersonal bank with outlets all over the country, do you? You want the personal touch. You want it from a person—a real, live flesh-and-blood human being. If you can't look your donor in the eye, can you really trust his sperm?

When you buy my sperm, you know exactly what you're getting—the magical little potion necessary to make another extraordinary human being just like me. As you can see, I'm tall and reasonably attractive. I have a college degree, and I'm a real entrepreneur, full of ambition and spunk. Catch that? *Spunk*?

So, what do you say? Do we have a deal here? Let me tell you, I'm probably going to lose money on this transaction, but that's okay by me. That's how much I want to make this deal happen. How about $300?

Not only do I personally hand-deliver each sperm sample directly to your door for no extra fee, but I'll happily bring it to its final destination. That's right, if you're looking to save money and eliminate hassle, leave the fertilization to me. I'm happy to deliver the sperm directly to your uterus, free of charge.

Not only do I personally hand-deliver each sperm sample directly to your door for no extra fee, but I'll happily bring it to its final destination. That's right, if you're looking to save money and eliminate hassle, leave the fertilization to me. I'm happy to deliver the sperm directly to your uterus, free of charge.

Just for a simple fertilization job, a doctor would charge you thousands of dollars. You're paying a fortune for a baster, a cup, and a few precious moments of some M.D.'s time. What's more, you're letting some guy you don't even know insert semen into your vagina. From me? Free, and we're already friends.

Still not sold? I can't go any lower on the price, but I can double your quantity for no extra charge. Yep, you heard me—no charge. I'll personally deliver a second batch of sperm to your uterus, absolutely free. And my product is 100 percent guaranteed, so if you are dissatisfied for any reason, I'll be more than happy to replace it with another of equal or lesser value. In fact, I'll even give you my home phone number so you can call me any time, night or day, for a refill. You won't get customer service like that from any of the big sperm banks.

Okay, you've got my back against the wall here. I'll go $250. Final offer, take it or leave it. Ø

Woman Doesn't Have Single Photo Where She's Not Hugging Someone

ST. CLOUD, MN—According to friends and coworkers, Krista Stoddard, 33, a St. Cloud-area paralegal, doesn't have a single photo of herself where she's not hugging someone.

"Everyone was having a nice time, and then someone broke out a camera," Bergtraum said. "Every time someone pointed it at Krista, she'd say, 'Ooh, get a picture of me and Marta!' or 'Hey, Jon, get in here!' I don't think she even knows she's doing it."

"It takes a while to pick up on the pattern, but once you do, it's really freaky," said Rebecca Donohue, a graphic designer and longtime friend who recently went through Stoddard's photo collection to assemble a collage for her. "If you go through all her pictures from grade school to the present, you won't find a non-huggy shot. With every photo, it's 'Here's me and Janine,' or 'Here's me and my friend Robbie—isn't he a hottie?' or 'Here's me and a statue of Michael Jackson at Madame Tussaud's—I did this one on a dare.'"

"I started seeing the pattern with the pictures she took in Greece with her friend Susan [Ortiz]," Donohue continued. "She's in a foreign country, so you'd think there would be at least one shot of Krista not hugging somebody, right? Wrong. In every picture, she's hugging a guy selling sunglasses on the beach or people in a bar or just some poor sap walking by that got suckered into the picture. It's like a compulsion with her."

More disturbingly, Donohue noted that even in the photos where Stoddard is alone, she is depicted in the act of hugging.

"She has a lot of photos where she's hugging her favorite stuffed rabbit, Señor Nose," Donohue said. "There are pictures of her with her arms around a statue of Abe Lincoln, and even one of her squeezing a yield sign. Maybe she doesn't know what else to do with her arms."

Jon Bergtraum, a coworker of Stoddard's, said he witnessed her hugging-compulsion firsthand last month at a company picnic.

"Everyone was having a nice time, and then someone broke out a camera," Bergtraum said. "Every time someone pointed it at Krista, she'd say, 'Ooh, get a picture of me and Marta!' or 'Hey, Jon, get in here!' I don't think she even knows she's doing it."

Above: Stoddard puts her arm around a friend in a 1999 photo.

Dr. Andrew Pulsipher, author of *True Exposure: The Psychology Of Photos*, said a hug-intensive photo collection is not uncommon.

"Many people find posing for a hugless photograph unnerving, like an awkward silence," Pulsipher said. "By not physically embracing another, we are forced to confront what frightens us most: ourselves. Another explanation is that hugging, as Krista puts it, is simply 'more fun!'"

Donohue said she has four more photo albums to analyze before she has seen all of Stoddard's photos. The media will be notified should she find a picture of her not physically embracing something or someone. Ø

NEWS IN BRIEF

Newsweek Editors Argue Over What To Make Readers Fear Next

NEW YORK—Having devoted cover stories to the threats of Hepatitis C, identity theft, and airport security, the editors of *Newsweek* spent Monday arguing over what they should stoke fears of next. "We could do the dangers of caffeine—that'd get people pretty worked up," managing editor Jon Meacham said. "Or how about daycare workers? There must be some alarming new study revealing just how few of them undergo background checks." Among the other ideas the editors proposed: the possible link between laptop computers and stomach cancer, the potential threat of water-supply poisoning by terrorists, and stunning new Biblical evidence pointing to April 4, 2004, as the date of the apocalypse.

Man Who Hasn't Moved In Six Hours Repeatedly Welcomed Back By TV

PADUCAH, KY—Despite not moving from his couch for more than six hours, Randy Kresge, 26, was repeatedly welcomed back by his television Monday. "Welcome back to *Blind Date*," said show host Roger Lodge, one of 12 different TV personalities to herald the return of the inert Kresge. "So glad you could join us." Kresge's obvious intention to remain seated did not keep the television from repeatedly urging him to "stick around."

Wisconsin Has Crush On Minnesota

MADISON, WI—After years of silent ardor, Wisconsin finally admitted Monday to having a serious crush on its neighbor Minnesota. "Dear Minnesota, I've been wanting to say this for a long time, but I've been too shy—I think you're cute," the Badger State wrote in a three-page letter it slipped under the door of the Minnesota State Capitol in St. Paul. "I think your Glacial Ridge Trail is so pretty. I'll be sitting between Illinois and Michigan if you want to talk to me." Minnesota, which harbors no romantic feelings for Wisconsin, is reportedly trying to figure out a polite way to let the state down easy.

Soldier Hoping We Invade Someplace Tropical Next

BAGHDAD—Sgt. Daniel Marshall, a member of the Army National Guard's 501st Infantry, is hoping that the next place he is ordered to invade has a tropical climate. "I'm proud to have served my country here in the Iraqi desert, but it sure would be nice if we got into a conflict with someplace nice," Marshall said Tuesday. "With any luck, President Bush is thinking about shocking-and-awing Cuba next—a little deep-sea fishing would really boost the morale of my men." Marshall said he is "so jealous" of his uncle Stephen, who got to invade Grenada in 1983.

Security Guard Makes Passing Women Feel Unsafe

DALLAS—The presence of security guard Frank Basso, 45, at the Lane Bryant store in Dallas' Valley View Mall makes female shoppers feel significantly less safe, sources reported Monday. "He just stands there by the door, staring at you while you shop," said customer Tracy Farr, 23. "Then he'll decide to wander around the store a bit, but he'll always wind up hovering somewhere around the lingerie section." Farr said Basso also has a creepy habit of tapping his club whenever an attractive woman passes by. Ø

MINISTER from page 175

Above: A board outside the church publicizes Sunday's sermon.

the church the moment the service ended, taking the side exit and making a beeline for the family minivan.

Genzler has made a habit of touting his unhappily virginal son as a symbol of chastity.

"It is not an easy road to virtue, but it is one that holds infinite returns," Genzler said during a recent Bible-study session. "I have seen my own son making the courageous choice of remaining abstinent while so many of his peers choose to turn their young bodies into vessels of immorality."

"I talk about these matters with my children, but not every parent does," Genzler said. "That's why I like to discuss Paul's virginity in sermons, at youth groups, on retreats, at church dinners... whenever possible."

Impressed and inspired by Paul's sanctity, members of the congregation have taken to lavishing him with praise at every turn. Last weekend, during an outing to the mall with some friends, Paul was approached by parishioners Roberta and Albert Voss.

"Hello, Paul!" Roberta said before the humiliated teen could conceal himself within his group of friends. "It was nice to hear what your father was saying about you on Sunday. Keep up the good work."

"Remember, Albert?" Roberta continued. "Reverend Genzler was saying Paul's still a virgin. Isn't that wonderful?"

Genzler said he wishes all parents would feel comfortable discussing sex openly with their children.

"A lot of parents have no idea the pressure today's teens are under," Genzler said. "Kids today need strong guidance. See, I talk about these matters with my children, but not every parent does. That's why I like to discuss Paul's virginity in sermons, at youth groups, on retreats, at church dinners... whenever possible. He's a living example of the power of self-respect and self-love."

During a June 12 catechism class, Genzler addressed his son along with 18 of his classmates, many of whom Paul sees every day at school.

"I know it's easy to become adrift in today's sea of sexually explicit imagery," Genzler said. "It's on the TV, it's in the magazines, it's on the album covers. But do not let it drive you to a life of vice. I've seen what my son Paul faces, and if he can resist it, so can the rest of you folks."

Added Genzler: "Some of your peers will try to tell you that it's 'cool' to break the rules. Well, my son doesn't. And he's cool... *very* cool."

Genzler has even attempted to enlist his son's help in educating his fellow teens. In addition to asking him to speak on virginity at a youth seminar this summer—an offer Paul declined—Genzler has encouraged his son to start a teen-abstinence group at his high school.

"It is not an easy road to virtue, but it is one that holds infinite returns," Genzler said during a recent Bible-study session. "I have seen my own son making the courageous choice of remaining abstinent while so many of his peers choose to turn their young bodies into vessels of immorality."

"Well, I'm going to be pretty busy with marching band this year, so I don't think I can," Paul told his father. "Then there's getting ready for the junior prom—you know, if I can find someone willing to go with me." ⌀

BUSH from page 175

when well-organized, coordinated attacks on his administration were carried out on a near-daily basis. But in spite of the National Criticism Alert Level holding steady at yellow (elevated), administration officials warn of severe impending attacks.

"We've become too complacent," Attorney General John Ashcroft said. "We've grown accustomed to thinking of criticism as something that only happens to people in other political parties. But this administration needs this funding to counter a very real threat to its reputation."

"As government officials, we have an absolute obligation to protect the leader of this country from future acts of criticism," U.S. Sen. Orrin Hatch (R-UT) said. "And it will not be cheap, easy, or quick."

Ashcroft said the Justice Department, working closely with the CIA and FBI, has identified more than 300 potential targets, ranging from the Bush Administration's inability to produce the weapons of mass destruction used to justify the war with Iraq to its deficit-ballooning fiscal policies.

"I doubt I could protect my ongoing Halliburton cronyism from critical strikes with just a few million dollars—especially if it was not accompanied by powerful preemptive legislation," Vice-President Dick Cheney said. "We need to build stronger anti-criticism defense shields in this country. And the time to act is now, *before* the media say something negative about us."

If the funding is approved, the Bush Administration will act swiftly to shore up numerous areas of vulnerability. Among the actions: ensuring that the White House is defended against verbal snipers, safeguarding the president's past illicit actions from biographical weapons, and sealing off the largest sources of domestic criticism by securing and patrolling the nation's newsrooms.

Congressional leaders are already pledging their support for the plan.

"As government officials, we have an absolute obligation to protect the leader of this country from future acts of criticism," U.S. Sen. Orrin Hatch (R-UT) said. "And it will not be cheap, easy, or quick."

"We're all in this together," Speaker of the House Dennis Hastert said. "You attack one American politician, you attack us all." ⌀

MATRIX from page 175

be a pretty funny twist."

The ad, as scripted, features Dieber bowling in a dark trenchcoat similar to the one worn by Laurence Fishburne's *Matrix* character Morpheus. After bowling a strike, Dieber turns to the camera, strikes a martial-arts pose, and says, "At Menasha Lanes, you are *The One*."

Though the commercial conveys the low prices, fun family atmosphere, and new bumper bowling one can enjoy at Menasha Lanes, Dieber said it lacks the "dazzling computer-y feel" of *The Matrix* and *The Matrix Reloaded*.

"Is there any way we can work in those falling green letters or something?" Dieber said. "And I'd love to throw in some of those levitating effects. There could be a shot of me in the snack bar, and I jump into the air and just stay there while the camera spins all around me. That'd grab people's attention."

Dieber's suggestions have caused headaches at Hot Spot Films, the local production house shooting the ad. Especially frustrated by his efforts to up the *Matrix* ante is director Andy Schuba.

"We pride ourselves on being *the* commercial-production house in the Fox River Valley area," Schuba said. "We have a state-of-the-art editing suite and a special machine dedicated to titling effects. But the things Bob wants to do would run 10 or 20 times over the budget for this project, if we could even do them at all."

In spite of his limited resources, Schuba has made every effort to satisfy his client, trying to closely replicate the multiple-camera "freeze" shots popularized in the *Matrix* films. With only one handheld Hi-8 video camera, Schuba attempted to slow down the ball as it approached the pins, then "pan around the other side

The ad, as scripted, features Dieber bowling in a dark trenchcoat similar to the one worn by Laurence Fishburne's *Matrix* character Morpheus. After bowling a strike, Dieber turns to the camera, strikes a martial-arts pose, and says, "At Menasha Lanes, you are *The One*."

of the ball quickly." The effort ended in frustration.

"[Cameraman] Derek [Gund] was supposed to run around the ball as it was rolling down the lane, but his shots were all too bumpy to use," Schuba said. "On the third or fourth take, he twisted his ankle in one of the gutters and had to take the rest of the week off. Normally, I wouldn't even try something like that, but Menasha Lanes is one of our biggest accounts, and we really want to keep them happy. It's been tough, though."

Schuba said that Dieber, though well-intentioned, does not understand the technical complexities of his ideas.

"He's really hands-on with his ads, but in the end, he doesn't really know what he's getting into," Schuba said. "He wants full CGI effects, multiple-camera stuff, stop-action filming. You just can't do that stuff on a $900 budget."

Spoofing hit movies is nothing new for Dieber: The *Matrix* spot is Menasha Lanes' fourth movie-inspired ad in the last decade. The first was a 1993 *Terminator 2*-inspired ad in which Dieber donned a leather jacket and said, "Bowl here once... and *you'll be back*."

"People really got a kick out of that one," Dieber said. "I can't tell you how many people would see me in the street or standing in line at the post office and shout, 'Hey, *Terminator*!' Years later, I still get that every now and again."

In the summer of 1995, the *Terminator* ad was followed by a *Wayne's World* ad, in which Dieber, wearing a long black wig and brandishing a guitar, invited viewers to "Party on at Menasha Lanes!"

"That was a good one, too," Dieber recalled. "The kids loved it."

In 1999, looking to tap into the *Austin Powers* craze, Dieber donned a purple paisley sports coat and shouted, "Menasha Lanes is shag-alicious, baby!" The ad, which has run for the past four years on local Milwaukee Bucks telecasts, will be retired in September when the Matrix spot is set to debut.

Schuba, who collaborated with

In 1999, looking to tap into the *Austin Powers* craze, Dieber donned a purple paisley sports coat and shouted, "Menasha Lanes is shag-alicious, baby!"

Dieber on those previous ads, said he always feels pressure to top the last commercial.

"The viewers have come to expect a lot from us, and we don't want to let them down," Schuba said. "We've got to continually raise the bar. I want to deliver a 30-second *Matrix*-looking bowling-alley ad more than anyone. But what Bob wants is a tall order, even for a production company like Hot Spot." Ø

VULVA from page 169

amounts of blood. Passersby were amazed by the unusually large amounts of blood. Passersby were

I'm sorry that I'm blind.

amazed by the unusually large amounts of blood. Passersby were amazed by the unusually large amounts of blood. Passersby were amazed by the unusually large amounts of blood. Passersby were amazed by the unusually large amounts of blood. Passersby were amazed by the unusually large amounts of blood. Passersby were amazed by the unusually large amounts of blood. Passersby were amazed by the unusually large amounts of blood. Passersby were amazed by the unusually large amounts of blood. Passersby were amazed by the unusually large amounts of blood. Passersby were amazed by the unusually large amounts of blood. Passersby were amazed by the unusually large amounts of blood. Passersby were

see VULVA page 186

PANDAS from page 171

amazed by the unusually large amounts of blood. Passersby were amazed by the unusually large

You may have one bite, and one bite only.

amounts of blood. Passersby were amazed by the unusually large amounts of blood. Passersby were amazed by the unusually large amounts of blood. Passersby were amazed by the unusually large amounts of blood. Passersby were amazed by the unusually large amounts of blood. Passersby were amazed by the unusually large amounts of blood. Passersby were amazed by the unusually large amounts of blood. Passersby were amazed by the unusually large amounts of blood. Passersby were amazed by the unusually large amounts of blood. Passersby were amazed by the unusually large amounts of blood. Passersby were amazed by the unusually large

see PANDAS page 183

COMMUNITY VOICES

It's Not Nice To Be Smarter Than Other People

By Helen Heep

I can't think of anything ruder than people who have to be all brainy and intelligent. As my mother used to say, if you can't say anything mundane, don't say anything at all. She was right: It's not nice to be smarter than other people.

Why did you have to say all that stuff about that book you're reading? Would it have been so hard to keep your love of literature to yourself? When you display your intelligence to the people you're talking to, you're really just telling them that you don't have enough respect for them to keep your smarts to yourself.

Reeling off a list of your favorite jazz artists may make you a good parrot, but it doesn't make you a good person. Good people hold their tongues, knowing they could hurt someone's feelings if they show knowledge the other person doesn't have.

I'm sorry to have to set you straight, but most people don't speak because they want to be educational. They speak because they want to be nice. They have an interest in interacting with other people in a non-confrontational manner that doesn't make them feel like dummies.

I'm sorry to have to set you straight, but most people don't speak because they want to be educational. They speak because they want to be *nice*. They have an interest in interacting with other people in a non-confrontational manner that doesn't make them feel like dummies.

In other words, they just want to be friendly. What's friendly about bringing up some article about the Mideast crisis you read in *The New York Times*? Not much, that's for certain. No, it's friendlier to say unchallenging things and let everyone feel like they know as much as you do.

There's more to life than being well-informed and cultured. There's good graces, good manners, and good old-fashioned horse sense—especially

Reeling off a list of your favorite jazz artists may make you a good parrot, but it doesn't make you a good person. Good people hold their tongues, knowing they could hurt someone's feelings if they show knowledge the other person doesn't have.

when it comes to knowing when to talk and when to keep your mouth shut. And, let me tell you, you may know something about astronomy, but you could certainly stand to learn a thing or two about politeness.

Do you think people want to hear your views on abstract art or the First Amendment? No one wants to hear things they don't already know, because that just makes them feel dumb.

I don't think it's your goal to try to make people feel stupid, but you seem to have this fixation with sharing your intelligence with others. That doesn't make any sense to me. Do you know how you sound when you do that? When you say something like "I'm a big Kubrick fan," what people hear is, "Look at me! I know things!" And nobody likes to hear that.

I don't know why you want to come off all smart and well-read, anyway. Sure, with your head full of facts, you may seem to have the world at your feet, but if you keep it up, you'll soon have no one to share it with. Smart people are the loneliest people in the world. They don't have anyone to talk to except other smart people, and who wants to join a conversation between two smart people? No one I know.

So, if you want to keep the friends you have and maybe even make some new ones, try being a little less of a know-it-all and a little more of a know-it-some. I mean, would it really kill you to think the capital of Illinois is Chicago? It could only help. Trust me. ⊘

HOROSCOPES

Your Horoscope

By Lloyd Schumner Sr.
Retired Machinist and
A.A.P.B.-Certified Astrologer

Aries: (March 21–April 19)
Your life's accomplishments will greatly enrich the human race, but 100 years from now, you'll mostly be judged by the crappy font on your tombstone.

Taurus: (April 20–May 20)
Your popularity skyrockets next week when you're smothered in barbecue sauce and bacon and offered as a Southwest Rodeo Whopper at Burger King.

Gemini: (May 21–June 21)
You'll finally get around to the important and long-delayed business of calling that toll-free number right now.

Cancer: (June 22–July 22)
You'll be indicted on seven counts of outsider trading this week. It's not a crime, but the SEC just wanted to see you sweat.

Leo: (July 23–Aug. 22)
The dread specter of your own mortality will loom over you all month, but you'll be so busy remodeling your kitchen that you'll hardly notice.

Virgo: (Aug. 23–Sept. 22)
You'll once again avoid becoming a household name this week, except in the more perverted households.

Libra: (Sept. 23–Oct. 23)
You've often compared your tribulation-filled life to that of Job, but as you'll soon discover, God gave a much better speech to him.

Scorpio: (Oct. 24–Nov. 21)
Rough times lie ahead of you in the financial and personal arenas when you're suddenly cut from 50 Cent's entourage.

Sagittarius: (Nov. 22–Dec. 21)
The ACLU will officially state that protected speech is all fine and good, but they're tired of jumping up every time you open your mouth.

Capricorn: (Dec. 22–Jan. 19)
It's time to rid yourself of the fallacious belief that kids or animals or anyone else likes you.

Aquarius: (Jan. 20–Feb. 18)
No amount of money can solve your current problems, which is really odd because they're mostly hunger- and shelter-related.

Pisces: (Feb. 19–March 20)
You will remember with bitterness the days when all you wanted were good seats at the airshow.

WOMAN ASTRONAUTS from page 177

amounts of blood. Passersby were amazed by the unusually large amounts of blood. Passersby were amazed by the unusually large

Let me just throw a blanket over that erection.

see WOMAN ASTRONAUTS page 186

NEWS

Rice Krispie Treat Eaten In 8" x 8" Square

see FOOD page 9D

Woman Seems Too Hot To Be Riding Bus

see LOCAL page 12B

First-Grader Wants Monkeypox

see LOCAL page 9B

Short Film Drags On

see MOVIES page 11C

STATshot

A look at the numbers that shape your world.

Top Reasons For Retirement, U.S. Carnival Workers

1. Phased out in favor of younger Tilt-A-Whirl operators
2. Lost enthusiasm, thumbs
3. Bumper-car lung
4. Finally gave away all the prizes in booth
5. Couldn't guess weight for shit
6. Total renal-system shutdown

the ONION®

VOLUME 39 ISSUE 26 AMERICA'S FINEST NEWS SOURCE™ 10–16 JULY 2003

Insecurities Laid Bare In Wal-Mart Shopping Cart

Above: A few of the items purchased by Dolger (left), a woman about to fall apart.

OWINGS MILLS, MD—The insecurities of Wal-Mart shopper Anita Dolger, 40, were laid painfully bare Monday, when her deepest fears and self-doubts manifested themselves in her purchasing choices.

"One look at [Dolger's] shopping cart betrays her deep-seated anxieties about everything from her family's financial outlook

see WAL-MART page 184

Giant Girl Forces Playthings Cheney And Rumsfeld To Wed

Left: Alice plays with Cheney and Rumsfeld on the White House lawn.

WASHINGTON, DC—The Bush Administration suffered another giant-girl-related setback Tuesday, when 60-foot-tall Alice Drury, 7, "married" Vice-President Dick Cheney to Defense Secretary Donald Rumsfeld before a crowd of cowering White House staffers in the Rose Garden.

Grasping Cheney and Rumsfeld tightly in her enormous hands, Alice forced the helpless leaders-turned-playthings to exchange vows of matrimony.

"Dick, do you take Donald to be your lawfully wedded wife?" Alice asked Cheney. "'Yes, yes I do!' And Donald, do you take Dick to be your lawfully wedded husband? 'Yes! Yes! Oh, yes!'"

After pronouncing Cheney and

see GIRL page 185

Lottery Winner An Inspiration To All Who Play The Lottery

SNELLVILLE, GA—After years of back-breaking ticket-buying, Teddy LeBarge's hard work finally paid off Monday, when the 36-year-old Snellville man won $193 million in the multi-state Mega Millions lottery, making him an inspiration to lottery players everywhere.

"I'm not going to be afraid to take risks anymore," said Teri Oswalt, a Paducah, KY, homemaker and one of the millions of Americans moved by LeBarge's remarkable rags-to-riches story. "I'm going to remember what Teddy LeBarge said: 'I just picked my numbers, and they finally done come up a winner.' If he can do it, so can I."

"This man didn't just hit the jackpot the first time he ever bought a ticket," said Carla Brooke of Batavia, NY. "He'd been going down to that gas station for years. It just goes to show you that there's no such thing as an overnight success."

The son of two factory workers, LeBarge grew up without the educational and economic opportunities most Americans take for granted. But that didn't stop him from striving to make something of himself.

"Yeah, I'd drive my old heap of junk down to the Amoco station near every Friday—Friday bein' payday—and buy myself a carton of cigarettes, six-pack of Busch, and a few lottery tick-

see LOTTERY page 184

Above: Lottery winner Teddy LeBarge.

Is The Economy Turning Around?

The Dow recently passed 9,000 for the first time in nearly a year, raising hopes that the economy is finally poised for a turnaround. What do *you* think?

"It's turning around? Hang on, I want to mention this to the guy repossessing my couch."

Lou Alessandro
Truck Driver

"They're just playing up the economy to distract us from the war."

Mary Bohnert
Homemaker

"As a hurdler, I must warn you: Even though the economy has cleared this hurdle, there will likely be more hurdles to hurdle soon."

Kathie Coombes
Hurdler

"Ah, the economy! How my soul stirs at the thought of discussing it! Sit! Sit! 'Tis a beautiful day, and we have all afternoon!"

Karl Edmonds
Systems Analyst

"Do we have enough for another war yet? How about an Olympics? Can I get another $300?"

Mark Adams
Shipping Clerk

"And with the low interest rates, there's never been a better time to buy a home. Oh, wait—I'm fucking *unemployed*."

Mike Ory
Unemployed

Summer Music Festivals

Summer's here, and that means it's time for music festivals. What are some of this year's big tours?

- Smuckers 2003 "Kick Out The Jams, Mothersmuckers!" music fest—*Tucson, AZ*
- "Monsters Of Abstinence" Christian Rock Fest—*Houston, TX*
- 2003 Citibank Counterculture Jamboree—*Brookline, MA*
- Sauk County Brat-Fest featuring surviving members of BoDeans—*Sauk County Fairgrounds, WI*
- Autoharpalooza—*Stone Mountain, GA*
- The Colossus Of Prog festival, featuring Yes, members of Yes, Jethro Tull, and Jon Anderson of Yes—*Charlotte, NC*
- Electrocash-in—*Brooklyn, NY*
- Radiohead Goes Outside festival—*Chicago, IL*
- The "Someone Forgot To Gas Up The H.O.R.D.E. Festival" festival—*Somewhere on I-70 between St. Louis and Kansas City*

the ONION®
America's Finest News Source.™

Herman Ulysses Zweibel
Founder

T. Herman Zweibel
Publisher Emeritus
J. Phineas Zweibel
Publisher
Maxwell Prescott Zweibel
Editor-In-Chief

Here Are Reviews Of Some New Shit

Hola, amigos. I know it's been a long time since I rapped at ya, but I been left standing with my dick in the breeze by a whole lotta bullshit. For example, I had my hours cut at work. I asked if they were mad at me, and they said I drove people to and from the airport like a champ, but that business was slow. I told them to just fire me so I could get unemployment, but they said they wanted to keep me for when things get better. Now I gotta get a second job, which totally blows. I'd quit, but it's one of the best jobs I've ever had.

The Cruise
By Jim Anchower

Anyway, there's been some things coming out lately, movies and music and stuff, that I thought I should let you know about. Think of it as a public service by yours truly.

I didn't think it would ever happen, but there's not just one but *two* new Zeppelin CDs out. Actually, one's a video. The CD's called *How The West Was Won*, and it isn't just one CD, it's three. That's right: three CDs' worth of gettin' the Led out. And, get this, it's got a 25-minute live version of "Dazed And Confused." Whenever I listen to the original version or see it on *The Song Remains The Same*, I wish it wouldn't end. Now, it almost doesn't! I always hate it when I go through a whole album before my buzz wears off, but now there's so much Zep, I have to light up again midway through.

There's not just one but *two* new Zeppelin CDs out. Actually, one's a video. The CD's called *How The West Was Won*, and it isn't just one CD, it's three. That's right: three CDs' worth of gettin' the Led out. And, get this, it's got a 25-minute live version of "Dazed And Confused."

I got the video, too, but I haven't seen it yet because I don't have a DVD player. Ron's friend Rob's got one, but he just got a girlfriend, so he's too busy dipping his wick to have us over. Anyway, I've seen a bunch of other Zep videos, and if it's anything like those, it's awesome.

CD: ★★★★★. Video thing: ★★★★★.

I saw *The Matrix Reloaded* twice. The first time I saw it, I went with Wes. See, we saw the original *Matrix* together, and we were so psyched afterward that we promised to see the next one together. I had to wait almost two whole weeks after it opened until Wes was free to see it, which really chafed me, but it was worth the wait.

There's been some things coming out lately, movies and music and stuff, that I thought I should let you know about. Think of it as a public service by yours truly.

We got super-baked in the Loews Stadium 24 parking lot before we went in. This was one of those awesome new theaters where you get the big-ass seats and you can see from everywhere in the house. There were plenty of open seats, so we plopped down in the middle, where Wes says you get the best sound. Actually, after 10 minutes, I fell asleep. I was pretty wiped out from busting my ass all day, and the weed was pretty much the last nail in the coffin.

Good thing Wes was there, 'cause he woke me up for all the fights. My favorite was the one in the park where that guy with the suit goes after Keanu, and then there's, like, a hundred of him. That rocked. And those twins fuckin' creeped me out. I saw it a couple days later on my own, when I was sure I wasn't going to fall asleep. I was just as baked, but it wasn't nearly as good. After the first half, I fell asleep and didn't wake up until five minutes before the end, so I missed the big car chase.

Matrix Reloaded if Wes is there to wake you up for the good parts: ★★★★★. Seeing it by yourself: ★★★.

I snuck into *Daddy Day Care* after the second time I saw *The Matrix*, but I got rousted by the usher after 15 minutes. Actually, I was kinda glad he did. That shit's not funny unless you like kids, and I sure the hell do not.

Daddy Day Care: ★

After hearing all about *American Idol*, I thought I should check it out. I mean, all the chicks at work were yapping about Ruben this and some-other-guy that. Since I love music, I figured I'd find something up my

see ANCHOWER page 185

BUSINESS

Kick-Ass Sales Proposal Written

FLAGSTAFF, AZ—Wayne Gorlin, 41, a sales associate for Air-izona Air Filtration Systems, has written a kick-ass sales proposal for the company's new line of Breathex air purifiers, sources reported Tuesday.

"I've been working my butt off to get this together so I can hit the ground running next week," Gorlin said, holding the seven-page document. "As summer comes, people are thinking

The killer proposal, jam-packed with information about Air-izona's entire line of Breathex air-purification systems, specifically targets businesses large enough to require an air-cleaning system servicing 4,000 to 6,000 square feet.

air conditioners and cooling systems, and an Air-izona air-filtration system is the next logical step."

Added Gorlin: "There's no way I'm not going to reel in some orders with this baby. It's got all the pertinent info, and it looks great, to boot."

The killer proposal, jam-packed with information about Air-izona's entire line of Breathex air-purification systems, specifically targets businesses large enough to require an air-cleaning system servicing 4,000 to 6,000 square feet. The purifiers would also be suitable, however, for someone with a very large residential home.

"This baby covers every possible use," said Gorlin, who spent nearly three weeks writing and refining the client-centered proposal. "Some of the other guys in the office don't take the time to put something nice together. Or maybe they just don't have the know-how. I've been working in sales for almost 16 years, so I do."

Gorlin said he likes to give prospective customers primo printed materials to help them make "as informed a decision as possible."

"These systems do not come cheap, so it's good to hand the customer a leave-behind," Gorlin said. "When someone is about to drop eight or nine grand on an air system, he's going to have a lot of questions. This little number will give him the answers."

"Got some nice full-color photos of the Breathex line, got some charts showing the effectiveness of air cleaners in reducing pollutant concentrations in indoor air," Gorlin said as he leafed through the proposal. "Ton of other great stuff. I did my homework. You gotta do your homework. There's no B.S.-ing your way through something like this."

"Look at this," Gorlin added, pointing to a section labeled "Pollutants Of Concern." "Someone reads what it is they're breathing in on a daily basis:

Above: Air-izona Air Filtration Systems sales associate Wayne Gorlin.

biological particles like animal and insect allergens, viruses, bacteria, and molds. Gaseous organic compounds. Radon. Well, they don't have to be an expert in air filtration to understand why they need the Breathex air purifier Model AXA central system. This bad boy rocks."

Gorlin said he can custom-tailor the proposal to the specific needs of a particular business by including brochures he feels are most appropriate.

"A hospital isn't going to need the same system as a bar or an office building," Gorlin said. "That's just idiotic."

Gorlin added that when he sends proposals to prospective buyers, he plans to enclose a letter addressed to the specific individual responsible for making purchasing decisions for a company.

"That kind of personal touch makes all the difference," Gorlin said. "If I'm

see PROPOSAL page 185

NEWS IN BRIEF

Millionaire Thinks Of Self As Upper-Middle Class

GROSSE POINTE WOODS, MI—Jim Blakeley, 43, a Ford Motor Company executive with personal assets totalling roughly $5.5 million, described himself as "upper-middle class" Monday. "I guess I'm pretty well-off. I make a decent upper-middle-class living, but I'm certainly not what you'd call super-rich," said Blakeley, whose annual salary of $675,000 puts him in the top one-half of 1 percent of Americans. "I know plenty of people who make way more than I do, but I get by with what I have."

Shape Magazine Declares July 'Let Yourself Go' Month

WOODLAND HILLS, CA—*Shape*, the women's fitness magazine, has officially declared July "Let Yourself Go" Month. "You've toned those abs and burned the flab in time for bikini season... Now it's time for a meatball sandwich," wrote *Shape* editor-in-chief Barbara Harris in her 'From The Editor' column. "Come on, live a little. Don't be a tight-ass with a tight ass. Eat, lounge, and slouch your way to a happier, more satisfied you." Features in the issue include "Girth Equals Mirth: Six Sure-Fire Techniques For Broadening That Belly," "Wrinkles: The More You Have, The More You've Lived," and "Reduce Unwanted Stress By Not Giving A Fuck."

Midwesterners Descend On Insurance Company's Free Nail Files

CHICAGO—At the Chicago Home Expo Monday, throngs of voracious Midwesterners descended on the State Farm Insurance booth to grab free promotional nail files. "Look—they have the State Farm logo printed right on them," said Beth Hoffman, 37, a Zion, IL, mother of four, as she clutched a handful of the complimentary items. "I'll grab a few extra for Mom. I'm sure she could use a couple, too." The horde of freebie-seeking Midwesterners then moved on to the Century 21 real-estate booth, where they plundered a basket filled with free business cards that turn into sponges when dunked in water.

Woman Masturbates To Concept Of Commitment

PORTAGE, MI—Soaking in her bathtub Tuesday, area resident Linda Marston, 32, pleasured herself over the thought of a long-term committed relationship. "Mmmm... oh, yeah, baby... I want to settle down with you forever," moaned the never-married Marston, as she gently massaged her clitoris with two fingers. "Oh, God, yes... two kids, maybe three... and a house in the country. Big swingset in the backyard." Several hours later, Marston masturbated again to the idea of loving someone unconditionally through good times and bad.

Man With Shitty Job Just Doing This Until He Gets Fired

EULESS, TX—Sub Shack employee Rory Graser, 25, reported Monday that he plans to keep his shitty job as a sandwich prep cook "only until I get fired." "Making turkey hoagies isn't what I plan to be doing long-term," Graser said. "I'm just doing this until I've stolen enough food and treated the customers rudely enough that [Sub Shack manager] Barry [Wheaton] cans my ass." Pondering the time frame for his next career move, Graser said he hopes to get caught sweeping trash under the bread rack sometime in the next three to four months. Ø

WAL-MART from page 181

to her ability to hold her husband's interest sexually," said psychotherapist and bestselling author Dr. Shari Berman. "From the looks of her cart, that poor woman is hanging on by a thread."

Roughly half of the items filling Dolger's cart were beauty aids, revealing a woman gripped by the fear that her looks are fading. In addition to a tube of Rembrandt whitening toothpaste and a bottle of L'Oreal shampoo for "flat, limp hair" were no fewer than six skin-related items. Among them: a container of Almay Kinetin Age-

"Looking into this blue plastic cart is like peering into her soul," Berman said. "I see fear for her future and shame over her current economic status in this roll of Sam's Club bargain-brand toilet paper. In these scented candles, I see a desire to escape life."

Decelerating Daily Lotion, a package of Biore pore-cleansing strips, and Tan In A Bottle bronzing spray.

"Based on these three items, it appears that Dolger feels her facial skin is not firm enough, clear enough, or tan enough," Berman said, nodding gravely. "If she feels this way about her skin, just imagine how she feels about the rest of her body."

Berman said that Dolger, despite being only a size 11, clearly feels insecure about her weight.

"Let's see... diet soda, sugar-free candy, low-carb meal-replacement bars. We've even got a pair of control-top pantyhose here," Berman said. "This is not a woman who likes what she sees in the mirror."

Judging from the presence of the book Personal Finance For Dummies, Dolger also seems to feel insecure about her family finances.

"Mrs. Dolger's choice of books would be unremarkable if her husband hadn't recently taken a pay cut at work," Berman said. "With two young kids and no real gameplan for paying for their college education, she can't be feeling too happy about that. Then there's her concerns about her own career, which has been nonexistent ever since the birth of Corey, her oldest child. Not good."

The various stresses appear to be taking their toll, as evidenced by Dolger's selection of a *Pure Moods* CD.

"*Pure Moods* is one of those 'As Seen On TV' CDs that's a compilation of all this really soothing easy-listening stuff," Berman said. "It's got [Enigma's] 'Return To Innocence' and that 'Sail away, sail away...' song by Enya. Basically, music for women about to lose their shit."

"Looking into this blue plastic cart is like peering into her soul," Berman said. "I see fear for her future and shame over her current economic status in this roll of Sam's Club bargain-brand toilet paper. In these scented candles, I see a desire to escape life."

"What's this?" Berman continued. "Do I spy a springform pan? Anita can just add that to all the others in the cupboard. I know she dreams of being a great chef, but that pan won't change the fact that she'll never muster the lifeforce necessary to cook a gourmet meal." ⌀

LOTTERY from page 181

ets," LeBarge said. "Some days during the week, I'd get me some scratch-offs, too, but I always made sure to buy that MegaPick ticket, 'cause that's where you get the big money."

"[LeBarge] was just a regular guy like me," said James Hale of Carthage, TN. "You don't need to be some fancy lawyer or doctor to win the lottery. You just need to be able to guess the same numbers as the ones that get picked a few days later."

Despite going years without winning a single lottery jackpot, an undaunted LeBarge bravely soldiered on.

"There was sometimes I thought I wasn't ever going to win, but I kept going," LeBarge said. "I knew I had to if I ever wanted a big TV and a boat and a Humvee and things like that."

"I didn't let [not winning] get me down, 'cause I knew what I wanted," LeBarge continued. "Sometimes, it wasn't easy to scrounge up those couple dollars, like when I was unemployed from '92 to '95, but I did it. And here I am today—a goddamn millionaire. Shit."

LeBarge, who will receive his jackpot in annual installments of $8.4 million over the next 23 years, quit his job as an unemployment-check collector hours after finding out he was a winner.

"[LeBarge] was just a regular guy like me," said James Hale of Carthage, TN. "You don't need to be some fancy lawyer or doctor to win the lottery. You just need to be able to guess the same numbers as the ones that get picked a few days later."

LeBarge's tenacity has even inspired some who have never played the lottery before.

"I thought the lottery was for other people," said Ralph Fischer, a Medford, OR, retiree. "Now I realize that if I want a check for millions of dollars, I have to get out there and do what it takes. I'm going to make my dreams come true."

As for LeBarge's dreams, he said his plans include paying off his many debts, taking a vacation to "someplace exotic," and doing some serious partying.

"The world can't help but look up to him," said Brenda Kenyon, a Brookfield, WI, daycare worker who buys about 20 scratch-off lottery tickets a week. "It's so wonderful what he did, such a beautiful story. He truly is a lottery winner."

"If I want a check for millions of dollars, I have to get out there and do what it takes," Fischer said. "I'm going to make my dreams come true."

"I see a lot of myself in Teddy LeBarge," Kenyon added. "He's someone who wanted to have a lot of money with little to no effort. And I do, too. More than anything else in the world." ⌀

YALTA from page 180

amounts of blood. Passersby were amazed by the unusually large amounts of blood. Passersby were amazed by the unusually large

Please, God, don't let me die without having seen *The English Patient*.

amounts of blood. Passersby were amazed by the unusually large amounts of blood. Passersby were amazed by the unusually large amounts of blood. Passersby were amazed by the unusually large amounts of blood. Passersby were amazed by the unusually large amounts of blood. Passersby were amazed by the unusually large amounts of blood. Passersby were amazed by the unusually large amounts of blood. Passersby were amazed by the unusually large amounts of blood. Passersby were amazed by the unusually large amounts of blood. Passersby were amazed by the unusually large amounts of blood.Passersby were amazed by the unusually large amounts of blood.Passersby were amazed by the unusually large amounts of blood.Passersby were amazed by the unusually large amounts of blood.Passersby were amazed by the unusually large amounts of blood.Passersby were amazed by the unusually large amounts of blood.Passersby were amazed by the unusually large amounts of blood.Passersby were amazed by the unusually large amounts of blood.Passersby were amazed by the unusually large amounts of blood.Passersby were amazed by the unusually large amounts of blood.Passersby were

see YALTA page 189

GIRL from page 181

Rumsfeld husband and wife, Alice ordered the trembling vice-president to kiss his equally frightened "bride," then bumped the two men's torsos against one another repeatedly in a crude simulation of kissing.

"Kissy kiss kiss," Alice said. "Dick and Donald love each other."

While not considered legally binding, the wedding is only the latest episode of giant-child's play to rock the Beltway. Since acquiring the White House as a birthday present from her colossal parents last week, Alice has repeatedly disrupted affairs of state, forcing key government officials to serve as dolls for her playtime flights of fancy.

During a Bush Cabinet meeting on the morning of June 9, Commerce Secretary Don Evans was unexpectedly hoisted from his chair and pulled through an open West Wing window by Alice's right hand. Eyewitnesses described how the young giantess, crawling on her hands and knees, "walked" Evans down Pennsylvania Avenue.

"She held him by the waist with her thumb and forefinger and sort of bounced him down the street," eyewitness Phil Urban said. "He never left her grip, but it must have been terrifying for him. His feet touched the ground only every 20 to 30 feet or so. It was sickening to watch."

After disappearing for nearly two hours, Evans was dropped unceremoniously on the White House lawn, minus his shoes, coat, and shirt. He also sported several bald patches on his head, the result of an apparent giant-girl-administered haircut.

Later that afternoon, Secretary of Health and Human Services Tommy Thompson nearly drowned after being "bathed" by Alice in the Lincoln Memorial reflecting pool. Stripped naked and dunked several times, the stunned Thompson was abandoned face-down in the pool when Alice's mother called her to dinner. Thompson was eventually rescued and revived by Capitol police.

Above: Alice peers into her playset.

Later that afternoon, Secretary of Health and Human Services Tommy Thompson nearly drowned after being "bathed" by Alice in the Lincoln Memorial reflecting pool.

National Security Advisor Condoleezza Rice has endured her share of punishment, as well. Three times in the past week, Alice has seized Rice and brushed her hair with strokes described by witnesses as "rough."

"She uses this huge plastic brush and practically rips Condi's hair out at the roots," Deputy National Security Advisor Stephen Hadley said. "And that dress [Alice] made out of gigantic Kleenexes and secured with rubber bands? Horrible. God knows where Condoleezza's original dress went. Probably lost forever, along with the Marine One helicopter and [Secretary of Veterans' Affairs] Anthony Principi."

While federal officials have remained calm thus far, many fear that Alice's play will become more violent if left unchecked. Beltway insiders point to Monday's switching of Energy Secretary Spencer Abraham's head with that of Labor Secretary Elaine Chao.

Asked if they had any plans to intervene, Alice's parents seemed unfazed.

"I agree that Alice should try to keep her things nice," 95-foot-tall mother Elizabeth Drury said. "But I'm more worried she might trip and bump her head on that nasty Washington Monument. There it is, jutting out in the middle of nowhere, just waiting for someone to get hurt on it."

"I'm not at all concerned," 110-foot-tall father Lawrence Drury said. "I say, let giant children be giant children. I remember all the fun I had with my Kremlin playset years ago, with the army men and the little nuclear missiles. I would take my little roly-poly Khrushchev doll to bed with me every night. But my mother made me stop playing with it because she didn't like war toys. Pity." ⌀

ANCHOWER from page 182

alley. Well, whatever they were doing on that show sure as hell wasn't music. The fat black guy just wailed about love and shit, and the skinny white guy did the same thing. The fat guy won, only they both sucked pretty much equally. Where's the guitars? Where's the drum solos? And does that British guy think he's funny? They should stick to the tried-and-true rule: "More rock, less talk."

Whatever they were doing on that show sure as hell wasn't music. The fat black guy just wailed about love and shit, and the skinny white guy did the same thing.

I wasn't gonna rate it, but since they'll probably have another show in a few months, I give it: ★

I got Animal Crossing from Blockbuster. It's this game for GameCube (the best) where you have a town, and you gotta write letters to animals and pick weeds and run errands. What a pain in the ass! I already have to get a second job that pays. Why the hell do I want a third job that doesn't? And on a videogame, yet.

Animal Crossing: ★★

Well, that's pretty much all I got for now, but you better believe I'm gonna give you the score on other stuff later. Like that fish movie. I definitely want to see that. Plus, there's some concerts I wouldn't mind checking out, like Ozzfest. I hate most of that nu-metal crap, but there's got to be something there I'd like. ⌀

PROPOSAL from page 183

a buyer, who am I gonna go with: The air-filtration company that sends me a letter addressed 'To Whom It May Concern,' or the one that actually knows my name? I think the answer is pretty obvious."

After weeks of preparation, Gorlin will finally put his kick-ass proposal to the test this coming Monday, when he will drive his Toyota Camry around Flagstaff, calling on potential clients from a prepared list.

"I did cold calls all week, finding out who might be interested, and now it's time to go face-to-face," Gorlin said. "I have to say I'm pretty excited. I'm coming armed and ready."

Gorlin then smiled and read aloud from the awesome proposal.

"Designed for larger residential and commercial applications, Breathex air purifiers work with your HVAC system to clean and circulate air throughout your building," Gorlin read. "It is especially beneficial for newer buildings, where improved sealing methods can reduce ventilation and cause a buildup of indoor air pollutants and..."

Gorlin will finally put his kick-ass proposal to the test this coming Monday, when he will drive his Toyota Camry around Flagstaff, calling on potential clients from a prepared list.

Customers interested in a Breathex system may contact Gorlin at his Arizona office, extension 487. ⌀

ADVICE

Ask The Back Of A Gourmet Potato Chip Bag

By A Gourmet Potato Chip Bag

Dear Back Of A Gourmet Potato Chip Bag,

Help! My kitchen is turning into an Internet café. My husband and kids have started to haul out their laptops right at the breakfast table, checking their e-mail or finishing up homework before we all rush off in the morning. I admit that breakfast isn't an elaborate affair around here, but what happened to sitting down to a nice meal together? What's your opinion?

Irked In Irvine

Dear Irked:

Take a moment to savor the delicious taste of Crackle Creek Farms old-world-style kettle chips. What makes them so good? Ever since my great-grandfather, Cyrus P. McVitty, brought the secret of taterliciousness to America from Bremen town way back in 1912, we've made them the very same way he used to. They're thick-cut from the finest Water Gap russets, hand-salted by master chipsmen, then slow-cooked using our special family recipe until they're good through and through.

I'm fully confident you'll enjoy them. That's why you have the Crackle Creek Farms Quality Guarantee Seal right on the front of every bag. If our potato chips aren't the best you've had, my name isn't Kevin J. McVitty.

Dear Back Of A Gourmet Potato Chip Bag,

Boy, am I steamed. My dry cleaner ruined one of my favorite blouses. Of course, he pointed to the "not responsible" clause on the ticket, but as a longtime valued customer, I think the shirt should be replaced out of common courtesy. My friend says I'm making a big deal out of nothing, but I think it's downright crummy of them not to at least offer a discount on future cleanings. Should I consider taking my business elsewhere, or am I overreacting?

Miffed In Middlebury

Dear Miffed:

According to legend, the Milwaukee potato chip was born in 1854 when steamship captain and restaurant patron Heinrich Van Der Linus sent his fried potatoes back to the kitchen, saying they were too thin and salty. Annoyed, the chef hacked a baking potato with his wife's pinking shears, tossed the angular chunks into carefully spiced saffroot oil, and fried them to a crisp... and the Munchwaukee Wunderkrunch was born!

Since 1996, our family has strived to recapture that spirit of adventure in every bag of our Munchwaukee Wunderkrunches. By using only all-natural ingredients, hand-stressing every batch, and testing at every stage, we ensure that the quality and taste of the original live on.

Enjoy.

Dear Back Of A Gourmet Potato Chip Bag,

My husband and I are in the midst of planning a family vacation for this summer, and we were thinking of inviting a group of my son's friends to join us. Troy has leg braces, and many of his friends have minor physical disabilities, as well. Any suggestions for great historical destinations that would be fun and accessible for special kids with special needs?

Planning In Plano

Dear Planning,

When Ellie founded Ellie's Chips more than 25 years ago, she wanted to bring her ancestral Lithuanian cooking secrets to the people of the Taos area. She succeeded beyond her wildest dreams!

Now, the folks here at the Desert Bloom Chip Foundry salute her achievements with the new Ellie's White Chili Earth-Apple Crisps. Only the finest native hybrid white chilis are hand-infused into the robust Cossack Golden potatoes. Then, they're slow-cooked in loom-pressed flaxseed oil and mineral water, and suffused with cilantro, sea salt, and peppercorns. Finally, they're sent to our quality-control specialists, who personally inspect each and every chip for imperfections. The handful of chips good enough to pass muster emerge into the light as our clean, clear, spicy Earth-Apple Crisps.

Sure, they might take a little more time and cost a little more than ordinary chips, but we think you'll taste the difference in every bite.

We know Ellie would approve. We hope you do, too.

Confidential To Lonely In Lodi:

Includes: Select Potatoes, Vegetable Oil(s): (Sunflower, Canola, Cottonseed, Corn/Cottonseed, Corn, Expeller-Pressed Oleic Canola), Salt, Sugar, Dextrose, Barley Malt, Citric Acid, Spice, Spice Extracts.

Gourmet Potato Chip Bag is a syndicated advice columnist whose weekly column, Ask The Back Of A Gourmet Potato Chip Bag, *appears in more than 250 newspapers nationwide.* Ø

HOROSCOPES

Your Horoscope

By Lloyd Schumner Sr.
Retired Machinist and
A.A.P.B.-Certified Astrologer

Aries: (March 21–April 19)
Don't take it personally: Someone had to be the cutoff point for who does and doesn't get on the Emergency Earth-Escape Rocket.

Taurus: (April 20–May 20)
You know you should really stop hurling fistfuls of hamsters out the window of your speeding car, but they're so darn cute.

Gemini: (May 21–June 21)
After weeks of deliberation, you have yet to hear a compelling argument for not beating most of the people you've ever met to within an inch of their lives.

Cancer: (June 22–July 22)
It's looking like they're not going to start calling you the Double-Dustpan Killer until you kill someone with a pair of dustpans.

Leo: (July 23–Aug. 22)
No one can understand you without first understanding the subtle-but-crucial difference between the terms "all you can eat" and "all you care to eat."

Virgo: (Aug. 23–Sept. 22)
You will finally learn the true meaning of fear this week. First of all, it's not a light minty flavoring.

Libra: (Sept. 23–Oct. 23)
That man who just wrapped a trombone around your neck was Jim Knepper, a Mingus sideman and notorious crank.

Scorpio: (Oct. 24–Nov. 21)
Polaris rising in Scorpio this week is deeply troubling, as it has to be millions of light-years out of position to do so.

Sagittarius: (Nov. 22–Dec. 21)
Your bossiness and predilection for minding other people's business are important parts of being the World's Best Grandma.

Capricorn: (Dec. 22–Jan. 19)
A little bird tells you that someone has a crush on you, but terrible secrets imparted by the giant birds hatched from the sun render this irrelevant.

Aquarius: (Jan. 20–Feb. 18)
The importance of a good night's sleep will be briefly overshadowed by the importance of a good set of shovels and entrenching tools.

Pisces: (Feb. 19–March 20)
You're the kind of person who considers himself open to all kinds of new experiences, as long as they involve eating buffalo wings.

EXPO CENTER from page 177

amounts of blood. Passersby were amazed by the unusually large amounts of blood. Passersby were amazed by the unusually large amounts of blood. Passersby were amazed by the unusually large amounts of blood. Passersby were amazed by the unusually large amounts of blood. Passersby were amazed by the unusually large amounts of blood. Passersby were amazed by the unusually large amounts of blood. Passersby were amazed by the unusually large amounts of blood. Passersby were amazed by the unusually large amounts of blood. Passersby were amazed by the unusually large amounts of blood. Passersby were amazed by the unusually large amounts of blood. Passersby were amazed by the unusually large amounts of blood. Passersby were amazed by the unusually large amounts of blood. Passersby were amazed by the unusually large amounts of blood. Passersby were amazed by the unusually large amounts of blood. Passersby were amazed by the unusually large amounts of blood. Passersby were amazed by the unusually large amounts of blood. Passersby were amazed by the unusually large amounts of blood. Passersby were amazed by the unusually large amounts of blood. Passersby were

This cactus sucks.

amazed by the unusually large amounts of blood. Passersby were amazed by the unusually large amounts of blood. Passersby were amazed by the unusually large amounts of blood. Passersby were amazed by the unusually large amounts of blood. Passersby were amazed by the unusually large amounts of blood. Passersby were amazed by the unusually large amounts of blood. Passersby were amazed by the unusually large amounts of blood. Passersby were

see EXPO CENTER page 199

NEWS

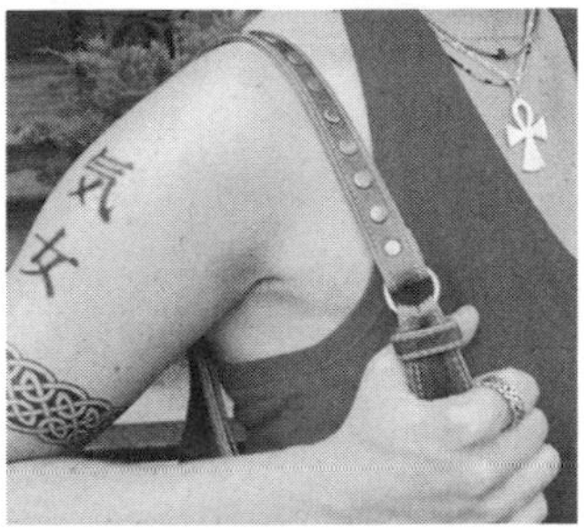

Woman's Body Confusing Jumble Of Celtic, Egyptian, Japanese Symbols

see LOCAL page 7C

Painting Of Jesus Totally Knows Area Man Is High

see LOCAL page 3C

Turkmenistan Whistles Casually, Moves Border A Few Miles East

see WORLD page 4B

STATshot

A look at the numbers that shape your world.

What's Sitting On Our Grand Pianos?

1. Finicky white longhair cat
2. Three-year-old note reminding us to tune piano
3. Creepy skull covered with candle-wax drippings
4. Other stuff we won on *Wheel Of Fortune*
5. Boom box playing that Nelly song
6. Forehead

the ONION®

VOLUME 39 ISSUE 27 AMERICA'S FINEST NEWS SOURCE™ 17–23 JULY 2003

Sen. Frist Receives High Bid In White House Bachelor Auction

WASHINGTON, DC—The 85th Annual White House Bachelor Auction closed Monday night with an impressive $9,310 raised for leukemia research. By a clear margin, Senate Majority Leader Bill Frist (R-TN) received the highest bid, netting an impressive $825.

"This isn't a competition, really," a blushing Frist said. "I'm just happy to do my part for such a worthwhile charity."

Dates with 18 different government officials were sold during the black-tie event, which was emceed by Secretary Of State Colin Powell.

"We look forward to these every year," Powell said. "The guys love to ham it up onstage, and the gals in the audience have such a fun time bid-

see AUCTION page 191

Above: Auction emcee Powell opens the bidding on the Tennessee Republican.

Left: Abbas and Sharon shake hands to commemorate their media spotlight-sharing agreement.

Israelis, Palestinians Agree To Share Headline

AQABA, JORDAN—In an agreement that marks a key first step in the Mideast news-piece process, Israeli Prime Minister Ariel Sharon and new Palestinian Prime Minister Mahmoud Abbas pledged to share a two-state Israeli and Palestinian headline Monday.

"This pact shows that Palestinians and Israelis can and will commit to sharing the column-inch space devoted to the Middle East region," said *New York Times* executive editor Joseph Lelyveld, who mediated the Jordan summit. "Given the state of affairs in the area, I am confident that we will see more headlines uniting these two countries in the future."

Under the terms of the agreement, Palestinians and Israelis will commit to "sharing together, side by side, a

see HEADLINE page 190

Unemployed Man Getting Really Good At Unemployment

PORTLAND, OR—Nicholas Higby, a graphic designer laid off in January, is on his way to mastering unemployment, the 34-year-old reported Monday.

"Yeah, I don't mean to brag, but I definitely have this down cold," Higby said. "Of course, I'd rather find another job, but until the economy turns around, I'm doing a pretty kick-ass job at the not-working thing."

Ever since losing his last job, Higby said he is enjoying all his city has to offer.

"I've eaten through my savings, but funemployment [sic] is enough to get by if you're careful what you do," Higby said. "I'm hitting all the free concerts and museums. I'm getting exercise at the park. I'm making repairs I've put off for years. It's amazing how productive I've been."

Higby has not always been so successful at not having a job.

"The first month, I was totally lost," Higby said. "I was either moping around the house or chasing leads for jobs that were ridiculously out of my reach. But now I have experience under my belt."

Through a months-long

see UNEMPLOYED page 190

Above: Higby, who strives to be "the best jobless person I can be."

Bush's African Tour

President Bush recently returned from a tour of Africa that supporters say signals U.S. commitment to tackling the continent's problems. What do *you* think?

"This trip demonstrates strong support for Africa in a way that adequate humanitarian aid never could."

Roland Sutton
Purchasing Manager

"All I ever hear is Bush, Bush, Bush. When are we getting a new president?"

Jay McDaniel
Conveyor Operator

"Did he get his picture taken next to a big pile of skulls? That'd be awesome."

Hector Castillo
Aircraft Mechanic

"*Africa*?! But that place is dangerous! What if he'd been *hurt*?!"

Helene Rhodes
Teacher

"I pray Bush steered clear of Anansi, the trickster spider-god. If not, the president may have learned a few lessons in a manner he didn't appreciate."

Duane Carr
Systems Analyst

"Thank God Strom Thurmond didn't live to see a member of the GOP do this."

Dena Hardy
Procurement Clerk

Kraft Goes On A Diet

Kraft Foods recently announced it will join the fight against obesity by cutting portion sizes and altering the recipes of many of its top products. What other changes is the company planning?

- Discouraging overeating by vastly reducing the quality of its products
- Introducing Half Stuf Oreos
- Making string-cheese packets out of unrippable Kevlar
- Throwing some of that Ginko Bilboa stuff into the hot dogs
- Removing fattening deli meats and cheeses from photos of Triscuits on box
- Retiring long-time Kraft Foods mascot Andy, The "I'll Eat Anything!" Boy™
- Reducing serving size of Velveeta to negative-two ounces per day
- Halting use of shortening derived from the neck and underarm wattle of old ladies
- Adding message to label, "Warning: Stop eating when no longer hungry"

the ONION®
America's Finest News Source.™

Herman Ulysses Zweibel
Founder

T. Herman Zweibel
Publisher Emeritus
J. Phineas Zweibel
Publisher
Maxwell Prescott Zweibel
Editor-In-Chief

Normally I Enjoy Your Pornographic Web Site, But This Time You've Gone Too Far

By Gerald Conroy

To the people at Sexxxotika.com, let me begin by saying that I thoroughly enjoy your pornographic web site. I have been a paying member since September, and since then have reveled in the graphic images of female nudity and hardcore sex. But I'm afraid this week your site went too far.

I know that Sexxxotika.com likes to push the envelope of sexual imagery, and I fully understand that you must cater to the peccadilloes of a wide range of subscribers. For example, though I harbor no foot fetish myself, I endure without complaint the occasional photo slide show of a man licking a woman's stilettoed heel. This is because I know your next posting likely will feature enough streaming video of tangy young nubiles experimenting with double-ended dildos to make my automatic credit-card deduction worthwhile.

You have no idea how much I look forward to your Thursday-afternoon site update. It is the high point of my week. So, it is as a longtime Sexxxotika fan that I feel obligated to share my outrage over this week's offering.

When I logged on and saw the headline "Bathroom!" I felt great excitement. The last time you used a powder-room theme was February's "Showering with Juli and Mindy," perhaps the most glorious pictorial in Sexxxotika.com history. But upon clicking on the "Bathroom!" link, I was not presented with more photographs of randy lesbian girlfriends soaping each other up or masturbating with the showerhead.

Instead, I was barraged with images of hot young barely legal teens squatting in the bathtub—not to reach for the bath gel, but to *urinate*, sometimes even on each other. Shame on you, Sexxxotika.

I come to your web site to be erotically entertained, not disgusted. Sure, there may be some perverts out there who enjoy the sort of thing featured in your "Bathroom!" gallery of last Thursday, but I'm sure I speak for the majority of Sexxxotika regulars when I say this montage goes way, way over the line. How could you?

To be honest, I've noticed a slip in Sexxxotika's quality control over the past few months. Take, for instance, your recent Quicktime movie "Luvving Sisters," which showed two luscious, nearly identical 18-year-old blondes in the act of mutual cunnilingus. Now, I am a huge supporter of graphic depictions of sapphic sex play, but your suggestion that these two women were related by blood made me more than a little uneasy. Perhaps it is my strong devotion to family values, but the offending caption nearly caused me to lose my erection. Granted, not every Quicktime movie can be *Citizen Came*.

I believe you owe your subscribers an apology. If you fail to use some editorial judgment in the future, I am afraid I will be forced to cancel my Sexxxotika membership and take my adult-entertainment dollar elsewhere. After all, there is no shortage of web sites featuring hot young cum-drunk gutter sluts who love 14" horse cocks rammed into their tight little assholes.

Yet about "Bathroom!" I cannot remain silent. After browsing through picture after picture of women peeing on the ground, on men, or on each other, I can honestly say that I did not enjoy it. Not in the slightest. You need to get back to the sort of straightforward sex we have come to expect from Sexxxotika.com: hot girl-on-girl action, blow jobs, anal sex, and facials.

I believe you owe your subscribers an apology. If you fail to use some editorial judgment in the future, I am afraid I will be forced to cancel my Sexxxotika membership and take my adult-entertainment dollar elsewhere. After all, there is no shortage of web sites featuring hot young cum-drunk gutter sluts who love 14" horse cocks rammed into their tight little assholes.

I anxiously await your reply. Ø

Before He Knows What's Happening, Man Belongs To $uper $aver's Club

ALTOONA, PA—Will Zimmerman stepped into a local supermarket Monday to purchase a pint of half-and-half, but before he could fully comprehend the situation, the 28-year-old repairman was a member of the Feltz Foods $uper $aver's Club.

"Yeah, I've got the card right here in my wallet," a pale and dazed Zimmerman said as he revealed the 3"x2" laminated induction into the $uper $aver family. "I guess I'm supposed to present it at any Feltz Supermarket for super savings."

Zimmerman, addressing a sudden shortage of creamer in the Altoona Advance Heating & Cooling breakroom, drove to the Highmarket Road Feltz and at 2:26 p.m. selected a pint of half-and-half from the dairy case without incident. He approached one of the checkout aisles at 2:28 p.m.

"I took out my wallet, and the girl at the register asked if I had a $uper $aver's card," Zimmerman said. "She must have interpreted my pause as a 'no,' because she started telling me all this stuff about the $uper $aver's Club."

The cashier, 22-year-old Dorothy Salgado, recited a standard description of the benefits of joining the $uper $aver's Club.

"Besides being able to take advantage of bigger discounts than non-cardholders, you can receive advance information on monthly specials, free check-cashing privileges, and the ability to participate in Double Coupon Tuesdays," Salgado said she told Zimmerman. "Best of all, there's no cost to join."

Above: A still-dazed Zimmerman poses with $uper $aver's Club card in hand.

Zimmerman can recall neither agreeing nor disagreeing to join.

"I heard 'discounts' and 'no cost to join,'" he said. "Then it gets fuzzy. The only thing I remember is the girl shoving a form and ballpoint pen in my hand and directing me away from her register."

A surveillance tape released by Feltz Foods confirms Zimmerman's recollection. At 2:30 p.m., he is seen leaving the checkout aisle and approaching the service desk.

"I didn't really want to fill out a long form because I had to get back to work, but the lady [Feltz Foods supervisor Joyce Epps] said it would just take a couple minutes and it was worth the time," Zimmerman said.

Zimmerman described the subsequent events as a "whirlwind of signing and laminating."

"I recall being told to fill out my address and phone number, and to 'press down hard,'" Zimmerman said. "Then I was given this little laminated card. No, wait—first I signed the card, then she laminated it. I'm sorry, it all happened so fast."

New card and half-and-half carton in hand, Zimmerman was told by Epps to return to the checkout aisle. More confusion followed.

"The half-and-half rang up at its regular price," Zimmerman said. "I asked if I got a discount, and [Salgado] said no, because the half-and-half wasn't a $uper $aver's Club Special Of The Week. So I asked why she made me join the $uper $aver's Club, and she said she didn't *make* me join anything."

Zimmerman's supervisor, Jack Thiele, noted his employee's condition when Zimmerman returned to work at 2:44 p.m.

"The color was drained from his face, and when I asked what was wrong, he mumbled something about a laminated card and 'they charged me full price,'" Thiele said. "I said that's it—no more ducking out of the office to get half-and-half or gum or whatever the hell."

Supermarket analyst Mark Ludovic said that while Zimmerman's case is extreme, customers, especially those with work or family concerns on their minds, are often unprepared for the opportunity to save.

"When you enter Feltz Foods or any other supermarket chain, you should

see CLUB page 190

NEWS IN BRIEF

Elaborate Sentence Construction Facilitates Omission Of Word 'Boyfriend'

BAKERSFIELD, CA—Local Target cashier Lori Spelmann, 23, told coworker Marsha Kimball about her weekend Monday using a winding sentence to facilitate omission of the word "boyfriend." "I didn't get home until late because my friend who is the guy I've been hanging out with a lot for the last five or so weeks locked his keys in his car," Spelmann told Kimball in the Target breakroom. Other words and phrases Spelmann managed to avoid during the run-on sentence included "went on a date," "relationship," and "had sex."

Pen Pal Becomes Pen Foe

CHUGWATER, WY—In light of their recent antagonistic correspondence, 8-year-old Ryan Werther has decided that 7-year-old Trenton, NJ, resident Dashiell Kudia has changed from his pen pal to his pen foe. "You wer [sic] so wrong when you said the Fairly Oddparents are as good as Spongebob," Kudia penned in a letter Werther received Monday. "You can go jump off a brij [sic] for all I care because you are no longer my friend." Kudia's letter ended with a tersely written "So there."

Secretary Of Agriculture Finally Gets Around To Reading *Fast Food Nation*

WASHINGTON, DC—Though insisting that she had been meaning to read Eric Schlosser's book *Fast Food Nation* ever since it was published in 2001, Secretary of Agriculture Ann M. Veneman finally got around to doing so just this month. "Wow, I had no idea that commercial beef ranches packed so many head of cattle into such a small space," Veneman said Tuesday. "It's disgusting! And all that about the flavoring from animal products being used to make McDonald's french fries—that was a real eye-opener. Mark my words, something must be done." Veneman vowed that, upon completing *Fast Food Nation*, she will immediately go out and buy Rachel Carson's *Silent Spring*.

Late-Working CEO Calls Out For Coffee In Vain

NEW YORK—While pulling a late-nighter at the office, Verizon Communications CEO Ivan Seidenberg repeatedly called out for coffee Tuesday despite being the only person in the building. "Would somebody please bring me some coffee?" Seidenberg shouted from his desk at approximately 11:30 p.m. "I need a cup of coffee—with two sugars. Dolores? Janice? Coffee?" Seidenberg alternated his requests for coffee with announcements that printer tray number two was out of paper.

Judge Totally Understands Where Defendant Is Coming From

CONCORDIA, MO—During a domestic-dispute case on Monday, Judge Peter Spiveck ruled that he could totally understand where 32-year-old defendant Samuel Werton was coming from. "Man, I totally hear what you're saying," Spiveck said, moments before handing down a sentence. "If my old lady stayed out drinking until 3 o'clock in the morning, I'd be tempted to run her over with the Dodge myself. But, dude, you can't do that. You've got to learn to keep it under control, see." Spiveck then warmly patted Werton on the shoulder and sentenced him to 90 days in the Lafayette County Lockup. Ø

UNEMPLOYED from page 187

process of trial and error, Higby has learned the tricks of the unemployment trade.

"Leaving the house every single day is very important, even if it's just to spend a few hours at the coffee shop

"If you think about how you need stamps, and you put getting stamps on your mental list of things to do the next day, when you do go get those stamps, you've achieved a goal," Higby said. "Another example: Thursday is *Sports Illustrated* Day. Now, back when I had a job, I also used to read *Sports Illustrated* on Thursdays, but Thursday was never *Sports Illustrated* Day."

organizing the MP3 files on your laptop," Higby said. "I try to be out the door by 2 or 3 in the afternoon—no exceptions. You have to get out and do something during the day in order to not feel guilty about going out drinking that night."

Higby warned strongly against going to bed too early.

"It's depressing to be out at 9 a.m., because you see everyone else being productive," Higby said. "Besides that, morning TV sucks. *The Rockford Files* starts at noon, so I try to be up, showered, and out on the couch by at least 11:55."

According to Higby, continuing the search for employment amid setbacks is key. Every day, Higby makes it a point to go out and apply for jobs, buy a paper and peruse the classifieds, or wait for his cell phone to ring.

"It's hard being rejected so many times, but you have to stick to your guns," Higby said. "I make sure to spend at least 10 percent of my day looking for work."

Another of Higby's tips involves assigning additional meaning to activities he once did as a matter of course.

"If you think about how you need stamps, and you put getting stamps on your mental list of things to do the next day, when you do go get those stamps, you've achieved a goal," Higby said. "Another example: Thursday is *Sports Illustrated* Day. Now, back when I had a job, I also used to read *Sports Illustrated* on Thursdays, but Thursday was never *Sports Illustrated* Day."

Higby said he considers himself a cut above other non-workers he knows.

"I have other friends without jobs, and they're pathetic," he said. "They get nothing done. They're always depressed or frustrated. I know it's rough the first couple months, but they should have their act together by now."

Conversely, Higby said he hit his stride about three months ago.

"I definitely can recommend doing your reading at Powell's City Of Books rather than the library," Higby said. "The library is filled with dregs, people who have no idea what to do with their surplus 40 hours a week."

Higby added that it is important to uphold the appearance of productivity.

"When I'm out during the day, I carry around some notebooks and papers and take them out whenever possible," he said. "It's no good to be just sitting there on a park bench staring off into the distance. It creeps people out."

"And don't burden others with your sad reality," Higby continued. "I used to complain to my friends that I was bored, but I quickly realized that, after busting their asses at work all week, they don't want to hear it. Now, I talk about 'working hard on my portfolio.'"

Additionally, Higby is careful to cycle through his companions so as not to become a social burden on any individual friend.

"Josh works weekends, so on Monday and Tuesday he's sitting at home

"Don't burden others with your sad reality," Higby continued. "I used to complain to my friends that I was bored, but I quickly realized that, after busting their asses at work all week, they don't want to hear it. Now, I talk about 'working hard on my portfolio.'"

looking for someone to watch a movie with," Higby said. "Kenny freelances, so I usually call him on Wednesday. If I drop by Beth's restaurant in the slow hours before dinner rush, I can usually kill a few hours and score some Pad Thai. You could definitely say I'm pretty proud of all the non-work I've been getting done." ⌀

HEADLINE from page 187

real and substantive presence" in the global foreign-disaster-based news media. The shared-headline commitment extends to news about massacres throughout Israel and the occupied West Bank and Gaza Strip territories, and covers both the destruction of Palestinian homes by Israeli air-to-surface rocket attacks and the killing of Israeli women and children in suicide-bombing campaigns by Palestinian extremists.

Although foreign correspondents said they regarded the agreement as a step forward, they stressed that it is only the beginning.

"From the 1979 Broadcast-News-Coverage Accord between Egypt and Israel to the 1989 Summit On Font Point-Size Minimums with the PLO, we have all heard this sort of thing before," said reporter Jeffrey Douglas-Miles of the London *Times*. "Can a successful end to more than 50 years of bloody conflict over headline domination be achieved in a single day? No. But this development is a positive one. There have been five more deaths in the region since Sunday, all of them newsworthy."

Given the region's history of violent headline-grabbing on both sides, the new agreement's limitations are many.

Historically, negotiations over the wording of joint headlines have been complicated by both groups' insistence on being portrayed as victims. In the latest round of talks, Abbas has okayed depictions of the *intifada* as an uprising of people oppressed by a modern apartheid state of superior military and economic strength, but will not allow portrayals of all Palestinian dissidents as fundamentalist terrorists.

Similarly, Sharon agreed to allow headline space describing Israel as a lone democratic state fighting to defend itself from constant attack, and will permit descriptions of Jews as victims of millennia of anti-Semitism. Sharon did not agree, however, to be portrayed as a hard-line hawk who repeatedly sabotages attempts at peace by moderates on both sides of the conflict.

No agreement was reached concerning reportage describing either side as unethical, racist, or oppressive.

"We will concede the necessity of a shared Israeli-Palestinian headline accompanied by a photo of civilian parents mourning recently killed

Abbas has okayed depictions of the *intifada* as an uprising of people oppressed by a modern apartheid state of superior military and economic strength, but will not allow portrayals of all Palestinian dissidents as fundamentalist terrorists.

children caught in the crossfire," Sharon said. "But no concessions regarding media depiction of Palestinian victimhood will be tolerated unless a commitment to Israeli victimhood is also maintained."

Abbas echoed this stance.

"Portrayals of Israeli victimization in the world media must only continue if equal headline space for the victimization of Arabs can be guaranteed by the press," Abbas said. "If such conditions can be met, headlines about explosions, machine-gunning crowds, religious death-cults that manipulate children into suicide attacks on innocents, economic deprivation, religious discrimination, race-based subjugation, and needless human tragedy can continue to be generated equally by both Israelis and Palestinians well into our children's children's future."

The first proposed shared headline, "Israeli, Palestinian Death Toll Mounts," could appear in newspapers worldwide as early as Thursday.

No agreement was reached involving the peaceable sharing of land. ⌀

CLUB from page 189

be aware that discounts can occur without warning," Ludovic said. "Often, these supermarkets play by their own

"Saving a few cents is not worth the stress and bewilderment," Zimmerman said.

rules, such as claiming to honor the lower prices of competitors when they are only referring to advertised prices. Unless you feel you can fully comprehend the fine print and are capable of membership in a savings club, the best way to handle these situations is to politely decline any offers and calmly exit the store. Saving a few cents on kidney beans is not worth the stress and bewilderment."

In the wake of the incident, Zimmerman said he remains unsure of whether he'll ever use his Feltz $uper $aver's card.

"I usually shop at Goodall's Grocery near my apartment," Zimmerman said. "It's more convenient. I don't think they have a savings club, either. God, I hope they don't." ⌀

AUCTION from page 187

ding against each other. Things get pretty heated."

Despite Powell's suggestion that Beltway females in attendance "get out those checkbooks," the evening began slowly. The first bachelor,

Frist's high price tag came as no surprise to those who know the handsome statesman. The senator was a practicing surgeon before his 1994 election to office and has saved at least two lives since then. A proponent of AIDS research and traditional marriage, Frist is widely considered among beltway insiders to be a good catch.

Above: Condoleezza Rice attempts to procure Frist with a cash bid.

White House Chief Of Staff Andrew Card, brought in a mere $168.

Bids for Frist also began low, stalling at a $275 bid by National Security Advisor Condoleezza Rice. Just as the auctioneer was about to close the bidding, however, Frist began to swagger comically and removed his tie, throwing it to U.S. Rep. Julia Carson (D-IN), who caught it with a scream.

Supreme Court Justice Sandra Day O'Connor quickly searched through her purse, raised her bidder paddle, and shouted, "I'll give you $400 for that man!"

Not to be outdone, Rice upped her bid to $425. This ignited a tough two-minute bidding war between O'Connor and Rice, with prices rising in $25 increments. Encouraged by a table of tipsy girlfriends, O'Connor emerged as the victor.

"You won!" said Ruth Bader Ginsburg, O'Connor's friend and fellow Supreme Court justice. "I can't believe you did it! Woo!"

Rice, who witnesses said was "more than a little mad" after losing the auction, snapped up a bargain-priced U.S. Rep. Jim DeMint (R-SC) later in the evening for $125.

The price for Frist marks the highest bid for a bachelor since former White House Press Secretary George Stephanopoulos brought in a staggering $950.75 for multiple sclerosis in the 1993 auction.

Frist's high price tag came as no surprise to those who know the handsome statesman. The senator was a practicing surgeon before his 1994 election to office and has saved at least two lives since then. A proponent of AIDS research and traditional marriage, Frist is widely considered among beltway insiders to be a good catch—a fact not lost on his wife Karyn, who lent him out for the event.

"I know it seems odd to auction off a married man, but everyone knows it's all in good fun," Karyn Frist said. "Married or single, my Bill is the hottest piece on the auction block."

As the winner, O'Connor will receive an evening with Frist that includes dinner for two at Chadwick's, a popular D.C.-area restaurant, followed by front-row seats to a touring production of Mamma Mia at the National

"You won!" said Ruth Bader Ginsburg, O'Connor's friend and fellow Supreme Court justice. "I can't believe you did it! Woo!"

Theatre.

Following Powell's announcement that Frist was "sold to the Supreme Court justice," O'Connor ran to the dais, looped her sash around Frist's neck, and said, "You're all mine, big boy," while winking at her tablemates.

Following the frenzied Frist sale, Powell sought to ride the wave of enthusiasm by putting twice-passed-over Secretary of Health and Human Services Tommy Thompson up for auction a third time.

"Come on! We're talking about a top member of the president's cabinet!" Powell said, as Thompson gamely flexed and posed for the assembled bidders. "This is Tommy Thompson, the original ladies' man. Don't you remember his calming presence during the anthrax scare, or the SARS outbreaks? Can I get $50? How about $30? Come on, ladies, this is for charity." ⌀

DISCHARGE from page 183

amounts of blood. Passersby were amazed by the unusually large amounts of blood. Passersby were amazed by the unusually large amounts of blood. Passersby were amazed by the unusually large amounts of blood. Passersby were amazed by the unusually large amounts of blood. Passersby were amazed by the unusually large amounts of blood. Passersby were amazed by the unusually large amounts of blood. Passersby were amazed by the unusually large amounts of blood. Passersby were amazed by the unusually large amounts of blood. Passersby were amazed by the unusually large amounts of blood. Passersby were amazed by the unusually large amounts of blood. Passersby were amazed by the unusually large amounts of blood. Passersby were amazed by the unusually large amounts of blood. Passersby were

This constitution sucks the big one.

amazed by the unusually large amounts of blood. Passersby were amazed by the unusually large amounts of blood. Passersby were amazed by the unusually large amounts of blood. Passersby were amazed by the unusually large amounts of blood. Passersby were amazed by the unusually large amounts of blood. Passersby were amazed by the unusually large amounts of blood. Passersby were amazed by the unusually large amounts of blood. Passersby were amazed by the unusually large amounts of blood. Passersby were amazed by the unusually large amounts of blood. Passersby were amazed by the unusually large amounts of blood. Passersby were amazed by the unusually large amounts of blood. Passersby were amazed by the unusually large amounts of blood. Passersby were amazed by the unusually large amounts of blood. Passersby were amazed by the unusually large amounts of blood. Passersby were amazed by the unusually large

see DISCHARGE page 196

HARVEY'S HOLLYWOOD

A Second Dose Of *Angels*? I Must Be In Heaven!

Item! Are you "2" pumped to see **Charlie's Angels 2: Full Frontal?** In light of all the super-duds in this blockbuster summer, I sure was. I needed a dose of **Drew Barrymore** more than ever, with the one-two punch of **Lucy Loo** and the beautiful but deadly **Carmen Diaz**. And, just when I thought I couldn't take any more, I got Moore...**Demi Moore**! Let me tell you, she kicked "2" much butt all over the screen.

The Outside Scoop
By Jackie Harvey

Speaking of the lovely Ms. Moore, the word on the street is that she's involved in a May-December romance with none other than future "Where Are They Now" candidate **Asheton Koosher**. Demi, didn't you get enough of him in the Dell computer ads? If you want a **Scott Baio** type, then go to the source and watch some of the classic episodes of **Joanie Loves Chacha**. Wise up, dear. You can do better—like your last husband, **Bruce** "Whatchoo talkin' 'bout?" **Willis**. Now, there's a man with class.

How is it that the **Swiss** got so famous for banking? In the movies, money is always being transferred to Swiss bank accounts, but the Swiss are about so much more than banks. They're also famous for **watches**, **army knives**, **iced tea**, and **chocolate**. Oh, and **the Alps**! Hollywood, it's high time you celebrate all things Swiss and stop portraying **Sweden** as a country full of greedy banking villains! Let them have their dignity.

Everybody's talkin' at me about the new CD from **Fifty Cents**, so I decided to pick up a copy at my local music store. Boy, was I in for an education! Did you know that music stores now sell **used CDs** at a discount? In fact, they had a bin of CDs marked down to under $2. I couldn't believe what I found: **Spice Girls**, **Alannis Morisette**, **Baha Men**. I forgot all about Fifty Cents and walked out with an armload of classics. I'd go back, but I'm afraid I might spend my whole paycheck!

Item! Adam Sandler, the Jewish **Jerry Lewis**, tied the knot with longtime fiancée supermodel **Jackie Titrone**. In true comic fashion, his little dog Meatball was all decked out in a dog tuxedo and served as best man. I wish I could have been a fly on the wall to see all the funny stuff that went on behind the scenes. Maybe **Rob Schneider** made some of his trademark crazy faces. Anyway, I hope the new Mrs. Sandler can settle him down without taking away his ability to make us laugh. Mazel tov!

It's **barbecue season**, and I love nothing better than to slap a slab of beef on the grill. For such a special occasion, I'll share my special recipe for **Jackie Harvey's Name In Lights Burger**. Ready? Take two pounds of ground beef. Add a small minced (that

Speaking of modesty, the hot song of the summer has to be "Camel Toe" by the band Fanny Pack. The subject of the song seems to be some sort of fashion problem of a female nature. Keep your ears open, because I'm sure you'll hear more from Fanny Pack in the coming years.

means chopped up very fine) yellow onion, two cloves of garlic, 1/4 teaspoon of salt, one tablespoon of dill, and no fewer than five twists of fresh ground pepper. That's fresh ground pepper, not the kind in a can. Now, roll up your sleeves, because you're going to be mixing it with your hands. Shape the beef into five patties and you're ready to dazzle! Serve some of these at your next cookout, and I guarantee you'll be the blockbuster of the block. (Don't worry, I'll never tell your secret!)

Item! The new season of **Sex In The City** is on, and if you don't have Sex In The City Fever, you must be living under a rock! I'm not sure what to expect, since I don't have **HBO**, and I only have the first three seasons on DVD. I hope **Chris Noth** makes a big splash as Mr. Big again. He's really the one for Carrie. Since I won't be able to follow the action, I'll just pop in the DVDs, watch one episode a week, and pretend they're new. By the season's end, they'll release a new season on DVD so I can get up to speed.

Are you as tired as I am of **thongs**, especially the ones you can see in the back because the girls wear those lowrider jeans and half-shirts? My grandmother used to say that you shouldn't sell the chicken when there's still eggs left in it. Have some modesty, ladies.

Speaking of modesty, the hot song of the summer has to be "Camel Toe" by the band **Fanny Pack**. The subject of the song seems to be some sort of fashion problem of a female nature. Keep your ears open, because I'm sure you'll hear more from Fanny Pack in the coming years.

I hate getting parked in by some insensitive jerk. It happened the other day, and I almost left a note under his windshield, but I decided I didn't want to stoop to his level.

Item! Everybody's buddy, Hollywood legend **Buddy Hackett**, is dead from undisclosed causes. You may remember him from the classic movie **It's A Mad Mad Mad Mad Life** or his years playing **Jed Clampett** on TV. On the comedy stage, he may have worked blue from time to time, but in the end he left me blue with his passing. Rest in peace, Buddy.

I hate getting **parked in** by some insensitive jerk. It happened the other day, and I almost left a note under his windshield, but I decided I didn't want to stoop to his level. I'm sure he'll get what's coming to him eventually.

Well, that wraps it up for **The Outside Scoop**. I have to take some time at the lake to recharge my batteries. It's a yearly ritual for me. I hope you also get a chance to cool down wherever you are, so we're all rested up for my next installment. I don't want to give away too much, but I have a hot lead about a certain **Jeremy Piven**'s weakness for that all-American delicacy, the **hot dog**. Until then, I'm Jackie Harvey, and you're a **treasured reader**. ⌀

HOROSCOPES

Your Horoscope

By Lloyd Schumner Sr.
Retired Machinist and
A.A.P.B.-Certified Astrologer

Aries: (March 21–April 19)
You will relinquish your title as president of acquisitions and finance after being forced to admit you're just the assistant office manager.

Taurus: (April 20–May 20)
You'll finally be able to build the home you've always dreamed of now that you have enough blankets and couch cushions.

Gemini: (May 21–June 21)
Venus is descending in your sign this week, but you're better off not knowing exactly what that means.

Cancer: (June 22–July 22)
That might have been the worst birthday you've ever had, but take note: It won't be the worst of your life.

Leo: (July 23–Aug. 22)
It will be hard to take on the dual role of teacher and parent, but that's the life you'll lead as the enchanted rabbit companion to two plucky orphans.

Virgo: (Aug. 23–Sept. 22)
You're nearly at the end of the longest, most difficult spirit-journey of your life. Be prepared for a difficult and boring period of spirit-unpacking.

Libra: (Sept. 23–Oct. 23)
You still don't understand what people tell you about getting along with others, but that's okay. You don't want to.

Scorpio: (Oct. 24–Nov. 21)
You'll experience a strange mix of random violence, stultifying boredom, and financial security after becoming an English Premier League soccer star.

Sagittarius: (Nov. 22–Dec. 21)
Engineers will soon restore power and water to your area, so you'll have hours of hard sledgehammer work ahead of you to get it back the way you like it.

Capricorn: (Dec. 22–Jan. 19)
People will come from miles around to seek your wisdom on all manner of things, which is proof that people will do anything for a good laugh.

Aquarius: (Jan. 20–Feb. 18)
Love may mean different things to different people, but you know that it usually means free meals for someone.

Pisces: (Feb. 19–March 20)
Frantic drivers will chase you around town for hours when a typo in the city charter mistakenly lists you as a free weekday parking spot.

the ONION®

VOLUME 39 ISSUE 28 AMERICA'S FINEST NEWS SOURCE™ 24–30 JULY 2003

NEWS

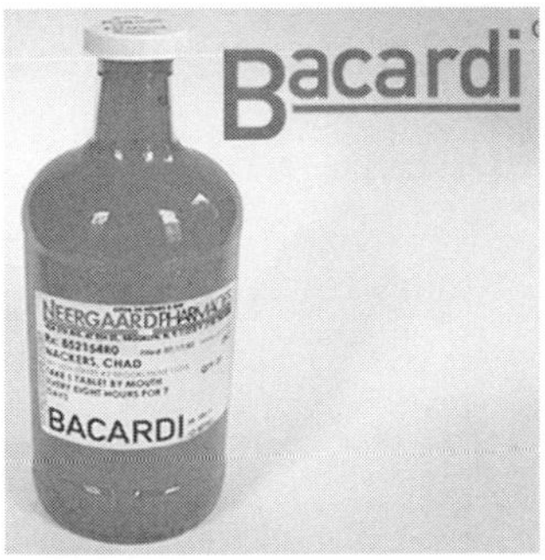

FDA Approves New Drug For Treatment Of Social Anxiety

see NATION page 4B

Gazebo Underutilized

see LOCAL page 3C

Schwarzenegger To U.S. Troops: 'You Guys Are The *Real* Genocidal Killer Robots From The Future'

see ENTERTAINMENT page 7E

STATshot

A look at the numbers that shape your world.

Least Favorite Household Chores

1. Shoveling path from bed to bathroom
2. Programming robot to dust
3. Making small talk with cleaning lady
4. "Husbandly duties"
5. Cleaning out duck trap
6. Recovering smokeable resin by straining bong water through coffee filter

LAPD Discovers Hidden Deformed Olsen Triplet

Above: Ethel, the previously unknown Olsen.

LOS ANGELES—A ragged and misshapen girl officials are calling a "third Olsen twin" was rescued from the basement of the residence of teen superstars Mary-Kate and Ashley Olsen Tuesday, Los Angeles police said.

"The girl has been positively identified as a sister of Mary-Kate and Ashley Olsen, born on the same day in June 1986," said LAPD Capt. Ellen Yanez, relating information provided in a confession by parents David and Janette Olsen, now divorced. "The monstrously contorted child was discovered living in conditions that could charitably be described as squalid."

Currently in custody at LAPD head-

see TRIPLET page 197

Above: A Baltimore-area interstate.

Deficit-Wracked Maryland Calls It Quits

ANNAPOLIS, MD—Citing mounting debt and a decline in tourism dollars, the state of Maryland will shut down for good on August 31, Maryland Gov. Robert L. Ehrlich Jr. told reporters Monday.

"I would like to sincerely thank everyone who has ever lived in or visited the great state of Maryland," Ehrlich said at a press conference held on the steps of a boarded-up Capitol Building. "You are the people who have made this such a wonderful place. Maryland will live on in the fond memories of each of you, even as

see MARYLAND page 196

Man Going To Taco Bell 'With Or Without You'

BOWLING GREEN, OH—After a series of delays, Josh Brooks, 29, reportedly informed his two roommates Monday evening that he was going to Taco Bell with or without them.

"I'm going," said Brooks, a distribution manager for the *Bowling Green Sentinel-Tribune*. "You guys don't have to come. But if you want to, I'm going, like, now. I'm grabbing my keys, then I'm out of here."

Brooks first proposed a trip to the Taco Bell restaurant on East Wooster St. at 6:13 p.m., echoing the popular ad campaign of the Mexican fast-food giant with his suggestion that the three friends "make a run for the border."

"Look, I don't have all night," Brooks said. "But if you guys want to come with me... to get some delicious hot Mexican food..."

Roommates Tony Solomon, 26, and Ron Alexander, 25, reportedly

Right: Brooks announces his departure to the Taco Bell on East Wooster St. (above).

expressed lukewarm interest in the excursion.

"Yeah, man—I guess I could go for a Steak Soft Taco or something," Solomon said, without looking up from the television. "Yeah, I guess I'll go."

Alexander's interest in the meal was

see TACO BELL page 196

Troops To Stay In Iraq

U.S. military officials recently announced that thousands of soldiers will remain in Iraq for longer than previously stated. What do *you* think?

"At least democracy's flowering over there. They could be here, where it's nearly fucking dead."

Arthur Rucker
Professor

"Good. Maybe it'll teach those weaklings some discipline."

Jessica Burrell
Salesperson

"As an employer of several U.S. reservists, I have one question: Who's gonna sell these motorboats?"

Edward Enriquez
Sales Manager

"I can't imagine why it's taking them so long to accomplish a simple little matter like stabilizing that particular geopolitical region."

Maude Wilkenson
Artist

"Boy, the Iraqis better develop a fun pop culture with cute cartoon animals and grown women in schoolgirl uniforms, or this will be a complete waste."

Sammy Marsh
Security Guard

"If our soldiers must be involved in a lengthy occupation, at least it's in a place without any dangerous weapons of mass destruction lying around."

Martin Stearns
Systems Analyst

The New *New York Times*

Effective July 30, Bill Keller will become *The New York Times'* new executive editor. What changes are in store for the nation's most respected newspaper?

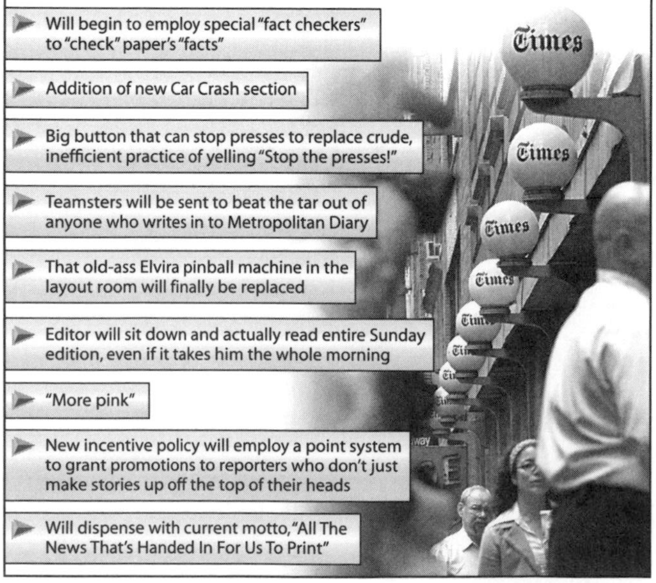

- Will begin to employ special "fact checkers" to "check" paper's "facts"
- Addition of new Car Crash section
- Big button that can stop presses to replace crude, inefficient practice of yelling "Stop the presses!"
- Teamsters will be sent to beat the tar out of anyone who writes in to Metropolitan Diary
- That old-ass Elvira pinball machine in the layout room will finally be replaced
- Editor will sit down and actually read entire Sunday edition, even if it takes him the whole morning
- "More pink"
- New incentive policy will employ a point system to grant promotions to reporters who don't just make stories up off the top of their heads
- Will dispense with current motto, "All The News That's Handed In For Us To Print"

the ONION®
America's Finest News Source.™

Herman Ulysses Zweibel
Founder

T. Herman Zweibel
Publisher Emeritus
J. Phineas Zweibel
Publisher
Maxwell Prescott Zweibel
Editor-In-Chief

Sitting Through This Boring Murder Trial Should Be Punishment Enough

By Donald Glenn Ehrman

I've heard all killers think this, but I really believed I was going to get away with it. Well, if I knew what was in store for me at the courthouse, I might have thought twice before offing that family. Day after day, hour after hour, there's more of the same tedious examining and cross-examining. And don't even get me started on Judge Sominex up there. I tell you, sitting through this boring murder trial should be punishment enough.

It's cruel and unusual the way prosecution goes on... and *on*... and on. I knew it wasn't going to be like it is on TV, or in my juvenile animal-cruelty busts. But I had no idea it was going to take this long. Is there no such thing as mercy? I thought I had committed my crime in a state without capital punishment, but I swear this trial has been designed to bore me to death.

In addition to prosecuting me for the murder of my idiot neighbors, this damn district attorney's in a politically sensitive position that requires him to capture the public interest. "Blah blah, I now introduce into evidence People's Exhibit Number 89, a wooden yardstick, blah blah, this will take 20 minutes for some reason, Your Honor." And I didn't even use Number 89 as a weapon, or to force my way into my neighbors' house, or even to beat their dog to death. It was present at the scene, I think—sorry, but I

You try to sit through this stuff for seven hours straight. I demand this time be subtracted from what I'm guessing will be multiple life sentences.

drifted off in the middle of the presentation—and I guess it has my prints on it or some blood spatter or some fibers or something. But come *on*! There was a .38 caliber revolver and a spade involved, too. Don't you think they could cut to the chase?

And my pro bono counsel is not helping. I asked him what the hold-up is, and he said the prosecution is trying to be thorough in establishing a chronology and a chain of evidence. Yeah, I could tell they were being thorough when they spent two hours establishing that I did, in fact, live next door to my victims. Sorry, "alleged victims."

Can I get a cup of black coffee over here?

Listen to this, if you have the

It's cruel and unusual the way prosecution goes on... and *on*... and on. I knew it wasn't going to be like it is on TV, or in my juvenile animal-cruelty busts. But I had no idea it was going to take this long. Is there no such thing as mercy?

stamina: "As a matter of fact, Your Honor, there was a real accusatory instrument in effect at the time, being my client's charge under Section 130, Sodomy with a Minor, so his absolute right to counsel had therefore been violated. It follows that anything said, even under the perception of Miranda waiver in connection with any other matter, does not alter the fact of the violation in the face of Absolute Right to Conviction, so whatever came from that is absolutely inadmissible on technical grounds." And that's my own lawyer! You try to sit through this stuff for seven hours straight. I demand this time be subtracted from what I'm guessing will be multiple life sentences.

Come *on*. Let's wrap this *up*.

Then there's the prosecution, who should have a pretty easy job since I kind of skipped the cover-my-tracks phase: "Even with a Miranda oversight, those rights are not considered a constitutional guarantee, but are merely meant to guard against self-incriminatory statements made involuntarily. Furthermore, even intentional violations of Miranda which result in evidentiary discovery do not render said admissions inadmissible."

Bo-ring!

It doesn't have to be this way. I mean, human beings were brutally and methodically butchered, for God's sake. That's nothing to yawn about. Let's get on to the crime-scene photos. That'll be enough to wake the jury up and make sure they never sleep soundly again.

Well, I regret nothing—except for pleading "not guilty" and dragging this thing out. Next time I'll know better. Ø

Goofy Guy Named Gary Enlivens Otherwise Intolerable Wedding Reception

MINOT, ND—At the outdoor wedding reception of Kevin Thomas and Elaine Schroeder on Saturday, a party guest identified only as "Gary" alleviated tensions and endeared himself to guests with his unpredictable and irreverent actions, turning the miserable event into one of marginal tolerability, sources reported Monday.

"I'm not sure who he is, but that Gary guy was the best thing about the wedding," said Warren Thomas, Kevin's father. "My wife must have invited him, because he sure couldn't have been a friend of sticks-in-the-mud like the Schroeders."

According to other guests, Gary, estimated to be in his late 50s, seemed to have attended the event alone. Although he made his biggest impression at the reception, witnesses said he was present at St. Paul's Catholic Church during the ceremony.

"The first time I noticed [Gary] was in the church," best man Joseph Farrel said. "The flower girl kept giggling during the vows. It took me a while to realize [Gary] was making faces at her. It was pretty funny, I guess. Then after the ceremony, I ran into [Gary] in the bathroom. He came up to the urinal next to mine and said, 'This must be where all the dicks hang out.' Normally, I'd punch out any guy who tried to talk to me in the john, but the joke was a relief after listening to those awful self-written vows."

According to guests at the reception, relations between the Thomases and the Schroeders have been strained since January, when Elaine

At the reception, however, Gary reportedly lightened the mood by telling jokes, singing, and repeatedly clinking his glass to make the bride and groom kiss.

announced that she was not taking Thomas as a last name. Additional tensions arose when the Schroeders learned that Kevin was not Catholic and did not want a church wedding. Guests said these factors, among others, lent the event an air of discord from the start.

At the reception, however, Gary reportedly lightened the mood by telling jokes, singing, and repeatedly clinking his glass to make the bride and groom kiss.

"There was this funny-looking guy

Above: Some guy named Gary.

[Gary] at the table next to mine," said Jeanie Schroeder, Elaine's cousin. "He was cracking people up by making a tie out of one of the streamers hanging from the ceiling. Meanwhile, at my table, everyone was just gossiping about how Kevin made so much less money than Elaine's first fiancé. I kept thinking, 'I wish I was sitting at the goofy guy's table.'"

After dinner, guests milled about the tent, making uncomfortable small talk about relatives and complaining about the middling quality of the buffet food and the cost of drinks at the cash bar. As the evening wore on, the children and more adventurous guests gravitated toward Gary, who told corny jokes, pretended to steal items from the gift table, and did impersonations of celebrities.

"That Gary was doing this impersonation of Father Spencer performing the service with a thick lisp," said Gilbert Szigmond, a friend from the Schroeders' parish. "I usually wouldn't stand for someone showing

see RECEPTION page 196

NEWS IN BRIEF

Man Trapped Under Boulder Braces For Possible *Good Morning America* Interview

YOSEMITE VILLAGE, CA—Rock climber Scott Prichard, 31, who has spent the last 48 hours with his legs pinned under a boulder on Glacier Point, is reportedly bracing himself for a possible interview on *Good Morning America*. "God, Katie Couric, that chubby weatherman with the wisecracks," a sweat- and urine-soaked Prichard said. "I pray Diane Sawyer doesn't ask me if I wanted to climb the Point 'because it was there.' I just would not be able to stomach that kind of inane chit-chat." Prichard then passed out from the intense pain.

Widower Misses Sex With Dead Wife Terribly

SCOTTSBLUFF, NE—Nearly one year after a car accident claimed the life of his wife Sarah, Lloyd Monreal still misses having sex with her "more than I can say," the 44-year-old reported Tuesday. "Even now, every room in the house reminds me of the times we had sex in it," Monreal said, fighting back tears. "I don't care if 40 years go by. I'll never forget her breasts, her ass, those thighs." In honor of the anniversary, Monreal will eat a quiet dinner at home, after which he will take out a box of old photographs and perform a one-hour masturbation vigil by candlelight.

Area Man Overly Proud Of Never Wearing Underwear

LITTLE ROCK, AR—Local record-store clerk Greg Oertel, 23, seems inordinately proud that he never wears underwear, Oertel's coworkers told reporters Tuesday. "I've heard Greg mention about 10 times that he never wears underwear," coworker Jake Hannah said. "He acts like he doesn't care what we think about it, but I'm beginning to suspect he does." According to his friends, Oertel insists that he gets hot when he wears underwear, so he "just doesn't bother," and that "it's no big deal."

Hot New Secretary Of Transportation To 'Shake Up' U.S. Highways

WASHINGTON, DC—In a press conference announcing the replacement of Norman Mineta, vivacious new Secretary of Transportation Kyla Damon unveiled plans Tuesday to "shake up" U.S. highways. "You think you've seen negotiation and implementation of international transportation agreements and the issuance of regulations to prevent alcohol and illegal-drug misuse in U.S. transportation systems?" Damon said. "Well, think again!" Damon added that her first order of business would be to "say so long to that dusty old fossil known as the Federal Highway Administration."

Bush Not Heard From For Over A Month

WASHINGTON, DC—Beltway insiders and members of the media expressed concern Monday that President Bush has not been heard from for nearly five weeks. "I hope he's okay," said Secretary of State Colin Powell. "It's just like him to go off on a fishing trip to Alaska or something and not tell anyone. Which is fine. I mean, he's the president and can do what he wants and all that, but we kind of need to wrap up this whole Liberia thing we started." White House Press Secretary Scott McClellan admitted that he was unclear about the president's whereabouts, but figured he must be "off somewhere busy with something." Ø

RECEPTION from page 195

disrespect for a man of the cloth, but the levity was welcome relief after that hostile toast by Kevin's mother. It was the only thing that kept me from ducking out before the cake was served."

An informal poll of the wedding guests and hosts revealed that no one was certain who invited Gary, but all were relieved that he was present.

"Everyone lined up for the cha-cha slide, and it was like 'Oh, boy, here we go,'" said groomsman Jeff Can-

The level of barely suppressed tension turned into outright hostility when the groom's brother, David Thomas, got into a fight with the DJ.

zanovia. "I had to dance with [bridesmaid and Elaine's sister] Erica Schroeder, who I can't stand, but we were all going through the motions to make Kevin and Elaine happy. Then this guy [Gary] comes onto the dance floor and acts like he can't dance, pretending to trip and fall. I usually hate ridiculous behavior like that, but I have to admit his antics were pretty much the only thing that made the night halfway bearable."

The level of barely suppressed tension turned into outright hostility when the groom's brother, David Thomas, got into a fight with the DJ.

"By the time we had to catch the bouquet, we were all pretty much fed up," bridesmaid Helen Perry said. "The fight really freaked everyone out—Elaine's family is pretty strict, and that's putting it nice. No one was mingling, and everyone was just sort of sitting quietly at their tables and waiting until they could slip out unnoticed. But when the DJ announced that all the single women should line up, that guy [Gary] ran over, jumping and clapping and pretending to be really excited to catch the bouquet. Elaine's dad gave him a look, but Gary didn't seem to care."

By the end of the reception, the room was nearly empty, except for a handful of stragglers and Gary, who wished the newlyweds well.

"Ordinarily, a guy like Gary would annoy the shit out of me," the bride said. "But between the fights and my little sister getting plastered and Grandma not showing up because Kevin's not Catholic, that Gary was the one thing stopping me from screaming at everyone to get out and let me start my new life with my husband."

Added Kevin: "Yeah, where did that Gary dude come from?" ⊘

MARYLAND from page 193

we liquidate the state's assets."

Ratified as the seventh state in 1788, Maryland has been a favorite haunt for a devoted group of fans. In addition to being the home of the Annapolis U.S. Naval Academy, Maryland is the birthplace of such notable Americans as surveyor Benjamin Banneker, singer Billie Holiday, baseball legend Babe Ruth, and former Supreme Court Justice Thurgood Marshall.

In spite of its rich history, Maryland has struggled with mounting debt since the '90s, as tourism and tax revenues failed to keep pace with rising expenses. The state has for years fought what many insiders considered a losing battle.

"We had a good run, but we just can't do it anymore," Ehrlich said. "The bad economy, increased spending on homeland security, and an increasing Medicaid bill were the final nails in Maryland's coffin. We are simply losing too much money to keep the borders open."

Ehrlich promised that Maryland would not shut down operations until the last day of August, giving longtime fans of the Old Line State an opportunity to visit.

"We wanted to give people a chance to say goodbye," Ehrlich said. "Since the rumors of a state shutdown began, I have received thousands of letters and small donations from people all over the country. This means so much—more than you can ever know—but despite all the love and devotion, I'm afraid it's just not going to happen."

Ehrlich told the crowd that he did everything he could to keep Maryland open, but in the end no effort proved successful.

"I made across-the-board budget cuts, restructured all of our social services, effected hiring freezes, and emptied out the state's rainy-day fund," Ehrlich said. "The last decade has just been exhausting. As much as I love Maryland, I can't say that I'm going to miss the 18-hour days trying to keep this state afloat."

Ehrlich said he received offers to buy out Maryland, but the bids were rejected.

"We had a deal with New Mexico that could have saved us, but it fell through," Ehrlich said. "The things [New Mexico Gov.] Bill Richardson wanted to change when he took over went against everything Maryland is all about. Rather than severely compromise our state, we decided instead to pass."

On Sept. 1, the government of Maryland will disband and all state employees will be laid off, a situation Ehrlich calls "extremely regrettable."

"Many of these workers have been in Maryland all their lives," Ehrlich said. "These folks are like family to me. In fact, some actually *are* family. The people are why we held on to statehood as long as we did."

Although current residents of Maryland will be allowed to stay in the state until they can arrange to relocate, they must do so without government services. Experts predict the state will become a vast vacant lot within five years.

In order to offset some of the debt accrued over the last few decades, Maryland is selling its assets, announcing that "everything must go" before the state closes. The most sought-after items to be auctioned off include the original first draft of "The Star-Spangled Banner," written by Maryland native Francis Scott Key.

The rights to Maryland's state flag, bird, and motto are also being sold to the highest bidder.

"Secret [brand antiperspirant] has put in a substantial bid for our motto, *Fatti maschii, parole femine*, which means 'Manly Deeds, Womanly Words,'" Ehrlich said. "I also think that Nevada might buy the rights to our state sport, jousting. When we sell the rights to our state song, 'Maryland, My Maryland,' that's when it's going to hit me that it's finally over."

For many longtime fans of Maryland, the closing strikes a deep emotional chord.

"It's just a shame," said Gene Tupper, a resident of Maryland since 1955. "I don't think anyone will really understand what it was like to visit the historic Antietam National Battlefield or walk along beautiful Chesapeake Bay back in the prime years. I guess all great things have to end sometime."

Many fans of the state said they hope someone purchases and revitalizes Maryland before it falls into disrepair.

"I don't want what happened to Oregon to happen here," said Jane Renski, a Maryland resident. "We drove by the place a few years ago and it was totally abandoned—really eerie. The whole state was infested with raccoons." ⊘

TACO BELL from page 193

coupled with serious reservations.

"I should get out of the house for a while, but I'm pretty broke," he said, walking to his bedroom. "I'll go look for some change."

After several minutes of watching his roommates' preparations, Brooks said again that he was in no mood to wait.

"Tone, you don't need the jacket," Brooks told Solomon, who had begun to search the floor around the couch for clothing. "Let's just go. It's 10 minutes away. We'll be in the car the whole time. Round trip'll take 30 minutes, tops. C'mon."

"You don't need your warm-ups, Beckham," Brooks added, sighing. "Listen, I'm out of here in two minutes whether you guys are with me or not."

Gathering his wallet and keys, Brooks relocated to the area by the front door.

"Ronnie, I'll buy you a taco there if you want," Brooks said, calling into the back bedroom. "I'm getting old here. I'm not going to bring anything back, so if you want it, you gotta come. Now."

Continued Brooks: "Or not. Whatever. I just thought we'd talked about how we all wanted to go. Just make up your minds, kids, 'cause the train's leaving the station."

"Okay!" Brooks said, clapping his hands as Alexander emerged from the bedroom. "It's TB time."

In spite of the announcement, the group did not leave.

"Just a sec," Solomon said, finally rising from the couch. "I gotta clean up, then we can go."

According to Brooks, this is not the

"Ronnie, I'll buy you a taco there if you want," Brooks said, calling into the back bedroom.

first time Solomon has further delayed the group by wasting time he could have been using to get ready.

"He just sits there and does nothing," Brooks said to Alexander. "Just lays on his ass until I make him move. If it weren't for me, that guy would never leave the house. I can't spend my day just waiting for him. If he isn't out here in two minutes, we're leaving without him."

In spite of the pronouncement, Brooks rarely, if ever, leaves the apartment alone after such a threat. According to Solomon, Brooks feels the need to "decide every last thing we do."

"It's like last month, when we were throwing this party," Solomon said later. "He begged me to go with him to the store to buy the beer. We got there, and before I knew it he was standing at the register with two cases of MGD in cans. He was like, 'Look, man, we're getting MGD cans. That's all there is to it.'"

Added Solomon: "I mean, I like MGD, but he didn't have to be a dick about it."

Dr. Janice Shoreham, a psychiatrist and adjunct professor at Bowling Green State University, said Brooks' behavior is characteristic of an altruistic dominant male in a household of twentysomethings.

"[Brooks] sees himself as the lighthouse, and his less-motivated friends as ill-fated ships, cruising toward the rocks," Shoreham said. "If he doesn't lead them to safety, or in this case a delicious Seven Layer Burrito, he feels he has let them down."

Brooks disagreed.

"I really don't care if you guys come or not," Brooks said, opening the front door. "That's it—I'm heading out. I'm vapor. I've been ready, and I'm leaving."

Added Brooks: "I'm not kidding. I'm leaving now. Are you guys coming or what?" ⊘

TRIPLET from page 193

quarters, the twisted, hunched, foul-smelling figure of Ethel Olsen, 17, is drawing both pity and horror from investigators.

"With hair covering over 60 percent of her diminutive body, teeth protruding through her bottom lip, and her only useful limb a prehensile claw, Ethel would make a poor slumber-party companion," Yanez said. "The

Said Yanez: "A reluctant sense of duty toward the infant forced her parents to bring her home, but pity soon turned to revulsion, and after a ghastly and traumatic attempt at nursing, the wretch was relegated to the cellar, where she was locked in a cage and fed through a garden hose."

Olsen family's actions are understandable, if ultimately unconscionable."

According to Yanez, the Olsen family was able to conceal Ethel's birth from public record because the triplets were born during a camping trip in an isolated area of the Sierra Nevada mountains.

"Ethel was reportedly the last to be delivered, and the family recoiled in horror to see such a deformed and unsightly creature emerge from a womb that had housed her two cherubic sisters," Yanez said. "A reluctant sense of duty toward the infant forced her parents to bring her home, but pity soon turned to revulsion, and after a ghastly and traumatic attempt at nursing, the wretch was relegated to the cellar, where she was locked in a cage and fed through a garden hose."

The Olsens' plans to anonymously abandon Ethel at a convent were thwarted in 1987, when Mary-Kate and Ashley Olsen, barely 1 year old, found fame sharing the role of Michelle Tanner on the ABC sitcom *Full House*.

"The parents didn't want to risk any chance of negative publicity," said Lieut. Ron Mudd, one of the detectives who questioned the Olsens. "Someone at an orphanage might have spotted the dim similarities the hideous mutant bore to her apple-cheeked siblings, who only grew in popularity as the years went by."

Continued Mudd: "It appears that Ethel was continuously kept on the cusp of survival, the family's tenuous

Above: A scene from Ethel's first film project, currently in production.

belief in the sanctity of life the only thing that kept her fed and sheltered. That she received no love is evident. To be fair, it is hard to love someone whose hairless body parts are covered with scales, half-inch-thick toenails, and a harelip that extends past her brow."

Although an investigation is still underway, some details of Ethel's 17 tortured years have been made public. According to the police report, her

"The parents didn't want to risk any chance of negative publicity," said Lieut. Ron Mudd, one of the detectives who questioned the Olsens. "Someone at an orphanage might have spotted the dim similarities the hideous mutant bore to her apple-cheeked siblings, who only grew in popularity as the years went by."

cellar dwelling had no heat or ventilation, and only a single grimy, barred basement window provided light. There was no plumbing, so Ethel was forced to scuttle into a corner and defecate in a drain.

When found, the girl was clad in mismatched, threadbare castoffs from Mary-Kate and Ashley's Wal-Mart clothing line. She slept on a heavily tarnished serving tray believed to have been taken from a craft-services table on the set of the 2001 straight-to-video release *Holiday In The Sun*. Police say she subsisted on rainwater, half-eaten bagels salvaged from talk-show green rooms, and any small rodents she was able to catch; she saved their bones in a corner, along with a pile of coughed-up pellets. The girl owned no toys other than a headless Mattel Ashley doll, onto which she had stuck hanks of her own body hair.

Investigators say that Ethel communicates in guttural grunts and wheezes, as well as the occasional piercing howl. She is fond of rocking on her haunches and humming the same tune fragment, which is believed to be an extremely off-key version of the song "I Am The Cute One," recorded by the Olsen Twins in 1992.

"Perhaps she heard the song emanating from upstairs and it made an impression in her twisted, imbecilic psyche," Mudd said. "The irony is annihilating."

Police rescued Ethel after receiving a tip from an aromatherapist employed by the Olsens. The woman alerted authorities that she had detected a "distinctly un-jasminelike" odor emanating from the basement door of the three-story home.

Ethel's condition has shocked even those on the battle-hardened LAPD.

"My daughter loves Mary-Kate and Ashley, and this is going to be hard to explain to her," Mudd said. "In a way, I wish we'd never found Ethel. As a cop, I see a lot of ugliness every day, but this devastates me. How could something so hideous be connected to something so pure and whole-

Police rescued Ethel after receiving a tip from an aromatherapist employed by the Olsens. The woman alerted authorities that she had detected a "distinctly un-jasminelike" odor emanating from the basement door of the three-story home.

some?"

The Olsen parents face multiple charges of child abuse and reckless endangerment of a minor, but they are also reportedly in negotiations with television executives to develop a sitcom starring Ethel.

"The parents who did this should be punished," said Linda Spassky, vice-president in charge of programming for ABC Family Channel, which airs the Olsen Twins sitcom *So Little Time*. "But there is no reason to continue to hurt poor Ethel with further sequestering. After all, she has that magical Olsen name, and that means guaranteed tween appeal." Ø

COMMUNITY VOICES

In Sex Sales, What You're Really Selling Is Yourself

By Traci Hoff

The younger women come to me nearly every day and ask, "Traci, what is your secret? How are you so successful, while I struggle every day just to make ends meet?" I smile, because I used to be like them: insecure and afraid. That was before I developed my patented Three-Point Plan™, the only sure-fire path to spectacular success. It starts with one simple lesson: In sex sales, what you're really selling is yourself.

Your prospective clients want to do more than just buy a service from you. They also want to buy your attitude, your style, your body. You are offering a service, but you are also offering *yourself*. What is really "up for sale" is *you*. Remember: Details matter, from the miniskirt to the perfume to the heels. You need to wear what makes you feel your best and also says to the customer, "I am a professional, sexy woman, and I'd like to spend part of the evening with you." When a man walks out of your motel room, he wants to feel like he's just fucked a hundred dollars.

The next point is just as important, but often forgotten: The customer *always* comes first. His needs and his desires must always come before yours, no matter what else is going on in your life. You can try to sell a man your body, but if you're preoccupied with thoughts about your own ego, your own fears, or the child you left home alone with the excuse that you were running out for cigarettes, you're not going to close the deal. If you're serious about success, you have to be focused on your prospect's needs at all times.

Your prospective clients want to do more than just buy a service from you. They also want to buy your attitude, your style, your body. You are offering a service, but you are also offering *yourself*. What is really "up for sale" is *you*. Remember: Details matter.

Remember this: Being sensitive to a client's needs sometimes means telling him what his needs are. He is paying for your expertise, so don't be afraid to take control of the situation if he seems to need guidance. Some customers, however, know exactly what they want. With those types, it's best just to listen. A little trick that has proved invaluable over the years is to repeat what the customer says. For example, if a man says, "I want to fuck you," I often repeat, more quietly, "Fuck me, yeah." This gives the buyer a sense of satisfaction. He is being listened to, and his needs are being met.

A customer can always tell if you are genuinely interested in satisfying him. Remember: A satisfied customer is a repeat customer. And repeat customers translate into less time on the street corner, more time in the bedroom, and more money in your pocket. It's not always easy, but I leave my troubles at the motel door. The more empty I'm feeling, the more pride I take in silencing my woe-is-me monologue and focusing on my customer's desires and the repetitive creaking of an old motel bed. There is a time for my own needs, but it is certainly not when I'm with a client.

It's not always easy, but I leave my troubles at the motel door. The more empty I'm feeling, the more pride I take in silencing my woe-is-me monologue and focusing on my customer's desires and the repetitive creaking of an old motel bed. There is a time for my own needs, but it is certainly not when I'm with a client.

Point Three is closely tied to customer satisfaction, and is the key to a long and prosperous career in the world's oldest profession. The best way to be financially secure is to rely on your personal contacts and connections. As a sex saleswoman, you are only worth as much as people are willing to pay for you. If you follow Points One and Two—that is, if you find customers, sell *yourself* to them, and make sure to satisfy each one—you'll end up with a strong client base, a network of valuable contacts in the business. That way, you don't need to fret if your pimp goes to jail, or if your corner gets busted by vice. No matter what, you'll be in business as long as your customers have your phone number.

A little trick that has proved invaluable over the years is to repeat what the customer says. For example, if a man says, "I want to fuck you," I often repeat, more quietly, "Fuck me, yeah."

Also, in sex sales, you need to learn how to take rejection *professionally*, not personally. When you approach trucks parked on a highway's frontage road and ask the drivers if they want to party, you're going to hear "no" a lot. But a good sex saleswoman understands that even the top sellers on the block get rejected more often than not. Even if you get rejected four times out of five, you were still able to sell yourself once successfully. And that one man, if you treat him right, will come back for repeat business, helping to ensure your financial future.

Now, let's review the Three-Point Plan. One: In sex sales, you're selling your whole self to a paying customer. Two: A customer's satisfaction must be your number one priority. And three: Good connections and contacts are the only way to judge your worth as a sex saleswoman, and to secure your financial future. Follow this simple plan, and you can be as phenomenally successful as I have been. Ø

HOROSCOPES

Your Horoscope

By Lloyd Schumner Sr.
Retired Machinist and
A.A.P.B.-Certified Astrologer

Aries: (March 21–April 19)
You will pass away next week at the age of 95, heralded as a beloved entertainer despite being in your late 20s and generally disliked at the moment.

Taurus: (April 20–May 20)
They'll soon put you in a secure, soundproof, knife-filled room where you can't hurt anyone but yourself.

Gemini: (May 21–June 21)
Although you honestly believe you do a better job of it than they could, finishing other people's sentences for them is still a real dick move.

Cancer: (June 22–July 22)
It's true that they say all is fair in love and war, but be advised that some still consider the use of nerve gas barbaric in either circumstance.

Leo: (July 23–Aug. 22)
The job market and the economy are both pretty dismal right now, but take heart: No one would hire you even if things were perfect.

Virgo: (Aug. 23–Sept. 22)
You've never believed that "love conquers all," but that will change when love invades the area, enslaves your subjects, and sows your fields with salt.

Libra: (Sept. 23–Oct. 23)
Police are forced to concede that the blowtorch really was for making crème brûlée after finding several of the desserts among the charred and smoking corpses.

Scorpio: (Oct. 24–Nov. 21)
All signs point to you having a quiet, uneventful week, but the stars' gut feelings nonetheless say different.

Sagittarius: (Nov. 22–Dec. 21)
This will be a very romantic period for Sagittarius, which beats the hell out of the weepy, self-absorbed pre-Raphaelite period you've been going through.

Capricorn: (Dec. 22–Jan. 19)
This is a great time to start new projects, as long as they don't involve a router, a band saw, or tungsten inert gas welding.

Aquarius: (Jan. 20–Feb. 18)
The doctors will tell you you're only in for a routine colonoscopy, but then the minor-key calliope music will begin.

Pisces: (Feb. 19–March 20)
This week will be a series of excruciatingly painful metaphorical and physical low blows for you.

the ONION®

VOLUME 39 ISSUE 29 AMERICA'S FINEST NEWS SOURCE™ 31 JULY–6 AUGUST 2003

NEWS

Genetically Modified Chicken Lays Its Own Dipping Sauce

see SCIENCE page 3A

Yearbook Committee Forced To Print Mug Shot

see LOCAL page 2C

Friend Who Can Play Law & Order Theme On Bass Asked To Do So

see LOCAL page 5C

STATshot

A look at the numbers that shape your world.

Least Favorite U.S. Highways

1. Interstate To Grandma's
2. M. Emmet Walsh Commemorative Middle-Of-Nowhere Stretch, East Texas
3. The Hershey Highway, Hershey, PA
4. America's Loneliest And Chattiest Road
5. [Your Name Here] Memorial Highway

THE ONION • $2.00 US • $3.00 CAN

Adorable Democratic Candidate Actually Believes He Has A Chance

WASHINGTON, DC—Democratic candidate John Kerry seems to truly believe he has a chance at winning the presidency in 2004, the adorable Massachusetts senator revealed Monday.

"The current administration's reckless approach to tax cuts is a huge fiscal gamble," the plucky politician said. "It benefits the wealthy, hurts the poor, and will never succeed in restoring broad-based economic growth and financial discipline."

"We must act now, before our nation plunges deeper into debt," added Kerry, sounding as cute as ever. "When George W. Bush took office, there was a projected budget surplus of $5.6 trillion from 2002 to 2011. Now, economists project hundreds of billions of dollars in deficits for the same time period."

The precocious Kerry is one of nine candidates in the race for the Democratic presidential nomination.

"That is so great," a beaming Dan Rather said following a report on *CBS Evening News*. "Kerry says he will beat not only all the White House hopefuls in the primary, but also President Bush in the election. Keep it up, champ!"

In spite of Bush's campaign war

see CANDIDATE page 203

Above: Kerry, looking very nice all dressed up.

Gigli Focus Groups Demand New Ending In Which Both Affleck And Lopez Die

HOLLYWOOD, CA—Focus groups at advance screenings for Gigli, a romantic comedy starring Ben Affleck and Jennifer Lopez set to open nationwide July 30, have demanded a new ending in which both stars die "in as brutal a manner as possible," sources at Sony Pictures said Tuesday.

"The movie is pretty good, I guess," read one comment card from a test-screening audience in Culver City, CA. "I liked the Al Pacino character, but I had a hard time buying Jennifer Lopez as a les-

see GIGLI page 202

Above: Focus-group participants suggest possible violent deaths for characters played by Lopez and Affleck (right).

Area Man Knows All The Shortcut Keys

Left: Turlock opens a new browser window without even touching his mouse.

NEW BRITAIN, CT—Catalog copywriter Roger Turlock knows all the keyboard combinations that execute a computer's common commands, the Comfort Uniforms employee said yet again Tuesday.

"You can just hit Command-P to print, you know," Turlock, 38, told a coworker who had just gone through the labor-intensive process of printing via the word-processing application's pull-down File menu. "Lot faster. Just Command at the same time as the letter P."

"Command-Q to quit a program," Turlock said to the air. "Command-X for cut. Command-C for copy. Command-V for paste. Those are biggies—Com-

see KEYS page 203

Uday And Qusay On Display

Last week, the U.S. military defended its decision to place the bodies of Saddam Hussein's sons on display. What do *you* think?

Patrick Herron
Computer Specialist

"I can think of no better way to win opposing Iraqi hearts and minds than by showing them some opposing Iraqis' actual hearts and minds."

Darcie Windham
Activity Director

"So, we've got Uday and Qusay. Now, how about the eapons-way of ass-may estruction-day?"

Juan Russ
Station Engineer

"Now the Iraqis will love us, like they were supposed to in the first place."

Marty Felder
Bus Driver

"My heart goes out to Saddam. I can't imagine what it's like to lose even one, much less two evil henchmen."

Terrance Fleck
Histopathologist

"Raise the heads on gilded poles! Roast the fatted calf! We need a rousing song—summon Toby Keith!"

Alisa Overstreet
Systems Analyst

"Super. Now, let's show those bodies to the economy and our problems are over."

Digital Music Piracy

The music industry recently filed lawsuits against hundreds of individuals it accuses of illegally sharing music on the Internet. How are music fans responding?

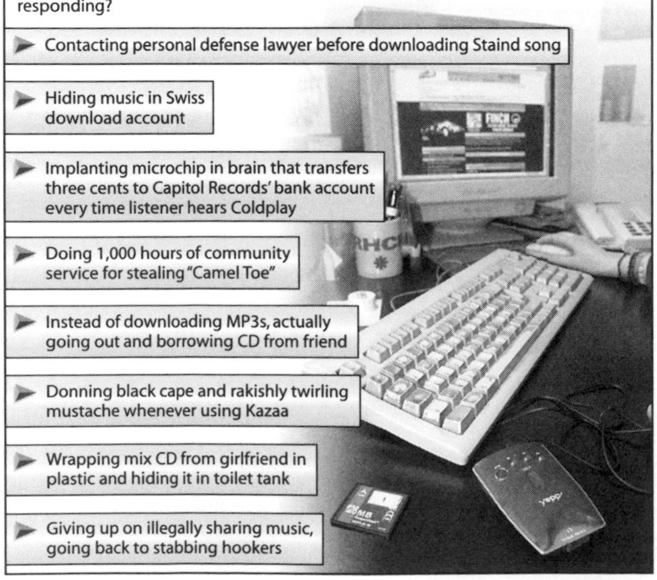

- Contacting personal defense lawyer before downloading Staind song
- Hiding music in Swiss download account
- Implanting microchip in brain that transfers three cents to Capitol Records' bank account every time listener hears Coldplay
- Doing 1,000 hours of community service for stealing "Camel Toe"
- Instead of downloading MP3s, actually going out and borrowing CD from friend
- Donning black cape and rakishly twirling mustache whenever using Kazaa
- Wrapping mix CD from girlfriend in plastic and hiding it in toilet tank
- Giving up on illegally sharing music, going back to stabbing hookers

the ONION®
America's Finest News Source.™

Herman Ulysses Zweibel
Founder

T. Herman Zweibel
Publisher Emeritus
J. Phineas Zweibel
Publisher
Maxwell Prescott Zweibel
Editor-In-Chief

You Shall Make An Excellent Queen

By Gorzo The Mighty Emperor Of The Universe

Grand Vizier Adrakus! Prepare a full report on the attempted siege of my palace! Spare no detail, and have the Royal Theater Guild prepare a full operatic dramatization for next month's Tyranny Day festivities!

And a cask of Venusian sapphires shall go to whoever finds the remains of my most hated enemy: Crash Comet, Space Commander from the Year 2000!

As for that most vaunted and foul Space-Yacht, the Star of Freedom III, fetch me every scrap of wreckage that can be found! I shall display its shattered hull as a trophy at the entrance to my Palace!

A survivor? You have found a survivor of this wreck? Unthinkable! Nevertheless, bring him so that I may mock his utmost defeat.

Who is this? The skinny, pale Earth-woman April Van August? The very mate of Crash Comet himself?

Well, how tragic for you that your beloved has been so violently incinerated by my Astro-Fleet this day.

Evacuated by life-pod, were you? How touching. Crash Comet—chivalrous to the end, that insufferable Earthling meddler.

Come closer, Earth-woman. I grow pleased by your presence. Yes, I see that for all his faults, Crash Comet was a connoisseur of beauty. Though you are obviously frail and unintelligent—typical faults of your primitive species—you shall make an excellent queen for the Universe's mightiest tyrant!

Come closer, Earth-woman. I grow pleased by your presence. Yes, I see that for all his faults, Crash Comet was a connoisseur of beauty. Though you are obviously frail and unintelligent—typical faults of your primitive species—you shall make an excellent queen for the Universe's mightiest tyrant!

Yes, my dear Earth-woman, as my bride, you shall sit at my side as I pass judgment on the cosmos, not to mention engaging me in more... pleasurable duties.

I decree it! The mighty Gorzo has found a bride! Bedeck the Great Courtyard! Prepare a magnificent feast! And dress the Bride of Gorzo in a gown of the sheerest gossamer!

Yes, my dear Earth-woman, as my bride, you shall sit at my side as I pass judgment on the cosmos, not to mention engaging me in more... pleasurable duties. I decree it! The mighty Gorzo has found a bride! Bedeck the Great Courtyard!

Assemble my armies in full formal ceremony! Arrange a salutatory fly-over of my fleet's mightiest vessels! I shall be wed by sundown!

Is all prepared? Has my ceremony been arranged? Then bring forth my bride! Let the betrothal commence! Signal the orchestra!

I advise you to stop crying, my lovely, if you wish to live to see the honeymoon. Be of cheer! You shall soon be queen of all you survey!

Speed it up, now. Yes, yes, yes. She does. She most certainly does. Yes. Well, of course I do, you imbecile! I ordered this ceremony!

And now, my dear, as I place this Magmazantium ring on your finger, you shall be bound by cosmic law as my mate for all eternity! So, I'll just place it right now—GAH!

What is this? Who has broken from the fly-over formation? Who dares disrupt my wedding with shenanigans?!

Why, that Valkyrie War-Jet strafing the courtyard! It dips and weaves in the trademark flying style of... CRASH COMET, SPACE COMMANDER FROM THE YEAR 2000? Curses!

But how could this be? His Space-Yacht flew to bits before my eyes! This is unthinkable! I demand justice! Bring down that shuttle, or the entire Navy shall be put to death!

Stop panicking, everybody! The ceremony is not finished! We must complete the ceremony!

No! Not the giant statue of the mighty Gorzo!

No... No! *Aiyeee!* ⌀

LOCAL

Dominatrix Seems Preoccupied

RENO, NV—Local submissive Jack Traden announced Monday that his dominatrix, Mistress Varla of DV8, seems to have more on her mind than his humiliation.

"Mistress Varla hasn't been herself lately," Traden said. "Last week, she commanded me to lick her boots clean, but when I finished, she just stared off into space."

"When she finally noticed I was waiting, she ordered me into the cage for no reason," Traden continued. "What's the point? Usually, before she puts me into the cage, she scolds me about how bad I've been or tells me that I need to learn a lesson. If she's punishing me for doing a bad job on her boots, I need to know that. It wasn't humiliating, just confusing."

Traden cited other examples of Mistress Varla's recent distraction.

"The whipping—it's all over the place," Traden said. "I don't know whether she's trying to whip my ass or my elbows. It's just not the same getting flogged by someone who's barely paying attention. And her ordering-around has been totally indecisive."

Added Traden: "I've seen her like this before—last year, when she lost her job at the bank."

Especially worrisome to Traden, however, is Mistress Varla's sudden inability to tie the simplest of bondage knots.

"When I first started seeing Mistress Varla, you can bet if she bound me to a rack I was staying there," Traden said. "Lately, the leather knots are either so loose that they come undone or so tight I get no circulation. I love it when she makes me suffer, but I don't want to lose a limb."

Traden then related what he termed the saddest example of Mistress Varla's recent lack of attention to his humiliation needs.

"[Mistress Varla] slapped a collar around my neck and started walking me around her basement like a dog," Traden said. "Usually, the collar is on nice and snug, but this time it started to slip right off. I felt bad for her, so I tried holding it on with my chin while I was crawling around, but she caught me. Man, she beat the holy hell out of me for that, which normally would be great, but in this case it seemed like she was just upset with herself for making a rookie mistake. Who wants a dominatrix with confidence issues?"

Also unsettling to Traden is the sloppiness of Mistress Varla's appearance.

"When I walk into her dungeon, Mistress Varla is usually the very image of sleek menace," Traden said. "Lately, though, her boots are all scuffed and there are runs in her black stockings. Last week, I noticed she'd even incorrectly tied her leather corset. I would've mentioned it, but Mistress demands that I put in my ball gag before I arrive."

Traden said he is also disappointed with the state of Mistress Varla's torture chamber.

"A month and a half ago, that place was spotless," he said. "The floor was so clean you could eat off of it, and believe me, I would know. Now, instead of looking like her slaves scrubbed it with toothbrushes, it's just another mildewy basement with a dust-covered iron maiden."

Above: Traden pauses outside DV8 after another disappointing meeting with Mistress Varla (inset).

Traden said he has no idea why Mistress Varla seems so distant, but noted that he is unlikely to find out.

"To ask about her personal life would be an inappropriate breach of the B&D code," Traden said. "But that doesn't mean I'm not worried about her. She's very special to me, but if I told her that, she probably wouldn't put me on the spanking rack for a long time."

Although he could find a new dominatrix, Traden said he believes in loyalty.

"I've been with Mistress Varla too long to call it quits," Traden said. "There's a bond that would be difficult to reproduce. When I'm under her boot, it feels like a second home to me. When she's focused, there's no one in the world who can make me feel more like a worm than she can."

In spite of this praise, Traden said he "can't keep paying top dollar for second-rate domination."

"I like to be debased, but I'm no chump," Traden said. "I might have to take a break from being her chattel while she gets her head together. After a little break, I'm sure before you know it I'll be lashed to the floor, covered in hot wax, and happier than ever." Ø

NEWS IN BRIEF

Congress Establishes Bill Suggestion Hotline

WASHINGTON, DC—House Speaker Dennis Hastert (R-IL) announced Tuesday that a new hotline will allow average Americans the chance to suggest new bills to the 108th Congress. "Do *you* have a great idea for an amendment, a revolutionary new tax bill, or just a few riders, but don't know how to turn it into law?" Hastert said at a press conference on the Capitol steps. "Call us at 1-900-NEW-BILL. We can help. Operators in the House and Senate are standing by." Hastert added that calls are just $3.99 a minute up to the first 10 minutes.

Playground Treated To Hot Pug-On-Pug Action

PROVIDENCE, RI—Children playing on the swingsets at Waldo Street Tot Lot were treated to a raw, uncensored display of hot pug-on-pug action, sources reported Tuesday. "First the one doggy got behind the other doggy," said Andy Haupert, 6. "Then the first doggy tried to get on top of the other doggy while the other doggy tried to run away. It was really funny." The canine copulation has been the most talked-about animal-related playground incident since June, when a pigeon crapped all the way down the slide.

Man Thinks Receptionist Is Hitting On Him

MEMPHIS, TN—Based on approximately two minutes of conversation and a series of polite smiles, chiropractic patient Jordan Walters earnestly believes that receptionist Mandy Pruitt is hitting on him, waiting-room sources reported early this afternoon. "Did you see how she offered to get me coffee?" an excited Walters said after Pruitt left to fetch him coffee. "I think she was just looking for an 'in' with me, if you follow me. One where she got to show me her legs." Earlier that day, Walters also caught the eye of an Applebee's waitress, a Goodyear service-center employee, and two different bank tellers.

That Knife Guy From High School Arrested In Knife-Related Incident

RILEY, OR—Thirty-year-old Daryl Wohlert, that guy who always had all the knives in high school, was arrested Monday for allegedly threatening a local storekeeper with a switchblade, Riley police reported. "Daryl always used to have a knife on him, and a couple lying on the top shelf of his locker, too," said Riley Police Department desk clerk Jeremy Dunbar, who graduated with Wohlert from Riley High School in 1991. "He used to flip that thing around and roll it around in his hands until [shop teacher] Mr. Adams told him to put it away. Even after he put it back in the sheath, he'd still hold it out to threaten us with the case." Wohlert's alleged victim, 58-year-old Clarence Sewell, declined comment.

NPR Listener Acquires Kick-Ass Tote Bag

VENICE BEACH, CA—An avid National Public Radio listener, 48-year-old bicycle repair-shop technician Steve "Hozzie" Hasaji pledged $30 to 89.9 KCRW and "scored a kick-ass tote bag," Hasaji reported Tuesday. "Check this out," he said, showing coworkers a navy denim bag emblazoned with the KCRW logo. "If I knew listening to *Morning Edition* every day before breakfast was gonna get me this cool bag, shit, I woulda sent them money a long time ago." Hasaji added that Renee Montagne's insightful interview with author Diana Abu-Jaber was "totally off the hook." Ø bian. I also really, really wanted [Affleck and Lopez's characters] Larry and Ricki to die, to get shot or blown up or run over by something. I would prefer to see the blood and the looks on their faces."

On Monday, 3,000 people in markets as varied as Dallas, Chicago, Albany, Atlanta, and Seattle screened *Gigli*, a gangster-themed romantic comedy written and directed by Martin Brest, in which lowly thug Affleck lets his

According to the exit cards, other popular methods of achieving Lopez and Affleck's on-screen demise included car bombs, multiple stab wounds, acid baths, rabid wolf attacks, lightning strikes, and, in one case, a "hammer party."

love for hitwoman Lopez get in the way of a high-risk mob assignment. Of those viewers, 2,965 "strongly agreed" that the ending should be changed to include a graphic scene in which its main characters die.

"Many participants wrote 'shot to death' in the space provided for comments, probably thinking that it fit in with the gangster characters' stated realities," Columbia Pictures director of marketing Peter Zitterman said. "Some comments showed a lot of careful thought, such as 'point blank through head from right side,' 'both at once with single shot from elephant gun,' and 'several hundred times, with multiple camera angles showing their bodies jerking as they're shredded with a heavy hosing of lead, spraying the lens with gobbets of meat and bone and blood, with the sheer number of fist-sized exit wounds obviously precluding any sequel.' And shootings weren't the only ideas suggested, believe me."

According to the exit cards, other popular methods of achieving Lopez and Affleck's on-screen demise included car bombs, multiple stab wounds, acid baths, rabid wolf attacks, lightning strikes, and, in one case, a "hammer party."

"We never expected this kind of reaction," Zitterman said. "We've had odd results from focus groups before, but I don't recall an audience ever agreeing on such a sweeping change. If only we had done this survey in pre-production."

Although the various test audiences differed on the preferred methods of death, they seemed unanimous on one point.

"We were very surprised at how many

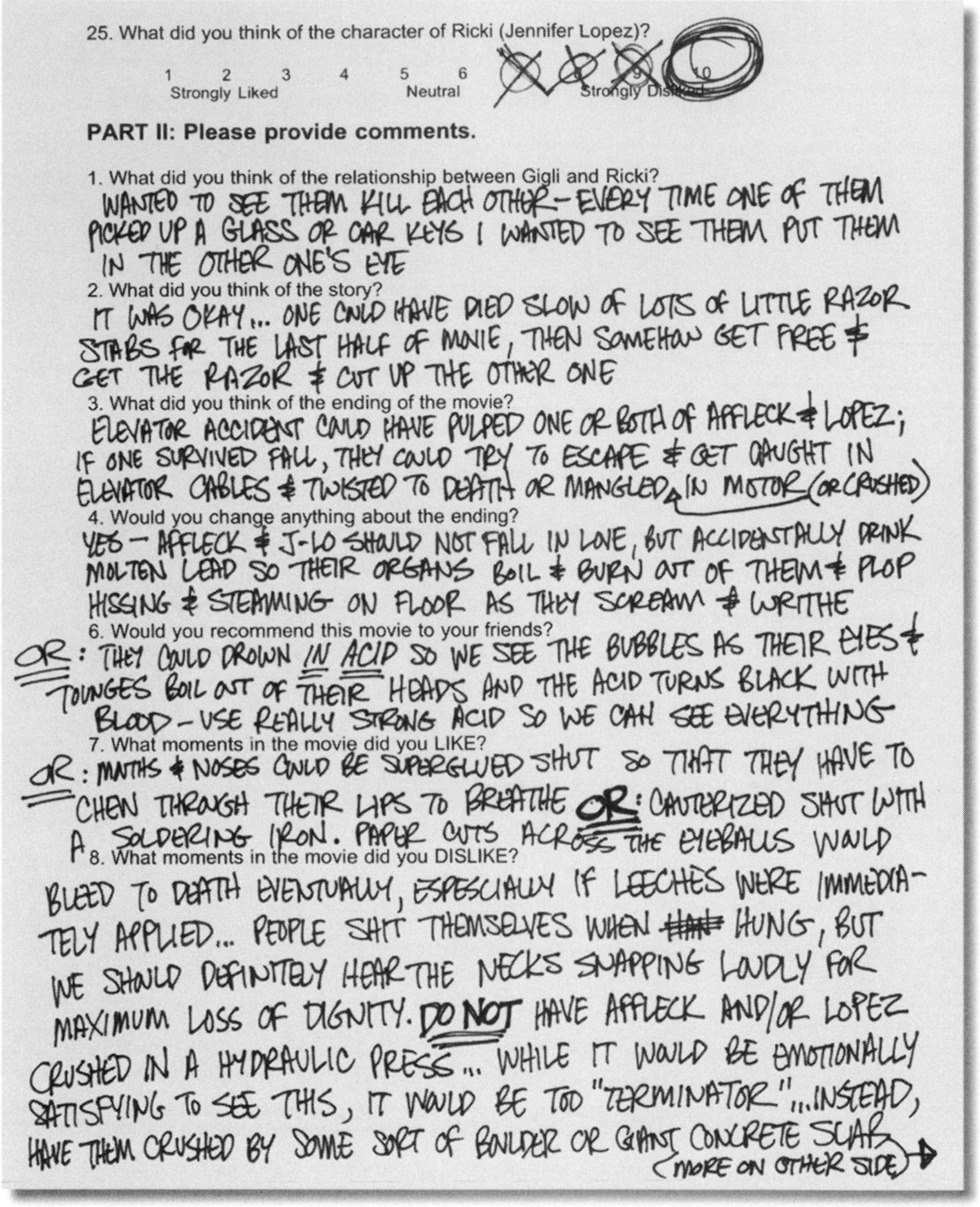

25. What did you think of the character of Ricki (Jennifer Lopez)?

1 2 3 4 5 6 7 8 9 10
Strongly Liked — Neutral — Strongly Disliked

PART II: Please provide comments.

1. What did you think of the relationship between Gigli and Ricki?
WANTED TO SEE THEM KILL EACH OTHER—EVERY TIME ONE OF THEM PICKED UP A GLASS OR CAR KEYS I WANTED TO SEE THEM PUT THEM IN THE OTHER ONE'S EYE

2. What did you think of the story?
IT WAS OKAY... ONE COULD HAVE DIED SLOW OF LOTS OF LITTLE RAZOR STABS FOR THE LAST HALF OF MOVIE, THEN SOMEHOW GET FREE & GET THE RAZOR & CUT UP THE OTHER ONE

3. What did you think of the ending of the movie?
ELEVATOR ACCIDENT COULD HAVE PULPED ONE OR BOTH OF AFFLECK & LOPEZ; IF ONE SURVIVED FALL, THEY COULD TRY TO ESCAPE & GET CAUGHT IN ELEVATOR CABLES & TWISTED TO DEATH OR MANGLED IN MOTOR (OR CRUSHED)

4. Would you change anything about the ending?
YES—AFFLECK & J-LO SHOULD NOT FALL IN LOVE, BUT ACCIDENTALLY DRINK MOLTEN LEAD SO THEIR ORGANS BOIL & BURN OUT OF THEM & PLOP HISSING & STEAMING ON FLOOR AS THEY SCREAM & WRITHE

6. Would you recommend this movie to your friends?
OR: THEY COULD DROWN IN ACID SO WE SEE THE BUBBLES AS THEIR EYES & TOUNGES BOIL OUT OF THEIR HEADS AND THE ACID TURNS BLACK WITH BLOOD—USE REALLY STRONG ACID SO WE CAN SEE EVERYTHING

7. What moments in the movie did you LIKE?
OR: MOUTHS & NOSES COULD BE SUPERGLUED SHUT SO THAT THEY HAVE TO CHEW THROUGH THEIR LIPS TO BREATHE OR: CAUTERIZED SHUT WITH A SOLDERING IRON. PAPER CUTS ACROSS THE EYEBALLS WOULD

8. What moments in the movie did you DISLIKE?
BLEED TO DEATH EVENTUALLY, ESPECIALLY IF LEECHES WERE IMMEDIATELY APPLIED... PEOPLE SHIT THEMSELVES WHEN HUNG, BUT WE SHOULD DEFINITELY HEAR THE NECKS SNAPPING LOUDLY FOR MAXIMUM LOSS OF DIGNITY. DO NOT HAVE AFFLECK AND/OR LOPEZ CRUSHED IN A HYDRAULIC PRESS... WHILE IT WOULD BE EMOTIONALLY SATISFYING TO SEE THIS, IT WOULD BE TOO "TERMINATOR"... INSTEAD, HAVE THEM CRUSHED BY SOME SORT OF BOULDER OR GIANT CONCRETE SLAB (MORE ON OTHER SIDE)

Above: One of the many focus-group comment cards calling for *Gigli* characters' deaths.

viewers thought that, no matter what, Affleck and Lopez should not be entwined in a romantic embrace at the time of their deaths," Zitterman said. "Everyone was perfectly clear on that."

Although Brest said he is satisfied with the final cut of *Gigli*, he briefly considered incorporating some of the test audience's ideas into the film.

"The danger here is succumbing to what people in the business call 'option paralysis'—being caught with so many good ideas that you're not sure which one to use," Brest said. "Getting shot is fine, but what about an automobile fire in which Ben and Jennifer are shown perishing in a slow-motion montage, their new-found love discarded as they try desperately to claw their way past each other's melting bodies, while slowly roasting to death in their own fat? You'd be surprised at how many people came up with that one. Or having them crawl through a field of broken glass while a safely booted and gloved Christopher Walken casually advances on them with a spray bottle of acid and a pair of bolt-cutters? I

"We never expected this kind of reaction," Zitterman said.

must say, a part of me loves the idea of them chewing each other to death during a 14-minute dolly shot."

Added Brest: "Believe me, after the singular experience of working with these two for several months, it would be a joy to get back together just to make these changes."

Even if time were not prohibitive, Columbia executives remained skeptical about the validity of the focus-group results.

"I find it hard to believe that audiences would harbor hostility toward such major media figures as J. Lo and Ben," Zitterman said. "With her magazine covers, clothing and perfume lines, and constant radio presence; his roles in *Daredevil* and *Project Greenlight*; and their recent joint appearances on *Dateline NBC* and numerous entertainment shows, how could anyone wish for anything but a resolution that unites these two attractive, highly visible celebrities?"

Insiders confirm that time constraints will prevent the much-requested death-scene additions to Gigli, which already underwent several days of fine-tuning when earlier focus groups noted a lack of romantic chemistry from the real-life couple. In light of the results, however, director Kevin Smith has said he will consider adding a gruesome double homicide to his Affleck-Lopez comedy *Jersey Girl*, due in theaters next year. Ø

KEYS from page 199

mand-X, -C, and -V."

Turlock knows the shortcut keys for not only Microsoft Word, Microsoft Explorer, and Outlook Express, the three programs he uses most frequently on his iMac at work, but also for the OS9 system software and a number of other programs on his home computer.

"It's not that hard to learn," Turlock said. "A lot of the keys are pretty much the same. In Explorer, if you hit Command-N, you're going to get a new browser window. In Word or Excel, you're going to get a new document, in Outlook Express a new message. In OS9, it'll be a new folder. See? Easy. Saves a lot of time. Command-N."

Turlock said he is "more than willing" to teach those who have been too timid to seek out the shortcut knowledge independently.

"Command-F for find," Turlock told human-resources secretary June Blise today after 1.5 seconds of scrolling had failed to produce his name on her screen. "Then just type 'Turlock' and hit return. Really, you could just type 'T-U-R' to find it even faster."

"What's 'Command'?" Blise asked.

"Sorry," Turlock said. "Same as Open Apple. Microsoft isn't going to want to say that dirty word, though, so on MS products it's called the Command key."

"What's 'Open Apple'?" Blise asked.

Despite years of hearing questions like Blise's, Turlock said he remains surprised by ignorance of basic key commands.

"I don't know," Turlock said. "They use the keyboard every day. You'd think they'd be curious about what F1 through F15 do. Those function keys aren't up there for someone else, after all."

Turlock insisted that his knowledge of all the shortcut keys, though an anomaly among his peers, is no special gift.

"It takes one second to learn a combo, then you have it," Turlock said. "People use these commands every day, and for some reason they never learn the shortcut. Amazing. It's so simple. Open Apple-S. Save. There you go. Done and done."

"Take Command-W," continued Turlock, in spite of a visible lack of interest among those present. "The same shortcut—that's Command and W—will close a window in Word, and in Explorer... in Adobe Acrobat, in Quark [XPress]. I'm pretty sure it closes a window in Quark. I'd have to check on that one. I'll check that out tonight at home."

Turlock said he is "shocked" by how many people do not know about Command-Z, the shortcut to "undo typing," or cancel the last action performed.

"Absolutely unbelievable," Turlock said. "Command-Z has saved my butt so many times."

While Turlock works on an Apple system, he said all of the "life-or-death combos" are available on every operating system.

"Roger is always saying, it's just this key and this key with this key held down," coworker Carlin Sampson said. "I think it's simpler to just go into the menu."

"But it's not simpler," Turlock said. "It's just one motion. It takes time to grab the mouse and pull down the menu. You can just hit the key without lifting your hands from the keyboard."

"Why wouldn't I want to lift my hands off the keyboard?" Sampson asked.

In spite of its usefulness, much of Turlock's advice will likely continue to go unheeded.

"You don't even have to go to the manual, guys," he said. "All the important ones are listed in the pull-down menu... Or hit the Help key to get a list... Or Command, question mark... Or you could look under the Help menu item on the right." ⌀

CANDIDATE from page 199

chest of more than $40 million, Kerry maintains a positive outlook.

"Our country cannot afford to stand behind a president who cuts taxes in the face of huge military spending," Kerry said on NBC's *Meet The Press* Sunday. "We must choose a leader who is not afraid to make economic decisions that make us stronger in the future, not just the ones he thinks will keep him in office."

"Yes, sir, 'Mr. President,'" interviewer Tim Russert said. "Whatever you say."

Kerry has campaigned tirelessly since announcing earlier this year that he wanted to run for president.

"I believe it's time to turn this country around," Kerry said at a campaign stop in Davenport, IA. "On virtually every issue, the president has moved America in the wrong direction: the budget busted, the economy down, the stock market down, unemployment up, the uninsured up, and an America increasingly isolated in the world."

"He looks so handsome," 68-year-old onlooker Iris Weum said. "It's so nice that he's trying to be president."

Kerry, looking very presidential in his nice new suit and clean white shirt, also criticized Bush's strategy for the war in Iraq.

"The truth is, the Bush Administration went to war without a plan to win the peace in Iraq," Kerry said. "Our troops should not be sent into battle like campaign props. We must demand more of our commander-in-chief."

Though the road to the presidency is a long one, experts report Kerry is "doing a great job."

"Kerry's presidential campaign had nearly $11 million in the bank at the end of June, which tops the field of Democratic hopefuls in terms of cash," said Candice Lowman, a political analyst with the conservative think tank American Enterprise Institute. "So, that's something. Heh heh. What a sweetie."

Lowman added: "Well, you know, though, as the White House scrambles to answer questions about disputed intelligence on Iraq's nuclear-weapons programs, at least one of those Democratic candidates might have a shot. Stranger things have happened. Aw, who am I kidding?"

While Kerry seeks to discredit Bush, he must also differentiate himself from the eight other campaigning Democrats. His main competition within the party comes from U.S. Sen. Joe Lieberman (D-CT), U.S. Rep. Richard Gephardt (D-MO), and Vermont Gov. Howard Dean, all of whom think they are going to win the election in 2004.

"Go get 'em, tigers," said Toby Nichols, a top advisor to Bush's campaign in 2000. "Go be president, guys."

Kerry shows no signs of slowing his cute campaign efforts.

"It is long overdue that America stops being the only industrialized nation on this planet that doesn't have health care available for all of its citizens," Kerry said in a conference call with reporters. "I'm running for president to make health care for all Americans a right and not a privilege, to bring costs under control, and to cover the uninsured."

"Awwww," said Adrian Tung, reporter for *The Baltimore Sun*. "That Kerry." ⌀

"Kerry's presidential campaign had nearly $11 million in the bank at the end of June, which tops the field of Democratic hopefuls in terms of cash," analyst Candice Lowman said. "So, that's something. Heh heh. What a sweetie."

Above: House Majority Leader Tom DeLay (R-TX) congratulates Kerry for making a "super-duper point" about Iraq.

COMMUNITY VOICES

They're Ruining My Favorite Soap!

My romantic worldview has taken some big hits lately. The first was the shocker that my fave-rave miniseries mega-hunk, Father Ralph de Bricassart himself, Richard Chamberlain, prefers the company of men. In all fairness, it's not like he could help it. But the second thing *can* be helped: the stinko storylines on my once-favorite soap, *Brink Of Destiny*!

A Room Of Jean's Own
By Jean Teasdale

The last straw came for me on Friday, when it was revealed that Krista was Helena's daughter. Never mind that Krista is a teenager and Helena's character graduated from high school only seven years ago! (I even remember the graduation-day episode—Helena finally lost her virginity to leather-jacketed bad boy Cutter, even though her father, Dr. Ted, despised him because he suspected him of making whoopee with his much-younger second wife Trish!)

Are we also to believe that Eve, the plucky girl from the wrong side of the tracks, is really an evil, spell-casting sorceress? And that Shannen of "Ash and Shannen"—the golden couple who kept their love intact through everything from paralysis to demonic possession—isn't really Shannen at all, but *Arden*, Shannen's laboratory-bred clone that kidnapped and hid Shannen shortly after she began seeing Ash years ago?

I suppose next we'll learn that saintly Sandy really *did* murder Annabelle, and that Luka's baby is actually a live bomb!

I'm telling you, Jeanketeers, I remember when this soap was great. Is this really the same show that pulled out all the stops for Nikki and Cash's long-awaited, mega-romantic Caribbean wedding? The show that touchingly wrote out Tarleton (the black lawyer guy) by making him terminally ill with cancer and floating him away in a hot-air balloon bound for parts unknown? (True, Daisy's rape was a bummer, but it was treated with great taste and sensitivity.)

If viewers have any sense, they'll join me in switching off their sets! (Well, I don't *really* switch off my set. I just flip to HSN, or Lifetime if there's a good Valerie Bertinelli movie on.)

The romance in *BOD* has been replaced with shock tactics, catfights, and a whole lot of weirdness. Don't *BOD*'s makers know stuff like that is ...oooo disrespectful to longtime fans? ...aps are supposed to be an escape, ... cause for more worry!

...be I'm coming off as a big com-... but I think I'm qualified: I've ... *Brink Of Destiny* religiously for nearly 25 years! Despite the rigors of marriage and holding down more than my share of part-time jobs, I've always deftly manipulated my schedule to accommodate my *BOD* viewing. Even in pre-VCR days, I watched nearly every episode.

My love affair with *BOD* started back in the 10th grade. This popular girl Wendi picked on me a lot in school, so much so that it made my stomach hurt, and I started cutting class and hiding in the girls' bathroom. One day, she cornered me and

> **Sometimes I think I was meant to be born a couple hundred years ago in the Age of Chivalry, or some other era when men courted women in beautiful parlors, or lived on the frontier and made passionate love in cabins.**

threatened to cut off all my hair with her boyfriend's butterfly knife, so I started skipping school altogether. In the morning, I'd pretend to leave for the bus, then when Mom went to her day job at Woolworth's, I'd sneak back into the house and watch my tiny black-and-white TV. That's how I discovered *Brink Of Destiny*. At first, I was confused by the complex storylines, but something told me I should stick with it.

This went on for almost two weeks, when the school finally phoned my mom and asked why I was absent. Boy, I really thought I was in the soup! Anticipating a grounding that would last into my 30s, I went to bed early. Then, a miracle: When I awoke the next morning, I felt so exhausted that I could barely move! Even my mom, with her sharply honed powers of suspicion, could tell I was actually ill. Dr. Kesselman's diagnosis revealed mono, which meant a month-long sabbatical from school. What's more, it happened to be May, the last month of the school year! I still look back on that time with fondness. I had 30 sweet, dreamy, languid days of sleep and daytime TV—something that, with my adult responsibilities, I'll probably never relive. Ah, youth! (Only drawback was, because my grades were already bad anyway, I had to take 10th grade over.)

But another close call soon threatened to jeopardize my new *BOD* habit. When summer vacation arrived, Mom wanted to put me in St. Benedict Summer Day Camp. (Yecch!) But then she learned that Dad was sleeping with his secretary at his roofing business, so between throwing out Dad's stuff and going to Mass, she practically forgot about me. My older brother Kevin had a summer job detasseling corn, and when he wasn't in the fields, he was tinkering with his dirt bike at his buddy (and my future hubby) Rick's place. I was all alone with no money and no driver's license, so I had nothing to do *but* watch *BOD* and sleep! By summer's end, I considered Francie, Dr. Ted, Gloria, and Stefan old friends. (By the way, when I say "Stefan," I mean the first Stefan—*that's* how long I've been a fan!)

The one thing that has me scratching my head is that, in spite of its drop in quality, *BOD* is more popular than ever! Unless the article in the Sunday TV insert is lying, *BOD* has been riding high in the ratings ever since the network insisted the producers improve their "boring" plots. Apparently, they brought in a new head writer and she set to work changing everything that made *BOD* so great! The result: *Brink Of Destiny* was rescued from the brink of cancellation, and the bold and beautiful soap-opera characters of my youth were reduced to shrieking nincompoops!

Sometimes I think I was meant to be born a couple hundred years ago in the Age of Chivalry, or some other era when men courted women in beautiful parlors, or lived on the frontier and made passionate love in cabins they built themselves, like pioneer Adams and Eves. (Instead, I have a hubby whose idea of intimacy is lifting the covers after passing gas. Har-dee-har-har, Rick!)

I invite anyone who agrees to please contact me. We could start a letter-writing campaign calling for a return to the old *BOD* we know and love. And we could include a list of demands. I vote to bring back Ash and Shannen, and have Nikki divorce Gunther and remarry Cash. Maybe we could even raise Harte from the dead. I hope so. The actor who played him was *soooo* hunky! ⊘

HOROSCOPES

Your Horoscope

By Lloyd Schumner Sr.
Retired Machinist and A.A.P.B.-Certified Astrologer

Aries: (March 21–April 19)
You could be bound in a nutshell and count yourself a king of infinite space, were it not for the fact that you have no imagination whatsoever.

Taurus: (April 20–May 20)
If you've ever regretted not pursuing a career in bullfighting, this week may bring an accidental chance to start over.

Gemini: (May 21–June 21)
It's still going to be muggy in the high 90s with occasional periods of wind as far as your personal forecast is concerned.

Cancer: (June 22–July 22)
Your actions this week will all be morally correct and without flaw, as long as you've correctly interpreted the Book of Numbers.

Leo: (July 23–Aug. 22)
You will certainly survive next week, but it won't be the kind of survival that sells a lot of inspirational books.

Virgo: (Aug. 23–Sept. 22)
More than anything, you want to mold and shape young minds. Unfortunately, most commercially available Jell-O molds are unsuitable for this purpose.

Libra: (Sept. 23–Oct. 23)
Although it's true that your spouse doesn't make you happy, keep in mind that nothing really ever does.

Scorpio: (Oct. 24–Nov. 21)
Please contact the service department at Scorpio Communications and explore options to restore your service.

Sagittarius: (Nov. 22–Dec. 21)
It may take extensive surgery to turn you into a Bond girl, but it's still a lot cheaper than hiring one of today's A-list actresses.

Capricorn: (Dec. 22–Jan. 19)
You will have a vision of peace, transcendent love, and infinite compassion, only to find it was all a dream. Also, your pillow is gone.

Aquarius: (Jan. 20–Feb. 18)
There are some things about the universe that you are simply not spiritually capable of knowing, such as its exact size, mass, and age.

Pisces: (Feb. 19–March 20)
Your fear that "your family doesn't care about you anymore" is incorrect. The proper phrasing is "your family no longer cares about you."

the ONION®
VOLUME 39 ISSUE 30 | AMERICA'S FINEST NEWS SOURCE™ | 7–13 AUGUST 2003

NEWS

Cheney Regrets Buying Bush Laser Pointer

see NATION page 1B

Fridge Magnet A Constant Reminder Of Arizona's Existence

see LOCAL page 4D

Sex Fantasy Becomes Action-Adventure Without Warning

see LOCAL page 8D

STATshot

A look at the numbers that shape your world.

Why Did We Enter Law Enforcement/Teaching?

1. Enjoy ordering people to put up their hands
2. Inspirational high-school English teacher was murdered
3. Have deep hatred of skateboards
4. Passed over for promotion at Target for last time
5. Like to wear short-sleeved shirts and necktie, yell

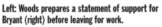

Kobe Bryant's Fantasy-Team Coach 'Saddened' By Allegations

CAPE MAY, NJ—Steven Woods, a claims adjuster with Midland Insurance and coach of the Midland Maniacs fantasy basketball team, announced Monday that he is "deeply saddened" by the sexual-assault allegations leveled against his team's star guard, Kobe Bryant.

"I can't believe this is the same Kobe I've worked with all these years," Woods said at a breakroom press conference. "I've won two Midland

see COACH page 209

Left: Woods prepares a statement of support for Bryant (right) before leaving for work.

Former President Carter To Be Tried For Peace Crimes

GENEVA, SWITZERLAND—An international peace-crimes tribunal commenced legal proceedings against former U.S. President Jimmy Carter for alleged crimes against inhumanity Monday.

"Jimmy Carter's political career includes a laundry list of anti-war-making offenses," said chief prosecutor Charles B. Simmons. "Carter's record of benevolence, diplomacy, and respect for human life is unrivaled in recent geopolitical history. For millions, the very sight of his face evokes memories of his administration's reign of tolerance."

The former president, whom Simmons described as "relentless in his naked pursuit of everlasting global peace," has been sought by peace-crimes officers in the international

see CARTER page 208

Above: Carter awaits trial for acts of peace committed between 1976 and the present.

Nation's Toddlers Critically Under-Photographed, Says U.S. Aunt Coalition

Above: Members of the NCA protest at the Capitol.

WASHINGTON, DC—Citing a desire to more closely monitor the growth of U.S. nieces and nephews, the National Coalition of Aunts denounced the severe under-photographing of the nation's precious toddlers Tuesday.

"These little treasures grow up so fast," said Linda Mirrin, chairwoman of the NCA and aunt to three adorable boys. "We aunts have a simple and reasonable request: Take more photos and send them to us, so that we can see how big those little darlings are getting."

Mirrin then dug into her wallet and pulled out photographs of her nephews to show to the assembled crowd of reporters and fellow aunts.

"This is Troy, this one is Michael, and this is David," said Mirrin, who lives three states away from her sister, Maggie Genz. "Aren't they just perfect?"

According to Mirrin, NCA statistics show that the number of photographs taken of a child declines by 42 percent when the child reaches his or her sixth month. The photograph-rate

see TODDLERS page 209

Embattled Liberia

The Bush administration is still unsure what role the U.S. military should play in war-ravaged Liberia. What do *you* think?

"If there's one thing I know about other countries, it's that they can't get enough of our troops."

Raymond Blair
Systems Analyst

"Why does it always have to be troops we send? Let's send them something nice, like a pretty candle."

Penny Harmon
LPN

"Ah, let's just strongly condemn the latest round of escalating violence and leave it at that."

Paul Doherty
Civil Drafter

"I don't understand why everyone's so up in arms about some unruly librarians."

Ethan Templeton
Gaming Dealer

"As an opponent of military intervention, I have a question: What sort of giant protest puppets are appropriate for the Liberian situation?"

Tamra Rider
Fitness Trainer

"Isn't this one of those situations we can just leave for our children?"

Rufus Moyer
EMT

The Davis Recall

California Gov. Gray Davis faces a recall election Oct. 7. What are the voters' complaints?

- Davis insisted on collecting "taxes" to pay for government "programs and services"
- Turns out they didn't elect the guy who drew Garfield, after all
- Under Davis' watch, Hollywood released worst summer blockbusters in a decade
- Davis lacks 20/20 hindsight of his challengers
- State can take care of its own self, don't need no governor bossing it around
- Davis stood idly by while Republicans deregulated energy industry, leading to blackouts across the state
- Davis unfit to handle imminent rise of the machines
- Being $37 billion in debt was funny, but $38 billion is just too much
- Just wanted do-overs

the ONION®
America's Finest News Source.™
Herman Ulysses Zweibel
Founder
T. Herman Zweibel
Publisher Emeritus
J. Phineas Zweibel
Publisher
Maxwell Prescott Zweibel
Editor-In-Chief

Get Ready, Folks, 'Cause This Is The Greatest Late-To-Work Excuse You've Ever Heard

By Matt Harnack

Okay, people. You are *not* going to believe why I'm late today. Sheila? Come on in here. Sorry about this, but you gotta get in here. Shondra? Harold? Can you hear me over there? Maybe you should move a little closer. Get Emmelyn in here, too. I don't want anyone to miss this. In fact, get Colleen on speaker phone. She's going to love this.

Okay. Is everyone here? Good. This shouldn't take long.

I know you thought you'd heard it all a couple weeks ago, when I was late because my fish flopped out of the tank. Then there was the time in February, when I was halfway to work, spilled hot coffee all over myself, and had to go to the doctor. Whoo! That was no fun. Oh, and last Monday: I forgot my work keys, went home to get them, got back to the office, and realized I had the wrong set.

I won't even mention the Bee Allergy False Alarm, the Zipper Crisis, or the now-famous Cardigan Incident. You've heard the rest, and now here's the best. I hope your shoes are tied, because this is going to knock

I know you thought you'd heard it all a couple weeks ago, when I was late because my fish flopped out of the tank. Then there was the time in February, when I was halfway to work, spilled hot coffee all over myself, and had to go to the doctor. Whoo! That was no fun.

your socks off!

Are you ready? You sure? Here we go, coworkers.

You all know how I get to work, right? Train to the bus, walk four blocks, and I'm there. Well, I've been thinking that I should get more exercise, so I decided to alter my route a little. Instead of taking the train to the bus, I decided to take the train to the Grant Avenue stop, transfer to another train, and then walk seven blocks.

Oh, come on in, Kyle. Grab a seat.

So, it's train a little farther, transfer, walk seven blocks. It would only take

You all know how I get to work, right? Train to the bus, walk four blocks, and I'm there. Well, I've been thinking that I should get more exercise, so I decided to alter my route a little. Instead of taking the train to the bus, I decided to take the train to the Grant Avenue stop, transfer to another train, and then walk seven blocks.

five minutes longer than my usual route, and I'd squeeze in a little exercise. At least, that's how it would go under perfect conditions. But when do things ever go perfectly?

Are you all still with me? I don't want to lose anyone and have to back up and repeat myself. That wouldn't be fair to everyone else.

Anyway, I was on the train headed downtown to Grant Avenue but, since I was breaking my usual routine, I got confused and a little panicky and went one stop too far. I don't know what was going on in my head. I got out and tried to transfer to the uptown train, but I wound up on the crosstown express. I must have been riding for 10 minutes before I recognized my mistake.

Hey, can I get a water over here? I want to be in top form for the finish. Thanks, Donna, appreciate it. Okay, back in.

By the time I realized what I'd done, I was already 10 minutes late. I decided, you know, screw the exercise, I've got to get to work. So I got off at the next stop and tried to catch a cab. But I was in a desolate part of town, and there weren't a lot of cabs, right? Just when I was about to give

see EXCUSE page 210

LOCAL

Everything On Menu So Tempting

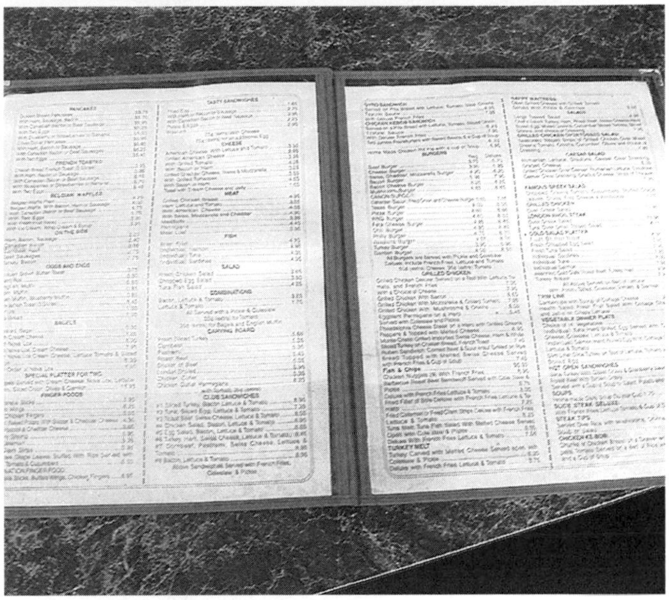

Above: The menu at the Cedar Tree Family Restaurant (left).

CHILLICOTHE, OH—Absolutely everything—*everything*—on the Cedar Tree Family Restaurant menu is so tempting that diners are going to be hard-pressed to stay on their diets, customers reported Monday.

"Oh, this is pure agony," said Lynette Macagnone, 43, a mortgage loan officer at Foremost Savings and a self-described weight watcher. "I just can't decide!"

No one in the 80-seat establishment seemed surprised by Macagnone's indecision after seeing the red-vinyl-jacketed menu's four columns of mouth-watering items like chicken marsala, fisherman's platter, turkey and bacon clubs, baked meatloaf, and 100 percent grade-A beef burger topped with Monterey Jack cheese, all served with a choice of soup or salad, as well as fries or baked potato.

Although the Cedar Tree diners knew they should be good, their original plans to stick to salad and soup flew out the window when they saw the menu's many offerings, from potato-skin appetizers to ribeye steak.

Dental technician Beth Arneson, 28, said she wished she hadn't turned to the back of the menu and read that Cedar Tree serves—get ready for this—an all-day breakfast.

"'Belgian waffle with fresh strawberries!'" Arneson read aloud to companion Keith Zuehlke. "'Eggs Benedict with Hollandaise sauce and Texas toast!' 'Chocolate-chip pancakes!' 'Huevos rancheros!' I'm afraid to look at this menu any-

Although the Cedar Tree diners knew they should be good, their original plans to stick to salad and soup flew out the window when they saw the menu's many offerings, from potato-skin appetizers to ribeye steak.

more—I'm going to gain five pounds just reading it!"

When Zuehlke read the description of the pigs-in-a-blanket as "link sausage cuddled in buttermilk pancakes, whipped butter, and syrup," Arneson let out a mock shriek.

"With the fried chicken 'tenderized overnight in buttermilk and rolled in specially prepared seasoned breadcrumbs,' it's amazing that [bus boy Mike Hatch doesn't] seem to have put on an extra ounce anywhere," observed local piano and voice teacher Richard Quincy, dining with his elderly mother.

"I'm not allowed to speak to customers," Hatch replied.

In addition to serving up such unexpected, tantalizing dishes as teriyaki chicken and shrimp stir-fry, the Cedar Tree also offers daily specials. Yes, specials.

"Smothered chicken, spinach quiche with French onion soup, baked pork chops with mashed potatoes, and our weekly $9.99 prime-rib special, which comes with a trip to the salad bar," waiter Sergio Arias said.

Macagnone had so much trouble deciding what to order that she sent Arias away twice.

"Even the salads are sinful," Macagnone told Arias. "Can I get a bread-bowl salad with half a bread bowl and no cheese and no ham chunks? I'm afraid if I order the whole thing, I won't be able to stop."

"No," Arias said.

To further complicate attempts at calorie control, Cedar Tree just had to have the best dessert menu this side of the Perkins on Frontage Road. Even though the majority of diners felt too full already, dessert-menu

see MENU page 209

NEWS IN BRIEF

Loser Can't Even Get Wife Pregnant

MARSHFIELD, WI—After three years of trying, pathetic loser Ron Dreschel can't even get his wife Marisa pregnant, sources at the Marshfield Clinic reported Tuesday. "Ha, poor Ronny Dreschel can't even knock up his own old lady!" fertility counselor Derek Vojtik said. "What's the matter? Problems with sperm motility?" Dreschel was unavailable for comment.

Gary Busey Nearly Drowns Recovering Pork Chop From Swimming Pool

LOS ANGELES—Actor Gary Busey was flown from his Malibu home to Cedars-Sinai Medical Center after he nearly drowned trying to retrieve a pork chop from the bottom of his swimming pool Tuesday. "We're eating on the patio, and Gary suddenly shouts, 'Let's have dinner in the pool!' and starts throwing baby red potatoes and hunks of meat into the water," said Lupo Risinger, Busey's friend and next-door neighbor. "Well, the pork chop he threw sank like a stone, and—you know Gary—he wouldn't come up for air until he had that sucker in his teeth." Busey is currently listed in "marginally stable" condition.

Milkshake Almost Ruined By Breakup

MINNEAPOLIS, MN—Local woman Janice Garnecki's blueberry milkshake was nearly ruined Tuesday when boyfriend Timothy Stover announced he was ending their relationship. "Six months together, and now he says he wants to see other people," a distraught Garnecki said immediately after the breakup, but before taking a long sip of her mouthwatering shake. "How could he do this to me? Doesn't he care? This is made with premium ice cream, isn't it?" Garnecki said she plans to spend the day crying on her best friend's shoulder and licking her fingers.

Half-Asleep Man Pauses 20 Minutes Between Socks

SANDPOINT, ID—Seated on the edge of his bed, Carl Thompson, 38, paused for 20 minutes with one sock on his foot and the other in his hand Tuesday. "Ugh, tired," said Thompson, who was otherwise silent from 6:30 to 6:50 a.m. During that period, Thompson stared at the wall and teetered perilously close to a reclining position six times.

Vice President Of Making Your Job Harder Given Raise

NEW YORK—According to the buzz around the office, Hank, the Vice-President Of Making Your Job Harder, received a sizable raise Tuesday. "Goddamn it," you said to yourself. "All Hank does around here is screw things up so bad that I have to stay late and fix them. Then he shows up in the morning and rides my ass when things aren't done." At this rate, you decided, you'll never get promoted from the position of Assistant Vice-President Of Cleaning Up Other People's Messes And Never Getting Any Goddamn Credit.

Drug Deal Goes Great

MIAMI—An exchange of five grams of cocaine for an undisclosed amount of cash "went off without a hitch" in Bayfront Park Monday night. "When I went to the park to buy some blow, I never expected anything bad to happen," said a 30-year-old drug buyer who identifed himself as John. "It didn't. I got some really good stuff, the guy didn't gyp me, and the whole thing only took, like, three minutes." Kold Kim, an area dealer, agreed with John, adding that the entire exchange was "cool."

CARTER from page 205

war-making community for decades. Police apprehended Carter on July 25 in South Florida, where he was building low-income housing as a part of a Habitat For Humanity project. Shortly thereafter, he was extradited to Geneva, where he will be prosecuted for "grossly humane acts against all nations."

"Carter is one of the worst enemies the forces of destruction have known since Dr. Martin Luther King Jr. and his non-violent rampages of the '50s and '60s," Simmons said. "Even today, in his capacity as an ex-president, [Carter] continues his pursuit of non-aggression. He must be stopped now, before more lives are saved."

Above: An unearthed 1978 photo shows a peace-mongering Carter with Menachem Begin and Anwar al-Sadat.

Yale University political-science professor Janet Hargrove said the evidence against Carter is overwhelming.

"Carter's defense team will have a difficult task defending him against these peacemaking accusations," Hargrove said. "Carter's signature is right there on the Camp David accords between Egypt and Israel. His decision to return control of the Panama Canal to Panama continues to impede U.S. military intervention in the region even today, and his influence on the SALT II treaty is a matter of public record. He may have been in part responsible for the temporary nuclear *détente* between the U.S. and the Soviets."

While much of his peacemaking took place during his term of office, the years following Carter's presidency have included peace-mongering missions in Ethiopia, Sudan, North Korea, and the former Yugoslavia.

"Carter is one of the worst enemies the forces of destruction have known since Dr. Martin Luther King Jr. and his non-violent rampages of the '50s and '60s," Simmons said. "Even today, in his capacity as an ex-president, [Carter] continues his pursuit of non-aggression. He must be stopped now, before another terrible war is avoided and more lives are saved."

Prosecutors have linked Carter to a number of international humanitarian organizations, including Red Cross and Amnesty International, both of which fund compassionate, non-military efforts around the globe.

"The former president has even been linked to an organization within Sweden known for promoting the peace agenda by remaining on the outside of the international political process," Hargrove said. "A medal commemorating a so-called 'Nobel Peace Prize' was seized from Carter's Georgia estate and will be used as evidence against him."

Vince Halloway, an expert in international law with the Brookings Institution, said he expects Carter's defenders to attempt to establish him as a propagator of international conflict by citing his mishandling of the Iran hostage crisis, his boycott of the 1980 Moscow Olympics, and his time served on a Navy nuclear submarine.

Halloway, however, said he considers this defense "thin."

"Prosecutors will have no difficulty establishing Carter's willful intent to pursue and maintain the aim of peaceful intervention in international affairs when they cite his formation of The Carter Center, an organization whose three *publicly stated* aims are 'Fighting Disease,' 'Building Hope,' and 'Waging Peace,'" Halloway said. "Carter will be forced to answer for his reign of tranquility before the entire world community."

If found guilty, Carter could face permanent exile in a nonviolent nation such as Norway.

On behalf of the Bush administration, Vice-President Dick Cheney expressed regret over Carter's alleged crimes.

"We are all aware of the missteps that occurred during the placid days of the Carter administration," Cheney said. "It was simply a matter of bringing the justice to light. Thankfully, the process has begun, and this chapter in our nation's history is finally being brought to a close." ⌀

APPLESAUCE from page 200

amounts of blood. Passersby were amazed by the unusually large amounts of blood.Passersby were amazed by the unusually large amounts of blood.Passersby were amazed by the unusually large

I can't believe that bitch served yams.

see APPLESAUCE page 213

COACH from page 205

Fantasy Basketball League championships with him. He's always handled himself with such class, both on and off the court."

"Obviously, Kobe has my full support during this difficult time," Woods added.

Bryant, 24, is charged with sexually assaulting a 19-year-old woman at a resort in Colorado. If convicted, he faces four years to life in prison or 20 years to life on probation.

"You expect this of the [Allen] Iversons and [Latrell] Sprewells of the league," Woods said, alluding to Iverson's firearms charge and a 1997 incident in which Sprewell choked his coach. "But Kobe... I thought I knew him."

Woods acknowledged that he was shaken by news of the allegations.

"I don't know what to think," Woods said. "Kobe's shown himself to be nothing but a responsible team member, ever since I took him in the 1996 Midland office draft. That was all the way back when we still figured everyone's rank on paper in a big blue binder."

"I thought I was getting a character player with solid stats," Woods continued. "For years, he never let me down. Last season, he was averaging 30 ppg and 5.9 apg. And now this?"

"You expect this of the [Allen] Iversons and [Latrell] Sprewells of the league," Woods said, alluding to Iverson's firearms charge and a 1997 incident in which Sprewell choked his coach. "But Kobe... I thought I knew him."

Since the allegations were made, Woods has followed the case by frequently logging on to the NBA's fantasy-basketball web page.

"One thing's for sure," Woods said. "Kobe is innocent until proven guilty, and I stand by my pretend player."

"Still, this sort of thing makes us question who our fantasy players really are," Woods said. "Kelly at the front desk has a Kobe replica jersey. I have a souvenir card with a scrap of his game-worn shorts on it."

Bryant's Midland Maniacs teammates—including Ray Allen, Vlade Divac, and Keith Van Horn—have yet to comment on the allegations.

"This is going to be tough on everyone who works with Kobe," Woods said. "There's no way a scandal like this is not going to affect the picks in next year's Yahoo! Sports Fantasy NBA competition."

Throughout the informal conference, Woods downplayed his needs as a fantasy-team coach and returned the attention of those assembled to Bryant and his family.

"This going to be a difficult time for Kobe and [his wife] Vanessa," Woods said. "I urge everyone to show some restraint. Let's give them some room."

In spite of Woods' entreaties, his fantasy coaching peers were outspoken in their criticisms of both Woods and Bryant.

"This is just what Steve needed," said Clarence Rispert, Midland Insurance policy manager and coach of the two-time division-champion Desk Demons. "Just a few weeks ago, he was acting all cocky about me signing Grant Hill right before [Hill] busted his ankle all to hell. Well, look who's crying now."

Midland Fantasy Basketball League commissioner and claims-department manager James DeMille refused to comment directly on the Bryant allegations.

"I plan to comply with any disciplinary action [NBA commissioner] David Stern takes," DeMille said. "Unfortunately, dealing with distasteful situations like this one has become a part of the reality of fantasy sports. Now, everyone, get back to work. The phones are ringing off the hook out there."

Although the pressures of his impending trial may hinder Bryant's

"Kobe's shown himself to be nothing but a responsible team member, ever since I took him in the 1996 Midland office draft," Woods said. "That was all the way back when we still figured everyone's rank on paper in a big blue binder."

performance on the court, Woods has decided that Bryant will play for the Maniacs when the NBA season opens Oct. 28.

"I just wouldn't feel right benching Kobe at a time like this," Woods said. "I think the best thing I can do is let him play basketball and hope for the best. I have to admit, though, that it would be pretty hard to see the Desk Demons claim the Midland Fantasy League title and all those Outback Steakhouse gift certificates two years in a row."

Bryant was unavailable for comment on Woods' show of support. ⌀

TODDLERS from page 205

declines another 26 percent at the end of the first year, and another 20 percent each subsequent year until the child starts kindergarten.

"True, I have *some* pictures," Mirrin said. "But they were taken a year ago, and from what Maggie tells me, David's hair is shorter now, and the little tyke's been growing like a weed. Sadly, I can neither confirm nor deny these statements because I have no photographic evidence. Maggie says she'll send the boys' new school pictures, but would it be so hard for her to take some photos this summer?"

"If you need some film or batteries, I would be happy to mail you some," Mirrin added.

An additional NCA goal, Mirrin said, is to increase the number of photographs taken in the weeks immediately following a toddler's first steps.

"We want that number up by at least 50 percent," Mirrin said. "It's true that toddlers are mischievous. It's also true that aunts would like pictures of the little rascals engaged in mischief. I hear Maggie's stories over the phone, but I would love to see pictures of David dumping dog food on the kitchen floor, or Troy drawing on the wall with crayons."

NCA research indicates an inverse relationship between a family's size and the rate at which its toddlers are photographed.

"We are doing everything we can to fight this trend, but we need cooperation between parents and the extended family," Mirrin said. "When more snapshots are taken, everyone wins."

Mirrin said the NCA was troubled to discover that disposable-camera purchases generally accompany only major events like a trip to Canada, or a child's first haircut.

"Is it so hard to buy a $5 camera and take some pictures of the kids watching TV?" Mirrin asked. "Michael looks so adorable in his pajamas."

"Maggie knows how much I love those little critters," she added.

In an effort to encourage the photographing of everyday life, the NCA is lobbying Congress to provide tax breaks totaling up to $200 for parents who purchase digital cameras, scanners, and high-resolution inkjet printers.

"We are doing everything we can to fight this trend, but we need cooperation between parents and the extended family," Mirrin said. "When more snapshots are taken, everyone wins."

"We're all connected to the Internet these days," Mirrin said. "With e-mail, parents have no excuse for failing to take and send pictures of their little ones."

The NCA hopes early intervention will prevent future photographic oversights.

"It's time to take a stand, before we aunts are denied photos of our nieces' and nephews' pre-teen and teen years," Mirrin said. "We implore all parents to redouble their efforts, because the sad fact remains that 80 percent of family photos taken never make it beyond the nuclear family's photo album."

The League of American Parents responded to the NCA's claims with a strongly worded message.

"We are sympathetic to the nation's aunts," LAP spokesman George Jarvis said. "No one should be deprived of adorable pictures of toddlers dressing the dog in a funny Halloween costume, or simply falling asleep on the living-room floor. However, our official statement on this matter is and always has been: Get your own damn kids. Then see how much you feel like driving to Walgreens and the post office with three screaming kids in the back seat." ⌀

MENU from page 207

items like the caramel cheesecake, the carrot cake, and the sizzling apple pie à la mode had them wondering if they could squeeze in just a teeny bit more.

"If I get the salad with the pork chops and eat half the mashed potatoes with no butter, I'll feel a little less guilty," Macagnone said. "And I can remove the bacon from the club and request no dressing. Plus, I'm having Diet Sprite."

"Just pick something. It's all good," Arias said.

"But you've made it so hard!" Macagnone said, adopting a mock pout.

Paying her check at the register, Arneson asked Cedar Tree manager Spyros Andropoulos how he sleeps at night knowing he's made countless people pounds heavier, if a lot happier.

"I sleep at night," Andropoulos said. "If customers afraid they get fat, they don't have to eat here. Please, I must work."

Perhaps due to its hard-working staff, the Cedar Tree remains a popular choice for no-fuss family celebrations and after-work get-togethers. It's also popular with patrons of the nearby go-kart track.

"I know, I know, I should really eat at home, especially since I just bought groceries," Macagnone said. "But it's on the way home, and I like to treat myself once in a while."

"Oh," she added, lowering her voice to a whisper. "But if you go, avoid the pork chops. Mine were a little dry." ⌀

COMMUNITY VOICES

I'm Sorry, But I Only Date Men My Friends Are Afraid Might Kill Me

By Julie Jacobs

Listen, Doug, you seem like a really nice guy. You're even kind of cute, in a well-adjusted sort of way. All in all, you seem really harmless, and that's the problem. I'm looking for someone with that special something that makes my friends worry I might suddenly disappear without a trace and never be heard from again.

You were nice to ask me out, but I have to say that the way you did it was a little weird. You said, "There's a movie I really want to see. Would you like to come with me?" *Huh?* How can you be assured you're going to have sex with me if the evening's plans do not specifically include drugs or alcohol?

Then you were all, "Let's go to dinner afterward." *Whoa.* What was *that?* Are we married now or something? Slow down! What is this, the '50s? Women aren't impressed by that "normal person" stuff anymore. I like to know there's at least a chance that a suitor will stuff my body into a car trunk and then toss it into a KFC Dumpster two towns over.

I'm sorry, but you're just not my type. I'm into guys who wear leather jackets, dirt-caked fatigues, or jumpsuits. I don't see any tattoos, piercings, scars, cigarette burns, missing eyebrows, open sores, self-inflicted wounds, blackened teeth, or incorrectly set bones. You don't even have an excessive number of fillings. You make eye contact when you speak to me and don't have any off-putting tics or compulsive, repetitive tendencies. You've never been to jail, and you don't have any addictions—not alcohol, heroin, cocaine, or even gambling or pornography.

God, I could take you home to meet my parents. You would never sneak off for three hours, leaving everyone to nervously glance at each other as we waited to open my sister's birthday presents. I'll bet you never once got up to go to the bathroom in a restaurant, then called half an hour later to say you "ran into some problems" and that you'd call the next day. No, I didn't think so.

I'm standing right next to you, and I can't smell a trace of body odor. Your hair appears to have been washed recently, probably just today. There's absolutely nothing feral about you. Your clothes are even unwrinkled. I'm sorry, but there's absolutely nothing to indicate that I might end up a statistic in the police ledger of some backwoods Oregon logging town, my family never giving up hope for my return until the day they die themselves.

Don't get me wrong, Doug. You'd be great for my sister, or maybe one of my coworkers. You're just not for me. You've got respectability coming off you in waves. If there's no chance one of my friends will pull me aside and ask me how I can stand you, I'm just not interested.

Are we married now or something? Slow down! What is this, the '50s? Women aren't impressed by that "normal person" stuff anymore. I like to know there's at least a chance that a suitor will stuff my body into a car trunk and then toss it into a KFC Dumpster two towns over.

You're nice, though, so let me help you out. Try something like this next time: "Hey, my friend's band is playing at the Red Shed this Friday. They're called Meatmagnet. They totally suck, but I get to hang out in the back and drink from the cooler, and those dudes always have weed. If you're at the bar, maybe I'll get you backstage." Now *that's* what I call a date.

See, all that dinner and wine stuff doesn't do anything for me. The kind of guy I'm into is big on going out to get eggs. Usually at Denny's, at 4 a.m., and I end up paying for the eggs. Here're some other things I like to do with the men I date: hang out on their friend's couch, rent porn, drive around looking for drugs, or sit at a kitchen table and drink.

I noticed you're in pretty good shape, but that doesn't impress me. It doesn't take a lot of muscle to drag a woman's corpse to the river's edge. It just takes that special inclination. Anyway, with all those muscles, my friends might respond when you proposition them. Oh, but you'd never do that.

Doug, you're very sweet, and I'm flattered by your attention, but unless you do something in the next minute that lets me know you might put me in the morgue, or at least the intensive-care unit, I think we need to end this. ⌀

HOROSCOPES

Your Horoscope

By Lloyd Schumner Sr.
Retired Machinist and
A.A.P.B.-Certified Astrologer

Aries: (March 21–April 19)
You are not noble in reason, infinite in faculty, like an angel in your actions, or especially moving in your form. However, you are a real piece of work.

Taurus: (April 20–May 20)
Be reasonable. Just because last week's horoscope was a wildly inaccurate prediction of your future is no reason to give up on the Zodiac forever.

Gemini: (May 21–June 21)
Your plans to find love, fortune, and happiness utterly ignore the Second Law Of Thermodynamics.

Cancer: (June 22–July 22)
You should have a relaxed week once you clear your calendar of all appointments except that strange one in Samara.

Leo: (July 23–Aug. 22)
This week could be exceptionally soul-crushing, especially if you finally complete work on that Soul Crusher.

Virgo: (Aug. 23–Sept. 22)
The stars know how this is going to sound, but trust us on this one: You are, in fact, fated to meet a tall, dark stranger.

Libra: (Sept. 23–Oct. 23)
Your problems in the bedroom are finally solved when you hire trained professionals to remove the raccoons.

Scorpio: (Oct. 24–Nov. 21)
For centuries, great thinkers have contemplated the purpose of life. It's best to just relax and assume they've figured it out.

Sagittarius: (Nov. 22–Dec. 21)
The Latin inscription on the amphora you found translates to "Insanity is not a necessity to work in this Senate, but helpful nonetheless."

Capricorn: (Dec. 22–Jan. 19)
The *Coq au Vin* will be a little astringent and the wine a bit audacious for the menu, but as last meals go, there have been worse.

Aquarius: (Jan. 20–Feb. 18)
You've always wanted a helper monkey, but your new harmer monkey will have to do.

Pisces: (Feb. 19–March 20)
The stars would love to influence your future, but they are powerless against your well-established patterns of behavior.

EXCUSE from page 206

up and go back to the train, a cab pulled up out of nowhere. I thought it was my lucky day—but no trip to work could ever be so lucky.

Now, hang on. It really gets sort of bizarre here. This is the part, on the way up in the elevator, that I was thinking no one would believe. Ready? Okay, let's do it.

We started moving, but I could tell the driver was in some sort of mood. He was on the phone with someone, and his voice kept rising until he was in a full yell. Suddenly, he jerked the wheel, pulled over to the curb, and started screaming even louder into his phone—not even words, just screams.

I thought I was going to be murdered by a cab-driving maniac!

Now, assembled employees, I assure you this is all true.

The driver hung up the phone, and we just sat there for a few seconds. I didn't say anything; he didn't say anything. Then he reached up, shut off the meter, and said, "No charge." I was still two blocks away from the office, but I sure as hell wasn't going to complain. I got out of the cab, and he peeled off.

So I walked the two blocks, and I'm here. And there it is.

Was that not an amazing series of events, culminating in my 70-minute lateness? Have you ever heard an excuse like that in this office, or in any other office, before? Has the 12th floor ever been graced with such a tale? I told you it'd be good. Was I right, or was I right?

Have you ever heard an excuse like that in this office, or in any other office, before? Has the 12th floor ever been graced with such a tale? I told you it'd be good.

Well, see you all at lunch. ⌀

the ONION®

VOLUME 39 ISSUE 31 AMERICA'S FINEST NEWS SOURCE™ 14–20 AUGUST 2003

NEWS

Asimo Tricked Into Falling Down Stairs

see SCIENCE page 6D

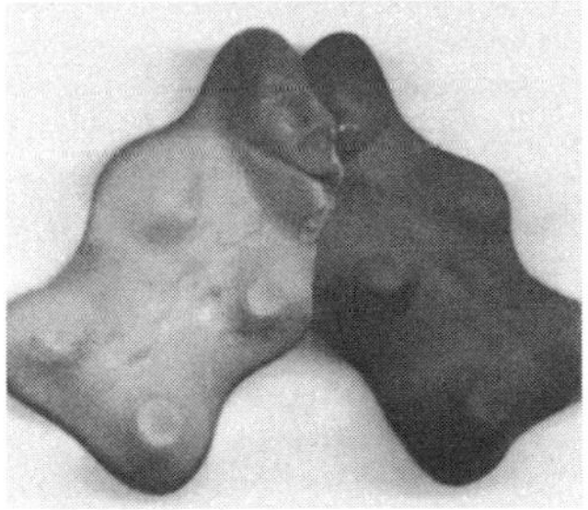

Gummy Bears Born Conjoined

see FAMILY page 3E

Seven-Foot-High Grammatical Error Displayed Next To Car Dealer's Head

see BUSINESS page 9C

STATshot

A look at the numbers that shape your world.

Daddy, Where Are You Going?

1. Daddy said stay by the vending machines
2. Easy on the D-word there, kid
3. Your mother's funeral... Oh, and your mother's dead
4. Candyland, but you're not invited
5. I'm... Just... Look! A plane!

Confused Americans Seek Steady No. 1 At Box Office

LOS ANGELES—Unsettled by U.S. military action abroad and economic struggles at home, Americans say they are desperate for the stability of an unchanging number-one movie at the box office.

"Although several summer blockbusters had successful opening weekends, only *Finding Nemo* has held the top slot for more than a week or two," said Andrew Kohler, chairman of the Citizens for Consistent Cinema (CCC). "This has caused unease and confusion for millions of Americans."

"With a new top movie every week, the average American can neither keep up nor move on," Kohler continued. "In times of national and international turmoil, we need a summer smash to calm our nerves. Unfortunately, few of the summer's major releases have had box-office staying-power."

The Matrix Reloaded and *Charlie's Angels: Full Throttle*, two highly anticipated sequels, both opened at number one, only to fall from the top slot the very next week. Kohler said this typifies the uncertainty at the box office this summer.

"After suffering a long spring of one-weekend hits, the nation was waiting for a single movie to emerge from the pack and take the lead," Kohler said. "That movie never came. Not *Hulk* or *T3*, and certainly not *The League Of Extraordinary Gentlemen*."

According to Kohler, no movie has topped the chart for more than

see AMERICANS page 214

Humanitarian Aid Check Blown Before It Arrives

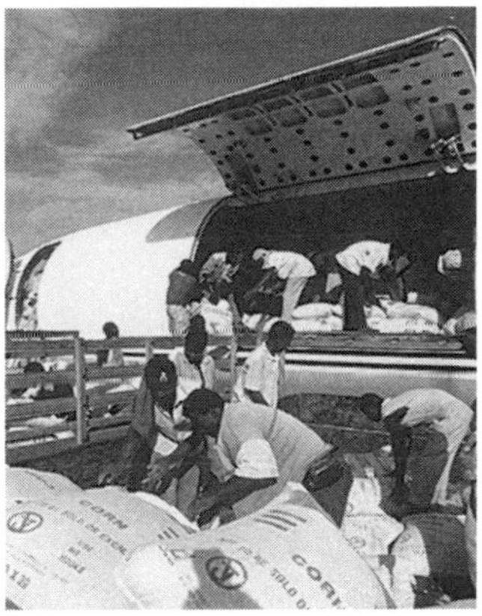

Above: Grain that Malawi never should've bought.

LILONGWE, MALAWI—A much-needed humanitarian aid check from the United Nations to Malawi was "totally blown" by the beleaguered South African nation before the actual payment arrived, government officials admitted Tuesday.

"We've been living so hand-to-mouth lately that, as soon as we received word that aid was coming, we began buying some necessary items," President Bakili Muluzi said when reached by phone at his home office. "We got a little out of control. Then again, we couldn't bear the thought of another dinner of bark."

The $50 million check, a combination of funds from UNICEF, World Food Programme, and other U.N. agencies, was intended to help alleviate disease and famine in Malawi, which has been devastated by recent flooding and the sub-Saharan AIDS

see CHECK page 215

Rise In Teen Sexual Activity Comes As Surprise To Area Teen

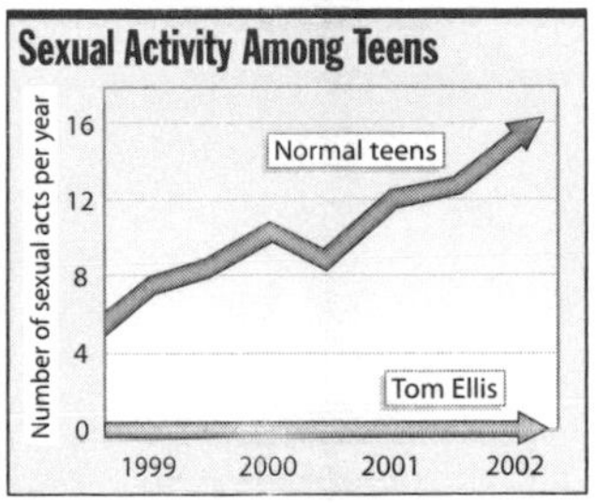

Left: Tom Ellis, who was surprised by statistics showing that other teens are having sex (above).

SALEM, OR—The Alan Guttmacher Institute released a report Friday that showed a dramatic increase in teen sexual activity, a finding that surprised policy-makers, public-health professionals, and 17-year-old Tom Ellis.

"So, more teens are having sex, are they?" Ellis asked Monday. "Well, I'm not sure where those guys got all their data, but it sure wasn't from me."

Ellis, a senior this fall at Sprague High School in Salem, learned of the trend while watching television at

see TEEN page 214

The First Gay Bishop

The Rev. V. Gene Robinson recently won confirmation as the first openly gay bishop in the Episcopal Church, prompting protests and walk-outs. What do *you* think?

Ryan Reiff
Systems Analyst

"Now that the church has been compassionate and reasonable about this, people are going to expect that all the time."

Carlos Ferebee
Welder

"Among the greatest mysteries of faith are why God allows people to die, why evil exists, and why the hell some gay guy would want to be bishop."

Larry Cody
Cook

"Isn't worrying about God stuff all the time kind of gay anyway?"

Marjorie Moyers
Bookkeeper

"What's next? *Black* ministers?"

Joseph Bogan
Tax Examiner

"Whoa, that church has really gone downhill since forming the ecclesiastical body with their own episcopate in 1789."

Katherine Millard
Musician

"Since when is it a crime to be gay? Oh, yeah. Up until a few weeks ago. Well, it's not anymore. Get with it."

Internet Social Networks

Friend-matching web sites like Friendster.com are gaining in popularity. What's the appeal?

- Online friends easier to cut loose than people who live in your building
- Great way to chip away at the remaining normal methods of human interaction
- Allow for meeting new people under predetermined arrangement that you like each other
- Wifester left, and have never been that close to familyster
- Face-to-face friends object to being put into spreadsheet form
- Lonely... Please, someone... So lonely
- Users can dodge and blow off people online and in real world
- People who use it testify it's not weird, even though it is

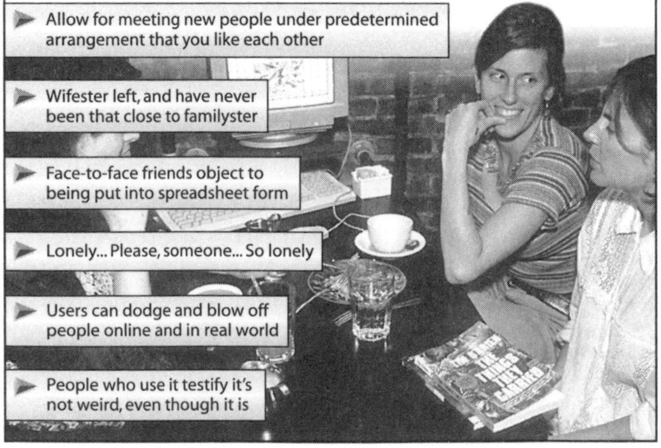

the ONION®
America's Finest News Source.™

Herman Ulysses Zweibel
Founder

T. Herman Zweibel
Publisher Emeritus
J. Phineas Zweibel
Publisher
Maxwell Prescott Zweibel
Editor-In-Chief

This Job Isn't Nearly As Exciting As The DeVry Institute Led Me To Believe

By Ted Lascowicz

When I was 18 or so, I used to watch Ricki Lake on Channel 9 every afternoon. During the commercial breaks, I always saw ads for the DeVry Institute Of Technology. One ad featured a group of mostly male students eagerly crowded around a single computer in a fluorescent-lit classroom, on the fast track to earning their degrees. Another ad showed a recent DeVry graduate striding into a windowless block of an office building like he had the world by the tail. Everyone looked ready to dive into a high-paying career, and I wanted that for myself. I was hypnotized by the fast-growing field of technology. But now, 12 years later, I'm stuck in a job that's not nearly as exciting as the one the DeVry commercials led me to expect.

Despite the allure of an exciting job in the field of technology, and even though the phone call to DeVry was free of charge and obligation, I didn't jump-start my career immediately. I'm not dumb, but I'd always felt bored in high school. I barely squeaked by with passing grades, and when I finally graduated, I was determined never to set foot in another classroom. I took a job bussing tables at Perkins, then moved to line cook and lead line cook. After years of barely making ends meet, I decided I didn't want to work in a restaurant for the rest of my life. It was time for a change, but I lacked the skills I needed to be a vital part of today's challenging job market.

Now, I'm part of the support team for Point of Sale Systems, Inc. At PSS, we manufacture and distribute computerized cash registers. I'm in charge of installing the hardware for our Flash Register systems at the client's site.

Then I remembered DeVry. The free brochure I received in the mail explained that the DeVry Institute Of Technology, under the umbrella of DeVry University, offered career-oriented undergraduate and graduate programs. After looking over the brochure, I decided I was ready for some workplace-relevant learning. I wanted more than anything to prepare for a career in an exciting area such as systems analysis and design, applications software support and maintenance, applications software consulting, or business applications programming. But was a job in the challenging field of technical and application support, or computer-related sales and marketing support, really mine for the taking?

I figured I didn't have anything to lose. I took out a few loans and applied for a degree in computer information systems.

The courses were pretty tedious, but I slogged through, believing that the benefits were down the road. After all, DeVry was providing me with the technical skills, business principles, and general education I needed to succeed in the field. I graduated well within the top half of my class.

Now, I'm part of the support team for Point of Sale Systems, Inc. At PSS, we manufacture and distribute computerized cash registers. I'm in charge of installing the hardware for our Flash Register systems at the client's site. After the system is installed, I spend a day training employees to use it. Most of our contracts are with restaurants, so the only thing that's really changed for me is my hours. At least I'm not alone: My company hired one of my classmates from DeVry for pretty much the same job, only he works on a freelance consulting basis for Joe's Crab Shacks across the country.

I thought that by going to DeVry, I'd become part of a team—a strike force ready to simplify people's lives with technology. Instead, I'm lucky if I can hold a waiter's attention long enough to teach him how to void a margarita sale. I have to pretend I don't hear the waitresses making fun of my bald spot while I'm crouched under the counter connecting wires.

When I'm not in a windowless back room stringing cable along a filthy, grease-splattered suspended ceiling, I'm stuck in traffic between suburbs, wishing I cared enough about my life to quit smoking. I've gained 15 pounds from the fried food I eat while setting up the Flash Register systems,

see JOB page 215

Prisoner Claims Cell Block D Was Much Cooler Two Years Ago

JOLIET, IL—Citing an increase in "leg humpers and peter-gazing diddlers," Joliet Corrections Center inmate Joseph J. Romans told reporters Monday that Cell Block D is not as cool as it used to be.

"When I first went down, D was straight," said Romans, who is serving an eight-year sentence at Joliet for armed robbery. "Minute I walked in, I knew it was a good stop. I don't know what happened."

Romans said that 2001, his first year in D Block, was his best year in prison.

"D used to have the toughest guys, pruno [homemade alcohol], and pearl handles [commercially manufactured cigarettes], and with my connections-man Willie G on block, we had Cadillac everything," Romans said. "I almost felt like I was in the world with my crew again. Now, all we got left is a bunch of punk-ass june bugs with nothing coming. I don't even know what name half these young kids go by."

New prisoners are often impressed by the severity of the facility, but Romans said it pales in comparison to that of the old Cell Block D.

"These bitches and dumb-ass crackheads come in all wide-eyed, losing their shit over how we got the corners worked," Romans said. "Well, what they don't know is that the old D used to have the straightest crew in [Joliet]. We weren't thugs. We did our own time. But if you crossed one of us, you got a pumpkin head. Everyone knew that and gave us our respect."

"These bitches and dumb-ass crackheads come in all wide-eyed, losing their shit over how we got the corners worked," Romans said. "Well, what they don't know is that the old D used to have the straightest crew in [Joliet]. We weren't thugs. We did our own time. But if you crossed one of us, you got a pumpkin head."

A pumpkin head is the injury that commonly results when a pillowcase is filled with heavy objects and used to beat an enemy's face until it is badly bruised.

"Yeah, things have gone to hell," Romans said. "These fools will sodomize a guy with a pipe for no good reason. Too young to know standards of conduct."

Above: Romans in his cell on the now-lame Joliet Corrections Center Block D.

According to Romans, Cell Block D's reputation has been hurt by a number of unsuccessful escape attempts by some of the newer inmates.

"See, if you rabbit and get away, you become a legend," Romans said. "If not, you get your ass beat by the hacks and put in the hole. The guys in the old D would never pull the half-ass stunts they pull here now. Well, 'Smokey' Hudson tried to make a break a few years ago, but he wasn't really solid with the D crew to begin with."

Recent behavior by the newer members of Cell Block D has resulted in punishment for all the inmates, said Romans.

"The last few weeks, the D's been in lockdown for some ignorant stunt," Romans said. "Somebody tried to make pruno in a bag, tie it up, and put it in the toilet. Shit, that's the first place they gonna look."

see PRISONER page 215

NEWS IN BRIEF

Last Great Party Of Life To Result In First Child

LAKE CHARLES, LA—Unbeknownst to him, 27-year-old Ron DuPree attended the last great party of his life Saturday, as a 3 a.m. coupling with girlfriend Tamara Harris will result in a child nine months from now. "That was the best party ever," DuPree said to friends on Monday, oblivious to the seed of life now growing in his soon-to-be-wife's womb. "I was so wasted! God, Tamara and I have to start getting out on the weekends again." In addition to enjoying his last great party, DuPree will also soon bid farewell to liquor, cigarettes, and most of his current friendships.

Avid Fisherman Forever Ruins Fishing For Son

MANKATO, MN—Thanks to his nitpicking, impatience, and insistence on absolute silence in the boat, avid angler Don Gillespie, 41, forever ruined fishing for his 10-year-old son Douglas Tuesday. "No, no, no—you're casting all wrong," said a visibly seething Gillespie after Douglas' line landed a mere three feet from the stern of the rowboat. "Forget it! Just let me do it, and I'll hand you the rod afterward." Douglas was further put off fishing when his father threw back the only fish the boy caught all day because it wasn't big enough.

Hussein Family Can't Bear To Throw Out Uday's Favorite Nutsack Shocker

AWJA, IRAQ—Relatives, sorting through boxes at Uday Hussein's home Tuesday, couldn't bear to discard one of the deceased tyrant's favorite torture devices. "Oh, how Uday loved his electric nutsack shocker," Uday's uncle Karim Suleiman al-Majid said, as he sifted through a box of clamps, cables, saws, and 8-volt batteries. "And here's that trusty little knife he would use to dig eyeballs out of their sockets." Al-Majid said he is sure that Uday would have wanted his favorite cousin Nawaf to have the roll of flensing wire.

Republicans Introduce Economic Equality Bill For Fun Of Shooting It Down

WASHINGTON, DC—Republicans in the House of Representatives proposed H.R. 2093: the Economic Equality Initiative, with the express purpose of shooting it down "just for kicks" Tuesday. "H.R. 2093 will level the economic playing field, spreading the wealth among the rich and poor," Majority Leader Tom DeLay (R-TX) said, visibly fighting back snickers. "We must pass this bill to stop the fat cats from getting fatter while the average Joe struggles to make ends meet. Also, I'm the Queen of Bavaria." Following 10 minutes of uproarious laughter, the congressmen stepped out of the chamber to smoke cigars lit with a bill that would allocate $115 million to clean up hazardous waste sites.

News Anchor Wonders Where All These Great Stories Come From

SALT LAKE CITY, UT—Midway through a story about new evidence in an unsolved area homicide, KTVX news anchor John Reesen wondered aloud where all the great stories come from. "Yet another gripping investigative report, right here on KTVX," said Reesen, during Tuesday's *News At Ten*. "Wow. Who comes up with this news?" Reesen posed a similar question to weatherman Gary Yount, wondering who could possibly know all that science stuff. Ø

AMERICANS from page 211

four weeks since Sept. 11, but in the last six months, even three-week reigns have been infrequent. The high rate of turnover at the box office has resulted in what Kohler terms "pop-culture vertigo."

"Not one of these movies has had any major impact on the national consciousness," Kohler said. "Yes, many people saw *Bad Boys II*. But who saw it twice? Who is quoting lines from it? Who is planning a Halloween costume based on one of its characters?"

In contrast, Kohler points to previous summers, when movies like *Batman*, *Independence Day*, and *Star Wars: Episode I* united us as a people.

"When *Jurassic Park* came out, everyone at work was talking about it, all the talk shows were doing skits about it, and the tie-in products were everywhere," Kohler said. "It wasn't a good movie, but it was a *huge* movie. We knew who we were and what we had to do: We had to see *Jurassic Park*."

Omaha elementary-school teacher Janice Daly fondly recalled the comfort reliable box-office charts gave her in 1998.

"Clinton was embroiled in scandals, the terrorists had attacked American military sites, and we were bombing suspected al-Qaeda camps in Sudan," Daly said. "But every weekend, I could open up the paper and see *Titanic* sitting right there at number one. We had something we could all believe in as Americans. In my time of need, that movie never let me down."

Few moviegoers have found such solace on the big screen this year.

"I was excited when *Anger Management* was number one for two weeks," said Richard Jackson, a master carpenter unemployed since February. "Then, along came *Identity* and knocked it off. The very next week, *X2: X-Men United* opened and knocked out *Identity*. Doesn't Hollywood know that the people of this country need some stability in our lives?"

Oliver Reynolds, an 18-year-old pizza deliveryman, was particularly stricken by the summer's jumble of one-week wonders.

"I was counting the days until *The Matrix Reloaded*'s opening night," Reynolds said. "After my folks split up, I needed something steady to rely on. After more than a year of hype, I thought it'd rule theaters for months. I thought my friends and I would go, like, 10 times."

"We all know how that ended," he added.

Some experts say the trend may have lasting effects.

"If no film manages to dramatically outdraw its competition before the end of summer, our national identity will be called into question," said Dr. Alison Weisgall, sociologist and author of *Hollywood Heartbreak: A Nation Abandoned By Its Entertainment Industry*. "If the world's dominant superpower can't produce a reliable, record-breaking hit at the box office, then what is it? And, by extension, who are we?"

But Weisgall said she sees no steady box-office front-runner in sight.

"With the next *Harry Potter* movie not slated until next summer, 2003 is shaping up to be the most chaotic box-office year of the new millennium," Weisgall said. "Unless America finds the anchor it so desperately needs in *S.W.A.T.* or *Freddy Vs. Jason*, I fear for us all." Ø

TEEN from page 211

home Saturday, as he does most weekend nights. A *20/20* story titled "The Teen Sex Epidemic" informed him that 82.6 percent of his peers aged 15 to 19 have engaged in some form of sexual contact with another person.

"Really?" Ellis asked. "Eight out of 10 teens? There's an *epidemic*?"

While excited by the findings on teen sexuality, Ellis has yet to observe the increase in his own life.

"I mean, it's summer, and I can't help

According to friend Doug Binder, Ellis' chances of joining the growing ranks of the sexually experienced are slim.

but notice all the girls wearing sexy dresses and tank tops and stuff," he said. "But, does that mean I'm one millimeter closer to getting some tail? No, sir."

"Doesn't matter that I've grown six inches this year, that I've been working out in my basement, or that I dress in Gap clothes, like everyone else," Ellis continued. "Girls like Kelly [Mehan] and Michelle [Lehrer] still totally ignore me. At this rate, I'll be lucky to French [kiss] a girl before college."

Although teen sexual activity is on the rise, the Guttmacher report indicated that the teen pregnancy rate has dropped to a 13-year low.

"More teens are engaging in sex, but a larger percentage of them are doing so responsibly," said Dr. Jerry Kendall, a senior researcher for the Guttmacher Institute. "There's an increased access to and acceptance of proper contraceptives, mainly the condom, even among the disenfranchised teen population. An additional factor is the marked casualization of oral sex, which is often substituted for full intercourse."

"Really?!" Ellis asked. "Blow jobs? Well, that national trend hasn't spread to Salem yet, because I'm about one blow job shy of joining that statistic. It would take a miracle to get a girl to go down on me."

Ellis did confirm that he would use a condom if he were to have sex.

"You have sex, you wear a condom," said Ellis, who has practiced proper condom use alone in his bedroom. "At least that's what everybody says. I certainly wouldn't know from experience because, clearly, I'm a freak. I'm one of the pathetic 18 percent who still haven't even seen, much less touched, a naked breast. Well, rest assured: When and if I ever get the chance to have sex, I will definitely know how to put on a condom."

Although Ellis has carefully documented his intense desire for a sexual encounter in his journal, that desire hasn't translated into sexual activity. Ellis insisted that this is not by choice.

"Hey, I'm not one of those weird abstinence kids," Ellis said. "There's nothing I would like better than to waste myself on the wrong girl. I just want to know: Where in the hell are all these millions of loose teenage girls? Because they certainly don't go to my school."

According to friend Doug Binder, Ellis' chances of joining the growing ranks of the sexually experienced are slim.

"Tom?" Binder asked. "He's doomed to virginity, just like me. But, hey, that doesn't stop us from talking and thinking about sex all the freaking time. For all our yapping about what we'd do if we were ever alone with a girl, neither of us is anywhere near getting some action."

Although he admitted he was startled by the report, Ellis said he remains hopeful for the future.

"I've still got two years to get laid and join the majority," Ellis said. "I mean, I've heard guys talking about all the girls they've slept with, but I thought they were just making it up. Turns out, everyone really *was* having sex all that time. Well, thanks, *20/20*. Now I know what a complete loser I am." Ø

Above: Teens who, unlike Ellis, are engaging in sexual activity.

CHECK from page 211

pandemic. Although the check wasn't due to arrive until Aug. 11, Malawi officials were promised the money on Aug. 4 and behaved as though the cash was already in their hands.

"When we found out money was on the way, we celebrated by immediately going out and buying 200,000 bushels of maize," Malawi Agricultural Minister Chakufwa Chihana said. "We even said, 'What the heck, let's throw in a little millet.' Big mistake."

Government officials also bought fuel and medical supplies, promising suppliers that a big check was on the way.

"When we flashed the letter from the U.N., our suppliers were more than happy to float us a few imports, just until the check arrived," Muluzi said. "Unfortunately, we didn't keep track of every little crate of AIDS medicine. When we added it all up, it came to, like, 40 million bucks."

A few high-ticket items sneaked onto the list of purchases, among

Malawi lent struggling neighbor Mozambique $1 million, under the express agreement that Mozambique was to repay the money Aug. 8, when its own relief check came in.

them a new computer system for an agricultural weigh station outside Chilumba.

"We told ourselves we would only get the things we really needed," Muluzi said. "But when we found out that the weigh station needed a new computer, we figured it was now or never."

Giddy with the promise of a large cash deposit, Malawi lent struggling neighbor Mozambique $1 million, under the express agreement that Mozambique was to repay the money Aug. 8, when its own relief check came in.

"Bad move," Muluzi said. "In terms of repaying loans, Mozambique is as bad as Tanzania. On payback day, [Mozambique Prime Minister] Pascoal [Mocumbi] called me and said that we still owed him money for the cashew nuts and sisal twine we imported in February 1996."

On Aug. 6, unanticipated events plunged Malawi further into debt. A mudslide outside Lilongwe devastated a shantytown and displaced hundreds of its residents. The problem was compounded by bandits in northern rural areas who prevented aid trucks from entering the disaster area until large payments of cash and food were made.

"Then, the goddamn fan belt on our newest food-distribution truck broke," Muluzi said. "Fixing it set us back a lot, even though it was less than two years old. What could we do, though? We needed to distribute the maize."

Deep in debt, Malawi officials resorted to tactics employed during past cash crunches. Government employees found their paychecks postdated two weeks. Interest payments to creditors were delayed by the deliberate transposing of addresses on envelopes. Creditors who phoned government offices were thrown off by deceptive outgoing voicemail messages claiming that the government was out of town and would be back Aug. 20.

Such tactics are common among countries receiving assistance, according to Malawi's U.N. humanitarian aid advisor Donna Roush.

"It's obvious what [Finance Minister Friday Jumbe] was trying to do," Roush said. "Malawi has been independent for decades, and he's written enough checks to know that if you owe somebody $74,000, you can't write in $47,000 and have no one notice."

"Although money is often tight right before a large aid check is due, countries must resist the urge to splurge," Roush added. "If you live off money that doesn't exist yet, you have to pay the piper at some point. Resist the temptation. The key is to create a budget for yourself and stick to it. Save money by eating your own crops, instead of imports, and make sure your coal plants are running as efficiently as possible."

Roush's advice provided little comfort to Muluzi.

"The humanitarian aid people always act like recipient countries are irresponsible, but we're trying very hard to keep our spending in check," Muluzi said. "For years, we've had our eye on a brand-new hydroelectric plant for a site outside Blantyre. It would be totally perfect, but we have put the project on hold yet again, because we just don't have the money."

Continued Muluzi: "This whole humanitarian aid thing can be a real bummer. It's our money to keep, but technically, it's not really our money. We have to spend it the second we get it. It feels like we're never going to get ahead. What can I say? Being poor sucks."

Above: One of the many small purchases Malawi officials failed to realize would add up quickly.

JOB from page 212

and the only people I ever talk to are restaurant managers.

Sometimes, I think what I'd like to do is find all those DeVry students from those ads and beat the living shit out of them. Then I'd move on to the president of DeVry, and the head of the studio that made those damn commercials. But I guess I have to admit that nobody put a gun to my head and forced me to enter the fast-paced world of technology.

If only I could turn back time and get a medical-technician degree instead.

If only I could turn back time and get a medical-technician degree instead.

PRISONER from page 213

Continued Romans: "I'm sick of taking heat for these kids. From here on in, I'm doing my own time. When I get called up [to the parole board], I'm walking up packed, bo-bos tied. D is dead."

New inmate Nathan Gold has an entirely different attitude toward Cell Block D.

"The D is dope and everyone knows it," said Gold, a convicted arsonist. "Even the hogs know if you're from D, you ain't to be fucked with. I can't imagine doing my bit in that punk-ass Cell Block A."

Other inmates questioned Romans' credibility. Thirty-year inmate Jerome Hughes said his fellow prisoner is a "cell gangster," someone who boasts in his cell but never amid the general prison population.

"Romans is a bitch," Hughes said. "If he didn't have Big Norman looking out for him, he wouldn't have lasted his first year. Yeah, people get out of line, but Romans doesn't do the correcting, tell you that much."

Continued Hughes: "I don't know

"Yeah, things have gone to hell," Romans said. "These fools will sodomize a guy with a pipe for no good reason. Too young to know standards of conduct."

why he's knocking his gums. Cell Block D's been a sandbox for 10, 15 years. Hasn't been the same since Stabbin' Jackie Kayne went on 10-10 furlough in '85. Yeah, '83 and '84. Those were the days."

COMMUNITY VOICES

You Gotta Be Careful With Fireworks

Hola, amigos. You all right? I know it's been a long time since I rapped at ya, but I've been in constant motion, dodging all the crap life's been shoveling my way. I had to put my car out to pasture, because the door fell off. I would've just re-attached it, but it was all rusted out, and I didn't want to fall out of my car while I was doing 75. Besides, the engine had about 170,000 miles on it and a bad knock. I'll be damned if I was going to replace the engine on an '88 Ford Festiva.

The Cruise
By Jim Anchower

It's too bad. I liked that car. It wasn't exactly a power machine, but it got 40 miles to the gallon, and it was a Ford. Plus, the tape deck worked, and that's half the battle right there. At least I got to take it on one last trip before it went south.

See, last weekend I went on a fishing trip up north with Ron and Ron's friend Rob. (That's a whole other story that I don't want to get into right now, or right *ever*. Fishing is for suckers, and that's my final answer.) Wes would've come, but he got stuck watching his little brother Zac while his mom was out of town for some convention. She's one of those people who cleans off your teeth at the dentist's and then hands the dentist tools and stuff. Not like any of that matters. The important thing is that, on the way back from this trip that sucked my bag, we picked up some fireworks.

I decided we had no choice but to buy a shitload of fireworks, so we pulled into a gas station/convenience store/Arby's/fireworks outlet.

I remember getting sparklers, Snakes, and Jumping Jacks as a kid. Even though they were totally babyshit fireworks, they were still pretty cool. Especially Snap-Pops, those rolled up pieces of paper that crack when you throw them against something. I'd save up and buy, like, three boxes. Then I'd unroll them all and put them in a paper towel to make one huge Snap-Pop. The giant Snap-Pop was still pretty weak, even after all that work, but when you're 8, you've got a lot more time to waste.

Back then, you couldn't get the big stuff around here. If you wanted the M-80s or Thunder Bombs, you had to wait until someone hauled back a trunkload from South Dakota, and then you had to deal with a serious mark-up. These days, all you have to do is drive north, and it's like you're in the lawless West. Once you're above Menomonee Falls, you can't blow a tire without crashing into a roadside fireworks store. I'm talking real stores with three, four aisles of fireworks packages like the "Fourth Of Surprise," "The Peacemaker Pack," and my personal favorite, "The Big Buttload Of Fireworks."

These days, all you have to do is drive north, and it's like you're in the lawless West. Once you're above Menomonee Falls, you can't blow a tire without crashing into a roadside fireworks store. I'm talking real stores with three, four aisles.

Well, I lost my stash on the trip and needed cheering up. Ron, Rob, and I decided we had no choice but to buy a shitload of fireworks, so we pulled into a gas station/convenience store/Arby's/fireworks outlet. Now, if the convenience store had carried any tapes other than *The Best Of Ray Stevens* and *Love Rocks: The 30 Greatest Love Ballads Of All Time*, it would've been the best spot on earth. I bought 25 Roman candles, the "Justice For All" bottle-rocket assortment, and five roast-beef sandwiches.

When I buy fireworks, I'm usually torn between setting them off as soon as I get home (which means wasting them) and saving them for a special occasion. But saving them usually amounts to sitting on them through two humid summers, setting them off some night when I'm drunk, and finding out they don't work anymore.

This time, I decided I was going to do it right. I loaded a pony keg into the back of my car, and me, Wes, Ron, and Rob headed out to the quarry.

After we tapped the keg, Ron got out one of his big tubes and lit it off. I tell you, it looked as good as a professional firework. Things were pretty quiet as we watched it, lost in thought. But then I felt something hot hit my arm. I looked over and there was Ron, 15 feet away, pointing a Roman candle at me. I grabbed a handful of Roman candles and took off running, before he could tag me again.

This time, I decided I was going to do it right. I loaded a pony keg into the back of my car, and me, Wes, Ron, and Rob headed out to the quarry.

Now, when you're having a Roman candle fight, Fireworks Safety Rule #1 is "Never aim above the neck." Fireworks are a little bit unpredictable, so it's best to aim for the ass and hope the firework doesn't stray too far north. But right away, Ron broke Rule #1 and hit me in the back of the head.

Good thing I was thinking fast, otherwise I would've lost all my hair, instead of just a patch of it. Ron said "Sorry, man," but I could see him laughing. That made me break Fireworks Safety Rule #2. ("Don't take it personal.") I lit up two Roman candles and aimed them both at Ron. I was all like, "Pow! Pow! Pow!" Pretty soon we were both laughing like mad.

But the dumbass had to run over by my car with his Roman candles shooting off every which way. There were still a couple loose fireworks sitting in the back of the car, and within seconds, the entire backseat was on fire.

The pony keg was right there, so we used it to put out the fire. Thankfully, when we were done, we still had about a quarter of the keg left. We sat and drank until the seat cooled down, then yanked out what was left of it and threw it to the bottom of the quarry. The car smelled like beer and burnt cat, but it still ran, so we drove it home.

When the door fell off of the car the next day, I knew it was time to give up. Sometimes, your car tells you things, and you've gotta listen. In this case, the Festiva was saying, "It's time to let go."

I'm gonna miss that car. Ø

HOROSCOPES

Your Horoscope

By Lloyd Schumner Sr.
Retired Machinist and
A.A.P.B.-Certified Astrologer

Aries: (March 21–April 19)
Things suddenly get awkward when your coworkers notice your resemblance to the Easter Island statues and put two and two together.

Taurus: (April 20–May 20)
You'll be damned if you know what those guys on the Spanish-language station are saying, but they're definitely having a much better time than you are.

Gemini: (May 21–June 21)
It's time to acknowledge that your "trusty right-hand man" is really just a little face you drew on your thumb and forefinger.

Cancer: (June 22–July 22)
When the credits roll at the end of your life, the words "Directed By Henry Jaglom" will go a long way toward explaining things.

Leo: (July 23–Aug. 22)
This week's events will give you cause to reconsider the wisdom of the phrase "Never give up."

Virgo: (Aug. 23–Sept. 22)
Stop telling everyone you are popular with the ladies. Only your magnificent body is popular with the ladies.

Libra: (Sept. 23–Oct. 23)
There is nothing morally wrong with anal sex, but your failure to exercise sufficient precautions has gotten you ass-pregnant.

Scorpio: (Oct. 24–Nov. 21)
You will abandon your attempt to make the world's largest pancake after finding out how depressingly serious other people are about it.

Sagittarius: (Nov. 22–Dec. 21)
There's nothing wrong with waiting tables while waiting for your big break, unless you're that girl Annette at the corner diner.

Capricorn: (Dec. 22–Jan. 19)
You are the very picture of goodwill, honesty, and social grace. Note that use of the word "picture" also implies a certain two-dimensionality.

Aquarius: (Jan. 20–Feb. 18)
You have many thoughtful questions about fate, destiny, and the future. It's a shame so many concern the Red Sox.

Pisces: (Feb. 19–March 20)
Sometimes, there are things a friend is too nice to tell you. Luckily, you don't have any friends like that.

NEWS

Skywriter Leaves Suicide Note

see OBITUARIES page 5G

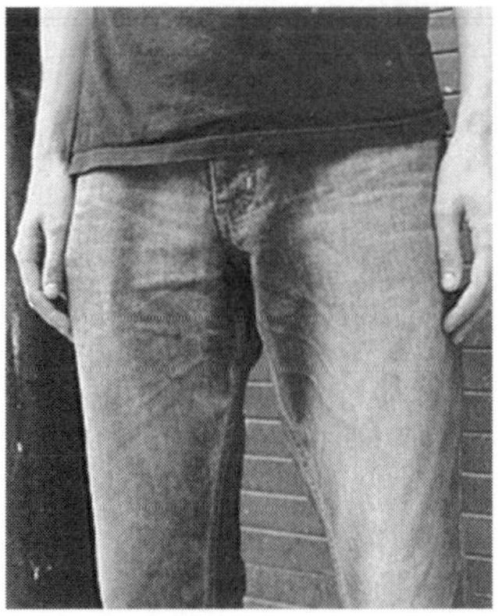

Heroic Pants Enter 19th Day Of Continuous Duty

see LOCAL page 3C

Blackout Survivors Tell Stories Of Harrowing Inconvenience

see NATION page 7B

Hollywood Accessed

see ENTERTAINMENT page 12F

STATshot

A look at the numbers that shape your world.

Top Regional Restaurant Chains

1. Captain Donut's Steakhouse
2. Church & Fried Chicken
3. More Meatloaf? The Restaurant
4. Formerly Sambo's
5. Bob Evans' Loose-Cannon Cousin
6. Friami International Fryport

THE ONION • $2.00 US • $3.00 CAN

the ONION®

VOLUME 39 ISSUE 32 AMERICA'S FINEST NEWS SOURCE™ 21–27 AUGUST 2003

The California Recall Candidates: A Focus On The 87 Front-Runners

see CANDIDATES in the ONION's 48-page ELECTION GUIDE insert

Above: Nielsen shows off her revolting suntan.

Woman Proud Of Horrible Tan

PORTAGE, WI—Local resident Stacy Nielsen takes great pride in her deep, dark, horrible suntan, the 28-year-old sales associate revealed Tuesday.

"I worked hard all summer to get this tan," Nielsen said, her wide smile threatening to crack her sun-dried,

see TAN page 220

U.N. Factoid-Finding Mission Discovers Liberia About The Size Of Tennessee

MONROVIA, LIBERIA—A U.N. factoid-finding mission sent to war-ravaged Liberia discovered that the West African nation is roughly the size of Tennessee, members of the U.S.-led team reported Tuesday.

"It's difficult for outsiders to comprehend the horrific proportions of the crisis in Liberia," said team leader Dr. Johann Sieber in his report to the U.N. Monday. "Our mission was to put things into perspective by collecting informational tidbits about the country—easy-to-understand snippets we can all relate to."

"Did you know that the flag of Liberia was modeled after the U.S. flag?" asked Sieber, who has eight years of factoid-finding experience with CNN Headline News. "The white star represents freedom, and the 11 red and white stripes stand for the 11 signers of the Liberian Declaration Of Independence."

Over the course of the mission, the team—composed of sound-bite engineers, fun-fact-checkers, and a trivia-pursuit squad—collected more than 300 informational tidbits about Liberia's geographical features, sports records, cuisine, and indigenous plant and animal life.

"The average U.S. citizen is woefully ignorant, not just about Liberia, but about the African continent as a whole," Sieber said. "For example, did you know Sapo National Park in Liberia is Western Africa's largest untouched tract of rainforest? Well, it is. It's also home to a great variety of animal species, including elephants, leopards, giant forest hogs, and

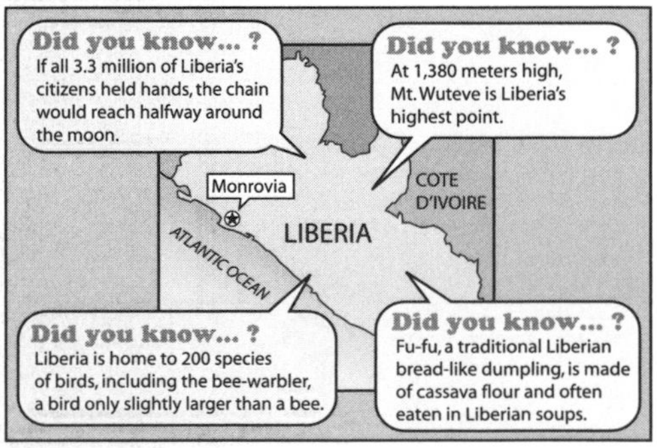

the rare pygmy hippo."

Did you know... ?
If all 3.3 million of Liberia's citizens held hands, the chain would reach halfway around the moon.
Did you know... ?
At 1,380 meters high, Mt. Wuteve is Liberia's highest point.
Monrovia
COTE D'IVOIRE
LIBERIA
ATLANTIC OCEAN
Did you know... ?
Liberia is home to 200 species of birds, including the bee-warbler, a bird only slightly larger than a bee.
Did you know... ?
Fu-fu, a traditional Liberian bread-like dumpling, is made of cassava flour and often eaten in Liberian soups.

Added Sieber: "The Black Spitting Viper, also at home in Liberia, can spit venom distances of up to 20 feet."

The team began the mission on Aug. 12, during a period of unrest following the resignation of Liberian President Charles Taylor. Members gathered at the U.S. embassy—which, they noted, is home to the country's very first pay-telephone. From that point forward, the mission was a flurry of measuring, comparing, and contrasting.

"The fun-facts started flowing as soon as we got into the helicopter," Sieber said. "The pilot told us the OH-6A Cayuse light observation helicopter was first used during the 1995 peacekeeping efforts in Bosnia. A minute later, he told us Monrovia was named after James Mon-

see FACTOID page 221

Canadian Prescription Drugs

Major drug manufacturers are attempting to stop Canadian pharmacies from selling discounted prescription drugs to Americans. What do *you* think?

"Look, Canada, stick to exporting that maple-sugar candy of yours. We'll take care of the obscenely expensive prescription drugs."

Caroline Lenhart
Transcriptionist

"Man, I got some primo Nexium when I was up in Vancouver last year."

Terry Yoder
Solderer

"Canada has already given us the best medicine—laughter. Thank you, Ottawa's Dan Aykroyd, for everything."

Phillip Settle
Systems Analyst

"Gay marriage, legal weed, and cheaper prescription drugs? Next they'll have donkeys painted like zebras, too."

Nicholas Perez
Paramedic

"I want to see these senior citizens jailed. I mean, I actually want to *see them* in the jail."

Allison Burke
Auditing Clerk

"As CEO of Abbott Laboratories, I think Americans should consider themselves lucky they're getting our medicine *at all*."

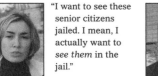

Jacob Harmon
CEO

Gay TV

Gay-themed television series like Bravo's *Queer Eye For The Straight Guy* and *Boy Meets Boy* are popular with mainstream audiences. What's the appeal?

- Viewers like their gays without all that cock-sucking and ass-fucking
- Better than Oxygen's *Lesbian OshKosh B'Gosh Outlet-Store Shopping Spree*
- 90 percent of Americans are latent homosexuals
- Fans can live fun-filled life vicariously through gay characters before having methodical sex with wife in Mobile, AL
- Explode myth that gay people are human beings just like the rest of us
- Homosexuals not so intimidating when they're only 22" tall
- Lost remote, accepting alternate sexuality easier than getting up and crossing room
- The Mexicans already had a network, why not the damned fruits
- Crocodile-huntersexuals, Osbournosexuals, and antiques-roadshowsexuals are old hat

the ONION®
America's Finest News Source.™

Herman Ulysses Zweibel
Founder

T. Herman Zweibel
Publisher Emeritus
J. Phineas Zweibel
Publisher
Maxwell Prescott Zweibel
Editor-In-Chief

I Have An iPod—*In My Mind*

I'm sure you've seen a lot of tech-savvy people smugly showing off that new hunk of entertainment hardware, the iPod personal stereo. Well, I might not have the scratch to get one, but frankly, I don't want the white-corded wonder. I have my very own iPod—*in my mind*.

By Ted Lascowicz

I hear those little things carry up to a month's worth of music. Well, so does *my mind*. I can call up any song I've ever heard, any time I want. And I never have to load software or charge batteries. There are no firewire cords or docks to mess with. I just put my hands behind my head, lean back, and select a tune from the extensive music-library folder *inside my brain*.

Thirty gigabytes? So what? I know 7,500 songs, maybe more. Some songs, I forget I even have until they come around on shuffle. Why, just the other day, my mind started playing David Naughton's "Makin' It," a song I hadn't heard in years. And the sound quality was great!

Easy downloads? You don't know the meaning of the word "easy." And I don't have to know the meaning of the word "download." You may get MP3s off the Internet, you smug scenester, but I can get music off the television, the radio, even a passing ice-cream truck. If I don't want to waste the memory space on a high-fidelity copy, I just don't pay very close attention. Now, *that's* what I call convenience.

There are no firewire cords or docks to mess with. I just put my hands behind my head, lean back, and select a tune from the extensive music-library folder *inside my brain*.

All I have to do is hear a song once or twice, and it's stored forever. I can call it up any time I want. Beach Boys. Beatles. How about some Bach? Or some Billy Joel? Sing me a song, piano man of my mind! And those are just the artists whose names begin with "B."

I can browse by artist, album, song, or music genre. Boom! I'm doing it right now! The "repeat" feature? Heck, songs from my iPod *don't ever have to end*. I swear, I had "Music Box Dancer" going through my head for three days straight last week.

You say those iPods have customizable playlists that allow you to line up songs of your choosing? Primitive! I can put together a playlist, say "Best-Ever Heavy Metal Anthems," while I'm sitting in traffic. My mind is light-years beyond that, though. Does your iPod have the "That Reminds Me Of Another Great Song" feature? Well, my mind does!

Does your iPod have a powerful feature that can play back the great songs of summer 1993, as they sounded coming out of Mike Tollefson's boombox in the back of the school bus?

Does your iPod have a powerful feature that can play back the great songs of summer 1993, as they sounded coming out of Mike Tollefson's boombox in the back of the school bus? Of course not. That particular playlist is in *my brain*, which your pitiful iPod will never be able to autosync with.

But wait, you say that my iPod isn't wrapped up in a pretty little white case? Oh, I guess you haven't heard of a pretty little white case I like to call my *skull*. There's plenty of room for all of my contacts, too. Check this out: Paula, 398-9172, 195 Webster Place. Ha! Take that, *Apple*.

Sure, it doesn't hold all the music I've ever heard, but if I can't remember a song, it's usually not worth having anyway. Except, I'll admit, that one by The Tubes that I think was called "She's One In A Million Girls." The file somehow got corrupted with part of that J. Geils Band song about the centerfold. But every product has its bugs, right?

Even so, my mind has features your iPod will never have. Does your iPod have real-time remixing? No?! Well, if I don't like the original lyrics to Kansas' "Carry On Wayward Son"—zip, zip, zing—my mind can change them! Adding a cool bass line or a rocking keyboard flourish to any piece of music? No problem! Adding images of myself performing on stage with the band? Done!

Does your iPod turn you from just another bus-rider into a lonely figure finding his way down Baker Street? Guess what? My *mind* can! And it does it all with no moving parts, man. None. 'Cause it's *my mind*. ⊘

Precocious 6-Year-Old Claims *Berenstain Bears* Book Changed Her Life

LITCHFIELD PARK, AZ—Since reading *The Berenstain Bears Get The Gimmies* last month, 6-year-old Melody Johnson has lived a changed life, the above-average reader reported Monday.

"*The Berenstain Bears Get The Gimmies* is my favoritest book ever," Johnson said, hugging the dog-eared book to her chest with both arms. "The

> **"I told Spencer he should read *Too Much Teasing*, and then he wouldn't tease anymore," Melody said. "But he just called me a rotten egg. I tried to give the book to him so he could borrow it. But he wouldn't take it. It's a good book. It's funny, and it'd teach him a lesson."**

Berenstain Bears taught me about not being greedy. I used to have the 'galloping greedy gimmies,' but not anymore."

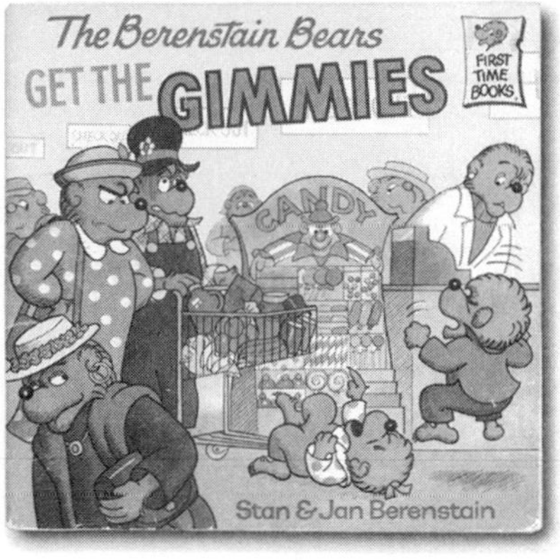

Left: Johnson reviews an underlined passage in her copy of The Berenstain Bears Get The Gimmies (above).

Johnson received the life-altering 32-page book, one in a series of more than 50 written and illustrated by Stan and Jan Berenstain, as a gift from her grandmother.

"Gramma Gloria gave me this book," Johnson said. "I used to go to the store with Mommy and want more and more. Now, I pick out one thing I really, really like."

"I know lots of stuff I didn't ever know before," added Johnson, who first began reading at age 3 and three-quarters. "You can ask Mommy or Daddy or anyone at school."

While she still looks at *Get The Gimmies* "every single day," Johnson asked her parents to buy her more books from the Berenstain series.

"I used to really like *Clifford* [*The Big Red Dog*] books," Johnson said. "I guess they're still good, sorta, but the Berenstain Bears are the best. I like the way the bears look, especially their noses."

Delighted by the positive influence of *Get The Gimmies*, Johnson's parents purchased their daughter 14 more books from the series.

"These books really speak to Melody," said Johnson's father Gordon. "We overheard Melody calling her brother's room a 'dust-catching, wall-to-wall, helter-skelter mess.' That's from *The Berenstain Bears And The Messy*. Melody's very bright for her age, you know."

"'You can't have fun or relax in a room that's such a terrible mess,'" Johnson recited. "I mesmerized [sic] that part, so I wouldn't forget it."

Johnson frequently offers others snippets of the Bears' wisdom.

"I was playing in the sandbox the other day," Johnson said. "Spencer was making fun of Kate's dress. I remembered when *Brother Bear* learned his lesson in *Too Much Teasing*. Brother thought it was fun to tease, until someone teased him. Then it was no fun."

"I told Spencer he should read *Too Much Teasing*, and then he wouldn't tease anymore," Melody said. "But he just called me a rotten egg. I tried to give the book to him so he could borrow it. But he wouldn't take it. It's a good book. It's funny, and it'd teach him a lesson."

Some of Melody's other friends have been more receptive to her testimonials about the life-changing power of the Berenstain Bears. Best friend Angie Bishop started reading the books after Johnson recommended them at a recent sleepover.

"I read *Get The Gimmies* as soon as Melody told me about it, and I really liked it," Bishop said. "I went to the

see BOOK page 221

NEWS IN BRIEF

Bob Hope Happy To See So Many Troops In Heaven

HEAVEN—Recently deceased entertainer Bob Hope announced Monday that he was happy to be reunited with the millions of U.S. troops currently stationed in Paradise, many of whom he entertained during his 50-year career. "It sure brings a smile to my face to see all you proud men and women in uniform," Hope said. "Let's hope the food is better here than it was in the mess tent." Turning to the Pearly Gates, Hope gave a thumbs-up to a soldier killed Monday in a guerrilla attack 20 miles west of Baghdad.

Bush Diagnosed With Attention-To-Deficit Disorder

WASHINGTON, DC—Pointing to massive war-time tax cuts, physicians from the Congressional Budget Office diagnosed President Bush with attention-to-deficit disorder Tuesday. "The president exhibits all the symptoms of ATDD: impulsiveness, restlessness, inability to focus on mounting U.S. debt likely to reach $400 billion by the year's end," Dr. Terrence Spellman said. "Failing to address his affliction could lead to serious long-term fiscal-health problems for future generations of Americans." To treat the president's ATDD, Spellman prescribed Ritalin and an introductory course in high-school economics.

Woman Assures Friend She Has Blackouts From Drinking All The Time

COLUMBUS, OH—When Yolanda Franks expressed concern that friend Becky O'Neill couldn't remember the second half of an apartment-warming party Saturday, O'Neill assured her that she has blackouts all the time. "It's no big deal," O'Neill said Tuesday. "Sure, I had a bit too much to drink, but I got to work Monday fine. No need to worry." O'Neill added that she just shakes off her frequent blackouts, as she does the occasional unplanned pregnancy.

Suicide Hotline Operator Talking To Ex-Boyfriend Again

ABERDEEN, WA—Volunteers at the Helping Heart ~~Crisis~~ Hotline announced Tuesday that Candice Knoff, 25, is on the phone with her attention-starved ex-boyfriend Tony Hewitt again. "Tony always calls right after he runs into Candy on the street," said Jeanne Teal, one of Knoff's coworkers. "He spends an hour going on and on about how he's been so depressed ever since they broke up, even though it's been like a year. I can always tell it's him, because Candy'll be over there rolling her eyes the entire call." According to the other volunteers, Hewitt has called the hotline at least once a week for the past year, except in March and April, when he was dating a waitress he met in Olympia.

Criminal Mad That Man Called The Cops On Him

OAKLAND, CA—Ben Patton, arrested Monday, said he was angry that a passerby reported him to the police. "I'm minding my own fucking business, crowbarring the door off of a Radio Shack, and some punk drives by and calls 911 on his cell phone," Patton said. "If it was his car I was breaking into, I could see him getting involved, but this is bullshit." While in custody, Patton added that he wishes he had noted the color and model of the informant's car, so he could express his irritation to the driver in person.

TAN from page 217

rusty-orange face. "It's not like you can just lay out whenever. To get an even tan, you have to know when to go tanning, and what to expose when."

Nielsen frequently offers coworkers advice on proper flipping procedures, tanning oils, and skin moisturizers.

"Stacy looks amazing," said fellow sales associate Judy Haskins, overlooking the obvious flaking and discoloration of Nielsen's epidermis, perhaps in an unconscious attempt to cope with her colleague's increasingly reptilian appearance. "I just don't see how she finds the time."

"I guess you could call tanning an addiction for me," Nielsen added, crossing a leg that resembled a hot dog forgotten on a gas grill. "But I just can't stand to look like a ghost."

Despite having taken no vacation this summer, Nielsen has managed to "get a little color," impressing her coworkers at Reliant Consumer Health Products.

"Stacy looks amazing," said fellow sales associate Judy Haskins, overlooking the obvious flaking and discoloration of Nielsen's epidermis, perhaps in an unconscious attempt to cope with her colleague's increasingly reptilian appearance. "I just don't see how she finds the time. I guess, unlike me, she has the type of complexion the sun loves."

Haskins is not the only one to unfavorably compare his or her own light skin to Nielsen's withered husk.

"I thought I had a tan, but I'm two shades lighter than Stacy," said Don Rourke, his eyes glued to the sandpapery skin revealed by Nielsen's clothing. "Well, if you ever need me to help put suntan lotion on your back, Stacy, just give me a call."

Stretching her arms over her head to reveal her ghastly burnt-ochre armpits, the sun-raped Nielsen related some tricks sunbathers can use to prematurely age their skin and increase their risk of skin cancer.

"I catch a few rays over the lunch hour if the sun's out," Nielsen said. "Then, if I have a little time after work, I drive out to the lake and relax on the pier with a Diet Coke. And, of course, I sun a lot during the weekends—at home and at the lakeshore. I make sure I'm out there during peak hours. I don't burn easily, so sunscreen isn't really necessary."

Nielsen said she looks forward to the Caribbean cruise she will take with her boyfriend in January.

"It's going to be so great getting out of Wisconsin," the leather-handbag-like Nielsen said. "By that time of the year, I'm so faded, it's embarrassing."

Stretching her arms over her head to reveal her ghastly burnt-ochre armpits, the sun-raped Nielsen related some tricks sunbathers can use to prematurely age their skin and increase their risk of skin cancer.

"I don't want to look horrible my first day on the beach, so I probably should use a sunless tanning lotion before I go," Nielsen added, twirling a hay-like stalk of blonde hair around her finger.

Dr. Helen Rasmussen, a Rochester-based clinical psychologist who specializes in sun-related psychological disorders, attributed Nielsen's ardent cultivation of her horrible tan to a broad phenomenon she calls "Climate Overcompensation Syndrome."

"People who live in cold regions are often beset with complexes over their climates," Rasmussen said. "Therefore, we see things like Wisconsinites who wear floral-print shorts during a brief snap of unseasonably warm February weather, and sorority sisters in Michigan whose keggers always seem to incorporate plastic leis and Wayfarer shades. Climate Overcompensation Syndrome results in the public nudity along mosquito-plagued Minnesota lakes, as well as the Key West screensaver popular with office workers in Illinois."

Statements made by Nielsen's boyfriend, hardware-store manager Curt Kleis, seem to support Rasmussen's theory.

"I'm going to spend as much time as possible outside with my beach bunny while we have the chance," Kleis said, using a moniker which would imply that Nielsen is a nubile, attractively sun-kissed maiden. "Before we know it, winter will be here and we'll be stuck inside with nothing to do."

"We're definitely going back to the nude beach at Mazomanie a few more times," Kleis said with a wink, oblivious to the sickening impact of his words. "Stacy wanted to work more on her 'all-over tan,' if you know what I mean."

the ONION presents:

Public-Speaking Tips

Speaking in public can be a nerve-wracking experience. Here are some tips to help you captivate an audience:

- Structure your speech to include a strong opening, a memorable conclusion, and at least six references to your wife sitting in the front row.
- Rehearse your speech in front of the mirror, if you are attractive.
- Imagining your audience naked is passé. Imagine them weak, emotionally vulnerable, and thirsty for a peer-shared breakthrough.
- Kids, if you are preparing to give a class presentation, remember to not be fat.
- Public speaking is a lot like riding your bike: It's tiring, you get sweaty, and sooner or later you take an iron bar to the nuts.
- The first step to great speech-giving is great speech-writing. And the only way to master speech-writing is to enroll in one of the many speech-writing courses at Newbury College. Newbury, where your dreams come to life.
- It's probably best to leave unverified allegations that Saddam Hussein tried to obtain uranium from Africa out of your State Of The Union address.
- Your audience is just as afraid of you as you are of it. Don't make any sudden movements.
- Posture is important! When speaking, insert your left hand into your toga and extend your right hand toward the heavens.
- As a public speaker, you should always be given snacks before speaking. Make this clear to the audience as soon as you get on stage: No snacks, no speech.
- "Weird Al" Yankovic performs in front of large groups of strangers all the time. If that freak can do it, you ought to be able to manage.
- Remember, girls: Pear-shaped vowels, crisp consonants. Inhale through the nose, delivering the air to the diaphragm. Exhale in a graceful, circular movement. (This tip courtesy of Miss Eleanor Carlton, headmistress of Miss Carlton's Finishing Academy For Exemplary Young Women, established 1932.)
- The oldest, best-known public-speaking tip still applies: Shut the fuck up, jackass.

FACTOID from page 217

roe, the fifth U.S. president. I thought, 'Wow. That's interesting, and also easy to remember.'"

"Liberia has 1585 kilometers of borders—with Cote d'Ivoire, Guinea, and Sierra Leone," Sieber continued. "But get this: That's only 72 more than the number of ships in the nation's merchant marine."

Václav Mikulka, the team's legal counsel, told reporters he unearthed

"I was completely unaware that, until 1999, Liberia had two different $1 bills: the JJ Roberts and the Liberty," Abdallah said. "I also didn't know that Liberian soccer player George Weah, named the World's Best Player in 1995, is known as the 'Lion King.'"

his first item of trivia shortly after landing in Monrovia.

"Liberian taxis are a bargain!" Mikulka said. "You can travel from downtown to Sinkor for 15 Liberian dollars or 38 cents American!"

According to spokesman Ahmedou Ould Abdallah, the U.N. was "pretty surprised" by the team's report.

"I was completely unaware that, until 1999, Liberia had two different $1 bills: the JJ Roberts and the Liberty," Abdallah said. "I also didn't know that Liberian soccer player George Weah, named the World's Best Player in 1995, is known as the 'Lion King.'"

Abdallah said the U.N. plans to act on the findings immediately, by distributing them to the media along with pictorial representations of the facts.

"To increase our understanding of

Above: The factoid-finding team collects data about Liberia's biggest, smallest, longest, and shortest.

the confusing situation in Liberia, we'll need to see some colorful icons," Abdallah said. "But for now, try this one on for size: Although Liberia has 47 airports, only two of them are paved. Isn't that interesting? Two of 47!"

After waiting patiently for Abdallah to complete his comments, Kenzo Oshima, Undersecretary-General for Humanitarian Affairs and a four-time *Jeopardy!* winner, provided a short list of his own favorite Liberia factoids.

"Well, some of the research team's findings were pretty good, but did you know..." Oshima said, pausing briefly for dramatic effect, "that the original settlement of Liberia was purchased for trade goods, supplies, weapons, and rum worth approximately $3,000? What a steal! How about this: Liberia's oldest known resident is Moriba Magassouba. He's a retired farmer living outside of Liberia's second-largest city Zwedru, and just turned 103!"

"Did you know... that last year, Liberia received 200 inches of rain?" Oshima added. "Oh, and watch out, because in Liberia, kissing is considered a dirty and disrespectful act."

White House Press Secretary Scott McClellan said he was excited both by the facts themselves and by their potential impact on Liberia.

"We're hoping this report leads to a better understanding of Liberia, so that we can move toward solving its many problems... and those of the rest of the African continent, too," McClellan said. "And get this: Hilary Johnson, elected in 1884, was Liberia's first native-born president. I'll bet you would've thought it was later."

"Look at this factoid: The youngest of the children who fought in Liberia's civil war were, get this, only 6 years old. Crazy world, eh? Truth is stranger than fiction, I say." ⌀

BOOK from page 219

library and got lots of other ones, too. I've been reading them all week. My favorites are *The Berenstain Bears Forget Their Manners* and *The Berenstain Bears Visit The Dentist*. Others are super good, too."

Added Bishop: "Melody found them first. But I think I understand them a little better. I'm like Sister Bear. She says something, and I think, 'That's what I would say.'"

Johnson, who has been reading above her grade level for the past two years, does not view reading as a contest.

"I'm happy to have the books," said Johnson, who reports she used to take things she was given for granted, but no longer. "Like in *Count Their Blessings*. There [are] lots of good things that you want to happen, but you probably already have a lot of good things, so remember to be happy about those. That is just so true."

Johnson's mother agreed that her daughter's outlook has changed for the better.

"Not only has she learned a lot of life lessons, but she also learned to ride a bike without training wheels," Carrie Johnson said. "She never fights naptime anymore, and she's making great strides with her violin playing. I haven't seen her this inspired since last year, when she was blown away by getting to shake hands with the Three Little Pigs at Storybook Gardens." ⌀

SILENT AUCTION from page 206

amounts of blood. Passersby were amazed by the unusually large amounts of blood. Passersby were amazed by the unusually large amounts of blood. Passersby were amazed by the unusually large amounts of blood. Passersby were amazed by the unusually large amounts of blood. Passersby were amazed by the unusually large amounts of blood. Passersby were amazed by the unusually large amounts of blood. Passersby were amazed by the unusually large amounts of blood. Passersby were amazed by the unusually large amounts of blood. Passersby were amazed by the unusually large amounts of blood. Passersby were amazed by the unusually large amounts of blood. Passersby were amazed by the unusually large amounts of blood. Passersby were amazed by the unusually large amounts of blood. Passersby were

I have an irrelevant personal anecdote for any occasion.

amazed by the unusually large amounts of blood. Passersby were amazed by the unusually large amounts of blood. Passersby were amazed by the unusually large

see SILENT AUCTION page 229

COMMUNITY VOICES

I'm Not One Of Those People Who Goes Around Having Fun

By Geoffrey Hebert

So, you're all going out tonight after work for a few drinks at the bar down the street? Well, thanks for the invite, but no, thanks. Fraternization with coworkers may be fun, but let me make one thing clear: I'm not one of those people who goes around having fun.

I know you people like to gather around Laura's work station and joke about the sign on the copy machine or the socks the FedEx man wears. I'm sure it's really enjoyable. I'm sure you all have a good time. As for me, I just can't relate to the way people attempt to enrich their lives with social interaction. I, for one, have better things to do with my time. You know, like the work we get paid to do?

While you're all chattering away, filling each other's heads with office gossip, I'm using my time constructively. I'm not running around, shooting my mouth off, telling jokes, and schmoozing. There are files to be filed, papers to be sorted, proposals to be written. Idle hands are the devil's tools, and I'm certainly not going to let them lead me down the road to delighting myself.

I notice you all seem to get a kick out of Larry's antics. That's fine for Larry,

I know you people like to gather around Laura's work station and joke about the sign on the copy machine or the socks the FedEx man wears. I'm sure it's really enjoyable. I'm sure you all have a good time. As for me, I just can't relate to the way people attempt to enrich their lives with social interaction.

I guess. But you won't see me running around, saying "Everyone, pay attention to me! I am not a robot! I have a need to interact with others." No, I will be in my office, in my chair, with both of my feet on the floor under my desk.

Why spend time frivolously when there are tasks and problems in the world? If everyone thought that having fun was a worthwhile endeavor, nothing of import would ever be accomplished. Everyone would be

While you're all chattering away, filling each other's heads with office gossip, I'm using my time constructively. I'm not running around, shooting my mouth off, telling jokes, and schmoozing. There are files to be filed, papers to be sorted, proposals to be written.

playing games or appreciating music or reading glossy four-color magazines. Meanwhile, the whole world would fall apart. Well, I won't be party to the downfall of mankind through wanton acts of indiscreet enjoyment.

My time is too valuable to be spent indulging in lighthearted activities that "increase the quality of my life." Life is meant for living meticulously, not for the trifles of gratifying amusement. So, no, I don't care to sign the card for Sheila.

Have you ever seen me goof off? No, you haven't. I don't go for that namby-pamby personal happiness. For me, there is nothing quite like an evening at home balancing my checkbook or scrubbing the grout between my bathroom tiles. That is what it means to be human: to finish chores.

True, you all seem to derive enjoyment from bonding with your fellow man. Well, leave me out of it. I'll take an evening of hard work and intense concentration any day.

You may have a need to form relationships with other humans, and participate in the community at large, but I am well above such trivialities. It's just not my style to engage others in a mutually enjoyable interchange of thoughts or ideas.

I know my words are falling on deaf ears. I don't expect to change any minds with my little speech here. I just want to give you something to ponder tonight as you're out there indulging in senseless, nonconstructive recreation. Perhaps someday you'll see the wisdom of what I'm saying. As for now, just go on without me and have your "fun." ⌀

HOROSCOPES

Your Horoscope

By Lloyd Schumner Sr.
Retired Machinist and
A.A.P.B.-Certified Astrologer

Aries: (March 21–April 19)
Your threats to the other bar-goers would have seemed a lot more frightening if your Vespa hadn't stalled while you were trying to race away.

Taurus: (April 20–May 20)
Whatever else happens this week, you should not miss the Taurus Summer Blowout Sale, going on right now.

Gemini: (May 21–June 21)
You will learn that he whom the gods would destroy, the gods first treat to a whole bunch of delicious pancakes.

Cancer: (June 22–July 22)
Three wonders will you see this week: seven falling stars, a rainbow 'round the moon, and a person drinking Stoli Vanilla whom you don't want to hit.

Leo: (July 23–Aug. 22)
Remember to take baby steps. There is no reason to rush something major like a trip to Miami.

Virgo: (Aug. 23–Sept. 22)
There are things that people weren't meant to know. In spite of what you think, however, that doesn't include everything.

Libra: (Sept. 23–Oct. 23)
Although you've certainly slept your way somewhere, no one would ever mistake it for the top.

Scorpio: (Oct. 24–Nov. 21)
You will magically transform yourself from the nice lady in human resources to the bad girl of goat porn.

Sagittarius: (Nov. 22–Dec. 21)
The "astronomers" say Mars is now closer to Earth than it will be for 60,000 years, but you know it's really rising in Sagittarius.

Capricorn: (Dec. 22–Jan. 19)
Take heart: The worst is over. Nevertheless, the fact remains that "life as normal" is nothing to write home about.

Aquarius: (Jan. 20–Feb. 18)
The fairness of destiny isn't ours to judge, but if you feed hot sauce to a Rottweiler, you deserve everything you get.

Pisces: (Feb. 19–March 20)
A little hard work never hurt anyone—unless, like you, they were trying to move 16 beef sides off an assembly line during a runaway meat-warehouse fire.

BLASTULA from page 214

amounts of blood. Passersby were amazed by the unusually large amounts of blood. Passersby were amazed by the unusually large amounts of blood. Passersby were amazed by the unusually large amounts of blood. Passersby were amazed by the unusually large amounts of blood. Passersby were amazed by the unusually large amounts of blood. Passersby were amazed by the unusually large amounts of blood. Passersby were amazed by the unusually large amounts of blood. Passersby were amazed by the unusually large amounts of blood. Passersby were amazed by the unusually large amounts of blood. Passersby were amazed by the unusually large amounts of blood. Passersby were amazed by the unusually large amounts of blood. Passersby were amazed by the unusually large amounts of blood. Passersby were amazed by the unusually large amounts of blood. Passersby were amazed by the unusually large amounts of blood. Passersby were amazed by the unusually large amounts of blood. Passersby were amazed by the unusually large amounts of blood. Passersby were

You can buy a soda for 10 cents less in a machine 18 blocks west of here.

amazed by the unusually large amounts of blood. Passersby were amazed by the unusually large amounts of blood. Passersby were amazed by the unusually large amounts of blood. Passersby were amazed by the unusually large amounts of blood. Passersby were amazed by the unusually large amounts of blood. Passersby were amazed by the unusually large amounts of blood. Passersby were amazed by the unusually large

see BLASTULA page 227

the ONION®

VOLUME 39 ISSUE 33 AMERICA'S FINEST NEWS SOURCE™ 28 AUG.–3 SEPT. 2003

NEWS

King Latifah Returns For Wife

see PEOPLE page 8C

Old El Paso Introduces Emergency Taco Kit

see BUSINESS page 3E

Scissors Kills Paper, Rock; Turns Blade On Self

see LOCAL page 6D

Rear End Justifies Means

see LOCAL page 5D

STATshot

A look at the numbers that shape your world.

With Whom Are We Avoiding Eye Contact?
1. Mr. Nicholson
2. Other undercover cop
3. Miss Hawaiian Tropic 1982
4. Friendly transsexual in bunny suit
5. Medusa
6. Puppy who saw the whole thing

THE ONION • $2.00 US • $3.00 CAN

Mad Scientist's Plot Thwarted By Budget Cuts

Above: Mortis packs up the lab he was forced to surrender.

UPTON, NY—In response to recent budget cuts, the National Science Foundation has reduced grants to individual recipients, including those of megalomaniacal researcher Dr. Edward Mortis of Brookhaven Laboratories.

"My positronic raygun was nearly complete," Mortis said at a press conference Tuesday. "With one gigagram of destructonium [a rare element mined from a meteor belt that passes Earth once every 29 years], I could have ruled the world!"

Days before the window of destructonium-mining opportunity closed, the "ignorant fools" at the NSF slashed Mortis' Armageddon Project funding by 90 percent. The cut in funding forced the mad scientist to halt work on his raygun, and set back his plans for world domination indefinitely.

"This is a dark day for mad science," Mortis said. "On this day, my evil plans are like the seed that lands on stone, unable to take root and blossom."

The principles of Mortis' Armageddon Project were explored in his doctoral dissertation, written and researched while he was a student at

see MAD SCIENTIST page 226

No One Makes It To Burning Man Festival

GERLACH, NV—The Burning Man festival, a prominent artistic and countercultural event that draws tens of thousands of people to the Nevada desert annually, is in danger of cancellation this week because "no one had their shit together enough to even make it," organizers said Tuesday.

"Jesus Christ, this is pathetic," event coordinator Ethan Moon said as he angrily gestured toward the empty Black Rock Desert basin expanse, known as the playa. "We've been promoting this thing all year. You can't start panhandling quarters for gas the week before the festival and expect to make it here in time, man."

Moon listed some of the most common no-show excuses, among them oversleeping, forgetting to request time off work, faulty van-borrowing arrangements, a shortage of ochre body-paint, and the last-minute realization that transportation to the Burning Man festival requires money.

"As of a few weeks ago, or even a few days ago, there

see BURNING MAN page 227

Above: The empty Burning Man festival grounds.

Graphic Artist Carefully Assigns Ethnicities To Anthropomorphic Recyclables

Left: Characters from the culturally sensitive Department of Sanitation leaflet.

PHILADELPHIA—Freelance graphic artist Chrissie Bellisle carefully delineated the ethnicities, genders, and sexual orientations of the Recycla-Buddies, a group of talking recyclables created for a public-service leaflet she submitted to the Department of Sanitation Monday.

"I assumed the Department of Sanitation would want the recyclables in its new leaflet to represent not only Philadelphia's recycling procedures, but also its diverse ethnic make-up," Bellisle said, flipping

Above: Bellisle in her studio.

see ARTIST page 226

The Ten Commandments Ruling

State Supreme Court justices recently ordered that a Ten Commandments monument be removed from the Alabama Judicial Building. What do *you* think?

"At the rate the liberals are going, it won't be long before our country has an official policy mandating the separation of church and state."

Stanley Welty
Systems Analyst

"I support its removal. A monument to the Ten Commandments is a graven image, and therefore blasphemous."

Opal Burch
Loan Counselor

"Alabama was just using that monument as a cheap, easy way to score some God points anyway."

Lawrence Petty
Program Director

"People can be so stupid about religion. I always have to explain my 'I'm A Fundament-tail-ist!' T-shirt to people. It means I like ass-fucking, all right?"

Jeff Rawson
Groundskeeper

"I know they have to take down the big granite monument at the Judicial Building, but what about the small tin sign tacked up in the Negro Courtshack?"

Kay Sines
Talent Director

"Let them have their statue. It's Alabama. No one there can read it anyway."

Arthur Serra
Order Filler

The New Energy Bill

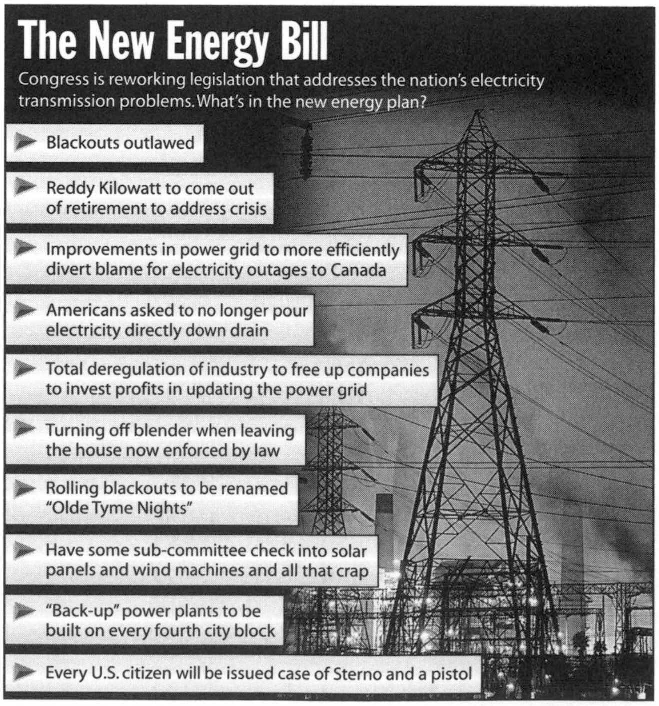

Congress is reworking legislation that addresses the nation's electricity transmission problems. What's in the new energy plan?

- Blackouts outlawed
- Reddy Kilowatt to come out of retirement to address crisis
- Improvements in power grid to more efficiently divert blame for electricity outages to Canada
- Americans asked to no longer pour electricity directly down drain
- Total deregulation of industry to free up companies to invest profits in updating the power grid
- Turning off blender when leaving the house now enforced by law
- Rolling blackouts to be renamed "Olde Tyme Nights"
- Have some sub-committee check into solar panels and wind machines and all that crap
- "Back-up" power plants to be built on every fourth city block
- Every U.S. citizen will be issued case of Sterno and a pistol

the ONION®
America's Finest News Source.™

Herman Ulysses Zweibel
Founder

T. Herman Zweibel
Publisher Emeritus
J. Phineas Zweibel
Publisher
Maxwell Prescott Zweibel
Editor-In-Chief

Perhaps I've Been A Little Too Tough On Crime

By Greg Shechtman
District Attorney

As district attorney of Grand Rapids, I've got a lot of responsibility. This job keeps me running day and night. But with all the prosecuting and sentencing I've been doing lately, I've started to think that maybe I've been a little tough on crime.

Now, don't get me wrong. I want to stamp out crime as much as the next D.A., but sometimes I think I've come down just a wee bit hard on it. I know we're supposed to be getting criminals off the streets, teaching them about consequences, and all that. But aren't there nicer ways of going about it, without all the arresting and incarcerating?

Just the other day, I was at the sentencing for Donnell Williams, a 22-year-old responsible for a string of burglaries on the West Side. The judge, a hard-liner, handed Donnell the maximum sentence: a two-to-five. Just like that. *Two to five years.* You should have seen Donnell's face as they led him away. He looked so disappointed. I said to myself, "Why do we have to give him jail time? Why can't we just tell him that this time we're *serious*, that this is his last chance *or else*?"

Heck, I've done some things I'm not proud of. I used to sell fireworks when I was a boy. In college, I sometimes skipped my afternoon classes to drink beer.

I firmly believe that lawbreakers should be held accountable for their actions. On the other hand, I'm kind of a softie. A couple aggravated assaults here and there—who's counting? The summers are hot here. I can't blame some of these guys for blowing off a little steam. Who am I to tell them what they should or shouldn't do? Sometimes, even I find myself being a little short with my wife, or raising my voice with my kids. It doesn't feel right to punish violent criminals every time they assault some landlord with a pipe. I get off scot-free every time I head down to the batting cages to release my tension. And let's not even talk about speeding. My Lumina doesn't know the meaning of the phrase "speed limit."

Instead of taking a bite out of crime, we should take a chance on a criminal. Let's give him the benefit of the doubt. Criminals live up to the expectations we have of them. If we treat criminals like criminals, that's exactly how they're going to behave: like criminals. What if, instead of writing up a ticket, we pulled over a reckless driver and told him that we weren't mad, just disappointed? We could tell him that we know he feels bad about his misdeeds, and then we could tell him that we're willing to give him the chance to right his wrongs on his own terms.

I firmly believe that lawbreakers should be held accountable for their actions. On the other hand, I'm kind of a softie.

People forget that criminals are people, too. When the police haul a guy in for holding up a convenience store with a handgun, I know I'm supposed to prosecute him for armed robbery. But sometimes, I can't help but think we'd all be a lot better off if I gave him a slap on the wrist, and then the two of us went for a drive through the nature conservatory.

At the end of the day, criminals will be criminals. Even with all the huffing and puffing down here at city hall, people are committing crimes as much as ever. So, I say, why not stop harassing the criminals? Let's loosen up a little. If we don't, it's only going to make these guys rebel.

Heck, I've done some things I'm not proud of. I used to sell fireworks when I was a boy. In college, I sometimes skipped my afternoon classes to drink beer. I was even late making a rent payment a couple months ago. I learned my lessons the hard way. No, I was never put in front of a court, but I was prosecuted by a much harsher D.A.: my conscience.

Maybe we should sit down with these felons and try to connect with them, instead of always getting on their cases. If criminals felt like they could confide in us, we'd probably stop a lot of crimes before they even happened. From now on, instead of "three strikes and you're out," I'm trying "three strikes and let's talk about it." Ø

Horrified Teen Stumbles Upon Divorced Mom's Personal Ad

NEWTON, MA—Derek Friedman, 16, was "shocked and disgusted" Tuesday, when he discovered a personal ad posted by his mother Susan on the popular online dating service Match.com.

Friedman, a junior at the Commonwealth School in Cambridge, MA, was in his room reading the personals listings with friends when he discovered his mother's ad.

"There were tons of hilarious personals for people right in my hometown," Friedman said. "All these pathetic people looking for 'friendship,' and these really horny people looking for 'a night of no-strings-attached passion,' and shit like that. But after I found Mom's ad, the other ads didn't seem so funny anymore."

SweetFunSue372's ad begins: "Attractive, divorced, 43-year-old woman who loves spending time outdoors, going to movies, and her 16-year-old son. Looking for a 40- to 50-year-old man to accompany me to museums, jazz clubs, and the beach. Afterwards, maybe we can come home and cuddle?"

James Phillips, Friedman's oldest friend, said he'd never seen Friedman so upset.

"Derek was reading the ad out loud," Phillips said. "To us, it sounded like a boring one—pretty standard. But we could tell something was up, because he kept reading more and more slowly. Then he started scrolling through the ad and shaking his head, as if he couldn't understand what he was reading."

When he clicked on the "See Picture" button, Friedman's worst fears were confirmed. Adding insult to injury, the photo of his mother was one Friedman had taken earlier this year.

According to Phillips, Friedman said "She hates the outdoors" three times, and then remained quiet for several minutes.

Friedman's friends were uncharacteristically circumspect about the disgusting ad. Their restraint was surprising, especially considering the teasing that Friedman has experienced in the past. Several of his classmates have repeatedly said that they consider Friedman's mother "bangin'."

The only remarks came from Jared Ricks, a fellow junior at Commonwealth, who heard about the ad from Phillips.

"Yo, D, I left a voicemail for your moms but she ain't called me back," Ricks said. "I told her I like long walks and hot fucking."

The ad seems to explain a recent increase in phone calls to the Friedman household.

"We started getting a lot of calls to the house," Friedman said. "These guys would ask for Susan, but when I asked for their names, they'd act real awkward about it and ask to talk to Susan again. When I asked Mom about them, she said they were friends."

"I knew the guys were asking her out, because she took the calls in the laundry room and laughed a lot," he added. "But I assumed [the callers] were people she'd met at work, or through friends or something. Even at the grocery store. I never thought she'd do anything like advertise herself."

Above: A "seriously freaked out" Friedman scrolls through the Match.com web site.

Although the revolting personal ad disturbed Friedman, it was not the first sign that his mother, who divorced his father Michael in August 2001, was jump-starting her dating life.

"A few months ago, I was flipping through one of those underwear catalogs that my mom gets," Friedman said. "She'd circled all this black-lace, strapless stuff, and a couple of thongs. Now I know she's gonna wear that stuff for some guy she met on the Internet. That's so nasty."

see TEEN page 226

NEWS IN BRIEF

Son In Iraq Or Something

VICKSBURG, MS—Fabric-store manager Bonnie Reedner told reporters Monday that her 18-year-old son, Pfc. Matthew Reedner, is "over there, fighting in Iraq, or something." "I guess he's stationed in Baghdad or Basra—some place beginning with a B," Reedner said. "I don't really know. I should check the return address on one of his letters. I think there's another one over on the microwave with the unopened mail." Though Reedner said she hopes for her son's safe return, she admitted she should probably pick up a newspaper one of these days to get an idea of when that might be.

Woman Only Dates On National Television Now

HOLLYWOOD—After stints on *Temptation Island*, *The Bachelor*, and *For Love Or Money*, 23-year-old bartender/model Angela Langdon announced Monday that she refuses to date anyone who's not courting her in a front of a national TV audience. "Unless there's the promise of a million-dollar payday, a romantic evening in the tropics, or a humiliating rejection in front of all of America, I'm not interested," Langdon told potential suitors. "Come with cameras, or don't come at all." Langdon also expressed a preference for network shows over those in syndication.

Public Urinator Gives Passerby Dirty Look

TALLAHASSEE, FL—While walking past a house party on Tripoli Avenue early Sunday morning, Howard Lipner, 20, received a withering look from an unidentified public urinator. "He was taking a leak right there in the front yard, not even behind a bush, or garbage can, or anything," Lipner said. "And he gives me this look, like, 'What are you looking at? Can't you see I'm trying to take a piss?' As if it's my fault for walking on a public sidewalk while he's out there taking a leak, like the king of Sheba." Lipner assured reporters that he intentionally avoided looking at the urinator's penis, because he's "not some kind of perv."

Great Lover Also Great At Slinking Out

MANITOU SPRINGS, CO—According to a number of area women, the lovemaking abilities of the handsome and gregarious Ken Millagro are matched only by his ability to quietly slink out the door after a night of passion. "I'll spare you the details, but Ken was really, really good in the sack," 35-year-old Heather Yorgrau said Sunday, the morning after meeting Millagro at a friend's birthday party. "He was also really, really good at getting out of the sack without waking me up. He was absolutely amazing at not tripping over the shoes on the floor, leaving the noisy fan in the bathroom off, and quietly managing the locks on the front door." Millagro was unable to be found for comment.

Japan Spotted Hovering Over Algeria

ALGIERS, ALGERIA—Japan continued to vex the world Monday, as numerous eyewitnesses saw the exotic and mysterious Pacific Rim country hovering over the mountainous coastal regions of Algeria. "I noticed it up there around noon," said Ahmed Boumediènne, a farmer whose land lay in the 1,744-mile shadow temporarily cast by the floating archipelago. "The schoolchildren were having a great time waving at it. But, when I came out after lunch, it was gone again. Must have moved on." Boumediènne added that no one was threatened by Japan's serene presence. As of press time, the Japanese islands were back in the Pacific Ocean. ⌀

MAD SCIENTIST from page 223

Berkeley in the late '70s. Mortis' three-tiered approach to conquering the universe so impressed Brookhaven Laboratories that he was hired out of graduate school and placed in the facility's dilapidated-castle wing.

"For a time, I had unlimited funding, free rein over a well-equipped lab, and eight henchmen at my disposal," Mortis said. "Then, when the economy went south, the NSF started chipping away at my allotment. First, it was a nosy question here, a rudely worded letter there. Suddenly, I was being asked to justify the purchase of every little dicantheum deoxidationifier or Anubis drill in my inventory."

Last week, a letter from the NSF informed Mortis that his annual grant will be reduced substantially, from $2 billion a year to a mere $200 million. According to Mortis, the budget cuts will effectively terminate both the Armageddon Project and his work on several outside efforts, including a hyperchronal disrupter, a polysonic transmogricon, and 100,000 killer robots.

"They expect me to work with $200 million?" Mortis said. "My legion of armed robots now sits in a storage center outside D.C. The robots have been denied the very function of their being! I ask, what good are killer robots if they will never be activated and set to killing? It's so typical that the buffoons at NSF stop me now, when I'm already half done. It's so frustrating."

"These pencil-pushers don't appreciate the purity of research," Mortis continued. "As Plato said, the love of knowledge is the purest form of love. I would go further and say that the greatest quest for knowledge is the quest for insane knowledge. All these bureaucrats see is columns of numbers on paper."

Mortis said his only option is to pursue his mad agenda independently, by working at a slower pace and paying for expenses out-of-pocket. To that end, Mortis has taken a position as an adjunct researcher on a longitudinal study of the effects of cholesterol in adolescents, and is proofreading a report on the distribution of freshwater mussels in the lower Great Lakes drainage region.

"That never would have happened if I'd had the funds to do a test run of the polysonic transformation process," Mortis said. "But I was forced to cut corners. I was the laughingstock of the mad scientific community."

Mortis said he is keenly aware of the effects a limited budget can have on mad scientific research. In May, he attracted national attention when he unleashed a horde of beast men in Denver, CO. The release was successful, until the hideous creatures' unstable molecular structure reacted with the city's low air pressure, and the beasts dissolved into gooey blue puddles.

"That never would have happened if I'd had the funds to do a test run of the polysonic transformation process," Mortis said. "But I was forced to cut corners. I was the laughingstock of the mad scientific community."

Mortis was not charged with any crime in the Denver incident, due to the vaporization of all evidence, and he returned to his lab with a new sense of purpose, vowing to "show them all." But Mortis had not anticipated the recent budget cuts.

"Mad-scientific progress has been set back 20 years," Mortis said. "If you want to see yet another boring paper on relativistic heavy-ion colliders or synchrotron radiation, by all means, drain my lifeblood! But don't come crying to me when you need technologies to enslave the human race."

Even in the current financial climate, the budget cuts surprised Mortis' colleagues.

"We all thought [Mortis] was untouchable," said fellow Brookhaven researcher Dr. Phillip Kondos. "Edward's genius for devising plans for world domination is second only to his genius for whipping up applications for funding. We always envied his ability to isolate himself in his dank lab and emerge days later with a hideously ingenious grant proposal all of his own creation." ⌀

ARTIST from page 223

through some initial sketches in her studio. "It turned out to be quite a challenge."

As the purpose behind establishing racial and cultural identities for the talking waste was one of celebration, not caricature, Bellisle found herself working within unusual limits.

"For reasons of basic sensitivity, you don't want to make the Chinese take-out container an Asian," Bellisle said, as she flipped past a crossed-out pencil sketch of an Inuit ice-cream carton. "But, if you make the same type of container represent two different races, people notice. It's a delicate balancing act. I discovered that there were negative connotations attached to a surprising number of the things people throw out."

Although she said she is satisfied with her decision to incorporate Asiatic epicanthic folds into the eyes of an age-discolored stack of newspapers, Bellisle admitted that infusing everyday household garbage with easily recognizable racial traits—while avoiding demeaning stereotypes—is difficult.

"It took me forever to get this trash can to look like a black guy, especially around the nose," said Bellisle, who noted that she discarded close to 30 preliminary characters, among them a Native American milk carton, a Filipino cereal box, and a stack of East Indian wire-hangers. "I finally made the green recycling drum a woman, which was great, since a garbage can is kind of husky, and I could get around the sexy-garbage/body-image

see ARTIST page 227

TEEN from page 225

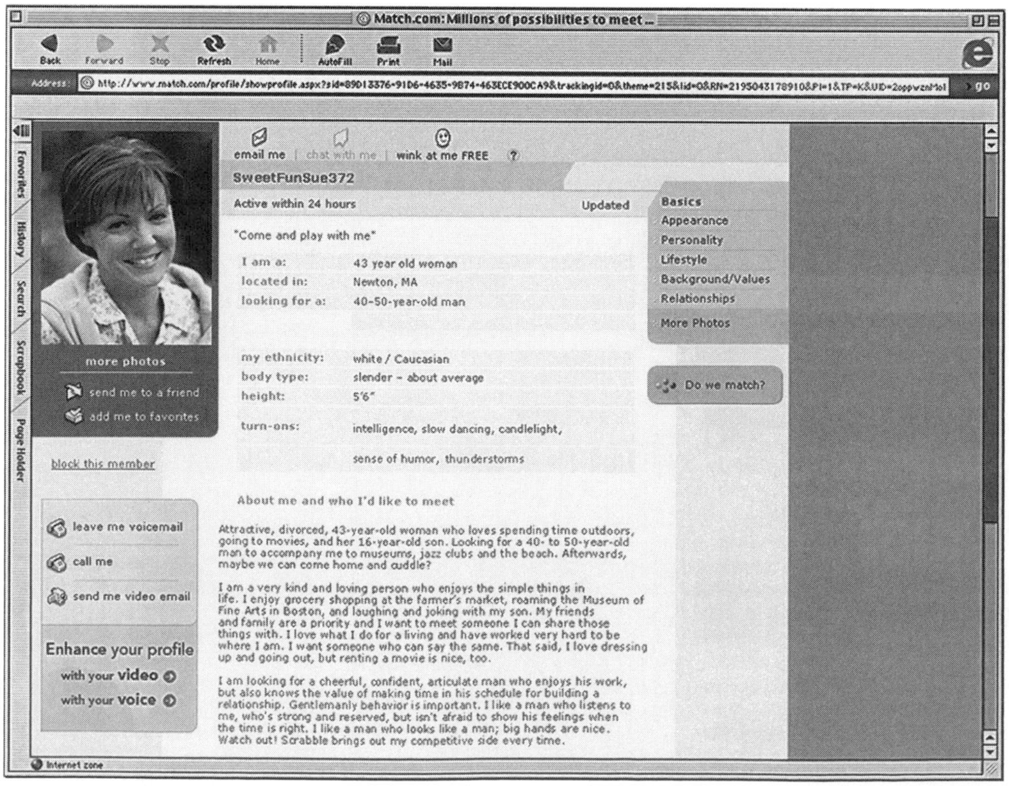

Above: The stomach-turning ad.

In spite of his initial shock, Friedman said he understands that his mother is an adult with a normal human desire for companionship.

"I know, I need to let her live her life and move on and everything," Friedman said. "And she's been lonely since she divorced Dad, but an Internet dating service? She must be *so desperate*. I never knew things were so bad for her."

According to psychiatrist Ann Cohen, author of *Post-Divorce, Pre-Death*, an event like Tuesday's discovery can shake a teenager's entire sexual worldview.

"A child's realization that his mother is a sexual being usually comes during pre-pubescence for boys, at around 11 or 12," Cohen said. "But that association fades quickly when the boy turns from an inexperienced child into a sexualized teenager. After that, the mother becomes an anti-sex-symbol, a purified ideal of womanhood who's above, or at least outside, the realm of normal animalistic impulses. For a teenager like Derek, it must be incredibly traumatic to see his mother put herself on the dating market like a side of beef."

Added Cohen: "Think about it—your own mom? Looking for sex? Disgusting!" ⌀

ARTIST from page 226

issue."

Added Bellisle: "That brings another problem to light: If you include one woman in the mix, no one cares what race she is. As if one female recycling drum can represent female recycling drums of all races, but male recyclables deserve further distinction."

Drawing friendly, nondescript male characters is not the answer, Bellisle said.

"Look at this grinning soda can giving the thumbs-up here," she said. "Everyone subconsciously assumes it's a Caucasian male."

As of press time, Bellisle was still struggling with drawings for a RecyclaBuddies poster to complement the leaflet.

"I have no idea how to make the

"And I'm really not looking forward to doing the page that explains the symbols on the bottom of plastic containers," Bellisle added. "Who am I to determine which RecyclaBuddy of color is a 1 and which is a 5?"

plastic milk jug look gay," Bellisle said. "I don't want to make him a bottle of water, for obvious reasons. Maybe I'll use a soy-milk container when I draw the gay jug. Or maybe they'll let me switch him with the Chicano, this tin can here. I wasn't too pleased with the Chicano tin can to begin with, especially because my first instinct was to put tomatoes or beans on the can. Not because he's Chicano, but because he's a can."

"And I'm *really* not looking forward to doing the page that explains the symbols on the bottom of plastic containers," Bellisle added. "Who am I to determine which RecyclaBuddy of color is a 1 and which is a 5?"

Heather Franks, a public-relations official with Philadelphia's Department of Sanitation, was quick to laud Bellisle's efforts.

"We're very pleased with Chrissie's work on the RecyclaBuddies so far," Franks said. "We haven't given final approval to anything, but we've liked the range and depth of the sketches we've seen. They really provide a sense of the cultural diversity that exists in the Philadelphia trash-collection zone."

Added Franks: "We especially love that soda can giving the thumbs-up. I don't know what it is about that little guy, but we're thinking of making him the boss of the whole crew." Ø

BURNING MAN from page 223

Above: Boulder resident Paul Sandley, who was halfway to Burning Man when his truck "totally konked."

were 30,000 people who honestly planned on coming," Moon said. "In every case, however, there were, well, you know—shit happened."

Although Burning Man festivals have had no-shows in the past, Moon said he's never witnessed absenteeism on this level.

"You have to figure out a way to get here, stock up on water and extra clothing for the cold nights, and make sure you have adequate shelter," Moon said. "Apparently, the advance planning it takes to arrange those three basic things was more than anyone could handle. Sorry to be on this uptight trip, but check out the playa. Not a single nude dude in a homemade papier-mâché tribal mask as far as the eye can see."

Although Burning Man is billed on its web site as a "temporary community dedicated to radical self-expression and radical self-reliance," it became evident that the no-shows were more capable of the former than they were of the latter.

Los Angeles silkscreen artist Goldi Trewartha was among the tens of thousands of Burning Man devotees who stayed home this year.

"Yeah, I was supposed to go with Ari and Shel, but they couldn't score [Ecstasy] in time for the trip, and I forgot my bartering beads at my friend Marnie's place in Los Feliz," Trewartha said. "Oh, and I forgot to get a dog sitter."

Added Trewartha: "Shel made this great suit out of old stuffed-monkey pelts and duct tape, and he was going to hop up and down on this old trampoline he found. But his ex, Nikki, made him babysit [their daughter] Gaia while she headed out to Big Sur for a few days. I love Nikki, but sometimes she can be real flaky."

Chaz Bullard, a University of Vermont undergraduate and veteran mud person, had multiple excuses for his failure to attend the Burning Man festival.

"I totally spaced that August is 8, and I wrote down 9 in my sketchbook," Bullard said. "Oh, and I got evicted. Yeah, fuckin' Dyl up and ditches me, right, and I'm stuck owing $700, because he wasn't on the lease."

Bullard added that he contracted hepatitis from his ex-roommate's tacos.

"I totally spaced that August is 8, and I wrote down 9 in my sketchbook," Bullard said.

Moon said he has received apologetic phone calls from a squadron of recumbent bicyclists lost somewhere in southern Nebraska, a Kentucky artist whose pet python was too carsick to continue the journey, and a group of Germans who uncovered a fatal structural flaw in their "Freak Harnesses" art installation at the last minute.

Hippies were not the only counterculture group to miss the Burning Man festival. Portland-area Linux user and self-described cyberconceptualist "Free" Lance Kaegle explained his absence in an instant message from his studio.

"I was organizing this boss techno-art project called 'Off The Grid,'" Kaegle wrote. "We were going to set up computer terminals in various parts of the playa and have people use them. Then we'd feed the binary data from those terminals into this fractals program that [Silver Lake, CA software designer] Ricky [Thomas-Slater] wrote. Those fractals would be sent, on the fly, to a group of exiled Buddhist monks I befriended online. The monks would transform the fractals into a temporal sand painting, the making of which we would webcast live to everyone on the playa."

Added Kaegle: "But I had to stop working on the monk thing to finish up this Pam's Country Crafts web site I'm working on. I really need the money."

While most absences were accidental, a few were not. Doug "Crazyroot" Pycroft, a former smoothie-stand employee, has a history of missing countercultural events.

"I thought about going, but then I decided I don't need some dudes pushing their rules down my throat," Pycroft said. "That's the problem with these things. If they're so nonconformist, how come you gotta obey some fascist wearing a lanyard just to use the Port-A-John? Same reason I refused to go to [The Church Of The Subgenius'] X-Day back in '98. Hell, I ditched the very first Lollapalooza one hour in."

As a cloud of sand whipped across the desolate playa, Moon could only shake his head. Although the week-long festival traditionally culminates in the igniting of the Burning Man, a 50-foot-tall wooden structure strapped with fireworks and other incendiaries, Moon wondered aloud whether he and the handful of other staffers should even bother.

"I guess we could burn what we've built, but it would just feel anticlimactic with no one around to watch," Moon said. "You gotta look at the bigger picture here, folks. You shouldn't think of Burning Man as a burden. Burning Man is about being part of a community. Unfortunately, it's a community of people who can't get up before 1 p.m." Ø

HARVEY'S HOLLYWOOD

Billy Crystal Passed Over... Again!

Item! According to my sources, the **Emmys**—the Oscars of television—are going to be hosted by no less than seven comedians. Before you get your hopes up, I checked, and none of the hosts will be funnyman **Billy Crystal**. Now, I ask you, the esteemed Academy, why waste a golden opportunity? I'm sure the other hosts are very funny, but have they proven themselves like Billy? I doubt it.

The Outside Scoop
By Jackie Harvey

Boy, I guess no one liked **Gigli**, huh? Wrong! Even though I've had enough of the **Ben-Lo Show**, I gave the movie a try, and you know what? It was pretty good. You can see the beginning of the real-life sparks flying on screen, just like you did with **Bogey** and **Bacall** in the song "**Key Largo**." I think people reviewed Ben and J-Lo's relationship, not their movie, and that's just not fair. For the first time, I'm ashamed to be part of the entertainment-journalism community.

(By the way, did you know that Gigli is pronounced "**zhee-lee**" and not "**giggly**"? Who says you can't learn things from the movies?)

I can't wait until October. Not only will it cool down, but also, the **scary movies** will come out. I confess that I love sitting in a dark theater getting the wits scared out of me by a scary-scary movie. Not just scary, the likes of **Freddy** or **Jason**, but scary-scary, like **Michael Mayers**. His **Dr. Evil** really gives me the willies! Those creatures of the night, what music they make...

It's true what they say. It's not the **heat**, it's the **humidity**.

Item! Fox is starting the fall season early this year with the steamy beach series **The OP**. That's shorthand for Ocean Pacific, and it stars **Peter Gallagher** as a fashion designer trying to re-launch his line of beach wear while raising a juvenile-delinquent kid. I haven't seen it yet, but as soon as I get a **Tuesday** night free, I'll be right in front of my television catching the waves. How Gallagher can be on a new series while he's running for governor of California and smashing vegetables with a **mallet** is a mystery to me. I wish I had one-tenth of that man's energy.

Speaking of **California**, how about that governor's race? I don't think it's right that a minority of voters can enact a recall of a sitting governor, particularly when you consider that it only takes 65 signatures and $3,500 to enter the race. It's also not fair that the sitting governor requires a **majority vote** to remain in office, as opposed to the **plurality** an opponent needs to unseat him. But personally, I'd vote for **Arnold** any day of the week. Who's going to say no to the **Terminator**? He'll "erase" that deficit like no one else can—that's for sure.

I felt like I needed to get back to nature, so I started planning a camping trip. Just after I bought all the gear, I saw this great documentary called **Wings Migration**. I went in thinking it was about one of my 10 favorite bands, **Paul McCarthy's Wings** (#6 on the list). Turns out, I was wrong,

Fox is starting the fall season early this year with the steamy beach series *The OP*. That's shorthand for Ocean Pacific, and it stars Peter Gallagher as a fashion designer trying to re-launch his line of beach wear while raising a juvenile-delinquent kid.

but joyously so—it was actually a nature documentary full of beautiful shots of migrating birds. That pretty much took care of the outdoor urge for me. Anyone want a good deal on a tent and sleeping bag?

Boy, that **blackout** sure had everyone in a tizzy! I wasn't affected, but I was glued to the TV news coverage. I'd like to personally thank *New Yorkers* for the heroism they showed by acting like human beings during the crisis. I blew a fuse once, and I had to sit and eat all my ice cream before it melted. I can only imagine what it must have been like for people in one of the affected states.

For the life of me, I can't understand the show **Banzai**. There's so much yelling and cruelty. I tell you, if I wanted a Japanese man to yell at me, I'd move to **Vermont** and marry a Japanese man, if I were gay. Just kidding. I do love Japanese people, though. Those I've met haven't shouted nearly as much as the ones on that show.

Speaking of shows, I can't wait for the new fall TV season to start. Tops on my list of **Appointment TV Shows**? One word: **Whoopi!**

There's a lot more going on in the world of entertainment, but I only have so much space. I'll leave you with a little teaser about **Julia Roberts**' next "role" as a baker looking for a new "sweet"-heart! Hungry for more? Stay tuned for the next installment of The Outside Scoop! ø

HOROSCOPES

Your Horoscope

By Lloyd Schumner Sr.
Retired Machinist and
A.A.P.B.-Certified Astrologer

Aries: (March 21–April 19)
You'll raise self-involvement to new heights by taking the discovery of a new species of insect as a personal affront.

Taurus: (April 20–May 20)
The way you relate to others will be only subtly altered by your new habit of carrying a constantly firing Gatling gun under each arm.

Gemini: (May 21–June 21)
This week will bring you a healthy, fulfilling romance in the workplace. That will motivate you to get a goddamn job.

Cancer: (June 22–July 22)
The siren song of forbidden love will ring in your ears this week when you become sexually attracted to your town's warning klaxon.

Leo: (July 23–Aug. 22)
The world's scientists will be excited when you tell them you're growing a vestigial tail, until they realize the scatological nature of your sense of humor.

Virgo: (Aug. 23–Sept. 22)
Enough about you. This week, Virgo will be unable to shake the feeling that you never listen to her.

Libra: (Sept. 23–Oct. 23)
You'll discover a great new diet that lets you eat whatever you want while ballooning up to 450 sexy, sexy pounds.

Scorpio: (Oct. 24–Nov. 21)
It's getting harder for your loved ones to believe that you never have any spare change.

Sagittarius: (Nov. 22–Dec. 21)
The movement of planets in your sign foretells amazing romantic events this week. The stars, however, just pour out endless amounts of electromagnetic radiation.

Capricorn: (Dec. 22–Jan. 19)
People often fall in love with the person who is worst for them, which is good news for you.

Aquarius: (Jan. 20–Feb. 18)
You will find yourself lost in a strange new world in which the hairless, vaguely simian natives seem to be trying to communicate with you.

Pisces: (Feb. 19–March 20)
Don't worry if you don't understand the complex, yet seemingly effortless, unfolding of the universe. After all, you're stupid.

SQUISHY BALL from page 199

amounts of blood. Passersby were amazed by the unusually large amounts of blood. Passersby were amazed by the unusually large amounts of blood. Passersby were amazed by the unusually large amounts of blood. Passersby were amazed by the unusually large amounts of blood. Passersby were amazed by the unusually large amounts of blood. Passersby were amazed by the unusually large amounts of blood. Passersby were amazed by the unusually large amounts of blood. Passersby were amazed by the unusually large amounts of blood. Passersby were amazed by the unusually large amounts of blood. Passersby were amazed by the unusually large amounts of blood. Passersby were amazed by the unusually large amounts of blood. Passersby were amazed by the unusually large amounts of blood. Passersby were amazed by the unusually large amounts of blood. Passersby were amazed by the unusually large amounts of blood. Passersby were amazed by the unusually large amounts of blood. Passersby were amazed by the unusually large amounts of blood. Passersby were

Who dares to defy the regional manager?

amazed by the unusually large amounts of blood. Passersby were amazed by the unusually large amounts of blood. Passersby were amazed by the unusually large amounts of blood. Passersby were amazed by the unusually large amounts of blood. Passersby were amazed by the unusually large amounts of blood. Passersby were amazed by the unusually large amounts of blood. Passersby were amazed by the unusually large amounts of blood. Passersby were amazed by the unusually large amounts of blood. Passersby were

see SQUISHY BALL page 238

NEWS

Bird's Nest 65 Percent Cigarette Butts

see NATURE page 4E

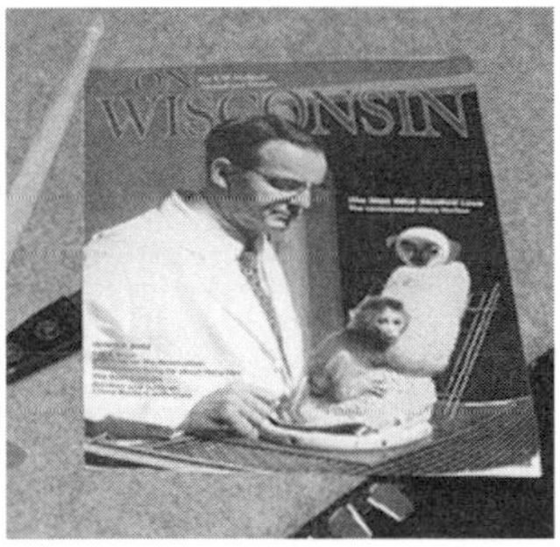

Local Band Finds Great Photo For Flier

see LOCAL page 12B

Woman Never Making Recipe From Back Of Gatorade Bottle Again

see LOCAL page 5B

Bush Calls Front Seat

see NATION page 3C

STATshot

A look at the numbers that shape your world.

How Are We Organizing The Closet?

- 10% By percentage polyester
- 16% Alphabetically, by item's use
- 8% With a cleansing fire
- 20% Promoting most-deserving stuffed animals
- 19% Cutting down backing wall, opening space into living room
- 27% Locking child inside, hoping he tidies up

the ONION®

VOLUME 39 ISSUE 34 AMERICA'S FINEST NEWS SOURCE™ 4–10 SEPTEMBER 2003

'Six Flags Killer' Still At Large, Say Souvenir-Bedecked Police

Above: Police launch a search of the Yukon Territory.

GURNEE, IL—Local authorities continue to search Gurnee's Great America theme park for a criminal dubbed "The Six Flags Killer," souvenir-laden police reported Monday.

"If you have any information that might lead to the capture of this vicious killer, please contact us immediately," a button-covered Gurnee Police Captain Jack Moynihan said at a press conference held in Carousel Plaza. "We have officers standing by on the Whizzer."

"Oh," Moynihan added. "And if you know where to get one of those blinking hats we've been seeing around, let us know."

Police began their search on Aug. 26, when ride operator Zack Lipton, 16, found a decapitated body behind the Fiddler's Fling control booth. Two days later, the remains of Six Flags employee Cory Reader were found in the bushes at the perimeter of the Yukon Territory, still inside his Wile E. Coyote suit.

Park-goers reported sightings of a blood-covered man in the vicinity of the crimes, leading police to believe that both murders were committed by the same 35- to 45-year-old Caucasian

see KILLER page 233

Above: One of four Tampa-area Tanzanias.

Tanzania Loses Name To Tanning-Salon Chain

TALLAHASSEE, FL—The country formerly known as the United Republic of Tanzania has lost the use of its name to Tampa-based Tanzania Tanning Salons, the Florida Supreme Court ruled Monday.

"Any use of my country's name constitutes infringement on the plaintiff's trademark," said Benjamin Mkapa,

see TANZANIA page 232

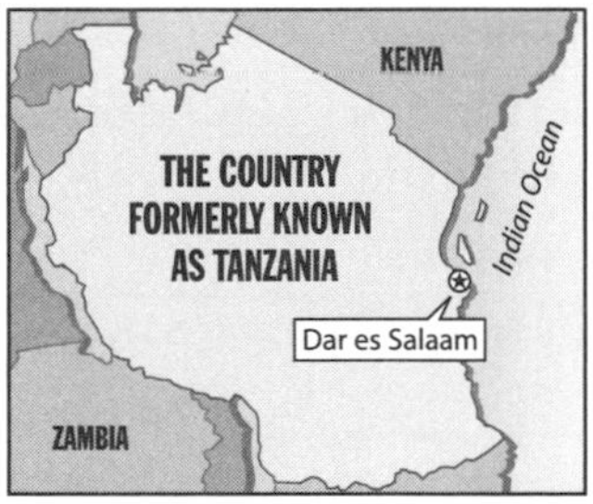

Entire Fourth-Grade Class Hates Jeremy Halcote

MUNCIE, IN—The entire fourth-grade class, everyone from Ashley Amberson to Corey Zoellner, hates Jeremy Halcote, sources at John Tyler Elementary School revealed Tuesday.

"The popular kids, the brains, even the bad kids who spend noon hour behind the groundskeeper's shed—they all hate that little pig," Indiana University sociologist Marian Newcomb told reporters Tuesday. "The consensus? Jeremy Halcote is just plain gross."

Halcote, who runs really slow, always looks sloppy, and forgets his schoolwork at home practically every other day, has been despised for as long as anyone at the school can remember.

"Last year, in Mrs. Swanson's class, Chad Vanderhof was in the bathroom with Jeremy Halcote," student Ivan Kinard said. "Well, Chad pushed Jeremy, and Jeremy's hand went right into the toilet. But Jeremy didn't even take his hand out! He just kept it in there for, like, forever."

"He started crying, too," Vanderhof added.

Students forced to stand next to Halcote in the lunch line will leave a four-foot gap between themselves and Halcote in an effort to avoid association with the undesirable fourth-grader, the report indicated. Similarly, no one wants to sit with Halcote on the bus, share an art cubbyhole

see HALCOTE page 232

Above: Miss Grant's fourth-grade class, including the hated Halcote (circled).

High U.S. Incarceration Rates

The Justice Department reports that one in every 37 U.S. adults has been in prison, giving our nation the highest incarceration rate in the world. What do *you* think?

Joe Wengert
Waiter

"Look on the bright side—36 of us are free. USA! USA! USA!"

Risa Woods-Tanouye
Receptionist

"I guess you can only talk about getting tough on crime for so long before you have to back it up with meaningless arrests."

Sarah Burns
Title Examiner

"Whoa. I'd better start cutting back on my citizen's arrests."

Anthony King
Sound Engineer

"We should privatize prisons! Not because it would help the rate of incarceration. I've just always wanted to own a prison."

Bret Christensen
Systems Analyst

"And did you know that half of the people currently serving time were prosecuted under the Anti-Skitching Act passed in 1978 to curb wintertime pranks?"

Lennon Parham
Underwriter

"But that can't be. I easily know 37 people and... Oh, wait. I forgot my stint for vehicular homicide in the '80s. Never mind."

The Shuttle Columbia Report

Last week's report by the Columbia Accident Investigation Board contained recommendations to improve the safety of future NASA missions. Among the suggestions:

- Double-check, or even triple-check, ballistics calculations
- Repair the floorboards on the shuttle Atlantis so deep space doesn't show through
- Eliminate mission control's snack- and juice-breaks during critical moments
- Stop blaring Europe's "The Final Countdown" across the pad on launch days
- Address NASA's alarming shortage of men in short-sleeved white shirts and crewcuts
- On next project, get much-needed production assistance from Pharrell Williams of The Neptunes
- NASA district managers make unannounced visits to command centers
- When a shuttle's mileage exceeds 250 million miles, it's no longer worth it to replace the engine
- Abolish mission control's shuttle-disaster office pool

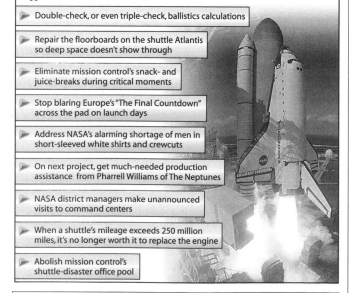

the ONION®
America's Finest News Source.™

Herman Ulysses Zweibel
Founder

T. Herman Zweibel
Publisher Emeritus
J. Phineas Zweibel
Publisher
Maxwell Prescott Zweibel
Editor-In-Chief

Living Out Of Your Car Is A Dying Art

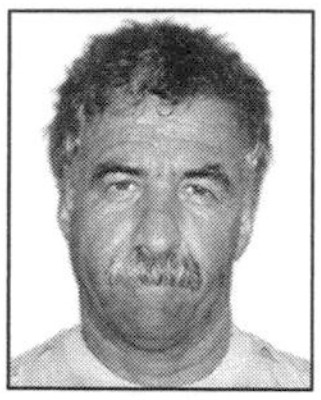

By Howard "Howie" Dassle

In the past 20 years, I've lived in nine different homes and 14 different cities. No, I'm not some fancy millionaire who jets around from place to place. I don't even own a suit for funerals. Rather, I'm one of a dying breed. I live out of my car, and I do it with pride.

Hell, there used to be legions of vehicle-dwellers like me, criss-crossing the country with no one telling us what to do, spending our nights parked next to a row of Dumpsters behind the Kmart. I still encounter people living in their Buicks, but how many of them take the time to do it with dignity anymore?

Used to be, even the young upstarts knew better than to just pull over to the curb and pass out in the driver's seat. If you do that, some cop is bound to see you and feel obligated to check your vital signs. There's a subtle science to picking a good lot to camp out in. People today don't seem to understand that. You have to consider local parking and street-cleaning ordinances, changes in seasonal temperatures, and which direction to face so the sun doesn't come beaming in on you at 6 a.m. But the real truth is that there is no formula. It's an art. When you've been living in your El Dorado for as long as I have, you can just sense which spot is the right one.

Yeah, it was different 10 years ago. Back then, vehicle-dwellers had finesse. Sure, fights would break out over a bag of hotdog buns, but we never shot or stabbed one another. We fought with our fists, and when the fists stopped flying, we watched each other's backs. Common decency—we let each other know what time a local grocery store threw out its expired milk. Now, all I see is loners who can't be bothered to share a tip about a gas station with a wheelchair-bound attendant, a busted security camera, and a pallet of motor oil waiting to be harvested. They don't give a care who you are or why you're on the road. They're a mean bunch, these new ones.

I've been in some of the cars they "live" in. I couldn't believe what I saw. One guy put his cigarette butts in the same coffee can he peed in. Have you ever smelled a cigarette that was put out in pee? That'll rank up your upholstery faster than anything. And what happens if you bring a Waffle House waitress back to that smell? She ain't staying the night, that's for sure.

I met a guy last week who didn't even have any napkins in his glove box. You can't live out of your car if you don't have the proper tools. Your glove box should contain all your vital small objects—napkins, Q-tips, disinfectant, plastic shopping bags, pens, a flashlight, your bottle, a jackknife, keys to your ex-girlfriend's son's apartment in Paducah, a few bottle openers, and your court papers. Once you've assembled the things you need, you have to take care of them. You can't leave your bolt-cutter in the trunk where it'll get rusty. It goes on the back seat, wrapped in a garbage bag.

The lack of napkins was the least of

Used to be, even the young upstarts knew better than to just pull over to the curb and pass out in the driver's seat. If you do that, some cop is bound to see you and feel obligated to check your vital signs.

this guy's problems, though. His car was filled with garbage, and not just on the floor of the passenger's side, where it belongs. When I told him that he needed to clean, he kicked the junk out the door, right onto the ground. When I'm at a rest stop, I have enough class to toss my trash under a bush, where no one has to see it.

Yeah, the old breed is dying. The new guys don't know how to look at an object and see the potential within. They don't even know how to use their clothes. Your duds deserve better than to be balled up and jammed in a plastic bag in the trunk. They're your mattress, your pillows, your blankets, your emergency coffee filters, and your towels. You gotta spread them around and have them ready for when you need them. Try telling that to these kids, and they'll just laugh at you.

Time was, we travelers took pride in our rides. Most people hang a sexy air freshener on the rear-view mirror and call that decorating. Man, this is your *home*. What's wrong with making a little effort to give the place some character? For instance, my radio busted, so I got a battery-operated one and taped it to my dash. Then, I took this picture of my kids—they're with their mom now, but I still get across town to see them a couple times a year—and hung it from the lighter knob with a rubber band. What happened to paying attention to

see CAR page 234

LOCAL

New Roommate Has Lots Of Big Redecorating Ideas

Above: Beckman (standing) suggests a decorating change to Linkater (left) and Kiely.

LAS CRUCES, NM—Dave Beckman, the newest tenant of a three-bedroom apartment in the Lincoln Crest complex, has offered numerous redecorating tips "to make the place more livable," longtime inhabitants Andrew Kiely and Marcus Linkater said Monday.

"Dave's only lived here six weeks, but he's had lots of ideas," said Linkater, who has lived in the apartment with Kiely for three years. "Like, he brought in this glass-topped coffee table to replace the old one from my parents' rec room. Other than the wobbly leg, the old table was fine. But I figured, if it mattered so much to him, so be it."

> **"Dave painted the bathroom orange," Linkater said.**

Linkater and Kiely said that Beckman has been very aggressive about "fixing the place up a little."

"Dave painted the bathroom orange," Linkater said. "We were fine with it, because he bought the paint and did all the work, but now he wants to paint all the rooms. He keeps saying, 'If we *all* pitch in, we can get it done in a weekend.' Yeah, that's true, but I don't want to waste a whole Saturday painting the stupid apartment."

Added Linkater: "One weird-colored room is fine, but doing all of them is just fruity."

Beckman has also nagged his roommates about replacing the weathered leather couch Kiely found on the curb three years ago.

"Dave said he saw this red-velveteen couch at Goodwill for $75 that he wants us to check out," Kiely said. "I keep telling him that the couch is fine. It sags a little, but we could stick a piece of plywood under the cushions, and it would be like new. This couch has history. I don't want to give up the place where I made out with Katie Linnon."

According to Linkater, Beckman began scoping out potential redecorating projects the day he moved in.

"I caught him staring at my Alice In Chains poster in the living room," Linkater said. "He said, 'Do people really care about having that poster there?' He said he had some artwork his friend Meg did that would look great in the living room. I've had that poster since I was in high school. I like it just where it is."

To date, Beckman has suggested numerous redecorating tips, including installing track lighting in the dining room, outfitting the toilet with a cushioned seat, fixing the hole in the hallway wall, and replacing the free-standing bookcases with wall-mounted shelves.

"Yesterday, he was talking about taking out the carpet," Kiely said. "I'm not spending a fucking week ripping up perfectly good carpet just because Dave thinks hardwood floors are the thing to have. Basically, we'd be working for our landlord for free."

Last week, Linkater and Kiely came home and found their dishes sitting in boxes outside their bedroom doors. According to Linkater, Beckman said his dishware "matched," unlike Linkater and Kiely's diverse collection of plates, bowls, and plastic containers. Beckman also replaced the coffee maker and the toaster with newer, more expensive models.

"So what if his stuff *is* better?" Kiely asked. "It's a dick-move to stick our shit in the hall without asking."

Beckman's most grievous suggestion to date involved the house's "Szechwan Horror Night."

"Every Tuesday, Andrew and I get takeout from Szechwan Gardens and watch horror movies," Linkater said. "At first, Dave thought it was fun, but the last two times, he suggested we try this new Cajun place. We've been getting Szechwan Gardens for two years. Why would we switch?"

"He can put candles on the end tables and hang posters of French movies in the bathroom all he wants, but you don't fuck with tradition," Linkater added.

According to Kiely, while previous roommates have been friends, Beckman was only a "friend of a friend."

"I know I barely know Dave, but the guy's kind of a jag-off," Kiely said. "We let him move in, and now he tries to give our apartment 'more character.' If I knew him better, I'd tell him to fuck off and that would be the end of it."

"I'm drawing the line here," Linkater said. "I'm not putting up with any more of his 'Wouldn't this look great here?' shit." ⊘

NEWS IN BRIEF

State Appoints Obviously Hungover Attorney

INDIANAPOLIS, IN—The State of Indiana appointed a nauseated Bill Fenniman, Esq., as legal counsel to suspected arsonist Tom Shilue Monday. "I reviewed your case, and I'd advise you that, since this is your first offense, that... ooh, man," said Fenniman, shielding his eyes from the fluorescent lights in the room. "Listen, why don't you just plead guilty? You're guilty, right?" Fenniman asked to be excused before the pretrial hearing so that he could grab some juice and a quick nap.

Hope Fades For Survivors In 1999 Turkish Earthquake

IZMIT, TURKEY—Rescuers acknowledged that hope is fading in the search for additional survivors of the massive earthquake that hit the area Tuesday, Aug. 17, 1999. "Tens of thousands of victims were pinned under the wreckage when the many poorly constructed three- and four-story commercial and residential buildings in the region collapsed in the quake," city official Ahmet Kocabiyikoglu said Monday. "Sadly, the sweltering heat and lack of water make survival chances slim for anyone still trapped in the rubble." The official death toll from the devastating earthquake reached 17,000 in November 1999.

Hog Executed Farmland Style

GRUNDY CENTER, IA—Police are investigating the vicious farmland slaying of a prize hog whose methodically gutted corpse was discovered Tuesday in the barn of local livestock farmer Lyle Whitman. "It appears the hit was done with a large butcher knife or some similar cutting implement," Grundy County Deputy Keith Angrim said at a press conference Tuesday. "The hog was hung by its feet with its belly sliced open and its head removed. In addition, all the blood had been drained from the animal's body, and its internal organs were missing." Given the meticulous but brutal nature of the killing, Angrim said he believes the hog was "taken out by a professional."

Suburbanite Shocked By Poor Condition Of Urban Mall

DEER PARK, TX—Forced to pick up a pair of shoes from a Famous Footwear at Sharpstown Mall in Houston Monday, stay-at-home mother Linda Hendrikson, 31, was reportedly shocked by the mall's condition. "It was just so sad," Hendrikson said. "The floors were dirty, the shoes were in disarray, and there didn't seem to be any management. I just can't imagine what it would be like to shop under those conditions every day." Hendrikson said she has more sympathy for the plight of the city's poor after witnessing their mall firsthand.

Jerky Boys Accidentally Prank-Call Last Remaining Fan

NEW YORK—Infamous crank phone-callers Johnny G. Brennan and Kamal Ahmed, better known as the Jerky Boys, unknowingly pranked 22-year-old videostore employee Jake Matson, their last remaining fan, Tuesday. "Hello, this is Frank Rizzo," Brennan said. "I'm throwing a bachelor party and I wanna come over there and rent some smutty animal videos. What kind you got there, sizzle-chest?" Matson, who, unlike his peers, still listens to his Jerky Boys CDs regularly, instantly recognized Brennan's voice and begged him to do a few seconds of Saul Rosenberg. ⊘

TANZANIA from page 229

president of the currently unnamed republic. "We've lost our national identity. This is a very sad day for the people once known as Tanzanians."

The United Republic of Tanzania, formed in 1964 from the union of African nations Tanganyika and Zanzibar, predates the tanning-salon chain, which opened its first store in Tampa in 1982. Nevertheless, after fewer than two weeks in court, the State of Florida granted legal rights to the name to Tanzania Salons founder and CEO Jerry Yeltzer.

"It was easy to establish that my client's company had a greater vested interest in the Tanzania brand name," Yeltzer's lawyer, Ben Knowles, said. "Tanzania, the salon chain, is a rapidly growing business, adding nearly 50 locations each year. Tanzania, the African nation, is languishing under a debt of $7 billion."

Tanzania Salons is also close to completing a lucrative deal that would put its moisturizing and replenishing cream on the shelves of retail stores across the nation, making the situation even more pressing, Knowles added.

Yeltzer said he didn't realize that the African country existed until July 2001, when a routine Internet search brought the nation to his attention. Yeltzer said he created the name for Tanzania Salons by merging the words "tan" and "zany" to suggest a lighthearted, fun approach to indoor-tanning retail.

"Tanzania, the salon chain, is a rapidly growing business," Knowles said. "Tanzania, the African nation, is languishing under a debt of $7 billion."

"When you come to a Tanzania location, you know you're in for an out-of-the-ordinary tanning experience," Yeltzer said. "Our salons are famous for their casual but professional atmosphere. Last year, four million customers visited Tanzania Salons. Can the country of Tanzania make that claim?"

Although Yeltzer refused to disclose the amount of money he spent to bring the trademark-infringement suit against the country, he said it was "sizable." His team of lawyers delivered the first cease-and-desist order to the nation of Tanzania in August 2001, but received no response from Mkapa until January 2003, when the letters were finally translated into Swahili.

"Had Mkapa changed the name when we asked, he could have saved his country all those legal fees," Yeltzer said. "Our lawyers know what they're doing. They're not afraid to take on a midsized African country."

"We are the third-largest tanning-salon chain in Florida," Yeltzer added.

Mkapa said he plans to raise funds to appeal the decision and blames poor preparation for his country's loss.

"We're in the right, but we simply didn't have the resources to assemble our case," Mkapa said. "Our government is dealing with an AIDS epidemic affecting an estimated 800,000 people and food shortages caused by this season's erratic rainfall. Also, I must admit, we didn't realize we might actually lose our name to a chain of tanning salons in Florida."

Lose they did, and changing the name of the former Tanzania is likely to cost millions of dollars, driving the country even further into debt.

"We're one of the poorest nations in the world," Mkapa said. "Changing all of our signs and official stationery is going to be expensive."

Tanzania Salons also filed a civil suit against the African country, demanding $85 million for court costs and damage done to the salon's brand.

"By using the name of my client's franchise, the United Republic of Tanzania did irreparable damage to the business' sparkling reputation," Knowles said. "As far as I know, their Tanzania doesn't have tanning salons. Still, my client wouldn't want his locations associated with a location where one in six children dies before the age of 5 as a consequence of poverty-related infectious disease and inadequate health-care provisions."

The former Tanzania will hold a referendum next week to vote on a new name for the country.

"We're considering a number of words in Swahili," Mkapa said. "So far, the people's top choices are Karibu, Rafiki, and Triscuit." ⊘

HALCOTE from page 229

with him, or collaborate with him in any class, for any reason, ever.

"I'm not going to share a song-time folder with Jeremy Halcote," Alexis Tyler said during music class Monday. "I'm not. I'll go to the nurse's office if [music teacher] Mrs. Cook tries to make me."

"At the Spring Concert last year, I had to hold hands with Jeremy Halcote, so I pulled my sleeve all the way down, so I wouldn't have to touch him," said classmate Christine Halley, commiserating with Tyler. "He didn't even sing. He just stood there breathing really heavy. And he had a cold sore on his lip that started bleeding, because he kept licking it. And he was wearing tennis shoes, even though Mrs. Cook said 'no tennis shoes.'"

Finding a classroom partner for Halcote is a task that usually falls to his teacher.

"Once, [fourth-grade teacher] Mrs. Grant sent Jeremy Halcote out of the room and yelled at us, because no one would be his flashcard buddy," Halley said. "But then Jeremy sneezed right in Kimberly's face during multiplication drill, and her mom called the school to complain."

Although Halcote is in Mrs. Grant's class, students in Mrs. Verkilen's and Miss Willie's fourth-grade classes, who encounter him on the playground and during field trips, also hate him.

"Remember the time Jeremy Halcote threw up when we went to the paper mill?" said Jen Lipner, of Mrs. Verkilen's class. "It was so gross. I hate him."

"I hate him, too," said classmate Hilary Taylor, making a sour face.

"Me, too," added classmate Winter Spalding.

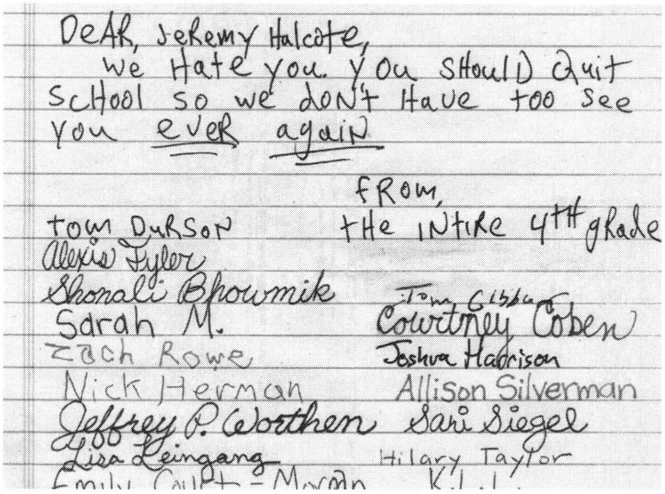
DeAR, JeRemy Halcote,
we Hate you. you SHould Quit
ScHool so we doN't Have too See
you eveR again
FROM,
tHe iNtiRe 4tH gRade
Tom DuRSON
Alexis Tyler
Shonali Bhowmik
Sarah M.
Courtney Coben
Zach Rowe
Joshua Harrison
Nick Herman
Allison Silverman
Jeffrey P. Worthen
Sari Siegel
Lisa Leingang
Hilary Taylor

Above: A note classmates presented to Halcote Monday.

Newcomb couldn't find one student who would admit to liking Halcote, who is also known as Germy Halcote, Jeremy Halitosis, and Snotnose.

"Jeremy Halcote's nose is always so full of snot that you can hardly understand what he's saying," Vanderhof said. "He talks like this: 'Mmr mmr mmr. I'm Jeremy Halcote.'"

The investigation revealed another disgusting thing about Halcote: his desk.

"Jeremy Halcote is such a slob," said Tom Durson, the fourth-grader unfortunate enough to have been seated directly behind Halcote. "He keeps wrapped-up cookies and fish sticks from lunch in his desk. His worksheets always have big grease stains on them."

Durson has devised a system for avoiding contact with Halcote-germs when he is forced to correct Halcote's papers.

"If Mrs. Grant puts his paper on my desk, I hold my breath the entire time," Durson said, describing a procedure that other students have begun to copy. "I only touch [the paper] with the tip of my pen, not my fingers. And, if the worksheet has a back-side, I use two pens, like chopsticks, to flip it over."

In addition to having perpetually sticky hands, Halcote earns barely passing grades.

"Today, Mrs. Grant asked Jeremy what a president's wife is called, and he just *sat there*, not saying *one word*," straight-A student Melanie Esteban said. "That happens *all the time*. He didn't even do a dinosaur diorama last week. He spent the whole class pouring glue on his hand and peeling it off after it was dry."

"Last week, Jeremy Halcote threw his own backpack on the roof of the school, and the janitor had to get it down for him," Esteban added.

"Germy will take a ball at lunch hour and then just sit there with it, even though he knows there are only six balls for everyone to use," classmate Karl Harding said. "Then, if you try to get the ball from him, he'll scream that weird Jeremy Halcote scream. The playground supervisor doesn't even bother coming over when she hears him, because he does it *all the time*."

Newcomb said she collected far more anecdotal evidence of Halcote's outbursts than she could possibly fit into her report.

"I'm not sure whether Halcote's eccentric behavior results from or is the reason for his ostracism," Newcomb said. "Frankly, I don't care."

Newcomb said he was sure of one thing: that Halcote is doomed to remain at the very bottom of the social ladder for the remainder of the school year, unless someone even grosser moves to Muncie.

"Even the kids who live in the Section 8 housing over by the interstate will not go near Jeremy," Newcomb said. "There isn't one fourth-grader who can tolerate the way he talks, walks, eats, smells, kicks at the chair in front of him, sniffs constantly—God, he *always* seems to be sick, doesn't he? He wipes his nose right on his hand. But if you offer him a Kleenex, he sticks his tongue out at you. He is *way* too old to be doing things like that. Ugh. Jeremy Halcote. Yuck." ⊘

KILLER from page 229

male.

Police have been combing the attraction for clues, thoroughly investigating every ride, game, snack bar, gift shop, and photo-sticker booth.

"We started our search in Yukon Territory and fanned out to Yankee Harbor and Orleans Place," Moynihan said. "We've got a whole squad on the SkyTrek Tower. If anything suspicious happens, we'll be sure to see it from our vantage point on the bridge by Splash Water Falls."

"We gather by the double-decker Columbia Carousel twice a day to compare notes, discuss leads, and eat funnel cakes," Moynihan said.

"I urge the public to cooperate with any officers forced to butt in line," Moynihan added, as he shifted his grip on a three-foot-tall, plush Bugs Bunny. "It's a lot of ground to cover in one day, as you all know."

Moynihan said his first priority is to ensure the safety of Great America employees and visitors. To that end, he has stationed an officer in the front car of every ride in the park.

"I have men working in shifts on rides, from 10 a.m. until the park closes at 8 p.m.," Moynihan said. "Officers from neighboring departments have volunteered to cover some of the more popular attractions, such as the American Eagle and Superman: Ultimate Flight."

Moynihan had to develop a unique system to oversee the patrol of a park as big and fun as Great America.

"We gather by the double-decker Columbia Carousel twice a day to compare notes, discuss leads, and eat funnel cakes," Moynihan said. "We also keep in constant radio contact with one another. Instead of the usual 'all clear,' we've been using an updated, site-specific check-in."

When pressed, Moynihan said, "The check-in signal is 'Wheeeeee!'"

Looking for a killer in a theme park has created its share of problems, Moynihan admitted.

"The crowds, the noise, and the overall jovial atmosphere have been distracting," Moynihan said. "We've limited our searches to weekdays, because on weekends, the lines here are nutso."

Cost has also hindered the daily patrols. The city of Gurnee bought season passes for 50 police officers, but the admission fee is far from the only expense the department incurs.

"We've been trying to stay within a budget," Moynihan said. "You'd think that once you paid admission, you'd be covered. But then there's parking, souvenirs, and game tickets. And food here is outrageous. Ten dollars for a burger and a Coke? If we didn't have to keep a constant presence in the park, our officers never knowing when or where the killer might strike next, we'd probably bring a cooler full of sandwiches and eat in the parking lot."

Above: A police sketch of the suspected "Six Flags Killer."

Moynihan said he hopes for a break in the case before the end of the season, but is willing to personally supervise the investigation through the Six Flags' Fright Fest, which begins Oct. 11.

"As adventure-filled as this investigation has been, we can't focus all of our man power on Great America," Moynihan said. "By now, the killer could be as far away as Magic Mountain."

Moynihan ended the press conference with an ultimatum, which was later broadcast over the park's public-address system.

"You will not get away with this," Moynihan said, shaking a fistful of cotton candy at the still-at-large assailant. "We will find you if we have to fingerprint every Skee-Lo game in the park." Ø

the ONION presents:

America's Best Zoo Exhibits

A trip to the zoo is fun and educational for the entire family. Here's a list of the top-rated animal exhibits around the country:

- **Snakes: Somewhere In This Room!**
  Zoo Atlanta, Atlanta, GA
- **The Fascinating World Of Dead Capybaras**
  Bronx Zoo, Bronx, NY
- **Why Sloths And Chimps Can't Have Babies**
  Chehaw Wild Animal Park, Albany, GA
- **Anaconda**
  San Francisco Zoo, San Francisco, CA
- **You Deal With This Sick Rhino**
  Fort Worth Zoo, Fort Worth, TX
- **Kanga-Roofied**
  Sea World/Busch Gardens, Orlando, FL
- **Inside The Digestive Tract Of The Mighty Boa Constrictor**
  Toledo Zoo, Toledo, OH
- **Nature's Videos We Rented**
  Birmingham Zoo, Birmingham, AL
- **Feed Twizzlers To The African Waterbuck**
  San Antonio Zoo, San Antonio, TX
- **Watch The Zookeeper-Mauling Polar Bear Get Euthanized**
  Memphis Zoo, Memphis, TN
- **Polaroids Of Koalas**
  Mesker Park Zoo, Evansville, IN
- **Peacocks And Turkeys: Nature's Unlikely Best Buddies**
  Fort Wayne Children's Zoo, Fort Wayne, IN
- **Suddenly There's Bears!**
  Wildlife Parking Lot
  Gladys Porter Zoo, Brownsville, TX
- **Mr. Hippo Loves Mrs. Hippo Very Much**
  Franklin Park Zoo, Boston, MA
- **Hamm's Bear Cardboard Stand-Ups Behind Bars**
  Lincoln Park Zoological Gardens, Chicago, IL

COMMUNITY VOICES

I'll Thank You Not To Call My Collection Of Sequential-Art Erotica 'Dirty Comics'

I've been called many unfair names in my day, Grygor, but I never imagined that someone I consider a friend would label me an "onanist" before the entire *Animatrix*-message-board community. The personal attack was beneath the dignity of an erstwhile standard-bearer of the fan community. I'll thank you, Grygor, to discontinue forthwith your practice of referring to the works contained in my collection of sequential-art erotica as "dirty comics."

By Larry Groznic

Although it may come as news to you, there is a long tradition of sequential artworks in celebration of the human love-act. The works in my collection are borne out of this tradition, and exist far afield from the base pornography you referred to in your posting of Tuesday. How dare you call the pieces in my extensive collection of erotic animated-film stills "girlie cartoons"? Do you honestly compare the masterful line drawings of Milo Manara's *Butterscotch* series to the pandering output of Wicked Pictures or Larry Flynt Publications? (Your stance on such lesser forms of erotica is well-known, Grygor. Or am I to suppose that the Nikita Denise "Stars Of Adult Cinema" action figure I saw in your merch-bag at San Diego Comi-Con got in there *by mistake*?)

Manara—not that you would be aware of this—is famed throughout the Continent, though sadly unappreciated on these shores, thanks to the ignorance of philistines like yourself. Are you familiar with Manara's collaborations with a certain Federico Fellini, a man who is seen in Italy as a filmmaker on par with our Lucas?

For your information, Grygor, breathtaking depictions of the female form are considered high art in Europe. But I'm willing to bet that Europe's finest comics lie entirely outside of your realm of knowledge, even though you call yourself a fan of "the ninth art." (The French rank comics equally among the other arts—ballet, opera, and the like. Comic artists there enjoy a level of respect that is, in this country, bestowed only upon such universally regarded masters as Rob Liefeld, Todd McFarlane, and Alex Ross.)

But *your* familiarity with comics is so limited, you couldn't identify Aquaman's wife without recourse to the Justice League FAQ! To think I believed you capable of appreciating the works of the finest erotic artists working in the medium today! Even your knowledge of *Metal Hurlant*'s internationally acclaimed Moebius is confined to the production sketches from *The Fifth Element*. (Perhaps you've heard of a little something called the *Incal* series? Oh, great suns of Krypton! Something Grygor doesn't know?!)

Grygor, there is nothing "dirty" about the nude female form, as explored in the Eros sampler *Submissive Suzanne #5*. I should not be publicly ridiculed simply because I, as a mature adult, have an appreciation for aspects of sexuality lost on an infantile ignoramus such as yourself.

I should not be publicly ridiculed simply because I, as a mature adult, have an appreciation for aspects of sexuality lost on an infantile ignoramus such as yourself.

I had no reason to take you into my confidence, Grygor, and show you my collection in the first place, save my evidently incorrect appraisal of you as someone who could appreciate the finer things of fandom. And how did you reward my trust? By calling me "Pervertimus Prime" before the entire online community.

Far from aberrant, my collection represents the full breadth and width of human sexuality. My works range from serious literary works like *Story Of O*, by Guido Crepax, to such playful fare as *Cherry Poptart*, by Larry Welz. And, for your information, the majority of the comics you so cruelly maligned are published by no less an authority on the form than Gary Groth. Had you behaved with more maturity, I might have shown you the crown jewel of my collection: a signed first-edition copy of the moving tale of an anthropomorphic cat's personal journey into sexual discovery, Reed Waller and Kate Worley's *Omaha The Cat Dancer*. Oh, but you'll never see that, Grygor.

Nor will you ever lay your eyes upon Frank Thorne's *Ghita Of Alhizaar*, *Lann*, or the timeless classic *Moonshine McJuggs*. The sophisticated sensibilities of works like the *Little Annie Fanny: Complete Hardcover Limited Edition* are beyond the scope of your intellect, as well. As, I am guessing, would be my extensive collection of the finest *mangerotica* available outside of Japan. No, those tender coming-of-age stories would be as pearls before swine.

I hope you realize now, Grygor—or shall I call you "trinitysbyfrnd," as I see that is what you're calling yourself on the Wachowski Brothers message board—that there is nothing "dirty" about my erotica collection, save what "dirtiness" you, in your benightedness, brought to it. Until you learn to show respect for that which you clearly know nothing about, consider your instant-message username blocked.

P.S.: I want my *Doctor Who: The Key To Time* TVD box set returned posthaste. ∅

HOROSCOPES

Your Horoscope

By Lloyd Schumner Sr.
Retired Machinist and
A.A.P.B.-Certified Astrologer

Aries: (March 21–April 19)
A revolutionary idea for a clean, economic mass-transit system will strike you in the middle of the night, powdering both your femurs.

Taurus: (April 20–May 20)
You'll finally lose your long and painful battle with stomach cancer for the hand of the beautiful Esther.

Gemini: (May 21–June 21)
Although your life has not assumed the lyrical beauty of Wallace Stevens' poetry, it's right on the money as far as the terrifying sense of loneliness is concerned.

Cancer: (June 22–July 22)
Your habit of insisting that "the future is now" is leading people to wonder what you think comes after this.

Leo: (July 23–Aug. 22)
It's hard to say this, especially in binary: 110111001000000011110010110111101110101001011101110000101 01000100110.

Virgo: (Aug. 23–Sept. 22)
You've learned a few things in your life, but as you'll soon see, looking both ways before crossing the street isn't one of them.

Libra: (Sept. 23–Oct. 23)
You'll trade a chance to be the talk of the cocktail-party circuit for a plate of fried chicken, proving that you're no dummy.

Scorpio: (Oct. 24–Nov. 21)
History remembers the inventor of the machine gun, but not its first victim. Your role as the recipient of the first ice-pick noogie will likewise be anonymous.

Sagittarius: (Nov. 22–Dec. 21)
You've made it your life's mission to find the best crab cakes in Boston. Truly, you're one of America's unsung heroes.

Capricorn: (Dec. 22–Jan. 19)
Your long-held belief that women are beautiful no matter what their size will continue to net thoughtful nods from everyone you meet.

Aquarius: (Jan. 20–Feb. 18)
You've been busting your hump at your thankless job for years, so it'll be a grave injustice when your company refuses to pay for life-saving hump surgery.

Pisces: (Feb. 19–March 20)
Everything you've ever believed will be called into question when it turns out that Cap'n Crunch is a real guy.

CAR from page 230

detail?

You can't forget about curtains, either. Who wants someone peering in while you're trying to take a piss or get off? It doesn't take but an old flag, a couple T-shirts, and some tape. A lot of these new guys don't care who's looking at them when they're taking care of business. That's just not right. It's guys like them who give guys like me a black eye.

Worst of all, these new guys are full of tall tales, always talking about how they're gonna move into an apartment any day. Used to be, everyone knew enough to keep things real. We kept our chins up and our hopes down. We'd drive from truck-stop to rest-stop chasing a meal or some hitchhiker. But at the end of the day, when we turned off the ignition and cracked the window just enough for air—but not so much that a hand could fit through—we knew who we were.

Guess I'd better move over to the right lane, because it looks like my kind is driving into the sunset. ∅

the ONION®
VOLUME 39 ISSUE 35 AMERICA'S FINEST NEWS SOURCE™ 11–17 SEPTEMBER 2003

NEWS

Sweatshop Laborer's Child Loves Her Irregular *Finding Nemo* Sweatshirt

see WORLD page 3B

Drug-Sniffing Dog Develops Taste For Bit-O-Honeys

see LOCAL page 11D

Alabama Man Wins Personal Victory Over Gun Control

see LOCAL page 7D

STATshot

A look at the numbers that shape your world.

Who's Dad Good At Imitating?
14% Snotty check-out girl at Pick 'n Save
13% Pat Summerall
22% Someone who could've been a contender
8% Bloated corpse
27% It's either Elmer Fudd or Joe Lieberman
16% Life, art

FBI Discontinues Witness Protection Parade

WASHINGTON, DC—FBI director Robert S. Mueller III announced Monday that, due to logistical complications and a lack of interest among participants, the annual Witness Protection Parade will be cancelled "for the foreseeable future."

"The feeling among organizers, participants, and sponsors was that the John Smith Memorial Witness Protection Parade—though a lot of fun—presented too many headaches for everyone involved," Mueller said in a press conference Monday.

The parade, scheduled this year for Oct. 4, has been a major event in Washington ever since the creation of the federal witness-protection program 30 years ago, and has historically garnered TV ratings second only to those of the Macy's Thanksgiving Day Parade.

"This event has been our way of recognizing the brave men and women

see PARADE page 238

Above: Participants in last year's Witness Protection Parade.

Relations Break Down Between U.S. And Them

WORLD FOCUS

WASHINGTON, DC—After decades of antagonism between the two global powers, the U.S. has officially severed relations with Them, Bush Administration officials announced Tuesday.

"They have refused to comply with the U.S. time and time again," Defense Secretary Donald Rumsfeld said, following failed 11th-hour negotiations Monday night. "It's always unfortunate when diplomacy fails, but we could not back down. We have to be ready to fight back, in the name of freedom, against all of Them at once, if necessary."

Rumsfeld added: "If They're not with

see RELATIONS page 239

Above: Rumsfeld announces that the U.S. has severed ties with Them.

Above: Hoagland, who one day will die.

Impending Mortality Influences Area Senior's Purchasing Habits

INDEPENDENCE, MO—Grace Hoagland's purchasing habits are increasingly influenced by her sense of impending mortality, sources close to the 73-year-old reported Tuesday.

"I offered to buy Mom a new fan, because hers is 10 years old and only works on 'low,'" daughter Nancy Seely said. "She said, 'Oh, don't bother. New things are only wasted on an old goat like me.' Like she's in the grave already."

Although she remains in good health and has a comfortable pension, Hoagland sees her golden years as a time to severely restrict her purchasing habits. This means sleeping on a sagging mattress with coils poking through the padding, watching a television with a drifting picture, and manually opening her heavy garage door.

"I said to her, 'Mom, don't pull those weeds in your tomato garden out by hand. Get a soil aerator, so you don't have to bend down,'" said Seely, 46. "She told me, 'Oh, honey, I'm used to doing it this way. Besides, you and [Hoagland's other daughter] Peggy

see SENIOR page 238

U.S. Seeks Help In Iraq

In a U.N. resolution last week, the U.S. sought troops and money from all nations to aide in Iraq's postwar reconstruction. What do *you* think?

Joseph O'Brien
Systems Analyst

"They weren't too keen on helping us invade, but now that we've shown them we can do it, I bet they'll fall all over themselves to pitch in."

Erin Rose
Interior Designer

"Finally, the U.S. is allowing other countries to contribute financially to Iraq's reconstruction. They were getting really pissed off that we weren't letting them do that."

Brett Gelman
Poet

"We must get the other nations of the world to commit troops in Iraq. Then they'll be weak at home—and we can strike!"

Don Moe
Translator

"There's trouble in Iraq?! Quickly! To the unilateral-invasion-mobile!"

Evan Foley
Lawyer

"When a nation sees a fellow nation going through troubled times, like Iraq is now, it's important to reach out and help. Together, through caring and sharing, we can make a difference."

Julie Brister
Social Worker

"Good heavens! So many problems and complications! I sure do miss having the old Iraq around, just the way it was."

Back-To-School Supplies

Schools are back in session across the country. What supplies are teachers recommending students bring?

- Compass with eight different fold-out blades
- 1,024-color Crayola crayon set
- Slipknot T-shirts (4)
- Any necessary prescription anti-spaz pill
- Three-pound hand ax
- Wooden yardstick for extracting Tater Tots from behind radiator
- Pencil not-all-that-sharpener
- Enough gum for the entire class
- $10,000 in unmarked, non-consecutively numbered, small-denomination bills
- Brand-name pencils
- Ritalin® (methylphenidate) Trapper Keeper
- A supply of Coca-Cola, the official sponsor of education

the ONION®
America's Finest News Source.™

Herman Ulysses Zweibel
Founder

T. Herman Zweibel
Publisher Emeritus
J. Phineas Zweibel
Publisher
Maxwell Prescott Zweibel
Editor-In-Chief

Well, Well, Well—If It Isn't A Family-Owned Retailer

By Wal-Mart Store #3297

Well, well, well—lookee here. If it isn't a small, family-owned retailer. How quaint.

Pretty nice shop you got here. Okay if I take a look inside? Don't mind me. I won't be long. Neither will you, but that's a story for another day.

I'm sure you must be real busy, but if you have a minute to spare, I could use a bit of help. I was hoping to buy the new Alan Jackson CD, but I'm having trouble finding your music section. I'd also like to pick up a bottle of scented bath gel. What's that? Really? Just a hardware store, huh? Well, I'm sorry. I do apologize. Seems like it'd be a whole lot more convenient to go to a single store for all of my needs, but what do I know?

My, oh, my. I really like what you've done with the place. It's so old-fashioned. Kind of cramped, but I guess you did your best. Takes a lot of persistence and elbow grease to keep a place like this open for... 53 years, you say! My, my, that's impressive! It's too bad how things will end up. Real shame.

But biggest isn't always best, they say. People probably love the character of this neighborhood store, how cozy it is. I just wonder if people will still want to scurry around this little shack after they've pushed a cart through our 48 spacious, well-lit, air-conditioned, perfectly organized, fully labeled aisles.

Bet you're *real* proud of your little store here, the way it's passed from one generation of your family to the next. Must mean a whole lot to you and your little lady and your two kids. How's high school going for those kids, anyway? Good to hear. Education is key. Incidentally, here's my number. When they graduate, have them call me. I'll see if I can't get them a job.

I love looking around these mom-and-pop places. It helps me get a feel for a town's local flavor. Just out of

My, oh, my. I really like what you've done with the place. It's so old-fashioned. Kind of cramped, but I guess you did your best. Takes a lot of persistence and elbow grease to keep a place like this open for... 53 years, you say!

curiosity, what do you tell your greeters to say around these parts? Oh, you don't *have* greeters? Then who greets the customers? Interesting. That certainly is *one* way of going about it, I guess.

It's also very novel the way you meet your customers' parking needs. Your customers must really get a kick out of jockeying for available spots on the street. I'm sure none of them would be interested in the convenience of three football fields' worth of parking. Then again, what use would you have for all those spaces, anyway? This little store probably couldn't handle more than three or four customers at a time, now, could it?

I see you have some nice items on sale there. A Black And Decker two-speed power drill for $23.99? Lowest price in town. Bet you can hardly keep them in the store. Hmm, I wonder how well they'll sell when some other store in town starts offering the same drill for $19.98. I wonder. Well, I guess we'll just have to wait and see.

Say, why *do* you charge so much for your products? Silly me, how could I forget? You pay wholesale, then mark up from there. Have you ever considered buying everything at prices well below wholesale? Not the only way to do things, I admit, but it's what we do. Just one of the benefits of being the biggest retailer in the world.

But biggest isn't always best, they say. People probably love the character of this neighborhood store, how cozy it is. I just wonder if people will still want to scurry around this little shack after they've pushed a cart

see RETAILER page 239

Take-Charge, Can-Do Guy Makes Horrible Decisions

Above: Stuart in his office, which he calls "mission control."

BOSTON—Matthew Stuart, an enthusiastic 33-year-old junior executive at Boston Tea Market, Inc., gets things done quickly, confidently, and terribly, sources at the tea supplier said Monday.

"Matt is always willing to take on new responsibilities," said Nellie Jordan, Stuart's direct supervisor. "In fact, just this week he was responsible for the boneheaded move of reorganizing the 500 items in our new catalog *alphabetically*, instead of by product group. Really screwed it up good."

Boston Tea Market distributes high-end teas and tea-brewing accoutrements to coffee shops, restaurants, and retail stores. Stuart decided that an alphabetical listing would make the company's catalog easier to use and took the initiative to redesign the winter issue.

"See, if you *work* here you'd want to be able to go right to 'S' to find the order number for Sunshine Organic Green Tea," Jordan said, scowling as she paged through the catalog printout. "On the other hand, *Matt*, if you're a customer, you might wish to find it by looking at a page of green teas."

"At least he got it done before deadline," Jordan added. "I know that when I make him change it, he won't complain."

Because of his positive attitude and boundless energy, Stuart's frequent errors in judgment are generally overlooked.

"Everyone here really likes Matt," Jordan said. "You never really notice what an idiot he is until you're cleaning up his mess. He loves to roll his sleeves up, get in there, and fuck all sorts of things up."

"Matt is usually the first one here in the morning," coworker Karla Groff said. "There's always a fresh pot of nasty, weak coffee brewing when the rest of us get in."

A graduate of Boston College's Carroll School of Management, Stuart said he has always enjoyed the "game of business."

"I love to get out there on the court and take the bull by the horns," Stuart said. "I'm not afraid of hard work, never have been. Leadership is in my blood."

Stuart, who has called himself the "king of multi-tasking," has shown himself to be a highly motivated employee ever since starting with the company four years ago.

"We're a small business, so a take-charge person can really wear a lot of hats," sales manager Ronnie King said. "That means there's plenty of work for which Matt is completely unqualified, like overhauling the company database or developing new teas in the test kitchen."

"He's wonderful at getting everyone going, often in the wrong direction," King continued. "Last week, he pulled a team of stockers off the warehouse floor and set them up in a conference room in order to come up with 10 ways to streamline product unloading. At 20 employees and four hours of discussion, it cost us about 80 combined hours of labor."

Jordan admitted that she was initially impressed by Stuart's enthusiasm.

"It's great to have someone who always volunteers to spearhead a project," Jordan said. "I thought it was great how he was excited to bounce ideas around. Very bad ideas, I soon noticed."

While many of Stuart's ideas are never used, some occasionally pass as "original," due to the strength and force of his hopelessly misapplied personal energy. Promotions coordinator Jane Eckerly detailed one of Stuart's recent projects.

"[Stuart] did this thing called the Tea & Toast mailer, where we mailed prospective clients samples of our tea along with toasters and a loaf of bread," Eckerly said. "I'm guessing everyone voted for the idea pretty much to give Matt something to do."

"Not my fault," Eckerly added. "I was on vacation."

Ultimately, the mailers cost the company approximately $10,000 and resulted in only two new clients. The connection between high-quality teas

see GUY page 238

NEWS IN BRIEF

White House Denied Third Mortgage

WASHINGTON, DC—In light of recent budget concerns, President and Mrs. Bush attempted to take out a third mortgage on the White House Monday, but were denied. "Unfortunately, we're unable to serve the president's needs at this time," Washington Mutual loan officer Judy Schamanski told reporters. "Within the next 30 days, Mr. Bush will receive an adverse-action notice in the mail, which will outline the specific reasons for the denial. But, for starters, I would suggest that he get current on his second mortgage before he even considers a third." Schamanski added that Bush is more than welcome to reapply in the future, should his credit profile improve.

Obituary Cites Teen's Love Of Music, Cars

PHOENIX—Patrick Pryde, beloved 17-year-old son of Charles and Elizabeth, loved music and cars, the *Phoenix Gazette* reported on page D-18 Monday. "Patrick's enthusiasm and passion for life touched all who knew him," the obituary read. "Whether waiting in line overnight for Kid Rock tickets or checking his car's oil level, Patrick showed an unshakable determination and insatiable curiosity, both of which will forever live on in our hearts and minds." Other items mentioned as being loved by Pryde include video games, the Internet, and cable television.

Woman Assures You She's Not Mad

CASPER, WY—Your girlfriend of four months, University Xerox employee Rebecca Kohler, assured you Monday that she was "not mad" about being unable to reach you on the phone Saturday night, even though you said you would probably be home. "For the last time, I'm not angry at you, goddamnit!" a furious Kohler said. "Christ, are you trying to *make* me mad?" The perfectly fine Kohler then proceeded to violently three-hole-punch stacks of photocopies and explain to her coworker, Annabelle Agneau, that the only person she was mad at was herself, for having thought you might be different.

New Desk Chair A Boring Dream Come True

BUCKLIN, KS—The arrival of a royal-blue Global Armless Task Chair at Allstate Insurance Monday marked an extremely mundane "dream come true" for human-resources aide Patty Keely. "I so love my life," said a giddy Keely, 31, without a shred of irony. "I've been wanting a chair with wheels for so long, but I never thought [office manager] Don [Frissel] would get me one. Now my chair won't make that horrible scraping sound every time I stand up to file something. Yes!" Now that she has a new desk chair, Keely said she fantasizes about one day buying a Chevrolet Cavalier or visiting her cousin in Branson, MO.

45-Year-Old Fails To Make Someone Very Happy One Day

NEW MEADOWS, ID—In spite of predictions to the contrary, Larry Naering, a 45-year-old research scientist, has failed to make someone very happy one day, his mother Nancy reported Monday. "He's always been such a handsome, responsible boy," said Nancy, who used to look forward to having grandchildren. "I always told him that some girl was going to discover a real hidden treasure if she took the time to look at him. I guess I was wrong." Nancy said her son's chances of finding that one-in-a-million love have dwindled to one in 50 billion. Ø

PARADE from page 235

whose legal testimony forced them to join the federal witness-protection program," Mueller said. "It was our way of putting these true patriots in the spotlight, if only for a few hours."

Nevertheless, Mueller said that dozens of last year's marchers, all of whom have asked not to be named, declined the invitation to participate in next month's parade. Most claimed that family matters, personal commitments, or the demands of their pool-cleaning jobs in Tempe wouldn't allow them to be in Washington over the weekend.

"You wouldn't believe how hard it was to track everyone down every year," Mueller said. "Even after we did, there was always trouble. We'd have a group all arranged to carry the big 'Star Witnesses Shining Bright' banner, and then, poof, all six men would disappear into thin air the day of the event."

Mueller said the parade has always been difficult to organize.

"You wouldn't believe how hard it was to track everyone down every year," Mueller said. "Even after we did, there was always trouble. We'd have a group all arranged to carry the big 'Star Witnesses Shining Bright' banner, and then, poof, all six men would disappear into thin air the day of the event."

Mueller said that an additional factor leading to the parade's cancellation was the rising cost of insuring it.

Over the years, the parade has seen an unusually high incidence of tragedy as it winds through 2.4 miles of downtown D.C. In 1977, a burning, driverless garbage truck, reported stolen earlier in the day from the Happy Haul-Away Sanitation Company, plunged into the "Telling The Tales Of Yesteryear" float, killing 17 men. In the '80s, the route was changed annually, in an attempt to circumvent the tendency of Colombian-owned businesses to detonate as the parade passed. Also, the "Boxes Of Nails From Around The World" limousine caravan sponsored by the Sons Of Italy Working Men's Association has exploded with dire consequences seven out of the past nine years.

"Even though the parade was cancelled, it was nice to have been invited," said John Smith, who would have been this year's grand marshal. Smith was granted the honor in celebration of his testimony in the Racketeer Influenced, Corrupt Organizations Act case against convicted Russian mafia boss Illyini Yutokarev last year.

"For poor boy from Ukraine, it is certainly dream come true," said Smith, who said he is not related to any of the 27 previous grand marshals of the same name. "But I never expect any special recognition for what I've done. In fact, I specifically ask for no recognition. Please, none. Please."

Longtime fans of the event expressed disappointment over the parade's cancellation.

"I always loved to watch the parade," said Jilly Messalini, 48, a small-business owner from New York. "I tell you, I'll miss it. Every year, I bring the boys from Brooklyn to see the sights, you know? I usually spot at least one old friend, or maybe even his kids, in one of the marching bands."

"Last year, I recognized a long-lost cousin on the 'Fun Fun Fun In The Arizona Sun' float," said parade attendee Herbert Tong, a prosperous dry-cleaner and importer from San Francisco's Chinatown. "I waved, but he must not have noticed me. I followed him for blocks yelling out his name, but he never waved back. He was probably just embarrassed about his missing fingers."

Although the FBI sponsored the annual parade, the cancellation will also affect other federal agencies that make use of the witness-protection program.

"The IRS and the DEA would always send a nice group out," Mueller said. "And the CIA would usually support us by collecting donations. But then, money was never a problem. In fact, I was shocked by how generous some of the anonymous donors were. You should have seen the rubber-banded rolls of cash we'd find in those coffee cans we placed around town. Clearly, some people really wanted to see these parades happen." Ø

"For poor boy from Ukraine, it is certainly dream come true," said Smith, who said he is not related to any of the 27 previous grand marshals of the same name. "But I never expect any special recognition for what I've done. In fact, I specifically ask for no recognition. Please, none. *Please.*"

SENIOR from page 235

don't like gardening, so it wouldn't be of any use to you once I pass on.' Good Lord."

In recent months, Hoagland has revealed that similar logic dissuaded her from buying a new car, a modern refrigerator, a decent couch, a grocery pushcart with working wheels, an alarm clock she wouldn't need to wind every day, and non-charred pot holders.

"Mom used to buy the most durable products available," Seely said. "Now, when she sees 'Five-Year Warranty' on a box, she says the thing is 'too nice' for her. A 60-day warranty is about all she'll accept."

Hoagland even considers the purchase of a new winter coat to be frivolous, given that she's likely to die before it wears out.

"I know my old coat isn't at the height of fashion anymore," Hoagland said, referring to her 20-year-old quilted stadium coat. "But it still serves its purpose just fine. Leave fashion to the young. I had some very beautiful coats in my time, like the lovely blue boucle one I wore when [late husband] Dick proposed to me."

Once an avid bulk-purchaser of items like pretzels, toilet paper, and sandwich cookies, Hoagland now only buys what she needs. Her refrigerator contains a pitcher of filtered water, a jar of mustard, several hard-boiled eggs, a bowl of waxed beans, a half-empty can of chicken broth, and a slice of pepperoni pizza from her grandson Carter's birthday party in July.

"I hate to bring more things into the house," Hoagland said. "The basement freezer is still full of sausage from the deer Dick shot before he passed six years ago. If something happens to me, all that venison will go to waste."

Seely said that she and her siblings don't buy Hoagland the things they think she needs, because the gifts usually go unused.

"I got Mom a coffeemaker, but it sits there on the counter all shiny while she makes her coffee on the stove," Seely said. "She said she wanted to keep the new coffeemaker nice, so whoever got it next could enjoy it. The box and all the instructions are in the kitchen closet. Plus, she said she didn't want to buy coffee filters for it, because they come in packs of 100."

Seely complained that her mother's frugality has had a deleterious effect on her own memories.

"I can't be nostalgic about my childhood home, because it's still right there in front of me," Seely said. "Mom will hold on to a throw pillow until it's just a frizzy, formless clump of feather-dust inside a worn-out sack, and then she'll still keep it."

"Mom used to buy the most durable products available," Seely said. "Now, when she sees 'Five-Year Warranty' on a box, she says the thing is 'too nice' for her."

Appraiser Jane Schallert of the firm Glover, Glover & Upham recently assessed the value of Hoagland's personal effects.

"I would be surprised if Mrs. Hoagland owns anything less than eight years old," Schallert said. "Her curtains are sun-faded to a sickly pale yellow, her area rugs have large holes produced by thousands of footfalls, and the vinyl tablecloth in the dining room was past its prime when her middle-aged daughters were still teenagers. I'm an appraiser, not a psychiatrist, but I'd say Mrs. Hoagland has all but handed in her cards."

Drying her hands with a dish towel Schallert characterized as "a handful of soiled yarn," Hoagland said she plans to maintain her thrifty ways, but insisted that she is "no miser."

"As my daughters will tell you, I'm very generous with the grandkids," Hoagland said. "I know little Aimee will adore the kitchen play-set I got her for Christmas. I know it seems premature to buy it so early, but you never know what will happen to me between now and December." Ø

GUY from page 237

and warm toast, while strong in Stuart's mind, didn't seem to translate to product-buyers at coffee shops, restaurants, and retail stores. Most thought the toasters were sent by accident.

"From a distance, Matt seems to be shaking things up," Eckerly said. "He's always briskly walking through the office, on his way to an important meeting. But when he stops and tells you how he wants to market sun-dried-tomato tea, the speed-walking seems less impressive."

Despite the failure of many of his campaigns, employees at the company still perceive Stuart as an ambitious go-getter.

"I don't know Matt very well, but it seems like he's really on the ball," president Gil Schneider said. "I always notice him signed up to use the boardroom, and I get a lot of e-mails from him. I'll have to keep him in mind next time I need a go-to guy." Ø

"From a distance, Matt seems to be shaking things up," Eckerly said.

RELATIONS from page 235

us, They're against us."

U.S.-Them relations have been strained for nearly three years, but disagreements came to a head last week, when two of Their leaders opposed a U.S.-drafted U.N. proposal

"The world's petrochemical supplies are nearly exhausted," National Security Advisor Condoleezza Rice said. "If we allow Them to control the only remaining fossil-fuel sources, how are we supposed to get our oil? By *buying* it from Them?"

Above: Crewmembers of the U.S.S. Constellation prepare for further diplomatic breakdowns with Them.

seeking cooperation from Them in important peacekeeping missions.

"We've tried reasoning, but Their agendas are in direct opposition to ours," Vice-President Dick Cheney said. "They stand in stark defiance of stated U.S. policy. We cannot and will not allow Them to dictate global policy."

Many current U.S. policies regarding Them are outlined in a recent State Department report titled "Long Term Organizational And Regulatory Governmental Procedures: U.S. vs. Them." According to the document, the standoff is a result of Their continued economic encroachment, Their ongoing reluctance to allow U.S. military bases on Their lands, and the refusal of many of Them to speak English.

"The U.S. is surrounded on all sides by Them," Rumsfeld said. "Over 90 percent of the planet's land mass is controlled by Them, and the territories immediately south, west, east, and north of the U.S. are all occupied by Them. Until we can correct this risky state of affairs, it is vital that we maintain our military readiness to intervene whenever and wherever They oppose us."

Another key factor in the standoff is U.S. dependence on Them-controlled resources.

"The world's petrochemical supplies are nearly exhausted," National Security Advisor Condoleezza Rice said. "If we allow Them to control the only remaining fossil-fuel sources, how are we supposed to get our oil? By *buying* it from Them?"

"They only think about what's good for Them, but we're concerned with the needs of *all* Americans," Rice added.

Bush political advisor Karl Rove said that the current situation is unfortunate but inevitable, given Their outdated governmental frameworks.

"Americans enjoy a modern, pluralistic, democratic society," Rove said. "They, on the other hand, have a weird mishmash of contradictory belief systems and agendas. It's really not even worth penetrating the whole mess."

According to military historian Wesley Crandon, problems between the U.S. and Them go back decades.

"They have shown themselves to be dangerously aggressive," Crandon said. "Tensions have come to a head between the U.S. and Them when Them factions attacked the U.S. in the Philippines, Central America, Europe, and Japan."

According to Crandon, many U.S. political analysts hoped Them-led resistance had finally come to an end after the Cold War.

"But now, even former allies have revealed anti-U.S., pro-Them sentiments," Crandon said. "This includes

One political expert stressed that, in spite of the ongoing climate of hostility, Americans have little to fear from Them.

the Them province of France and its lack of support for Operation Them Freedom, and England, who—despite having helped the U.S. fight Them in the past—has recently been revealed as un-American by the ongoing Tony Blair investigation."

Experts remain unsure how long the current U.S.-Them rift will last, but President Bush said Tuesday that the U.S. will stand tall.

"We're Americans and They are not," Bush said. "We will not, under any circumstances, allow some alien, foreign one-of-Them to dictate how we're going to run our, or Their, lives. It's us and Them now, people."

One political expert stressed that, in spite of the ongoing climate of hostility, Americans have little to fear from Them.

"I wouldn't worry," Harvard political analyst Gregory Peters said. "Sure, the U.S. makes Them mad, but since we have unilateral military supremacy, it's not as if They can do anything about it." Ø

RETAILER from page 236

through our 48 spacious, well-lit, air-conditioned, perfectly organized, fully labeled aisles.

But you have a real nice line of goods in here, too. Very select. Probably picked it yourself, hmm? Must've been real tough deciding which handful of things to keep in stock. Now, just what are these handmade cards on the counter? The girl down the street made those, and she's selling them to make money for her cheerleading uniform! My goodness! And you get nothing out of the deal? How sweet. Do you think she could make 10,000 cards a month? Why don't you ask her and get back to me? If she can produce, I might know a retailer that could help her and her team out.

Yes, sure would be a shame if you lost the tiny, local customer base that's kept your store in business for half a century. I mean, how would you pay your mortgage? Where would that leave you and your family? Just what *will* you do to survive?

Loyal customers, you say? Loyalty is a funny thing. You never really know

Yes, sure would be a shame if you lost the tiny, local customer base that's kept your store in business for half a century. I mean, how would you pay your mortgage? Just what *will* you do to survive?

what people are going to do until they're tested. I guess we'll see soon enough. Personally, I don't know the people of this little hamlet too well. I'm new here. But if they're anything like the people of the 8,420 other small towns I've seen, I expect to see quite a few of them at our grand opening in four weeks. We'll be handing out free balloons and soda pop, you know. Hot dogs will be two for a dollar in the deli.

Well, I honestly hope everything turns out well for you. I like you. It'll pain me to see you out of work, but what can I do? I can't force people to keep patronizing your little shop. I can't convince people to slog from one specialty store to another when they can find everything they need conveniently located in one place. I can't make customers pay anything more than the lowest price.

If I could, believe me, I would. Ø

COMMUNITY VOICES

Daddy H. Day Care

By Herbert Kornfeld
Accounts Receivable Supervisor

Yo, this is foe tha day-care peeps who tend to mah shortie, Baby Prince H Tha Stone Col' Dopest Biz-ook-kizeepin' Muthafuckin' Badass Supastar Kornfeld Tha Second. (His mama call him Tanner, but she a bitch.)

First off, I wanna say that I ain't down wit' this lame-ass daycarin' bullshit. Agnes—that's Baby H's moms—decide she wanna get educated. So, she said either I tend to tha shortie durin' tha day while she at school, or he gots to go to this Little Britches place on Commercial Road. So I said, "Shit, you high? Days I spend tendin' to bidness at Midstate Office Supply. Can't that fuckin' mama o' yours, who always hatin' on tha H-Dog, look afta tha Prince?" An' she said her mama have corns, or cancer, or somethin' beginnin' wit a 'C,' an' so she can't look afta tha shortie no more.

So, whut that mean is, a bunch o' muthafuckin' strangers be lookin' afta my son an' heir to tha storied Kornfeld accountz-reeceevin' legacy. Tha H-Dog don't play that shit. But I ain't gonna give up my sweet, sweet gig at Midstate. Tha place be givin' up tha mad scrilla, plus I just got one o' those desktop fridges you can keep yo' lunch in. Y'all best believe it goin' to good use, muhfuckaz. Besides, who gonna keep tha Prince in Pull-Ups if I don't keep krunchin' those numbahz?

He can watch tha show wit tha freaky puppet bloodsucka that counts off tha numbahz.

You daycarin' amateurs ain't in tha clear wit' me, though. Y'all got a shitload o' shortiez in tha hizzy, but I don' want nobody forgettin' who Daddy H's boy be. I don't wanna come collect tha boy one day an' find him wit' a load in his pants an' about to stick his tongue inna 'lectric socket, 'cause all y'all off in anothah room playin' some candy-ass game wit' chutes an' laddaz. So I come up with this list o' rulez y'all best heed. 'Cause y'all workin' foe me now. An' if y'all don't like it, go find a betta payin' gig wit' Blu Kross/Blu Shield benefizets, where y'all get treated wit' some respect. Feel me?

Make sure he wear his goddamn sweata. He got this li'l acrylic sweata-vest just like his Pops, an' I keeps it in his backpack next to his solah calculata. I know how you muhfucks like to keep tha thermoshizat down 'cause you figure all tha shortiez create they own heat when they runnin' around. But ain't no boy o' mine gonna catch his death 'cause some pencil-pusha wanna cut corners. Yo, an' check this: Y'all gots my permishizzon to trash that ill doll his moms keeps in his backpack. You know, that freaky-lookin' thing wit' tha red yarn hair an' check shirt. Thing got a tattoo on its chest sayin' "I love you." Tell her some other kid shit all ovah it or somethin', so you hadda torch it.

A bunch o' muthafuckin' strangers be lookin' afta my son an' heir to tha storied Kornfeld accountz-reeceevin' legacy.

Don't feed him none o' that nasty-ass strained-carrot shit his mama give him. He almos' 2 now, and he ol' enuf foe Skittles an' Slim Jims an' Andy Capp Hot Fries. If it good 'nuf foe tha Midstate employee-breakroom vendin' machine, then it good 'nuf foe mah shortie. I better not hear no muhfuckaz dissin' tha office eats, not evah.

Rolez he can play wit' his li'l shortie homiez durin' playtime: CPA, bank tella, collections rep. If they play house, he can bust in an' audit 'em. Huh. That'll teach the li'l muhfucks. If they play store, he can play cashier, but he gotta be all bidness: no sleepin' on tha job or quittin' his post an' goin' shoppin' like a li'l pussy girl. An' he can't claim no employee discount. An' if they play office, I betta not see him workin' tha accountz payabo. Give that shit to one o' tha weaker shortiez.

I best never see mah boy in one o' them huge-ass strollaz that carry a dozen or so shortiez. I got mah reasons.

He can watch tha show wit tha freaky puppet bloodsucka that counts off tha numbahz. Back inna day, that same show used to have a pinball-machine cartoon wit numbahz in it, too. That wuz dope. But my boy can't watch nothin' else, 'specially not that wack sponge wit' no dignity.

Don't let none o' tha shortiez use his special sippy-cup, neither. It gotta blue top an' somethin' on its side—uh, what's the shit—oh, yeah. A duck. It a gift from my ol' faculty advisa at Eastech Bidness & Technical College, Mr. Sherman. He wuz mad proud when he find out his supafly protégé got his freak on an' made a shortie. That don't happen too often in tha accountin' profession. But mah accountz reeceevin' posse gonna change that, no doubt. That remind me...

If all y'all daycarin' peeps spot some officin'-lookin' homiez kickin' back an' drinkin' wine coolahz on yo' property, don't call tha 5-0. That jus' mah posse. They used to chill in tha H&R Block parkin' lot, but them tax foolz decided they had enuf an' called tha pigz. The homeboys got they asses outta there befoe they could be busted foe vagrancy, but all this pig harassment mean they runnin' outta places to hang. So I tol' 'em about Little Britches, how y'all got this big-ass parkin' lot y'all hardly use and those def monkey-barz an' shit. Yo, don't hate. They peaceable, they got crazy love foe Baby H, an' they ain't lookin' to brawl. Although tha monkey-barz might come in handy if the homiez go toe-to-toe wit' tha pigs, an' they gotta do some freaky mystical Shaolin shit. You know, twirlin' aroun' an' as they dismount, they kick in a sucka's head somethin' like 60 times in a half-second befoe touchin' the ground. Jus' sayin.'

Shee-it. Writin' up this list be somethin' no self-respectin' A.R. bruthah should evah do. Daycare. Huh. Back inna day, mah moms an' pops both led tha Workin' Life, but they didn't put me in no day care. I wuz straight-up latchkey. Got my ass off tha schoolbus, let myself in, stripped down to my Underoos, fixed me a bowl o' Quisp, an' sat down to a aftanoon o' *3-2-1 Contact* an' *Tic Tac Dough*. I ain't lookin' foe yo' goddamn sympathy. I wore that house-key bling aroun' my neck wit' mad pride. Even then, tha H-Dog took care o' bidness, an' didn't need no daycare sucka chasin' afta him wit' a ass-wipin' cloth an' a juice box. Solitude good foe a shortie; it build characta an' shit. Peep this: Soon as tha Prince in kindergarten, he gonna kiss muhfuckin' daycare goodbye an' wear his own house key on a bright orange shoelace, jus' like his pops. I'll see to it. H-Dog *out.*

HOROSCOPES

Your Horoscope

By Lloyd Schumner Sr.
Retired Machinist and
A.A.P.B.-Certified Astrologer

Aries: (March 21–April 19)
You'll garner praise you don't deserve when you carefully manipulate the facts concerning your late phone bill to make yourself look like a hero.

Taurus: (April 20–May 20)
Your recent decision to adopt the warrior code of *bushido* to guide you through life will lead to a tragic confrontation with your inept pet groomer.

Gemini: (May 21–June 21)
You insist that there is nothing wrong with the American educational system, but the person who reads this to you isn't quite so confident.

Cancer: (June 22–July 22)
That old joke about the blind woman who answered the hot iron won't seem so funny when you're hospitalized after talking on one for 45 minutes.

Leo: (July 23–Aug. 22)
Trial by jury is fine, but not when all 12 jurors insist on chanting "Guilty!" throughout your entire testimony.

Virgo: (Aug. 23–Sept. 22)
You should have seen it coming when, out in the West Texas town of El Paso, you fell in love with a Mexican girl.

Libra: (Sept. 23–Oct. 23)
You're living proof that a sordid and unhealthy sexual relationship doesn't have to involve other people.

Scorpio: (Oct. 24–Nov. 21)
Before you can truly grasp the principle behind the zero-sum game, you will have lost all your money playing Texas Hold 'Em.

Sagittarius: (Nov. 22–Dec. 21)
Letting tomorrow take care of itself isn't really a bad philosophy, if you're pretty sure there are more than eight tomorrows left.

Capricorn: (Dec. 22–Jan. 19)
Your life story will be called "a *Lord Of The Flies* for the fat and lonely" by a local newscaster who has obviously never read *The Yellow Wallpaper*.

Aquarius: (Jan. 20–Feb. 18)
Things aren't so rosy at the moment, but take heart: Someday, you'll be able to look back and laugh at all those nurses you had to kill.

Pisces: (Feb. 19–March 20)
Filing off the numbers and reselling the hot goods would be a workable plan, if you didn't deal in stolen credit cards.

NEWS

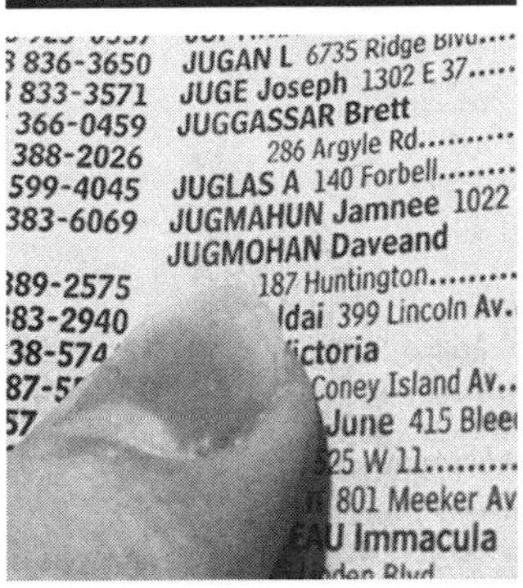

Stripper Not In Phone Book

see LOCAL page 3B

Vacationing Family Visits World's Biggest Asshole

see TRAVEL page 9E

God Grants John Ritter's Wish To Meet Johnny Cash

see OBITUARIES page 5H

Pancakes 'Famous'

see NATION page 14C

STATshot

A look at the numbers that shape your world.

What Are We Lying About To Barb?

- 10% Quality of her watercolors
- 15% That revolting banana bread
- 17% How realistic her new arms look
- 22% Her raggedy-ass azalea bushes
- 6% What dipshit son did to economy
- 30% How life's not the same without her

the ONION®

VOLUME 39 ISSUE 36 AMERICA'S FINEST NEWS SOURCE™ 18–24 SEPTEMBER 2003

D.C. Once Again Murder Capital, Mayor Brags

WASHINGTON, DC—Washington Mayor Anthony Williams bragged Monday that, after nearly a decade, the city has resumed its rightful place as the U.S. murder capital.

"Hey, it only makes sense," Williams said at a press conference Monday. "We're the capital of the United States, so we should also be the capital of murders. But the thing is, if you're *from here*, you know how to take care of yourself in a city as big and bad as D.C."

According to the latest crime statistics provided by the FBI, Washington led the nation in murders per capita in 2002 with 45.8 per 100,000 citizens, edging out 2001's murder capital, Detroit, by 3.8 murders.

"I knew we'd come back," Williams said. "These other cities are pretenders. Detroit doesn't have what it takes to keep up with the real champ. They talk a good game, but that's all it is: talk. We don't mess around here. We're for

see D.C. page 244

Above: Williams boasts of Washington's dangers.

OUR CULTURE

History Of Rock Written By The Losers

Above: Dana Harris spends a Friday night cataloging his CD collection on a computer spreadsheet.

BOSTON—Fifty years after its inception, rock 'n' roll music remains popular due to the ardor of its fans and the hard work of musicians, producers, and concert promoters. But in the vast universe of popular music, there exists an oft-overlooked group of dedicated individuals who devote their ample free time to collecting, debating, and publishing the minutiae of the rock genre. They are the losers who write rock's rich and storied history.

"The city of Boston is about more than just Mission Of Burma or Galaxie 500, and it's certainly about more than Boston or The Cars," said 28-year-old Dana Harris, a rock historian. "The scene in Boston is full of history, but it's also vibrant right

see ROCK page 245

FDA Approves Sale Of Prescription Placebo

Science & Health

WASHINGTON, DC—After more than four decades of testing in tandem with other drugs, placebo gained approval for prescription use from the Food and Drug Administration Monday.

"For years, scientists have been aware of the effectiveness of placebo in treating a surprisingly wide range of conditions," said Dr. Jonathan Bergen of the FDA's Center for Drug Evaluation and Research. "It was time to provide doctors with this often highly effective option."

In its most common form, placebo is a white, crystalline substance of a sandy consistency, obtained from the evaporated juice of the *Saccharum officinarum* plant. The FDA has approved placebo in doses ranging from 1 to 40,000 milligrams.

The long-awaited approval will allow pharmaceutical companies to market placebo in pill and liquid form. Eleven major drug companies have developed placebo tablets, the first of which, AstraZeneca's Sucrosa, hits shelves Sept. 24.

"We couldn't be more thrilled to finally get this wonder drug out of the labs and into consumers' medicine cabinets," said Tami Erickson, a spokeswoman for AstraZeneca. "Studies show placebo to be effective in the treatment of many ailments and disorders, ranging from lower-back pain to erectile dysfunction to nausea."

Pain-sufferers like Margerite Kohler,

see PLACEBO page 245

The Ban On Travel To Cuba

The House of Representatives recently voted to end the decades-old restriction prohibiting travel to Cuba. What do *you* think?

"But if we impose sanctions for just one more year, we could still win the Cold War."

Charlie Todd
Financial Examiner

"What flake thought up this stupid bill? Oh, U.S. Rep. Jeff Flake (R-AZ)."

Mary Regan
Appraiser

"Tom DeLay claims lifting restrictions will support Fidel's 'thugocracy.' And who would know better than an elected Thugocrat?"

Porter Mason
Podiatrist

"Our country should not recognize the tyrant Castro until the land that belonged to the tyrant Batista is returned to its rightful mob owners."

David Berman
Paramedic

"Making Cuba accessible to Americans would encourage reforms there, as it did in the once-oppressive republics of the Bahamas, Aruba, and South Padre Island."

Jane Borden
Systems Analyst

"We all know imposing sanctions doesn't work. It seems our only option is to *strike now*."

Rob Webber
Sales Agent

Eco-Vandalism

The Earth Liberation Front recently made headlines by defacing SUVs. What other actions have radical environmentalists taken to further their cause?

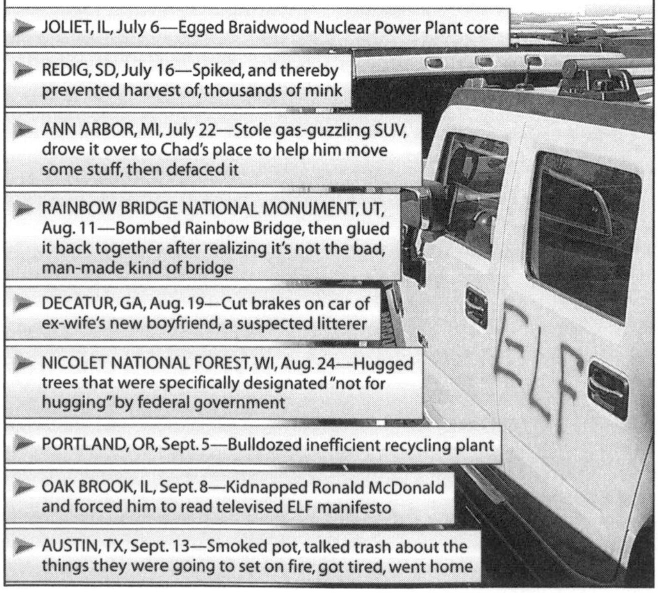

- JOLIET, IL, July 6—Egged Braidwood Nuclear Power Plant core
- REDIG, SD, July 16—Spiked, and thereby prevented harvest of, thousands of mink
- ANN ARBOR, MI, July 22—Stole gas-guzzling SUV, drove it over to Chad's place to help him move some stuff, then defaced it
- RAINBOW BRIDGE NATIONAL MONUMENT, UT, Aug. 11—Bombed Rainbow Bridge, then glued it back together after realizing it's not the bad, man-made kind of bridge
- DECATUR, GA, Aug. 19—Cut brakes on car of ex-wife's new boyfriend, a suspected litterer
- NICOLET NATIONAL FOREST, WI, Aug. 24—Hugged trees that were specifically designated "not for hugging" by federal government
- PORTLAND, OR, Sept. 5—Bulldozed inefficient recycling plant
- OAK BROOK, IL, Sept. 8—Kidnapped Ronald McDonald and forced him to read televised ELF manifesto
- AUSTIN, TX, Sept. 13—Smoked pot, talked trash about the things they were going to set on fire, got tired, went home

the ONION®
America's Finest News Source.™

Herman Ulysses Zweibel
Founder

T. Herman Zweibel
Publisher Emeritus
J. Phineas Zweibel
Publisher
Maxwell Prescott Zweibel
Editor-In-Chief

I Totally Outlived Jesus

By Ian "Kersh" Kershaw

Well, as you know by now, today's my birthday. A big happy birthday to me! Oh, yeah! Everyone knows what this day means: Pabst Blue Ribbon pitchers at the Fuzzy Duck Inn. This year, I *better* see you there, because this isn't going to be just any birthday celebration. This year, my birthday will be a deeply meaningful, almost humbling occasion. See, I'm turning 34. That means I totally outlived Jesus!

You know, 33 was good. I had a pretty decent year, all in all. I started seeing Melissa, I moved into an apartment complex with a pool, and I solidified my position of authority at the car-stereo installation shop. But there was one thing I couldn't say that I'd done, until today: outlive Jesus Christ. Well, check the calendar. See that circle around today's date? See that '34' written there? In your face, Jesus!

Don't get me wrong. I'm not badmouthing Jesus. He's our Savior and the Son of God, and He has all of those churches dedicated to Him and books written about Him. He did a lot of amazing things, like that walking-on-water business. I'm just saying there's at least one area in which the ol' J-Man failed to outpace a certain birthday boy standing before you now.

Jesus and I have a lot in common, but we're different, too. I know how to draw a crowd, but I'd rather tell my great stories from the summer I

You know, 33 was good. I had a pretty decent year, all in all. I started seeing Melissa, I moved into an apartment complex with a pool, and I solidified my position of authority at the car-stereo installation shop. But there was one thing I couldn't say that I'd done, until today: outlive Jesus Christ.

worked at the water park than talk about Adam and Eve. He liked wine; I like my Pabst Blue Ribbon. What can I say? Kersh is a man of the people. At the end of the day, though, I think my accomplishments, miracles aside, pretty much measure up to Jesus'. Jesus was a carpenter, right? Carpentry is pretty cool, but the installation of mobile audio is cool, too. I know how to put the decks in, like, a hundred differ-

I'm not badmouthing Jesus. He's our Savior and the Son of God, and He has all of those churches dedicated to Him and books written about Him. I'm just saying there's at least one area in which the ol' J-Man failed to outpace a certain birthday boy standing before you now.

ent cars. So Jesus and I are pretty even there. And without question, I beat Him, hands down, when it comes to not kicking the bucket before 34! Hey, take that, Jesus, you numbnuts!

Oh! I didn't go too far, did I? I'm just kidding around! No disrespect intended there, young, dead Jesus.

I can kid, can't I? It's my day, after all! On my birthday, I'm like the king for a day, right? The king has come! Tonight, I'm going to score a big table for us at the Duck, and we can all sit on one side, just like they did at the Last Supper. If it's good enough for Jesus, it's good enough for us old fogies, too.

I can put up a little sign over my chair that says "INRI," just like the one Jesus had. No one knows what Jesus' damn sign even meant, but mine will mean "Ian Needs Ribbon Immediately!" Oh, but His sign wasn't over His favorite booth in the back, the one right by the jukebox. Nope, his sign was over His head when He died—younger than Kersh!

Kersh 1, Jesus 0.

Okay, fine. He died for my sins. Well, you can bet I've made some real good ones lately. Because I figured something out a year ago today: You're only as old as Jesus once, and then you're older than Jesus for the rest of your life!

Yeah, I outlived Buddy Holly, James Dean, and now, the big one: Christ Almighty, Himself! That's no small thing. I might not have done as much good in the world, but if I want to, I totally have the time! Shit, I'm probably going to live twice as long as Jesus!

Boo-yah! Burn on you, Jesus! Ø

FAMILY

Mother-Daughter Heart-To-Heart Devolves Into Bitching About Dad

GARBERVILLE, CA—A frank discussion of dating gave Elizabeth Kurden and her 15-year-old daughter Claire an opportunity to discuss the failings of husband and father James Monday.

"You're too young to be dating a boy so seriously," Kurden said to Claire. "I don't want you to get in over your head. Look at me. I married your father when I was 20. He was so sweet then. I had no idea how much things change when you settle down."

"Mom, isn't how you feel about someone all that matters?" Claire said. "Troy is really cool, and he wouldn't ask me to do anything I wasn't ready to do. Don't make *me* suffer just because Dad never wants to do anything but sit and watch football all weekend."

No topic is too large or too small for the Kurden women to discuss, nor is any topic so far removed from the family patriarch that he can't be brought into the conversation and disparaged.

"Right now, some boys might seem attractive because they have the right clothes or the right haircut, but don't get fooled by that," Kurden said. "If you pick someone who has personality and intelligence, instead of someone who looks good in jeans, you'll be much better off. Speaking of jeans, I'll be taking you to the mall today because your father decided it was more important to fix the rototiller than it was to spend time with his daughter."

Even more mundane interactions between Kurden and Claire occasionally devolve into discussions of James and his many irritating flaws.

Above: Sloppy, insensitive James Kurden.

"The right skin moisturizer might not seem important now, but you need to start taking care of your skin early," Kurden told Claire on a recent grocery-shopping trip. "You really have to start when you're young, if you want to look nice when you get to be my age. Your father, on the other hand, seems to have forgotten all about keeping himself up, as I'm sure you've noticed."

"I've noticed," Claire said.

"And let's not even discuss those yellow marks on the armpits of his dress shirts," Kurden said.

Claire said she used to consider herself "Daddy's little girl," but in recent years, she's grown closer to her mother.

"Lately, Mom and I have been talking more about life and stuff. We've been a lot more honest with each other," Claire told reporters. "Before, if I complained that Dad broke his promise to help me with my homework or something, Mom would say something like, 'Your father is a busy man.' But now, Mom and I talk like friends. Sometimes she really goes off on him."

Above: Kurden discuss life, love, and the shortcomings of her husband with daughter Claire.

Between Kurden and Claire, no subject is taboo.

"I feel like I can tell Mom anything," Claire said. "I was telling her how it ticks me off when boys stop talking to you after you tell them you like them. Then, Mom told me how Dad used to tease her about her butt being too big until finally, one day, she went nuts and threw a lamp at him."

Psychologist Anthony Wieland, author of *Divided Parents, Conquered*, said bonding over the shortcomings of a fellow family member is common.

"As happens with mothers and daughters all over the country, Claire and Elizabeth's talks bring them closer together, and allow the elder Kurden to pass on life wisdom," Wieland said. "How else would Claire learn how idiotic men can be sometimes?"

According to Wieland, husbands and sons bond in a similar manner. However, because men are less likely to verbalize their feelings, the teaching of life lessons and gender roles often takes place through role modeling.

"A man is less likely to openly discuss his spouse with his son," Wieland said. "Instead, he'll act out his feelings. If, for example, a father is interrupted in the middle of the Raiders game with some stupid question, he'll cast an unmistakably annoyed and condescending glare at his bitch wife. Then, leaving this expression in place, he'll turn so his son can see it. It's basically the same thing." Ø

NEWS IN BRIEF

Indian-American Couple's Accent Makes Fight Adorable

SAN DIEGO—A witness to an argument between Indian-Americans Soumitra and Vineeta Chattergee reported Monday that she thoroughly enjoyed the vicious fight. "They were at each other's throats, arguing about which one wrote the check that caused an overdraft," said eyewitness Shelly Knight, who was delighted by the heated exchange while standing in line at Citibank. "Usually, I can't stand it when couples go at it in public, but that accent made them sound so cute." Knight added that she was slightly disappointed when Soumitra stormed out.

School Friends Don't Find Camp Songs Funny

SIOUX FALLS, SD—Friends of fourth-grader Kendra Tyler failed to find her songs about Eagle Waters Junior Camp funny, 9-year-old classmate Tanya O'Doole reported Monday. "Kendra kept singing this one song that sounds like 'Camptown Races,' but it's about some guy named Counselor Bob," O'Doole said. "She was acting like it was so great, but it didn't even make any sense. I mean, what's a Prospect Peak, anyway?" Tyler's friends were similarly uninterested in doing the Eagle Wing Dance.

Revised Patriot Act Will Make It Illegal To Read Patriot Act

WASHINGTON, DC—President Bush spoke out Monday in support of a revised version of the 2001 USA Patriot Act that would make it illegal to read the USA Patriot Act. "Under current federal law, there are unreasonable obstacles to investigating and prosecuting acts of terrorism, including the public's access to information about how the federal police will investigate and prosecute acts of terrorism," Bush said at a press conference Monday. "For the sake of the American people, I call on Congress to pass this important law prohibiting access to itself." Bush also proposed extending the rights of states to impose the death penalty "in the wake of Sept. 11 and stuff."

Supreme Court Gets Free Box Of Shoes After Mentioning Nike In Ruling

WASHINGTON, DC—The nine justices of the U.S. Supreme Court were treated to a free crate of athletic shoes Monday, following an offhand mention of Nike during a ruling in the case of *McBrayer & Company v. The City Of Detroit*. "All I did was say that the claims made by the defendant were similar to those made by Nike when defending labor conditions in its Asian footwear factories," Justice Ruth Bader Ginsburg said. "Next thing you know, we get this big box of red Air Zoom Spiridons in the mail. Inside the box was a form letter from Nike's publicist. Sweet!" The Supreme Court will begin its new session Oct. 6, with Case 03-130: *Sony High-Definition Widescreen Televisions v. Fossil Sterling Silver Multifunction Watches v. Bombay Sapphire Gin.*

Change In Bus Seats Taken Personally

ST. LOUIS—Bus passenger Dan Pohl was offended by 26-year-old fellow rider Lana Peters Monday when she moved from the bus seat beside him to a seat closer to the door. "What? I'm not good enough to sit next to?" Pohl thought. "Go on and move then." Peters was unavailable for comment, as she exited the bus at the next stop. Ø

D.C. from page 241

real."

Washington was one of a handful of cities that didn't follow the nationwide trend of decreasing homicide rates.

"Yeah, we're not big trend-followers here in D.C.," Williams said, puffing out his chest slightly. "We have our own way of doing things. Our murder rate has always been high. Just because folks over in L.A. or Miami start settling down, that doesn't mean we will here."

One possible explanation for the increase in the murder rate is the implementation of new homeland-security measures. Many Washington police officers have been reassigned from their regular duties in order to protect government buildings and public monuments. However, the FBI report noted that New York, which faces similar safety concerns, experienced a slight decline in the murder rate for 2002.

"I'll admit, it's a little rough here," Williams said. "This city isn't for everyone. You gotta have street smarts to get by. You can't carry yourself like some tourist from Cowtown, USA. You gotta watch your back."

"Even so, it's still the best place on earth," Williams said. "I wouldn't live anywhere else. Washington has so much to offer: history, culture, entertainment. A few murders won't change that. They just bring those of us who live here a little closer together. You see, we look after our own here. We got one another covered."

At the mention of community spirit, Williams appeared downcast.

"We would like to express our condolences to the families of the victims who made us number one," Williams said. "Our hearts go out to those who have fallen. We're like family, so it's always sad to see one of our own die. Unfortunately, that's the risk of life in the fast lane."

Although Washington led the nation in murders per capita, detractors were quick to point out that it ranked fifth in overall homicides. While Washington counted 262 murders in 2002, both Chicago and Los Angeles tallied more than 600.

"Yeah, Chicago thinks it's so great with its 647 murders," Williams said. "Believe me, if Washington had as many people as Chicago, we'd have more than twice their murders. Do the math."

Karla Rose, spokeswoman for the public-watchdog group Safe Streets D.C., expressed dismay over what her group called Williams' "cavalier attitude toward crime."

Above: One of the 262 homicides that made Washington, D.C. number one.

"I expected the mayor to address these disturbing statistics with sobriety," Rose said. "This city doesn't need a show of bravado. It needs a show of grave concern and nebulous promises to improve things."

Should the crime rate continue to rise at the current rate, analysts predict that Washington could see as many as 325 murders next year. For those who expressed concern, Williams had a suggestion.

"If you think it's too tough for you, and you want to move out to [Washington suburb] Silver Spring, then don't let me stop you," Williams said. "Seriously, I think we can get by without you. Me, I'll take D.C. every time."

Rose characterized Williams' comments as "more ridiculous posturing."

"It's absolutely outrageous that a graduate of Yale, who earned degrees in law and public policy at Harvard, would talk this way," Rose said. "See, I'm *from* D.C. I grew up right in [the inner-city neighborhood of] Anacostia. I think Williams better watch himself. You go around shooting your mouth off like that here, you're liable to get yourself hurt."

Although Washington led the nation in murders per capita, detractors were quick to point out that it ranked fifth in overall homicides.

the ONION presents

Rush-Week Tips

Pledging the Greek system is a great way to enhance your college experience. Here are some tips to help you get into the fraternity or sorority of your choice:

- The Greek system isn't all about partying. There's that basketball-toss thing for charity, or whatever.
- Rush week can be stressful if you're an insecure young person seeking the acceptance of an elitist social community. That's the point.
- Just because you don't have the most expensive clothes and you're not the prettiest, you will not make it into the sorority of your choice.
- If anyone tries to make you drink more than you think you should, remember: Alcohol can't kill you, unless you're a pussy.
- Sororities and fraternities create leaders. Did you know that Kirstie Alley, John F. Kennedy, and Matthew McConaughey were all members of the Greek system?
- Get to know the other girls who are rushing with you. When you get in and they don't, it'll be fun to walk past them like you don't know who they are.
- Rent the movie *Old School.* My friend Matt is in one of the scenes. You can totally see him.
- If some geek tries to tell you that fraternities are born out of a classical Greek tradition that embraced sexual relations between men, punch him in the face. If you hit him hard enough, you can finger him while he's still passed out.
- Don't be discouraged. If you aren't asked to join a fraternity, you can still tie a brick to your penis.
- If you have any questions about the programs, benefits, and leadership opportunities the fraternity offers, ask Lance. He's the one with the "Whassup Bitch?" T-shirt and the big foam cowboy hat.
- Be selective. There are dozens of different fraternities to choose from. Pick the chapter that best meets your personal binge-drinking and date-raping needs.
- Just so you know, *Animal House* was a satire, not an endorsement, of Greek life.
- Before you decide to participate in rush week, be aware that there's a chance you'll wind up in a fucking fraternity.

ROCK from page 241

now. Someone needs to record all the amazing things going on here, even if it means that person will never have a social life."

For Harris, rock is the only topic of conversation and the only form of entertainment. While other men his age go on dates or enjoy the sunlight, Harris haunts the rear corners of local rock clubs like The Paradise, where he sits alone, hunched over a notebook. During the day, he works in his windowless bedroom compiling facts about the city's rock history for his web site, BostonRockScene.com.

"Rock is so important to me," Harris said, gesturing to a cabinet where he files articles concerning all of the live shows he attends and detailed transcriptions of interviews with artists who live only blocks away. "If I couldn't write about music and collect music, I have no idea what I'd do instead."

The social misfits who chronicle rock seek not only to log facts, but also to influence public opinion about obscure rock issues, something most people care little about.

"Joe Lunchpail would say 'Rock Around The Clock' by Bill Haley & His Comets was the first rock single, but that's dead wrong," said Dave Rinkin, a line cook in Chapel Hill, NC, who occasionally writes for *Roctober* magazine and has a collection of more than 10,000 records. "Haley's song just brought the sound to the

The social misfits who chronicle rock seek not only to log facts, but also to influence public opinion about obscure rock issues, something most people care little about.

mainstream. Anyone who knows anything will say the first single was either Roy Brown's 'Good Rockin' Tonight' or 'Rocket 88' by Jackie Brenston And His Delta Cats."

Added Rinkin: "Brenston And His Delta Cats was actually Ike Turner's Kings Of Rhythm under a different name, in case you didn't know."

From covering concerts for a local newspaper to distilling rock's history into an 800-page book, the historians of rock 'n' roll soldier on, in spite of their negligible impact on the direction or quality of rock itself.

"When you're writing rock's history, you have to make some hard choices," said Anthony DeCurtis, one of the editors of *The Rolling Stone Illustrated History Of Rock*. "Do you give equal space to influential artists like Jonathan Richman, Gang Of Four, and Fugazi, even though they're not as well known as Madonna or Elton John? Making a decision like that can take an entire weekend of soul-searching."

"I don't mind, though, because I love music," added DeCurtis, slipping a Cream CD just to the left of one by The Creation in the British Invasion section of his music collection. "Rock is just so spontaneous and full of life."

Not all rock history is comprehensive. Many rock historians choose to focus on individual artists who can barely tolerate the authors when they meet. In-depth rock bios have been written about acts ranging from Bruce Springsteen to Captain Beefheart, with biographers desperately trying to attain coolness by association with their subjects.

"Talking Heads was a crucial band for its time," said David Bowman, author of *This Must Be The Place: The Adventures Of The Talking Heads In The 20th Century*. "Their quirky brand of music brought African and funk flavors to American pop, both in the underground and on Top 40 radio. David Byrne's influence can still be heard in modern hip-hop. If you have a couple hours, I'd be happy to talk at you about it."

Although rock historians provide a valuable service to music fanatics, Princeton sociology professor Henry Yates said that their focus on music hinders their accumulation of knowledge in other areas.

"From discussing long-defunct record labels to analyzing the impact of a band's personnel changes, rock historians cannot see beyond their acne-scarred noses to realize that there are interesting subjects in the world besides music," said Yates, a self-professed "ex-music-nerd." "If you ask them who the U.S. attorney general is, or what's going on in the park around the corner, you'll get a blank stare. But ask which member of The Doors produced *Los Angeles*, the debut album by X, and you'll have to dodge all the flying spittle from everyone trying to be the first to answer."

Added Yates: "It was Ray Manzarek."

PLACEBO from page 241

who participated in a Sucrosa study in March, welcomed the FDA's approval.

"For years, I battled with strange headaches that surfaced during times of stress," Kohler said. "Doctors repeatedly turned me away empty-handed, or suggested that I try an over-the-counter pain reliever—as if that would be strong enough. Finally, I heard about Sucrosa. They said, 'This will work,' and it worked. The headaches are gone."

Researchers diagnosed Kohler with Random Occasional Nonspecific Pain and Discomfort Disorder (RONPDD), a minor but surprisingly pervasive medical condition that strikes otherwise healthy adults.

RONPDD is only one of many disorders for which placebo has proven effective, Bergen said.

"Placebo has been successful in the treatment of everything from lower-back pain to erectile dysfunction to nausea," Bergen said. "That's the beauty, and the mystery, of placebo. It's all-purpose. Think of it like aspirin, but without any of the analgesic properties."

The FDA is expected to approve the drug for a wide range of mood disorders later this year. According to Bergen, initial research has shown placebo to be effective in the treatment of bipolar disorder, depression, dysthymia, panic disorder, post traumatic stress disorder, seasonal affective disorder, and stress.

Above: An advertisement for AstraZeneca's placebo Sucrosa.

As industry analysts predict the drug's sales will top $25 billion in the first year, the approval of placebo is expected to unleash one of the pharmaceutical industry's biggest marketing battles to date.

GlaxoSmithKline expects to have two versions of placebo on the shelves in late December. One, a 40-milligram pill called Appeasor, will be marketed to patients 55 and over, while the other, Inertra, designed for middle-aged women, is a liquid that comes in a 355-milliliter can, and is cola-flavored. Eli Lilly plans a $3 million marketing campaign for its 400-milligram tablet, Pacifex.

"All placebos are not the same," Eli Lilly spokesman Giles French said. "Pacifex is the only placebo that's green and shaped like a triangle. Pacifex: A doctor gave it to you."

In spite of such ringing endorsements, some members of the medical community have spoken out against placebo's approval, saying that the drug's wide range of side effects is a cause for concern.

"Yes, placebo has benefits, but studies link it to a hundred different side effects, from lower-back pain to erectile dysfunction to nausea," drug researcher Patrick Wheeler said. "Placebo wreaked havoc all over the body, with no rhyme or reason. Basically, whichever side effects were included on the questionnaire, we found in research subjects."

Added Wheeler: "We must not introduce placebo to the public until we pinpoint exactly how and why it works. The drug never should have advanced beyond the stage of animal testing, which, for some reason, was totally ineffective in determining its effectiveness."

In spite of the confusing data, drug makers say placebo is safe.

"The only side effect consistent in all test subjects was a negligible one—an almost imperceptible elevation in blood-glucose levels," French said. "It's unfair to the American people to withhold a drug so many of them desperately think they need."

ADVICE

Ask A Man Who's Had One Hell Of A Long Day

By Arnold Cardwell

Dear Man Who's Had
One Hell Of A Long Day,

My roommate and I have been best friends since college, but lately she's been getting on my nerves! Although we've happily shared an apartment for years, I'm starting to think we need some time apart. How can I break the news that I want to get a new roommate without hurting her feelings?

At The End Of My Rope
In Raleigh

Dear Rope,

Huh... what? Oh, I'm sorry, I was a million miles away. I just... Whew, what a day I've had. Cody, go get Daddy his mug from the kitchen. Oh, *man.*

Sorry, honey. I didn't mean to ignore you. I apologize. It's just... Look, I've had a really long day, okay? I can't even begin to tell you. I just... I mean, oh boy.

What *didn't* happen is more like it. Believe me, you don't even want to know. Seriously. Don't even ask.

Do we have any aspirin? My eyes are going to pop right out of my skull. It's a throbbing, this intense throbbing, right behind my eyes. Feels like a jackhammer back there.

Trust me. The last thing you want to hear about is all the crap I had to put up with today. I don't even want to go into it. *Please.* Don't get me started. Don't even.

Dear Man Who's Had
One Hell Of A Long Day,

I recently babysat my neighbor's kids while they were on a weekend getaway. I can understand why my neighbors needed to get away! Those kids were a real handful. Long story short, the little terrors cut down the bushes in my backyard. They said they were "playing lumberjack." Are my neighbors responsible for the damage, or am I stuck with the landscapers' bill?

Delicate Situation In Scarborough

Dear Situation,

Oooh, *God.* Man. Are my dogs barking. My thigh muscles are even doing that jerky, jumpy thing. Whew. It's just been one hell of a long day, okay?

Ooh, God. Well... Okay. So first off, I had to go pick up the car this morning, right? It was supposed to be done before the weekend, and today is *Tuesday.*

So I get up early and drive down there before work. Kids hadn't even gotten up for school when I left the house. Six bells in the friggin' a.m., and I'm down at the garage already. But I *needed* that Dodge *today,* because I had to drive all the way down to Plainfield to meet a client. I sure as hell didn't want to take the damned Toyota, that old thing. I mean, ask yourself: How would *that* look?

So *finally,* they've got the car ready. I go to pay up, and there's an extra $120 on the bill for a new muffler. I say to the guy, I say, "New *muffler?* I brought this cocksucker in for..." I'm sorry, honey. You're right. Sorry, Cody. Daddy has had one doozy of a day.

Do we have any aspirin? My eyes are going to pop right out of my skull. It's a throbbing, this intense throbbing, right behind my eyes. Feels like a jackhammer back there.

So I said, "I brought this so-and-so in for lousy leaky *brake* fluid, not a new *muffler,* for chrissakes. I just bought..." Cody, stop it with the light. I said, "I just bought a new muffler, like, five *months* ago!" And then *he* said that their work order must've gotten screwed up, and... Cody, stop switching the light on and off like that, please. It hurts Daddy's eyes. My pounding, aching... Cody, *away* from the light switch. Please just go. Go play. Daddy's tired, son.

Dear Man Who's Had
One Hell Of A Long Day,

I recently bought my dream house. I couldn't be happier with it, except for one small thing: My neighbor insists on intervening in all sorts of decisions. She tries to tell me where I should build my deck, how often to cut my grass, and where to plant my trees. It's a real case of "trouble in paradise." I've worked hard to build my new home, and I don't want to let this thorn in my side ruin my enjoyment. What should I do?

Hassled In Harristown

Dear Hassled,

I don't know. My brother? I don't know. I don't have any opinion. I don't *know.* Don't ask me questions about birthday presents. Do whatever. Get him whatever you want. You make the choice. I don't *care.* Look, I know we said we'd talk about it this week, but... please. Oh, God. I can't even think straight right now, and you're talking birthday presents.

I've had a really long day, all right? *Sheesh!*

I don't know. My brother? I don't know. I don't have any opinion. I don't *know.* Don't ask me questions about birthday presents. Do whatever.

Look, I work hard, don't I? Don't I bust my ass for those mother... those so-and-so's, every day of the *week?*

Well, so I drive all the way to Plainfield and back—and let me tell you, this Plainfield bastard, I mean, talk about your brick-wall situations. This guy, *complete* wash. I couldn't sell him a bucket of water if his dick was on fire.

So I get back to work, and what happens? Schermerhorn calls me into his office and tells me they're making Koepp regional manager. He's all, "Sorry, we know you've been at the company for six years, blah blah blah, but the head office says they want Koepp." Koepp is some kid wet behind the ears. Doesn't know a sprocket from his own asshole. Lemme tell you, what that kid doesn't know you couldn't fit into Yankee fuckin' Stadium, that pissant cocksucking goddamn... Samantha, don't... oh, great. Sammy, don't cry. Daddy's sorry.

Yes, I know, honey. It's not the table's fault. You're right, you're right. Look, I said you're *right! Christ!*

I've had a really long day, okay? It's been a real whopper. That's all I'm going to say about it. I don't even want to go into it.

Arnold Cardwell is a syndicated advice columnist whose column, Ask A Man Who's Had One Hell Of A Long Day, *appears in more than 250 newspapers nationwide.*

HOROSCOPES

Your Horoscope

By Lloyd Schumner Sr.
Retired Machinist and
A.A.P.B.-Certified Astrologer

Aries: (March 21–April 19)
You'll be exonerated when the grand jury admits that you had no choice but to set fire to Grandma.

Taurus: (April 20–May 20)
You must admit that you're sleeping better than ever, but it's kind of unpleasant to wake up every morning with a blowgun dart in the back of your neck.

Gemini: (May 21–June 21)
You'll feel faintly embarrassed about your decision to release the beast within when you see how fuzzy and cute it is.

Cancer: (June 22–July 22)
Those who fail to learn the lessons of history are doomed to repeat its mistakes, which is why the Japanese will launch a bombing raid on you Sunday.

Leo: (July 23–Aug. 22)
Once again, you'll drink yourself into insensibility while watching the videotape of your 1997 *Where Are They Now?* segment.

Virgo: (Aug. 23–Sept. 22)
You will have a violent argument with a pastor, a congressman, and a judge over how many wrongs make a right.

Libra: (Sept. 23–Oct. 23)
You'll try to maintain a healthy perspective, but you can't shake the feeling that $87 billion is a whole hell of a lot of money.

Scorpio: (Oct. 24–Nov. 21)
You'll always have someone standing at your side to love you, no matter how many times you try to escape by skipping town in the middle of the night.

Sagittarius: (Nov. 22–Dec. 21)
You like to think of every day as a fresh new challenge, which would be inspiring if you didn't fail each challenge.

Capricorn: (Dec. 22–Jan. 19)
In today's high-tech business world, it's good to pause a moment to remember that you're there to sell truckload after truckload of dildos.

Aquarius: (Jan. 20–Feb. 18)
In spite of what the doctor says, you don't have a heart problem. You get excited, your heart stops, you fall down—no problem!!!

Pisces: (Feb. 19–March 20)
Well, the stars tried, but somehow, you've been left more or less in control of your own destiny this week.

NEWS

Wildfire Somehow Rages Back Into Control

see NATURE page 13E

25-Pound Ham Wedged In Parents' Refrigerator

see LOCAL page 7B

Black Eye For The White Guy Cable's Newest Hit

see ENTERTAINMENT page 5D

Eiffel Tower Washes Up On Delaware Beach

see LOCAL page 5B

STATshot

A look at the numbers that shape your world.

Why Are We So Late?

- **21%** Wife was bugging us to beat Grand Theft Auto
- **19%** Had to deal with a bunch of bullshit down at the cop shop
- **13%** Bus explosion blew us in wrong direction
- **20%** Definitely not because we're having an affair
- **27%** Are tremendous fuck-ups

0 74470 94595 6 00

THE ONION • $2.00 US • $3.00 CAN

the ONION®

VOLUME 39 ISSUE 37 AMERICA'S FINEST NEWS SOURCE™ 25 SEPT.–1 OCT. 2003

U.S. Government To Discontinue Long-Term, Low-Yield Investment In Nation's Youth

Above: President Bush explains the nation's new investment strategy at an inner-city school in Baltimore.

WASHINGTON, DC—In an effort to streamline federal financial holdings and spur growth, Treasury Secretary John Snow announced Monday that the federal government will discontinue its long-term, low-yield investment in the nation's youth.

"For generations, we've viewed spending on our nation's young people as an investment in the future," Snow said. "Unfortunately, investments of this type take a minimum of 18 years to mature, and even then, there's no guarantee of a profit. It's just not good business."

Snow compared funneling money into public schools, youth programs, and child health-care clinics to letting the nation's money languish in a low-interest savings account.

"This is taxpayer money we're talking about," Snow said. "We can't keep pouring it into slow-growth ventures, speculating on a minuscule payout some time in the future."

"Federal expenditures are recouped when a child grows up and becomes a productive, taxpaying member of society," Snow said. "But we don't see a sizable return on our investment unless a child invents something profitable, or cures a costly disease, like cancer. The wisdom of making such

see GOVERNMENT page 250

Actress Excited To Land Eating-Disorder Ad

Above: Astor at a recent casting call.

NEW YORK—Actress Bianca Astor, 22, was excited to be cast in the role of a woman who suffers from anorexia nervosa for a filmed public-service announcement Monday.

"I can't believe it!" Astor said upon receiving the call from her agent. "I honestly didn't think I was going to get the part. I'm pretty thin, but I didn't think I was eating-disorder thin. I guess I am!"

The spot for the National

see ACTRESS page 251

Canada, India Sheepishly Resolve Border Dispute

OTTAWA—Canadian Prime Minister Jean Chrétien and Indian Prime Minister Atal Behari Vajpayee held a subdued press conference in the Canadian Capitol building Monday to announce that the two nations have peacefully and sheepishly resolved a dispute over their common border.

"We are—well, I guess proud isn't the word—relieved, I suppose, to restore friendly relations with India after the regrettable dispute over the exact coordinates of our shared border," said Chrétien, who refused to meet reporters' eyes as he nervously crumpled his prepared statement. "The border that, er... Well, I guess it turns out that we don't share a border after all."

Chrétien then officially withdrew his country's demand that India hand over a 20-mile-wide stretch of land that was to have served as a demilitarized buffer zone between the two nations.

Above: Chrétien and Vajpayee restore diplomatic relations.

"Really, I think the best thing for us to do is forget

see DISPUTE page 250

Should Arafat Be Removed?

Many see Palestinian President Yasser Arafat as a roadblock to Mideast peace. What do *you* think?

"Arafat needs to be taught a lesson he'll never survive to forget."

Scot Armstrong
Systems Analyst

"These brutish Palestinians need to learn that democracy is about choosing a leader who can speak for all Americans."

James Eason
Lawyer

"Hey, there's nothing like martyring a leader to calm the Palestinian extremists."

Jason Mantzoukas
Deliveryman

"Arafat should get out of politics. It would give him time to focus on his Baby AraPhat line of Palestinian urban wear."

Jon Daly
Waiter

"Arafat should be replaced with someone younger and cuter, like that dreamy Hamas hunk Hafiz Mahmet al-Bahri. Oh, he was assassinated?"

Tara Copeland
Legal Assistant

"The question is not 'Should Arafat leave Israel?' The question is 'Why hasn't *everybody* left Israel?'"

Christine Walters
Loan Counselor

Ben And J-Lo Break Up

Jennifer Lopez and Ben Affleck are rumored to have split. What are the reasons?

- Lopez tired of director Kevin Smith always hanging out in the living room eating chips and wearing that stupid hoodie
- Affleck blamed Lopez for the commercial failure of *The Curse Of The Bambino*, the HBO Babe Ruth documentary he narrated
- Lopez insisted on signing cards from the pair "Bennifer"
- Lopez found out Affleck bought her pink engagement ring for $39.95 through a mass e-mail offer
- Each secretly thought the other was too stupid
- Felt critics of *Gigli* reviewed their relationship instead of their movie, realized the critics were right
- Now that Affleck thinks about it, Lopez has kind of a big ass
- Suddenly realized that they're a total media creation and not actually dating

the ONION®
America's Finest News Source.™

Herman Ulysses Zweibel
Founder

T. Herman Zweibel
Publisher Emeritus
J. Phineas Zweibel
Publisher
Maxwell Prescott Zweibel
Editor-In-Chief

I Assume My Reputation For Arrogant Presumption Precedes Me

By Carl Underberg

Okay, everyone, I'd like to begin. We're running rather late because I just showed up. Although I'm aware that you've all been standing around waiting for me for at least an hour, now that I'm here, it's me being inconvenienced. So, if you'll all please take your seats immediately—*pronto*, people!

Finally, we can get started.

I assume my reputation for arrogant presumption precedes me, so I'll be anything but brief. Surely, you're all familiar with much of what I'm about to say, but I'll say it anyway, because, as I'm sure you're all aware, I'm in love with the sound of my own voice.

We'll be working together—and by "working together," I mean that you'll be working for me—for the next six to eight weeks. Now, I know how much you've been looking forward to meeting me, so it's only fitting that I make a few remarks that will allow you to get to know me better than you could while breathlessly observing my career from afar.

I'm going to skip over some of my better-known, but still deeply fascinating, attributes, simply because I know you're well aware of them. Why wouldn't you be? I'm clearly the most interesting person you've ever heard of, let alone had the opportunity to meet in person, so I'm going to basically do this exactly as my whims instruct me.

Ahem. I hate to interrupt my own self-aggrandizing monologue, but what's the problem with this coffee? I always take cream and two sugars. I assumed you would know that without being told, but evidently you pinheads have some kind of, I don't know, some kind of sugar shortage. Hello? Are you people deaf? Coffee? Snap to it! I can't believe what I'm forced to put up with. I'm the only guy in the room worth a goddamn nickel, and you backwoods hill people can't even show enough consideration to do some research on how I take my coffee. Preparation, people. But I digress. We were talking about me.

A few quick words on the subject of my egotism, since I know how much you all must admire it. Ah, my precious egotism. What can be said that has not already been said by others, albeit less mellifluously? My ostentation is truly without parallel. I was placed on this earth by the loving hand of God as a gift for lower gentry to look up to and emulate.

But I'm sure you all knew that, as my characteristics are often the subject of others' conversations.

Boastful and self-important? I've bragged of everything from my golf game to my ludicrously expensive automobile to the size of my perfect dick. Maybe someday, I'll let you curl up at my feet, and I will delight your eager ears with talk of such matters.

Rude and insensitive? Ha! You'll never meet anybody less sensitive than I am. Can you hear me?

Base? Fuck yes!

Patronizing? Indubitably. (That means 'yes,' in case I lost you there.)

Inappropriate to the point of being downright sexist? Believe it, sweet-cheeks.

But these are only a few facets of the rare and beautiful gem that is Carl Underberg. For I am a gem that can

I'm going to skip over some of my better-known attributes.

be held up to the light, turned over and over, and admired for hours on end by a jeweler—as you are looking forward to doing in the coming weeks, no doubt.

It's inevitable that some of you will find yourselves attracted to me, so I might as well get this next part over with now. Regarding short-term office romance: Do not attempt to date me unless I initiate. Look, unless you are one of the tiny fraction of young, beautiful colts whom I look down upon with favor, *don't bother me.*

For the next six to eight weeks, my needs are more vital than your needs. Let me put it in terms simple enough for dullards like you to grasp: I am more important than you. Therefore, you and I both care much more about me than we do about anybody else, especially you. Do not impart to me, even unintentionally, any sense of your own existence at any time. I want to particularly stress this point. Let's say I should forget your name, or incorrectly blame a mistake on you, or have an irrational mood swing and throw something at you. I not only expect you to tolerate it; I expect you to have anticipated and dealt with it before it even happened. Got it? Think of this as your chance to be happy by helping to make me happy. That is your primary concern.

Well, I think I've wasted enough of my time explaining things that you should already know. I look forward to the exciting opportunities this team will face in the coming weeks. Let's hope things go smoothly. They will, provided that you cater to my every whim while I work my magic. Ø

CRIME

Idaville Detective 'Encyclopedia' Brown Found Dead In Library Dumpster

IDAVILLE, FL—Police are currently investigating the death of police detective Leroy "Encyclopedia" Brown, 49, whose body was discovered in a Dumpster behind the Idaville Public Library Monday.

"Detective Brown's death is a great loss," said Idaville Police Commissioner Rupert "Bugs" Meany, a longtime critic of Brown's unorthodox investigative technique who nevertheless appeared to be shaken by the murder. "Thanks to him, Idaville has the highest arrest-to-conviction-due-to-obscure-trivia rate in the nation. I believe I speak for everyone in Idaville when I say that Encyclopedia Brown was truly the greatest sleuth in sneakers."

Police discovered Brown's badly beaten, nearly decapitated body after the detective failed to respond to routine radio check-in calls. Pages from Brown's battered casebook, which contained such cryptic entries as "Whales are *mammals*, not fish" and "Dinosaurs and cavemen did *not* live at the same time," were found stuffed in the detective's mouth.

Police said the only other evidence found at the crime scene was a pair of "disgusting sneakers" and a damaged floral-patterned cookie jar that held dozens of human teeth.

According to friends, Brown spent hours at the library each evening memorizing facts—blooming cycles of house plants, the notes of the harmonic scale, America's state capitals—that often proved crucial to his violent-crime-unit investigations.

Above: The trash bin inside of which police found the mangled body of Detective Brown (inset).

"Leroy taught me everything I know about investigative police work," said Capt. Sally Kimball-Brown, Brown's friend since childhood and wife until their divorce in 1986. "You can be sure we'll use the technique that bears his name to track down his killer."

"Encyclopedia was a good man who helped a lot of people," Kimball-Brown added. "For him, no case was too small."

Brown, the only son of former Idaville Police Chief Brown, is survived only by Kimball-Brown. Brown's salary, $.25 per day plus expenses, will be placed in a fund to establish a criminology scholarship in his name at Idaville University.

Kimball-Brown said Brown was so respected that even several criminals he helped convict have stepped forward to assist investigators.

"Thanks to him, I got a new start," said parolee Margaret "Maggie" DeLong, who was convicted for intellectual-property theft late last year in Case 03-823: *The Case Of The Stolen Tape*, but was later released on Brown's recommendation. "You can bet your bottom dollar I'll be working closely with the cops on this one."

"Looks like Brown finally ran up against a case he couldn't crack," said a caller who identified himself to police only as "Stewie." "But everything isn't what it seems here. Check out a gang called the Tigers. See who really runs it. There's your clue."

Officers from the Florida Department of Law Enforcement's Internal Affairs Division are investigating the lead by making a long list of all the facts they know about tigers. They are also investigating wildcats, the jungle, zoo history, and rumors of unrest within the Idaville Police Department.

"Leroy and Commissioner Meany butted heads before," Kimball-Brown said. "Leroy knew he was the better detective, and it bothered him that Bugs' smooth-talking and glad-handing got him the commissioner's seat, in spite of his spotty past. It's also common knowledge that Bugs resented Encyclopedia's cleverness, which often made Bugs look like a clumsy, no-necked bully."

Tensions between Brown and Meany came to a head in 1999 when, against Meany's wishes, Brown testified before the Florida Supreme Court in *The Case Of The Slippery Salamander*. Meany publicly threatened Brown several days after the *The*

see ENCYCLOPEDIA BROWN page 251

NEWS IN BRIEF

Church, State Joyfully Reunite After 230-Year Trial Separation

WASHINGTON, DC—Following a two-and-a-quarter-century-long trial separation, Church and State reunited in the U.S. Department of Justice press room Monday. "Even through all the bad times, I knew there had to be a way to get these two old friends back together," Attorney General John Ashcroft said. "With a little counseling and faith-based intervention, I knew Church and State would work it out. It was meant to be." Effective Oct. 15, prayer will be mandatory in public schools and congressional sessions will open with Holy Communion.

Area Woman Can't Bring Herself To Pardon Store's Appearance

THOUSAND OAKS, CA—In spite of the prominent sign posted outside a Nordstrom department store asking shoppers to "Pardon Our Appearance," Gina Calvert, 56, could not bring herself to do so Monday. "This is inexcusable," Calvert said. "There are exposed beams and hastily built temporary walls everywhere I look. I'm sorry, but this is just too far out of line." Calvert said she will take her business to Macy's until Nordstrom begins to show its customers some respect.

U.S. Invades Non-Oil-Rich Nation To Dispel Criticism

LUXEMBOURG VILLE, LUXEMBOURG—In an effort to quiet criticism of U.S. military policy, 50,000 U.S. troops invaded and soundly defeated the non-oil-rich Grand Duchy of Luxembourg Monday. "Once again, the U.S. claims victory over a rogue nation," President Bush said after the 45-minute war. "The people of Luxembourg, although prosperous and living in peace, have suffered under the tyranny of a monarchy for centuries. And allow me to point out that Luxembourg has not one drop of crude oil." Troops will return home Friday, following the public hanging of Grand Duke Henri de Luxembourg.

Tenants Forced To Clean Apartment Before Telling Landlord About Mice

BILLINGS, MT—The three roommates residing at 320 Sycamore Ave. #4 were forced to thoroughly clean up their living space before they could inform landlord George Hayton that it was infested with mice, the tenants said Tuesday. "We don't want slumlord George acting like the mice are our fault," said Keith Paucek, 20, as he hauled four garbage bags to the curb. "He's just the kind of guy to make some comment about there being three weeks' worth of dishes in the sink." Paucek last avoided the landlord's criticism by removing the grill and charred couch before asking him to replace the porch.

Double-Entendre Doesn't Stand Up To Scrutiny

BALTIMORE—Though the risqué comment provoked giggles from coworkers, a double-entendre made by Natural Land Foods cashier Don Mallard Monday failed to hold up upon examination, linguistics expert Randolph Cox said. "The group was thoroughly pleased when Don told Gary [Pickard], 'I'll *bet* you'll water her plants while she's away,'" Cox said. "But let's look at the phrase 'while she's away.' If she's not physically present, how could sexual relations occur between Gary and his attractive young female neighbor?" Cox called Mallard's attempt at wordplay "a good try." ⌀

GOVERNMENT from page 247

long-range, long-shot investments is questionable at best, especially when you consider inflation. America would do better to invest in profitable business ventures. It's just that simple."

In the first quarter of 2004, the U.S. will scale back such youth-market investments as Head Start, a federal preschool program for the poor, and D.A.R.E., a drug-use prevention program for minors. Snow said such programs focus on preparing tomorrow's leaders at the expense of turning a profit today. The extensive federal public-education system will also experience major cutbacks.

"With the economy showing signs of recovery, now is the time to cut away the dead wood," Snow said. "As the stock market turns around, we have a real opportunity to make some money. But that's only if we shift the nation's funds into high-yield, short-term investments."

Snow said he plans to support the private sector with corporate subsidies, and to invest overseas.

"This nation needs something really big to turn it around, something like the '90s tech bubble," Snow said. "We need a winning business model, something that after-school art workshops and inner-city basketball programs simply do not offer."

Federal Reserve Chairman Alan Greenspan expressed cautious support for the divestments.

"Investments in our nation's young people have never yielded very impressive gains," Greenspan said. "On the other hand, as the market improves, disinflation is a major concern for future quarters. The education system is a huge employer in this country, and consumer spending could be affected."

Jack Carpenter, a financial consultant for Deloitte Touche Tohmatsu,

A Sound Investment?
Fact: In 2002, the expenditure per pupil in public elementary and secondary schools averaged $8,000.
Fact: Five out of every 100 young adults enrolled in high school in October 2001 left school before October 2002 without graduating.
Fact: In 2002, education programs received an estimated $109.5 billion in federal funds.
Fact: In the last decade, between 347,000 and 544,000 10th- through 12th-grade students left school each year without successfully completing a high-school program.
Stop Throwing Away Our Money.
Paid For By Citizens For Immediate Profits (CFIP)

Above: An advertisement that supports divestment of our stake in the nation's youth.

said he is excited by the prospects for the nation's financial future.

"In such tough markets, the federal government should be putting its money in fliers, but instead, it's wasting it all on crawlers," Carpenter said. "Right now, we should focus on high-growth industries. Professional and technical services, finance and insurance, and information management are hot right now. Inner-city community youth programs—not so much."

Carpenter noted that not all investments in America's youth are low-yield, pointing to several youth-targeted efforts in the private sector that have generated immense returns.

"Coca-Cola and Microsoft," Carpenter said. "Both organizations have done very well in the youth market. Coke markets their beverages largely to children and young adults, showing steady gains. And Microsoft, maker of the X-Box, has increased profits and beat earnings expectations in each of the past eight quarters. The federal government has a lot to learn from these businesses."

In spite of an outcry from teachers and union leaders, Snow insisted that the divestment will be a boon for all Americans.

"Taking a student through high school costs the federal government nearly $100,000 in taxpayer money," Snow said. "If that figure upsets you, then think about the times that we invest in a child and then he pulls out of the program before he matures."

Secretary of Education Rod Paige, whose post has historically been strongly committed to investment in youth and the bridges from one century to the next, surprised many when he came out in favor of the controversial plan. Paige said data collected over the past five years shows that there is reason to divest our stake in the nation's youth.

"Look at our recent graduates," Paige said. "So many recipients of years of federal investments are laying around in a state of unemployment. It's just not reasonable to continue to invest billions of dollars in such risky ventures."

Paige was quick to add that the new investment strategy doesn't involve dismantling the public school system, just restructuring it.

"The proposed plan actually includes *increased* investments in vouchers for private schools," Paige said. "Through the years, we've seen consistent returns from blue-chip schools."

In addition, Paige said Republican leaders are investing record levels of federal money in support of President Bush's No Child Left Behind program, which calls for expanded testing, higher-quality teachers, and greater achievement among students, particularly those in poor districts.

"Testing is exactly the sort of research the government should do before making spending decisions," Paige said. "How else will we know which individuals are sound investments and which are likely to waste our time and money?" ⊘

DISPUTE from page 247

about the whole thing as quickly as possible," Chrétien added. "Please."

Vajpayee echoed Chrétien's sentiment.

"India is, likewise, pleased that the situation has been resolved," said Vajpayee, who just last week demanded that Canada remove all long-range weaponry from the Western Yukon. "The news is greeted by all the people of India as a great... you know... a very great [inaudible]."

"Can this press conference be over now?" Vajpayee asked.

The two leaders then exchanged a brief, fumbling handshake.

No one is sure how the conflict began, but once it was set into motion, the two countries' demands became increasingly forceful. Last week, India insisted, under threat of war, that Canada withdraw its troops from the "disputed zone." Canada responded with a counter-demand that India remove its own troops from the "disputed zone."

Tensions neared the flash point Sept. 20, when units of the Indian 77th Light Infantry and the Canadian 44th "Wild Geese" Armored Cavalry assembled and glared across the borders, in each other's directions, for several hours. Throughout the standoff, both nations

With relations restored, both nations have declined to address specific accusations or the manner in which the conflict was ultimately resolved.

rejected U.N. offers of counsel.

With relations restored, both nations have declined to address specific accusations or the manner in which the conflict was ultimately resolved.

"India has always been a peaceable nation. We accept the peaceful solution whenever possible," said an Indian government official who declined to give his name. "Likewise, we are glad that our Canadian allies have joined us in seeing reason. The end."

"The people of Canada have put the matter behind them, and hope that in the future, disputes of this kind can be resolved peacefully," said Assistant Foreign Affairs Minister Gerard Tollifer, who didn't take questions. "Actually, come to think of it, the Canadian people hope disputes of this kind don't ever happen in the future. And that is all we will ever need to say on this again, okay? Right. This never happened."

World leaders have met news of Canada and India's peaceful resolution with a mixture of relief and sly amusement.

"We are all pleased that these two nations were able to resolve their differences," U.N. Secretary General Kofi Annan said, hiding his mouth behind a manila file folder. "We congratulate Canada and India on whatever they did to solve the conflict over their... their... *border.*" ⊘

ACTRESS from page 247

Association of Anorexia Nervosa and Associated Disorders is part of a campaign designed to raise the public's awareness of eating disorders. According to ANAD statistics, 1 in 100 adolescent girls suffers from anorexia.

"The cool thing is that I'll be helping to make a difference," Astor said. "Besides appearing in the TV ads, I'll also be on billboards and the sides of buses. Everyone in the country will see me as the super-skinny girl."

"This will look really good on my résumé," Astor added. "I tried to pick glossies that were flattering, but this will definitely help drive home the point that I can play thin."

Astor has struggled to get her acting career off the ground ever since she moved to New York four years ago. She has modeled sporadically and worked as an extra on several daytime soap operas, and also appeared in two commercials, portraying Smiling Woman #4 in a Gap ad and a fungicidal-cream user for Lamisil.

The anorexia spot marks her first starring role and the first to highlight her extreme boniness.

"I was really nervous when I went in for the audition," Astor said. "When I got to the waiting room, I thought, 'I'll never be able to compete with all these girls.' I was checking out their hips, and mine were definitely wider than a couple women's. But I guess that in the end, I was the one with the right combination of talent and physique."

Astor said she doesn't suffer from an eating disorder, but is lucky enough to have been born with a slight build.

"I've just always been thin, ever since junior high," Astor said. "I'm blessed with a fast metabolism. Plus, I work out at the gym for three hours a day. And I'm careful to watch what I eat. And I dye my hair because my agent said it makes my face look more defined."

Astor's agent, Allied Arts' Debra Fayhill, said she's proud of her 5'8", 101-pound client.

"I'm so excited for her," Fayhill said. "I called her up and told her that the producers thought she was perfect for the role of Gretchen, the wholesome 20-ish woman who's starving herself to death. I've never heard anyone scream so loud."

Continued Fayhill: "Not many actresses get a chance to have this sort of impact on young girls. Hopefully, she'll really make a big difference in girls' lives, and stick in casting agents' minds when they need a beautiful, hollow-eyed wraith."

"Bianca was all, 'Do you really think I'm thin enough to play an anorexic?'" friend Fiona Lin said. "All of us kept saying 'Yes, totally.' She shouldn't doubt herself. She looks fantastic."

Although few PSA actresses have gone on to great success, Fayhill said she is optimistic.

"Look at Rachael Leigh Cook," Fayhill said. "She starred in the 1998 'Frying Pan' anti-drug spot from Margeotes, Fertitta + Partners, and she went on to play skinny women in the movies. Bianca is on the same track."

Astor is already practicing her line for the role.

According to the script, her ad will open with a close-up on a "frail, emaciated hand." The hand will reach across a restaurant table toward a piece of bread. The camera will pull out to reveal Gretchen sitting in a restaurant with a friend. Gretchen will change her mind and drop the piece of bread. The friend will ask what's wrong, and Gretchen will say, "Nothing." The word will echo eerily as the scene fades out to reveal a grave.

"Emaciated," Astor said, smiling and examining her hand held at arm's length.

After she was selected for the role, Astor called her friends to celebrate with a night on the town.

"Bianca was all, 'Do you really think I'm thin enough to play an anorexic?'" friend Fiona Lin said. "All of us kept saying 'Yes, totally.' She shouldn't doubt herself. She looks fantastic. Out of all of us, she *so* has the most visible rib cage."

Not all of Astor's friends say she's thin enough for the part.

"Bianca's thinner than most of us, but she's not very proportional," friend and fellow actress Tia Rialto said. "Personally, I'd buy her as a bulimic, but never an anorexic. Have you seen the flab under that girl's arms? Ugh." Ø

ENCYCLOPEDIA BROWN from page 249

Above: Brown's office, which now stands empty.

Miami Herald lauded "ace case-cracker Encyclopedia Brown" for his expert testimony on a dead cockroach, a runaway judge, a peacock's egg, and a stolen surfboard.

"It's true that Detective Brown and I didn't see eye to eye, but I would never do something so downright dirty rotten as murder him," Meany said.

Because of the long-standing mutual enmity between Meany and Brown, Meany was named among the suspects in *The Case Of Encyclopedia Brown's Mangled Corpse*. Meany denied the allegations.

"It's true that Detective Brown and I didn't see eye to eye, but I would never do something so downright dirty rotten as murder him," Meany said. "Besides, it's a matter of public record that, at the time the crime was committed, I was at the North Pole watching the penguins."

While no solid leads have surfaced, Kimball-Brown said she has a hunch that Brown knew his killer.

"The bitter irony is that Brown would have easily cracked a case like this one," Kimball-Brown said. "I just can't help but wonder: WHAT DID ENCYCLOPEDIA KNOW THAT WOULD HAVE HELPED HIM SOLVE HIS OWN MURDER?"

For the answer to this story, turn to page 76. Ø

FASTLANE from page 249

amounts of blood. Passersby were amazed by the unusually large amounts of blood. Passersby were

I want a refund on this rape whistle.

amazed by the unusually large amounts of blood. Passersby were amazed by the unusually large amounts of blood. Passersby were amazed by the unusually large amounts of blood. Passersby were amazed by the unusually large amounts of blood. Passersby were amazed by the unusually large amounts of blood. Passersby were amazed by the unusually large amounts of blood. Passersby were amazed by the unusually large amounts of blood. Passersby were amazed by the unusually large amounts of blood. Passersby were amazed by the unusually large amounts of blood. Passersby were amazed by the unusually large amounts of blood. Passersby were amazed by the unusually large amounts of blood. Passersby were

see FASTLANE page 256

COMMUNITY VOICES

Personal Magnet-ism

What do the following things have in common: a witch on a broomstick, a smiling carrot, a pig wearing a chef's hat, Tweety Bird, a vase of violets, a clam with googly eyes, a genie, Mr. Peanut, and a butterfly with plastic wings? No, they're not the names on the roster of some crazy baseball team. They're all magnets on the trusty Teasdale refrigerator!

A Room Of Jean's Own
By Jean Teasdale

I don't know how novelty magnets originally came about, but let's just say that I'm very *attracted* to them! Not only do magnets have healing properties, but they hold things to metal objects, as well. And let's not underestimate their ability to beautify. Our fridge would look pretty boring without them. For a sensitive person who likes to surround herself with the things she loves, an unadorned fridge is a major bummer (unless there's a chocolate cake lurking inside!).

I'm very particular about how I use my fridge magnets. For example, when I put up dessert recipes, I secure them with chocolate-kiss magnets. If I'm displaying Thanksgiving recipes, I use my little plastic cornucopia. A clipping from a women's magazine that points out how one size does *not* fit all is held up with a high-heeled shoe. And the Claritin magnet I got from my doctor is the only one I'll use for medical appointment cards and prescriptions—no exceptions!

I don't know how novelty magnets originally came about, but let's just say that I'm very *attracted* to them! Not only do magnets have healing properties, but they hold things to metal objects, as well. And let's not underestimate their ability to beautify. Our fridge would look pretty boring without them.

I have more magnets than I have things to put up, though, so most of my magnets rarely see active duty. But that doesn't mean I don't have fun with them! I've divided the fridge's surface into several distinct zones, each based on a general theme. The area by the freezer handle has a nautical motif, with magnets shaped like Noah's Ark, a life preserver, and a whale. The top-left corner of the main door has a North Woods theme: a black bear, a canoe, a rainbow, and a Minnesota Golden Gopher. And the left side of the fridge is a shelter for the 16 kitty magnets I've collected—but these little cuties will never be put to sleep! (That handicapped girl in the play I read in high school had her glass menagerie; *I* have my *magnet* menagerie!)

Then there's hubby Rick's lone contribution to the collection: a boring black two-inch rectangle labeled "Haines Tire Center" that he brought home from work. It's so drab and ugly that it clashes with my other magnets.

Then there's hubby Rick's lone contribution to the collection: a boring black two-inch rectangle labeled "Haines Tire Center" that he brought home from work. It's so drab and ugly that it clashes with my other magnets. Couldn't someone have made it in the shape of a tire, or a cute little jalopy? Even though I hate it, Rick insists on keeping it up so the fridge doesn't look so "fruity."

Maybe I shouldn't even bother telling you about Rick's boring tire-center magnet, because you readers will probably side with him anyway. Judging from my mail, Rick's a real scene-stealer. (Hmph! More of a fly in the ointment, if you ask me!) In a previous column, I made the mistake of describing how Rick threw a geode at our TV set. (He did it after some Sunday-afternoon sports show prematurely cut away from a Winston Cup race to the Dinah Shore Golf Classic.) I received more letters about that stupid geode story than I've received for anything else I've ever written. Almost everyone demanded that Rick take over my column. Now, wait a second, people! I'm not even sure Rick *can* write! Besides, destroying a television is hardly admirable behavior—it was rent-to-own, and we still had eight payments left!

I've never understood the sway Rick has over my readers. When I offered to mail my heavenly recipe for Chocolate-Caramel-Raspberry-Peach-Mint Trifle With Whipped-Cream Garnish to anyone who sent me a SASE, I got zero takers. Yet people *still* stop me on the street to ask if Rick is okay after falling off his buddy Craig's pontoon boat. Folks, it happened way back on the Fourth of July, 1999, and he suffered only a hairline fracture to his left shin. He only fell three feet, and it was onto solid ground, because the boat was still on the trailer. He was so looped on Old Milwaukee when it happened, he didn't even *notice* that he was hurt until the next day!

The only things consistently named after me are the tickets I get for parking on the wrong side of the road on street-cleaning days!

I don't get it. Rick's a far bigger screw-up than I am, but he's the one who has the love and respect of total strangers! He's about as sensitive to people's problems as a wood chipper, yet he's the one invited to be the first to drive his pickup through WSTR-FM's Morning Zoo Kroo Charity Bikini Car Wash For Muscular Dystrophy! Then there's the monthly "Rick Teasdale 2-for-1 Taps Nite" at Tacky's Tavern. The only things consistently named after me are the tickets I get for parking on the wrong side of the road on street-cleaning days!

Anyway, decorating with magnets is one of life's simple pleasures. You can't stop and smell the magnetic roses, but they can brighten a drab day—like when your hubby goes hunting with his drinking buddies, and you wake up to find a dead, half-plucked pheasant in your sink! (And, no, Oswego Ice-Fishing Club, Rick is *not* available for speaking engagements!)

HOROSCOPES

Your Horoscope

By Lloyd Schumner Sr.
Retired Machinist and
A.A.P.B.-Certified Astrologer

Aries: (March 21–April 19)
You'll be thrilled all the way down to your toenails this week when electrodes are planted in the appropriate pleasure centers of your brain.

Taurus: (April 20–May 20)
You're not evil for contemplating murder. Everyone's done it at one time. You are, however, weak for not having the guts to actually go through with it.

Gemini: (May 21–June 21)
You'll once again lead the field in crashworthiness tests, but they're starting to take a toll on your health.

Cancer: (June 22–July 22)
This is a great week for romance at work, which is a mixed blessing for all of you down there at the old slaughterhouse.

Leo: (July 23–Aug. 22)
While there are certainly many qualities that you'd change about yourself if you could, it's telling that most of them are physical.

Virgo: (Aug. 23–Sept. 22)
You can understand why the guy would be proud, but all the same, you're glad that you're not an Okie from Muskogee.

Libra: (Sept. 23–Oct. 23)
Try to take the long view: It'll be really cool for the kid who eventually finds your charred skull.

Scorpio: (Oct. 24–Nov. 21)
It's not true that your best days are behind you. It's true that almost all of your days are behind you, but the best ones are yet to come.

Sagittarius: (Nov. 22–Dec. 21)
You will discover a sound historical reason why we drive on parkways and park on driveways, but people will choose to cling to smug ignorance.

Capricorn: (Dec. 22–Jan. 19)
As one who wonders how the world came to be, you're excited to meet your maker. A gentle warning: The person who proposed the trip may have bad intentions.

Aquarius: (Jan. 20–Feb. 18)
You don't mind having a girlfriend who likes to talk after sex, but the collect-call charges are really starting to add up.

Pisces: (Feb. 19–March 20)
The stars could reveal your future, but they'd just be repeating what the Love Tester at the fair already told you.

NEWS

the ONION®

VOLUME 39 ISSUE 38 AMERICA'S FINEST NEWS SOURCE™ 2–8 OCTOBER 2003

Cheney Suspects Bush Listening In On Other Phone

see NATION page 7B

More Cats Made

see NATURE page 15D

History Channel Devotes Entire Day Of Programming To Footnotes, Bibliography

see ENTERTAINMENT page 10D

STATshot

A look at the numbers that shape your world.

What Are We Refusing To Buy For Our Children?

- 16% Enormous Scooby-Doo tin of caramel corn
- 37% Black-market Jarts
- 8% Thong diaper
- 20% Top-shelf liquor
- 19% Anything asked for in that baby voice

SPECIAL REPORT

48-Hour Internet Outage Plunges Nation Into Productivity

BOSTON—An Internet worm that disabled networks across the U.S. Monday and Tuesday temporarily thrust the nation into its most severe maelstrom of productivity since 1992.

"In all my years, I've never seen anything like this," said Price Stern Sloan system administrator Andrew Walton, whose effort to restore web service to his company's network was repeated-

see OUTAGE page 257

85 Percent Of Public Believes Bush's Approval Rating Fell In Last Month

WASHINGTON, DC—According to a Gallup public-opinion opinion poll released Monday, a solid 85 percent of the American people strongly believe that the American people no longer strongly believe that Bush is performing effectively as president.

"Due to perceived dissatisfaction over the economy, a strong majority of Americans believe that a strong majority of Americans believe that Bush's reputation has taken a hit," said Paul Mallock, a spokesman for Gallup. "In addition, we discovered a small but growing minority that believes a small but vocal minority is dissatisfied with the way the president is handling the situation in Iraq.

POLL WATCH

The small but growing minority we found believes that a small but vocal group of Americans thinks that reconstruction is messier and more expensive than Bush originally said it would be."

Of the 10,577 U.S. adults polled, 8,891 "strongly agreed" that more Americans "strongly disapproved" of the president's current performance.

Mallock said the poll, in which public perception of Bush's popularity fell to its lowest point since he took office, may be a cause for worry among GOP leaders.

"This is a potentially devastating public commentary on the perceived public opinion that Bush will use to guide his re-election campaign," Mallock said. "In fact, some see this as the most dramatic midterm shift in the public's perception of popular opinion of the presidency since Carter was in office. The Carter Administration was, as you may recall, believed to be very poorly regarded."

Of those polled, 68 percent said that "at least half" of Americans think that

see POLL page 256

Above: A photo from August shows Jaynes and Loemer in happier times.

Breakup Secretly Hilarious To Friends

ATHENS, GA—The inevitable breakup of Henry Loemer and Frieda Jaynes, which occurred publicly on Sept. 25, left almost a dozen local residents secretly amused Monday.

"There's nothing funny about this situation—except everything," Jaynes' best friend Deanna Vodak said. "They were a terrible couple and never should've been together in the first place. They fought constantly and had nothing in common, other than they were both lonely and liked fucking. Not that I'd ever say that to their faces."

Jaynes and Loemer met two years ago at the University of Georgia, where they developed a flirtatious friendship based on a shared interest in Tom Robbins novels. The two launched their strained relationship in July with a drunken kiss at a bar, and the subsequent coupling

see BREAKUP page 256

Iran's Nuclear Program

Iran faces an Oct. 31 U.N. deadline to prove that it has no secret atomic-weapons program. What do *you* think?

Matt Donnelly
Editor

"If armageddon devices of biblical proportion don't belong in the hands of fundamentalist religious extremists, where *do* they belong?"

Steve Buck
Cashier

"A standoff over nuclear weapons? Fun! My father told me about those!"

Bob Wiltfong
Revenue Agent

"We have bigger things to worry about in the Mideast than nuclear weapons."

Jessica Allen
Systems Analyst

"If Iran breaks the deadline, they'll be in direct conflict with the U.N., which is a really big deal if you're not America."

Rachel Biello
Paralegal

"I know how Iran feels! Deadlines, deadlines, deadlines! Ack!"

Kurt Braunholer
Parking Attendant

"Everyone always says Halloween is going to be scary, but when the International Atomic Energy Agency says it, you can believe it."

The NYSE Overhaul

In the wake of the forced resignation of chairman Richard Grasso, the New York Stock Exchange plans to make major reforms. Among the changes:

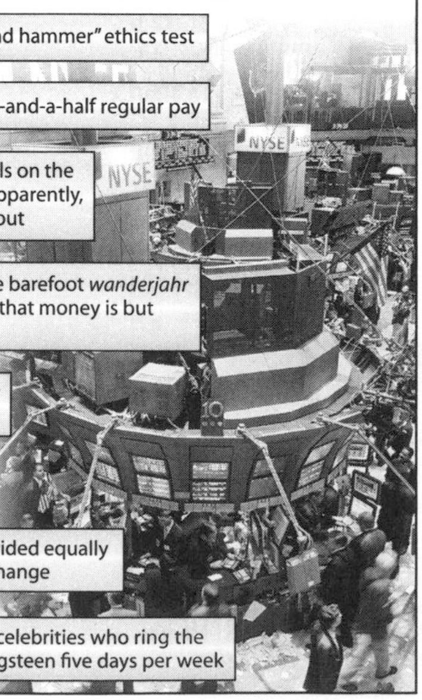

- Directors must pass basic "kitten and hammer" ethics test
- Overtime wage no longer 40-times-and-a-half regular pay
- Those arcane alphanumeric symbols on the animated board will be changed; apparently, people are starting to figure them out
- Future chairpersons must complete barefoot *wanderjahr* across Europe to better appreciate that money is but one of life's elements
- Traders no longer allowed to throw peanut shells right on floor
- Illegal trading now illegal
- Henceforth, stock profits will be divided equally among all companies listed on exchange
- No more revolving-door policy for celebrities who ring the closing bell; from now on, it's Springsteen five days per week

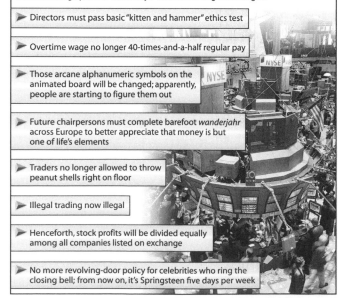

the ONION®
America's Finest News Source.™

Herman Ulysses Zweibel
Founder

T. Herman Zweibel
Publisher Emeritus
J. Phineas Zweibel
Publisher
Maxwell Prescott Zweibel
Editor-In-Chief

Thank You, But That Was Siegfried's Idea

By Roy Uwe Ludwig Horn

Well, thank you! I'm so glad you enjoyed the show. Thank you so much! We've been doing this for a long time, but I never get tired of hearing that.

Your favorite part of the show? Hmm... I really couldn't guess.

Oh, really? The giant mechanical dragon? Thank you very much. But actually, that was Siegfried's idea.

I do appreciate the kind words. If Siegfried were around, I'm sure he would appreciate them even more than I do. He loves to meet fans. Unfortunately, he had to rush home, because he's having work done on his indoor waterfall. It's really too bad he isn't here. He loves to talk about that dragon.

No, I had very little to do with it, to be perfectly honest. But of course, it takes the two of us to really make it come alive on stage. If I remember correctly, I helped to choreograph the number. I was influenced by the motion a cobra makes when it strikes... But the larger dragon concept really was Siegfried's. Though it was my idea to give the dragon laser-beam eyes.

At the end, lasers shoot out of its eyes. It's really quite dramatic. I'm surprised that you don't remember.

Well, you might be interested to know that it was my idea to kill the dragon with a sword at the end. Siegfried wanted to use a battle ax. He thought it would look better for those sitting in the back rows, but I maintained that a sword was more traditional.

Did you enjoy the white tigers? Most people love the white lions and the white tigers. Siegfried and I often fight over which of us should get the spotlight, but in the end, the star of the show is always the cats. Everyone assumes that they work for us, but it's more the other way around! Luckily, I've always had a great rapport with those beautiful creatures. My home is filled with jungle cats of all kinds. It's truly a wonderful way to live. So, if you loved the cats, then that's thanks enough for me.

Well, I suppose that we have been "doing the tiger thing" for some time, yes.

The woman in the basket? Yes, quite a trick. Yes, Siegfried really gets everyone's attention with that one... Even though it's pretty much just a new take on the old sawing-the-woman-in-half trick.

No, she's never been hurt.

Did you like Akasha? She's my favorite. I like to find new ways to fit Akasha into the show. Oh, she's the tiger. Remember, when the evil queen transforms into a tiger?

The rope trick?

No, Siegfried hadn't met the volunteer beforehand. Yes, straight from the audience. I agree.

He does, I agree.

Do you have any other favorite parts?

Uh-huh, I see. It's too bad that Siegfried isn't here—he seems to have a real fan. Yes, that was Siegfried's idea, too. Yes, it was me inside the giant suspended smoke-filled bubble, but still Siegfried's idea. Don't worry about it, please. I'm not offended.

If I remember correctly, I helped to choreograph the number. But the larger dragon concept really was Siegfried's. Though it was my idea to give the dragon laser-beam eyes.

Not to toot my own horn, but I pick out most of the music for the show. Did you have a favorite song?

Well, if it were up to Siegfried, every song in the show would be jazz-fusion. Sometimes, Siegfried can be a little gauche. I'm only joking, of course. Siegfried is brilliant. But he doesn't know how to set an act to music to save his life.

"SARMOTI"? It stands for "Siegfried And Roy, Masters Of The Impossible." Well, that was a team effort, if I remember correctly. Siegfried didn't want to say "hocus pocus" or "ala kazaam." He wanted us to have a trademark incantation. Yeah, Siegfried—more the magic guy. Me—more the cat guy.

What is it like working with him? Well, Siegfried and I make a wonderful team. We have a very long history together. Of course, we have our disagreements from time to time, but every conflict brings us to a better way of doing things. Just the other day, Siegfried was talking about a flying horse that would swoop down and save a dancer from that precious dragon of his. We had quite a fight about that one! But in the end, we came to an understanding and... Well, I'm sure it sounds like a good idea to

see SIEGFRIED page 257

THE ARTS

Mournful Irish Flute Used In Documentary About Loss Of Senior Lounge

GREENWICH, CT—In a documentary that the *Greenwich High School Gazette* called "daring and evocative," 17-year-old director Brad Harrison used a plaintive Irish-flute melody to underscore what he described as the "tragic nature of the loss of the senior lounge."

"It wasn't easy to find the right soundtrack for my film," Harrison said as he smoked a cigarette in the school parking lot. "I knew it needed to be profoundly emotional. Luckily, when I was at Best Buy, I heard this CD called *Celtic Moon*. The third track, 'Dark In Dublin,' totally sucked me in."

Todd Fackler, cinematographer of the 11-minute short, *Paradise Lost: The Story Of Room 114*, said he approved of the mournful flute music.

"This whole movie was shot with tone in mind," Fackler said. "I spent two hours getting the perfect skateboard-dolly shot of the lounge. I wanted the audience to feel that. When Brad had Elton John's 'Goodbye Yellow Brick Road' in there, it just wasn't doing it."

"But that wooden flute is dead on—it's so monumentally sad," Fackler added. "Everyone's been looking forward to using that lounge for the past *three years*."

Harrison said he has looked forward to using the lounge for even longer.

"My older brother told me about the lounge when I was in seventh grade," Harrison said. "He told me how each new senior class would decorate it however they wanted, and how you could hang out in there during lunch hour or whenever. That lounge was a *tradition*."

Through the years, students furnished Room 114 with items brought in from home: a couch, two bean-bag chairs, a television, and a rug. But upon returning for the new school year on Sept. 8, Harrison and his classmates found the furniture replaced by stacks of chairs, desks, and various janitorial supplies.

Students later found out that Principal Richard Ventzian had cruelly repurposed Room 114, filling it with the contents of Room 232, the former furniture-storage room, now the science laboratory. A single upholstered chair is all that remains of the old lounge.

"We didn't even get any say in the matter," Harrison said. "It was so unfair. I couldn't just stand by and watch it happen."

Harrison said he began work on *Paradise Lost* "immediately." The movie took two weeks to shoot and another four days to edit.

"I didn't do this just for me, or even for my classmates. I did it for future generations of GHS students," Harrison said. "Homecoming week will never be the same without that lounge."

According to the documentary, Ventzian was the one who officially designated the room as a senior lounge in the spring of 1995, when the school district cancelled its drivers education program.

Reached at his office, Ventzian said students were given use of Room 114 with the caveat that the room could be used as a lounge "only until it was needed for other purposes."

Grainy pans across Room 114's furniture-stacked west wall feature prominently in *Paradise Lost*. The documentary also includes testimonials from outraged students and an interview with Ventzian. It's all tied together by the dramatic voiceover narration of Dan Phelan, the senior with the deepest voice.

Above: Harrison in the school library. Inset: The *Celtic Moon* CD that he purchased for $6.99.

The documentary opens on a black-and-white, slow-motion shot of feet walking down a tiled hallway.

"They say people can survive as long as they have hope and water, or see a light at the end of the tunnel," Phelan narrates. "But what happens when that light is snuffed out?"

Harrison shot several student interviews in his darkened bedroom, with subjects cast in silhouette so that they could speak with impunity.

"They're just mad because we toilet-

see **DOCUMENTARY page 257**

NEWS IN BRIEF

Regular Citizen Heroically Enforces Park's 'No Glass Containers' Rule

LINCOLN, NE—Courageous citizen Gail Wendell went above and beyond the call of civilian duty when she enforced Irvingdale Park's "no glass containers" rule Tuesday. "Excuse me, that bottle is not allowed in this park," Wendell said to Rich Cavanaugh, who was drinking a Snapple. "Read the signs." Wendell last intervened for the common good Monday, when she glared at a Target shopper who failed to use the cart corral.

Plan To Live In Storage Facility Voiced

LOUISVILLE, KY—Just Sunglasses employee Eric Thorp intrigued coworkers Monday with his ingenious plan to live in a storage-facility unit. "The rent would be, like, 50 bucks a month," Thorp said. "Those things are totally heated in the winter, you know. For another $50, I could join a gym and shower there." Coworkers could find no significant downside to Thorp's idea, which no one in the world had ever thought of before.

Schwarzenegger Running Out Of Movie-Related Campaign Slogans

LOS ANGELES—Two months after he announced his candidacy for the California gubernatorial recall election, Arnold Schwarzenegger is running out of movie-related campaign quips. "Government and special-interest groups should not be '*Twins*,'" the actor said during the Sept. 24 debate. At a fundraising breakfast Monday, the actor told a confused group of business leaders, "I will '*Jingle All The Way*' to Sacramento!" Breakfast attendee Ken Straus said Schwarzenegger "really hit the bottom of the barrel" minutes later, when the actor announced, "In the movies, I played Hercules going bananas. But it's the tax-and-spend Democrats who are really going bananas."

Frustrated Sycophant Can't Figure Out What Boss Wants To Hear

EL PASO, TX—Associate vice-president Barry Ackerman has been struggling to determine exactly what West Texas Bank CEO William J. Holloway wants to hear, the shameless toady said Monday. "I thought for sure he'd be against Proposition 13, because it allows home-equity lines of credit," the bootlicking Ackerman said. "But when I started slamming it, he told me he supported giving the public greater spending power. I just can't read him." To repair any damage his comment may have done, Ackerman sent Holloway two tickets to *The Producers*.

Satan Depressed All Weekend After Man Opts Out Of Casino Trip

UNCASVILLE, CT—Satan, The Father Of Lies, suffered a dispiriting blow Saturday, when potential sinner Jeffrey Kremer chose to forego a soul-polluting trip to the Mohegan Sun Resort Casino, The Prince Of Darkness said Monday. "I had hoped that the allure of the bright lights and the promise of instant wealth would tempt Kremer into the mortal sin of avarice," a despondent Lucifer said. "Alas, he told his friends that he felt like spending the day hanging out around the house, instead of joining them at the casino. Curses!" Satan said he hopes that Kremer will at least watch softcore pornography on cable before the week is over. Ø

BREAKUP from page 253

ended a six-month sexual dry spell in each of their lives.

Loemer and Jaynes' torrid relationship came to a hilarious end in front of seven of their friends.

"A group of us went out for drinks at McGarvey's [Tavern]," said Jerry Pittman, a mutual friend of the couple. "We were all having a good time until Frieda took offense at some joke Henry made about the waitress. She sat and glared at him for 10 minutes. It might have made everyone uncomfortable if Frieda hadn't scrunched her face up like a 6-year-old to let everyone know she was mad."

When Jaynes could no longer contain her anger, she chastised Loemer for his failure to acknowledge her feelings. Loemer said he'd be more attentive to her feelings if she'd communicate them, "instead of shutting up like a fucking clam all the time."

"Even that might have slipped under the radar if Henry hadn't turned to Jerry, asked if he looked like a mind reader, and rubbed his temples like a psychic," friend Emily Solie said. "The next thing I knew, Frieda chucked a salt shaker at [Loemer]. But it was a totally weak sidearm throw and the salt hit an empty table to the right of us."

When Jaynes screamed, "There! Can you read that?" the assembled friends could barely conceal their amusement.

The small argument escalated into a screaming match. Jaynes expressed her disgust for Loemer's body, and he called her under-educated and spoiled. The fight ended when Loemer pulled Jaynes' photo out of his wallet, ripped it in half, and stormed out of the bar.

The fact that Loemer and Jaynes had been dating for less than three months heightened friends' enjoyment of the frivolous *sturm und drang*.

"Frieda was devastated," Vodak said. "She kept saying, 'It's over, it's over,' as if we hadn't caught that. Then she called the breakup 'tragic.' We tried to console her, but the moment she went to the bathroom, we all cracked up."

"Frieda was devastated," Vodak said. "She kept saying, 'It's over, it's over,' as if we hadn't caught that. Then she called the breakup 'tragic.' We tried to console her, but the moment she went to the bathroom, we all cracked up."

Pittman spent Friday with Loemer to provide his hilariously heartbroken friend with companionship. When the two friends walked past McGarvey's, Loemer choked back tears, while Pittman choked back laughter.

"Henry said he could never set foot in that 'tainted place' again," Pittman said. "I can understand why Henry wouldn't want to go back, but 'tainted'? He acted like nuns had been slaughtered there. And the night they broke up was only the third time we'd ever even been there. I mean, give me a break."

Frequent phone calls and visits have kept friends abreast of the ex-couple's daily tribulations.

"I was talking to Frieda yesterday and she said, 'How could this happen? We were so right for each other,'" Vodak said. "Luckily, I passed off my gasp as a cough. My favorite part was when she said she threw the mix CD Henry made her into the river, as a symbolic rejection of their life together. Oh, man. What a riot!"

Ever since the breakup, the ex-couple's friends have surreptitiously called one another to trade ludicrous details.

"When I was at Henry's house, I heard this message from Frieda demanding $20 for Blockbuster late fees,'" Solie said. "It was this diatribe about how he was going to have to find someone else to support his 'secret *Sex And The City* habit.' I thought I was hallucinating when I heard that one."

"Henry said he could never set foot in that 'tainted place' again," Pittman said. "I can understand why Henry wouldn't want to go back, but 'tainted'?"

Solie said she and her friends can justify their behavior.

"I'd understand if they'd been soulmates, but they were terrible together," Solie said. "Frieda's a bit of an introvert, and Henry's pretty cocky. When they got together, he transformed into a loud asshole, and she turned into a spiteful, controlling harpy. We like them fine apart, but together, they were ridiculous."

"I still don't know how I've managed not to laugh right in their faces," Solie added. "I'm sure this is going to get old in a week or two, but in the meantime, it's funnier than anything on *Conan*." ⊘

POLL from page 253

consumer confidence has dropped by "at least 50 percent" since Bush took office. One out of every three participants also noted that one out of four Americans believed that Bush was at least partially to blame for the perceived drop.

"I'm not surprised," said Barry Amodale, a Plano, TX, systems analyst. "I had a feeling that Americans were feeling that way. I heard that the voters were wondering how the average citizen thought Bush would explain his $87 billion request to the taxpayers, too."

Amodale's opinion seems to reflect a recent rise in the popular regard of general opinion.

"I saw something on CNN about the White House response to a *Time* magazine story about Congress' reaction to Bush's tax cut," Mammoth Falls, PA, schoolteacher Robert Brinley said. "I guess that story really made people think about how people think."

The opinions of Bush's approval rating, as revealed by the poll, are already beginning to affect public opinion.

"Until last week, I didn't know that people had such strong opinions about public opinion about Bush," said Greg Simon, a Chicago-area realtor. "I may have to reconsider my feelings about the president. I wouldn't want people to think that I don't think that what they think is important."

"Until last week, I didn't know that people had such strong opinions about public opinion about Bush," said Greg Simon, a Chicago-area realtor. "I may have to reconsider my feelings about the president."

Such public reactions to Gallup-poll findings are typical, Mallock said.

"We often see a desire to acquiesce among survey participants," polling-analysis analyst Tamara Bello-Dockett said. "There's a pendulum effect to the feedback loop generated by the see-saw aspect of how people form their opinions about their perceptions of others' beliefs. This does make it somewhat difficult for us to know exactly what the American people are actually saying about how the public is feeling about popular thinking, if you see what I mean."

Gallup-poll results are accurate to within plus or minus 3 percent. ⊘

Above: Nearly 65 percent of Americans polled said citizens will respond favorably to seeing Bush with this cute doggie.

DOCUMENTARY from page 255

papered the school and egged Ventzian's car last year," an anonymous student said. "That lounge was ours, man. They can't just take it away from us."

"But I guess they can and did," added the subject, who was identified on the screen as a National Honor Society member. "It's a bunch of *bullcrap*."

Senior Jennifer Shouse expressed her frustration openly. As student council president, Shouse proposed a resolution to return Room 114 to the seniors. Although the act passed unanimously, it was ignored by GHS staff.

"It's a travesty," Shouse said. "They're infringing on our rights. America is all about freedom, and I used to think that GHS was, too. I guess I was wrong."

The movie ends with a slow-motion shot of Room 114's door closing. The shot is accompanied by the sound of a prison door slamming shut.

After several seconds of blackness, Harrison's cell-phone number appears on screen, alongside a plea for viewers to "get involved." At this point, the Irish-flute music takes the movie through the credits.

Harrison shot his documentary on a Sony Mini-DV camcorder that he received for his 17th birthday. The project received an "A-minus" Tuesday in Harrison's audio-visual art class. Ø

SIEGFRIED from page 254

you, but there are many reasons, complicated reasons, why it's not right for the dragon to take on a greater role in our show. I don't really have the time to explain it, but trust me. It simply wouldn't work.

It simply wouldn't work.

Actually, I think I've added a great deal to the show. Without me, Siegfried would just be some magician with a bunch of dancing girls, laser lights, and fog machines. I was the one who added the cats, starting with our beloved Chico.

The cheetah. Everyone knows it's the cheetah, for God's sake.

Well, it may not seem like much now, but back when we started, it was something that hadn't been done before.

Like I said before, we're a team, a fusion of two separate entities. You couldn't split us up. It just wouldn't work. We create the magic in our minds and then bring it to life in front of the audience, as a team.

Making an elephant disappear? Mine. Having Siegfried transform me into an owl? Also mine. I don't know if you were listening, but it was *my* idea to bring in the white tigers and the white lions. It's not a big deal, of course. Contributing what sets us apart is "not a big deal." To you. But I *would* call it a big deal.

Well, I'm sorry that you feel that way. It was nice to have met you, but I really must go. I'll pass on your comments to Siegfried.

Yes, I promise. Ø

OUTAGE from page 253

ly hampered by employees busily working at their computers. "The local-access network is functioning, so people can transfer work projects to one another, but there's no e-mail,

Shortly after office workers found their web, e-mail, and instant-messaging capabilities disabled, reports of torrential productivity began to reach corporate offices nationwide.

no eBay, no flaminglips.com. It's pretty much every office worker's worst nightmare."

According to Samuel Kessler, senior director at Symantec, which makes the popular Norton Antivirus software, the Internet "basically collapsed" Monday at 8:34 a.m. EST.

The Gibe-F worm, an e-mail-transmittable virus, initiated cascading server failures. Within an hour, Internet service to more than 90 percent of the U.S. was disabled, either by the worm or by network firewalls that initiated security protocols.

"Unlike SoBig or Blaster, this worm didn't harm individual computers; it just used them as a gate to attack the Internet at the ISP level," Kessler said. "Computer technicians at most offices couldn't do anything but sit by helplessly as people worked through stacks of filing, wrote business-related letters they'd put off for months, and sold record amounts of goods and services over the phone."

Shortly after office workers found their web, e-mail, and instant-messaging capabilities disabled, reports of torrential productivity began to reach corporate offices nationwide.

"My first thought was 'My God, this has to be some kind of mistake,'" said Prudential Insurance executive vice-president Shane Mullins of San Francisco. "My e-mail wasn't working. Nerve.com wasn't working. I eventually found out that the company web site wasn't working, either. But by that time, my inbox was filling up like you wouldn't believe."

"My actual physical inbox," Mullins added. "It's this gray plastic thing on my desktop—the top of the desk I sit at."

With workers denied access to ESPN.com, Salon, Fark.com, and Friendster, employers struggled to keep up with the sudden increase in efficiency.

"Our office was working at roughly 95 percent efficiency," said Steven Glover, an advertising executive and creative team leader at Rae Jaynes Houser. "It's problematic to have the

Above: The Internet outage forced a Minneapolis couple to tackle a task they'd put off for months.

rate jump like that—it sets a precedent that will be impossible to maintain once the Internet comes back."

Glover said his department failed to reach 100 percent productivity only because employees stopped work

"In the absence of that information, I've been forced to go about my job," Lewison said.

every few minutes throughout the outage to see if Internet service had been restored.

"This is terrible," said Miami resident Ron Lewison, an employee at Gladstone Finance and an Amazon.com Top 500 Reviewer. "For two days, I've been denied access to the vital information I need to go about my workday. In the absence of that information, I've been forced to go about my job."

According to Labor Department statistics, companies affected by the Internet outage generated an estimated $4 to $6 billion in extra revenue.

"Losses to online retail companies will be considerable," said Jae Miles, senior financial economist at Banc One Capital Markets in Chicago. "Nevertheless, the outage's overall impact on the national economy will be a positive one. The losses should be easily offset by the gains to companies that depend primarily on people finishing actual work."

As of press time, many administrators had begun to apply a patch that combats the Gibe-F worm.

"Thank God, Earthlink service is back, and with it, online shopping and entertainment news," office worker Emily Jaynes said at 7 p.m. Tuesday. "I'm ready to head home now. I couldn't bear to spend another evening repainting furniture and using my pool."

Financial experts say they hope to have detailed data on the economic impact of the outage within the next 24 hours.

"When American office workers are denied access to vast, complex streams of ever-fluctuating and evolving information, they tend to get a lot done," said Nicole Dansby, a business-information analyst employed by the New York Stock Exchange. "The extended Internet outage may or may not have had something to do with the Dow's 278-point jump Tuesday. I'll have to, you know, check the web for a few hours and get back to you." Ø

COMMUNITY VOICES

Pizza Hut Doesn't Know What It's Missing

You know what? I don't care if they don't think I'm right for the job. I went in there and put my best foot forward. I said I was excited about joining the team and laid out exactly how hiring me would benefit the operation. If they're too narrow-minded to see what I have to offer, then that's their loss. All I can say is, Pizza Hut doesn't know what it's missing.

By Jack W. Dunst

I won't deny it—I wanted that position. When I read the want ads, I carefully considered the type of work, the commute time, the meal benefits, and the starting wages offered by the various restaurants in the area. Then, I factored my skill and experience levels into my decision. Out of all the options, the Pizza Hut on Pflaum Road next to the Costco had the most to offer me.

And I brought a lot to the table to offer them in return. Upbeat, can-do attitude? Check. Fast-learning self-starter? Check. Willingness to work weekends and night shifts, regardless of the inconvenience? Check. How many prospective employees can say all that?

I thought I did pretty well in the interview with that assistant manager—Greg, I think was his name. But if

I won't deny it—I wanted that position. When I read the want ads, I carefully considered the type of work, the commute time, the meal benefits, and the starting wages offered by the various restaurants in the area. Then, I factored my skill and experience levels into my decision.

Greg thinks somebody else is a better candidate for the job, then he's entitled to his opinion. He's the one who's going to have to live with his decision. For his sake, I hope whomever he hired over me is good. If that other guy doesn't work out, Pizza Hut better not come crying to me. I've moved on.

Pizza Hut's short-sightedness will be their undoing, because I'm about to take my talents to one of their competitors. Only after I'm already settled in making burritos at Taco John's or squeezing out cones at TCBY will Pizza Hut recognize its error.

And I brought a lot to the table to offer them in return. Upbeat, can-do attitude? Check. Fast-learning self-starter? Check. Willingness to work weekends and night shifts, regardless of the inconvenience? Check.

Still, what a heavy blow.

No, I'm not going to cry. I won't give Pizza Hut the satisfaction.

Maybe in some strange way, the rejection is for the best. I probably wouldn't have worked out at Pizza Hut, anyway. A guy like me can't be happy working for people who don't appreciate quality. Look what happened at Dunkin' Donuts. You'd think that good customer service and a positive attitude toward the challenges of the job would be enough, but it's all politics. The brass at Dunkin' Donuts needed to make cutbacks. I didn't have the seniority, so I got my walking papers.

Did I bemoan Dunkin' Donuts' egregious mistake? I did not. Okay, I was devastated for a few weeks. Why wouldn't I be? I gave my all for five months, only to see it slip right down the drain. But I've put it behind me. I've picked up the pieces and moved on. That's the nature of the fast-food biz. You've gotta roll with the punches. Adaptability is the key. The dinosaurs couldn't adapt, and look where they are now.

I'm only upset because I know that I would've been a real force at Pizza Hut, if they'd given me a chance. I would've grated the hell out of that cheese. I would've poured my heart and soul into that sauce. And there wouldn't have been any shortages in my till, because I'm a professional.

I'm not perfect, but I do believe that if something's worth doing, it's worth doing well. Good luck finding another guy like me, Mister Fancy-Pants Greg The Assistant Manager. I hope you got a good look at me, because I'm the one that got away.

Okay, maybe the interview didn't go as well as I thought. Maybe I didn't get hired because I lack some insignificant surface-level qualities that Pizza Hut evidently looks for in a second-shift cook.

Well, I'll let you in on a little secret that the Pizza Hut powers-that-be don't know: Pizza Hut isn't the only place that received an application signed Jack W. Dunst. That's right, I just happen to have a few other applications out there. So, just because Pizza Hut can't see the skills that I have to offer, that doesn't mean I'm going to deprive someone else of them.

I'll recover from this setback. It may seem overwhelming now, but I'll survive. I'm young. I've got my whole life ahead of me. Whatever doesn't kill me makes me stronger, Pizza Hut! Just wait until I start getting phone calls about all those back-up applications. Then we'll see who picked the winning horse and who missed out. I wonder how you'll feel, Pizza Hut, when Jack W. Dunst doesn't even remember your name. Ø

HOROSCOPES

Your Horoscope

By Lloyd Schumner Sr.
Retired Machinist and
A.A.P.B.-Certified Astrologer

Aries: (March 21–April 19)
Later, you'll realize that there was no need to rearrange the opossum to make it look like an accident.

Taurus: (April 20–May 20)
The chaos of Fashion Week is over, but one truth has surfaced: Both you and Betsy Johnson should be forced into exile.

Gemini: (May 21–June 21)
You will cry because you have no shoes, despite being told some sappy "footless man" story that doesn't make your shoeless condition any more acceptable.

Cancer: (June 22–July 22)
You have grown fat on the blood of the innocent, which, as it turns out, is the main ingredient in that white cream inside Twinkies.

Leo: (July 23–Aug. 22)
Please stop using the "check please!" hand gesture to get the attention of the waitstaff, you insufferable prick.

Virgo: (Aug. 23–Sept. 22)
Your life's longtime correspondence to country-music lyrics will become terrifying when you hear Red Sovine's "Phantom 309."

Libra: (Sept. 23–Oct. 23)
You can either be part of the problem or part of the solution, but in the end, being part of the problem is much more fun.

Scorpio: (Oct. 24–Nov. 21)
Your belief that the earth is carried on the back of a giant turtle will seem silly, until you receive panicked, late-night phone calls from NASA herpetologists.

Sagittarius: (Nov. 22–Dec. 21)
The worst of it all seems to be behind you, especially if you were serious about that whole "death would be a mercy at this point" thing.

Capricorn: (Dec. 22–Jan. 19)
Stretching before exercise does not require a medieval rack and the services of two shirtless, hooded men, but that couldn't hurt.

Aquarius: (Jan. 20–Feb. 18)
Self-employment has a lot of advantages, but one thing that hasn't changed is your fierce desire to shoot your fucking boss.

Pisces: (Feb. 19–March 20)
You're not the kind of man who can limit himself to just one woman bringing him pancakes.

ELECTROLUX from page 244

amounts of blood. Passersby were amazed by the unusually large amounts of blood. Passersby were amazed by the unusually large amounts of blood. Passersby were amazed by the unusually large amounts of blood. Passersby were amazed by the unusually large

They don't make knock-off items like they used to.

amounts of blood. Passersby were amazed by the unusually large amounts of blood. Passersby were amazed by the unusually large amounts of blood. Passersby were amazed by the unusually large amounts of blood. Passersby were amazed by the unusually large amounts of blood. Passersby were amazed by the unusually large amounts of blood. Passersby were amazed by the unusually large

see ELECTROLUX page 260

the ONION®

VOLUME 39 ISSUE 39 | AMERICA'S FINEST NEWS SOURCE™ | 9–15 OCTOBER 2003

NEWS

Gorillagram Employee Shot By White House Security

see NATION page 3B

Chaps Unnecessary

see FASHION page 15H

Goths, Vandals Invade Rome, IL

see LOCAL page 5C

Package Tracked Doggedly

see LOCAL page 8C

STATshot

A look at the numbers that shape your world.

What Do We Regret?
13% Getting caught
33% Spending so much time with kids
21% Genetically engineering humoctopus
8% Failing to pop Doug on the schnoz
1% Dying for their sins
24% Not selling out

0 74470 94595 6 00

THE ONION • $2.00 US • $3.00 CAN

IBM Emancipates 8,000 Wage Slaves

ARMONK, NY—In a move hailed by corporation owners as a forward-thinking humanitarian gesture, IBM emancipated more than 8,000 wage slaves from its factories and offices Monday.

"You are all free, free to go!" IBM CEO Samuel J. Palmisano said to the 600 men and women freed from the corporation's Essex Junction, VT, location. "No more must you live a bleak, hand-to-mouth existence, chained to your desks in a never-ending Monday-through-Friday, 9-to-5 cycle. Your future is wide-open. Now, go!"

The 600 newly freed workers cleared out their desks and were escorted from the building within an hour. In spite of Palmisano's jubilance, the emancipated wage slaves were strangely quiet as they filed into the parking lot, carrying their work possessions in cardboard boxes.

"I'll miss them," said Jim Tallman, manager of IBM's plant in Rochester, MN.

Tallman, who was ordered to set 150 of his factory's wage slaves free, added, "They were hard workers. Many of them were extremely intelligent. Some were like members of the family. But I know in my heart that having them here was a crime against human resources. The world is chang-

see SLAVES page 263

Above: Palmisano abolishes 600 jobs at the Essex Junction, VT, location.

Celine Dion Secluded In Lab Developing New Perfume

LAS VEGAS—Sequestered in her private laboratory near Goodsprings, Celine Dion has demanded that no one disturb her until the next scent in her perfume line is complete, her manager and husband René Angelil announced Monday.

"Celine has been in that lab for 27 days so far, and judging from the jasmine-smeared birthday card I received yesterday, she has no intention of taking a break any time soon," Angelil said. "She calls once a week to ask how our son is doing, but otherwise, she leaves the phone off the hook, unless she's ordering essential oils or equipment."

Angelil continued: "Celine has to replace her lab equipment quite frequently. She works so intensely that the machines burn out."

see DION page 262

Above: Dion inspects 300 mL of Anise hyssop essence.

Teens 'Going To Town' With Restaurant Comment Cards

Above: Malkus, McIntosh, and Konkel really get into those cards.

TRAVERSE CITY, MI—Three teens eating at the North Henderson Street Country Kitchen diner "really went to town" with the restaurant's comment cards Sunday, third-shift manager Rick Wehl reported.

"Yeah, there was a group of kids in that back booth last night," Wehl said Monday. "They sure were getting their jollies filling out those comment cards. Must have been at it for an hour and a half."

The 17-year-olds—Christine Konkel, Aaron Malkus, and Jeffrey McIntosh—reached Tuesday at the same Country Kitchen location, said they entered the 24-hour family restaurant at 12:15 a.m. Sunday, after spending several hours driving up and down Central Avenue.

According to Malkus, an hour after the teens sat down, shortly before they ordered food, he spotted the comment-card display near the register. He brought a stack of cards to

see TEENS page 262

CIA Leak Probed

The FBI has launched an investigation into whether White House officials leaked the identity of an undercover CIA officer. What do *you* think?

"The White House needs to assure the American people that, in the future, more interesting things than this are leaked to the press."

David Martin
AV Technician

"We must do more to safeguard our covert operatives, even if that means never allowing them to spy and forcing them to work at Cinnabon instead."

Christine Kula
Music Director

"It's important to compromise national security every now and again, to keep the CIA on its toes."

Will McLaughlin
Systems Analyst

"This is just like Karl Rove. Last year, before the White House Christmas party, he leaked the true identity of my Secret Santa."

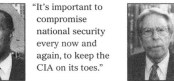

Charlie Sanders
Information Specialist

"The Karl Rove I know would never commit such a nefarious act. Then again, the Karl Rove I know runs Rove's Auto Body out by the interstate."

Jeff Hiller
Coach

"You know who else is a CIA agent? My asshole ex-boyfriend Dave Fredericks at 2102 Leavitt St. Go get him, terrorists."

Katie Dippold
Law Clerk

$87 Billion For Iraq

The White House has requested $87 billion to help rebuild Iraq. How would the money be used?

- Healthcare for working-class soldiers who can't afford medical insurance
- Construction of al-Iburton headquarters
- Xerox copies of Iraq's new constitution
- Costly dismantling of more than 150 solid-gold palaces
- Giant "HELP" sign that points toward Europe
- Pilates lessons for the Iraqis
- Neon sign over gates of Baghdad that flashes "Bag," then "Dad," then "Bagdad"
- Brand-new team jerseys for all Iraqis
- Roadwork ($500 million for materials, $2.5 billion to pay American supervisors)

the ONION®
America's Finest News Source.™

Herman Ulysses Zweibel
Founder

T. Herman Zweibel
Publisher Emeritus
J. Phineas Zweibel
Publisher
Maxwell Prescott Zweibel
Editor-In-Chief

Parrot Care Is Actually Quite Time-Consuming

By Capt. Crimson Bannister, Pirate

Ahoy thar, mateys! I see ye be gazin' upon me parrot Isabelle. Quite a keen fair lass, she be! Aye, but mark well me words: Thar be quite a lot o' work in carin' for a likely creature as she. Why, some scurvy swabs think a bowl o' seed an' a friendly shoulder be enough to please a bird from Gibraltar to Macao, but that be a d--n sight from truthful, I assure ye. What ho—I espy a calm driftin' in from the nor'-nor'-east—strike the mizzensail, me tars, an' lay-to as I tell ye what ye need to keep yer parrot a healthy an' happy crewmate.

Firstly, stock yer ship's hold with a handsome cargo o' pellets. Be ye one o' those who think seed the best diet for a bird? Heave to, ye poxy dog! Seed be high in fat an' low in nutrition. An' don't give her salt or cow's milk or foods high in sugar. Wean a bird on this witches' brew an' ye be consignin' it to Davy Jones' locker before the poor bastard's time.

Yer bird needs fresh water, as well. The briny blue won't do—find ye a gran' solid bowl, barnacle-free, an' treated with pitch, mayhaps, so it won't leak—an' replace it twice daily with clean drink. To fill the bowl with bilge is a crime o' the darkest dye, an' I'll give no quarter to avian abuse upon me brig: Any blackguards caught in the act shall have the ears lanced from their very heads an' parboiled before their eyes!

Ye also must supply yer parrot with a great deal o' provisions. If ye be in doubt as to where to procure this kit, thar be many pet-supply stores throughout the torrid zone an' parts north. In Port-Royal, thar be a bloody fine pet-supply store. Likewise in Nantucket, an' I hear tell thar be a right bounty o' stores with many convenient locations on Long Islan'.

When yer bird cannot perch upon yer shoulder, ye will need a fine sturdy cage. Mind that the bars be not so far apart that she can slip through or can lodge her feathar'd head 'twixt 'em. An' don't ye be usin' a san'paper perch, lest ye wish yerself clapped in irons an' sharin' yer grog with the hold-rats! Yer parrot needs a natural branch perch so as to not have irritated feet, me salts.

Provide a goodly calcium an' mineral supplement an' treat her to a cuttlebone, as it helps to keep her beak from growin' too long. Or, ye can let her play with Cookie's wooden spoon, or such-like simple fare, an' through this amusement the beak shall be trimmed.

If yer bird be pluckin' out her plumage, why, shiver me timbers, that could mean she be beset with a pox! Examine her for parasites, fungus, or signs o' skin irritation or infection. An' bathe yer bird once a fortnight. 'Tis important for healthy skin an' feathers. The creature may protest, but ye need to be firm. If the parrot ceases not in her pluckin', drop anchor an' visit yer veterinarian.

Ye likewise need to be keepin' yer parrot's nails trimmed. But let this serve as a warnin': Ye must be careful not to cut 'em too short, especially if yer parrot be but a fledglin'. Birds be

Firstly, stock yer ship's hold with a handsome cargo o' pellets. Be ye one o' those who think seed the best diet for a bird? Heave to, ye poxy dog! Seed be high in fat an' low in nutrition. An' don't give her salt or cow's milk or foods high in sugar.

usin' their claws for climbin', now, an' cuttin' 'em too short can lead to falls. An' no bird shall go overboard on me watch.

Wing-clippin' be the most important aspect to parrot-groomin'. Ye don't want to have the rascal flyin' around the ship starboard to port, prow to stern, an' back. But don't be tryin' this for yer own self. Espy that passel o' skulls danglin' on tenterhooks from the bowsprit? 'Tis the remnants o' lowly crimps what tried to do their own wing-clippin'. So grievous were the results, I had those d--nable rogues keel-hauled, lashed to the gunwhales, an' blown to bloody bits by cannon-shot, then their heads cut loose from what remained an' strung up thusly. Aye, swabs, 'tis best to have the wings clipped by an experienced professional upon dockin' in port.

Parrots be sociable creatures, an' chances are, as yer bird sails the seven seas imbibin' o' the bracin' salt air, she will miss her old flock back in Africy. It rends this old buccaneer's heart to think upon such matters, but 'tis proof ye need to hold fast to yer

see PARROT CARE page 263

LOCAL

Area Man Institutes T-Shirt Purchasing Freeze

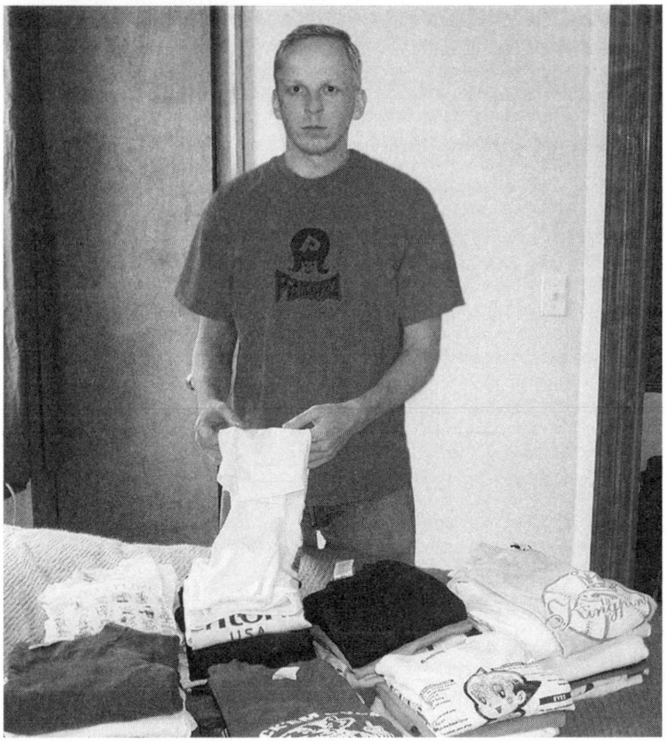

Above: Ciszek and some of his favorite T-shirts.

PORTLAND, OR—While standing in front of his open closet, Ken Ciszek announced Tuesday that he is instituting a T-shirt purchasing freeze until further notice.

"Although I love and have always loved T-shirts, the time has come to halt their acquisition," Ciszek said. "This includes T-shirts that feature bands and movies I like, locations I have visited, sports teams I support, causes I endorse, and phrases I find funny."

Ciszek said he has been buying T-shirts since high school.

"When I was a kid, I'd pick one up at every concert," Ciszek said. "Then, in college, I started buying them from thrift stores or getting them at political rallies."

The 29-year-old restaurant manager instituted his T-shirt-buying freeze when he realized he had so many T-shirts that he had lost track of his holdings.

"I found a great Cheap Trick *Dream Police* tour shirt at a garage sale," Ciszek said. "I couldn't believe my luck, but then I got home and realized I had one exactly like it buried under my other band T-shirts. Until I can figure out what to do with these things, I'm cutting myself off. It'll be hard, but I gotta do it."

Ciszek keeps the T-shirts that he wears most frequently hung in his closet. His second-tier T-shirts are kept folded on top of his dresser, which is filled with third- and fourth-tier T-shirts. Ciszek also has a box of T-shirts under his bed.

"There are ones I haven't worn in, like, four years," Ciszek said. "Some of them are riddled with holes. Some are so old that they're practically translucent. I have a 'Don't Mess With Texas' T-shirt that's so faded, the logo isn't even there anymore. It's just an outline of the state."

Added Ciszek: "But I love it, and I just can't bring myself to throw it out, until it falls completely apart or is ripped from my back."

Ciszek first recognized his problem in August, when his washing machine broke and he was able to go six weeks without needing to wash a T-shirt. Though he could easily donate his less-favored shirts to charity or throw them away, Ciszek said he is at a loss.

"Which ones can I get rid of?" said Ciszek, standing over a pile of shirts on his bed. "I mean, they all have sentimental value. This Old Milwaukee shirt I got to cheer myself up after I broke my leg in 2000. Here's one from a Fun Run I got roped into doing once. This one has a fish on it—I got it at a gas station. This one says 'We're All Earnest.' I have no idea what that even means, but the old telephone on it looks really cool."

Ciszek received some of the T-shirts in his wardrobe as gifts.

"This one is from the camp that my friend Jake worked at over the summer," Ciszek said. "My sister bought me this one at Disney World—I don't even like it, really, but I keep it because it was nice that she thought of me. Oh, wow. There's still a price tag on it."

At last count, Ciszek said he owned 132 T-shirts. The glut has gotten so out of control that he has been forced to turn down free T-shirts.

"I was at a sneak preview for *Kill Bill*, and they were tossing free stuff into the audience," Ciszek said. "Just my luck, instead of a hat or a poster or something, a T-shirt landed right on my head. I gave it to the guy sitting next to me. That's something I never would have done a year ago."

Ciszek's girlfriend, Faye Bullington, called the T-shirt purchasing freeze "a step in the right direction."

"If only I could just get him to start wearing shirts with buttons," Bullington said. "He's almost 30, but he still dresses like a 16-year-old. Is it really necessary for him to alert everyone on the street that he's been to San Diego?" Ø

NEWS IN BRIEF

Girlfriend Dumped After Forwarding Stupid Link

GREAT FALLS, MT—Amanda Manis was dumped Monday after forwarding boyfriend Anthony Madrid a link for the humor web site LunaticLobsters.com. "I was convinced that I had found my soulmate, my kindred spirit, the woman I could grow old with," Madrid said. "Then, out of nowhere, Mandy e-mails me this stupid link. When I saw those Flash-animation cartoons, I knew it was over." Madrid has previously dumped girlfriends for owning roller blades, buying Vegemite, and watching Craig Kilborn.

Thank-You Note Passive-Aggressive

LEWISTON, ME—According to Nancy Britt, a card she received Monday from friend Colleen Merissee, 46, resembled a thank-you note, but subtly expressed underlying hostility. "Thank you so much for providing the mini quiches for Michael's going-away party," Merissee's note read. "Everyone certainly did try them. Many people commented on how unique they were." Merissee added that the gift was very generous, considering that Britt stayed at the party for less than an hour.

8 Simple Rules Laugh Track Replaced With Somber String Arrangement

LOS ANGELES—ABC announced plans Monday to replace the laugh track of *8 Simple Rules For Dating My Teenage Daughter* with a somber string arrangement. "Following the untimely death of John Ritter, it's only appropriate that we repackage this madcap parenting comedy as a very special tribute to a man whose life touched us all," producer Tim Sharbarth said. "I mean, the episodes are in the can. We've gotta air them. Luckily, with the addition of new music by cellist Yo-Yo Ma, the episodes offer a chance for the viewing public to say goodbye to John, a beloved legend of physical comedy." Promos for the show, which used to feature choice sexual wisecracks, now contain a message from Ritter's "TV family" and clips of the sitcom's characters hugging.

Bartender Refuses To Acknowledge Patron's Regular Status

DAYTON, OH—Hurley's Pub bartender Don O'Hagan once again refused to acknowledge Henry Wells' status as a regular patron, the disappointed customer reported Tuesday. "I've been coming here for nearly two years, and I don't get so much as a nod of recognition when I sit down," said Wells, who estimated he's ordered a Bushmills with a splash of water from O'Hagan nearly 500 times. "I don't expect this place to be like *Cheers*, I just think that I deserve to be treated like a human being, is all." Wells said he seriously considered not leaving a tip on his next round.

Frustrated FCC Unable To Stop Use Of Word 'Friggin''

WASHINGTON, DC—The government agency responsible for enforcing broadcast-decency laws can do nothing to stop rampant use of the word "friggin'," Federal Communications Commission Chairman Michael K. Powell said Monday. "Everyone knows what it really means when someone uses that word," Powell said. "Still, we hear it all over the morning radio shows, all the time. Oooh, it burns me up. Those DJs aren't fooling anyone, certainly not us here at the FCC. But sadly, our hands are tied." Powell suggested that users of the non-profanity just grow up. Ø

DION from page 259

Dion, who holds doctoral degrees in botany and chemistry from the University of Montreal, has instructed her bodyguards not to allow anyone other than her 12 assistants into the lab.

"Celine built her lab outside of town so that she wouldn't be disturbed," Angelil said. "When I visit—just to make sure she's eating—she throws beakers at me. She says I destroy her concentration."

Added Angelil, "Have you ever been hit in the face with a beaker of pure essence of neroli oil?"

Angelil said he has worried about Dion ever since she announced that she would launch a new fragrance, tentatively called One Heart, as a follow-up to Celine Dion Parfums, the collection of *eau de toilette*, body lotion, and shower gel that she developed last year.

"Developing the first scent nearly killed her," Angelil said. "She's such a perfectionist. It was after months of non-stop work and a 46-hour stretch of not sleeping that she finally hit upon the perfect blend of fresh florals—lily, orange blossom, and exotic Tiare flower—balanced with rich amber, sheer musk, and creamy blonde woods. Why is she putting herself through this again?"

Although Dion has not been home since she began work almost a month ago, Angelil said she sporadically sends him terse e-mails.

"I get e-mails at all hours of the morning," Angelil said. "They'll say, 'Huge breakthrough... eucalyptus is showing promise, if centrifuge can hold,' or 'Discovered three new maceration techniques... patent pending.' She never responds to my e-mails, but at least I know she's alive."

"I got another one today," Angelil said. "She said, 'Closer, but still not there. Scent must be ideal for everyday use, yet sophisticated enough for special occasions.'"

Although Dion herself refused to comment, she allowed one of her assistants, molecular biologist Dr. Deborah Lasser, to speak to the press about Dion's $46 million, state-of-the-art laboratory.

"Celine's lab is a research scientist's dream—33 rooms with all the best equipment," Lasser said. "When she developed her first fragrance, Celine employed labor-intensive, 17th-century techniques like enfleurage and used jojoba carriers. But for her follow-up fragrance, she's using only the newest techniques, like hypercritical carbon-dioxide extraction and chromatographic photography, to isolate the various elements in the oils. It's a complete 180. Celine doesn't rest on her laurels."

Continued Lasser: "She pushes us to the limit, but no one works as hard as she does. I've worked both the day and night shifts, and she's always here. Every eight hours, she lies down in a hermetically sealed room to let her olfactory glands rest, but it's half an hour, two hours at most, and then she's back in the lab."

Lasser said she's amazed both by Dion's work ethic and by her "God-given talent" for dissecting and analyzing various scents without the aid of equipment.

"I've never seen anyone with such an acute olfactory sense," Lasser said. "Last week, a delivery came in. It was supposed to be an order of fresh pine needles from a white fir tree in Stockholm. Without even opening the box, Celine told the FedEx man that someone had made a mistake, and that the box contained Douglas fir needles. When we opened the box, we found out that she was right."

Earlier this year, Dion took several weekend-research trips to remote locations around the world to forage for exotic flowers.

"In February, we passed up an amazing touring opportunity so that Celine could go to Argentina and cultivate a patch of rare indigo *Tillandsia diaguitensis*," Angelil said. "It's really important to her that this scent be even more special than the last. I just hope she doesn't do lasting harm to her mental or physical well-being."

In a July interview with the *Toronto Sun*, Dion said she was confident that her new perfume would be better than her first.

"I know so much more now," Dion said. "In retrospect, I feel that using peppercorn poppy as a top note was a mistake. I'd say, also, that the amber base note seems out of place. It's too aggressive, too young and self-indulgent. Now, when I smell the bath gel, it screams, 'Look at me, see how I adapted Hobson's Isles of Sicily cold-soap method.' It doesn't have that classic, confident feel, like Chanel's blend of sandalwood, vetiver, musk, vanilla, chive, and foam of oak."

Lasser said that before Dion locked herself in her laboratory, she researched the work of 18th-century perfumer Francois Coty, the man widely recognized as the first great perfumer of the modern age.

"Celine knew that getting into Coty's head would help her with her own work," Lasser said. "She said, 'It's not just about the fragrance. It's also about the bottle and presentation.' I guess that's why those men showed up today and asked where they should build the glass-blowing oven." ⊘

TEENS from page 259

the table, at which point the teens immediately began to fill them out, reading their comments to one other as they wrote.

"The first spot was 'name,' so I wrote 'Oliver Clothesoff,'" McIntosh said. "I thought about writing 'Jack Hoff,' but I decided on 'Oliver Clothesoff' in the end. My dad's name is Oliver."

"I wish I'd been *served* by Cameron Diaz instead of some Country Kitchen asshole," Malkus wrote. "Or Anna Kournikova. She's hot."

Malkus wrote "Seymour Butts," while Konkel wrote "George W. Bush."

"For age, I wrote 'to perfection'—you know, 'aged to perfection,' like wine," Malkus said. "And for zip code, I wrote in my regular zip code, because I couldn't think of anything funny. I could have written '666' and then '69,' but that would have just looked like four sixes and a nine."

Despite the comment cards' lack of sex-related questions, the teens found a way to work the topic into their evaluations.

The teens provided a number of risqué answers—phone numbers like "555-TITS" and "ASS-FUCK" and e-mail addresses such as "blowme@yahoo.com" among them.

The question "Who served you today?" proved especially provocative.

"I wish I'd been *served* by Cameron Diaz instead of some Country Kitchen asshole," Malkus wrote. "Or Anna Kournikova. She's hot."

In the blank that requested the server's name, Konkel wrote "Dick Whale," in reference to Wehl, with whom the teens are familiar from their many recent trips to Country Kitchen.

"Remember that time Jeffrey brought over a booster seat and sat in it?" Konkel asked. "And then [Wehl] came over and told us to 'cool it.' Wasn't that hilarious? He was like, 'Cool it, guys.'"

"Remember the time we asked The Whale for the crayons, and he wouldn't give them to us, but then we got some from the other table?" asked Malkus, who has hung a Country Kitchen placemat featuring sexually explicit crayon drawings in his locker.

Konkel merely nodded, her attention focused on recounting the lengthy answers she provided to such simple multiple-choice questions as "What meal did you share with us?"

"I wrote, 'Sharing is caring, and I don't care to share my damn pancakes with anybody,'" Konkel said. "Then I got a better idea, so I put an asterisk next to the question and wrote 'Christmas fucking dinner' on the back."

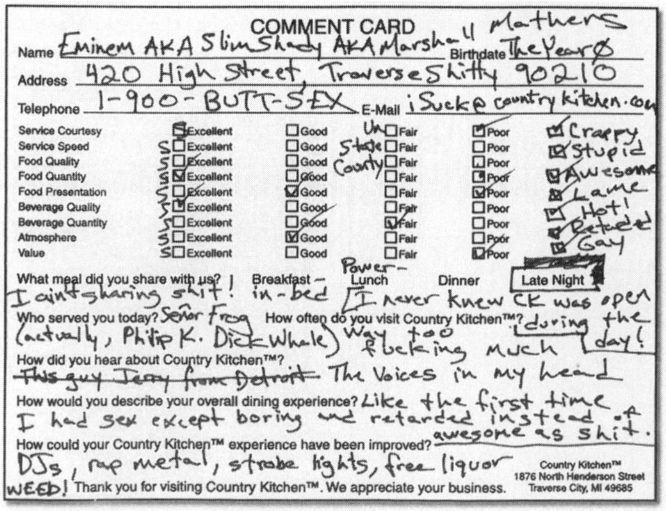

COMMENT CARD
Name Eminem AKA Slim Shady AKA Marshall Mathers Birthdate The Year Ø
Address 420 High Street, Traverse Shitty 90210
Telephone 1-900-BUTT-SEX E-Mail iSuck@countrykitchen.com
Service Courtesy ☐ Excellent ☐ Good Un ☐ Fair ☑ Poor ☑ Crappy
Service Speed S ☐ Excellent ☐ Good State ☐ Fair ☐ Poor ☑ Stupid
Food Quality S ☐ Excellent ☐ Good County ☐ Fair ☐ Poor ☑ Awesome
Food Quantity S ☑ Excellent ☐ Good ☐ Fair ☑ Poor ☑ Lame
Food Presentation S ☐ Excellent ☑ Good ☐ Fair ☑ Poor ☑ Hot!
Beverage Quality S ☑ Excellent ☐ Good ☐ Fair ☐ Poor ☑ Retarded
Beverage Quantity S ☐ Excellent ☐ Good ☑ Fair ☐ Poor ☑ Gay
Atmosphere S ☐ Excellent ☑ Good ☐ Fair ☐ Poor
Value S ☐ Excellent ☐ Good ☐ Fair ☑ Poor
What meal did you share with us? I ain't sharing shit! Breakfast-in-bed Power-Lunch Dinner Late Night
Who served you today? Señor Frog (actually, Philip K. Dick Whale)
How often do you visit Country Kitchen™? Way too fucking much [I never knew CK was open during the day!]
How did you hear about Country Kitchen™? ~~This guy Jerry from Detroit~~ The Voices in my head
How would you describe your overall dining experience? Like the first time I had sex except boring and retarded instead of awesome as shit.
How could your Country Kitchen™ experience have been improved? DJs, rap metal, strobe lights, free liquor WEED!
Thank you for visiting Country Kitchen™. We appreciate your business.
Country Kitchen™
1876 North Henderson Street
Traverse City, MI 49685

Above: One of the comment cards Wehl called "very funny."

To answer a question about the frequency of her trips to Country Kitchen, Konkel wrote that she visits Country Kitchen "way more than [she] should, considering what a shithole it is." In response to the same question, Malkus wrote "(2x - 50) y."

The group also provided creative answers to such open-ended questions as "How could your Country Kitchen experience have been improved?"

The teens agreed that Konkel's answer was the best: "Country Kitchen? Oh, shit, I thought I was at Red Lobster!"

In spite of the good time they seemed to have had Sunday, the teens' appraisals of their overall dining experience were overwhelmingly negative.

"It was a nightmare... a waking hellscape... of crappiness," McIntosh wrote. "It sucked more ass... than the whole... gay-ass staff combined."

The comment cards' last question solicited suggestions for improvement, and the teens happily complied, their responses sharing an undercurrent of sexual frustration.

"You want to know what you could do?" Malkus wrote. "Put in a stripper pole and have nude waitresses... You should also have edible food, lower prices, and free blow jobs."

Konkel said the restaurant "should have midgets bring you the food and

see TEENS page 263

SLAVES from page 259

ing, especially the economy, and no decent businessman could look at the cost-benefit analysis and not see that turning them loose was the only thing to do."

Palmisano explained that, while IBM posted profits for its second quarter, its microelectronics sector lost money due to a sharp downturn in the industry. The corporation also freed wage slaves from plants in Endicott, NY; Austin, TX; and Raleigh, NC.

"In these days of streamlined, modern business, wage slavery is an increasingly peculiar institution," CNN national business correspondent and arbitrage guru Mike Boettcher said. "We owe these poor, exploited people a chance to try to make it on their own merits. It's not right to work them to their deaths, or even to the usual retirement age of 67."

Public response to the emancipation has been largely positive, particularly among the company's shareholders. Value of IBM stock jumped 7.5 percent in the hours following the historic corporate-emancipation proclamation.

Business leaders have enthusiastically praised the wage-slave release.

Above: The remaining IBM wage slaves toil in Endicott, NY.

"In these days of streamlined, modern business, wage slavery is an increasingly peculiar institution," CNN national business correspondent and arbitrage guru Mike Boettcher said. "We owe these poor, exploited people a chance to try to make it on their own merits. It's not right to work them to their deaths, or even to the usual retirement age of 67."

Palmisano said the move, although sudden, came at the right time.

"There is no reason for a modern-day John Henry to spend his life trying to out-spreadsheet an IBM business machine," Palmisano said. "Especially since our computers, properly programmed and equipped, can handle the accounting workload of hundreds of human beings."

Upon hearing the news, many of the liberated wage slaves expressed trepidation over their uncertain futures.

"I don't know what I'm even supposed to do now," said Essex Junction's Anne Porter, 36. "I was born into a family of wage slaves. I've never known anything but wage slavery. I barely own anything more than the clothes on my back and the other, almost identical business-casual pantsuits hanging in the closet of my studio apartment."

"On the other hand, I'll never have to see that whip-cracking quality-assurance overseer again," Porter added.

President Bush hailed IBM's decision in an address to the White House press corps Monday.

"No one said freedom was easy," said Bush, who in recent months has praised wage-slave-emancipation programs initiated by Eastman Kodak, Sun Microsystems, AT&T, General Motors, Daimler-Chrysler, Ford, Boeing, General Mills, and Oracle. "But doing what's best for the corporation as a whole eventually benefits us all. This is what America is all about. I wish all the newly freed wage slaves the best of luck in their bright new futures."

Wall Street Journal analyst J. Craig Hoffman praised the emancipation.

"In a truly modern capitalist nation, letting people go is the only right thing to do," Hoffman said. "Certainly, IBM could have kept those poor wretches slaving away for the company, as some have been doing for the past 30 *years*. But, we must ask, at what cost?"

"Actually, $47,643 average annual overhead per worker, counting salary, benefits, and projected cost of pension or 401K co-payments, adjusted for inflation over the wage-slaves' useful lifespan, as it turns out," Hoffman added. ⌀

TEENS from page 262

then they should sit in your lap and feed it to you."

McIntosh's response was the group's favorite. He wrote, "This place needs way less depressed truckers, and way more 16- to 20-year-old single girls who like to get high."

At 2:45 a.m., the teens finished their seventh pot of coffee, hid the tip under a plate, and got up to leave the restaurant. On the way out, Malkus slipped 11 comment-filled cards into the box near the front register.

"I knew those kids were filling out comment cards over there," Wehl said, emptying the box at the end of his shift. "As long as the things don't end up on the floor, I don't care how many anyone takes. We've got a box of 5,000 in the back."

Wehl looked at one of Malkus' cards, which happened to be on top, for several seconds before dropping the stack in the trash. ⌀

PARROT CARE from page 260

bird an' provide her love an' companionship. A spry, talkative sort is a parrot, an' a keen scholar, as well. Knew ye, mateys, 'tis in the throat, not the mouth, that the parrot be makin' the words she speak? Aye, a fun fact, indeed! Ye can teach her to say words like "jolly-boat" an' "square-riggin'" an' "ahrrrrr!" Or instruct her in the riding o' a small bicycle.

Mind, also, that the parrot be a spirited squab, an' ye must forbear her caprice. If she nip yer hand, or yer hook as the case may be, resist the impulse to flense her to meat with yer cutlass, or even to growl "Avast!" Nay, punishment only sets her mind against ye, so do yer level best to ignore the rascal an' scold her not.

Long ago, me swabbies, I consecrated me life to the devil so that I might swash an' buckle fearlessly as a high-seas desperado. To this day, the British Navy deman's me head with a bounty o' one pound per hair. The life o' a pirate be nasty, brutish, an' short, so it be for that reason that ye should provide some means for the parrot's well-bein' after ye have departed this dismal realm. For ye see, parrots can live upwards o' fourscore years, an' can survive many a privateer. Arrange for yer parrot to be entrusted to an obligin' caretaker, or contact yer home port's humane society for assistance.

A parrot requires a d--ned goodly lot o' preparation, foresight, an' what the lan'lubbers call "TLC."

See ye, then, the importance o' proper parrot care? A parrot requires a d--ned goodly lot o' preparation, foresight, an' what the lan'lubbers call "TLC." Aye, 'tis time-consumin', indeed, but worth its weight in booty. An', should ye ever have a question about the parrot-raisin', fail not to flag me down to ask. It be what Capt. Bannister be here for, ye poxy salt.

Now, dampen those pipes an' rouse yerselves from the poop deck, ye scurvy layabouts, an' weigh anchor! Me yarn be spun, an' thar's work to be done! For tomorrow we dock at Port-Au-Prince, a city whose bounteous treasure be ripe for the plunder. Why, I hear tell the governor's daughter has the richest dowry in all the Indies! Also, Isabelle be due for her five-year check-up. ⌀

COMMUNITY VOICES

Please Don't Be Mad

Please don't be upset, baby.

Although I don't know what made you mad, rest assured that I didn't mean it. Smoove would never hurt you.

By Smoove B
Love Man

Was it my words? My words should only be used to describe your beauty and to express the deep feelings that I have for you. If some of my words somehow went astray and hurt you, please accept my apologies.

Was it one of my actions? Was it when I lit a fire in the fireplace after you said you were chilly? Maybe instead, you wanted Smoove to wrap you in a blanket and hold you close.

Perhaps you were upset by the sliced fruit that I brought to you. I brought you those slices of fruit because I thought that you might be hungry. If those fruit slices were not fresh enough, I will go to the 24-hour supermarket all the way on the other side of town and hand-select the store's ripest kiwi, in hopes that you will find it acceptable. If you don't like kiwi, I will seek out a farmers market and purchase fresh fruits of the finest local varieties.

Perhaps you became angry when I caressed your neck and shoulders. Was I too rough? Maybe you didn't want the muscles in your neck eased at that moment. If that was the case, then I am sorry.

Was it one of those things that made you upset? Please talk to me. Smoove can't read minds.

If you would tell me what angered you, I could make it better, either by correcting my error or by treating you in so sensual a manner that you would forget all about it.

If you remove that scowl from your beautiful face, Smoove will make everything right. Let me put on a D'Angelo CD, and I will pull you close, and we'll slow-dance on my white bearskin rug. The fire is still going, so it will be romantic. While we are grooving together slowly, I will whisper into your ear and say things like, "Mmm, I love the way you move," or "Your embrace feels like heaven to me," or "You have beautiful calf muscles." Or I may sing song lyrics in your ear. Whatever I choose, you will be overcome with emotion and desire for me.

You look so fine when you're upset. I want to get freaky with you right now on the kitchen counter. Please give it to me.

Tell Smoove what is bothering you. I know I can make it all better, if you give me a chance. Let me rub your back and neck. This time, I will use my exotic oils and massage your muscles until they are the loosest that they have ever been. You will feel much too good to be mad at me.

If you prefer powder, please tell me before I get my oils.

To help you forget your troubles, I could kiss you softly on your forehead and on your cheeks. Once your passion has been brought to a desirable level, I could pick you up and let you wrap your beautiful legs around my waist. My back is strong, and I will not falter one bit as I support your weight. We will kiss like that, until your desire overwhelms you. Then I will gently lower you onto the bearskin rug, put your legs onto my shoulders, and ride you like you've never been ridden before. I will take you to a new dimension of pleasure. This dimension, full of scented candles and rose petals, is where all of your wild sexual fantasies will be realized. This is a dimension that Smoove has visited often, but now I want to take you there.

While we are grooving together slowly, I will whisper into your ear and say things like, "Mmm, I love the way you move," or "Your embrace feels like heaven to me," or "You have beautiful calf muscles."

Aw, don't play me like that.

You know I would do anything if you would only smile for me. If there is something you want, please just ask for it. If you would like an exotic drink, allow me to travel around the globe and sample the various drinks of indigenous cultures. I will write down the recipes carefully. I will bring back all the ingredients, and then I will make the drinks for you. I will bring the glasses to your lips one by one, and you can tell me which exotic drink is your favorite. Your pleasure is all that matters to me. If you do not like the exotic drinks I make, I will go back to even more exoticer locations and find drinks that you do enjoy.

I will also garnish the glasses appropriately.

If you could only put aside your anger, I would caress your hand and look deep into your eyes. You would be able to feel the bond we share all over your beautiful self.

Damn, girl, why you gotta be that way? ø

HOROSCOPES

Your Horoscope

By Lloyd Schumner Sr.
Retired Machinist and
A.A.P.B.-Certified Astrologer

Aries: (March 21–April 19)
You'll slip a notch in the estimation of your peers when they find out that the Statue of Liberty was a gift from the French, not from you.

Taurus: (April 20–May 20)
Your eyes will soon meet the tender gaze of a handsome stranger, thanks to your decision to check the "organ donor" box on your driver's license.

Gemini: (May 21–June 21)
There is a time and place for everything, except for your loud and incompetent scat singing.

Cancer: (June 22–July 22)
Whether or not the pig learns to sing, you should keep trying to teach it. You have ample time, and no one cares about the pig's annoyance.

Leo: (July 23–Aug. 22)
You're never fully dressed without a smile, but in this era of office casual, a nice pocket square will do.

Virgo: (Aug. 23–Sept. 22)
Some will say you're incapable of loving anything in this world, but they've forgotten about the little baby ducks.

Libra: (Sept. 23–Oct. 23)
You'll be able to cross "See the Mona Lisa" off your list of things to do before you die, but that's about it.

Scorpio: (Oct. 24–Nov. 21)
You knew that girl on the billboard wasn't real, but you still hoped it was at least a picture of an actual 40-foot-tall woman.

Sagittarius: (Nov. 22–Dec. 21)
Being able to understand the language of the birds and the beasts sounded great, before you knew what self-centered little shits they all are.

Capricorn: (Dec. 22–Jan. 19)
You're finding it harder and harder to sleep at night, knowing that Wilford Brimley and his horse are still out there somewhere.

Aquarius: (Jan. 20–Feb. 18)
No one at the public library will be able to answer your question about whether anyone in America has normal old sex anymore.

Pisces: (Feb. 19–March 20)
It turns out that Andy Warhol overestimated the duration of your fame by about 14 and a half minutes.

POTTY MOUTH from page 257

amounts of blood. Passersby were amazed by the unusually large amounts of blood. Passersby were amazed by the unusually large amounts of blood. Passersby were amazed by the unusually large amounts of blood. Passersby were amazed by the unusually large amounts of blood. Passersby were amazed by the unusually large amounts of blood. Passersby were amazed by the unusually large amounts of blood. Passersby were amazed by the unusually large amounts of blood. Passersby were amazed by the unusually large amounts of blood. Passersby were amazed by the unusually large amounts of blood. Passersby were amazed by the unusually large amounts of blood. Passersby were amazed by the unusually large amounts of blood. Passersby were amazed by the unusually large amounts of blood. Passersby were amazed by the unusually large amounts of blood. Passersby were amazed by the unusually large amounts of blood. Passersby were amazed by the unusually large amounts of blood. Passersby were amazed by the unusually large amounts of blood. Passersby were amazed by the unusually large amounts of blood. Passersby were amazed by the unusually large amounts of blood. Passersby were amazed by the unusually large

Let's set fire to some shit out back.

amounts of blood. Passersby were amazed by the unusually large amounts of blood. Passersby were amazed by the unusually large amounts of blood. Passersby were amazed by the unusually large amounts of blood. Passersby were amazed by the unusually large amounts of blood. Passersby were amazed by the unusually large amounts of blood. Passersby were amazed by the unusually large amounts of blood. Passersby were

see POTTY MOUTH page 271

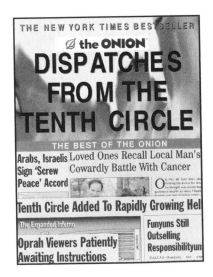